THE NEW
CAMBRIDGE MODERN HISTORY

ADVISORY COMMITTEE

G.N.CLARK J.R.M.BUTLER J.P.T.BURY

THE LATE E.A.BENIANS

VOLUME IX

WAR AND PEACE
IN AN AGE OF UPHEAVAL
1793–1830

THE NEW CAMBRIDGE MODERN HISTORY

VOLUME IX

WAR AND PEACE
IN AN AGE OF UPHEAVAL
1793–1830

EDITED BY
C. W. CRAWLEY

CAMBRIDGE
AT THE UNIVERSITY PRESS
1965

PUBLISHED BY
THE SYNDICS OF THE CAMBRIDGE UNIVERSITY PRESS

Bentley House, 200 Euston Road, London, N.W. 1
American Branch: 32 East 57th Street, New York, N.Y. 10022
West African Office: P.O. Box 33, Ibadan, Nigeria

Printed in Great Britain at the University Printing House, Cambridge
(Brooke Crutchley, University Printer)

LIBRARY OF CONGRESS CATALOGUE
CARD NO. 57-14935

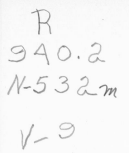

CONTENTS

CONTENTS

CONTENTS

CHAPTER VI

RELIGION: CHURCH AND STATE IN EUROPE AND THE AMERICAS

By JOHN WALSH, *Fellow of Jesus College, Oxford*

CHAPTER VII

EDUCATION, AND PUBLIC OPINION

By JOHN ROACH, *Fellow of Corpus Christi College and Lecturer
in Education in the University of Cambridge*

CONTENTS

CONTENTS

CHAPTER XI

THE NAPOLEONIC ADVENTURE

By FELIX MARKHAM, *Fellow of Hertford College and Lecturer in Modern History in the University of Oxford*

CHAPTER XII

FRENCH POLITICS, 1814–47

By G. DE BERTIER DE SAUVIGNY, *Professor in the Institut Catholique de Paris, and in the University of Notre Dame, U.S.A.*

CONTENTS

CONTENTS

CHAPTER XVII
THE LOW COUNTRIES AND SCANDINAVIA
A. THE LOW COUNTRIES
By J. A. VAN HOUTTE, *Professor in the Faculty of Letters in the University of Louvain*

B. SCANDINAVIA
By T.K. DERRY, *formerly Taberdar of The Queen's College, Oxford,*

CHAPTER XVIII
RUSSIA, 1789–1825
By J.M.K. VYVYAN, *Fellow of Trinity College, Cambridge*

CONTENTS

CHAPTER XIX

THE NEAR EAST AND THE OTTOMAN EMPIRE, 1798–1830

By C.W. CRAWLEY

CHAPTER XX

RELATIONS WITH SOUTH AND SOUTH-EAST ASIA

By K.A. BALLHATCHET, *Reader in Indian History in the University of Oxford*

CHAPTER XXI

EUROPE'S ECONOMIC AND POLITICAL RELATIONS WITH TROPICAL AFRICA

By J.D. FAGE, *Director of the Centre of West African Studies and Professor of African History in the University of Birmingham*

CONTENTS

CHAPTER XXII

THE UNITED STATES AND THE OLD WORLD, 1794–1828

By F. THISTLETHWAITE, *Vice-Chancellor of the University of East Anglia and formerly Fellow of St. John's College, Cambridge*

CHAPTER XXIII

THE EMANCIPATION OF LATIN AMERICA

By R.A. HUMPHREYS, O.B.E., *Professor of Latin American History, University College, London*

CHAPTER XXIV

THE FINAL COALITION AND THE CONGRESS OF VIENNA, 1813–15

By E.V. GULICK, *Professor of History at Wellesley College, Massachusetts*

CONTENTS

CHAPTER XXV
INTERNATIONAL RELATIONS, 1815–30
By C.W. CRAWLEY

CHAPTER I

INTRODUCTION

A N age so full of dramatic reversals of fortune and so big with consequences as that of 1793 to 1830 may seem to defy any attempt to
compose in one volume a survey of Europe and some of its links
with distant regions. Yet the very effort to survey the field in perspective, astride the 'natural frontier' of 1815, presents a challenge and
provokes questions sometimes obscured. This volume is intended to
offer a portrait or survey rather than a compressed record. Stirring
episodes, locally decisive battles, commanding personalities may receive
no more than passing mention or may even be sought in vain in the
index. But the problem of compression is not the only or the most
interesting one. More surprising is the uncertainty about some of the
foundations. There is still plenty of room for debate. The printed records are bulkier than for the eighteenth century, but many of them
relate to kaleidoscopic changes, blurred for us by political scene-shift-
ing and by the fog of war. Moreover, the voices of articulate contemporaries were more strident, more at cross-purposes with each other,
than in the apparently calm and confident age before 1789, more even
than in the short period when the Revolution in its first stages seemed,
not only in French eyes, to signify clearly a few universal principles
applicable to all Europe and perhaps to all mankind. On the other
hand, in the following period after 1830, aptly described as the
zenith of European power (Vol. X), the records, though even bulkier,
were becoming more systematic, and the basic social data were either
more regularly collected or at least collected in ways more capable of
statistical analysis.

In spite of recent efforts to test sweeping assertions by detailed
sampling, many central questions about this age of wars and revolutions
in Europe are still not precisely answered. How exactly was the widespread growth of population connected with some fall in the rate of
mortality and with increases in food supply or in commercial and
industrial activity? What was the balance-sheet for 'liberated' peoples,
materially and in their own generation, between release from old
obligations and violent subjection to spoliation by new armies and new
officials? How many men fought in the wars, how many of them died
by battle or disease, and how many just disappeared as deserters? Could
any general statement be made about the effect of compulsory military
service in the field upon the outlook of thousands of survivors who were
not disabled, or did individuals react to it as variously as to any other

experience in life? Was the peace-settlement at Vienna just an episode in power politics, or did the attempt to stabilise it foreshadow a lasting change in the conduct of international relations? Did the hostility between the French Republic and traditional religion help or hinder the survival of each? How far did Napoleon's treatment of the Pope effectively, through the clergy, alienate masses of people from the imperial regime towards the end? And what were the long-term effects of these conflicts upon Church and State alike? Did they indeed reflect irreconcilable differences between religious and secular philosophies, or did they rather spring from the fact that the higher clergy were in 1789 almost everywhere so inextricably embedded in the old social order that the Churches were still only beginning to disentangle themselves from it around 1830? Such questions might be multiplied.

The fall of Napoleon has often been a watershed for historians whose special field of study either reaches from 1789 (rather than 1793) to 1815 or else leads on from 1815 to 1848 (rather than 1830). Either peace becomes a preface and an epilogue or else the wars are only the background. It may be held that the 'unsullied' and truly significant ideas of 1789 would best be studied in the previous volume, while the enduring consequences of the great upheaval are revealed more clearly in the succeeding one: in short, that the period from 1793 to 1830 is only the filling of a sandwich, unevenly spread with violent stimulants and artificial tranquillisers. Yet a sandwich has no flavour without its filling. It has been said that from 1789 to 1815 France 'made war on history', and also that after 1815 the conservative alliance tried to 'put back the clock'. If so, both attempts were bound to fail; but the contrast is of course much over-simplified. The claims of tradition began to mingle with those of innovation very early in the first period; and, conversely, many conservatives after 1815 understood that history, on which it was dangerous to make war, included the history of the 'enlightenment', and now that of the past thirty years too. The metaphor of the clock is not really very apt, for it suggests a regularity which restoration governments might be excused for not recognising in the 'parties of movement' at that time. They saw themselves as trying rather to lower a feverish pulse of revolutionary conquest than to put back a clock of progress. Their diagnosis and their remedies were often crude, but during these years a process was going on of filtering and digesting rather than totally rejecting the mixed fare with which a whole generation had been forcibly fed.

This age of wars and their immediate aftermath has a character of its own, even if it is not that of fulfilment. Apart from its dramatic qualities, it presents us with the question whether we are to see in it, prevailingly, ideas at the mercy of violence or violence in the service of ideas, and with the problem of the role of war itself in shaping the direction of change and determining its extent. Technically, this was not a revolutionary age in warfare by land or sea (Chapter III); but the scale and persistence of warfare, and the methods used to meet these conditions (conscription, blockade, fiscal devices, propaganda) were ominously capable of much greater exploitation in future. Some chapters in this volume may help to bridge the barrier of 1815, and this may be salutary even if nobody would pretend to erect new barriers in 1793 or in 1830. The choice of a period which begins with a state of general war on the execution of Louis XVI, and ends with the avoidance of war on the abdication of Charles X, echoes the preoccupation of Europe with France in that age, and possibly also marks a stage in the inoculation of Europe to internal revolutions. Later revolutionary changes have mostly been initiated during or after wars and have not directly caused wars by intervention from outside.

In Chapter II some facts and figures are presented which mark the changing economic structure, together with an estimate of the forces which were changing it, rapidly in England, but unevenly and even still obscurely on the continent. The connection of these changes with political developments is indicated in chapters on the several countries. In retrospect, the most striking fact was the continued, accelerated and almost universal growth of population—a process not everywhere open to accurate measurement and still not fully explained. All over Europe agriculture still predominated, overwhelmingly in the south and east and much of the centre. The age of farm machinery was not yet, and the pattern of life in the country was everywhere traditional. Yet changes in methods, though not dramatic, were various, widespread and cumulative; yields were improved, crops were more varied and markets were becoming less local. It seems difficult to place in any definite order of cause and effect three concurrent facts—rising prices, more food, more mouths to feed.

Communications, too, were traditional, but again with a difference. Governments could now use the semaphore system in clear weather for signalled messages between important centres. Some roads were better, and passage over these was quicker and smoother for mails, for officials and for travellers who could afford it; but merchandise hardly moved faster by road than before. Some waterways were improved, and in a few industrial regions a web of new canals meant something like a local revolution in transport. In the twenties, the use of steam in harbours and for coast-wise shipping had begun. In and around some mines, the stationary steam engine for pumping water, and the horse-drawn railway truck, were already separately familiar before 1790; by 1830 the steam-locomotive, marrying the engine to the railway, was a proved experiment and was certain to go further and faster. The long haul for passengers or freight was still untried, and even in 1837

Parisians seem to have regarded as little more than a new toy their first suburban passenger line, just opened to St Germain; but five years earlier the *Globe* carried articles prophesying that steam would not only obliterate ocean barriers and barriers between oceans (Suez and Central America) but also reduce the frontiers between nations to mere municipal boundaries (Vol. X, pp. 434–5).

The same optimism was expressed by some writers as to the levelling of barriers between nations and between classes that would accompany the expansion of commerce with its attendant division of labour and redistribution of resources in the most economical way. Industrialists themselves were more apt to fix their attention on securing protected markets within the reach of their own government's influence; they favoured breaking down protective walls only if their own home markets were too small, or if their own methods of production were so far in advance of their neighbours' that they had, for a time, little to fear from foreign competition as a result of reciprocally freer trade. It was natural that English manufacturers should try by every means to penetrate the self-blockade imposed on the Continent by Napoleon, and to take advantage, when peace came, of the expected opportunity to flood the continental market. It was equally natural that French and Belgian industrialists, lately accustomed to having an open market over half the Continent, should seek protection after 1815 against this flood, and they were not slow in securing it. Yet the big start enjoyed by British coal, iron and textiles was not in the long run a threat but a stimulus to industrial change in Europe.

It is impossible to summarise the evidence for Britain's lead or the discussion of some of the explanations for it (Chapter II, pp. 39–43). In any case, the lead was already established before 1790; what needs explaining in this period is that it was maintained and even increased. Other countries were not lacking in inventiveness—science and technology were given more official recognition in France than elsewhere— nor lacking in commercial or industrial enterprise. But, if no country was so continuously at war as was Britain, most countries suffered greater dislocation by war when it came, and greater uncertainty about the future. To catch up quickly with Britain, they needed much more financial stability than they ever achieved during the wars. Whatever the combination of reasons may be, it would be wrong to speak of an industrial revolution in Europe before 1830, except in Belgium and in a few but important French and other scattered centres. Some governments were in no hurry to promote industries which might disturb the social order (as in Vienna and Rome). Most were still mercantilist rather than industrial in their policies, even if academic economists were almost everywhere disciples of Adam Smith and J. B. Say. Only one ruler, Muhammad Ali in Egypt, was experimenting, not very happily, in development of commerce and industry by thorough-going state monopolies intended to finance his army and navy. Although governments were usually keen to encourage new sources of wealth and revenue, they might well be concerned about the social consequences of headlong change and sudden fluctuations arising from the introduction of the new machines, especially in the manufacture of textiles. Traditional craftsmen could not be expected to see the virtues of new methods which might throw them out of work and replace them by women and children as minders of machines in factories. They might resort to violence like the Luddites, or become helplessly dependent on public or private charity. Country people, crowding into cities growing faster than their housing, might be affected in health or morals and might easily become destitute during a commercial slump. One of the earliest detailed studies of these conditions outside Britain was made in 1829 by a conservative and Catholic *préfet*[1] of whom Louis XVIII had said that he wished he had such a man for every department. He was not, like some royalists, a romantic advocate of a return to the old guilds and corporations, nor a critic of manufacturers from social prejudice, but he was shocked as an administrator. In France, relief of poverty had been regarded largely as a work for the Church, and there was nothing like the tradition of public assistance from local rates that had followed the dissolution of the monasteries in England in the sixteenth century. That system was now under fire in England, and in any case the survival or revival of charitable religious orders in France after 1790 could not cope any better than the old English poor-law with problems arising unpredictably in rapidly growing centres of population. The prevailing school of economists sincerely believed that attempts to moderate the speed of change or smooth the transition would only prolong the agony and delay the eventual distribution of the fruits of ever-growing opulence over the whole people. Soon, in the 1830's, Louis-Philippe's ministers were to be studying, with the help of the English economist Nassau Senior, the new English poor-law of 1834. It was not until 1839 that Prussia did something to mitigate the evils of children's labour in factories, on lines that had already been traced in England from 1801 but with effective inspection only after 1833.

One mechanical invention threatened in this age to create a more than temporary problem for a nation and even for its civilisation: Eli Whitney's cotton-ginning device directly caused an extension of the slave trade (Chapter XXI), and of slavery in the United States, as startling as the leap in production that went with it. And this happened at the moment when both the trade and the institution were being condemned by the French Constituent Assembly in the name of reason and natural

[1] F.P.A. de Villeneuve-Bargemont, *Économie politique chrétienne, ou recherches sur la nature des causes du paupérisme....* 3 vols. (Paris, 1834). Based on a report made in 1829.

rights, by philanthropists in the name of humanity and, most effectively in England, by zealous Christians in the name of religion. In the long run, economic arguments were to chime with the others in predicting the decline of slavery; but in this age the impetus came from men who were insisting that right should prevail in spite of private vested interests or national economic gain.

Some of the fluctuations in industry were due to changes in fashion or in the tariff policies of governments, or to transitions between war and peace; but many were caused, or their violence was increased, by the difficulties of both state and private banks in coping with any sudden crisis of confidence. These problems were very far from solved, and the potentially stabilising influence of great financial houses was seen not so much in commerce and industry as in transactions with governments, legitimate and revolutionary. Ouvrard, the most spectacular of the *fournisseurs* (army contractors), had big contracts with the Directory and was alternately employed and imprisoned by both Napoleon and the restored Bourbons. His own larger schemes for financing governments were too speculative to make for stability; but after 1815 there were moments when both the Bourbons in France and some of the South American republics may have owed their survival to foreign bankers, whose profits were commensurate with the political risks. Metternich acknowledged his own and his emperor's debt to the House of Rothschild by supporting in the German Diet an improvement in the status of the Frankfurt Jews (1817) and by helping to secure the title of baron for all five Rothschild brothers (1822).

Measured by every economic test, Britain emerged from the wars as the richest and most stable of the great states of the world—with London as the great international centre for banking and insurance, with the most powerful navy protecting the largest number of merchant ships, which in turn carried the most varied commerce all over the world, including the swelling output of the first modern industrial revolution and the primary produce of her expanding empire overseas. At the same time, British agriculture, partly protected by the corn laws from the possible effect of peace upon prices, could boast of high farming as well as high rent-rolls. The farm labourer shared even less than the unskilled factory worker or the ordinary seaman in all this prosperity, but perhaps few of these would have been pleased to change places with their counterparts on the continent; and the engineering artisans of the mechanical age were a new class of men, numerous enough already in England to be conscious of their importance, and made more aware of it by the demand for their services abroad. Josiah Wedgwood had great difficulty in persuading his skilled potters not to be tempted by glittering offers of employment on the continent. No wonder that the spirit of enterprise would soon be matched in England by a general spirit of complacency; many were completely left behind in the race, but most economists and men of substance believed that this was the price of progress. Britain had been more fortunate than most other countries in tackling the problem of a balance between liberty and authority; she was faced, earlier than others, with that of creating a balance between over-all economic progress, as measured by statistical averages, and those hardships of individuals, groups and even classes, which would be concealed in works like Porter's *Progress of the Nation* but must fill the whole horizon for those who had to endure them throughout their lives. In short, the upward surge in production of wealth was not yet matched by much skill in regulating its pace or distributing its material benefits so as to promote stability. Nor was much attention yet paid by 'practical' men to these problems, which therefore became the happy hunting ground of Utopian or fanciful men like Charles Fourier. The acuteness and relevance of many points in their diagnosis was obscured by the ridicule showered upon the quaintness of some of their remedies. Much more effective, up to a point, was the demonstration by Robert Owen at New Lanark that in certain conditions successful business could be married to humane considerations.

In 1830–1, the political map of Europe was surprisingly like that of forty years earlier. French conquests proved to be as impermanent as they had been dramatic, and few traces remained of French experiments like the Kingdom of (northern) Italy, the Confederation of the Rhine or the Saxon Duchy of Warsaw. The frontiers of France itself were almost the same as before, and so were the outer lines which enclosed the states of Germany. If Italy was still only a 'geographical expression', it was not differently bounded; the disappearance of the proud republics, Venice and Genoa, was the most radical change that survived the war. Spain and Portugal had lost most of their overseas empires, but their own frontiers were unchanged. The outward shape of Switzerland was hardly altered, and the newly united Kingdom of the Netherlands was breaking up into nearly the same two components that had been familiar on the map for more than 200 years. In the north, Sweden had lost Finland to Russia (1809) and gained Norway from Denmark (1815), but these were transfers of areas that had long been dependent and did not lose their identity by a change of sovereign; and Sweden was merely recognising the end of an era when she failed to recover in 1815 her last small foothold across the Baltic in Pomerania. Within Germany, an old and decayed framework which had for centuries been too rotten to bear renovation, though it might still give a little shelter, had suddenly collapsed at the touch of Napoleon. The Germans were by no means ready for political unification, for their thinkers and reformers mostly combined soaring universal ideas with an extremely limited, often parochial, outlook in current politics; but nothing could reverse the radical change of 1803–6, by which the big fish had swallowed up most of the smaller fry, so that Austria and Prussia, in their potential rivalry for domination, were confronted by a manageable collection of less than forty states instead of more than 300.

Austria, more securely based than ever outside Germany, with her apparently unshakable hold on northern Italy and the opposite Adriatic coastlands, planned to prevail in Germany (at least in foreign policy), not by direct rule or by reviving an elective imperial title which she had agreed to discard as obsolete in 1806, but by the kind of influence that she also exerted in central and southern Italy, and by her presidency of the new Germanic Confederation. Prussia, on the other hand, radically dismembered by Napoleon after Jena and compensated fully but differently in 1815, could only hope to prevail by further direct acquisitions or by very close control. Her provinces consisted of a large eastern block, thinning out to the west, and a smaller western block, the two separated by Hanover, Brunswick and Hesse in a belt nowhere less than 30 miles wide and mostly much more. She had problems of reinstatement in those parts of her shares in the partitions of Poland that she recovered in 1815, after losing them in 1806 before they had been fully digested; problems, too, of new rule in the northern part of Saxony, and in a large Rhineland province made up of former ecclesiastical and secular principalities which had all undergone the direct influence of France. Many of these new Prussian subjects were Roman Catholics; like the Silesians (now Prussians of the third generation), they were not readily absorbed into a Lutheran–Calvinist state which until the time of Frederick the Great had never since the Reformation been diplomatically represented at the Vatican. A government which could in 1817, by royal decree, make an administrative union between the Lutheran and Calvinist Churches in Prussia (Chapter VI, pp. 176–7), would not find it easy to treat the Roman Catholic hierarchy in the same brusque fashion.

Nobody dreamed in 1815 of restoring the political map of old Germany; and, even if Rome publicly deplored the injustice of secularising the great ecclesiastical principalities (Cologne, Mainz and Trier had provided three of the seven or eight Electors to the imperial title), yet the Pope's secretary of state, Cardinal Pacca, had not failed to recognise that they would, if restored, be an embarrassment rather than an asset, embedded as they had been in the aristocratic social order, with privileges which Rome was beginning to see as an obstacle to the unity and discipline of the Church. The German bishops had lately been inclined to Josephist ideas of a national state church, but 'if they are less rich and powerful they will lend a more willing ear to the voice of

Rome'.[1] But neither Rome nor her friends were yet ready to consider whether her own temporal power in Italy (other than a necessary *pied-à-terre*) might soon be an embarrassment too: the bulk of the papal states was restored almost without question in 1814.

Russia's apparently formidable resources had been swollen in all directions. Finland was a small but strategically important gain. The Congress Kingdom of Poland (1815) embraced the Austrian and Prussian shares in the partition of 1795, and about half the Prussian share in that of 1793, while the whole of the Russian shares remained within Russia. Until 1831, the kingdom was not yet fully part of Russia: it was separated by a customs frontier and it had a national army whose commander-in-chief, the tsar's brother Constantine, refused in 1828–9 to send any Polish troops for the war on Turkey; but other powers were virtually excluded from any influence there, and Polish patriots were very soon to provide the excuse for a harsher policy of Russification. In the south, Russia now planned, by necessity more than by choice, to preserve Turkey in Europe as a weakened and dependent client rather than directly to advance her own frontier on that side. But in 1812 she had annexed Bessarabia (a part of Moldavia), and the Treaty of Adrianople (1829) was the last of a long series which completed the administrative separation of Wallachia and Moldavia from Constantinople; whatever the eventual fate of these 'Danubian Principalities'—the future Roumania—might be, a Russian army was in occupation until 1834. On the Asiatic side of the Black Sea, Russia's European allies could not so easily impede her expansion—at the expense of Turkey in the Caucasus (1801) and in Armenia (1829), and of Persia around the Caspian Sea (1813, 1828). Her gradual penetration through Siberia had continued to the eastern sea; in 1799 the tsar granted a monopoly to a 'Russian-American Company' to control existing and future settlements (mostly for seal-fur) on both sides of the Bering Sea. Conventions with the United States (1824) and with Britain (1825) defined the southern boundary of the Alaskan settlements at 54° 40': and the Company's settlement much further south, in San Francisco Bay, was not formally liquidated until 1839. But difficulties of supply, friction with other powers, and mismanagement ('it was fine to be a director, but very dangerous to be a stockholder'), were already by 1830 disappointing any hopes of a great future in this region. The Company lingered on until the sale of Alaska to the United States in 1867.[2]

For Turkey, the direct cessions to Russia had been less alarming than in the time of Catherine II. Even the restrictions on sovereignty

---

[1] J. Schmidlin, *Papstgeschichte der neuesten Zeit*, (1800–46), 2nd ed. (Berlin, 1933), vol. I, p. 207, n. 5.
[2] S. B. Okun, *The Russian-American Company*, English translation. (Harvard, 1951.)

in the Principalities were tolerable, for these were hardly made as yet in response to an effective Roumanian national movement. Much more ominous for the future were the facts that the sultan had been obliged to allow a real autonomy to the Serbs (1817) and to recognise the existence of a small but ambitious Greek kingdom (1830). And, although Mahmud II had some success in tightening his control over his Asiatic provinces, he was now no more than a nominal suzerain in Egypt. Yet the long northern frontier in Europe was unchanged, and all the European powers paid at least lip service to the principle of the 'independence and integrity' of the Ottoman Empire (Chapter XIX).

If the frontiers of Russia and Turkey reached far outside Europe, those of British rule had been mightily extended, far beyond the reach of Napoleon. At the nearest point, the legislative Union of Ireland with Great Britain (1801) hardly affected the political map, though its indirect cause was the war and the influence of the Revolution on the rising of 1798. The genuine prospect of a healing effect was clouded by a long delay in granting the expected political rights to the Roman Catholics (1829), and the redress of agrarian grievances was hardly yet being considered. Time was to show the full unhappy effect of the union on British domestic politics, and also on the reputation of Britain in Europe and the United States; already Metternich had been countering Canning's arguments for Greece by reference to Ireland; and belief in Palmerston's sincerity as a champion of national and liberal causes was not to be enhanced by the fact that he was an Irish landlord. Nevertheless, the enthusiasm of Belgian (and some French) Catholics for O'Connell's successful new method of agitation was indirectly a tribute to the fact that British institutions were adaptable enough eventually to respond to opinion or bow to necessity.

Britain's sea power was much reinforced: in European waters by possession of Malta (1800) and Heligoland (1815), and by occupation of the Ionian Islands (1815–64) as a 'Septinsular Republic', with complete strategic control over this protectorate; along the approaches to India, by footholds and treaties at the mouth of the Red Sea and in the Persian Gulf (Chapter XIX), or again by her possession of the Cape Province and the islands of Ascension and Mauritius (1815); and still further east, by the acquisition of Ceylon (1815), Singapore and the Straits Settlements (1819), and by the gradual development of her recent settlements in Australia. The spectacular growth of British power in India is described in Chapter XXI. Across the Atlantic, short-lived hopes during the wars of footholds in South America were abandoned before the peace, but a part of Dutch Guiana gave Britain one small colony south of the Isthmus (1815). The war with the United States (1812–14) produced no change in the frontier with Canada, and the way was open for settling (1818) an artificial but stable boundary westwards to the Rockies before settlement had proceeded far on both sides of it. Britain's West Indian islands, with the addition of Trinidad, St Lucia and Tobago (1815), were strategically important to her in forestalling unwelcome schemes of European powers in Central or South America—and they were indirectly valuable to the United States also while its own navy was still weak. Commercially, the startling expansion of Britain's trade with the United States after the separation, and soon the more speculative but substantial growth of her exchanges with South America, meant that the West Indies were not so much as of old the hub of Atlantic trade; but, still in 1830, they were more important to Britain than India was as yet, and their own trade with the United States, restricted since 1783, had just been made easier by British legislation (Chapter XXII).

Thus, broadly speaking, the age presents a contrast in political map-making. Within Europe, the bewildering changes of the war years left comparatively few traces and, except in Germany, and to a lesser extent in Italy, did not point clearly along the lines that were to be followed in the next half-century. In the outer world, great changes were also seen, but most of them were more permanent or led on to further changes in the same general direction (India, Malaya, Australasia, South Africa, North and South America). But the force of the French explosion is not to be measured in Europe by its effects on the map. Even though a balance of power was achieved in 1815 along lines foreshadowed by Pitt at least ten years earlier (Chapter XXIV), and even though several fallen dynasties were restored, yet 'restoration' is a misleading description in all other respects for the condition of Europe after 1815. Much of what the French, and the wars, did to Europe, by direct action or by the stimulus of provocation, proved to be irreversible. The generation after 1815 is usually said to have lived in a period of reaction, associated with the name of Metternich. It is true that there was a strong reaction against 'irregular' governments, and some attempt to link government not with experiment or opportunity but with traditional supports. But some of this goes back to 1799 or earlier, to Burke and his admirers, to the quick disillusionment of the intellectuals in the 1790's, to the young de Maistre and Bonald, and to General Bonaparte recalling and employing *émigrés* and ordering a Te Deum of thanksgiving in Milan Cathedral for French victories in Italy (1800)—a gesture which shocked some members of the Directory and led on by stages to the Concordat (April 1802) and all that it seemed to imply. With the Consulate and Empire, the brief age of the revolution militant began to look like an interlude between systems of continuous power relying in part upon tradition for their stability. On the other hand, most of the administrative and social changes that were made effective before 1815 survived, while those which had only been initiated did not lose their impetus. None of the rulers of this generation would have been described as 'reactionaries' in the eighteenth century: the new currency of the word implies a radical change in the criteria commonly applied to government. Before 1776/89, acquiescence in government was normal, upheaval exceptional. The word 'revolution' was used to describe a turn of the wheel of fortune in politics, and another turn of the wheel might bring something familiar or something different to the top; the word 'reaction', if used at all, had a neutral meaning, as a pendulum 'reacts' by swinging to and fro. Those who believed in the improvement of mankind did not as a rule connect it with a crusade against the established order. After 1789, however, 'revolution' was generally held to be an uncompleted process which could hardly be reversed and could perhaps continue indefinitely; 'reaction' was anything that would impede this process, and commonly took on a sinister meaning. 'Conservatives', themselves newly so labelled, who resented this stigma of 'reaction', were preaching resistance to change regarded as a *process*, not just asserting their right or power against an enemy of the moment.

This new vocabulary, which still colours much of what is written (not only about politics), may be connected with the notion of the perfectibility of man and the revolt against it (Chapter IV): without insisting that any such doctrine was widely prevalent, we may detect a hint of Utopia round the corner in much political thought and action of the early nineteenth century. It is true that a subtle transition seems to have been under way by 1830: 'reaction' is contrasted, not so much with 'revolution' as with 'liberalism'. This implies that the goal is not to replace one regime summarily by another, but to ensure that in any regime the process of reaching decisions is conducted by means of public discussion and not simply by decree or by violent subversion. Nevertheless, most early nineteenth-century liberals carried a Utopian flavour about with them; so did some romantic conservatives who idealised the past, and some of the earliest 'socialists' (still in 1830 not so labelled). Even the Utilitarians, contemptuous as they were of natural rights and natural duties, saw at first hardly any limits to the benefits which the principle of the 'greatest happiness of the greatest number' might bring to mankind. This principle was a most effective engine—from Cesare Beccaria to Jeremy Bentham and his disciples—for attacking institutions which might appear to common sense to be obstacles to happiness, particularly in the fields of law and fiscal policy; to inflict unnecessary pain is as senseless as to impose self-contradictory taxes. Unfortunately, it was easier to detect pain and even to mitigate its causes than it was to define or create positive happiness; but the shallowness of the Utilitarians' philosophy need not obscure the vigour of their weapons, at least negatively, in removing hindrances to well-being. Their assumption that 'institutions make the man' is untenable; but, although good institutions cannot make men good or happy, we may allow that bad or obsolete or ill-functioning institutions make it more difficult for men to be good or happy. The question 'what is the use of it?' was more effective than the question 'what are the rights of it?' for clearing what appeared to be an administrative jungle.

In France itself, the Constituent and Legislative Assemblies (Vol. VIII) had demolished, along with privilege, most of the existing institutions in army, navy, local government, taxation, church, schools and universities—and had left a builder's yard in which, along with much rubbish, some materials for new construction were being assembled, at least on paper. What followed is told in Chapter X. Unhappily, of the Constituent's most impressive constructions, one—the elective system of local government—was overtaken by war and emergency methods until Bonaparte took over the framework of the new *départements* (with their neutral names intended to obliterate historic provincial loyalties) and himself appointed the eighty or more *préfets*; these were shorn of the judicial and fiscal power of the old provincial *intendants*, but all the powers of local government were more formidably centralised than of old. The other construction, the Civil Constitution of the Clergy (1790), was based on the principle of an elective national church, incompatible with Roman hierarchy and universality; it never won wide acceptance, and was replaced, first by a kind of separation between Church and State (1794–1801), uneasy because born in hostility, and then by Napoleon's Concordat (1802), which, just because it reflected the gallican Catholicism of 'the majority of Frenchmen', outlived the Restoration and lasted for a century.

The men of the Convention (1792–95) concentrated power at home as much as their predecessors had dispersed it, but their inoperative Constitution of 1793 showed that dispersion was still the aim, and that concentration was regarded only as the means of survival in emergency: 'without Virtue, Terror is useless; without Terror, Virtue is powerless' (Robespierre, 5 February 1794). The emergency was partly created by the Convention itself; it attempted too much in 'making war on history' not only at home but at the same time beyond the frontiers by offering 'succour to all peoples who wish to recover their liberty'. Out of the conflicts which followed, arose the fierce patriotism of Frenchmen, at first revolutionary in sentiment but soon just militant and acquisitive. With the collapse of the paper currency (*assignats*), the Directory had to leave its armies to live by private plunder and public exactions in liberated countries; with the fading of exalted hopes at home after Thermidor, the national pride of civilians too in France came to be centred in the exploits of the armies and their generals. The Directory needed a civilian-minded general as a mascot, and found in Bonaparte a master.

The Napoleonic adventure is sketched in Chapter XI, Napoleon's rule in France as consul and as emperor in Chapter X. These were years of fulfilment for administrators, whether soldiers or civilians, whether new men enjoying the 'carrière ouverte aux talents' or men to whom more prosaic careers would have been open under the old regime, including many men of noble family, often royalists at heart, who rallied to the Republic of the First Consul, to the republican Empire of 1804-8 or finally to the hereditary dynastic Empire of the last years. In 1814, very little was restored except the dynasty, which made, inevitably, far more use of men who had served Napoleon than of 'pure' royalists. Louis XVIII himself had never bowed the knee to the 'usurper', but many of his ministers and *préfets* and magistrates had done so, and those who submitted again during the Hundred Days were mostly not disturbed after Waterloo if they had not positively abetted Napoleon. Political debate, and the public exchange of ideas in the press, in pamphlets and in books, were much more free than they had been at any time during the wars; and the constitutional charter of 1814, with all its limitations in the eyes of later generations (and in those of contemporaries who wanted nothing less than the overthrow of the dynasty, or would not be shocked by that), was no sham. In the words of a constitutional lawyer of the Third Republic: 'our administration dates from the empire, our politics date from the Restoration. . . . The role of the Revolution has been immense, but it has remained negative. It destroyed the old regime; it cleared the ground for modern institutions, and on that ground Napoleon erected his edifice of despotism. . . . To the Restoration belongs the honour of having introduced in practice that fundamental principle of modern constitutions: the alliance between liberty and authority. Its work has endured.'[1] The experiment of constitutional monarchy in France, before and after 1830, is sketched in Chapter XII.

Elsewhere, except in some of the smaller states, the practice of representative government made little headway before 1830, or indeed before 1848; but neither had it made any real headway before 1815. The great majority of men in Europe were still occupied in traditional agriculture, and many of them were illiterate. The men of science and learning were not much impeded by forms of government, so long as these were fairly stable, although the prestige of the exact sciences and of technology was much increased in France, while that of philosophy and philology

---

[1] J. Barthélemy, *L'introduction du régime parlementaire en France sous Louis XVIII et Charles X* (Paris, 1904), Avant-propos.

was higher than ever in Germany (Chapter V). The demand for constitutional liberties came from men of the administrative, professional and commercial classes; it was to be made irresistible, more by the gradual revolution in industry and the transfer of wealth (or the creation of new wealth) associated with it, than by the active political agitation which itself reflected the contrast between new facts and old tradition. The work of adapting institutions so as to fit a changing social pattern was inevitably slow. Political seers like Saint Simon and his often dissident followers (among whom Auguste Comte was originally numbered) might announce the coming of a technocratic, positivist, era in place of the long ages when land had been the prevailing source of wealth and power and also (as it still was) the most desirable evidence of wealth derived from other sources; but such prophets seemed eccentric or fanciful to men engaged in the hurly-burly of current affairs. Nor were these seers prophets of democracy in the sense in which the 'Jacobins' had understood it. Among those who had 'learned nothing and forgotten nothing' since 1789 were not only the survivors of the age of privilege (and the inheritors of privilege where it had been little disturbed), but also the 'men of 1792', who constantly expected, in vain, to rehearse anew the scenes of the Revolution, if possible without its violence at home but not without its glorious adventures abroad.

The 'new look' given to Prussia from 1807 (Chapter XIII) was not effaced after 1815, even if constitutionalist hopes were disappointed more than in some of the other German states; but the emancipation of the serfs proved initially to be of less benefit to them than to the greater landowners, some of whom foresaw at the time that, if the peasant was no longer bound to the soil, neither would the soil be bound to the peasant. A strict administration, and a prospect of economic advantage, were the greatest attractions that Prussia could offer to her old or new subjects and to her weaker neighbours. The first of these advantages was rooted in earlier tradition and was reinforced by the products of the Prussian universities, administering the Prussian *Landrecht* (state law) which had been codified in 1794 (but commercial law was not codified until 1845). The second advantage was provided by the moderate Prussian tariff of 1818 and by the tariff union now beginning (from 1828) to be offered to neighbours willing to be included. The law of 1818 reversed the old system of discouraging exports of corn, and lowered tariffs all round. It also gave Prussia for the first time a single system for all the provinces, but the ratio of frontier-line to area was still very high. Tariff unions would therefore give an immediate saving of expense in addition to the prospect of positive gain and perhaps more distant political advantage. At the same time, roads were designed to avoid or minimise tariff barriers: for example, from Halberstadt to Cologne between Hanover and Hesse (1819), with a branch from Paderborn southwards (1829), and from Magdeburg to Hanover (1829).

Among the provincial Diets set up in Prussia from 1823, that of the Rhineland province was the most active, but no central system of representation existed. Hanover was oddly 'reactionary' after 1815, considering its long connection with England; but many of the states of central and south Germany had constitutions based (as in France) on a narrow franchise but protecting civil rights, for example Nassau (before 1814), Weimar, Bavaria, Baden, Württemberg and Hesse (all these 1816–20). The keynote of these, especially the Bavarian, was that of the enlightenment rather than of liberalism. The Federal Act (1819) did indeed envisage constitutional systems in each state; but very soon the state governments and the Federal Diet were confronted by movements which seemed to them not constitutional but revolutionary. There was indeed a good deal of froth on the beer of these early German liberals or radicals, but the governments of states which had working representative constitutions were not, on the whole, more dangerously threatened than those of states which had none.

The doctrine of immobility was partly imposed on the Confederation by the presidency of Austria. This was not uncongenial to Metternich in constitutional matters, resourceful and pliant though he was in diplomacy and administration; but in any case the personal views of the emperor, and the peculiar situation in the monarchy, left little room for any alternative to immobility (Chapter XIV). The peculiarity of Austria was that none of the historic 'nations' in it coincided with the just emerging racial and linguistic nationalities; moreover the emperor's government had no experience of a working constitution except that of the kingdom of Hungary, designed to preserve the ancient privileges of the Magyar nobles, whose ideas were more like those of the barons of Runnymede than those of contemporary liberals. It is not surprising that the emperor avoided summoning the Hungarian Diet from 1812 to 1825. Above all, it was in his interest after 1815, financially and politically, to avoid wars, for the 'parties of movement' in Europe generally were likely to profit by war: the Greeks counted on a Russian war against Turkey in the 1820's, and the French Left in 1830–1 wanted to push Louis Philippe towards intervention in Italy or Belgium or Poland. Revolutionary movements might also provoke war by neighbours fearing infection: Metternich felt obliged to intervene in Naples, while Russia offered, and France decided, to intervene in Spain. Metternich also held that rulers could help to forestall such embarrassing situations. It is well known that King Ferdinand of Naples promised him not to make constitutional changes without Austrian approval, but less well known that the king was also warned against trying to undo the changes introduced by Murat in law and administration (Chapter XV, p. 429). The Austrian government in the north did not compare badly with those of the rest of Italy (except perhaps for a 'liberal oasis' in Tuscany). It was not more foreign than French government had been, and the number of those who objected to foreign rule as such was small, even if they held the future. It was difficult to judge the government of the papal states by current standards, with its unique blend of easy-going paternalism and cruel inefficiency; but while Cardinal Consalvi was secretary of state, its intentions could hardly be called 'reactionary'. Consalvi was well aware of the danger of looking backwards; in a letter of August 1814 to the future Charles X of France, he was already urging the king and his brother to imitate Solon's work of reconciliation, and not the example of Charles II, 'who, after promising to forget the past, forgave nobody, poisoned his own reign, and prepared for the Stuart dynasty a new downfall, which came about under his brother—this time irrevocably'.[1] But, on the death of Pius VII (1823), Consalvi made way for the zealots in Rome, and throughout Italy the movements of 1821 in Naples and Piedmont intensified police activity, which most directly affected comparatively small but well-to-do and vocal groups of educated men (Chapter XV).

Although it was Spain (Chapter XVI) which gave to the name 'Liberal' a specifically political significance, the character of liberalism in the Peninsula was from the first peculiar, determined by the unique position of the Church and connected with officers in the army and soon with rival groups within the royal families and at court. Between 1812 and 1830 the reluctance of all parties to let go of overseas empire over-shadowed all other issues. The Spanish constitution of 1812—uni-cameral, cumbrous and without any provision for amendment—was a rallying cry for Liberals in the twenties, but after 1830 the much more viable constitution of Belgium began to fill that role.

The smaller states of Europe had the best opportunity after 1815 of developing parliamentary institutions, and some of them used it, though in different ways (Chapter XVII). Their relative freedom from the over-riding preoccupation of other governments with international politics had varying effects. The state constitutions within Germany have already been mentioned. The Baltic was no longer so much a focus of great rivalries, and the Scandinavian countries were all hard hit economically by the peace. In Denmark, the tranquillity of a bureau-cratic but not reactionary government was hardly disturbed until the problem of Schleswig and Holstein began later to create a popular agitation; but both the Swedish estates under the system of 1809 and the

[1] Consalvi to Artois, August 1814. P. Rinieri, *Il Congresso di Vienna*, pp. 271–2, cited in Fliche et Martin, *Histoire de l'Eglise*, vol. xx, by J. Leflon (Paris, 1949), p. 309.

single popular Chamber of Norway (1814) had a genuine existence within the union under their tactful foreign ruler Bernadotte, first as crown prince and then as Charles XIV (1818–44). The independence of the Netherlands and Switzerland was secured by the interest of their greater neighbours in a balance of power and in the containment of France, although both countries underwent the pressure of foreign governments against the activities of political refugees within their borders. Swiss politics were still mainly municipal and patrician until 1847–8, but in the Netherlands the uneasy marriage between Protestant Holland and Catholic Belgium was a spur to organised political parties, and this impetus survived the crisis of separation which was beginning before 1830. Belgium, already the spearhead of the industrial revolution in Europe (Chapter II, pp. 54–5), was soon also to be regarded, under its sagacious king Leopold I, as the model constitutional monarchy on the Continent (Vol. X, p. 191). Its unique separation between Church and State worked tolerably well, and its French culture (after twenty years as part of France) concealed as yet the popular Flemish founda-tion which (in more than half the country) underlay the politically educated classes. William I, during the period of Union (1814–30), found no popular response when he tried to promote, as a counter to French influence, not the Flemish language but the Dutch, which the Flemings of that day could not readily use or even understand.

The significance of the reign of the emperor Alexander I of Russia (1801–25), and of the 'Decembrist' episode on his death, is discussed in Chapter XVIII. The reign began, like several earlier ones, with a palace revolution in almost oriental style, and ended in a mystery deepened by unnecessary, but again not unprecedented, secretiveness within the imperial family as to the succession. Yet during this reign Russia became more than ever before a part of Europe. At home the Slavophil reaction against the 'westernisers' was only just beginning in the 1820's and was officially suspect; abroad, Russophobia was still the exception, not the rule, at least until the Turkish war of 1828–9. As a young man Alexander was steeped in the ideas of his tutor La Harpe, a French-Swiss republican; for some years he leaned on the advice of the Catholic Polish *grand seigneur*, Prince Adam Czartoryski; in the last period he wavered, in foreign policy, between the counsels of other non-Russians: Nesselrode, a professional diplomatist of German origin; Capodistrias, a Corfiot educated in Italy, Greek in sentiment but also feeling more at home in Switzerland than in St Petersburg; and, intermittently, Metter-nich, whose influence on Alexander always faded on the emperor's return to Russia. All these were comparatively young men—well under fifty in 1815—and Alexander himself was only forty-seven when his reign ended in 1825.

In spite of all these 'western' influences, or perhaps *because* they were foreign influences on a man whose environment was Russian, there was another side to Alexander—autocratic, wilful and misty; in the internal government of the Empire his chief personal advisers, though far from being elder statesmen, were wholly Russian. Speranskii, son of an Orthodox priest and himself educated in a seminary, was inclined to administrative reform within a traditional framework; but after his disgrace in 1812 the stage was held by the strange and violent Arakcheev, whose character has never been very intelligible to western observers. Catherine II, a German princess, had been cheerfully cynical enough to keep her balance in an alien world; but a Russian ruler who took himself as seriously as did Alexander I was likely to be mentally divided between his mainly western education and the primitive realities of life around him. When the Russian armies swept across Europe in 1813–14, the current image in the West was that of savage hordes and the 'rule of the knout'; but Russia could no longer be represented as the 'giant with the feet of clay' (Diderot); and soon Parisians, who in any case wanted to cultivate the tsar's good will, were astonished by his own captivating charm and by the intelligent good manners of his entourage. The Russian occupying army was not specially unpopular after the first months; many of its younger officers were welcome in the most 'advanced' salons, and some of them carried home ideas and hopes which led them after December 1825 to the scaffold or to Siberia. Joseph de Maistre's posthumous *Soirées de Saint Pétersbourg* (1822) was a best seller (not only in France), with its brilliant and intimate picture of aristocratic society and its prophecies of an eventual revolution which would make Russia far more powerful than before. The first solid background was provided by the seven volumes (each quickly translated) of Karamzin's *Histoire de l'empire russe* (1819–26).[1] There was some force in Metternich's comment on the death of Alexander I, before the succession was settled: 'the history of Russia will begin where the romance of Russia ends.'[2]

In republican North America (Chapter XXII) constitution-making followed a successful revolution instead of preceding it or being entangled in the process. The direct influence of the United States upon Europe was less noticeable during the wars and their aftermath than in the previous twenty years or in the twenty years after 1830. Frenchmen were immersed in the stream of their own revolution and no longer needed to cite an example which was less relevant in its detailed

---

[1] R. T. McNally, 'Das Russlandbild in der Publizistik Frankreichs, 1814–43', in *Forschungen zur osteuropäischen Geschichte*, Bd. 6 (Berlin, 1958), pp. 82–169.
[2] Metternich to Ottenfels, 18 December 1825. *Memoirs* (Engl. trans., 1889), vol. IV, p. 261.

course than it had been in the general inspiration. Americans were equally preoccupied, and their feelings of goodwill towards France faded in disillusionment. The long sea war hindered their contacts with Europe, and their feelings about the contest from time to time turned largely on the question which side was most interrupting or molesting their overseas trade. On balance, the things that were done or planned in Europe strengthened the federal government at the centre, simply because it had to make big decisions—purchasing Louisiana, protecting its merchants, deciding on war and peace with England (1812–14), and then reacting against rumours of European intervention or even colonisation in Central and South America.

The history of these more southerly Americas, in contrast, was closely connected with that of Europe in this period (Chapter XXIII). 'It would be almost as true to say that Spain fell away from the Indies as to say that the Indies fell away from Spain.'[1] Certainly, the fact that the viceroy of each great province had been linked with Madrid more than with his not very accessible neighbours meant, first that the abdication of Ferdinand VII (1808) left each province bewildered and isolated, and secondly that the independent states formed out of these provinces had no strong foundations for the federal union of which Bolivar and some other leaders dreamed. The movements for independence were ambiguous—partly, at first, in the name of the king against a French usurper in Madrid, but soon (and in some minds from the first) with the declared object of permanent separation from any European political sovereign. Yet there was no break away from the civilisation of the mother countries. By the 1820's, there was no future in the British government's idea of encouraging hereditary monarchies in those provinces which could not be reconciled with Spain by mediation—in spite of the example of Brazil, ruled by the heir to the Portuguese throne, who preferred the troubles of the new world to those of the old. Nevertheless, the constitutions of the new Republics, though showing a mixture of influences from France and from the United States, completely rejected both French Gallicanism and American separation between Church and State; they one and all made the Roman Catholic Church the only publicly recognised religion.

The shifting alignment of the Powers during and after the wars is described in Chapters IX, XXIV and XXV. How far did differing regimes and rival ideologies determine these patterns? In 1793, it seemed that the governments of France's neighbours, and several others that were less nearly threatened, were banded together in defence of the old order against the ideas, the example and the missionary aggression of

---

[1] *Cambridge Modern History*, vol. x (1907), p. 277.

revolutionary France. But their activity was half-hearted: two years later, Prussia, Holland and Spain had made peace (April–July 1795); and Catherine II, though nominally allied to Austria, Prussia and England, kept Russia out of the war while she was completing the partition of Poland. Her successor, Paul I, seems to have been moved by resentments and enthusiasms more than by cool policy; his personal interest in Malta, and his anger at British treatment of neutrals at sea, warred against his disapproval of France and the desire, which inclined him towards Britain, to check French power in Italy and the Mediterranean. Nevertheless, in 1799 a Russian army in Italy and a Russian squadron at Corfu were new portents, almost equally alarming to the governments of France and Britain.

With the consolidation of Napoleon's power as consul and then as emperor, it was only the disinherited princes like the king of Sardinia who never ceased to regard him as a revolutionary usurper. The future Louis XVIII might protest against the recognition of Napoleon's titles by the Pope and later by the sultan, but France was no longer subject to any ideological boycott by governments. They might fear the excessive power of the French Empire, as they would later fear that of the Russian, but their course was mapped by the exigencies of the moment. They might feel doubts about the permanence of Napoleon's power, but in January 1806 the king of Bavaria gave his daughter in marriage to Napoleon's stepson. Four years later, another of the oldest dynasties (and the first to have been at war with revolutionary France) was directly linked by marriage to Napoleon as the founder of a new dynasty; and Austria was reluctant in 1814 to exclude the heir. Even Englishmen, most consistent in their enmity, welcomed the Peace of Amiens in 1801–2, and could not know for certain in advance, for all their suspicions, that it was to be no more than a short-lived truce; nor did the government make a Bourbon restoration into an official aim of the renewed war, as Pitt had virtually done until then. For Alexander I, the alliance with Napoleon at Tilsit (1807) needed no more to be excused than the coalition against him two years earlier; it is true that the ensuing negotiations which dragged on between them only showed how deep and unresolved were the differences in their ideas about Turkey and the Straits, but these differences were not advertised as ingredients in a 'cold war'. The tsar, after rebuffing Napoleon's overture for a Russian princess, resented both his abrupt success in winning an Austrian one instead, and also soon the deposition of Alexander's own brother-in-law by the French annexation of Oldenburg; but almost until the coming invasion of Russia was evident, the forms of friendship and alliance were outwardly preserved.

The campaigns in Russia, and then westwards across Germany, sealed Napoleon's fate, but they also (along with the apparent popularity in

Spain of Wellington's successes) revived in the tsar's mind, for a time, his inclination to confide in popular support. In 1804, he had talked of 'a widespread opinion that the French cause is that of the liberty and prosperity of the nations'.[1] Ten years later he remarked that Napoleon was overthrown not by cabinets but by peoples, and that an outlet must be found for a new spirit in Europe that was at once constitutional, warlike and national.[2] The Prussian government, in escaping from subservience to France, was still much less inclined to put faith in appeals to the people, and in fact Napoleon was defeated by professional armies, not by patriotic volunteers; but not all Prussian officers wanted to return to bureaucratic monarchy—Gneisenau, for example, was as keen for liberal regimes in Germany as he was for unsparing revenge against France. The tsar's mood, combined with his distrust of the Bourbons and the Prussians alike, disposed him to insist on a constitutional charter for France in 1814.

The diplomatic history leading up to the settlement made at Vienna in 1814–15 is sketched in Chapter XXIV, and that of the following years in Chapter XXV. It is generally agreed that 'legitimacy' played only a small part in the minds of the peace-makers, compared with the desire to ensure a fairly stable equilibrium among the powers. Historians still disagree about the precise relation of the Quadruple Alliance for the containment of France to the tsar's notion of an alliance of the powers on a wider basis, with a general guarantee of the settlement and of existing regimes. It has been argued that Alexander looked to France and Spain as maritime powers, and beyond Europe to the United States, to create a global equilibrium under Russian patronage, offsetting both the supremacy of Britain at sea and that of Austria in Central Europe; and that the defeat of his repeated proposals for widening the Alliance was the real triumph of Castlereagh and Metternich in these years. The importance of the United States in the tsar's mind has perhaps been exaggerated,[3] but his conception in September 1815 of a 'Holy Alliance' was certainly not that of a police force of sovereigns against their peoples. Holland and Württemberg were among the first of the smaller states to adhere to it, Switzerland and the Hanse cities did so in the summer of 1817, and an invitation to adhere was not rejected by the United States until as late as June 1819. Nor was it intended as a plan for a crusade against the Turk, for the tsar

---

[1] 11 September 1804. Cited by M. Bourquin, *Histoire de la Sainte Alliance* (Geneva, 1954), p. 19.

[2] K. Waliszewski, *Le règne d'Alexandre I*, vol. II (Paris, 1924), p. 378.

[3] M. Bourquin, *op. cit.*, p. 183, n. 1, casts doubt in this matter on the work, which he for the most part endorsed, of J. H. Pirenne, *Histoire de la Sainte Alliance*, 2 vols. (Neuchatel, 1946, and Geneva, 1954). See also a note on Pirenne's thesis in *Clio*, vol. IX. 1, bk. IV by J. Droz (Paris, 1953), p. 583.

had lately not been averse to a guarantee, including the frontiers of Turkey, provided that Russo-Turkish disputes about the Treaty of Bucharest (1812) were first settled.

The tsar's wider plans were first obscured by their vagueness, then killed by Castlereagh and Metternich, and finally buried by his own change of mood. In the autumn of 1820, he came disillusioned from Warsaw to Troppau, and there had news, before the final Protocol was signed, of a mutiny of his own Semenov regiment. His Holy Alliance of 1815 was not revived, but he was now prepared to use the narrower Alliance for counter-revolutionary ends, while France stood aside and Britain protested. A few months later, the news from Greece put him in a fresh dilemma. He could disavow the revolt, but he could not be indifferent to its consequences. He could be induced to patch up the rupture of relations with Turkey and to part with his now embarrassing servant Capodistrias (July 1822); but the conservative Alliance could not survive this eastern complication or the use which Canning made both of that and of the Spanish American issue to discredit the very conception of a general Alliance of any colour. The Alliance was dead in effect before the tsar himself died (December 1825); within two years it was publicly repudiated by the combination of Russia, England and Bourbon France to settle the Greek question independently of it (Treaty of London, July 1827), and nine months later by the Russian war on Turkey independently of that very combination.

Although the relations between governments, both before and after 1815, were determined by their ambitions, fears and interests rather than by any ideology, the attitude of all rulers (not excluding Napoleon and Alexander) towards their peoples was certainly affected by the fear of 'Jacobinism'. Such fears had not been unreasonable in the 1790's, and were reflected as much in London as in Vienna. The fear of anarchy and violence may have been much exaggerated, and it is true that Napoleon sent many more men to their deaths than did the French Republic (including the Terror) and all its short-lived sister republics. There may be cases where civil strife is in the end more fruitful than foreign war: the American and French Revolutions, and the American Civil War, may be among them. Yet the 'Great Schism' between Frenchmen created by the events of the 1790's was not easily healed; in politics, the memory of heads severed by the guillotine was longer than that of bodies lying on foreign battlefields. From 1800 to 1815, wars and the demands of war everywhere blocked internal reform or gave it a feverish look; after 1815, the fear that radical change might lead to civil strife, and so to foreign war too, certainly made for immobility in politics. Conservatism came not only from the side of governments, for the radicals in Europe (and even in the mobile societies

23

of America) were numerically few, though correspondingly vocal. Secret societies and masonic lodges were not reliable pillars of a 'Holy Alliance of Peoples' against that ascribed to monarchs.

Moreover, not all radicals were admirers of the French example. Some of the reaction to it in thought and literature is described in Chapter IV. It may be added that Mazzini, much as he owed in thought to the Revolution, constantly reproached the French for giving priority to rights over duties; that the acute if eccentric Charles Fourier denounced their conception of liberty and equality in which political and economic power was still reserved to a minority, and to one sex;[1] and that Jeremy Bentham and the early Utilitarians, while they shared the French lack of respect for tradition, had no greater respect for the 'anarchical fallacy' of natural rights. Their campaigns for ruthless lopping off dead wood often made them the allies of political democrats in Europe; but, like Saint-Simon and his disciples, they were bound also to look to technical administrators and even to enlightened autocrats for the diffusion of happiness by 'improvement'. Bentham himself in old age wrote flattering letters to Muhammad Ali, the autocrat of Egypt, and the influence of the Utilitarians upon English administrators in India was conspicuous (Chapter XX).[2]

Probably the strongest link between radicalism after 1815 and the eighteenth century (whether of the Enlightenment or of the Revolution) was that of anti-clerical sentiment, which had become (what it had not been to Joseph II) a sentiment of suspicion against all institutional religion, especially that of Rome. This sentiment, fostered by the privileged position of the higher clergy in many countries, was expressed at all levels, from philosophic doubt, or the refined mockery of Stendhal, to the vulgar abuse of Paul-Louis Courier. The indirect method of Diderot, partly dictated by the censorship, and the polite scepticism of Voltaire or Gibbon, were now replaced by frontal attacks; but the old appeal to 'common sense' rationalism or deism, presenting the Christian religion as irrelevant or ridiculous for educated men of taste, was still in this period commoner than the painful quest of the serious agnostic confronted by unwelcome new difficulties (stemming from biblical criticism or natural science) in accepting the traditional expression of revealed religion (Chapter VI). In between, a high minded man in public life, who was repelled by hedonism or materialism and felt the immense social value of Christian tradition, might adopt, in effect, a position of 'Christian deism', not unlike that of Benjamin Jowett a little later. Guizot, nursed in the Geneva school, was occupied to the end of his life in trying to find, within the Huguenot church, an

---

[1] R. C. Bowles, 'The reactions of Charles Fourier to the French Revolution', in *French Historical Studies*, vol. I, pp. 348–56 (North Carolina State College, 1960).
[2] Cf. E. T. Stokes, *The English Utilitarians and India* (Oxford, 1959).

eclectic confession which would avoid the most thorny questions, and he never spoke disrespectfully of serious Catholics. Tocqueville, whose Catholic upbringing never lost its attraction for him, felt no sense of liberation when he ceased about 1820 to be a practising or believing Catholic. His acceptance of the sacraments at the end of his life was probably a gesture against the militant critics of Rome rather than a sign of total re-conversion.[1]

In any case, the vast majority of men (not to mention the other half of the human race, whose disposition was much neglected by male thinkers) were not apt to find religion irrelevant or ridiculous in their personal lives, even if they often treated it with the neglect of familiarity except on the occasion of birth, marriage and death. Literate or illiterate, satisfied or hungry, they might, like their betters, find the precepts of religion inconvenient to their desires; but they were not likely to find intellectually unacceptable a religion which taught that the illiterate and the simple were as capable as the learned of reflection and of spiritual insight. For most people, the pattern of living was still governed by the seasons, among the neighbours in the village or small town; if they had any leisure, it was not occupied, or distracted, by daily newspapers or by organised sport and entertainment. It seems likely then that, where anti-clerical radicalism met with a popular response, that response was not a considered rejection of Christian teaching as such, but rather a protest against the failure of churches and their clergy to live up to it— and in passing judgment on the clergy many people were apt to expect of them a standard of conduct which they would never dream of applying to themselves. The momentary popularity of the clergy, even in Paris, in February to March 1848 was to suggest that republican or at least popular sentiment was not necessarily anti-clerical.

However that may be, the most spectacular movements of the 1820's —the Greek revolt and the struggles for independence in South America —were not as radical in their aims as in their methods. Simple Orthodox sentiment against the infidel Turk, and a very simple notion of political freedom, were the driving popular forces among the fighting men in Greece; and the same sentiments were more or less shared by most of their native leaders. In South America some of the leaders were perhaps more separated from their people in their religious and political aims, but the new republics, however unstable, seemed much less revolutionary in the event than in their origins. Metternich no doubt understood this: he seems to have been more concerned in South America about the method and the example than about the result; and, again, to have meant what he said when, as early as 1825, he suggested a small independent Greece in preference to a larger one dependent nominally on

[1] D. S. Goldstein, 'The religious beliefs of de Tocqueville', in *French Historical Studies*, vol. I, pp. 379–415 (North Carolina State College, 1960).

Turkey but actually upon Russian good will. If political immobility was still the watchword in Metternich's Austria until 1848, and in Russia over Alexander I's last years and the whole reign of Nicholas I (1825–55), that may be ascribed not only to the ruling personalities but even more to the peculiar problems of those two Empires, problems which the shock of 1848 in Austria and that of 1856 in Russia made evident to the world but did little to solve.

From about 1828, however, the mounting discontent in France and Belgium, which led men of such conservative temper as Guizot or Louis de Potter to skate (for quite different reasons) on the edge of revolution; in Britain, the relief of Protestant dissenters and Roman Catholics (measures hitherto politically impossible) and the growing agitation for parliamentary reform; in Germany the implications of the Prussian tariff unions for the future; in the United States the election of Andrew Jackson as President—all these, with the muted revolutions of 1830, seem to announce the advent of a new generation, less unwilling to face unwelcome changes, or less Utopian in demanding or prophesying change. Tories and Whigs were to become conservatives and liberals. There is something novel in the enormous success in many languages of Tocqueville's *Democracy in America* (2 vols., 1835, 1840), or in Bentinck's decision to introduce western education in India (1835). Both these men were of aristocratic birth and leanings, but the one took an open-eyed plunge in thought, and the other a bold plunge of policy, neither of which can easily be imagined twenty years earlier. Gregory XVI was to give way to Pius IX, bringing hopes, for a time, to liberal Catholics. Proudhon (the first social-revolutionary writer of working-class origin) and Karl Marx were to go much further than their predecessors, but both claimed to be more interested in facts than in the moral foundation of rights, and to be no Utopians. The building of a heavenly city on earth was to give way to social engineering.

'If state power was advancing, the power of public opinion was advancing too' (Chapter VII, p. 180). The freedom of the press, proclaimed in 1789, was strictly limited, not only by governments of all shades which either suppressed or manipulated news and opinion, but also by small circulations, lack of financial independence and consequent venality. Yet the principle was reaffirmed in the French and other constitutions after Napoleon's fall, and the growing importance of the newspaper press was seen, despite fluctuating restrictions, in the public controversies over principles throughout the restoration period in France and in its direct influence on politics in England, especially in the debate about parliamentary reform. Deeper currents of opinion in literature and thought were, naturally, reflected less in newspapers than in periodical reviews, which abounded in England and France after the wars; although often the ephemeral organs of small groups, they were the forum for the battles between the classical and the romantic in literature, the utilitarian and the idealist in philosophy and to some extent also between the traditional and the critical in religion.

But the key to victory in these contests was seen to be in the school and the university; in both, the question of the method and purpose of education was central. The followers of Rousseau looked first to the release of individual powers, Pestalozzi and Robert Owen to the promotion of social utility and purpose in popular education. In secondary and higher education, Wilhelm von Humboldt gave great impetus in Germany to the gospel of classical humanism; philologists set the tone in the gymnasia, historians also and jurists in the universities. But the role of the state in organising a lay teaching profession gave it a commanding position in Prussia after 1815 (at least above the primary level), while in France the tradition of regimentation introduced by Napoleon was continued, with a different emphasis, during the Restoration. Napoleon's University was not hostile to Catholicism, provided it was loyal to the Concordat and the imperial regime. Fontanes, its grand master, was continued at first under Louis XVIII, and the aristocratic royalists failed to get rid of the Concordat or the University, those twin monsters created by the usurper. The clergy soon had much more power in primary and secondary education, but hardly succeeded in penetrating very deeply into the University, either in filling posts or in reorienting its tone. Lamennais and the crusaders continued to see in it the stronghold of 'indifferentism'.

The influence of religion in education was greater at all levels in England than in France or probably in Germany. This was in spite or even because of the denominational rivalry at the primary stage between Church and dissent, represented by Andrew Bell's National Society and the British and Foreign Society whose founder, Joseph Lancaster, was also the apostle of his peculiar but economical 'mutual system' of instruction by the pupils. Neither party enjoyed state aid, though governments took for granted a close link between education and religion. In the endowed grammar schools, both the many local ones and the few that catered for the upper class, Latin and Greek were the stuff of education, often with very little mathematics; but languages and even some science were taught in some of the private unendowed schools, including the dissenting academies which reached into higher education too. Oxford and Cambridge were notorious for laxity in observing their statutes. At least, able young Anglicans could and did educate each other and find intellectual stimulus among some of their seniors in these close societies; but the minimum standard required could hardly have been lower. The wind of reform breathed very gently until the middle of the nineteenth century. In the absence of any real system of higher education, scholarship and culture had been nourished mainly in the reading habits of those English gentlemen who used and added to their private libraries, and in their patronage of exceptionally gifted men who were noticed locally and found their way to a literary or legal career in London, or through the universities into the established Church. The results were sometimes eccentric, but could also be exceedingly fruitful.

Behind the dramatic reversals of fortune in politics and war, and not demonstrably connected with them or with the dispersed operation of new economic forces, individuals or very small groups of men were making discoveries or influencing thought in ways which pointed to even greater changes in the pattern of men's lives, or in their outlook on life. Scientific discoveries must be individual and sometimes lonely; the great men had worked in relative isolation, linked only by a common passion for measuring, explaining and reducing to order what they found in nature, or in elaborating the mathematical tools which could help them to do so. Such individual intellectual enterprise was not new, but discoveries were now becoming cumulative. Some of these men were diffusing knowledge as teachers and in systematic treatises. The organisation and dissemination of knowledge was beginning to produce a profession of scientists and a more widespread readiness to embrace new scientific ideas. In Paris and in the centres directly influenced by French 'cultural imperialism', the State honoured and aided scientists, especially those who could be of service to it. The French *Institut* and *École Polytechnique* gave impetus to similar developments elsewhere, above all in the Prussian Academy and the new University of Berlin (1810), nursed by the Humboldt brothers, and in other German centres, whose fame was later to outstrip that of the French models.

This process of organisation, with the prospect of careers open to scientific talent, is described in Chapter V, along with a survey of achievements such as those of Laplace in mathematical analysis, of Lagrange and Joseph Fourier in the abstract analysis of mechanics and heat, of Volta, Ampère and others in electricity, of Dalton and Berzelius among others in physical chemistry, of Lamarck and Cuvier (from different angles) in systematic biology, of Bichat and Magendie in experimental biology, of Hutton and Smith in geology. Geology and biology were soon to impinge on traditional beliefs about the antiquity of life on earth and (with much continuing debate among scientists) about the origin of different species.

'Theoretical science still had little to offer to industry', but in the rational and empirical 'coercion of opportunity . . . the behaviour of the engineers and industrialists resonates with that of men of science' (Chapter V, p. 141). The steam-engine and the infant chemical industry, for instance, owed more to experience than to theory, but there were links between invention and theory in Sadi Carnot's reflections on heat, or in Faraday's experiments, which gave birth respectively to thermodynamics and to the dynamo. The metric system is a legacy of the Revolution, launched in 1799 but not widely used for forty years. The use of uniform and interchangeable parts for machines, awards to inventors and patents for their protection, technical dictionaries and journals—all these began or multiplied in this age. In technology, England naturally played a big part, and there the period ends, fittingly in this field, with the spread of Mechanics' Institutes and the foundation in 1831 of the British Association for the Advancement of Science.

'Cross and tricolour had become opposing symbols for millions of Europeans in 1793' (Chapter VI, p. 146). That chapter surveys the conflicts and reconciliations between governments and organised churches during the next forty years, and suggests some of the internal questionings within the churches, springing not only from Catholic doubts about the marriage of throne and altar but also from deeper challenges to traditional apologetics, especially among the Protestants. Schleiermacher claimed that religion was 'not a set of propositions or an ethical code, but an inward experience, direct, intuitive, existing in its own right as a central part of human life' (Chapter VI, p. 169); Christian doctrines expressed Christian experience; they were historically conditioned, and their expression could alter as the nature of that experience altered through time. Thus theology would be prepared to meet the challenge of new knowledge and of new experiences too.

The political controversies of the age were less directly reflected in the arts (Chapter VIII) than in literature, education and ecclesiastical affairs. The confused battles between ancients and moderns, between classical (or pseudo-classical) and romantic, between the supremacy of form acceptable to cultivated common sense and that of personal feelings movingly expressed—these battles were not fought by armies in clearly contrasted uniforms but by mingled individuals and groups in motley dress and varying postures. A 'classical' battle-scene of the empire could be as sensational in its effect as a 'romantic' landscape could be discreet and elegant. It is even more rash to pin simple labels on to the great music of this period. But the place of music in society was changing in a way not unlike that of science, in that it was taking a more professional shape, with public concerts appearing alongside private chamber music; and composers were concerned, like authors, with publishers and the public.

The developments in science and technology, in educational theory and practice and the marshalling of opinion through the press, in theology and church life, or again in music and the visual arts—these did not all point in the same direction. Pure science and technology were not very closely linked either in method or purpose. Each, by concentrating on measurable and manageable knowledge, would give rise to new powers: intellectual power, bringing its own special kind of satisfaction; empirical power, insatiable and apparently uncontrollable in its social effects. Neither science nor technology had power to bring order into the lives of individuals or into the affairs of men in society. Paradoxically, the 'enlightened' idea of education for efficiency and opportunity—of the career open to talents—went along with Rousseau's notion of education to liberate the generous sentiments of the man and the citizen. Both rational deism and the revolutionary cult of civic patriotism, with its quasi-religious symbolism, could become as much the hand-maids of power politics as could older ecclesiastical systems. The rational and the intuitive were not bound to cross swords if they could keep to their autonomous paths. Could they not indeed be different activities of the same person—why should he not delight both in ordering knowledge or improving practical devices and also in cherishing an image of himself and his relations with other persons or in finding a clue to the wonder and the pain of man's existence? Yet the two did cross swords when each was apt to claim a monopoly. Like empire and papacy, they were not easily contained in a Gelasian theory of autonomous co-existence. The rational and positive spirit would slip into a rationalist and positivist strait-waistcoat, mistaking it for an imperial robe; and the intuitive spirit would wade into a treacherous bog of subjective romanticism, mistaking it for a glorious ocean plunge. Possibly the music of Beethoven came nearest to harmonising the two for this age.

CHAPTER II

ECONOMIC CHANGE IN ENGLAND AND EUROPE, 1780–1830

IN 1834 it seemed to Chateaubriand that 'Europe is racing towards democracy. . . . France and England, like two enormous battering-rams, beat again and again upon the crumbling ramparts of the old society.' Certainly the powerful influences of political and economic liberalism, stemming largely from the French Revolution and the English Industrial Revolution, had already begun to affect Europe. By 1830 England was transmitting to Europe and overseas—by direct influence or by example—new methods of production, new economic policies, and new social attitudes that favoured rapid economic growth. England, indeed, was 'the engine of growth' that forced European and world development, mainly by the expansion of international trade and by the emigration of men and capital. The long-term result was increased international specialisation and interdependence, and the creation of a world network of trading and financial relations, but national changes by 1830, except in England and in Belgium, were not dramatic. In spite of focal points of development in the coal fields of England and Belgium, and in spite of universal pre-occupation with industry, still over the vast area of Europe men's way of life and men's way of earning a living remained much the same as they had been for centuries, especially in southern, central and eastern regions. In 1826 a Belgian deputy, with his eyes on the growing industries of his own country, proclaimed that: 'All nations have turned their eyes towards industry, the sure and inexhaustible source of wealth; and toward foreign trade, which can give immense extension to industry.' In 1830, however, the European economy was predominantly agricultural. Even in England, where in 1760 agriculture employed between 40 and 50 per cent of the population, it still accounted for 35 per cent in 1800 and 25 per cent in 1830. Nowhere else was this proportion as low: in Italy and France 60 per cent of the population was rural in 1830, in Prussia over 70 per cent, in Spain 90 per cent, and in Russia and generally in eastern Europe 95 per cent.

Nevertheless, cities and towns were growing in size, and were slowly absorbing an increasing proportion of total population. By 1830 there were in Europe perhaps twenty-five cities of over 100,000 people (including four in England and one in Scotland), and London, with almost a million in 1800, had now a million and a half; Paris had over three-quarters of a million; Constantinople perhaps half a million;

St Petersburg and Naples more than 300,000; Vienna, Moscow, Berlin, Amsterdam and Dublin over 200,000; and Hamburg, Warsaw, Milan, Rome, Madrid, Palermo, Venice, Lyons, Budapest, Marseilles and Barcelona more than 100,000 each. The distribution of towns and of population in Europe, however, was little different in 1830 from what it had been in the middle of the fifteenth century. Towns were spread fairly evenly over the countryside, and served mainly as centres of industry, commerce and administration for their surrounding districts. Only in three areas was there marked concentration—in northern Italy, in the Low Countries, and in England—and only in England in this period was there a marked change in distribution (towards the midlands and north) together with a marked increase in town population. In Europe the distribution of towns and of population was still largely determined by agriculture; in England concentration was already linked closely to coal. In Europe the main urban growth was in capital cities; in England, it was widely dispersed. In Europe there remained the tendency, that had been general in 1750, towards uniform population density over wide areas, varying in most countries between sixty and ninety persons per square mile (with Belgium and Italy higher, and Spain lower); in England distribution was concentrated, outside of London, in the Birmingham–Liverpool–Hull triangle, without depopulation of agricultural counties in this period but with a noticeable drift of the increasing population to this growing industrial area.

The continued dependence on agriculture and the slow growth of cities, however, is no measure of economic change before 1830. Perhaps the outstanding economic fact of the previous century had been the increase in Europe's population. This grew from about 100 to 140 millions between 1650 and 1750, to 187 millions by 1800, to 274 millions by 1850. The average annual rate of growth had been 0·3 per cent before 1750; by 1900 it was 1·2 per cent. Although the increase was general throughout Europe, it varied in degree from country to country: between 1750 and 1850 England grew fastest—on average 1 per cent per annum; Prussia, Italy and Spain, for example, grew at about half that rate. Between 1800 and 1850 the rate of growth in England reached 1·5 per cent per annum, and in the period 1780 to 1830 a large part of Europe's population was growing at a rate that would have doubled population by 1900.[1] No certainty exists about the immediate causes of this increase—increasing fertility and/or decreasing mortality—or about the ultimate social and economic factors that determined those social indices. As a European phenomenon, and one that began early

[1] Population (in millions):

Year	Russia	Austria	France	Germany	Britain	Italy	Spain
1800	c. 40	28	28	23	15	18	15
1830	c. 57	36	35	35	28	25	18

in the eighteenth century, it cannot be explained, as English historians have often explained it, by industrialisation. If it was due to declining mortality, it was certainly not due to improvements in medicine and hospitals, for these had little effect before the third quarter of the nineteenth century. If it was due to increasing fertility, it was not due to a significant change in the age of marriage, for the modern marriage pattern was already established before industrialisation and urbanisation. Most demographers would agree, however, that there was a significant reduction in mortality during the eighteenth century, and that this was the primary cause of population increase. The expectation of life, where the statistics allow estimates, was certainly increasing: in Sweden between 1755 and 1840 from 33 to 40; in the United States of America between 1789 and 1850 from 35 to 41. Expectation of life in France by 1832 was 38 and in England by 1841 was 40. In particular, more children were surviving, and infant mortality rates were gradually reduced from their former terrifying levels. After centuries of stable or slowly growing populations the limits to growth were lifted in the eighteenth century. The amplitude of the cycle of mortality was diminished as plague and famine lost their intensity, and populations in consequence no longer underwent periodical decimations.

The gradual decline of plague was perhaps fortuitous—the unexplained disappearance of the black rat from Europe?—but the lessening impact of famine was the result of improvements in agriculture. Adam Smith had argued that 'the cultivation and improvement of the country ... must necessarily be prior to the increase of the town'. The long-run equilibrium of food supply and population (later so pessimistically analysed by Malthus) meant that the progress of agriculture was essential for industrial development. The large increase in population, and the long-run diversion of labour to industry, was possible only because food production expanded, because both the area and productivity of cultivation increased. In the eighteenth century the relationship of population to resources began to change: before 1700 the size of population was determined by the food-production possibilities of a traditional agriculture, and towns and industry were concentrated where there was abundant food; after 1700 there was increased agricultural productivity that, in combination with improved communications and industrialisation, and increased international and inter-regional trade, made it possible for Europe to feed its rapidly growing numbers. The supply of food, hitherto so inflexible that every harvest failure meant famine and the Malthusian check to population, was becoming more flexible. The economic conditions that hitherto had made progressive agriculture profitable only in regions of higher population-density were changing, and an increasing demand for food and raw materials was stimulating increasing production.

33

The market force in this change was a sustained upward movement in prices, especially of grain, after 1750, to a high war level after 1790 that was maintained until 1815. The technical changes that enabled increased production were: enclosures, the reduction of fallow with better crop rotations, and the related cultivation of fodder crops; land reclamation and additions to the area of tillage; and improvements in techniques and changes in organisation (in the farm unit and in property and tenurial rights) that increased productivity. Thus, reclamation in Italy, the Netherlands and France, beginning in the seventeenth and continuing into the eighteenth century, added arable in the west and south of Europe; the colonisation of the Ukraine steppes and of the Caucasus and Transcaucasia in the late eighteenth and early nineteenth centuries added vast agricultural areas to Russia in the east; and in England enclosures and the conversion of pasture added arable in an area of progressive agriculture.

But not only was more land cultivated, it was cultivated more efficiently in more places. No period in the history of European agriculture is richer in innovations.[1] The most important invention was the Brabant plough and its English counterpart the Rotherham plough— prototype of modern ploughs—that allowed deeper ploughing and the intensive farming of large estates. Appearing early in the eighteenth century, it was in wide use by 1800. Deeper ploughing, more manuring (provided by more livestock) and bed-and-row cultivation (made easier by the seed drill) made for better crops; better harvesting (with the increasing use of the scythe, the threshing block and the winnowing machine) made yields even greater. Equally important were inter-related crop and livestock improvements: the increasing use of forage and root crops (for example, clover, lucerne, turnips and potatoes) in better rotations, more leys (*prairies artificielles*), and better crop care. All these increased productivity sufficiently to allow more winter feeding of livestock, while selective breeding and better animal husbandry increased carcase weights and yields of wool and milk. The increase in the weight of sheep and cattle slaughtered at Smithfield in London is well known; equally striking, however, was the increase in milk yields in Germany and the Netherlands, from less than 150 gallons per cow during lactation in 1750, up to 220 and even 400 gallons in 1800, with associated improvements in butter churns and cheese presses.[2] Good rotations with forage crops had been used for some time in advanced agricultural districts like Flanders, but they came into more general use only after 1750.

[1] G. E. Fussell, *The Farmer's Tools 1500–1900* (London, 1952) has shown that there were only seven important agricultural inventions in the seventeenth century, eight between 1701 and 1750, thirty between 1751 and 1814, and sixteen between 1815 and 1848.

[2] B. H. Slicher van Bath, *De agrarische geschiedenis van West-Europa (500–1850)* (Utrecht/Antwerp, 1960); translated by O. Ordish (London, 1963).

Broadly speaking 'the old agriculture' was associated with common field farming, servile tenures for the cultivators, and subsistence crops: villages and open fields were the bases of rural life, and in 1750 from north-east France to the Urals there was little but open fields worked on a three-field rotation, with common pastures and woodlands and with primitive equipment. 'The new agriculture' tended to be the profit farming of cash crops (food or industrial raw materials) on small or medium-sized consolidated farms held on tenures determined by a free market. Agricultural surplus in the eighteenth century came mainly from large estates; in the early nineteenth increasingly from the small farm. In the century 1750 to 1850 the modern pattern of European agriculture—that of small intensively worked family farms—was established. 'The most general spontaneous tendency' was the spread of the dispersed farmhouse and the accompanying dissolution of nucleated villages; for example, the intensive cultivation of small farms in Belgium, Holland, French Flanders, around Paris, in Tuscany and Lombardy, and in parts of Portugal and Spain. In Spain, it was said, 'where small farming prevails, the land is a garden; where estates are large, a desert.' England was the exception where the best farming was on large estates, and where peasant farming was assumed to be, generally, as wretched as in Ireland. Elsewhere in Europe the persistence of large estates—in Prussia, Poland, Russia, Roumania, Hungary, southern Italy and southern Spain—was due both to geographical conditions that made intensive farming difficult or uneconomic, and also to socio-political conditions that strengthened the proprietary rights of the feudal landlord.

Generally there were moves throughout western Europe to strengthen the cultivators' rights to the land, to remove feudal obligations and to convert 'inferior' rights to land into 'full' ownership. By 1850 serfdom had disappeared from Europe except in Russia and Roumania. In this disappearance the French revolutionaries set a striking example by the abolition of feudal rights without compensation. This new liberalism, however, only carried forward what had been partly achieved already by eighteenth-century princes in their attempts to strengthen royal authority by pruning the powers of the land-owning aristocracy. And even earlier feudalism had disappeared from England, and much of it from France. Between 1790 and 1815 territories dominated or influenced by France also passed anti-feudal legislation—Holland, Prussia, Spain and Italy—but the extent of reform, and the compensation to the feudal landowner, varied. Moreover, there was some restoration of feudal rights after 1815, for example in Italy and Spain, with the result that quasi-feudal tenures persisted in southern and eastern Europe throughout the nineteenth century.

Indeed generalisations of any kind are difficult. Not all land passed, by ownership or tenure, into the hands of the peasants; nor were all farms consolidated; nor were all efficient or even improving. The large estates of England and of northern France were efficient, as was much common-field agriculture in south-west Germany; the consolidated farms of Spain and of south-west France were generally inefficient. The distribution of land-ownership broadened with the relaxation of feudal tenures and the commercialisation of farming, but more land was held in 1830 by *métayers* or tenants (and short tenures were common) than by owners. In Belgium the tenant farmer dominated, in Switzerland the small land-owner, in Lombardy the *métayer*. *Métayage*[1] was probably the most common and the least satisfactory tenurial arrangement. 'The *métayers* never get rich,' J. C. Loudon wrote of Lombardy, 'and are seldom totally ruined; they are not often changed'. Fragmentation of estates also continued in spite of the breakdown of communal farming. In Prussia, for example, legislation was more effective in promoting consolidation than it was in France where this occurred mainly in the large farms in the north. In the period 1780 to 1830 the only countries where fragmentation was disappearing were the United Kingdom and Scandinavia. Elsewhere in Europe farms were often made up of one or more plots, and even as late as 1900 more than one-third of Europe's farms were fragmented. Similarly, the size of farms varied even in the same area, although there was a tendency for medium-sized farms, usually consolidated, in north-west Europe (for example in Scandinavia), and for a combination of very large estates and very small farms, with considerable fragmentation, in the south and east (for example in Sicily). And within national boundaries differences were often striking; for example, the contrast between northern and southern France. Regional differences extended also to the goods produced, for these reflected the organisation as much as the fertility of farming units. By 1830 the south of Europe was tending to specialise in horticulture, the north in animal production, the east in grain. Generally agriculture was less intensive moving from north-west to south-east, and this intensity could be measured by the amount of capital and labour employed, and by the concentration of livestock that was possible only with intensive fodder-production. In all areas the stimulus from growing towns was evident. As J. Caird noted later: 'The production of vegetables and fresh meat, forage, and pasture for dairy cattle, will necessarily extend as the towns become more numerous and more populous.' Grain, requiring less capital, less labour, less care and more land, was increasingly grown on the periphery of Europe and shipped inwards and westwards.

[1] *Métayage* is a system of land tenure in which the cultivator pays a proportion (usually half) of the product as rent to the owner of the land, who furnishes the stock and seed, or part thereof.

As tenure, size, intensity and products varied, so did efficiency. In spite of widespread progress, with notable increases in productivity, the process was well under way by 1830 that would make European farms too small, and that would also make generally true the equation of peasantry and poverty. Acute, even desperate food shortages still occurred although improved communications made their effects less deadly. In the south and east there was still dire poverty as agricultural labourers and peasants eked out subsistence livings on *latifundia* and on minute farms. And in those areas the concentration of land-holding was 'a sort of provocation of levelling legislative measures' and the future source of revolution.

An important stimulus for agricultural development was the increasing demand for agricultural products in international trade. For example, British imports contained only 30 per cent of 'groceries' and raw materials in 1700 and 60 per cent in 1800, while between 1814 and 1845 foodstuffs averaged 28 per cent and raw materials 67 per cent of total imports. The significance of growing home markets for agricultural products in this period is well illustrated by the rapid increase in the production of sugar-beet and potatoes; and that of a growing international market by the increase and improvements in wool production, especially from the spread of the Merino sheep. The first sugar-beet factory was built in Silesia in 1801; by 1836 European production totalled 750,000 tons. Potatoes were first grown extensively outside Britain in the last quarter of the eighteenth century: after 1800 their production increased rapidly in France and Germany until by mid-century they were becoming part of the staple diet of west Europeans. Increasing wool production can be measured by British imports, Britain being the largest manufacturer of woollen cloth: imports averaged 2·5 million lb. annually from 1776 to 1799 and 35·2 millions from 1830 to 1834, the main suppliers being Spain until 1820 and Germany thereafter. Introduced into France and Germany in the eighteenth century, the Merino also provided in both these countries the essential raw material of a growing domestic wool textile industry.

To support the growing population of Europe, improved communications were just as necessary as the increase in the production of food. Larger towns and more industry involved the transport not only of food but of raw materials and manufactured goods; there was an increase both in the exchange of goods and also of the distances goods travelled. 'Railways, express mails, steamboats, and all possible means of communication are what the educated world seeks,' Goethe observed in 1825. And these means of communication had to be cheaper, especially for the movement of commodities like minerals that were heavy in bulk and low in value, so that the value added by transport costs was not so great as to make specialisation unprofitable. Agricultural specialisation in the Netherlands after 1816, for example, meant increasing exports of butter to the United Kingdom, and increasing imports of grain from the Baltic. In industry massive specialisation before 1830 was confined to Britain, which could still almost feed herself although she was increasingly dependent on imported raw materials: in 1830 wheat imports were 2·2 million quarters, cotton imports 261·2 million lb., and wool imports 32·3 million lb.

Within Britain (and to a lesser extent in Europe) the increasing use of coal was the most powerful stimulus to improved communications. While the consumption of coal was small, it was transported in small quantities by pack animal and cart, and in larger quantities by river and sea where pit and market were as fortunately situated as Newcastle and London. As consumption increased, waterways were first improved and then constructed specifically to carry coal. The first modern canals of England were the Sankey Brook from St Helen's coalfield to the Mersey (1757) and the Duke of Bridgewater's from the Worsley mines to Manchester (1761). Canal building was, of course, an old art in Europe, but the English canal system was built between 1750 and 1850 in response to new incentives, and after the main river improvements of the previous century. The canals of England were an essential part of the increasingly intricate and roundabout processes of manufacture and distribution. The map of English canals is the map of industrial England; in 1750 there were only 1000 miles of navigable waterways; by 1850 4250 miles of canals linked the main rivers and industrial towns with the ports and London.

In Europe also there was a great extension of waterways, but nowhere except in France and in the Low Countries was there a canal system so intimately related to economic development as in England. Outside those areas there was more river improvement than canal building in the first half of the nineteenth century. In France by 1830 Paris was linked to the south with the Loire, and to the north with the growing industries and coal mines of Belgium. In Belgium an elaborate network, partly ancient but greatly extended in the late eighteenth and early nineteenth centuries, joined the coal mines of Mons and Charleroi southwards to Paris and northwards to Brussels, Ghent and Antwerp. Holland, however, although equipped with many canals, was not linked with the Belgian system until after 1830, and until then was deprived of Belgian coal as a vital raw material of development. Elsewhere in Europe canal building before 1830 was sporadic and nowhere formed part of a national system of transport as in England.

The improvement of roads was more widespread and economically less significant than the construction of canals, and the motives for it were also different. Road improvement, like anti-feudal legislation before 1789, was very much the product of enlightened despotism, of absolute monarchy and economic nationalism. Thus, for example, the need felt by central authorities for good roads, the creation of administrative and technical bodies to make and maintain roads, the improvements in wheeled vehicles and increased traffic, produced in France by 1780 25,000 miles of classified roads. The French road system, a model for Europe, was maintained and extended by the military ambitions of Napoleon beyond the borders of France, into the Low Countries, Germany and Italy. In Scotland, as in France, the need for roads was partly military; but in England the motives were more economic, and the solution more piece-meal. Responsibility for roads after 1750 passed increasingly from local authorities to *ad hoc* statutory Turnpike Trusts of which 3783 existed in 1829. British roads were improved, and the road-making techniques of Telford and McAdam were widely used outside Britain; but with the rapid growth of canals, roads played only a minor role in the bulk transport of food, raw materials and manufactured goods. In Europe since the eighteenth century road improvement had advanced little by 1830, and transport remained a bottleneck to economic expansion until the development of railways.

But better roads and more canals were not the only transport improvements before 1830; important developments in the techniques of carrying commodities culminated after 1830 in the locomotive and the steam ship. There were locomotives by 1830, but their existence was an example for the future, not an illustration of present realities. Similarly, although there was a steam ship on the Clyde in 1812 and one on the Seine in 1822, the last great age of wood and sail lasted into the thirties, and ship development reached its perfection, not in size but in design, in the fast clipper. In ship making, copper sheathing of ships' bottoms and the increasing use of iron in structure and equipment were important developments, but in 1830 there were only thirty-nine steam ships, averaging 87 tons net, registered in the United Kingdom. The change in shipping was in quantity not in kind, and Europe's merchant fleet expanded rapidly between 1780 and 1830. Some measure of this increase can be gauged from the number of ships (British and foreign) employed in the foreign trade of Great Britain; these increased from 5182 vessels (average 180 tons) to 19,907 (average 146 tons) between 1783 and 1830. There were many more ships on the world's oceans in 1830, even if their design and size had changed little in fifty years.

'The central problem of the age,' T. S. Ashton has written of England, 'was how to feed and clothe and employ generations of children outnumbering by far those of any earlier time.'[1] In retrospect the population increase is the most startling feature of the period 1780 to 1830, but to contemporaries in Europe it was the industrial advance of England that impressed. In the eighteenth century English superiority

---

[1] T. S. Ashton, *The Industrial Revolution, 1760–1830* (Oxford, 1948), p. 161.

was attributed to a superior political system, to limited as against absolute monarchy; in the early nineteenth century almost entirely to machine technology. In 1740 the phrase 'à l'imitation de l'Angleterre' was already common, but by 1830 England was 'the schoolmaster of industrial Europe', visited continuously, and sending forth entrepreneurs, engineers, foremen and operatives to found and to work industrial concerns throughout Europe. In France the foundations of most of the great metallurgical enterprises were preceded by visits to England; in Belgium an English family, the Cockerills, had created by 1830 the largest industrial firm in Europe; the puddling process was introduced into Germany in 1824 by the Remy and Hoesch families (two of whose members had studied it in England) with the help of English puddlers.[1] There was envy of and desire for 'the marvellous machines' of England (as J. A. Blanqui called them in 1823), and the prohibition on the export of British machinery and on the emigration of British artisans was widely ignored long before it was repealed.

Britain was the first country to experience an industrial revolution, but the causes of this revolution and the reasons for British leadership have never been adequately explained. The sharp upward movement that marked the revolution in industrial production in England occurred in the decade 1780–90, but this was after eighty years during which production had been increasing at a rate of 2 per cent per annum and international trade had quadrupled. By 1780 French development was also impressive, with a similar rate of growth of industry and, also, a quadrupling of trade. But there were two important differences. First, since 1660 British coal mines had been producing five times as much coal as the combined output of European mines; production exceeded that of France thirty times in 1700 and still twenty times in 1800. On the Continent coal was little used before 1750, and its general use after 1800 came 150 years later than in Britain. Britain's annual consumption was already one-half ton *per capita* in 1700, and had doubled by 1800. Coal in Britain was the first raw material in history to be measured in millions of tons; its bulk transport justified massive investment in canals; the problems of its mining stimulated the perfection of the steam engine; it was the fuel essential for the mass production of iron—without which there could have been no industrial revolution, and of bricks— without which housing could never have kept pace with population. A second difference was less tangible, but even more decisive. In Britain industrial and commercial development was spontaneous; in France, and in other countries, it was tinged with artificiality, the result of the efforts of absolute monarchs for conspicuous consumption and economic nationalism. In France, for example, varying degrees of State ownership

---

[1] See W. O. Henderson, *Britain and Industrial Europe, 1750–1870* (Liverpool University Press, 1954), for a detailed account of the activities of the British in European industry.

or aid created a hierarchy of manufacturing concerns.[1] In Britain there were also privileged companies, but generally the market and not the government determined the profitability and hence the survival of industrial concerns.

Freedom of enterprise, however, was only one characteristic of a social environment in Britain that was more favourable to economic change than elsewhere: an environment in which there was political stability and social mobility, the general acceptance of a secular and individualist philosophy, a widespread knowledge of science and technology, and greater security for person and property than in Europe. Although other countries had shared in the secularisation of life and in the advance of science, and, with the enlightenment, in the liberalising of economic and social affairs, yet Britain, compared with France, had progressed much farther in the breakdown of economic regulation and of corporate enterprise; compared with Germany, she had the advantages of a national unity—and hence of an integrated market—that had been already maintained for centuries; compared with Holland, she had coal and iron in abundance. The English, declared Montesquieu, 'had progressed farthest of all peoples in three important ways, piety, commerce, and freedom.' Not one of Britain's advantages over her potential rivals for early industrialisation was unique, but together they formed a constellation that was. Given a social and political climate that did not impede innovation, industry and commerce that were already advanced, geographical advantages (coal and iron ore, a favourable location, short hauls for all transport), the economic pre-requisites of sufficient capital and expanding markets, then the siting of the first industrial revolution in Britain is not surprising.

A list of advantages, however, is not an explanation, and the general rise in productivity that characterised the industrial revolution was bewilderingly complex in causes, sequence and composition. Only one thing is reasonably certain: the turning point. After 1780 the production of industrial goods increased markedly, and the technological bases of this increase can be identified: the rapid introduction of the puddling process, the rotary motion steam engine, and improved cotton spinning machinery. On the long-term causes of the English industrial revolution, contemporary and nineteenth-century explanation stressed four factors: the change in economic policy from mercantilism to *laisser faire*, attributed largely to Adam Smith; the expansion of British commerce; the increase in productivity that came from the new machines, and, hence, the engineers and artisans who invented and applied them;

[1] W. C. Scoville, *Capitalism and French Glassmaking, 1640–1789* (University of California, 1950), p. 125, identifies four groups: *manufactures du roi* (state-owned and operated), *manufactures royales* (with monopoly privileges and taxation exemptions), *manufactures privilégiées* (crown chartered, with some privileges), and below these, establishments without official recognition or patronage.

the thrift and dedication of the early entrepreneurs who made available the capital and hard work necessary for pioneering new industrial processes. 'This country was the first manufacturing state in the world', Frankland Lewis declared in the House of Commons in 1816[1] 'not because labour was cheaper here than elsewhere, but because our persons and properties were secure—because we had good government—because we possessed some peculiar national advantages—because we had coals in abundance—because we had machinery and mechanical ingenuity—because, from our situation, we were not liable to the devastations of war which interrupt the progress of all improvement in countries exposed to its fury—and, above all, because we had a vast accumulation of capital, in which no other country could compete with us, and which would not seek employment under laws that yielded a more uncertain production.'

Adam Smith's arguments for *laisser faire* certainly influenced eighteenth-century politicians, and were the declared bases of public policy in the nineteenth century, but it is not possible to attribute to him any direct influence on industrialisation in 1780. At this time he was but one of many, in England and on the Continent, who were proclaiming that more liberal economic policies were necessary for economic growth. More important, certainly, were capital accumulation and inventions. It is T. S. Ashton's thesis, for example, that 'the lower rate of interest at which capital could be obtained' was the reason 'why the pace of economic development quickened about the middle of the eighteenth century'. Interest rates fell from 7 or 8 per cent at the beginning of the century to 3 or 4 per cent in 1750, and this was certainly important for land-owners who wished to enclose, and for canal and road builders, even though the new industrialists increased their capital assets mainly by ploughing back profits. The development of English banking was also remarkable, with 52 private banks in London and 400 in the provinces by 1800, which between them were responsible for much of the working capital of industry. Capital was necessary for development, and capital was more plentiful and cheaper in Britain in the second half of the eighteenth century than in any other country except Holland.

The immediate cause of increasing productivity, however, was undoubtedly technical progress: the use of power-driven machinery; the replacement of wood by coal as a fuel, and by iron as construction material; the transfer of production to the factory; improved communications. The effect of better machinery on productivity during the industrial revolution was both large and rapid in impact. 'In my establishment at New Lanark,' Robert Owen declared in 1816, 'mechanical powers and operations superintended by about two thousand

[1] Hansard, xxxiv, 778.

young persons and adults ... now completed as much work as sixty years before would have required the entire working population of Scotland.' Such improvements explain the shift between 1760 and 1830 from a situation where incomes and population were rising very slowly to one where population was increasing at the annual rate of 1·5 per cent, and average real incomes at the same rate.

'The greatest stimulus to English engineering,' Samuel Smiles declared, 'has been Trade—the increase of our commerce at home, and the extending of it abroad.' The industrial revolution with its great increase in production would not have been possible without the existence of large and accessible markets, at home and abroad, of consumers willing and able to buy the new products of industry. This extension of markets was made possible, particularly, by reduced prices, for the goods of the industrial revolution tended to be cheap and plentiful. Perhaps the most important discovery of the British entre-preneurs was the mass market in which sales of machine-made cheap goods at low profit-margins proved to be a more general foundation of wealth than the higher profits on the smaller sales of quality goods.

The process and sequence of growth in Britain can now be described. Starting with a stable but relatively advanced economy that was mainly agricultural—but with a significant industrial sector, especially textiles, and a mature commercial organisation biased towards international trade—Britain in the early eighteenth century was slowly changing its production methods in both agriculture and industry, but was saving little more than was required to meet depreciation and modest additions to fixed capital. With a slowly increasing population, and no other great impulse to change, entrepreneurial talent found its main outlet in commerce, and the merchants became, as P. Mantoux described them, *les excitateurs de l'industrie*.[1] They accumulated capital and exploited the home and foreign markets for agricultural produce and domestic manufacturers. At this stage, between 1740 and 1780, large-scale investment in agriculture, and to a lesser extent in communications, greatly enhanced the industrial potential of the economy and made possible the cumulative expansion after 1780. The population increase and the expansion of domestic and international trade after 1740 gave further stimulus, and the application of radically new production methods and the increasing proportion of the national income devoted to productive investment, enabled the economy to yield a rise in real output *per capita* that was sustained. Whereas total output was in-creasing after 1740, output *per capita* moved up sharply only after 1780; whereas the rate of growth of real income *per capita* had increased 0·3 per cent per annum between 1700 and 1750, it increased to 0·45 per cent between 1750 and 1800, to 1·1 per cent between 1801 and 1831, to

[1] P. Mantoux, *La révolution industrielle au 18ᵉ siècle* (Paris, 1906).

1·5 per cent between 1831 and 1851. Between 1782 and 1855 the rate of growth of industrial output varied from 2 to 4 per cent per annum, more than double the rate before 1780, and between 1800 and 1830 real national income *per capita* increased 50 per cent. The growth of domestic income, evident after 1730, provided the main market stimulus for growth, and, through the demand for colonial produce, the impetus for increasing colonial trade after 1740. The volume of international trade doubled between 1780 and 1800, and, after a slower growth during the wars, doubled again by 1840. No wonder G. R. Porter could introduce his book *The Progress of the Nation*, published in 1836 to 1838, with reference to Britain's 'eminence among nations' and to 'the greatest advances in civilisation that can be found recorded in the annals of mankind'. Much of this progress must be attributed to agriculture, for although the contribution of manufacturing industry to national income increased from 20 per cent in 1770 to 25 per cent in 1812 and to $33\frac{1}{2}$ per cent in 1831, still between 1780 and 1830 agriculture contributed, on average, one-third of the national income. This is not surprising: an agricultural revolution that began in the eighteenth century allowed the same number of people on the land to feed a total population that by 1830 had nearly doubled.

In industry the important advances were in the production of textiles and iron, and in the mining of coal. The growth of the cotton industry can be measured by the import of raw cotton, by employment (500,000 in 1831, of which about half were in factories), by exports, and by the use of machinery (10 million spindles and 80,000 power looms by 1831).[1] The iron industry was revolutionised by the use of coke for smelting, the puddling and rolling processes, and the steam engine: in 1788, when total production was about 70,000 tons, at least one-fifth came from charcoal furnaces; in 1806 there were 162 coke and only 11 charcoal furnaces, producing 260,000 tons; by 1830 there were probably 300 coke furnaces in operation with a total yearly production of 700,000 tons. Coal mining productivity was markedly increased by the steam engine—for both drainage and haulage—and by the railway: production, already 2·6 million tons in 1700, was 6·4 million by 1780, 10·1 million by 1800, and 30 million by 1830. A marked feature of British industrialisation, also, was its concentration on the coal fields, with practically all cotton manufacturing in Lancashire, and 40 per cent of iron making in South Wales and another 30 per cent in Staffordshire by 1830. Iron and cotton manufactures provided probably less than 5 per cent of the national income in 1780, more than 10 per cent

---

[1] (i) Raw cotton imports (million lb.): 1771, 4·8; 1785, 17·9; 1790, 31·4; 1800, 56·0; 1811, 90·3; 1821, 137·4; 1831, 273·2.

(ii) Cotton exports: 1820, 250 million yards cloth, 23 million lb. yarn. 1830, 445 million yards cloth, 65 million lb. yarn.

in 1810, and about 20 per cent by 1830; cotton goods were 13 per cent of exports in 1796–8 and 40 per cent in 1815–25. By 1830 the manufacturing industry was as important in the national economy as it was to be for the rest of the century; and in Lancashire, the West Riding and the Black Country a new society was being formed, a society that was predominantly urban and industrial and whose standard of living, in spite of many ills and some injustice, was slowly rising.

Britain's international trade after 1780 increased at a faster rate than industrial production. More significant for the European economy, however, was the greater growth, relatively and absolutely, of imports: for most years after 1796 Britain had an unfavourable commodity trade balance (averaging £9 millions annually to 1830), which was matched by an expansion of invisibles, the earnings of the merchant marine (Britain had 40 per cent of the world's shipping in 1820), commercial and financial commissions, the savings of Britons abroad (entrepreneurs, artisans, officials), and the income from foreign investment (assets abroad totalled £25 millions in 1817 and £113 millions in 1832). Britain's import surplus underlines two important factors: the fall in British export prices that followed from mechanisation (and thus the unfavourable barter terms of trade, and the export to foreigners of some of the advantages of the industrial revolution in the form of cheaper manufactured goods); the importance of the British market to foreign producers of raw materials and foodstuffs both in Europe and overseas. British trade constituted about 27 per cent of world trade in 1800 and 24 per cent in 1840; of non-British exports in world trade Britain provided a market for 42 per cent in 1800 and 36 per cent in 1840; of imports into all other countries Britain provided about 40 per cent in 1800 and 25 per cent in 1840.[1]

In direction of trade, both before 1780 and after 1830, Britain was oriented predominantly towards America and Europe: generally over this period Europe provided one-third of British imports and a market for more than 40 per cent of her exports, while North America (including the West Indies) provided over 40 per cent of British imports and a market for more than one-third of her exports. In composition British trade established a pattern that later characterised the trade of Europe with the rest of the world: exports mainly of the new manufactures—cottons, woollens, iron-ware; imports of raw materials and foodstuffs—with wheat, wool and cotton constituting 21 per cent of net imports by volume, and tea, sugar, tobacco, molasses and wines totalling 30 per cent over the period. In Britain between 1800 and 1830 raw materials increased from 40 to nearly 70 per cent of the volume of imports, foodstuffs from 20 to nearly 30 per cent, while manufactures sank to 5 per cent; in exports manufactures increased from 83 to 96 per

[1] A. H. Imlah, *Economic Elements in the Pax Britannica* (Harvard, 1958), ch. 2.

cent, with cotton goods forming over 40 per cent of exports by 1815. With Britain as yet the only rapidly industrialising country and by far the largest trader, a pattern of international specialisation was established on the basis of Britain's demand for primary products. And imports, at a time when bilateral payments in international trade were common, were directly reflected in exports; thus, the large north European market for British manufactured goods fluctuated directly with British grain imports from the Baltic. Nevertheless, without a fully developed multilateral system of payments, the eighteenth-century triangles of trade were extended towards multilateral settlements. Britain, with an unfavourable trade balance in the United States and Northern Europe, had a favourable balance elsewhere, in Southern Europe, South America and Asia. The United States had a favourable balance with Europe offset by an unfavourable balance with the rest of the world. Within Europe, for example, Russia and Sweden had favourable balances with Britain to offset purchases from Southern Europe; Belgium, France and Germany had a surplus within Europe to offset deficits overseas, especially with the United States.

Increasingly, since so much of world trade was with Britain, the complicated pattern of deficits and surpluses that resulted was settled in London without large flows of bullion. In 1832 Nathan Rothschild declared that England was in general 'the Bank for the whole world. . . . All the transactions in India, in China, in Germany, in the whole world are guided here and settled in this country.' Already in 1800 London was the commercial-financial capital of Europe, providing services of short- and long-term credit, marine insurance, shipping, merchanting and *entrepôt* facilities that were unique, even though some continental cities, Paris and Amsterdam for example, remained important clearing houses for international settlements. European banking services were catered for in 1780 by a number of chartered public banks, some large private merchant banks, and numerous small private deposit banks. Banking, which had developed initially for the deposit and loan of money, became increasingly involved during the eighteenth century in the international transfer of funds, and in the issue of bank-notes. After 1750 the old deposit banks were giving way to note-issuing banks of a semi-public character and after 1800 governments were restricting the right of issue wholly or partly to them: for example, the Bank of France was given the monopoly of issue in Paris in 1803, and in provincial towns where it had branches in 1806. By 1830 England, the United Netherlands, Sweden, Norway, Denmark, Prussia, France and Spain all had privileged national banks of issue. At the same time commercial and investment banks, and the English country banks, were emerging to provide for, and profit by, the increasing demand for currency and credit caused by economic development. The need for trade credit and improved machinery for the remittance of trade balances was the main stimulus; but also important were the needs of governments for funds, both short and long, to bridge the time-lag between the spending and collecting of revenue, and to fund state debts caused by the persistent and universal imbalance between revenue and expenditure, especially during war. Indeed banking developed largely in this period on the business of accepting deposits and buying commercial or government bills to hold against them. English banks usually avoided long-term commitments to industry, but on the Continent there was also the beginning of investment banking, for example in Belgium.

Equally significant for the future was the establishment of international banking houses, centred in London and concerned particularly with the growth of national debts. The Ouvrard–Baring–Hope combine managed the loan of 350 million francs to France in 1817, and the Rothschilds arranged the first Prussian external loan of 1818. By 1825 France, Prussia, Russia, Austria, Portugal, Spain and even the still unfree Greece all had external debts; and overseas the first large loans had been made to the impecunious free governments of South America. The Rothschilds were among the first to respond to the opportunities afforded by the growth of international finance, having five members of the family strategically placed in London, Paris, Vienna, Frankfurt and Naples in 1815. The approximate total of Europe's national debts increased from £500 millions in 1780 to £1500 millions in 1820 and, more slowly to £1730 millions by 1848.

These various financial developments had their own particular problems, intensified by the war, of inflations and crises. Inflation not only raised an important theoretical issue—largely explained by the postulation of the quantity theory of money—but also the practical problem of the control of the note issue. Periodical crises, including extensive bank failures, led to a consideration of the role of banks in booms and depressions, and to the practical problems of protecting the public from the instability of financial institutions. The systematic theorising about monetary problems in England, for example, finally led in 1844 to an attempt in the Bank Charter Act to control banking and currency and thus to prevent crises.

The amount of British foreign trade was far greater than that of any other country. French exports, the next largest, were less than half the value of British exports in 1830; those of the United Netherlands less than one-quarter, and those of other European countries much less. Similarly with the development of industry. Industrialisation in Europe nowhere matched that of Britain. Generally the amount of trade and the degree of industrialisation diminished with the distance from Britain, and the impact of British development was felt most by her nearest neighbours. Southern, eastern and northern Europe remained, in contrast, areas of little change before 1830. In the south—in Spain, Italy and European Turkey—economies remained agricultural and primitive, and there was little industrial development except in Catalonia. In Turkey there was some growth of enclosed farming and craft production, stimulated by increasing international trade and a very liberal trade policy. The *Moniteur Ottoman* reported in 1832: 'Good sense, tolerance, and hospitality have long ago done for the Ottoman Empire what the other states of Europe are endeavouring to effect by more or less happy political combinations. . . . Liberty of commerce has reigned here without limits. . . . The extreme moderation of duties is the complement of this regime of commercial liberty.' The possible good effect of such policy, however, was more than offset by a system of government that resulted in universal tyranny and insecurity, and made the main producer of wealth, the cultivator of the soil, the helpless prey to injustice and oppression. Only a break-down into nation states would bring quicker development.

Italy's economic ills, in contrast, stemmed largely from fragmentation, and until unification she remained 'a stationary and backward civilisation'. In the eighteenth century, political divisions, trade barriers, poor communications, guild restrictions, small markets, currency differences and the persistence of privilege had reduced a once great economy almost to subsistence agriculture. Conquest and unification by Napoleon did bring some positive benefits but these were offset by the blockade and by French exploitation. After the war, when some of these benefits could have been realised, the uneasy restoration of privilege and of the old political boundaries further delayed development. Only in Lombardy and Piedmont, the natural gateways to the rest of Europe, was there agricultural and industrial progress that contrasted with the rest of Italy, and even here agriculture overshadowed all other activities, including the feeble beginnings of factory production in textiles. Elsewhere there was some textile manufacturing (machinery was introduced into Prato in 1820, and even in Naples the first cotton mills were built after 1830), but in the whole of Italy iron production was small, and coal production nil. Nowhere before 1830 was there an agricultural revolution; and, although irrigation and consolidation, and the decline of feudalism, produced some increase in agricultural production, this growth barely kept pace with that of the population. The condition of the peasantry was everywhere wretched. When Sir John Bowring visited Italy in the 1830's he reported on the illiteracy, ignorance, superstition, hostility to innovation and 'the universal isolation' of the peasantry. 'In innumerable cases families have occupied the same farms for hundreds of years, without adding a farthing to their wealth, or a fragment to their knowledge.'

Similarly in Spain, where in spite of the Enlightenment with its reforming civil servants who believed that the economy could be improved by legislation, and in spite of the eighty economic societies of 'Friends of the Country' and, in consequence, much progressive economic thinking and some liberalisation of commercial life under Charles III, the old ills that had reduced her from a leading to a minor power persisted. Spain remained primarily an agricultural economy, a producer of raw materials for export—wine, oil, wool, silk and minerals —in return for grain and manufactured goods, even handkerchiefs from Manchester on which, as Gautier noted, the faces of celebrated matadors were garishly printed. The deficit in grain was the most striking irrationality of the Spanish economy, the result of the seigneurial system with its poorly farmed *latifundia* and of the absence generally, except in the north, of small or medium-sized farms. There was prestige in stock-breeding—and the power of the pastoral interest was reflected in the privileges of the *Mesta* with its wandering and destructive sheep flocks, not abolished until 1836—but little prestige in tenant farming. There were 25,000 'dispirited villages' but few towns that were large enough to stimulate intensive agriculture or that could form the focus of industrial advance. Thus industry languished, partly because of the smallness of Spanish towns and the failure to exploit the colonial market, but also because of restrictive guilds lately revived. The urban middle classes were small in number and held in low esteem by the nobility; their preference for guilds and protection is understandable in an economy where there was little agricultural and even less industrial surplus, poor communications and limited markets. Government patronage of industry was not important, as it was in France. Much of the external commerce was in foreign hands, for example in Cadiz, and its profits were drained abroad. The empire, 'a vast closed territory where commercial relations rested on the strictest exclusiveness which mercantilist concepts could conceive', had a larger and more rapidly expanding economy in 1800 than did Spain, but its demand for manufactures was met, not by industrialisation in Spain, but by foreigners, and specially by the British. The war made things worse: it disrupted government, increased inflation, and interrupted the wool trade; it finally established Britain in the market for manufactures both in Spain and in the empire. The empire—a source of bullion and a market, an avenue of employment for the nobility in a society where one person in twenty was a noble—had been the bulwark of Spanish fortunes. The British, in command of the sea and already established illicitly in the South American market, were alone in the position to take advantage of colonial independence when it came. To loss of empire was added an inflation which aggravated existing monetary problems: prices increased 60 per cent between 1770 and 1800, and more rapidly after 1800. And although the French invasion led to the formation of a liberal government—and to the drafting of a liberal constitution in 1811 —the war was followed by the restoration of noble privileges and the retardation of growth. The liberal revolt of 1820 was ineffective, but by 1830 Spain was simmering once more into violence. By this time only Catalonia, and especially Barcelona, had any substantial industry, mainly textiles.

In eastern Europe the rate of economic growth was also slower than in the west. In Russia there was a remarkable five-fold increase in population between 1720 and 1851, partly due to an extension of territory in all directions—an extension whose long-term economic importance lay in acquiring new potential resources and in giving direct access to the expanding economy of western Europe. There was, also, considerable industry. Indeed Russia was the scene of perhaps the most spectacular development of the iron industry in the eighteenth century: in the Urals by 1800 production was 65,500 tons, half of which had to be exported, mainly to Britain, because of the lack of domestic consumers. But this impressive output masked technological backwardness, with charcoal furnaces (eighty-seven in 1800) and hand forging. And, considering the size and population of Russia, the aggregate effort in industry was less impressive than it seemed, with perhaps 50,000 'factory' workers in 1770 and 210,000 in 1825. The trend in factories was away from serf and towards free labour, but by 1830 only the cotton industry was using a majority of free workers. The growth of factory production was accompanied by a decline in estate production which gradually destroyed a self-sufficiency of feudal estates that was probably unique in Europe. By 1830, also, there had developed a noticeable regional specialisation. In the north serfdom was already disappearing and an increasing percentage of the new industrial crops (for example, flax, potatoes and hemp) was coming from free peasant production. On the black soil of the centre and south, serfdom was maintained although it also produced increasingly for the market, partly to satisfy the increasing demand of the land-owners for industrial and particularly imported goods; and this was forcing agricultural change, for example the wider use of a three-course rotation. Russian exports were few—iron, flax, tallow, timber, grain; imports were varied—textiles, metal goods, sugar, wines, oil, and numerous consumer goods, and a favourable trade balance with Britain allowed the import of the southern European luxuries that increasingly adorned the noble household. But the economic advance before 1830 was slow and uneasy, and until the liberation of the serfs development was inevitably retarded.

In the Austrian Empire enlightenment and reform that might have engendered economic advance were abruptly halted in 1789. Thereafter a feudal reaction followed that, under Francis II, went so far as to restrict the building of factories, especially in Vienna. In consequence industry developed slowly; and, although the blockade stimulated mechanisation in the cotton industry, peace and cheap English imports brought crisis and halted production until the late twenties. Progress in the thirties was rapid: in Bohemia by 1840 hand-spinning had almost disappeared and the steam engine was widely used. There was change also in agriculture where the extension of the market stimulated the greater production of grain (for example in Hungary) and the growing of new products (for example potatoes, beet and fine wool). But the restoration of feudal rights by Francis in 1798, and the fact that so much noble land, especially in Hungary, was entailed, made commercial farming difficult and left wide areas of rich land under-developed until after 1848. Nevertheless, noble landowners in the chief agricultural areas did push profitable large-scale farming and agrarian reform after 1815. By 1830 the use of machinery in Austrian territories was confined to the textile industry (and mainly to cotton spinning in Bohemia); and mechanisation in other industries—iron making and sugar production—only commenced in the following decade.

In northern Europe the Baltic, once one of the great centres of European commerce, had declined in importance, with a trade now in iron, timber and grain. The Scandinavian economies were mainly agricultural, but there were marked improvements in agriculture during this period, with changes in land tenure, and the establishment of dispersed farms with yeoman-like freeholds and efficient medium-sized farming units. Industry, however, except for the Swedish iron industry, remained small in scale, and guild power, though reduced, was still strong throughout the period. British example in iron making and British demand for iron and timber were important incentives to industrial production. Swedish development was the most impressive: production of grain increased so that by 1830 the country hardly needed to import it; iron production grew from 60,000 tons in 1750 to 80,000 tons per annum between 1781 and 1830, although Sweden's percentage contribution to European iron production fell from 10 to 2 per cent between 1800 and 1850. Though the Swedish iron masters led in enterprise, rapidly adopting the puddling process, introducing the first steam engine in 1804 and making increasing use of water power, they could not compete with British coke-smelted iron. Second in importance was timber milling, with exports increasing 60 per cent between 1780 and 1830. Both iron and timber found their chief market in Britain, and growth would have been faster had it not been for the war, the rapid development of the British iron industry, and the British protection of Canadian timber. Nevertheless, the impression of Sweden in 1830 is of a country that was politically stable and moderately progressive in its economy (tariffs were liberalised in the twenties), with an improving agriculture, the beginnings of better communications (for example the Gotha canal), two metropolitan centres of importance, and two growth sectors in timber and iron that would later stimulate more rapid expansion.

Norway, transferred from Denmark to Sweden in 1814, had an agricultural economy, exporting timber, fish and some metals. Its resources, except timber, were more limited than those of Sweden, and the development of the timber industry was hampered by monopolies and by the restriction of output through fear of deforestation. Already by 1800, however, the greater part of the land was owned by the farmers, and the civil administration was in the hands of men of non-noble descent. After the war there was an expansion of arable (though the country remained dependent on grain imports), of timber felling, and of seal and whale fishing, but no signs of real growth by 1830. The prosperity of Denmark lay already in the export of food, especially grain, although in this period commerce and the carrying trade were also important. Denmark controlled the entrance to the Baltic, exacting a toll for transit that was maintained until 1857; she had also 700 ships in 1800 and 1600 in 1839; Copenhagen was an important centre for Baltic trade; the reform of the tariff and the early establishment of bonded warehouses (1793) encouraged a transit trade. The end of the war brought the inevitable British competition, but Denmark's need for the British market led in 1824 to a commercial treaty on the basis of reciprocity. Agricultural advance, with the process of farm consolidation practically completed by 1830, gave Denmark a relatively prosperous if not progressive economy by that date.

The greatest economic advance in continental Europe was in Belgium, although France and Germany also made significant progress. The economic greatness of Germany, however, was barely apparent in 1830. Voltaire's prophecy that Germany was doomed to eternal poverty seemed to be justified by the wars and the Prussian depression of 1815 to 1828. And although the reduced number of states and the great size of Prussia mitigated German atomism, industrialisation was not possible without a customs union as the minimum step towards unification. Competition from the new industries of Belgium and Britain discouraged growth in those old German industries, linen and iron making, that were the most progressive and had the widest markets. The dominance of the Junkers in agriculture, and of the guilds in industry, reinforced an institutional structure inimical to growth. Yet increasing industrialisation after 1815 was the result of agrarian reform and of the removal of customs barriers. The changes that abolished serfdom and the guild-regulation of industry were initiated before 1815; the breakdown of inter-state customs barriers came with the formation of the *Zollverein* between 1818 and 1834. Germany had coal and iron resources that would later provide the raw materials for the greatest heavy industry of Europe, but before 1830 they were little exploited. Of her two largest coal-fields, the Ruhr was little developed in this period because its wealth was unknown and because of its proximity to Belgian coal-iron works, while that of Upper Silesia, isolated as it was, would not have developed at all without the patronage of the Prussian government. Iron smelting, in consequence, remained mainly dependent on charcoal. Coke smelting and puddling were introduced into Upper Silesia as early as the 1780's, but not extensively elsewhere before the middle of the nineteenth century. And even there coke smelting was used only near the coal mines; elsewhere in Silesia, because of the abundance of timber, charcoal smelting survived even longer than in other parts of Germany. The hills east of the Rhine were the most important for the manufacture of metal goods and in 1840 still provided one-third of German blast furnaces. An iron industry that had been widely spread throughout central Germany suffered competition and decline in the early nineteenth century owing to cheaper iron from the Ruhr, Silesia and abroad. If Germany's future lay with coal and iron, however, her past and present lay with woollen and linen textiles. Linen was the main industry in 1800, when Prussian exports contained 75 per cent of textiles, including 60 per cent of linens, and only 4 per cent of metal goods. The Silesian–Westphalian linen, in particular, was esteemed throughout Europe. The basic exports from the Baltic ports—cereals, timber and cloth—all suffered in the post-war period. Linen exports, which had gone mainly to Spain, England and America, were competing after 1815 with cheap British linens and cottons, and declining exports led to continuous social distress among the hand-loom linen weavers. But the manufacture of woollens was also an ancient German industry that increased considerably after the introduction of the Merino sheep in the eighteenth century. Even so there were large exports of raw wool to Yorkshire between 1820 and 1840. Cotton manufacture, a new industry, grew rapidly after 1800, with increasing mechanisation in spinning after 1815 and 150,000 spindles by 1835. Three great institutional reforms—the abolition of serfdom, the curtailing of guild power, and the formation of the *Zollverein*, together with the immigration of Belgian and British entrepreneurs and artisans, and state enterprise and patronage—explain the economic advance of Germany before 1830. At that date, however, the economy remained predominantly rural, even in those states (Rhineland, Westphalia and Saxony) where industry was most advanced. Economic unification was necessary to create an internal market large enough to support specialisation, and to prevent, as a supporter of unification argued in 1814, the creation of 'vineyards along the Baltic, cornfields in the Harz Mountains, or sheep farming on the hills of the Rhine'.

In 1783 the area known as the Low Countries consisted of the Austrian Netherlands (Belgium), the United Provinces (Holland), and the Principality of Liège. Belgium was the first European country to have an industrial revolution and was the gateway through which England's industrial revolution first entered the Continent. The basic reasons for Belgian industrial eminence were a favourable location that gave access to three great and increasing markets (France, Germany and Great Britain); navigable rivers supplemented by canals to provide in 1830 over 1,000 miles of internal waterways, giving Belgium a unique link with the Great Plain of western Europe; easily exploited coal and iron ore which, though not rivalling the resources of Britain or Germany, were sufficient to begin and sustain an industrial revolution; an ancient industrial tradition in both textiles and metallurgy that provided a skilled labour force; and in Antwerp a great commercial and financial centre. To these advantages were added successive benevolent governments: incorporation with France brought better roads, the opening up of the Scheldt, and a long period of 'peace' in a protected market at a time when demand for textiles and metal goods was increasing rapidly; incorporation with Holland after 1815 led to judicious industrial expansion in the twenties under the wise patronage of William I. Government patronage of industry was both direct—loans by William and the state, and indirect—a moderate tariff and financial institutions to aid industry; such encouragement, for example, did much to establish a prosperous iron industry by 1830. Belgium in 1780 already had a large urban community and, to feed it, a Flemish agriculture as efficient as that of England. Although the peace in 1815 led to the separation from Belgium of the French and Rhenish markets and to the opening up of European markets to British goods, there was compensation after 1820 with modest tariffs, government grants to industry, and canal development. Rapid technological advance was assured in 1821 by the sending of Lieutenant Roentgen to report on the English iron industry and to compare it with that of Belgium. Roentgen found only one Belgian ironworks—that of John Cockerill at Seraing near Liège—as good as those of England, and advised a state-owned and operated factory equipped with English plant and worked initially by English technicians. Instead Cockerill was twice given large government loans to expand his works. The Cockerill establishment, one of the first vertically integrated organisations in Europe, was expanded by an *entrepreneur* of outstanding talent into an industrial empire that in 1830 was the largest in Europe. Belgium, like England, was also a large coal producer, and production increased after 1790 with the general expansion of industry, reaching 2·5 million tons by 1830. The textile industry also expanded rapidly, with twice as many cotton spindles and three times as many looms in 1829 as in 1810. However, it was the combination of coal and iron ores along the Meuse that provided the main bases for Belgian expansion. Even so, charcoal smelting gave way to coke smelting only slowly, the first coke-fired blast furnaces being built after 1820 at Grivengée by Orban and at Seraing by Cockerill. Even in 1842 only 45 of Belgium's 120 furnaces were coke-fired. Important for industrial development was the expansion of banking to provide credit and capital, anticipating the close link between industry and banking that was later characteristic of Germany. In particular, the establishment in 1822 of the *Société Générale des Pays-Bas pour favoriser l'industrie nationale* (to give credit to industrialists) and the *Nederlandsche Handel-Maatschappij* (to foster exports) prevented any financial bottlenecks to industrialisation and commerce. By 1840, again in spite of the dislocation caused by the secession, Belgium was technologically the most advanced country on the Continent, producing steamboats, locomotives and textile machinery as well as consumer goods, 'the one country in Europe', as J. H. Clapham pointed out, 'which kept pace industrially with England'.

Whereas Belgium prospered under France and under William I, Holland on the whole suffered. The Dutch commercial economy was already falling behind in the eighteenth century. The last Anglo-Dutch War began the final decline, by harming the still important American and Oriental trades and by reducing the Dutch mercantile marine; the Napoleonic period saw the loss of colonies and more ships, and the permanent eclipse of Dutch commerce. It was the aim of William I 'to make the Netherlands once more the stapling place for a not inconsiderable part of world trade, to which this Kingdom has a claim by virtue of its location', but his benevolent policy was doomed to failure. Irreconcilable differences in policy between Belgian interests for protection and Dutch interests for free trade made a unified policy for the combined countries impossible. The roads, canals and harbours built by William I benefited Belgium immediately, and Holland only in the long run. The idea of a unified state—with an industrial Belgium and a commercial Holland, and a useful empire—might well have succeeded had political unity been maintained. But the 1830 revolution left Belgium temporarily without markets, and Holland more permanently without industries. The attempt to revive Holland as an *entrepôt* had only small success: in the nineties Hamburg monopolised the commission trade in British merchandise; from 1800 to 1815, though trade continued behind the blockade, Holland was deprived of her traditional products of commerce; after 1815 tariffs and English competition made former markets difficult to regain. William's solution—to channel trade through a monolithic trading company—was a failure. The old staples—spices and sugar, herrings and linen—were being replaced by coal, iron and cotton, and these were not Dutch preserves. The future of Rotterdam and Antwerp was assured, but that of the smaller ports lay more as market towns for agricultural areas than as international emporia. Holland turned inevitably from commerce to agriculture, and the French abolition in 1801 and 1804 of feudal privileges aided the growth of a commercial agriculture that was already contributing substantially to Dutch trade by 1830.

France, the most populous and richest country of western Europe in the eighteenth century, was outstripped by Britain after 1780. Even before this, greater capital accumulation, more productive investment in industry, and better-developed financial institutions had put Britain ahead. In France the strength of the guilds, burdensome taxation, and a restrictive system of commerce and navigation had also hampered development. War widened further the gap between the economies of the two countries. Looking at the Europe of 1800, Michelet saw the masses streaming in France towards the barracks, and in England towards the factories. In agriculture, which continued to dominate the French economy, the most striking characteristics were 'stability and immobility'. Nevertheless, although basic food crops remained most important, the demand of metropolitan centres began an agricultural revolution—with its artificial pastures, root crops, enclosures and animal improvements—starting near Paris after 1750 and spreading slowly without radically affecting agriculture until the building of the railways. The Physiocrats, holding that 'the wealth of a country is in direct proportion to the fertility of its land', had stimulated agricultural improvements by the government and by large land-holders. Indeed, many of the rural nobility of the eighteenth century built their wealth on the proper management of their estates, in response to the increasing market, rather than on seigneurial rights. But markets seldom extended beyond provincial borders, and the only great specialisation was in wine-growing. In the poorer soils of the south biennial rotations were maintained beyond 1830; elsewhere rotations were triennial but not advanced except near Paris and in French Flanders. Even before 1789 proprietorship of land was widely spread, with peasant owners numerous everywhere. The Revolution, being concerned mainly with legal and proprietary relationships, led to a great exchange of property, but did not greatly affect the methods of farming. Indeed, except in the cultivation of potatoes and sugar-beet, there was no great change in agriculture before 1830. The story in industry is the same. Until the railways, and notwithstanding road and canal building, the economic provincialism of France with its dispersed small-scale domestic industry persisted. In the eighteenth century coal production was relatively large, but it was obtained from scattered fields and was used locally, mostly on the Massif Central and its borders. After 1760 St Étienne coal was reaching Paris by way of the Loire, and total French production was 500,000 tons in 1789 and 1,800,000 tons in 1830. But the slow adoption of the steam engine, the continued use of charcoal for iron smelting (aided by tariffs after 1819 that aimed at keeping up charcoal prices in the interest of landowners) and easy access to Belgian coal restricted output before 1840. Iron manufacture was hampered in the eighteenth century by fuel shortage and administrative caprice, and most works were small, although the industry was widespread from the Pyrenees to the Belgian border. This geographical diversity still existed in 1827, when there were 424 blast furnaces spread over 45 departments; the units were small, producing 340,000 tons including only 40,000 tons by the puddling process. In 1830, 86 per cent of iron was still charcoal-smelted. There was greater change in the textile industries—for example in the manufacture of cotton and woollen textiles in the northern departments—but no revolution except in the cotton industry of Mulhouse between 1815 and 1830, when there were half a million spindles and 2000 power looms in operation. French cotton consumption totalled 70 million lb. by 1830. Change in woollen manufacture was slower; in silk, slower still. The general technical backwardness of French industry can be measured by the fact that there were only 2803 steam engines in France in 1840. Whereas the war had helped Britain's industrialisation, it had deprived France of her colonial markets without compensating her with permanent European markets, and had encouraged protected industry behind the Continental System and within the administrative framework of the Napoleonic empire. In the competitive post-war world, with British goods freely entering Europe, only the French cotton industry grew quickly.

Thus the period 1780 to 1830 was not one of general European industrialisation, although there was significant and widespread development in the coal, iron and textile industries. An industrial revolution outside of Britain occurred generally only in cotton textiles, and here continental consumption of cotton was almost three-quarters that of Britain by 1830. At this date, however, Britain was still producing 80 per cent of Europe's coal and 50 per cent of Europe's iron, and almost all Europe's steam engines. Generally, therefore, this was a period of increasing population and trade rather than of industrialisation, and it was 'the devouring principle of trade', especially British trade, that was the main stimulus to economic growth. 'Where there is no English commerce', it was said, 'there is no commerce at all.' It was a period also of expectations; and Britain, envied and copied, encouraged that optimism and belief in progress that became characteristic of the nineteenth century. The French Revolution had raised acutely the problem of class relations and the threat of class conflict; the industrial revolution, although it underlined the contrast between rich and poor, promised plenty for all. Both revolutions helped to break down the stratified social hierarchy of the *ancien régime*, and both encouraged a political and economic liberalism that led to the replacement of juridical by economic distinctions as the bases of social roles, and to *laisser faire* as the basis of public policy. Rearguard actions by old interests to maintain the *status quo* might delay, but they could not prevent, the change that freed and expanded private interests against the old protecting and restrictive authorities. Economic liberalism resulted in the withering away of the guild system in industry (assisted by legislation), the greater freedom of the individual (to own and dispose of property, and to move from place to place in response to economic opportunity), and the freeing of trade. Manufacturers and merchants were soon organised into pressure groups to influence public policy, and two famous petitions for freer trade, from the German 'Commercial and Industrial Union' in 1819 and from the 'Merchants of London' in 1820, were characteristic of their efforts. At the beginning of the period, 1783 to 1793, the whole of Europe was negotiating for trade concessions, and after interruptions by the wars negotiations continued after 1815. The advantages of free trade and of *laisser faire* were 'proved' by the new science of political economy, as expounded by Adam Smith and the classical economists. The liberal influence of Smith was universal, with French, German, Italian, Spanish and Danish translations of *The Wealth of Nations* appearing before 1800. Smith not only attacked mercantilism, but also gave to the liberals the theory of the harmony of economic interests in a world of free competition in which an 'invisible hand' could operate. Smith's optimism was reinforced by J. B. Say's law of markets that emphasised supply, postulating that production finances consumption, and supply creates its own demand. The influence of T. R. Malthus and D. Ricardo was less optimistic. They believed that all costs could be reduced to labour costs, and explained how capital accumulation and population increase would raise the rent of land until the law of diminishing returns reduced profits and savings and resulted in a static subsistence-wage economy. Thus, although the classical economists justified *laisser faire*, they also provided the theoretical basis, in the conflict of interests between landlord, capitalist and worker implicit in the Ricardian system, for Marxian economics and for the theory of class war. And since there was working-class discontent and violence, the theory seemed proved.

Social unrest, however, was the product of discontent with status and with the distribution of wealth in societies in which the working class was gradually attaining economic and political self-consciousness. Ability as well as birth was now more generally a means of advancement, and never in history were so many humble men raised from poverty to riches and power. Yet never was there so much questioning of existing ideas and institutions; never more plans for the future ordering of society. Urbanisation, factories and better communications made working-class association easier. Civil disorder, partly the result of economic discontent—for example the fear of machines, and partly the result of revolutionary ideas—for example from Babeuf, Saint-Simon and Fourier, led to reaction and suppression; but it helped also the radicals and humanitarians of the middle and upper classes who argued for social reform and for a more active role by government to regulate conditions of work in the new industry. By the 1830's there was general agreement with Lamartine, that 'the proletarian question is one that will cause the most terrible explosion in present-day society, if society and government decline to fathom and resolve it'. Already the first factory acts had been passed in England, and these provided an example for other countries soon to follow. In any case the condition of the working class was improving: real wages in England in 1830 were 50 per cent higher than they had been in 1780, and in 1840 a committee set up by Louis Philippe showed also that the French working class was certainly better off than it had been before the Revolution. Elsewhere, except in Belgium, the improvement was not marked; but, wherever there was an increasing proportion of the occupied population in industry and commerce, the standard of life and the way of life were changing for the better. As Macaulay declared of England in 1830: 'Yet is the country poorer than in 1790? We firmly believe that, in spite of all the misgovernment of her rulers, she has been almost constantly becoming richer and richer. Now and then there has been a stoppage, now and then a short retrogression; but as to the general tendency there can be no doubt. A single breaker may recede; but the tide is evidently coming in.'

CHAPTER III

ARMED FORCES AND THE ART OF WAR

A. ARMIES

IN the eighth book of his classic *On War* Clausewitz describes what he understood to be the revolution in warfare which had taken place in his own lifetime. The wars of the eighteenth century, he says, were wars of kings not of peoples. National existence was not at stake (as certainly it was for Prussia after Austerlitz and Jena) but simply the conquest of an enemy province or two. Wars of this kind were affairs of the State, an autocratic State, and entirely separated from the interests of the people. Violence was restricted by calculation. In fact, this was what the twentieth century has come to call 'limited war'.

After 1789, however, there was a profound change. Clausewitz goes on:

Whilst, according to the usual way of seeing things, all hopes were placed on a very limited military force in 1793, such a force as no one had any conception of made its appearance. War had again suddenly become an affair of the people, and that of a people numbering thirty millions, every one of whom regarded himself as a citizen of the State. . . .

After all this was perfected by the hand of Buonaparte, this military power, based on the strength of the whole nation, marched over Europe, smashing everything in pieces so surely and certainly, that where it only encountered the old-fashioned Armies the result was not doubtful for a moment. A reaction, however, awoke in due time. [Elsewhere] the War became of itself an affair of the people. . . .

Therefore, since the time of Buonaparte, War, through being first on the one side, then again on the other, an affair of the whole Nation, has assumed quite a new nature. . . .[1]

In military, as in other matters, a basic problem for the historian of the years after 1789 is to distinguish between what was genuinely revolutionary and what had been developing gradually in the eighteenth century or even earlier. Clausewitz, as an eye-witness of the wars of the Revolution and Napoleon, had no doubt where the line of distinction lay. For him the contemporary armies of the Great Powers were, as they had been generally throughout the eighteenth century, much alike in discipline, training, equipment and general fitness for service. What, as he saw it, had transformed the limited wars of the eighteenth century into the total war of his own time was the infusion of a national spirit into fighting and the consequent warring of whole nations, one against the other. The objects of war, the size of armies, and the geographic scale of operations had all, as it were, been inflated by the

[1] C. Von Clausewitz, *On War*, trans. by Col. J. J. Graham, 3 vols. (London, 1873), vol. III, pp. 54-5

new spirit. War had become an affair of the whole nation. As a result, the restrictions of limited war had been overthrown. The object of fighting had now become 'the downfall of the foe; and not until the enemy lay powerless on the ground was it supposed to be possible to stop or to come to any understanding with respect to the mutual objects of the contest'.

It is difficult to disagree with Clausewitz's view. What was revolutionary in the wars of this period arose not from changes in weapons and only to a limited extent from new tactical forms and methods. It arose from the appearance of the 'nation in arms'; from the great increase in the size of armies which that phenomenon made possible; and from the new national rather than the frontier or dynastic policies of which the 'nation in arms' was the military instrument.

It would, of course, be wrong to imply that the impact of patriotism upon warfare, and its practical application in the form of military conscription, had been unknown, or at least not contemplated in pre-Revolutionary years. de Sade had argued that conscription would avoid the combination of force and fraud which produced nominally volunteer forces by press-gang methods. The French military reformer, Guibert, argued not only in favour of universal military service, but also for military training methods based on national characteristics. And Rousseau had claimed that only a national militia, in which every citizen would serve as a soldier, would be adequate for the defence of a free nation. But none of these had written hopefully. Guibert, in particular, had foreseen that only political revolution could make military revolution possible.

And even the Revolution, when it came, did not at first suggest that a new type of army and new ways of fighting would develop out of it. The *cahiers de doléances* of 1789 had, in many cases, called for the abolition of provincial militias, with the implication that political reform would make armed forces less and not more necessary. Then followed a series of actions which broke up the old royal army without, at any rate for the moment, putting any other effectively organised military force in its place. The most serious element in this temporary disorganisation was the loss of some two-thirds of the army's officers. Out of an establishment of nearly 10,000 officers in 1789 about 7000 were noblemen. Not all of these, let alone the officers who came from a *roturier* background or were officers of fortune, were against the Revolution. But many of them were, and quickly threw up their commissions to join the *émigrés* at Trier or Coblentz. The fall of the Bastille, the formation of the National Guards, the fundamental decree of the new military constitution of February 1790, which laid down that every citizen was admissible to every military rank and employment, the imposition of new oaths which subordinated traditional loyalty to the king to loyalty to the State and the constitution, all promoted the process of disruption. Emigration of officers continued throughout 1791 and into 1792.

Already, in December 1789, Dubois-Crancé had pleaded for universal short service and a small regular army. He argued that citizenship and the obligations of military service should go together. But the Constituent Assembly decided to retain the system of voluntary enlistment for pay. Theoretical objections to conscription, however, were of no avail against the practical need for national armed forces, particularly as the increasing violence of the Revolution appeared to be antagonising the other monarchies of Europe. From June 1791, therefore, successive and substantial increases of size took place in the French army. In that summer it was decreed that 158 new battalions, over 100,000 men in all, should be raised on a departmental basis by volunteers from the National Guard. In May 1792 the Legislative Assembly called for another 74,000 volunteers. This time, however, the voluntary principle was limited in application. Each department and district was allotted its quota and, if volunteers did not fill the list, then the rest were to be forcibly enrolled by ballot. The same method was tried the following spring. Many volunteers had terminated their engagements since the end of 1792, and it was estimated that some 300,000 new recruits were needed. It was highly unlikely that such a number would be forthcoming from volunteers alone. And so the Convention agreed to the requisition, by ballot among unmarried men between the ages of eighteen and forty, of men to fill gaps not filled by volunteers. Commissioners were sent out into the provinces to urge on the recruiting campaign.

Nevertheless it was clear that the voluntary system had completely failed. The *levée en masse*, wholesale compulsory enlistment, was in sight. On 23 August 1793 the Convention passed Carnot's decree. Five hundred and forty-three new battalions were to be raised by conscription, were to be administered directly by the Minister of War and to be distributed among eleven armies in the field.

All Frenchmen [it was announced] ... are called by their country to defend liberty.... From this moment until that when the enemy is driven from the territory of the republic, every Frenchman is commandeered for the needs of the armies. Young men will go to the front; married men will forge arms, and carry food; women will make tents and clothing, and work in hospitals; children will turn old linen into bandages; old men will be carried into the squares to rouse the courage of the combatants, to teach hatred of kings, and republican unity.

This was the proclamation of the modern nation in arms. Nor did its appeal fail. Young men between the ages of eighteen and twenty-five, the first class of *réquisitionnaires*, provided over 400,000 conscripts and, together with volunteers, satisfied the needs of the armies of the

Republic for the next five years. By the spring of 1794 France had about 750,000 men under arms. Moreover, in the winter of 1793–4 there had occurred the first *amalgame*, the merging of the remnants of the old army with the new, a process which the earlier suspicious governments of the Revolution had so strenuously resisted.

Napoleon continued, in principle, both the methods of recruitment and those of promotion which had become established in the Republican armies. At the same time the army of the Consulate and Empire illustrates admirably the practical limits which prevented the full application in this period of the principle of the 'nation in arms'.

A law of the year VI (1798) rationalised the rules of recruitment already in force, although those rules were not finally codified until 1811. Military service was legally due from all Frenchmen between the ages of twenty and twenty-five. But there were limits upon universality even within these ages. First, the law itself expressly exempted many groups from military service: married men; those, whether married or not, with dependants; and later, priests. Next—and this for financial and economic reasons—it was normal, until the last critical years of the Empire, to call up only a proportion of those named on the lists. Finally, it was possible for those chosen to find a substitute or replacement, a privilege already established in practice and made legal in May 1802.

Under the Directory, and at first with Napoleon, the size of the annual contingent was approved by the Legislature, which also decided the allocation among departments. Each municipality then provided for the medical examination of those summoned, decided who were actually to be called up and dealt with the business of replacements. Such an arrangement was clearly open to abuses, with the possibility of bribery and corruption at many stages. So Napoleon attempted to bring the whole system more directly under central control. In 1802 he ordered the setting up, within each department, of a recruiting committee comprising the prefect with some officers to help him, and their task was to examine all cases of those who claimed exemption from military service. Three years later local councils were deprived of all their responsibilities in connection with recruitment, and their functions were taken over by the prefect and sub-prefects. It was now the task of these officials to draw up the list of those eligible for military service, to draw out strictly by lot the names of those actually required, to arrange for the medical examination of recruits, and to deal with the whole business of replacements. Regimental officers were also present on these occasions, partly to provide their professional advice if necessary, and then to deal with the transfer of the selected recruits to their depots.

One revolutionary principle quite clearly infringed by this whole process was that of equality. However fairly the original selection was made by lot, the subsequent privilege of providing a replacement worked all too obviously in favour of the rich. In the Côte d'Or, for example, during the middle years of the Empire the cost of a substitute varied from about 2000 to 3500 francs, and only a very small percentage of the total contingent could afford that price. Moreover, it seems doubtful whether Napoleon's attempts to control the earlier stages of enlistment and examination proved entirely successful in eliminating corruption.

If, however, the principle of equality was denied in this particular way, it was continuously observed by the Convention, by the Directory and by Napoleon in one respect perhaps even more important. From the beginning the armies of the Revolution had offered ambitious and enthusiastic young men *la carrière ouverte aux talents*. Napoleon never broke with that tradition. It really was possible to rise from the lowest to the highest rank, and the biographies of Napoleon's marshals amply prove that. These were essentially fighting armies. And it was prowess in battle rather than birth or intellectual qualities which led to promotion. Honour was to be bought, but bought only by action in battle. And although Napoleon dealt lavishly in ribbons and distinctions of all kinds, and in the formation of *corps d'élite* within his armies, it was fighting qualities which determined the choice between those who succeeded and those who failed. Officers were thus much closer to their men than in the armies of the *ancien régime*. The relationship was much more like that which exists in some of the specialist arms of today where a crew, whether in a tank or an aeroplane, tends to ignore distinctions of rank. And the absence of distinction in the French armies of the Revolution and Empire was made the more possible because these armies developed no specialist general staff.

It would be wrong to suppose that man-power was recruited in this period with the systematic thoroughness of the twentieth century. Between 1800 and 1812 Napoleon enlisted little more than 1,100,000 Frenchmen; and even the crisis call-up of the years 1812 and 1813 took well under 50 per cent of the men whose names appeared on the lists of those eligible for military service. As Napoleon's needs increased so he used first foreign regiments and then the armies of allies and vassals. But behind this façade of apparent moderation there were excesses within the system which gradually changed military service from an honourable obligation into a widespread hardship, and especially as fighting became virtually continuous after 1805. For example, in 1803 over 170,000 men of the classes of 1792 to 1799 were retained with the colours and remained there more or less indefinitely. Those who had never been called up, and those who had already found substitutes for themselves, could never count on complete security; for there was nothing to prevent such elements of an old class from being called to the colours at a later date. This, for example, was done in 1805. Finally, in times of dire need the call up of a class could be anticipated. For instance, the conscription class of 1815 had been *appelée en activité* in October 1813 in a desperate attempt to offset the losses suffered in Russia and in the Leipzig campaign. These youths were legally too young for military service. Nevertheless, about 80,000 of them were training in the barracks during the final stages of the war in 1814. It was evils such as these which eventually made conscription seem insufferable to many Frenchmen. So much so that many of his strongest supporters tried to dissuade the emperor from reintroducing conscription during the critical days of 1815.

Prussia was the most important country, outside France, where in this period the process of social and political emancipation was accompanied by the military conscription of national man-power. In the months after Tilsit Stein and his co-reformers agreed that the liberation of Prussia demanded a national, a people's army, and that such an army could be created in Prussia only by the grant of basic social and political privileges to all Prussian subjects. As in France, political emancipation and military conscription were to be the twin pillars of the nation in arms.

The reformers, it is true, were for a long time baulked both by the suspicions of Frederick William III and by the restrictions imposed by Napoleon. The king's attitude was important because typical of conservative thinking in many European countries throughout the nineteenth century. Frederick William saw in a conscript army, or in a militia, a threat to the efficiency of a professional force and also a potential threat to royal authority. Napoleon, by the Treaty of Paris of September 1808, imposed an overall limit of 42,000 men on the Prussian army, and forbade the raising of a civil guard. It is clear now that even the Krümper system of replacements was organised on a very limited basis and did not, in fact, produce a massive national liberation army in 1813. On the other hand, much was done both to sow the seeds of new ideas and to make possible the harvesting of a successful crop in happier times. The new Ministry of War, under Scharnhorst's control from 1809, helped to break down that divorce between the army and the nation which had contributed so much to the collapse of 1806. Reforms in the recruitment and the training of the officer corps tended in the same direction. And when the time of crisis arrived in 1813 the idea of mobilising national man-power had been sufficiently debated and planned to make it possible to act in a very short space of time. First the East Prussian *Landtag* decided to mobilise a *Landwehr* of all able-bodied men between the ages of 18 and 45. Then in February 1813 universal conscription was applied to Prussia as a whole. All men between the ages of 17 and 40, if not already in the army or its volunteer Jaeger detachments, were to be formed into a *Landwehr* on the East

Prussian model or into forces for home defence and guerrilla operations. Here was the same spirit as that which had inspired the *levée en masse* in revolutionary France. By the end of 1813 Prussia had about six per cent of the population, nearly 300,000 men, under arms, a force nearly twice as large as the standing army of Frederick the Great.

One other military reform in this period emphasises the temporary similarity between developments in France and in Prussia. After Jena the Prussian reformers, particularly Scharnhorst, were anxious to put an end to the aristocratic monopoly of the officer corps. In Grolman's words—'In order to fight it is not necessary to belong to a special class.' A royal order of August 1808 declared that 'a claim to the position of officer shall from now on be warranted, in peace-time by knowledge and education, in time of war by exceptional bravery and quickness of perception. . . . All social preference which has hitherto existed is herewith terminated in the military establishment, and everyone, without regard for his background, has the same duties and the same rights.'

The king and his close associates soon began to limit this freedom, even before 1815, and more decisively afterwards. But some of the institutional reforms which accompanied it, for example the establishment of new military academies for the selection and training of officers, left a permanent mark upon the Prussians. The value of intellectual qualities in an officer was formally recognised, even if the old social requirements still, in large part, remained.

The most obvious sign, then, of the introduction of the period of people's wars—what we in the twentieth century have come to call total war—was a vast increase in the number of men under arms and of the size of armies in the field. The generals of the eighteenth century, from Marlborough onwards, had fought their battles with armies of 50,000 to 75,000 men. Indeed, Frederick the Great's battlefield numbers were little over 40,000 at Leuthen and Kunersdorf, and lower at Mollwitz. Napoleon appears to have had about 35,000 men at the start of his brilliant campaign against the Austrian and Piedmontese forces in 1796. For Marengo his numbers were up to 50,000. But for Ulm in 1805 and for Jena in 1806 Napoleon manoeuvred armies totalling some 180,000 to 190,000 men on each occasion, while the forces assembled for the invasion of Russia in 1812 rose to three times that number. Nor did Napoleon's enemies fail to conform to this general pattern of development. True, when fighting alone no one of them could match him. But the Austrians assembled some 85,000 men for the Ulm campaign and even more for Wagram. In 1806 Prussia put nearly 150,000 men into the field for the fighting which culminated at Jena. And in 1815 Russia, Prussia, Austria and England agreed to produce a total of nearly 600,000 to march by converging routes on Paris.

When the fighting at Ligny and Waterloo took place in June of that year nearly 250,000 troops, French, British and Prussian, were massed together for the final decision. Thus was the age of the 'armed horde' ushered in.

If war, looked at from the point of view of man-power, had changed its character, this was far from true of the weapons those men used. The weapons of this period were those which had been slowly developed during the eighteenth century and which remained in use until the second half of the nineteenth. While the political Revolution had released moral forces of incalculable significance, the early Industrial Revolution—despite all it did to enable Britain to wage war for over twenty years—did nothing comparable for the material and technical aspects of war.

The musket was the basic infantry weapon. It was the smooth-bored, muzzle-loaded flintlock which had come into general use early in the eighteenth century and which was to remain the standard infantry weapon for another generation after Waterloo. The advantages of grooved or rifled barrels had been known since the sixteenth century. There had been riflemen in the British Army as early as the war of American Independence. But rifling was expensive and was not easily combined with muzzle loading. The flintlock musket therefore remained in general use throughout this period, and was normally fitted with a bayonet. The infantry was thus provided with the modern combination of missile and shock weapon in one.

The musket or fusil of any European pattern was not a particularly efficient weapon. Flints wore out, barrels became fouled by the burning of coarse powder, and the powder itself was difficult to keep dry in wet weather. The complicated process of loading and priming meant that even highly trained and disciplined soldiers could not achieve a much higher rate of fire than about a round a minute, or two rounds a minute at the most. The ball so discharged was not normally effective beyond about 200 yards and then only when fired at a large target. At that distance, for example, the French musket was subject to an error of about 9 feet. Infantry therefore usually held their fire until the target was much closer.

All the technical limitations which prevented the development of a really effective hand weapon in this period also barred the way to the production of accurate artillery. The science of ballistics had already been well developed in the seventeenth century. It was the practice not the theory of gun-fire which lagged behind. So long as guns were smooth-bored, muzzle-loaded and clumsily fired by coarse powder mixtures, neither speedy nor accurate fire was really possible. Guns, like muskets, were fired once, perhaps as much as twice a minute with a skilled crew. Since there was no way of absorbing recoil action, pieces

5-2

had to be re-laid after each round. And although a 12-pounder could achieve an extreme range of about 3500 yards, its effective range was half that or less, and a much closer range was normally used.

Military reformers since the time of Gustavus Adolphus had attempted to improve their field artillery both by standardising types of guns and by making them more mobile, particularly on the actual field of battle. The French reformer Gribeauval, who became inspector-general at the end of the Seven Years' War, had done much in this direction in the mid-eighteenth century. He made guns lighter by shortening their barrels and he also made improvements in the process of boring, reducing the windage and thus improving accuracy. He reduced the calibres of field guns to three—4-, 8- and 12-pounders, and he also favoured the use of horse artillery. Moreover, his practical reforms were the basis of a well-known book published in 1778, *Sur l'usage de l'artillerie nouvelle dans la guerre de campagne* written by the Chevalier du Teil, an artillery officer in the regiment in which Napoleon was to be a subaltern.

In artillery almost more than in any other arm we can see the slow but continuous development in French military thought and practice throughout the last years of the old regime and into those of the Revolution and Empire.[1] For all his genius Napoleon was no more of a tactical innovator in artillery than in other arms. There was in general, during these years and virtually independent of Napoleon's own career, a development of artillery along three lines. First, a gradual organisation of artillery into separate regiments instead of being distributed in 'penny packets' among infantry and cavalry. Despite some changes made by Napoleon, in Egypt and later in Russia, the division remained the smallest unit to which artillery was normally attached during this period. Second, an increasing use of horse artillery, as evidenced by a law on the subject passed by the Legislative Assembly in April 1792. Third, a concentration of fire power on the battlefield, so that artillery ceased to have merely a nuisance value in hampering the enemy as he assembled on the battlefield and became, instead, a weapon with which to blast holes in his ranks before launching an infantry or cavalry attack to complete the process of disruption. Du Teil, whom Napoleon almost certainly read, had written:

In reconnoitring positions for the batteries the first objective should be the enemy's troops, not his artillery. No notice must be taken of his artillery except when his fire greatly disturbs the troops which we are protecting. It follows as a principle that we ought never to engage in artillery duels, except when it is indispensable for the protection of our troops, but that on the contrary our principal purpose must be, as has been said, to fire on the enemy's troops, when we can destroy them or the obstacles which cover them.

[1] For this development, see Matti Lauerma, *L'Artillerie de Campagne française pendant les guerres de la Révolution* (Helsinki, 1956).

The relative strength and importance of artillery tended to increase throughout the wars of the First Empire. To some extent this was a compensation for the deteriorating quality of man-power, to some extent perhaps a sign of Napoleon's own waning genius as brute force slowly overtook subtlety. During the campaigns of 1805 and 1806 the Grand Army had two artillery pieces for 1000 men. This figure was slightly increased for the 1809 campaign. By 1812 the figure had risen to 3½ pieces per 1000 men and, at some stages in that campaign, to an even higher figure. In 1796 Marmont broke the enemy's front at Castiglione with 19 cannons; at Wagram in 1809 and at Moscow in 1812 more than 100 pieces were assembled for a similar task. At Waterloo Napoleon began the action with a similar concentration.

Since Waterloo has been mentioned it is also interesting to note that at that battle the horse artillery of the British proved itself superior to the French, from whom this particular lesson in mobility had originally been learned. Indeed, a committee of enquiry set up by the French Ministry of War in 1818 reported that by their improvement in the organisation of horse artillery '. . . the English have made the Field Batteries a new arm'.

Apart from their vital functions of reconnaissance, providing cover whether in advance or retreat, and dealing with small independent operations at a distance from the main body of an army, cavalry had always had an important function on the battlefield itself. Ideas about the nature of that function and the weapons proper to it had varied a good deal since the introduction of fire-arms. At various periods cavalry had been equipped with fire-arms, often a short carbine, which generally proved of little fighting value to them. At other times commanders such as Gustavus Adolphus, Cromwell and Marlborough had insisted that the battlefield value of cavalry was as a shock weapon with cold steel, the sword. Certainly cavalry had a most important function in protecting the flanks of the otherwise vulnerable infantry line. Their value in attack against an unbroken line of infantry was much more questionable.

The early years of the Revolution found the French army extremely weak in cavalry. Many *émigrés* had been in cavalry regiments, and sometimes whole regiments went over to the enemy. This was too specialised an arm to build up again quickly. Moreover, the gradual development of the division, a small unit of all arms capable of fighting independently, led to an increasing tendency to use cavalry in smaller units than hitherto, and in a more intimate and at the same time more flexible relationship with the infantry. There was also a clear tendency to look upon the sabre and not fire-arms as the proper cavalry weapon.

Napoleon made several important changes. First he reduced the number of heavy cavalry regiments by about a half, from 25 to 14.

But those he kept were made into genuine heavy cavalry, with breast-plate and back-plate. These were never dispersed as divisional cavalry, but were kept as a reserve for shock battle service, and were organised and fought in homogeneous brigades and divisions. It was cuirassiers in massed formation who, under Ney's command, charged Wellington's squares in the afternoon of Waterloo.

Secondly, Napoleon greatly increased his regiments of medium and light horse, gradually converting dragoons from mounted infantry into cavalry proper, and making them much more like his chasseurs and hussars. This conversion of dragoons from a separate arm into regular cavalry was a process going on throughout Europe during this period. Napoleon used most of his light cavalry, chasseurs and hussars, to provide army corps cavalry, a corps having between two and four cavalry regiments attached to it. The remainder of the light cavalry were brigaded and, together with the dragoons, formed the cavalry reserve. Such a reserve, if not needed for shock action in battle, was then available for the sort of pursuit which could sometimes turn an indecisive battle into a rout. In both the Ulm and the Jena campaigns a decisive cavalry pursuit of this kind occurred.

Infantry were the principal arm of all military forces in this period, as indeed they had normally been since the days of sixteenth-century pike-men. It was easier to equip and to instruct large numbers of infantry rather than cavalry or artillery, and the part played by infantry in the development of tactics in this period was, in general, decisive.

By the time of the War of the Spanish Succession and for a good deal of the eighteenth century the accepted method of engaging infantry in battle was in line form. The infantry part of the line consisted of two or three ranks of musketeers, sometimes firing simultaneously, sometimes independently, sometimes firing as a complete line, sometimes in com-panies or even platoons. Because, as has already been pointed out, the musket was comparatively inefficient, the whole object of infantry fire was to achieve fire by volleys and that as continuous as possible. In addition, even volley fire was comparatively harmless unless dealt at fairly close range. All this meant an infantry the inefficiency of whose weapons was compensated for by a high degree of formation discipline which, in its turn, was the product of long training.

For some time before the Revolution, certainly in France, there had been much discussion about the best way to deploy infantry in battle, for the line was by no means accepted by all military writers as the right solution. One of its most serious disadvantages was that the drawing up of a line on the battlefield took valuable time, often hours, and troops were normally in no position to fight effectively while this was going on. Guibert, for example, had held that while the infantry line was the best tactical deployment for controlled fire-power and for defensive purposes, the massed column was sometimes more effective offensively, particularly for fighting over broken ground. Further, Guibert argued that infantry in battalion columns could deploy more easily on the field of battle, before forming into line, and move more quickly from one part of the battlefield to another, while fighting was in progress.

In the tactics of thirty years ago, [he wrote] and of some armies today, the movements for forming a line of battle were so slow and complicated that they took hours. The line had to be formed at a safe distance from the enemy, and once the formation had been taken up it was dangerous to attempt to change it. But with my system it will be safe to take the formation of battle as late and as near to the enemy as possible, and also to change that order after it has been taken, in other words to make counter-manoeuvres.[1]

The advocates of line and column fought out their verbal battle in France during the last twenty years before the Revolution. The result, embodied in a new infantry drill manual of 1791, was a compromise roughly as Guibert had advocated. This manual, which remained in use until 1831, showed some preference for the line in many conditions; but the usual way of forming the line was to be from close column by deployment, and it was admitted that the column had certain advantages in attack. In other words, commanders were given discretion to use the line or the column as they thought best.

One other related matter had also been the subject of much debate during the same period—the advantages and disadvantages of skirmishers operating in front of the main line. The nuisance value of elusive skirmishers against the disciplined line was well known in the eighteenth century, and was certainly employed by the Austrian army. The Austrians had used Croat bands for this purpose, and Marshal Saxe, learning from that example, had added light skirmishing troops to his own army. The British had used Rangers, corps of riflemen, in a comparable capacity against the backwoods marksmen during the War of American Independence. And although the Rangers had been disbanded after 1783, light infantry or rifle corps were in existence again in the British Army by 1800. Indeed, here lay the origin of the famous Rifle Brigade. These light infantry were organised in picked battalions, armed with a light-weight musket, and were specially instructed in skirmishing work. In their drill manual of 1791 the French made no mention of this particular matter. But modern French authorities claim that this was less from any official opposition to the practice than from a wish, again, to leave commanders free to act according to their own discretion.

What had been very largely subjects for discussion before 1789 became of very great practical importance from 1792. There was no sudden break with tradition when revolutionary France first went to

[1] Comte J. A. H. de Guibert, *Essai général de Tactique* (London, 1772), vol. I, p. 183.

war against the monarchies of Europe. French generals in 1792 and 1793 tended to hold to the line formation, since the veterans in their armies had been trained in this way and the new recruits at first fitted into the old system. This is what happened at Valmy. The massed column for attack was tried out once or twice, for example at Jemappes, but not with very satisfactory results. By 1794, however, and particularly in the *Armée du Nord* where the necessarily large reinforcements of new levies greatly lowered the discipline—though not the spirit —of the French troops, fighting in line became practically impossible. As a result, the French infantry in large numbers fought dispersed as skirmishers, using cover for their harassing fire and withdrawing when counter-attacked. This is what happened at Hondeschoote. Wallmoden's Hanoverians fought for four hours against a swarm of French skirmishers. The latter withdrew to the cover of trees, hedges and buildings when attacked, and gradually crumpled the line in front of them by shooting it to pieces.

This loose formation was the natural response of courageous but ill-trained enthusiasts. But the French levies were rapidly gaining experience all the time and effective skirmishing was, in fact, as much a job for a skilled soldier as fighting in line. The next step came when skirmishers, trained specifically for the job, prepared the way for a demoralising attack by infantry in column. This happened, for example, at the battle of Sprimont in September 1794, when the assaulting column went in with the bayonet. These columns which came in behind the skirmishers were formed either of companies or of divisions, i.e. with a depth of either twenty-four or twelve men. In either case only the first two ranks could use their firearms; the rest performed their task by sheer mass, but very effectively against a thin line which had already been disorganised and depleted by skirmishing fire.

By 1795–6 the French armies had really perfected fighting in *ordre mixte*. This was a combination of skirmishers, line and column— supported of course by artillery and cavalry. In this fashion a number of different tactical combinations could be used for a variety of conditions of terrain and opposition. But, basically, skirmishers harassed the enemy line; battalions still in line contained the enemy and prevented him from achieving a decisive concentration, and the column broke through at the chosen point.

Whether it was morale engendered by revolutionary fervour or, in fact, superior tactics, French armies with their skirmishers and massed columns did sweep across Europe. The column proved itself master of the line in many an engagement. Nonetheless, the new tactics were still vulnerable to the old, given trained troops in the line, or *ordre mince*, and a general in command who was willing to adapt the use of the line to the new conditions. This is what happened with Wellington, both in the

Peninsular War and at Waterloo. The column was dangerously defenceless against an unbroken line of musketeers. Trained fire-power was, as always, bound to prove superior to sheer *élan*. The essence of the problem can perhaps best be stated by two quotations. The first is from an anonymous English pamphlet published in 1802.

The French Army was composed of troops of the line without order, and of raw and inexperienced volunteers. They experienced defeats in the beginning, but war in the meantime was forming both officers and soldiers. In an open country they took to forming their armies in columns instead of lines, which they could not preserve without difficulty. They reduced battles to attacks on certain points, where brigade succeeded brigade, and fresh troops supplied the place of those who were driven back, till they were enabled to force the post, and make the enemy give way. They were fully aware that they could not give battle in regular order, and sought to reduce engagements to important affairs of posts. This plan has succeeded. They look upon losses as nothing, provided they succeed in the end; they set little value on their men, because they have the certainty of being able to replace them, and the customary superiority of their numbers affords them an advantage which can only be counterbalanced by great skill, conduct, and activity.

The second quotation, and with it the opposite side of the picture, is from Bugeaud's well known account after 1815.

The English generally occupied well-chosen defensive positions, having a certain command, and they showed only a portion of their force. The usual artillery action first took place. Soon, in great haste, without studying the position, without taking time to examine if there were means to make a flank attack, we marched straight on, taking the bull by the horns. About a thousand yards from the English line the men became excited, spoke to one another and hurried their march; the column began to be a little confused. The English remained quite silent with ordered arms, and from their steadiness appeared to be a long red wall. This steadiness invariably produced an effect on the young soldiers. Very soon we got nearer, shouting '*Vive l'Empereur! en avant! à la baionnette!*' Shakos were raised on the muzzles of the muskets; the column began to double, the ranks got into confusion, the agitation produced a tumult; shots were fired as we advanced. The English line remained still, silent and immovable, with ordered arms, even when we were only three hundred paces distant, and it appeared to ignore the storm about to break. The contrast was striking; in our inmost thoughts, each felt that the enemy was a long time in firing, and that this fire, reserved for so long, would be very unpleasant when it did come. Our ardour cooled. The moral power of steadiness, which nothing shakes (even if it be only in appearance), over disorder which stupefies itself with noise, overcame our minds. At this moment of intense excitement, the English wall shouldered arms; an indescribable feeling rooted many of our men to the spot; they began to fire. The enemy's steady concentrated volleys swept our ranks; decimated, we turned round seeking to recover our equilibrium; then three deafening cheers broke the silence of our opponents; at the third they were on us, pushing our disorganised flight.[1]

But the superficial tale of British successes should not be accepted without some qualifications. In the first place, Napoleon realised that

---

[1] Cited by Spencer Wilkinson, *The French Army before Napoleon* (Oxford, 1915), p. 58.

the column succeeded only when the ground had been carefully prepared for it. 'Even in the open,' he once said, 'columns do not penetrate lines unless they are supported by overwhelming artillery fire preparing the attack.' And Wellington, despite his confidence in the line, knew that it needed protection. A study of his campaigns against the French shows that, within the limits of the possibilities open to him, he always protected his line of musketeers first by some natural cover, second by a forward screen of skirmishers and, lastly, by flank cover from artillery or cavalry.

There is one other respect in which the armies of this period broke with the tradition of the previous one hundred years. The lack of mobility in most eighteenth-century armies is to some extent explained by the fact that they normally depended for their supplies upon prepared magazines. Whether this was part of a general reaction against the brutality and devastation of the Thirty Years' War, or whether it was part and parcel of that original sin of caution which besets so many soldiers, it is impossible to say. The fact is that magazines determined lines of communication and therefore the scope of operations.

Guibert, in this as in so much else, foresaw the advantages in mobility and surprise which could be gained by breaking with tradition and thus gaining the chances of decisive action if an army could move along lines of its own choosing without being hampered by the provision of its own supplies.

It is astonishing how much a good military administration can extract from the resources of a country. I speak of a populous and fertile country such as Flanders and the greater part of Germany. I am not exclusive nor excessive in my opinions. I will not say to an army; 'Have no supply trains, no magazines, no transport; always live on the country; advance if need be into the deserts of the Ukraine; Providence will feed you.' I want an army to have provision wagons, but as few as possible, proportionate to its force, to the nature of the country in which it is to operate, and to the means required in ordinary operations. If it starts from a river or a frontier, let it have on this base magazines and *dépots* well situated with a view to their defence and to the plan of operations. But if it is necessary to undertake a bold operation and forced marches the army must be able to discard the precise methods of routine. The enemy, I will assume, takes an unexpected position in which I cannot and will not attack him; I am sure to dislodge him or to take him in rear if I march towards his flank. According to our actual routine I shall require for this change of direction to form new *dépots* and new *rayons* of communication. I shall be asked for fifteen days to form these new magazines. What I want to avoid is that my supplies should command me. It is in this case my movement that is the main thing; all the other combinations are accessory and I must try to make them subordinate to the movement. The enemy must see me marching when he supposes me fettered by the calculation of my supplies; this new kind of war must astonish him, must nowhere leave him time to breathe, and make him see at his own expense this constant truth that hardly any position is tenable before an army well constituted, sober, patient, and able to manoeuvre. The moment of crisis past, my movement having fulfilled its purpose, then the supplies can return to the usual system of order and precision.[1]

The armies of the French Republic developed the system of requisitions as much by the necessity enforced upon them by administrative chaos at home as by any theory of war. And the tone was set by Bonaparte when he took over the ragged and half-starved Army of Italy in March 1796, and promised them that their reward lay in the conquest of Milan and the rich plain of Lombardy. Clearly this was a method of subsistence for victorious armies, and provided they fought in fertile and populous areas. Poland and Russia in 1812 showed the reverse side of the coin. And, as Clausewitz later pointed out, individual scavenging was no way for an army to support itself. If 'living off the land' was to be worth while, then it must be done by ordered requisitions through the normal machinery of local administration.

This survey would be incomplete without some attempt to assess the place of Napoleon, as a general, in the developments which have been previously outlined. The first point to be made clear is that Napoleon was not a great military reformer. In this respect he is not fit to rank with Gustavus Adolphus or Frederick the Great. He made no important contribution to the development of weapons or of tactics. Even in his own professional arm, artillery, it was not until the battles of his middle and later years that he produced the massed artillery barrage; and, even then, his use of guns does not show a steady evolution towards a new tactical concept. In all arms the types of weapon used, and the tactical views about their employment, owed more to the reformers of Louis XVI's reign and to the practice of the early revolutionary armies than to Napoleon himself. And the same generalisation applies to the development of the large armies of 'the nation in arms'. At St Helena Napoleon is reported to have said—'I have fought sixty battles, and I have learned nothing which I did not know in the beginning.' It was an entirely accurate comment on at least one aspect of his generalship.

What, then, was Napoleon's distinguishing mark as a 'great captain'? It was his ability to move very large armies, sometimes of 200,000 men and more, across great stretches of the continent at speeds far greater than had hitherto been thought possible; to manoeuvre these armies into positions best calculated to meet his enemies separately or break them apart if they had met; and to produce, on his side, a decisive superiority of force at the critical moment. Napoleon developed to their peak the fervour and military unorthodoxy of the Revolution. The 'blitzkrieg' was as truly a feature of Ulm, Austerlitz and Jena as it was of the first Italian campaign; and those later battles reveal the same ability to break his enemies apart before fighting them separately. Indeed, the Waterloo campaign, for all its ultimate failure, began on the

[1] Guibert, *op. cit.* vol. II, p. 58.

same high note and with the same recipe for success. The campaign in Russia failed partly because the area over which Napoleon operated from the start was too large for the necessary degree of personal control to be effective; partly because the roads and state of agriculture were too far below western European standards to make the necessary swift movement and living off the land possible; and partly because the Russians could withdraw, and chose to do so, rather than stand and fight.

This entirely personal quality of generalship, the art of the commander to detect the weak point in the enemy's deployment and to strike there with a swift and overwhelming concentration of force, had one further result. Napoleon planned and conducted his own campaigns. He felt that he could not trust even his most experienced marshals to understand his strategy unless he dictated all its details. He therefore developed no permanent staff organisation and bequeathed no staff tradition. The Prussian reformers of his own time, whatever their defects, knew better. They had seen the harm caused by purely personal leadership and now sought to perpetuate the lessons of experience in a permanent organisation. In that, as much as anything else, lay the secret of the greater success of Prussian arms in the nineteenth century.

B. NAVIES

The period of warfare when it was possible for Gibbon to speak of forces as being employed in 'temperate and undecisive contests' came to an end in the era of Nelson and Napoleon. Wars in which decisive victories were won were now fought on an unprecedented scale. Nelson, who embodied the art of the admiral, and Napoleon who embodied that of the general, agreed on the fundamental tactical principle of the concentration of force because under prevailing conditions, as Nelson said, 'Only numbers can annihilate'. Moreover the tactical freedom which he enjoyed now that the old Fighting Instructions had been replaced by the new signal books (notably Sir Home Popham's *Marine Vocabulary*) enabled him to improvise brilliantly as he did at the battle of the Nile, or plan with minute care an unusual mode of attack, as at Copenhagen and Trafalgar. His successes were made possible by the high number of officers of unusual ability in the British navy at that date. The fleets which he led to victory had been trained by Lord St Vincent, and his 'band of brothers' had already seen service in the War of American Independence. A new spirit of leadership atoned for whatever shortcomings there were in the administrative machine, whereas the efficiency of his enemies was impaired by their lack of combat experience and the consequences of earlier revolutionary excesses.

If sea power under sail may be said to depend on the three factors of an efficient battle fleet, a flourishing merchant marine, and overseas bases from which attacks on colonial possessions could be launched, Britain was in a favourable position at the start of the war. Nevertheless the traditional strategy adopted by Dundas (who was responsible for the general direction of the war) was increasingly criticised by naval authorities because of its dissipation of resources. As regards the policy of colonial conquest, good dividends were paid by the acquisition of such places as the Cape of Good Hope in 1795 and Ceylon the next year; but after eight years of war no foothold had been secured on the continent of Europe, from which British landings were ignominiously expelled on several occasions. Not until the latter part of the war were amphibious tactics perfected, first in Egypt and southern Italy, and then in Spain. The offensive uses of sea power, which lay in the ability to land and maintain an army at any spot on the long periphery of the enemy's defences, were then successfully demonstrated. 'If anyone wishes to know the history of this war,' Wellington told a naval officer, 'I will tell them that it is our maritime superiority gives me the power of maintaining my army, while the enemy are unable to do so.'[1]

As Napoleon's power spread over the whole continent, a greater concentration was required for the blockade of the enemy's fleets and the destruction of his commerce. The strategy of blockade had evolved over the past century, but its tactics continued to vary between the 'open' or distant blockade of Howe and Nelson, and the 'close' blockade favoured by St Vincent, Cornwallis and Collingwood. The success of the former policy was jeopardised by the risks of French fleets escaping (as indeed they did) when the British were off station. The 'close' blockade of Brest, Rochefort, Cadiz and Toulon decided the issue of the war; but it was a slow means of victory which required enormous powers of endurance on the part of the ships and men engaged in it, as well as expensive logistical support in the form of reserve ships to replace and replenish those on station. Nevertheless, as Mahan said, it was indeed 'these far distant, storm-beaten ships, upon which the Grand Army never looked, which stood between it and the dominion of the world.'[2]

The supreme test of this strategy, whether carried out by line-of-battle ships or by cruising frigates, came with Napoleon's Continental System after the battle of Trafalgar had eliminated any chance of a successful invasion of Britain. It was argued that, if Britain could be exhausted by the strain of maintaining a blockade of almost the whole

[1] *Letters of Sir T. Byam Martin*, ed. Sir R. V. Hamilton (Navy Records Society, 1898), vol. II, p. 409. Cf. *Keith Papers*, ed. C. Lloyd (Navy Records Society, 1955), vol. III, pp. 259 ff.

[2] A. T. Mahan, *Influence of Sea Power in the War of the French Revolution* (London, 1893), vol. II, p. 118.

coastline of Europe, while at the same time her overseas trade was denied her, national bankruptcy would ensue. But by the extension of the credit system, by developing new patterns of trade and organised smuggling from such bases as Heligoland, the 'real' value of British exports actually increased from £11 million in 1805 to £43 million in 1811.[1]

Privateering was the more traditional form of commerce destruction adopted by the French. This was countered by the Act of 1798 which made convoy compulsory for all ships except licensed 'runners', for which higher insurance premiums were paid. Only one or two frigates accompanied the huge convoys which sailed from the West Indies or the Baltic, but support squadrons were provided in dangerous areas and by the end of the war the risk of capture in convoy was negligible. Privateers continued to haunt the Channel, causing the underwriters of Lloyd's to put pressure on the Admiralty for better protection, but this form of warfare had evidently ceased to pay; on the other hand, there was almost a complete cessation of imports from overseas into continental Europe owing to the activities of British warships.[2]

France declared war on Britain in February 1793, without a navy worthy of the name. In order to fight an enemy possessing some 400 warships, of which 115 were of the line, she could muster only 246, of which 76 were of the line and of these only 27 were in commission. These ships were a legacy of the navy of the *ancien régime*, but such was the hostility felt towards the officer class by the Jacobins that very few of the *grand corps* remained in service. The ports were in a state of chaos. The ordinance of 1791 had removed all distinction between the merchant and the professional navies; the corps of marines had been disbanded, and all the bonds of discipline loosened in compliance with the egalitarianism of the day. On his first short cruise from Brest, Morard de Galle complained that he could never persuade more than fifty men to be on deck at a given time.[3]

The most violent critic of the old navy was Jeanbon Saint-André, a demagogue who had but slight acquaintance with the sea. Since he was possessed by a fanatical hatred of the 'insolent pride' of such an aristocratic profession, it was to him that the Committee turned in September 1793 to organise a republican navy. It was too late to save the Toulon fleet, of which 42 ships of all classes were burned or captured

[1] E. F. Hecksher, *The Continental System* (Oxford, 1922), pp. 42, 166, 245.

[2] Of 327 accounts studied for the war period, 200 show no profit; between 1803 and 1813, 156 St Malo privateers took only 170 prizes. L. Vignols in *Revue d'Histoire Économique* (1927), and H. Malo, *Les Dernières corsaires* (Paris, 1925). But the evidence of *Lloyd's List* suggests that British losses were heavy in the early part of the war—3466 vessels in seven years; many of these were retaken.

[3] E. Chevalier, *Histoire de la Marine Française sous la Première République* (Paris, 1886), p. 51. W. James, *Naval History of Great Britain* (London, 1837), gives comparative statistics of the two navies in vol. I.

by Hood before the English evacuated the port in December; but at Brest, Jeanbon, though he was no Carnot, succeeded by his energy in creating a new fleet. The incompetent Morard was replaced by Villaret de Joyeuse, a lieutenant in 1791 and an admiral of the fleet in 1794. Other members of the old navy, though all of bourgeois birth, whose rise to flag rank was equally rapid, were Van Stabel, Nielly and Ganteaume, while Sané, the great naval architect, continued to build ships for the new navy as he had for the old. The fanatical courage with which Villaret's fleet fought at the Glorious First of June in 1794 is a tribute to Jeanbon's work, but the experience taught him that revolutionary ardour without training or discipline was not enough. A marine artillery corps of 25,000 men was re-formed, officers ceased to be elected by their men, and the *inscription maritime* was revised so that 88,000 seamen became liable for service. To symbolise the new spirit, the tricolor replaced the white flag of the Bourbons in February 1794.[1]

The tendency towards the centralisation of naval administration, which the Convention began because of its distrust of the loyalty of the ports, continued under the Directory. Steps were taken to re-establish a professional *marine militaire de la république* of 1300 officers and 60,000 men. More officers of the old navy were re-employed, such as Brueys, Villeneuve and Decrès. Similarly, under the Napoleonic regime, a military flavour was imparted to the fleet. Sailors were organised into battalions and a hierarchy of admirals, *capitaines de vaisseaux*, *capitaines de frégates*, lieutenants and ensigns was established on a broader basis of entry than of old; training ships for boys, who passed out as *aspirants*, were opened in 1810. Drill, whether on shore or on board ships in harbour, was intensive, but it never compensated for the lack of experience at sea or in action. The French navy, in fact, never experienced that revolution in the art of war which we associate with Nelson or Napoleon.

An unenterprising strategic attitude marks the whole period of Decrès' Ministry of Marine from 1801 to 1814. Apart from the Egyptian expedition and the fleet movements of 1805, the occasional cruises which escaped the blockading forces were futile because the commanders were anxious to avoid battle. Decrès did his best to restrain any offensive use of the fleet by the emperor, so that the latter was justified in complaining that he could not find an admiral who was willing to risk the loss of a few ships in order to gain a victory. The strategic doctrine was that of a 'fleet in being'; in the minister's view, the strength of the British navy could be worn down, provided sufficient ships were built in all the main ports of France and her allies. Hence the big building programme after the main fighting force had been destroyed

---

[1] Cf. L. Lévy-Schneider, *Le Conventionnel Jeanbon Saint-André* (Paris, 1901), and N. Hampson, *La Marine de l'An II* (Paris, 1959).

at Trafalgar. No less than 83 of the line and 65 frigates were built, so that in 1814 the fleet consisted of 103 of the line and 157 frigates, in spite of the heavy losses suffered during the war. These losses amounted to 377 ships captured or destroyed in action, 24 by shipwreck. The equivalent British figures—10 and 101—are sufficient commentary upon the nature of the war at sea.[1]

Another strategic policy which Napoleon inherited from his predecessors was the invasion of Britain. The Jacobins had begun the war with the intention of planting 50,000 caps of liberty on British soil. Hoche came nearest to this ideal in 1796 when an invasion force reached Bantry Bay in the depth of winter, but so bad was the weather that not a man could be landed. The various schemes with which Napoleon amused himself cannot be described here; suffice it to say that by August 1805 there were 2343 boats capable of transporting 167,590 men from the Channel ports, and the grand diversionary plans for the use of the combined fleets of France and Spain looked like maturing; but the number of men ready for immediate embarkation was less than 100,000. So successfully were the emperor's schemes forestalled that even before Trafalgar he began to switch his strategy to one of land conquest, disclaiming that he ever had any intention to invade.[2]

Except for a brief period in 1827, when the title of Lord High Admiral was revived for the Duke of Clarence, the administration of the British navy was in the hands of the Board of Admiralty and the Navy Board, until the latter (together with subsidiary boards such as those for victualling, transport, sick and wounded etc.) were all abolished in 1832. The relation between the military or executive functions of the Admiralty and the civilian or supply services of the Navy Board were happiest when Sir Charles Middleton was comptroller of the latter board (1778–90) and when as Lord Barham he was first lord in 1805–6. He considered the system of dyarchy unsatisfactory because, as the office of comptroller—'the mainspring belonging to everything that is naval'—was second only in importance to that of the first lord, he should therefore have a seat on the Board of Admiralty. When his recommendations for reform were rejected he resigned, though he continued for some time to act in an advisory capacity.[3]

Relations were worst when St Vincent was first lord between 1801 and 1804. As an executive officer he had long been convinced that 'the civil branch of the navy is rotten to the core'. As soon as peace was signed he turned his formidable energies to a personal investigation of the dockyards, against the wishes of the Navy Board. He found

[1] Michael Lewis, *A Social History of the Navy, 1793–1815* (London, 1960), p. 348.
[2] E. Desbrière, *Projets et Tentatives de débarquement aux Iles Britanniques, 1793–1805* (Paris, 1902), vol. IV, pp. 464–6.
[3] *Barham Papers*, ed. Sir J. K. Laughton (Navy Records Society, 1910), vol. III, p. 33. Cf. Sir O. Murray in *Mariner's Mirror*, 1938.

the situation worse than he imagined. 'Portsmouth was bad enough, but Chatham beggars all description.' As a notorious disciplinarian, it was easy for him to break a strike of shipwrights under John Gast, one of the early trade unionists; but when the Addington cabinet 'mutinied' (as he put it) at the prospect of taking action against such a powerful body as the timber trust, he forced them to set up a commission of enquiry by the threat of resignation. In 1804, however, what his fellow Whig, Fox, called 'an insurrection of jobbers' found a mouthpiece in Pitt, whose attack on the alleged inefficient state of the navy resulted in the fall of the government. St Vincent had certainly restricted the building of small craft and had not made full use of the merchants' yards, because he mistakenly thought that the peace would last; but when the reports of the Commissions of Naval Enquiry appeared in subsequent years, his allegations of plunder and peculation were fully justified.[1]

Such was the legacy he bequeathed to Lord Melville. When the Tenth Report on the office of Treasurer was published in April 1805, Melville found himself charged with misappropriation of funds when he held that office in 1792. A vote of censure was passed, but in the actual impeachment (the last of its kind in history) he was acquitted on the grounds that he was not knowingly responsible for the losses incurred.[2] It was this trial which turned Cobbett into a critic of the government and made Lord Cochrane, the most brilliant frigate captain of the age, the radical member for Westminster.

Melville's fall brought Barham back as the last naval officer to hold the post of first lord of the Admiralty. The consequence was the virtual unification of the two boards during a term of office which, though brief, was of exceptional importance. Besides planning the Trafalgar campaign, the eighty-year-old Admiral found time for many administrative reforms. He departmentalised the work of the sea lords and prohibited serving officers from taking time off to attend sittings of Parliament, though they were not yet prevented from becoming members. Regulations of every type were brought up to date, so that the enlarged edition of the *Admiralty Regulations and Instructions for Officers* of 1808 was largely his work. Finally, a new office of Civil Architect and Engineer was created to replace that of Inspector General of Naval Works instituted in 1796.

The man who filled these posts until their abolition in 1813 was General Sir Samuel Bentham, brother of Jeremy Bentham, and a man of long administrative experience in the Russian service. He did much to

---

[1] *Letters of St Vincent*, ed. D. Bonner Smith (Navy Records Society, 1922, 1927), vol. I, p. 378, vol. II, p. 33. Cf. J. S. Tucker, *Life of St Vincent* (London, 1844), vol. II, pp. 123, 208.
[2] *Parl. Debates*, vol. IV, pp. 255 ff.; *Annual Register* (1806), pp. 112 ff.; *Letters of St Vincent*, vol. II, p. 37.

modernise the dockyards by introducing the steam engine in 1795 for pumping work and for driving the machinery invented by Sir Marc Brunel for the mass production of blocks. Similarly, he employed Rennie to build the breakwater at Plymouth, which thenceforth replaced Torbay as the principal anchorage of the Channel fleet. He anticipated his successor, Sir William Seppings (Surveyor from 1813 to 1832), in strengthening the build of ships by the use of diagonal trusses and watertight compartments, though the *Howe* of 1815 was the first big ship to be built under the new system.[1]

Apart from the introduction of the elliptical stern and a slight increase in dimensions, there was little material change in the build of ships during this period. Since the number of carronades carried on the upper deck had much increased, the old system of rating ships according to the number of guns became so confused that in 1816 new rates were standardised as follows: First Rate, three-decker line-of-battle ships (over 100 guns and 800 men); Second, Third and Fourth Rate, two-deckers (of 80, 74 and 50 guns); Fifth and Sixth Rate, single-decked frigates (of 36 and 24 guns). The latter did not lie in the line of battle, their function being that of cruisers. Smaller craft such as gun brigs and sloops were not post ships, i.e. they were commanded by officers under the rank of captain. A comparison of the size of the royal dockyards in 1803 may be made from the number of shipwrights employed—420 at Deptford, 360 at Woolwich, 640 at Chatham, 180 at Sheerness, 900 at Portsmouth and 800 at Plymouth. A few of these men were selected for education at the Royal Naval College, Portsmouth, in order to form a corps of naval constructors.

The building and repair of the huge fleets employed produced an even more serious timber shortage than in the previous century. To build a 74-gun ship of 1730 tons, 1977 loads of oak, 570 of elm, 139 of fir and 2500 of deal were required at a cost of £47,000. Before the war, annual timber consumption amounted to some 25,000 loads in addition to about 80,000 consumed by the merchant service. Foreseeing a shortage of English oak, a commission recommended the use of fir, so that during the war a number of ships were built of this material imported from Canada. Another hitherto untapped source was teak from India, where Bombay shipwrights built the first frigate of this material in 1805 and before the end of the war several first rates. Other methods adopted to conserve supplies were the building of 'wall sided' ships to save the pieces of curved timber required for the old-fashioned 'tumble home', and the use of iron supports instead of wooden 'knees'. What chiefly altered the pattern of trade was Napoleon's attempt to close the Baltic, so that between the beginning and end of the war North American

---

[1] See Lady Bentham, *Life of Sir S. Bentham* (London, 1862), and *Third Report of the Commission of Enquiry* (1805).

imports had risen from one to fifty-four per cent of the total. A particularly serious timber crisis occurred in 1803, when St Vincent attacked the whole system of contracts. The merchants, backed by the Navy Board and a section of the House of Commons, withheld supplies until they had secured the fall of the government, thereby jeopardising the safety of the realm as much by their own selfishness as by the policy of the enemy.[1]

After the introduction of the short-range carronade in 1779 there were no notable improvements in gunnery until the war was over. British crews were far better trained in the exercise of the 'great guns and small arms' than their enemies, so that their rate of fire was reckoned at three rounds in two minutes, though the effective range was not much above a quarter of a mile. Most actions, however, were fought at even closer range. 'I shall of course look at it,' wrote Nelson to a correspondent who suggested a new type of gunsight, 'but I hope we shall be able, as usual, to get so close to our enemies that our shot cannot miss the object'.[2] Naval officers, in fact, still manoeuvred their ships rather than their guns in order to bring a full broadside to bear, and most ships were captured by boarding rather than by sinking, since solid shot was incapable of sinking a wooden ship unless an accidental explosion occurred on board. This is the chief reason why naval casualties were far less than those suffered on land: even at Trafalgar only 449 British were killed, and of the 4408 enemy losses most were incurred by drowning in the storm which blew up after the battle. But the reliance on close range fighting failed when British ships came up against the American 'colombiad', a compromise between the carronade and the long range gun. Nor was there any uniformity in training, since responsibility for arming ships lay with the Ordnance Board. Little use was made of Shrapnel's invention of an explosive shell in 1787 except with mortars, and the standard of gunnery definitely fell off during the last ten years of the war. Nevertheless an officer who was also a gunnery enthusiast could achieve a spectacular success, as Broke did in the *Shannon's* victory over the *Chesapeake* in eleven minutes. Colonel Sir Howard Douglas was so much impressed with the low standard of naval gunnery that in 1820 he published a treatise on the subject, which was adopted in France but neglected in England until he and some influential friends founded the gunnery school of H.M.S. *Excellent* in 1832, one consequence of which was the disbandment of the Marine Artillery Corps, to which all gunnery problems had previously been referred.

Two inventions which were to transform naval warfare (though not

---

[1] R. G. Albion, *Forests and Sea Power* (Cambridge, Mass., 1926), pp. 115, 356. Cf. *Letters of St Vincent*, and *Naval Chronicle*, vol. XII, p. 34.
[2] *Despatches*, vol. IV, p. 292.

for a hundred years to come) were those of the rocket and the submarine. What its inventor, Sir William Congreve, called 'the soul of artillery without the body' was the incendiary rocket used against Boulogne in 1804 and on subsequent occasions both by sea and land. Like the rocket, the submarine was born at this time, but it also failed to develop on account of the propulsion problem. An underwater attempt had been made by Bushnell in the American War, but it was the *Nautilus* which Robert Fulton, another American, built for the French in 1803 which was the first 'plunging boat'. His services were later bought by the British Admiralty, who employed him in the construction of various forms of mines and 'torpedoes' (as he called them) which were used against the Boulogne flotilla, though most officers regarded them as contrary to the rules of war.[1]

Fulton's name is more generally associated with the development of the steamboat. If William Symington, with his *Charlotte Dundas* of 1802, may be regarded as the father of marine engineering, Fulton's *Clermont* (1807) was the first commercial paddle steamer in America, and his double-hulled *Demologos* (1814) was the first steam warship, though she was never in action.[2] Since the British navy emerged from the war with an overwhelming superiority under sail, the Admiralty was not predisposed to encourage the development of the steam warship, for which the paddle steamer was ill suited, though tugs do appear in the Navy List from 1822 onwards. The first steam warship to be used in action was the *Diana* in the Burmese War of 1824. The first in European waters was the *Karteria*, commanded by Abney Hastings in the Greek War of Independence. Both Hastings and his superior officer in the Greek navy, Lord Cochrane, were enthusiastic about the future of steam and it was their operations in 1827 which precipitated the battle of Navarino, the last battle to be fought under sail.

The demands on the manpower of the nation made by a war of unprecedented length and scale may be illustrated by the figures of seamen voted in 1793 (24,000), in 1797 (120,000) and in 1814 (140,000), from which the total dropped to 23,000 in 1820. The census of 1801 gives 135,000 seamen voted for the navy and 144,000 employed in the merchant service, out of a population of only eight million. The methods of obtaining such numbers remained much the same as before, though they had to be expanded and supplemented as the strain intensified. There was little difficulty about obtaining the 3500 officers required, since the service was more lucrative than the army on account of the chances of prize money, head money (£5 for each prisoner taken)

---

[1] On Congreve, see *Naval Miscellany*, vol. IV, pp. 423 ff., and on Fulton see *Keith Papers* (Navy Records Society 1955), vol. III, pp. 7 ff.

[2] Cf. H. P. Spratt, *The Birth of the Steamboat* (London, 1958); C. J. Bartlett, *Great Britain and Sea Power, 1815–53* (Oxford, 1963), p. 197.

and freight money for the conveyance of public treasure. Frigate captains naturally benefited more than those employed in the blockading fleets, but flag officers enjoyed 'eighths' of all ships captured on their station. Thus a commander like Lord Keith received £64,000 for the capture of the Cape, and for four years' service in the Mediterranean (during which he never fought a battle) his share in prize and freight money was £112,678. Sir Hyde Parker is said to have gained £200,000 on the West Indian station, and Lord Exmouth £300,000 in the East Indies.[1] At the beginning of a war an Act 'for the encouragement of seamen' laid down the scale of distribution. Though much money found its way into the hands of the lawyers of the Vice-Admiralty courts where prizes were condemned, great fortunes could still be made by naval officers. Hardship began with the peace, when officers were put on half pay; since there was no retired list, competition in the upper ranks of the list became so serious that many found employment outside the service as soon as the war was over.

The age and source of entry remained much the same as before, the profession being largely hereditary in families from the south of England and in the lowlands of Scotland. Although the regulations continued to be circumvented in order to gain fictitious sea time which rendered boys eligible for more rapid promotion, the normal age of entry was about twelve. From 1794 the old style of 'captain's servant' was replaced by that of 'volunteer, first class', the second class consisting of future masters and the third of boy seamen. Patronage was still largely in the hands of captains, though the Admiralty alone nominated those attending the Naval Academy which in 1806 was renamed Royal Naval College, Portsmouth. The great majority of boys, however, went straight to sea.

The order of precedence in a ship was laid down as captain or commander, lieutenant, sub-lieutenant, master, gunner, boatswain, carpenter, master's mate, midshipman. There were many varieties of midshipman popularly distinguished into youngsters and oldsters, the latter (who might be of any age) being those who had either failed to 'pass for lieutenant' or were waiting for their commissions. In order to provide junior officers for the numerous small craft employed, those of the former class who acted as master's mates were given the temporary rank of sub-lieutenant to distinguish them from the real mates who assisted the master in the navigation of the ship. To reach the rank of captain, interest was invaluable, and on a distant station astonishing promotions could be made—the sons of two successive commanders-in-chief in the East Indies becoming post-captains at the age of seventeen; thereafter, however, seniority alone counted.

[1] C. N. Parkinson, *War in the Eastern Seas, 1793–1815* (London, 1954), p. 349; *Keith Papers*, vol. III, p. 218; Lewis, *Social History of the Navy*, pp. 316 ff.

Sea officers, as they were then called, were distinguished between the commissioned (or executive) and warrant (or specialist), the latter being divided between civilians such as the surgeon, purser and chaplain, and those promoted from petty officer, such as master, gunner, boatswain and carpenter. By a number of changes which were finalised in an Order in Council of 1816 the status of the warrant officers (including the master) was improved in order to attract the right type of man. They became eligible for promotion to lieutenant and to wear uniform. Even the chaplain, who alone failed to benefit from the increase of pay made early in the war, was in 1812 given a larger salary instead of depending on seamen's groats to supplement his official pittance. This upgrading continued, but opportunities for promotion from the lower deck diminished.[1] At the same time as the ratings of coxswain, yeoman and cook were confirmed, such obsolete ratings as trumpeter and swabber were abolished. A section of the ship's company which stood somewhat apart from the crew because of their distinctive uniform and police duties were the marines, called 'Royal' from 1802.

'The People' (as the seamen were called) either volunteered, attracted by the generous bounties offered in wartime, or were impressed by the Impress Service which in 1793 superseded the old method of sporadic gangs. Nevertheless, if a ship was short of complement a captain sent out his own gang, or pressed men out of ships he met at sea. Hitherto only seafaring men could be legally impressed, but the two Quota Acts of 1795 (35 G. III. c. 5) specified the number of men to be provided by the counties and towns of England, e.g. Cambridgeshire 126, Devon 393, London 5704, Dartmouth 394. Magistrates were told to conscript from parish lists, to offer bounties to be paid out of the rates, and to accept substitutes; in practice, if the number was not forthcoming, they combed the gaols to provide 'landmen' who were often quite unfit for the service. A letter written by Admiral Collingwood shortly after the mutinies of 1797 expresses the widely held view that these 'quota men' were at the bottom of the trouble by reason of their connection with the Corresponding Societies, United Irishmen and the like (though no direct Jacobin influence has ever been traced): 'Billy Pitt's men, the county volunteers, your ruined politicians, who having drunk enough ale to drown a nation, and talked nonsense enough to mad it, are the fellows who have done the business, the seamen who suffer are only the cat's paws. . . . What were you to expect from the refuse of the gallows and the purgings of a gaol, and such make a majority of most ship's companies in such a war as this?'[2] It may be added that

---

[1] Lewis, *Social History of the Navy*, pp. 44 ff.

[2] *Correspondence of Collingwood*, ed. E. Hughes (Navy Records Society, 1957), p. 85. Cf. C. Gill, *Naval Mutinies of 1797* (Manchester, 1913), and G. E. Manwaring and B. Dobree, *The Floating Republic* (London, 1935). The men's petitions are in P.R.O. Adm. 1/5125.

such men (Parker, for example, the leader of the 'floating republic' at the Nore, and Joyce at Spithead) were also responsible for the good organisation of the outbreaks in April and May 1797.

The neglect of the men's petitions and the long period of uninspired leadership in the Channel fleet were the immediate causes of the outbreak, since the demands were based on long-standing grievances. The pay of an ordinary seaman had remained unchanged at 19s. a month since the Commonwealth. It was now raised to 25s. 6d. a month, but various deductions continued to be made for the support of Greenwich Hospital, the chaplain on board, the issue of slop clothing (there being as yet no uniform), and men still had to wait until a ship was paid off before they received their wage tickets, which were usually exchanged at grossly unfair discount at the ports. Dishonest victualling was chiefly responsible for the bad food and the inadequate medical treatment of which the men also complained. Two improvements in this respect may be noted—the compulsory issue of lemon juice to combat scurvy, and the introduction of canned meat in 1813. But it was not possible to comply with the demand for shore leave on account of the dangers of desertion, which achieved staggering proportions towards the end of the war. Nor could there be much relaxation in the severity of discipline until the war was over. By that time a tendency to humanise conditions in the service had begun which is illustrated by the cessation of the more brutal forms of punishment such as 'starting' with a rope's end and running the gauntlet. Furthermore, the methods of pensioning wounded seamen (the Royal Hospital at Greenwich reached its highest number of 2700 pensioners at this date) and of taking care of widows and families worked better than hitherto. For the latter, a number of fictitious 'widows' men' were carried on the books of a ship, their pay being devoted to charitable purposes. But that mutiny did not again break out is due chiefly to the way Nelson had taught his officers the art of leadership and had, by the example of his victories, raised the status of seamen in popular esteem.

The strain on the country's manpower made by the necessity of maintaining great fleets at sea was intensified by the losses due to disease and to desertion. An analysis of the 103,660 deaths recorded during the war suggests that 82 per cent died of disease, 12 per cent by shipwreck or accident and only 6 per cent by enemy action. To these losses should be added the 113,273 men who deserted.[1] The fatality due to disease would have been higher, had it not been for what was virtually a revolution in naval medicine during the last ten years of the century. Owing to the persistence of Sir Gilbert Blane and Dr Thomas Trotter, most of the reforms suggested by James Lind forty years earlier were now adopted. These included better treatment of the sick on board, the

[1] Cf. Lewis, *op. cit.*, p. 442, and W. B. Hodge in *Journal of the R. Statistical Society* (1855).

adoption of a 'divisional' system which enabled officers to keep a closer eye on their men, and the elimination of scurvy by the general issue of lemon juice in 1795-6. Smallpox was also brought under control after the introduction of vaccination a few years later; but the two major scourges of typhus and yellow fever remained undefeated. In 1805 the status of naval surgeons was at last improved when they became quarter-deck officers with uniforms and increased pay, thereby attracting a better type of practitioner to the naval service.[1]

Two forms of employment which added to the difficulties of recruitment were privateering and the Sea Fencibles. The former was always frowned on by the authorities because it deprived the service of a valuable source of manpower. Between 1803 and 1806 some 47,000 men were engaged in privateering, though they cannot have gained much profit owing to the ubiquity of cruisers.[2] Again, in order to guard against the dangers of invasion a corps of Sea Fencibles, composed of fishermen and coastal volunteers, was established in 1798 as a sea militia to man the chain of Martello towers and signal stations around the coast, and to provide a last line of defence with their boats. It was never an effective force, and it provided an escape for many who would otherwise have been enlisted for service at sea. It is significant that the force reached its greatest strength of 23,455 men in 1810 when the danger of invasion was long past.[3]

An analysis of the average ship's company would show about the following proportions: volunteers 15 per cent, pressed men 50 per cent, quota men 12 per cent, boys 8 per cent, foreigners 15 per cent.[4] Some of the latter were there of their own free will, but most had been impressed at sea and were unable to obtain their release through the normal consular channels. The most important element among such men were the Americans, partly because of the expansion of their merchant marine with the decline in the number of ships belonging to belligerent powers, partly because the number of forged citizenship papers made it difficult to distinguish between genuine Americans and British deserters. It was probably this which accounts for the small proportion of Americans released on official request—273 between 1803 and 1805 out of 1500 applications. In 1812 it was estimated that over 6000 Americans were serving in British ships, of whom 2500 were imprisoned for refusing to take up arms against their own country.[5] According to J. Q. Adams, it was the insistence on the right of search

---

[1] See C. Lloyd and J. L. S. Coulter, *Medicine and the Navy*, vol. III (Edinburgh, 1961).
[2] J. Barrow, *Life of Anson* (London, 1839), p. 467. Some 4000 letters of marque were issued during the course of the war; see Register of Issues, Adm. 7/325.649.
[3] *Keith Papers*, vol. III, pp. 133 ff. [4] Lewis, *op. cit.*, p. 139.
[5] J. F. Zimmerman, *Impressment of American Seamen* (New York, 1925), p. 106. Cf. A. Steel in *Camb. Hist. Journal*, vol. IX (1949), pp. 331–51; and T. Roosevelt, *The War of 1812* (New York, 1882), p. 42.

which was the principal cause of the war of 1812-14, though the root of the trouble probably lay in the demand for the conquest of Canada. The British claim to search neutrals not only for contraband but also for deserters rested on the view expressed by Lord Stowell that 'the fundamental principle of maritime jurisdiction is that ships upon the high seas compose no part of the territory of the state'. Diametrically opposed was the American principle of 'free ships, free goods', or as their pendants proclaimed, 'free trade and sailor's rights.' This long-standing quarrel might easily have resulted in war in 1806, when a party from H.M.S. *Leopard* took off a deserter and three others whose citizenship was ambiguous from the U.S.S. *Chesapeake* only ten miles off Cape Henry. Reparations were refused and the situation remained unaltered until 1812. On the eve of the war the obnoxious Order in Council which compelled neutrals to trade under British licence was revoked, but while the government might forego some of its pretensions it never surrendered the right to reclaim deserters. Nor was the subject mentioned in the peace treaty.

The obstinacy of the British government was based on a supremacy at sea won by a navy now rendered negligent by success. To the vast fleets which ringed the coasts of Europe, the Americans could only oppose eight frigates and eight smaller ships. But this force was of surprising efficiency, considering the neglect of the American navy before 1798. In that year the Navy Department was established, and also a Marine Corps of 720 men. The necessity of protecting the growing commerce of a young nation had, in fact, made the revival of a navy essential, in spite of the fears entertained in some quarters that the establishment of armed forces on a permanent basis might prove a threat to the democratic way of life. By 1812 man-power had increased to 4000 men (all volunteers) and 500 officers, many of whom had experience during the 'quasi-war' with Republican France or against the Algerine corsairs. But the chief reason for the successes during the first year of the war with Britain was the fact that their three 44-gun frigates were designed by Joshua Humphreys to be superior to any European frigate. Ships of all nations were underrated at this date owing to the increase in the number of upper deck guns, so that a 44-gun frigate carried in addition some 22 carronades. Such well-armed, well-fought ships proved more than a match for 38-gun British frigates. Nevertheless as the Peninsular war drew to a finish the massive weight of British sea power was transferred to the American coast to enable landings to be made (one of which burned Washington) and coastal traffic to be strangled, from which Mahan drew the strategic conclusion that 'not by rambling operations, or naval duels, are wars decided, but by force massed and handled in skilful combination'.[1]

---

[1] A. T. Mahan, *Sea Power in its Relations to the War of 1812* (London, 1905), vol. I, p. v.

Privateering, however, still flourished on that side of the Atlantic. Whereas in the course of the war American warships took only 165 prizes, American privateers made 1344 captures, some of which were extremely valuable. Nor were the Nova Scotians backward in this form of activity, though a comparison of the number of prizes condemned at Halifax shows the more important part played by naval commerce destruction, 200 prizes being brought in by privateers as compared with 490 by cruisers.[1] Had not an efficient convoy system been instituted by this date, British losses at the hands of American privateers would have been considerably greater.

Britain emerged from the twenty years of naval war on a world scale with unchallenged superiority at sea. Though conquests such as Java were restored in the interests of future peace, a chain of bases now secured the route to the East: Ascension, St Helena, the Cape, Mauritius and Ceylon. In spite of war losses, the number of registered merchant vessels had increased from 16,079 to 24,418, representing a tonnage increase of over a million tons.[2] At the same time her naval force of 1168 warships, 240 of them ships of the line, was vastly superior to that of any other nation. The navies of France, Spain, Holland, Denmark and the United States had been defeated, while those of Sweden and Russia were at this date of small account. The era during which British naval power reigned almost unchallenged had begun, although the age of warfare under sail was closing and that of the iron steamship and the explosive shell was about to dawn.

[1] Lists printed by Essex Institute, Salem, 1911. Cf. J. Maclay, *History of American Privateering* (1899).

[2] C. E. Fayle, *The Trade Winds*, ed. Parkinson (London, 1948), p. 83.

CHAPTER IV

REVOLUTIONARY INFLUENCES AND CONSERVATISM IN LITERATURE AND THOUGHT

THE fact that the French Revolution was something unprecedented, exceptional, and portentous for the future of Europe and perhaps the world did not escape the notice of some contemporaries. Edmund Burke, its fiercest antagonist, perceived as early as 1790 that he was witnessing the first 'complete revolution'. Kant predicted in 1798 that such a phenomenon could never be obliterated from the memory of mankind. Some twenty-five years later, Stendhal declared: 'In the two thousand years of recorded world history so sharp a revolution in customs, ideas, and beliefs has perhaps never occurred before.' Even so critical an observer as the German nationalist Arndt had to admit in retrospect: 'I should be very ungrateful and also a hypocrite if I did not avow that we owe an immense amount to that savage and crazy revolution . . . and that it has put ideas into people's heads and hearts which twenty or thirty years before the event most men would have shuddered to conceive of.'

From the very outset the Revolution had a profound impact on Europe's intellectuals. At that early stage delight by far prevailed upon dismay. Indeed, it was widely felt that a new world was opening to the astonished sight. William Wordsworth immortalised that frame of mind in *The Prelude*:

> Bliss was it in that dawn to be alive
> And to be young was very heaven.

And Coleridge, his friend and collaborator, vividly recalled how 'from the general heart of human kind Hope sprang forth like a full-born Deity'. The young poet Southey, Thomas Holcroft the dramatist, and the radicals Thomas Paine and Sir James Mackintosh, no less ardently embraced the principles of the Revolution. Burke's attack was followed within a few months by Mackintosh's warm apologia in *Vindiciae Gallicae* (April 1791).

In Germany intellectual circles were deeply moved by the Revolution. Forty years later Hegel compared that era to a marvellous sunrise. Other leading thinkers of his generation such as Fichte and Schelling, but also the aged Kant, the poets Klopstock, Wieland and Hölderlin, and the historians Herder, Johannes Müller and Schlözer, to name but a few outstanding examples, all welcomed the Revolution in no uncertain terms. This attitude was further disseminated by German eye-witnesses in Paris who sent back long and glowing reports. Elsewhere the Austrian reformer Sonnenfels, the Swiss educationalist Pestalozzi, the Italian poet Alfieri, the young Spanish writer Marchena, the Swedish publicist Thorild, as well as a host of others, helped to swell the almost universal echo. Indeed, Arthur O'Connor was not exaggerating when he declared in a speech to the Irish Parliament in May 1795 that 'the whole European mind had undergone a revolution neither confined to this or that country, but as general as the great causes which had given it birth and still continued to feed its growth'.

This widespread enthusiasm was based upon a variety of motives at the root of which lay the amazing social and political optimism of the age. Belief in the perfectibility of man and society, that central dogma of the Enlightenment, had by now reached its greatest intensity. In 1784, Kant had confidently asserted: 'By each revolution the seed of enlightenment is more and more developed.' Now in 1792, he still firmly believed in the inevitability of human progress towards ever increasing intellectual and moral perfection. The widespread and fervent acclaim of the Revolution was itself proof to Kant that there existed an altruistic moral fibre in mankind, at least in its basic make-up; for, as he pointed out, it needed courage and unselfishness to manifest pro-revolutionary sympathies.[1]

In France, the chief apostle of the idea of man-made progress was the Marquis de Condorcet, author of the celebrated *Esquisse d'un tableau historique des progrès de l'esprit humain*, composed during the troubled days of 1793–4. Even at the height of the Terror, while himself in mortal danger, Condorcet firmly clung to his belief in the indefinite moral improvement of mankind, and in April 1794 died a martyr to his secular faith. The brightest prospects for mankind firmly set before his eyes, he had concluded his *Esquisse* with the brave if pathetic words:

Such contemplation is for him an asylum, in which the memory of his persecutors cannot pursue him; there he lives in thought with man restored to his natural rights and dignity, forgets man tormented and corrupted by greed, fear or envy; there he lives with his peers in an Elysium created by reason and graced by the purest pleasures known to the love of mankind.[2]

In his *Inquiry Concerning Political Justice and Its Influence on Morals and Happiness* (1793), William Godwin, whose influence in England was seminal, envisaged a secular paradise hardly distinguishable from earlier Christian millenarian expectations. His prophecy, 'in that blessed day there will be no war,' harmonised well with the still prevalent ideal of cosmopolitan Fraternity, that secularised version of the

[1] Kant's essay, *Whether the Human Race is continually advancing towards the Better*, written in 1792, could not be published until six years later.
[2] *Sketch for a Historical Picture of the Progress of the Human Mind*, translated by June Barraclough (London, 1955), p. 202.

ideal of Christian brotherhood. Closely akin was the widespread belief which Montesquieu had formulated in the words: 'The spirit of the republic is peace.' For not only in revolutionary France but elsewhere too, it was expected that, once the absolute dynasties, those age-old troublemakers, were overthrown, war itself would cease to plague mankind; at least, war, as the Sport of Kings, would never be waged again. It was tempting to infer that the peoples, in their novel capacity as rulers, would sweep war aside since it could not be in their interest to become involved in it. This is why Kant, for example, was so greatly impressed by the striving on the part of the French for a representative regime which he maintained 'cannot be bellicose'. For the same reason he interpreted the fall of the absolute monarchy as the first step towards a federation of States ruled on representative lines. Kant had by now come to regard war as the greatest obstacle to morality, but was realistic enough not to share the fairly widespread illusion that the abolition of that supreme social evil lay just round the corner. What he envisaged in his famous essay *On Perpetual Peace* (1795) was rather a gradual process which would be characterised by an ever-growing respect for public international law. Little by little wars would be rendered more humane, then less frequent, until aggression would be abolished altogether.

Another aspect of the faith in progress was the hope that the French Revolution would usher in the longed-for Age of Reason. Although anti-rationalist doctrines, never extinct in the eighteenth century, were by now visibly gaining ground, the adoration of reason in general, and of rationalism in politics in particular, was still very much *en vogue*. William Godwin held reason to be an infallible guide to truth and goodness. Having been brought up on a particularly stern version of the Calvinist faith, he soon came to reject all religion as fettering the free use of man's rational faculties, and ended by idolising the intellect itself. Unalloyed human reason, systematised in a body of rational laws, was to be the panacea for all the political and social afflictions of mankind. Kant and Hegel, Condorcet and Godwin, and many kindred minds, were all dreaming of a Kingdom of Reason, and many felt confident that their generation was experiencing the first stages of its establishment on earth. Hegel, in his *Lectures on the Philosophy of History* (1830), drew this enthusiastic picture of their state of mind at the time of the first constitutional experiments of the Revolution:

All of a sudden, the Idea, the conception of Right, asserted its authority, and the old framework of injustice could offer no resistance to its onslaught. In this way, a constitution was established in harmony with the idea of Right, and everything was henceforth to be based on this foundation. Never since the sun has stood in the firmament and the planets revolved around him had it been perceived that man's existence centres in his head, that is in thought, inspired by which he builds up the world of reality. Anaxagoras had been the first to say that νοῦς governs the World, but not until now had man advanced to the recognition of the principle that thought ought to govern spiritual reality. . . . All thinking beings shared in the jubilation of this epoch.[1]

Paradoxically, it was on precisely opposite grounds that the French Revolution was hailed in other quarters. Among those affected by the romantic movement, now unfolding, the idea was prevalent that the Revolution had inaugurated the establishment of human life on a basis of pure feeling. Nor could it be denied that strong irrational forces, hitherto kept in check by the hierarchic society of the past, had been unleashed by the revolution, a turn of events which the romantics, critical as they were of the excesses of rationalism, could not but regard as highly auspicious. In a sense it might even be said that the eruption of irrational, or subconscious, impulses that characterised so many aspects of the French Revolution was the signal for the romantic battle against reason. Both movements were also united in their impassioned striving for freedom. The ideal of *Liberté* which enjoyed pride of place in the tripartite war-cry of the Revolution blended naturally with the subjectivist attitude that characterised European Romanticism especially in its initial stages. The emancipation of the self, as this trend has been called, was comparable to, but far in excess of, a similar tendency in the Renaissance. Time-honoured bonds of allegiance and belief had been loosened for some time past, but the Revolution had brought that process to a head. Suddenly, all ideas and ideals were once again in the melting pot, and thus the individual self appeared to some of the early romantics to be the only firm anchor. Fichte not only developed an epistemological system on highly subjectivist lines, but even declared that virtue and vice existed only in so far as the individual's conscience conceived them. This extreme view influenced Friedrich Schlegel, the young daredevil thinker, and some of his associates. Nor was the romantic quest for freedom confined to the individual. According to Friedrich's brother August Wilhelm, each national community had its own genius and must therefore be free to develop its own artistic mode of expression in literature as well as in the other arts. Clearly the time was over when all cultured nations could be expected to conform to the rigid standards of classical French taste. Cultural patriotism thus became one of the chief by-products of romanticism. Nevertheless, it will be seen that the attitude of the romantics to the Revolution was complex and by no means unequivocally favourable.

Whereas the revolutionary aspirations for liberty and fraternity, after a promising overture, soon met with disappointment and frustration,

[1] *Vorlesungen über die Philosophie der Geschichte*, in *Werke* (Berlin, 1840), vol. IX, pp. 535–6.

the great and embittered struggle for equality had a more lasting impact. The egalitarian zeal, which according to Chateaubriand (who deplored it) had become the dominant political passion in France, spread like wild-fire to other European countries and eventually to the four corners of the globe, passing in the process through all kinds of vicissitudes without exhausting its impetus. Like all great human ideals, the principle of equality was capable of several divergent interpretations. It could for example signify the dignity possessed by all human beings regardless of their social rank. This was the theme of Robert Burns's song *A Man's a Man for a' that* (1795). Or it could mean the gradual abolition of economic inequality. Thus Thomas Paine, in *The Rights of Man*, as early as 1791, advocated the public provision of educational services and a system of taxation which, in the cause of social justice, would lead to the redistribution of incomes. It is in the same vein that the *Déclaration des droits de l'homme et du citoyen* (1789) asserts that all men, by virtue of their humanity, have an equal right to well-being and the pursuit of happiness, an idea which the famous French scientist Lavoisier—who later fell a victim to the Terror—was probably the first to proclaim as a political doctrine.[1] Taking the idea one stage further, Kant went so far as to reject all hereditary privileges, so that everybody might start life with an equal chance. He also pointed out that the citizens' equality before the law should be regarded as one of man's fundamental and indeed inalienable rights. Unless it were given effect, his ideal of a *Rechtsstaat*, a State where the rule of law prevails, could never be established. Babeuf, self-styled Tribune of the People, and some of his fellow conspirators of 1796 carried egalitarianism to its logical conclusion by including in their social programme the community of goods, and the establishment of 'a true society where there should be neither rich nor poor'. On the political plane, the idea of equality also implied the right of the citizen, simply as a member of the community, to take part in the formation of the general will. In this way the political centre of gravity came to be shifted from the monarch to the people or the nation as the source of all sovereignty. In this respect the American and French Declarations of the Rights of Man mark a momentous phase in the world-wide movement towards democracy. In Paine's *Rights of Man*, these democratic achievements are recorded in a challenging manner. Ranke expressed the opinion that no other political idea of the last century had an impact comparable to that exerted by the idea of popular sovereignty which he described as 'the perpetually mobile ferment of the modern world'.[2]

[1] In the *Instructions* drafted in 1789 by Lavoisier, as a deputy, for his own constituents. *Oeuvres*, tome VI (Paris, 1893), p. 335.
[2] *Englische Geschichte, vornehmlich im sechszehnten und siebzehnten Jahrhundert* (Berlin, 1861), vol. III, pp. 287-8. English edn. (Oxford, 1875), vol. II, p. 542.

The idea of equality once conceived could not fail to lead to the demand for equal treatment and equal opportunity for the sexes. Thus Condorcet argued in 1790: 'Either not a single individual of the human species has any true rights, or else all have the same, and he who votes against the rights of another, whether on account of religion, colour or sex, henceforth renounces his own rights.'[1] Support for the cause of female emancipation was certainly not lacking from the side of the hitherto privileged sex. Jeremy Bentham, Friedrich Schlegel and Theodor Gottlieb von Hippel are examples of men who greatly helped to propagate the movement. Hippel, in his treatise *Über die bürgerliche Verbesserung der Weiber* (1792), voiced his astonishment that France, despite her preoccupation with equality, had not yet raised the legal status of women. The National Assembly in Paris indeed refused a petition for women's suffrage, and on 30 October 1793 the Convention forcibly suppressed all women's clubs that had sprung up in the earlier stages of the Revolution. It has been suggested that this anti-feminist turn of events may have been connected with the trial and execution of Queen Marie-Antoinette which took place in the same month.

In this context the fate of a woman pioneer of the movement is worth recording. Shortly before the Revolution, Olympe de Gouges, illegitimate daughter of a poet and herself a minor playwright, published her novel, *Prince Philosophe*, in which she pleaded that women be granted equality in education. Once the turmoil had started she threw herself into the fray. Her journal *L'Impatient*—one of many activities—was followed in September 1791 by her bold *Déclaration des Droits de la Femme et de la Citoyenne*. Soon, however, alienated by her feeling that female emancipation was being shelved and by her abhorrence of the king's trial, she became a violent critic of Jacobin dictatorship. On 3 November 1793, having dared to write an open letter to Robespierre, she paid under the guillotine the current price for such audacity. Her defiant feminism is poignantly expressed in Article 10 of the *Déclaration*: 'Woman has the right to mount the scaffold; she must also have the right to mount the tribune'.

In England—later to be in the van of women's emancipation—Mary Wollstonecraft, who was of Irish extraction, caused a stir by *A Vindication of the Rights of Women* (1792). Here she advocated equal educational opportunities, including even co-education, and pleaded that men and women should meet on the ground of their common humanity. The background of this treatise is revealed in the fragment of her novel *The Wrongs of Woman*, found among her posthumous papers. Unhappy marriages, drunkenness, squalor, poverty, childbirth, but above all the tyranny of the brutal male over the helpless female, all these were

---

[1] 'Sur l'admission des femmes au droit de cité,' published in 1790 in the *Journal de la Société de 1789*.

actual recollections woven into the work of fiction. Towards the end of her short and tempestuous life she became the wife of William Godwin, though both of them disapproved of the institution of marriage. The birth of her child Mary, who was to become Shelley's second wife, proved fatal to her, and she died in 1797.

In other directions too the principle of equality was extended as a result of the Revolution. The conception of common citizenship made it impossible to maintain the disabilities of the Jews. The age-old prejudice against these humiliated outlaws of European society had already been softened during the Age of Enlightenment. John Locke and John Toland had pleaded for the toleration of the Jews, and in 1740 the British Parliament had passed a naturalisation act for the American colonies which greatly advanced the general cause of equality for the Jews in that part of the world. When the colonies broke away from the motherland, the Virginia Declaration of Rights of 1776 established general equality without specifically mentioning the Jews. In Germany, the humanitarian idea of religious toleration found expression in Lessing's drama *Nathan der Weise* (1779). Significantly, its hero was drawn from Lessing's friend Moses Mendelssohn, born in the ghetto of Dessau, but by now a philosopher of wide renown. Two years later, the high Prussian official Christian Wilhelm Dohm published in Berlin his influential treatise *Über die bürgerliche Verbesserung der Juden*.

France was the first European country to grant the Jews full civil rights. Mirabeau's work *Sur Moses Mendelssohn et sur la réforme politique des Juifs* (1787) put their case eloquently, regretting that so gifted a nation should for so long have been deprived of the chance of developing its powers. 'Once its members are in full possession of civil rights,' Mirabeau concluded, 'they will soon be raised to the level of useful citizens'. In the same year a Jewish spokesman declared: 'We ask neither grace, favour nor privilege, but a law which will enable us to participate in the Rights of Man, which all men should share without exception. We demand also that the barrier that separates us from other citizens be removed, for we are no longer prepared to endure the humiliating distinction between ourselves and other men.' While the issue of Jewish Emancipation was discussed in the National Assembly, two other Jewish writers, Cerf Berr and Salkind Hurwitz, did their utmost to propagate the cause. Among those who supported it in the Assembly were Mirabeau, Robespierre and, most emphatically, Abbé Grégoire. On 28 September 1791 Jews were declared equal citizens in France. Thus the signal was given for the gradual emancipation of European Jewry, a process which seemed, deceptively, to have been completed by the Russian Revolution of 1917.

Finally, the idea of equality proved utterly incompatible with the toleration of slavery. It was on egalitarian grounds that the French *Société des Amis des Noirs* came into being and that the Constituent Assembly declared the slaves in French colonial possessions to be citizens of France. The final abolition of slavery owed as much to French revolutionary principles as it did to the strong religious feeling which characterised the English abolitionist movement.

As for the odious slave trade, it was fitting that Britain should take a leading role in its abolition, for during the eighteenth century she controlled more than half its total volume. The degradation of human nature involved in it had been denounced by a host of Christian and humanitarian writers and poets, notably John Wesley, Baxter, Thomson and Cowper, but also by Adam Smith, Dr Johnson and David Hartley, son of the author of *Observations on Man*. However it was the Quakers who first took concerted political action. Again, as in the case of Jewish emancipation, the movement originated in America where its chief exponents were John Woolman (1720–72) and Anthony Benezet (1713–84), the latter the son of a French Huguenot who left France after the revocation of the Edict of Nantes. It was largely due to Benezet's efforts that a universal effort of propaganda on both sides of the Atlantic was launched in favour of abolition. In England, the Quakers in 1783 founded an association 'for the relief and liberation of negro slaves in the West Indies, and for the discouragement of the slave trade on the coast of Africa'. Three years later, young Thomas Clarkson published the English version of a Latin prize essay suggested by Dr Peckard, vice-chancellor of Cambridge University, under the title *Essay on the Slavery and Commerce of the Human Species*. Clarkson, who was the most indefatigable champion of abolition, had for his collaborators a group of humanitarian evangelicals, the so-called 'Clapham sect', led by Henry Thornton, Zachary Macaulay and Granville Sharp, whose parliamentary spokesman was the influential William Wilberforce. The abolitionists refrained from an all-out attack on the institution of slavery itself as they were of the opinion that the ending of the slave trade would not only compel planters to treat their slaves more humanely, but would also lead in the long run to emancipation. Opposition to the proposed reform on the part of West Indian planters as well as other vested interests was formidable, and some politicians who had originally supported the abolitionist movement abandoned it when, influenced by the events in France, they had come to regard it as 'a shred of the accursed web of Jacobinism' (Burke).

Although gradual abolition had been agreed upon in the Commons in 1792, it was not until 1807 that Wilberforce carried a bill in Parliament which forbade British subjects and British ships from taking any part in the slave trade. Similar legislation was enacted in the United

States in the same year. It was with a deep sense of satisfaction that, in 1808, Thomas Clarkson brought out his well-documented history of the British abolition.[1] But it was not until 1811 that the British prohibition was given greater effect by the stipulation that henceforth offences were to be treated as felonies. Under considerable pressure from Britain, involving among other things a naval patrol off the African coast, the other slave-trading European countries (with the exception of Denmark which had preceded Britain) followed the British example in the course of the first decades of the nineteenth century. This was in due course followed by the abolition of slavery itself.

It was suggested above that the upsurge of cultural patriotism was connected with the romantic quest for freedom of expression. The political doctrine of nationalism was, however, more complex in its origins. Although cultural patriotism with its marked emotional overtones was certainly one of its ingredients, another equally important one was the democratic idea of popular sovereignty. Springing from the combination of those two ideas in the French Revolution, nationalism soon showed its explosive force in other parts of Europe and beyond. States that were not homogeneous in their institutions and culture were undermined under its revolutionary impact when oppressed national communities were clamouring for a redress of their grievances. Wolfe Tone was not unjustified in calling Ireland 'an oppressed, insulted and plundered nation'. As a disciple of Danton and Thomas Paine and founder of the society for the United Irishmen (1791), he drew his principles from the French example. His views, uncompromising from the first, came to be adopted by most of his followers, once they realised that a liberal measure of parliamentary reform in Ireland could not be attained by constitutional methods: Edmund Burke's perspicacious *Letters to Sir Hercules Langrishe*, advocating the admission of the Irish Catholics to the franchise, had fallen on deaf ears. Wolfe Tone's attempt in 1798 at an armed rebellion for an Irish republic ended in failure and the execution of the leader. His posthumously published autobiography is the most remarkable work of this era of Irish life. This and other nationalist insurrections, mostly abortive, threatened to break up some larger political units, and the same was true of national resistance against the Napoleonic regime in Europe. But nationalism could act in precisely the opposite sense when, for the sake of unification, a host of smaller political entities were attacked and eventually destroyed. Thus the drastic changes wrought by Napoleon in Germany and Italy paved the way for the future unification of the German and Italian nations.

[1] *History of the Rise, Progress, and Accomplishment of the Abolition of the African Slave Trade by the British Parliament.* 2 vols. (London, 1808).

The Dutch historian Johan Huizinga has drawn a useful distinction between patriotism and nationalism. With the former the prevailing sentiment, he suggests, is one of attachment, whereas with the latter the feeling of pride prevails, which only too often leads to overweening arrogance and aggression. In reality the two sentiments, though sometimes clearly distinguishable, were apt to merge into one another; for example, Jacobin patriotism soon degenerated into an aggressive nationalism which produced or at any rate reinforced a patriotic reaction among its victims. In any event, nationalism as it developed during this era not only clashed with the ideal of cosmopolitan fraternity, but increasingly also with that of the individual's liberty. Jacobins such as Barère or Carnot, and later Fichte in his *Addresses to the German Nation* (1807), extolled the nation at the expense of the individual. This sentiment, natural in a time of crisis, became a settled dogma when Hegel insisted that the individual had real liberty only through merging his will into that of the historical will of the community. Thus two of the basic ideals of humanitarian Enlightenment were already in full retreat at the time of the Jacobin dictatorship. If the outbreak of the Revolution in France coincided with the highwatermark of enlightened expectations, the wave began to ebb in the critical years from 1793 onwards. The resulting mood of disenchantment has aptly been described as 'The frustration of the enlightenment'.[1] Against this background the origins of conservatism may be studied.

Naturally, the protagonists of the Enlightenment were loath to admit their disappointment. Kant, in his essay *Der Streit der Fakultäten* (1798), tried to console himself with the reflection that the misdeeds of the Jacobins were nothing to those of the tyrants of past time. Admitting that the Revolution had outwardly been a failure, he still insisted that in the long run it was bound to prove a blessing to mankind. Similar views were expressed by Fichte. More generally, however, the Terror and French aggression engendered feelings of consternation and bitter disillusionment. The grim and relentless work done by the guillotine, on the Place de la Concorde, could hardly fail to act as an eye-opener. Jens Baggesen, the Danish poet, who had previously hailed the Revolution with a *Hymn to Freedom*, now composed his powerful ode *To the Furies*. In Germany, Friedrich Schiller and other idealists realised that the idea of liberty too could be abused and that reason as well as religion could be prostituted to hideous purposes. France, so it now seemed to Schiller, was not sufficiently educated for equality. Soon after accepting French citizenship as the author of the impetuous drama *Die Räuber*, he grew violently antagonistic to the Revolution. Like Giambattista Vico before him, he now concluded that

[1] Alfred Cobban, *In Search of Humanity. The Role of the Enlightenment in Modern History* (London, 1960).

a decaying culture produces a worse state of anarchy and corruption than does barbarism. The deepest insight was perhaps shown by the poet Hölderlin: 'What has transformed the State into a hell is precisely that man has tried to transform it into his heaven.'

In England, too, many former admirers of the Revolution now became its adversaries. Wordsworth was plunged into profound dejection by its horrors and expressed his mood in *The Prelude*:

> And now, become oppressors in their turn
> Frenchmen had changed a war of self-defence
> For one of conquest, losing sight of all
> Which they had struggled for: and mounted up
> Openly, in the view of earth and heaven
> The scale of liberty.

Coleridge's political conversion is marked by the magnificent ode *Recantation* (1797). A year later it seemed to him that 'rulers are much the same in all ages, and under all forms of government; they are as bad as they dare to be'. His reaction was however less violent than that of his friends. Many years later he declared that, though he had never been a Jacobin, there was much good in their creed and that the errors of the opposite party were equally gross and far less excusable. It was only after 1815 that he became more alarmed at the growth of what he still called Jacobinism. Southey, on the other hand, already before the turn of the century completely discarded his earlier views and became a rigid conservative. It has been suggested that he may have been the first to use the term 'Conservative' in its modern sense.[1]

Before it was possible for a conservative outlook on politics to be developed, it was necessary that the dangers of the Revolution should be fully appreciated. No other thinker had done so much in this direction as the Dublin-born Whig statesman Edmund Burke. Already in his celebrated *Reflections on the Revolution in France* (1790) Burke realised that an element of tyranny was inherent in mass democracy, and also that the Revolution, because of its quasi-religious character, was imbued with the spirit of proselytism. He used the whole armoury of the conservative onslaught against revolutionary doctrines, dwelling above all on the benefits of political and social continuity. Society, he insisted, is a partnership between those who are living, those who are dead, and those who are yet to be born. Of all the great traditions of the past, the spirit of chivalry found in him its most fervent champion. The characteristic passage bears quotation in full: 'The age of chivalry is gone. That of sophisters, economists, and calculators, has succeeded; and the glory of Europe is extinguished for ever. Never, never more shall we behold that generous loyalty to rank and sex, that proud submission, that dignified obedience, that subordination of the heart,

---

[1] Geoffrey Carnall, *Robert Southey and His Age* (Oxford, 1960).

which kept alive, even in servitude itself, the spirit of an exalted freedom. The unbought grace of life, the cheap defence of nations, the nurse of manly sentiment and heroic enterprise is gone! It is gone, that sensibility of principle, that chastity of honour, which felt a stain like a wound, which inspired courage whilst it mitigated ferocity, which ennobled whatever it touched, and under which vice itself lost half its evil by losing all its grossness'. Like most early exponents of a creed, Burke certainly overstated his case. Consequently, it was easy for his opponents—Philip Francis, Thomas Paine, Mary Wollstonecraft and others—to charge him with callous indifference to the misdeeds of the *ancien régime* and to the sufferings of the French people before 1789. Nevertheless, Burke's thought exerted a wide influence in England and abroad.

From rulers downwards came a chorus of praise. Catherine the Great and Stanislas, the last king of Poland, were as enthusiastic as was King George III. In Germany, Novalis hailed the *Reflections* as a revolutionary book written against the Revolution. A German translation, with numerous notes and appendices, was undertaken by the Silesian-born Prussian publicist Friedrich Gentz, who had at first welcomed the events of 1789 in glowing terms, but had changed his opinion, on the second or third perusal of the *Reflections*, just at the time when Prussia shifted from alert neutrality to outright war. Gentz inscribed his version to King Frederick William II, and also addressed a letter to the king on 23 December 1792, declaring that his steadfast intention of opposing French sophistry had led him to translate 'the strongest refutation of the revolutionary ideas which had appeared in any language' and that in an appended volume he himself 'sought to develop on political and philosophical grounds a complete theory of the anti-revolutionary system'. Soon afterwards Gentz duly received the long-coveted title of *Kriegsrat*. In a powerful reply to Mackintosh, he elaborated with the zeal of a convert his theme of the contrast between the early ideals and the grim realities of the Revolution.

Goethe, like Burke, rejected the Revolution from the very outset. Already then a man of forty, he illustrated his own general rule that, if youth inclines to democratic views, middle age is apt to see worth in aristocracies. His administrative experiences at the model court of Weimar, where he had settled in 1776, strengthened his conviction that reforms must come from above, and that order was more precious than liberty. Though no apologist of the old regime, Goethe was deeply disquieted by several aspects of the Revolution, particularly the tendency of politics to become all-pervading. The resulting state of perpetual unrest made people 'as on a sick-bed' throw themselves incessantly from one political side to the other. The proliferation of political parties and journals seemed to him unhealthy, and his comedy

Der Bürgergeneral (1793) expressed his strong dislike of propaganda. Most of all, the Frankfurt patrician dreaded an uprising of the inchoate masses who, he predicted, would fall an easy prey to unscrupulous demagogues and ruthless tyrants. As a result, European culture, the growth of centuries, might one day be swept aside. These forebodings resemble those of Erasmus during the upheaval of the Reformation.

The positive contribution of the romantics to revolutionary thought has already been noticed briefly. It was the idea of liberty that appealed to revolutionaries and romantics alike. On the other hand, some leading romantic thinkers were among the earliest critics of revolutionary egalitarianism, at least in its more far-reaching implications. They feared that the educated classes might one day become swamped by the masses. European culture, in the process of being levelled down, might thus become vulgarised out of existence, a fate which according to some ancient historians had overtaken the ancient Roman civilisation. Coleridge on one occasion scornfully spoke of mob-adulation which attributed wisdom to the majority of mankind. In Germany Hölderlin, Friedrich Schlegel, Görres and Schelling, in France Stendhal, Alfred de Vigny and others all lamented the horrid prospect of a mass civilisation with its progressive encroachment on individual freedom. Madame de Staël, too, foresaw an age when the victorious masses would demand that superior individuals should debase their standards to please their inferiors, now the masters. And her admirer Benjamin Constant—a liberal—wrote to a friend: 'You and I were not meant to live in this century.... Today there are no more individuals, only battalions in uniform'. And he added pathetically: 'We poor devils, who go on wearing our own clothes instead of a uniform, no longer know where we belong.'

Those who like Alfred de Vigny or the Silesian poet Joseph von Eichendorff belonged to the *élites* of the past naturally tended to deplore the passing of the age of feudalism and chivalry. So too, Adam Mickiewicz, in his great epic poem *Pan Tadeusz*, depicted nostalgically in glowing colours the traditional but vanished life among Polish gentlefolk in his own Lithuania. Indeed, so marked was the anti-egalitarian *leitmotif* in the European romantic movement, at any rate before 1830, that some historians have interpreted romanticism as the swan song of the European nobility. To be sure, there is more than a grain of truth in this view; to the list of romantic noblemen could be added, in the front rank, Chateaubriand, Lamartine, Musset, Byron, and Leopardi. Among other romantics who had no claim to nobility, some also felt nostalgia for the bygone age of relatively fixed social hierarchies. Here the originator of the Waverley novels springs to mind. True, Goethe's drama of the *Sturm und Drang* period, *Goetz von Berlichingen*, had already inaugurated the tradition of chivalry plays, but the genre of the chivalry novel began later and owed its widest appeal to Scott's imaginative gifts. The whole of his work, ingeniously combining feudal and patriotic sentiment, was steeped in the traditions of the past, and was brought to life by the fact that the age of heroic ideals was far less remote in Scotland than in most other European countries.

Among the anti-revolutionary intellectuals who had an axe to grind, the influential group of French *émigré* writers deserve special attention. Of these the Breton Vicomte de Chateaubriand showed remarkable detachment. Already in his early *Essai historique, politique, et moral sur les Révolutions*, published in 1797 during his exile in London, he declared that the French Revolution had been inevitable. In his great autobiography, the *Mémoires d'Outre Tombe*, on which he first embarked in 1809, the unbiased analysis of the main causes of the Revolution is resumed. Aristocracy, we are told, passes through three successive stages. At first there is the glorious age of superiority; this is succeeded by the age of privilege during which the aristocracy degenerates; finally, during the age of vanity, it dies out. Yet loss of faith in the ruling classes of the decadent *ancien régime* did not mean that he had much confidence in the people, that upstart sovereign of the post-aristocratic age. In France where, after the July Revolution of 1830, the political centre of gravity seemed to have shifted further than elsewhere, he lamented the complete disappearance of respect for authority of any kind. 'Nothing more exists,' he complains in his *Memoirs*, 'authority of experience and age, birth or genius, talent or virtue: all are denied, contested, and despised.' What he saw around him was 'a world without consecrated authority'. In one thing the romantics of every shade were agreed—their dislike of the rule of the middle class.

The self-styled Comte de Rivarol, who spent the last nine years of his life (1792–1801) in Brussels, London, Hamburg and finally in Berlin, stood out as a shrewd observer of the revolutionary scene. Burke, who had read Rivarol's account of the early stages of the Revolution in the *Journal politique*, called him the Tacitus of the French Revolution. Like Burke, but independently, Rivarol was struck by the similarity between the Revolution and earlier movements of religious reform. Since 1789 political struggles, he noted, tended to turn into religious, or quasi-religious, contests—and this in spite of the fact that the anti-Christian character of the Revolution was manifest. The new revolutionary political philosophy was taking over the function of a religion, albeit of a purely secular character. Rivarol was of the opinion that this was a highly dangerous phenomenon. He also perceived, as did his fellow-*émigré* Mallet du Pan, that the new political fanaticism was even more cruel than its religious counterpart had been. To combat the new ideas, gunfire was ineffective; it was new ideas that were needed. He bemoaned the fact that the Allies, in their campaign against the Revolution, were always in arrears 'by one year, by one army, and by one idea'. Rivarol also observed that man was after all not so rational a creature as the enlightened philosophers had tried to make out. Only too frequently, it seemed to him, human beings were swayed by a non-rational and even anti-rational quest for power. Political science would have to find room for a theory of the human passions. Even the most highly civilised nations were far less removed from barbarism than was generally believed. For the mob the century of Enlightenment did not exist and, moreover, would never come about. Rivarol was certainly among the first to make a psychological study of mass behaviour. Appalled by the atrocities of the Revolution, he reached the height of his powers as a writer in his famous indictment of the Terror,[1] which later made a deep impression on the literary critic Sainte-Beuve.

Rivarol also foresaw, as early as did Burke, that the Revolution would one day be ended 'by the sabre', and that its heir was bound to be a despot. His own preference was for a strong constitutional monarchy. Some kind of social *élite* seemed to him to be indispensable, but he was under no illusion about the nobility of his own time who, he declared, were but the spectres of their ancestors. Rivarol was also among the earliest champions of the conservative alliance between throne and altar.

In the polemical writings of the dogmatic and intransigent Joseph de Maistre religion and politics are inextricably interwoven. The French invasion of his native land of Savoy had driven the former liberal into exile in 1792. His conversion to an extreme anti-revolutionary attitude was rapid, indeed his *Considérations sur la France*, published in Neuchâtel in 1796, soon became the bible of the *émigrés*. Even more strongly than Burke, de Maistre emphasised the social function of religion. 'The greatest crime a nobleman can commit is to attack the Christian dogmas,' he wrote in a letter to a friend. He argued as follows: 'The patrician is a lay priest: religion is his paramount and most sacred property, for it preserves his privilege which is lost together with it.'[2] Accordingly, the Revolution, in all its Satanic frightfulness, appeared to de Maistre as God's punishment for the impiety of the French ruling class. When the sin had been atoned for, France would again raise her head; with the monarchy, order and religion would be restored. In some of its aspects de Maistre's political thought appears

---

[1] *Discours préliminaire du Nouveau Dictionnaire de la Langue française* (Paris, 1797), tome I, pp. 231–5. The above estimate of Rivarol's originality was perhaps not shared by contemporaries, but is evident to us in historical retrospect. Cf. Hans Barth, 'Antoine de Rivarol und die Französische Revolution', in *Schweizer Beiträge zur Allgemeinen Geschichte*, vol. XII (Bern, 1954).

[2] *Lettres et opuscules inédits* (Paris, 1851), vol. II, pp. 262–3.

to be theocratic, for he insists that the existence of the social order is the result of divine decree. However, closer analysis reveals that in his eyes the function of religion—to use Max Weber's phrase—is the domestication of the lower classes. What de Maistre is most concerned with is the necessity of order and subordination in the State. This is why all written constitutions and in particular the modern parliamentary system are roundly condemned by him, and why he insists that the ruling class should always be separated from the people by birth or wealth, for, once the people at large have lost the respect for authority, all government, he fears, will come to an end.

Less radical and more traditionalist was the political thought of the French *émigré* Vicomte de Bonald who returned and gave passive support to the Empire, even accepting a position as a councillor of Napoleon's University. He attributed the anarchic tendencies of the Revolution to the corroding power of the rationalist philosophers. Bonald's *Théorie du pouvoir politique et religieux*, published in Constance in 1796, contains a fierce attack on the ideals of the Revolution, especially those of political equality and the sovereignty of the people. The state should and must always be divided into the three categories of the sovereign, the ministry or nobility, and the subjects or the people. He abhors the independent expression of individual thought, and invests tradition with a halo glorifying the ideals of the past simply on account of their antiquity. In the midst of the revolutionary turmoil and its aftermath, he longs for stability, and finds it in the French society of the seventeenth rather than the eighteenth century. Moreover, rejecting eighteenth-century optimism about human nature, Catholic traditionalists like Bonald reverted to the Christian concept of original sin. The contrast with revolutionary thought could hardly be more glaring.

In German-speaking countries, and especially in Prussia, the counter-revolutionary doctrines of the Swiss Karl Ludwig von Haller caused a considerable stir. In essentials, they were contained already in his *Handbuch der allgemeinen Staatenlehre* (1808). A fuller exposition of his ideas is to be found in his main work, *Restauration der Staatswissenschaft*, published in Winterthur from 1816 onwards. It was from the title of this book that the period 1814–30 came to be described as that of the Restoration in Europe (though the period of Restoration in England from 1660 to 1688 may also have served as a model). Haller, a patrician of Berne, the social structure of which had been little affected by the French Revolution, made feudal or corporate tradition the pivot of his political thought. He was full of blind admiration for the Middle Ages, although on his own admission he had never read a single work on that epoch. Political power, provided it is exercised by long-established monarchs or aristocracies or civic oligarchies, is surrounded by Haller with an aura of sanctity. He even goes so far as to postulate a 'natural law of the stronger', an ominous idea reminiscent of the sophist Callicles or, indeed, Hobbes, and presaging Nietzsche and the social Darwinians. Even more markedly than Joseph de Maistre, Haller used religion as an *instrumentum regni*. His conversion to Catholicism (1820) seems to have been due mainly to political motives.

Although conservative ideologies, often more subtle than Haller's, naturally thrived during the Restoration period in Europe, the same era also witnessed the momentous rise of a second wave of revolutionary fervour. Here Shelley deserves pride of place. To a man born in 1792 the Revolution was a tradition and not a personal experience. Already at Eton Shelley rebelled against the school's rituals. It was then that he first came to read Godwin's *Inquiry Concerning Political Justice* which made a deep and lasting impact on his susceptible mind. *Queen Mab*, an early work, in parts reads almost like a versification of the philosopher's prose. The mature poems too, such as *The Revolt of Islam* and *Prometheus Unbound*, propagate Godwin's ideas: perfectibility of the human race, egalitarianism, anarchism, and non-resistance. Godwin's violent anti-clericalism was revived in a provocative pamphlet on *The Necessity of Atheism*, composed by the young firebrand during his undergraduate days at University College, Oxford, and bringing them to an end by his expulsion. Since Shelley rejected all organised religion, marriage meant nothing to him as a sacrament, and, again in Godwin's footsteps, he declared that the existing system of marriage was hostile to human happiness. 'A husband and wife', he writes in a note to *Queen Mab*, 'ought to continue so long united as they love each other: any law which should bind them to cohabitation for one moment after the decay of their affection, would be an intolerable tyranny and the most unworthy of toleration.' In his own tempestuous life Shelley acted accordingly. In France the novelist George Sand was to profess and act on similar principles. Arguing for legal methods of divorce, which had been introduced in 1792 but abolished in 1816, 'I can find but one remedy,' she wrote in 1837 to Lamennais, 'for the barbarous injustice and endless misery of a hopelessly unhappy marriage. That remedy is the right to dissolve such a marriage with liberty to marry again.'

Shelley made more than one excursion into contemporary politics. Thus he travelled to Ireland to forward the cause of Repeal and Catholic Emancipation, and worked out a scheme of parliamentary reform to be submitted to a referendum. He also championed the cause of equal rights for women. To Shelley, the aristocracy of his time were 'the drones of the community' who 'feed on the mechanics' labour'. His abiding passion, a strong aversion to cruelty and tyranny, inspired the bitter poem *The Mask of Anarchy* (1819). He had begun as the apostle of reason. Later however he deviated from Godwin's doctrinaire rationalism, for he had now come to realise that 'until the mind can love, and admire, and trust, and hope, and endure, reasoned principles of moral conduct are seeds cast upon the highway of life'.[1]

Shelley's friend Lord Byron gained an even wider reputation as standard-bearer of political radicalism. It is true that revolutionary movements all over the world had his outspoken sympathy, and those of Italy and Greece even his active support. Yet Byron felt no attachment to democracy, which he once called 'an aristocracy of blackguards'.[2] Had the French Revolution not shown that mobs too could turn oppressors? In the same vein he wrote to John Cam Hobhouse in 1820: 'Pray don't mistake me: it is not against the pure principles of reform that I protest, but against low, designing, dirty levellers who would pioneer their way to a democratical tyranny.'[3] Byron was intensely proud of his noble origin, and it is hard to avoid the impression that his hatred of oppressors exceeded his sympathy for the oppressed. His radicalism may have been sharpened by the social ostracism that clung to his name since the days of his separation from Lady Byron (1816). Whatever the motives, Byron's satirical poems certainly helped to inflame revolutionary sentiments both in England and abroad, particularly the last cantos of *Don Juan, The Age of Bronze*, and last but not least *The Vision of Judgment*. His death in the cause of Greek Independence inspired political idealists all over the world. It was in Italy, Poland, Russia and the Balkans, as well as in the politically minded Germany of Heinrich Heine and the Young Germany movement, that Byron's posthumous impact was felt most strongly. 'The day will come,' Mazzini wrote in 1835, 'when Democracy will remember all that it owes to Byron.'

As for Byron's Russian admirers and emulators, it is enough to mention the name of Mikhail Lermontov, the only genuine and at the same time significant Russian romantic. Like his great idol, Lermontov too regarded himself as being in a state of war with the society that surrounded him. For the stifling regime of Tsar Nicholas I and the social strata that supported it he had nothing but contempt, shown in his *Ode on the Death of Pushkin* (1837). Pushkin himself, whose early poems were mentioned specifically at the trials of 1826 as having influenced some of the Decembrists, had made a strong appeal in *The Village* (1819) for the abolition of serfdom. Both poets had to pay for their audacity by being exiled from Moscow to the outlying provinces.

[1] Preface to *Prometheus Unbound* (London, 1820).
[2] *Letters and Journals*, ed. R. E. Prothero (London, 1898–1901), vol. v, pp. 405–6.
[3] *Correspondence*, ed. John Murray (London, 1922), vol. II, p. 148.

The generations born during the last third of the eighteenth century witnessed also the early stages of the great Industrial Revolution that was destined to transform the entire face of the earth. No wonder that some contemporaries tended to look with alarm at changes whose ultimate consequences are still hard to estimate. Often the romantics' sense of beauty was offended by the hideousness of the districts in which the new industry had arisen. In England, Southey in his *Colloquies on the Progress and Prospects of Society* (1829), anticipated much of Ruskin's and William Morris's later campaign against the deformity of a mechanised world. The American writer George Ticknor, who in 1819 visited Newcastle-on-Tyne and its surroundings, thus described his impressions: 'At the appearance of every coal-pit a quantity of the finer parts that are thrown out is perpetually burning, and the effect produced by the earth, thus apparently everywhere on fire, both on the machines used and the men busied with it, was horrible. It seemed as if I were in Dante's shadowy world.' A journey through the Black Country in the dead of night inspired the background of John Martin's powerful painting *The Great Day of His Wrath*; he told his son that he could not imagine anything more terrible even in the regions of everlasting punishment. The romantics also recoiled from the growing artificiality of urbanised life. Some, too, and notably Southey, feared that the balance between agriculture and industry might one day be irrevocably upset. Southey's pseudonymous *Letters from England* (1807) contain some of the earliest critical observations on the human aspect of the Industrial Revolution. The conclusion is sweeping: 'In commerce, even more than in war, both men and beasts are considered mainly as machines, and sacrificed with even less compunction.' Coleridge, too, pondered much about the interdependence between economic problems and those of a social, moral and religious character. The teaching of the dominant school of political economists repelled him because of their purely economic approach to the problem of human labour. Thus he never ceased to condemn the system which considered 'men as things, instruments, machines, property'. In *The Friend* (1809) he declared explicitly: 'The economists who are willing to sacrifice men to the creation of national wealth (which is national only in statistical tables) are forgetting that even for patriotic purposes no person should be treated as a thing.'

Similar views were expressed by the Genevan historian and economist Simonde de Sismondi. He too felt that the economists were abstracting too much from reality, and he also pointed out that they tended to view things essentially from the point of view of the producer instead of that of society in general. As a counterblast to David Ricardo's *Principles of Political Economy and Taxation* (1817), Sismondi gave to his main work in this field the title *Nouveaux principes d'économie politique, ou de la richesse dans ses rapports avec la population* (1819). Part of his polemic was directed against Adam Smith's French disciple Jean-Baptiste Say, who had categorically declared that any increase in industrial productivity was bound to be beneficial, as every product would find its consumer. In Sismondi's view, this meant putting the cart before the horse. His study of the post-Napoleonic crisis in England, made during his visit to this country in 1818–19, had led him to the conclusion that the root cause of the crisis lay in under-consumption on the part of the working classes, whose purchasing power was insufficient to absorb the increased industrial output. Similar crises, he predicted, would recur unless the prevailing economic structure was overhauled. Among his proposals for social reform were legislative acts protecting the workers against unemployment and allowing them to form unions for the purpose of resisting oppression. His concern about the chaotic phase of the Industrial Revolution is epitomised in his warning that the interest of humanity should not be sacrificed to 'the simultaneous action of all industrial cupidities'. In short, 'the rich must be protected against their own greed.'

The three last-mentioned thinkers—Southey, Coleridge and Sismondi —to whom the Bavarian Franz von Baader might be added—clearly anticipated one of Karl Marx's fundamental indictments of capitalism, namely that it transformed human beings into things. It is therefore not surprising to learn from the posthumously published papers of Marx that in his youth he had been strongly influenced by romantic ideas. Yet the romantics were also protesting against the spirit of materialism and eudaemonism which was to penetrate Marxism. Moreover, Sismondi, though he advocated far-reaching social legislation, was as much opposed to socialism as he was to capitalism, because both systems appeared to him to be centralisers and, for that reason, oppressive.

It was only after 1815 that the ideas of the eccentric social reformer Charles Fourier began to attract much attention even in France. Although himself anything but a romantic, Fourier, too, was deeply alarmed by some features of the Industrial Revolution. Disliking centralisation and large-scale production, he strongly deplored the fact that the new industrial age must constitute a threat to smaller enterprises. His ideal, based on an agrarian handicraft economy, was in many ways retrospective, but he had some fresh and forward-looking ideas, such as the need to render labour as attractive and joyous as possible. More outspokenly than any previous thinker he fastened upon the waste involved in a competitive organisation and opposed to it his own peculiar conception of a so-called *phalanstère*, a community composed of about 1600 persons on some 5000 acres of land. Fourier resembled Godwin not only in his ardent rationalism, but also in his marked contempt for the institution of marriage, that bugbear of so many reformers. He also shared with Godwin and Condorcet the confident hope in the physical perfectibility of man and a spectacular extension of the span of human life, venturing a specific forecast—an average of 144 years.

In Britain, Robert Owen had the unusual distinction of being in a position both to preach and to practise social reform. A Welshman by birth, Owen worked for several years in Manchester where he became thoroughly acquainted with the seamy side of the factory system. Soon after becoming manager and part-owner of the textile mills of New Lanark in Scotland, he began to transform that enterprise in a truly unprecedented manner. In the teeth of stubborn opposition from his partners, he increased the workers' wages and reduced the working day in the factory from 16 to $10\frac{1}{2}$ hours. Child labour under the age of ten was abolished, and all children living in the village received free education from the age of five. By the end of the Napoleonic Wars, New Lanark had become a model establishment, at any rate by contemporary standards. Owen next proceeded to press for a more general improvement of industrial conditions. In *A New View of Society* (1813) he contrasted, as Southey had done before him, the care given by the superintendents of factories to the inanimate machines with their neglect of the animate ones; and in an appeal *To the British Master Manufacturers* (1818) he strongly underlined the baneful effects of the premature employment of children. Some but by no means all of Owen's proposals became incorporated in Peel's Act of 1819, the first effective Factory Act. It was at about this time that Owen began to mobilise public opinion abroad. He invited foreign statesmen to inspect New Lanark, and established further contacts when he visited the Congress of Aix-la-Chapelle and submitted *Two Memorials on Behalf of the Working Class*. There too he met the now ultra-conservative Friedrich von Gentz, whose reaction to Owen's schemes was cynical: 'We do not want the mass to become wealthy and independent of us. How could we govern them if they were?'[1]

Dissatisfied with the somewhat meagre success of his campaign, Owen in 1825 left the Old World for the New. His fame had preceded him, for a few years previously a Society for Promoting Communities based on his principles had been started in New York. Owen now bought the village of Harmony in Indiana from the Rappites who, like several other religious communities, had conducted their settlement along communist lines. The idea of Owen's settlement, renamed New Harmony, differed from that of its predecessor, in that 'it aimed at teaching the whole world a new way of life rather than at the withdrawal of a chosen few from the contamination of human wickedness' (G. D. H. Cole). No such aim was fulfilled: whereas the Rappites had

[1] *The Life of Robert Owen. Written by himself* (London, 1857), vol. I, p. 183.

apparently lived a frugal but contented existence, New Harmony was from the start beset with inner dissensions which were in part due to the haphazard composition of its members. Faced with the collapse of the settlement, which cost him four-fifths of his fortune, Owen concluded that men could not be fitted to live in community save by previous moral training. After his return to England in 1828, he took for a time a leading part in the Trade Union movement. The mainspring of his reformatory zeal lay in his unflinching humanitarianism. He rejected all established religion and denounced the Christian Churches, although he admitted that the seventeenth-century Quaker John Bellers had anticipated some of his ideas.[1] Believing as he did that the formation of man's character was due entirely to outward social influences, Owen felt unable to accept the Christian view that moral responsibility attaches to each human individual. For the most part of his life he remained a staunch rationalist, until at the end a long repressed urge for the supernatural made him a convert to spiritualism.

Claude Henri, Comte de Saint-Simon, one of the most original if also most eccentric thinkers of his time, enthusiastically welcomed the dawn of the Industrial Age, even declaring that the whole of history had been heading towards this consummation. Though himself the scion of a famous noble family he apostasised as it were from his class by giving up his title during the Revolution and then by including the nobility in the 'idle classes' who in his opinion deserved to be thrown off. These included also the officer class, despite the fact that in his youth Saint-Simon himself had fought bravely in the American War of Independence. The class that mattered most in his eyes was that of the *industriels* whom he thus defined: 'all those who labour to produce, or place within the reach of the members of society, one or several means of satisfying their needs or their physical tastes.' This definition comprised the three categories of agriculturalists, manufacturers and merchants. He proposed not only that the Chamber of Deputies should contain a larger proportion of *industriels*, but also that members of that class, aided by expert advice, should plan public affairs and projects of public works on a grand scale. He further suggested that the executive be composed of bankers. As for the conception of the new system as a whole, that should be entrusted to a single head, a suggestion that savours of Enlightened Despotism but has also a sinister modern ring of totalitarianism about it. Indeed, Saint-Simon was fully prepared to jettison the ideal of individual liberty which 'would eminently tend to hamper the action of the mass over the individuals'. Time and again he opposed to the 'critical, destructive and revolutionary' eighteenth

[1] *Proposals for raising a College of Industry of all useful Trades and Husbandry with Profit for the Rich, a Plentyful Living for the Poor and a Good Education for Youth* (London, 1696).

century his vision of the nineteenth as marked by 'organisation, cohesion and integration'. It was not surprising that he repudiated the idea of popular sovereignty. In a characteristic effort to sweeten the authoritarian pill, Saint-Simon tried to convince himself and his followers that under the new industrial system the function of government would no longer consist in the objectionable rule of men over men, but instead in the administration of things in response to the needs of any given situation. A similar illusion was to lead Frederick Engels to envisage 'the withering away of the State'.

The prospect of the social millennium, lately expected to be the fruit of the French Revolution, was now linked to the Industrial Revolution (if a term not then invented may be used). Previously republic and peace had as it were been identified. Now Saint-Simon trusted that, under the new dispensation, the administrative and industrial system would automatically be pacific. In retrospect the political revolution of 1789 still appeared as a turning point of great significance, but it had to be completed by a scientific revolution of comparable dimensions. Apart from physics, Saint-Simon attached the greatest importance to that new branch of science to which his famous disciple Auguste Comte was to give the name of sociology. Unlike some later idolaters of science, Saint-Simon was by no means blind to the spiritual *malaise* of his time, but in his view a return to any of the old established religions was impracticable, mainly for the reason that the clergy, since the sixteenth century, had not kept abreast of the scientific spirit of the age. Nor was he altogether uncritical of the men of science, who had been too readily harnessed to Napoleon's military despotism. Yet he was confident that scientists and scholars could be entrusted with the intellectual and even the spiritual leadership for the society of the future. A so-called Council of Newton was to function as the central authority for this purpose.

In his earlier writings Saint-Simon had not paid much attention to the harmful effects of the Industrial Revolution, but the grave and widespread crisis of 1817 and his study of industrial conditions both in England and France made him realise the urgency of that problem. His diagnosis presages that of Karl Marx: 'The workers,' he wrote, 'see themselves deprived of the enjoyment of their labour, which is the aim of their labour.' The first priority therefore must be to improve the lot of the working class. Indeed, Saint-Simon put forward the strikingly modern idea that society should be organised for the promotion of the well-being of the most numerous and poorest class; this carried him far beyond his earlier insistence on equality of opportunity and the suppression of hereditary privileges. The new doctrine forms the essence of his last work, *Nouveau Christianisme*, written shortly before his death in 1825. It suddenly struck him that his ambitious scheme of social reform could be justified on the basis of Christian ethics.

Without subscribing to that system as a whole, or to other aspects of the Christian doctrine which, indeed, he regarded as outmoded, he was still impressed by Christ's injunction that human beings should behave to each other as brothers. Thus Christian charity, shorn indeed of so essential an element as man's love for God, came to be linked to a purely secular religion.

Soon after Saint-Simon's death, some of his disciples issued a statement entitled *La Doctrine saint-simonienne* (1828), in which the Master's ideas were expounded systematically and new ideas added. This stressed the importance of work for all, or full employment as it was called later, and advocated ambitious projects of public works, such as the cutting of canals at Suez and Panama and the development of a world-wide network of railways. It was a particularly modern touch that these schemes were designed to unify the entire globe. In order to carry them through it was proposed that gigantic industrial companies be established. If the doctrine thus included some unmistakable features of a highly developed capitalism, it also anticipated some socialist postulates, such as the abolition of inheritance, on the basis of the motto 'To each according to his needs, from each according to his capacities'. This and other distinctively socialist ideas came to be included under the influence of the editor of the statement, Saint-Amand Bazard, who had previously been connected with the secret society of the Carbonari. Later on, Pierre Leroux became the ideologist of the left-wing Saint-Simonians. Not long after its inauguration, the movement—often in a grotesque manner—assumed the outward trappings of a Church, with Bazard and Barthélemy-Prosper Enfantin as its spiritual leaders. After the inevitable schism, the bizarre Enfantin remained in sole charge. The Saint-Simonian religion, as it came to be called, attracted many followers, among them a striking number of Jews, notably Saint-Simon's favourite disciple Olinde Rodrigues who many years later edited the Master's complete works, and the brothers Emile and Isaac Pereire who during the Second Empire were to distinguish themselves in the world of banking. It was largely the Messianic flavour of Saint-Simonianism that appealed to some newly emancipated Jews.[1] While clinging to that part of their inherited tradition, they had travelled so far from the religion of their ancestors that they could take Saint-Simon for their Messiah. The attitude of the Gentile followers of the sect was perhaps no less astonishing, for here were lapsed Christians whose religious yearnings found fulfilment, or so it seemed, in Saint-Simon's testament *Nouveau Christianisme*.

If Saint-Simon points in one direction to Comte's positivism, in another he and the two social reformers previously mentioned may be linked to the next generation by quoting the tribute paid by Frederick

[1] J. L. Talmon, *Political Messianism. The Romantic Phase* (London, 1960), pp. 80–1.

Engels to the men whom he regarded as his own and Karl Marx's precursors: 'German socialism,' he wrote, 'will never forget that it rests on the shoulders of Saint-Simon, Fourier and Owen—three men who, however fantastic and Utopian their teachings, belonged to the great minds of all times and by the intuition of genius anticipated an incalculable number of truths which we now demonstrate scientifically.'[1]

In the history of political and social thought, the period from 1789 to 1848 constitutes an entire whole. In France, above all, the February Revolution marks the close of an epoch, whose beginning and end are linked midway by the Italian-born Buonarroti's account (1828) of Babeuf's *Conspiration pour l'égalité* of 1796. Buonarroti, who had himself taken part in the conspiracy, helped to surround *Babouvisme*, as it came to be called, with a kind of mythical aura. His foremost disciple, Auguste Blanqui, was the eternal conspirator, and spent fully thirty-three of his seventy-six years in prison. A 'leading lady' in the revolutionary drama was Flora Tristan, the daughter of a Peruvian-Spanish father and a French mother, who was the first to conceive the idea of a workers' international union, described in the year before her death in her book *Union Ouvrière* (1843).

Among the more pacific advocates of social reform, Étienne Cabet and Louis Blanc deserve special mention. The former, influenced by Thomas More's *Utopia* no less than by the ideas of Babeuf, described, in his pseudonymous *Voyage en Icarie* (1839) a communistic Utopia in which the State exercises absolute control over all essential activities. All property is abolished and complete uniformity of dress is enforced as one of the symbols of equality. The indoctrination of the citizens is carried on from the cradle to the grave. Like Owen, Cabet too experimented with his ideas in America, where the Icarian settlement in Nauvoo, Illinois, eventually met with the same fate as Owen's New Harmony. Louis Blanc, son of a French *émigré* and of a Spanish mother, sprang into fame by his *Organisation du Travail* (1839). Unlike most of the socialists, he shared the belief of the radical democrats that universal suffrage, once achieved, would become an instrument of social progress. The idea of a powerful and benevolent State strongly appealed to him, for he believed that socialism could not be first established in any other way, though co-operation would then replace competition by its own greater efficiency.

It was precisely the role which Cabet and Blanc respectively assigned to the State in the transformation of society that was repugnant to the mind of Pierre-Joseph Proudhon. Almost alone among the social reformers of his time, that great anarchist revived the worship of Liberty which many of his fellow reformers had been ready to sacrifice on the

[1] Supplementary Preface for the 3rd edn. of *Der Deutsche Bauernkrieg* (Leipzig, 1875).

altar of Equality. Again Proudhon was almost the only social reformer of genuinely plebeian origin. This fact helps to explain the marked distrust he felt towards socialist intellectuals who did not originate from the common people. Any discussion of his thought and influence belongs outside this volume.

In the later stages of his tortuous intellectual career, that truly Protean character, the Abbé de La Mennais, also inveighed against the authoritarian schemes of many reformers and revolutionaries. Moreover he differed from them, not only by giving (like Mazzini) as much emphasis to man's duties as to his rights, but above all in his conviction that egalitarian views can only be defended on the basis of the idea of God as the common Father. For him (though not for Mazzini) the ideal of human equality was derived from Christianity and had no future without it. Through the vicissitudes of his career he clung to the belief that a Christian foundation was indispensable for the task of social reconstruction. Already in 1817, in his *Essai sur l'Indifférence en Matière de Religion*, that had been his chief argument in favour of a return to Christianity, which he commended principally as a means of regenerating French and, indeed, European society. La Mennais was not entirely alone in his bold attempt at reconciling revolutionary ideas with Christianity. Buchez, the founder of the co-operative movement in France, and later Constantin Pecqueur, were working in the same direction; and in Bohemia, the Catholic philosopher Bernard Bolzano in 1831 composed a social Utopia, *Von dem besten Staat*, which was not published until several decades after his death. None, however, wrote with the same millenarian fervour as did La Mennais. His *Paroles d'un Croyant* (1834), where radical social ideas were couched in biblical language, went through eight editions in less than a year. Pope Gregory XVI condemned the book in his encyclical *Singulari nos*, and there can be no doubt that the Vatican had discovered serious flaws in the Abbé's theological armour. Nevertheless, La Mennais was not wrong in suspecting that the Pope had yielded to strong pressure from Tsar Nicholas I, and also from Prince Metternich who even, it seems, influenced the very wording of the encyclical.[1]

Deeply mortified in his pride, La Mennais reacted with an astonishing *volte-face*: he discarded the Church, and Christianity in general, and took refuge in a vague blend of deism, pantheism, and idolatry of 'the People'. Henceforth he signed his name 'Lamennais', thus repudiating any aristocratic connections. For many years he had acted as the herald of a Christian revival; now the same man became one of the protagonists

---

[1] Cf. A. Boudou, *Le Saint-Siège et la Russie, 1814–47*, 2 vols. (Paris, 1922–5); Liselotte Ahrens, *Lamennais und Deutschland* (Münster, 1930); and Andreas Posch, 'Lamennais und Metternich', in *Mitteilungen des Instituts für österreichische Geschichtsforschung* (Vienna, 1954).

of a deistic humanism. La Mennais's instability was reflected also in his frequent change of profession. He had started as a teacher, had then somewhat reluctantly assumed the priesthood, next he had acquired European renown as the author of profound politico-religious works, afterwards he had become a journalist and now, in the late 1830's, ended as a political pamphleteer. The brilliance which distinguished his writing still shone in his treatise *De l'esclavage moderne* (1839), in which he drew a striking picture of the antagonism between capitalists and proletarians. Marx and Engels were most probably influenced by that work when, eight years later, they drew up their epoch-making *Communist Manifesto*. Altogether, Lamennais's immediate impact was more radical than his social thought; and, although he was a gradualist who believed in the suffrage rather than in revolution, he came to sit, in 1848, with the extreme Left on the Mountain of the National Assembly. Long after his death (1854), many of his ideas were revived in the political programme of Christian Socialist parties in several European countries. The posthumous controversy over this daring, if erratic, thinker has continued for well over a century.

CHAPTER V

SCIENCE AND TECHNOLOGY

IN the generation between the Revolutions of 1793 and 1830, the community of science and technology outgrew the posture of the Enlightenment and assumed the stance of the nineteenth century. The old rationale of Condillac and the associationist psychology developed into that of Comte and positivism, which would know in order to predict and predict in order to control. Condorcet, last of the *philosophes*, left the testament of the eighteenth century to appear in 1795 after his death—*Sketch for a Historical Picture of the Progress of the Human Mind*. In that moving little book, science figures as the bearer of progress. It is the instrument which educates the human understanding in the order of nature. But the revolutionary generation was more messianic than naturalistic, and it transmuted this benign educational mission into something closer to engineering—civil engineering, social engineering, and perhaps the engineering of humanity itself. The Encyclopedists had already prided themselves on freeing science from metaphysics. Now the positivists would consummate the emancipation by liberating science even from ontology and, indeed, from every pretence to lay hold on a reality beyond observation, experience and act. Comte wished to abandon absolute in favour of relative statements. And for this reason, he looked to human history rather than to some outer reality as the repository of experience. In his philosophy, rationalism turned attention to historical thinking, which had hitherto been the resort of romantics hostile to exact science. Man in history replaced matter in motion as the natural process *par excellence*, and science, rising in history, served it also as dynamic motor, the factor which made all the difference between one age and another, and which, graduating into knowledge of its own methods, held the promise of regeneration.

What thus transformed the expectations held of science was the extreme politicisation wrought by the Revolution in all aspects of culture. Positivism in scientific thinking was a proper creation of the Revolution, not of this or that faction or party, but rather of its consciousness and action, whether directed left or right. It was the philosophy of that thrust which Revolution and Empire made in common. In a generation which would make over the world in the interests of talent, science would fulfil itself in sociology applied. Nor did the new cast appear in words alone. It formed institutions. It styled and ordered the sciences themselves (though not their findings, which could only be about nature). It brought the Baconian dream to within one step of realisation, the old democratic dream of a common man's technology ennobled by science and nourishing it with problems.

Cultural leadership still was French. But not for long—virtue was at last going out of France after 1815. The pattern of French institutions and the impulse of French teaching would outlast the vigour of French science in the nineteenth century. For scientific affairs also may be illuminated by Tocqueville's perception of the Revolution as the culmination of civic tendencies in the old regime—an explosion inward down to the Year II, and thereafter outward. Napoleon is sometimes represented as an enlightened despot. The epithet takes on flesh when one reflects that the persons who actually administered the affairs of science and learning had been formed in the school of Turgot, minister-*philosophe* of the expiring monarchy, whose projects pre-figured the revolutionary reform of science (as of much else). In the 1790's the influential schemes for education—notably Talleyrand's and Condorcet's—contemplated constructing a national system around a core of science. Citizens at once handy and virtuous would be trained up in science and useful skills, and the Academy of Sciences would graduate from the role of privileged and honorific corporation into that of collective headmaster to all France, the scholarly apex of the nation.

Plans for an orderly institutionalisation of science failed when the Academy instead paid the price of the elements of privilege and intellectual aristocracy in its corporate personality. On 8 August 1793 the Convention abolished all academies as incompatible with a Republic. The scientific community ceased to exist during the Terror. Its members went into war-work or retreat, and in either case away from science. Indeed, the scientific and intellectual history of the Revolution is bound to put a value upon its phases different from that of political or military history. In the opinion of the intellectuals of the 1790's, the creative period of the Revolution began, not with the Bastille, nor with the night of 4 August, nor with the October days, nor with the exaltations of the Year II—all that they saw as anarchy tempered by one last burst of fanaticism—but with the fall of Robespierre and the preparation of the moderate, the politically despised Directory.

The great creation of the intellectuals—the *idéologues*—was the *Institut national de France*. A revival of the academies in republican guise, the Institute carried over into the new order that responsibility of the state for patronage of science, arts and letters, which, conceived as embellishments due to a great monarchy under Louis XIV, were now become handmaids of civic welfare. The existence of the Institute was prescribed by the Constitution of the Year III. Its regime was regulated by the law governing public education. Thus would science and learning serve under two masters, a co-operative body to which election meant arrival in an élite, and an educational system bound to become a department of state. Internal dispositions reflected the altering scale of values. There was no replacement for the *Académie française*, formerly (and again after the Restoration) the supreme embodiment of French cultural distinction. Instead, the Institute consisted of three 'classes', science coming first in precedence with sixty resident members, moral and political science second with thirty-six, and literature and fine arts third with forty-eight. Each class was subdivided into sections according to disciplines—mathematics, mechanics, astronomy, etc. The Institute opened in a ceremonial meeting at the Louvre in the *Salle des Cariatides* on 4 April 1796. Thereafter, the First Class resumed the functions of the old Academy: to serve the scientific community as a Mecca for ambition and the guardian of standards, and the state as high court of technical resort. The annual volumes of *Mémoires* continued the great academic series of the old regime, the repository together with the *Philosophical Transactions* of the finest fruits of research into nature. Already, however, the honorific was the more functional of the two aspects. Specialisation would draw the sciences apart rather than together in the nineteenth century, and the proliferation of societies and journals peculiar to each was already out-stripping the capacity of any institution to epitomise the work of all.

Nevertheless, the Encyclopedic ideology flowered in the Institute. It is a pity that the word 'ideology' has come to signify the intellectual content of some (discreditable?) political cause. To the original *'idéologues'*—Destutt de Tracy, Cabanis, Volney, Dupont de Nemours —the word meant rather right psychology, knowledge of how we come by ideas, which in their view was by way of sensation. Their starting point was Condillac's philosophy of science, according to which man is what he makes of his experience. If so, then the way to improve him is to give him a better one. They would form political and social sciences on this empiricism, and achieve the scientific idea of progress in the politics of liberalism. They have not, it is true, won a commanding place in the history of ideas or philosophy. They have been judged, perhaps, by their words and not by their works. But they were the men who drew the plans for the Institute—a 'living Encyclopedia' Daunou called it—and in them the scientific inspiration of the enlightened view of man passed over into political liberalism.

Indeed, the touch of *idéologie* reached far below the peak, revivifying the whole body of science and channelling its life into educational forms. In 1795 France had seen many educational schemes, but no schools, since the suppression of religious foundations four years before. The law of 25 October 1795, which founded the Institute at the summit, had as its main objective a system of universal education. An *École centrale* would furnish secondary education in each department. These schools, forerunners of *lycée* and *Gymnasium* alike, actually began work under the Directory. Science was the staple, taught, not for some moral value (as the *idéologues* had fondly hoped), but simply for its practical importance in the affairs of a modern nation, busy with conquest, commerce and industry, and rife with opportunity. Design, mathematics, physics and chemistry, natural history—those were the favourite subjects, and that the order of demand.

That order was determined by the prospect of careers, which lay through the professional schools. In higher education, the Directory followed eclectic and pragmatic principles, adapting what had proved itself in the old regime to the technical necessities of the new. The *Observatoire de Paris* was retrieved from the revolutionaries and restored to the astronomers. A new *Bureau des Longitudes* took over responsibility for the astronomical almanac, the *Connaissance du temps*. The ancient *Collège de France* alone had gone through the Revolution untouched, its prestige enhanced by its hospitality to science. Two useful and much less theoretical institutions were revived, the *École des mines* and the *École des ponts et chaussées*. The *Conservatoire des arts et métiers* housed objects of technical value expropriated from enemies of the people. It built around this nucleus the first national museum of science and technology, and offered technical courses for tradespeople and artisans. New medical faculties were erected upon the corpses of the old Universities of Paris, Strasbourg and Montpellier. The *Muséum d'histoire naturelle*, formerly the *Jardin du Roi*, emerged flourishing from the Terror, its regime nationalised, rationalised, and actually favoured by the Rousseauist preference for the humble, the seemingly more democratic sciences of field and flower, bird and beast.

Finally, the expiring Convention authorised the two nurseries of the intellectual élite of nineteenth-century France, the future *École normale supérieure* and the *École polytechnique*. The former proved abortive in its earliest effort to be born. Provision for training teachers must obviously accompany a system of schools, but the *École normale* of the Year III was conceived in too generous a fit of enthusiasm. Nearly 1400 pupils from all France crowded into 700 places in the auditorium of the *Muséum*, ranging in qualifications from near illiteracy to the virtuosity of the young physicist, Fourier. All were to become teachers in a four-month course. It could not work. The opening of a normal school restricted to setting standards had to await 1812 and Napoleonic consolidation. What is more significant than this setback was the faculty assembled—Laplace and Lagrange, Berthollet and Monge—the great names, in short, of French scientific leadership.

Temporary failure did not undo the commitment of scientists to education, though it did separate them institutionally from the *idéologues*, who would have staffed the courses in moral and political philosophy, and who, thereafter, what with their humane and psychological bent, gathered round the School of Medicine. The physical scientists, for their part, found full scope in the earliest, and always one of the most exacting, institutes of technology, the *École polytechnique*, first called *École des travaux publics*. That famous school, the nursery of all engineering science, opened for classes on 21 December 1794. It succeeded immediately because it was founded on two solid blocks of pedagogical experience. First, there was a democratic element in the 'revolutionary courses' devised for the *levée en masse*. Second, there was a professional element, drawn from the former school of military engineering at Mézières. In the military emergency of 1793, the regime had looked to scientists for leadership in war production. It had not looked in vain. For the first time, a scientific community mobilised to serve the nation in arms. Supply, ordnance, communications, gunpowder—France became a national workshop serving her armies. And though the technical problems were of no theoretical interest, theoretical scientists proved the best persons to see through and solve them. In particular, the supply of salt-petre for gunpowder required instructing masses of people in a new and simple technique of extraction. The guiding hand in the whole war effort was Lazare Carnot's. The guiding spirit in technology was Gaspard Monge. The one was a graduate of Mézières, and the other his former teacher. Both had endured the slights which the old regime knew how to visit on mere ability, and both burned to vindicate, or rather to secure, professional dignity to technicians, men who know and do something, as against men who simply are something.

Thus did *Polytechnique* become one channel by which the great sea of bourgeois grievance and idealism broke through into passionate practice, a rivulet in the perspective of the Revolution as a whole, perhaps, but the main stream for conveying scientific culture through great events into the nineteenth century. The school long bore the marks of its origin. Its regime was paramilitary. The numbers were manageable, 392 pupils at the outset, an élite chosen by competitive examination. The course required four years of intensive application. Here for the first time, students went through a systematic scientific and mathematical curriculum, directed toward practice to be sure, but under the foremost scientific minds, all formed in the rigorous tradition which implants in the French intelligentsia something of the Cartesian spirit, something of its mathematical imperative toward order, unity, and elegance in doctrine. The students were able and eager. They lived their days at *Polytechnique* exhilarated by the sense of being conducted to the very forefront of scientific conquest, and there told that the future of mankind, of the Republic, and not least of themselves depended on how they performed in so exposed a situation. And they responded. Among the early graduating classes will be found many names attached to the fundamental quantities and analytical devices in nineteenth-century science—Cauchy, Coriolis, Poncelet, Poisson, Gay-Lussac, Sadi Carnot, Fresnel. Among them, too, were young, dreaming engineers, who would soar in imagination with Saint-Simon far beyond technology to technocracy, beyond public works to public regeneration, and who would in fact construct railways and canals, among them Suez. And in the class of 1814 was Auguste Comte, who founded in positivism the most influential modern philosophy of science and thus reduced the spirit of this institution to system.

Polytechnique and the other schools had an equal influence upon the teachers. The attention of the historian of science is arrested by the great clustering of systematic treatises in the first decades of the new century. The explanation is that scientists were communicating, not for the moment with their colleagues, but with their students. They published their courses—Lagrange his theory of analytical functions, Monge his descriptive geometry, Laplace his essay on probabilities, Cuvier his comparative anatomy, Lamarck his zoological philosophy. And parallel to this movement of rationalisation and generalisation in the literature, the necessity to reorganise for teaching made science into the profession it has become, a profession bottomed in educational institutions and in return imparting to them the norms which make for research and discovery. Scientists, in short, became professors. It is difficult to exaggerate the importance of this seemingly so natural development, which was a special case of the professionalisation of function in the Revolution as a whole. For until then, science had been simply an avocation, like literature or philosophy, dependent on the wealth or favour of patrons, private or public.

Thus, France endowed herself almost at a stroke with a modern set of scientific institutions. Their educational form, and the quality of the men who taught and studied there, made her the scientific schoolmistress of Europe. It may be that extreme centralisation, basing higher learning upon a city rather than a nation, is what ultimately cost her the scientific leadership which was indisputably hers through the first third of the century. For the French way was to train an élite rather than a people, quality rather than quantity. It may be, too, that the very involvement of scientific education with Paris and the revolutionary heritage lost to French science the talents of the bourgeoisie once that class turned safe and defensive. The mood of science is to dare, and that was no longer the mood of bourgeois France.

But if these were flaws, they were hidden in the brilliance of the light from Paris. In Weimar on 2 August 1830, Soret paid a call on Goethe. Had he heard the news from Paris? cried the ageing sage: 'Well, and what do you think of this great event? The volcano has exploded.'[1] Nor did he mean the Revolution of July, but the open rupture in the Academy of Sciences (again its name since the Restoration) between Cuvier and Geoffroy Saint-Hilaire over fixity versus metamorphosis of species. When in 1804 Alexander von Humboldt returned from four years amid the jungles and upon the mountains of Latin America, it was to Paris that he hurried with his collections and his specimens, gathered during this, the pioneering geographical, botanical and anthropological exploration of the nineteenth century, that second age of great voyages. There he disposed his findings under the eyes of the Institute, ranged them among the collections of the *Muséum*, and compared them with the resources brought thither by the cultural raiders attached to the republican armies as representatives on mission to the museums of the Low Countries, Germany, and Italy. In 1801 Alessandro Volta and his assistant, Brugnatelli, were 'called to France' (such was the language of the Institute) to evoke the electric current from a Voltaic pile, ancestor of all batteries. On 15, 21 and 25 October, Volta demonstrated the essential experiments before the First Class. Laplace observed every particular, with utmost narrowness. On 7 November Volta began reading his famous memoir, 'On the Identity of the Electrical Fluid with the Galvanic Fluid'—i.e. current and static electricity. This time the first consul himself attended. It was his right as a member since 1797 in the section of mechanics. Nor did this august presence fail in attendance at two further sessions which Volta required to get through his memoir, after which Napoleon himself moved the award of a golden medal, and the creation of a prize for further discoveries with this new phenomenon. In 1807 Humphry Davy won the prize for his isolation by electrolysis of the alkaline metals, sodium and potassium, and in 1813 received a safe conduct to cross to Paris for his day of glory before the Institute.

'All men of genius,' so ran General Bonaparte's decree of 19 May 1796, authorising transfer (among other things) of certain Leonardo manuscripts from Milan to Paris, 'all who have won distinction in the republic of letters are French, whatever be the country which has given them birth.'[2] But it was rather a republic of science than letters of which Napoleon would make Paris the forum, fulfilling in the realm of culture her role as capital of Europe. Indeed, the Napoleonic variation on enlightened despotism would supplant *philosophe* by scientist. Letters fell into limbo, or into exile, insofar as the man of letters would be *politique-et-moraliste* in the fashion honoured both before and since in France. Napoleon started that contempt for the *idéologues* in which,

---

[1] Johann Eckermann, *Gespräche mit Goethe*, ed. H. H. Houben (Leipzig, 1925), p. 596.
[2] Quoted in Edward MacCurdy, ed., *The Notebooks of Leonardo da Vinci* (New York, 1955), p. 46.

for all their liberal aspirations, their reputation has languished. In 1803, he suppressed the group by reorganising the Second Class out of the Institute they had founded. Thereafter (as beforehand), he chose his intellectual courtiers from among the scientists. Berthollet and Monge were favourites. From organising victory, Carnot went back to creative mathematics for a time, but was minister of the interior during the Hundred Days. Laplace served briefly as minister of the interior, and then honorifically as president of the Senate. Later, Chaptal was minister of the interior, and Cuvier minister of education. Fourcroy had a post as inspector of education. Joseph Fourier and Ramond were departmental prefects. Expert and non-political, the behaviour of the scientific community exemplifies a remark made by André Malraux, pointing out that an effective regime by definition finds its technicians. In the afterglow of Empire, the Academy of Sciences continued to dominate the European scene until the Napoleonic generation wore out. The Restoration brought no interruption in the dual principate under which it had flourished since the Consulate. Laplace and Cuvier remained the lawgivers until their deaths in 1827 and 1832, new men with new titles, the mathematical marquis and the biological baron—indeed Louis XVIII, not Napoleon, issued their patents of nobility.

Those were the twin stars of the first magnitude; nor was their attraction, or that of the entire constellation, political. It was educational and institutional. In 1823, Adolphe Quetelet, the founder of statistics as an analytical rather than simply a descriptive science, came to Paris to qualify himself for a post at the Observatory of Brussels. He found himself more interested in Lacroix's course in probability than in celestial mechanics, and he returned to make his observatory the centre of statistical rather than astronomical science. Young German chemists, impatient for the last word, divided their studies between Berzelius in Sweden and Gay-Lussac in Paris, and bore off to their own universities the leadership of nineteenth-century chemistry. Their successors would not need to travel. The pattern of *Polytechnique* may be followed across Germany in the foundation of *Technische Hochschulen*: Prague in 1806, Vienna in 1815, Karlsruhe in 1825, Munich in 1827, Dresden in 1828, Stuttgart in 1829 and Hanover in 1831.

In the ordinary doings of scientists, and of other men beyond the Anglo-American island of avoirdupois, the metric system remains the most positive legacy of the French Revolution. The decision to base the metre in nature, one ten-millionth part of the quadrant of a meridian to be surveyed from Dunkirk to Barcelona, belonged to the naturalistic universalism of the early Revolution. By 1799 the measurements were complete, after difficulties both political and geodetic and not a few compromises with the element of arbitrariness in the choice of any system of units. And representatives of Europe were summoned to the first metrical Congress, 'To receive the metre from the hands of France.' But nowhere—not even in France—were the new units in daily usage before the 1840's.

From the outset, Napoleon perceived the possibilities in the Institute as an instrument for transmuting French universalism into cultural imperialism. He was not only a captain of the armies, he was a member of the Institute, who descended upon Egypt in 1798, accompanied by a whole staff of scientific camp-followers—mineralogists, archaeologists, cartographers, naturalists—headed by Monge, Berthollet and Geoffroy Saint-Hilaire. Upon arrival they organised themselves into an Institute of Cairo. The Rosetta Stone is their most famous find. The science of Egyptology is their legacy. Its foundations were laid in the long months following their desertion by its patron (by which default the British Museum became residual legatee).

French institutions had already begun to reproduce themselves in Italy. Article 297 of the Constitution of 1797 of the Cisalpine Republic created at Milan an *Istituto de Scienze, Lettere ed Arti,* in three classes. This body became an *Istituto della Republica Italiana* in 1802, moving its seat to Bologna, and turned into the *Imperiale Regio Istituto* when Italy became a kingdom in 1805. Napoleon exercised a beneficent patronage over Italian science. The Florentine Academy revived under Elisa, with the sciences in first place, and the mission of protecting the purity of the Tuscan tongue. Bemedalled in Paris, Volta became a count in Italy. It was at Napoleon's own initiative that Eugene decentralised his Institute in 1810, establishing branches in Venice, Padua and Verona, and returning the scientific class to Milan, the foyer in Italy of the spirit of progress and industry. Elsewhere in the Grand Empire, the surviving scientific bodies of the capitals sank to the level of provincial academies. At the centre in Paris, Cuvier reached out in his correspondence as Permanent Secretary of the First Class, and embraced the science of Western Europe in its ambit. Everywhere these bodies reverted to the legitimate sovereignties after the Restoration; but everywhere the novel emphasis on science in public service carried over into nineteenth-century progressivism, and technical careers beckoned young men of talent.

And all the while there survived on either flank of the Empire two systems of scientific bodies influenced from Paris by scientific attraction and political repulsion. Around the Royal Academy of Sciences of Berlin gravitated its satellite of St Petersburg, both conceived in the French image. For eastward the force of France bore on Prussia and Russia through the continuum of Europe. But to the west, across the temporary void of war and the deeper discontinuity which the sea and history always bring between Anglo-Saxon and continental institutions, the infant societies of Philadelphia and Boston looked rather to the Royal Society of London, and repeated its pattern of private and voluntary effort improvising what on the continent had seemed, since Colbert at least, to be functions of state.

Of the great cities, the most portentous scientifically was Berlin. 'The State must make up in intellectual force what she has lost in physical,' declared Frederick William III in his traumatic winter of 1806, his army shattered at Jena, his capital the prey of the French, and his patrimony the spoil of war.[1] And indeed, the rise of German science and learning to their nineteenth-century predominance may properly be celebrated as a glorious accompaniment to the progress of the Prussian phoenix. Throughout the Enlightenment, French had remained the language of Prussia's Academy as of her king. Many members of the Prussian Academy were French (and many in the Russian Academy were German). The movement to Germanise stirred in the romantic dawn of literary self-consciousness. From the beginning, it expressed the yearning for national distinction in the peculiarly German idea of *Wissenschaft*, wherein art, scholarship and science become components of the highest capacity for creativity and awareness.

Reorganisation of the Prussian Academy completed a series of reforms in which the brothers Humboldt took the lead when, after Jena and Tilsit, it became a question, not only of scholarship, but of retrieving a national disaster—through scholarship. Wilhelm von Humboldt, the humanist, was in Berlin. Alexander von Humboldt, the naturalist, was in Paris, and their collaboration epitomised the partnership of philosophy and science in German culture. Alexander von Humboldt knew the workings of the *Institut de France* and had actually experienced what its imposition of standards achieved in rigorous analysis. He would renovate the Prussian Academy in this same spirit and practice of exact science. But this was a vision ampler than that of the *idéologues*. He and his brother grafted their Academy upon the stout stem of the German university tradition.

The University of Berlin was founded in 1809–10 to replace, in the first instance, the lost and much mourned Universities of Halle and Erlangen. But this was to be more than an affair of faculty and students. It was to incorporate all the learned institutions of Berlin into a single great foundation, which should associate the quest for truth in observatory, botanical garden, museum, and library with its communication to young patriots by old philosophers. Every member of the Academy, moreover, would be a member *ex officio* of the University, licensed and encouraged to lecture in its halls. It is difficult to exaggerate the importance of this new turn. It carried science out to the educated

[1] A. Harnack, *Geschichte der königlich preussischen Akademie der Wissenschaften zu Berlin* (2 vols., Berlin, 1900), vol. II, p. 556.

class of a whole nation. For German culture—this was its peculiarity and strength—spoke, not like French in the accent of the capital alone, but with a hundred voices in the many universities scattered all across the land and among the many states. The University of Berlin never extinguished the older, smaller, and prouder centres of learning— Heidelberg and Göttingen, Marburg and Giessen, Königsberg and Tübingen, Leipzig and Würzburg. Instead, writes the historian of the Academy, 'The creation of the University of Berlin glows like a burning point whereon all rays stream together.'[1] For in universities science could become popular and diffused as it never could be when associated in the French fashion with academic hauteur and the specialised schools of a technical élite.

That dissemination lay not very far in the future. Philological and historical studies led the scholarship of the German revival, and by the 1830's the yield was far greater there than in scientific reaches of research. Nevertheless, the foundations were laid down on which by mid-century Germany would construct her scientific pre-eminence. In Germany the cause of science, scholarship and the universities was also the cause of the most liberal and progressive elements in society and politics. Whatever the fate of political liberalism east of the Rhine, its scientific home is Germany. The method of the seminar, in which advanced students are taught by employment on research itself, developed out of the technique of German university studies in philology, classics, diplomatics and history. The scientific laboratory may not itself be described as a German invention. Already in the 1790's, laboratories had developed beyond the personal to the institutional stage. They no longer pertained typically to a man—Lavoisier, say, or Priestley. The *École polytechnique*, the *Muséum d'histoire naturelle*, the Royal Institution in London—all maintained laboratories. But it was in the German university that the laboratory became an adaptation to science of the seminar technique, an instrument of research and instruction combined, and the foyer of the doctorate.

And the first fruits do belong to our period. In 1826 Justus Liebig, back from his studies in Paris under Gay-Lussac, opened the laboratory of research and instruction at the University of Giessen which is always, and properly, taken to symbolise the migration of chemical leadership across the Rhine. In 1828 Friedrich Wöhler accomplished the synthesis of urea, the first product of metabolism to be reproduced experimentally in the laboratory. Biological studies had already flourished, in the somewhat idealistic, not to say mystical, vein encouraged by Goethe. The school of *Naturphilosophie*, led by Schelling, would contemplate the unity of nature in some universal metamorphosis, and address biology to the study of archetypal, almost Platonic, forms. Their mood was

[1] Harnack, *op. cit.*, vol. II, p. 557.

that of Herder and historicism, of Hegel and the sense of process up through time. But now biology would also be tempered and hardened by the analytical spirit, and given body in the laboratory. Starting from Goethe's subjective and idealistic colour theory, which was wrong and quite unscientific, Johannes Müller built up the physiology of sense-perceptions and the specificity of reaction of the sensory organs—the eye reporting light when struck as well as when open. The German climate had not as yet proved hospitable to a mathematical school. Gauss lived and worked in self-taught eminence and wilful loneliness at Göttingen, like Euler before him a European figure who often wrote in Latin. In 1825, however, Carl Gustav Jacobi opened a seminar at Berlin in the analytical methods of the French school. Out of it he formed his own following. To contain their findings, and to free themselves from dependence on the *Journal de l'École polytechnique*, they started in 1826 their own journal, *Crelle's Journal*, perhaps the most distinguished of the specialised periodicals now springing into print in every land to meet the need for communicating every science each to his own kind. And finally, on 12 May 1827, Alexander von Humboldt left Paris after a residence of a quarter of a century, to spend the thirty years that remained to his astonishing career in Berlin, now at last fit to be a capital of science as well as of Prussia.

Scientific Britain, down to 1830, presents quite another prospect, her science, like her public life, traversing the belated last chapter of her old regime. There were notable achievements, of course, always in the practical, empirical and individualistic, not to say idiosyncratic, style which was the English counterpart to Gallic rational rigour or to Teutonic metaphysical depth. Thomas Young and the wave model of light, Humphry Davy and the inauguration of electrochemistry, John Dalton and the atomic hypothesis of chemical combination—all that argues vigorous scientific effort during the Napoleonic era. So, too, do the almost exclusively British foundation of stratigraphical geology down to 1830, and Faraday's discovery how to induce the electrical current by magnetism. Nevertheless, even if told in detail, this would be an episodic story, inseparable from the personal chances of inventive men, a story of scientists and not of science. And so it was that active and critical minds, appreciative of the ingenuity of British scientists, agreed upon the unwholesome and self-defeating state of British science. Charles Babbage's *Reflections upon the Decline of Science in England* appeared in 1830. The tract was a summons to carry the pattern of liberal and utilitarian modernisation into science. But the answer to the summons belongs to the reform period and after. In England the French Revolution came late to science as to politics.

There was as yet no such thing as a scientific profession in England, nor any institutions in which to lead a scientific career. (In Scotland there were the universities, but they were small and poor.) Dalton was a schoolmaster, Young a jack-of-all-trades, and Davy a careerist. Geology was the hobby of clergymen and men of means. The Royal Society was less the governor than the showplace of British science, which went quite ungoverned. Unhappily, the Royal Society had fallen ill of the place-seeking rot which afflicted corporate life in the eighteenth century, in Church, in Municipality, in University, in Parliament. By the nineteenth century the patrician patron of science had become a stultifying anachronism in societies which his seventeenth-century forebears had helped by joining. Figures tell the tale. In 1830 the membership of the Academy of Sciences in Paris was 75, of the Prussian Academy 38, and of the Royal Society 685. The majority of this horde pretended to no scientific qualifications. The society lived on their dues, that they might write F.R.S. after their names.

The cleavage between science and the springs of power went deeper into the social structure than the division between scientific and aristocratic Fellows of the Royal Society. Science had grown up quite outside the Establishment since the Restoration of Charles II. It had become a ward of the Nonconformist rather than the Anglican community. The public schools taught neither science nor any modern subject. No more did Oxford, and scarcely more did Cambridge. Cambridge remained faithful less to mathematics than to the memory of mathematics. Until the mid-1820's the tutors taught synthesis rather than analysis, and employed a fossilised Newtonian notation that disqualified graduates from reading writings from the Continent. Thus was British science thrown back upon those taught in dissenting academies, in Scottish universities, or by themselves. The poverty, amounting to destitution, of British mathematical achievement was one consequence. Mathematics was already the language of theory and the arbiter of taste in physics. And quite generally the literature of British science betrays that want of elegance which is too often the penalty attaching to the worthiest of radical self-educations. England, indeed, had divorced vigour of mind from urbanity of taste when she excluded the dissenting community from attendance at Oxford and degrees at Cambridge. That she achieved so much against this handicap attests rather to the vigour of her minds than to some virtue of self-help in science. It is difficult to think that Davy, Faraday, and Young would not have done even more had they been trained in mathematics.

Meanwhile, out on either extremity of the ambit of European culture, Russia and the United States addressed contrasting institutions to comparable scientific opportunities and resources. Virtually suppressed under Paul, the Imperial Academy of Sciences of St Petersburg was reorganised and granted a certain autonomy in 1803, but recovered its vitality only after 1815. It published in French now, rather than in the

Latin of the eighteenth century, and Russians began to displace the Baltic and German majority in its chairs. Russia has consistently practised the scientific *étatisme* of the Continent. In America, on the other hand, the Napoleonic wars had intensified the tendency created by common language and a common metric to depend primarily upon British scientific associations, and upon the voluntary pattern. Physicians, professors, and enlightened clergymen and men of affairs in Philadelphia and Boston continued the American Philosophical Society and the American Academy of Arts and Sciences as mildly honorific service organisations. The colleges—Harvard, Yale, Columbia, Princeton, Pennsylvania—modelled themselves rather on eighteenth-century dissenting academies or on the Scottish universities than on Oxford and Cambridge, and made increasing room for natural history and natural philosophy. Both in America and in Russia, however, the major scientific problem was one of acquisition rather than advancement. Both looked back to a recent culture-hero, an eighteenth-century polymath and *philosophe*—to Lomonosov or to Benjamin Franklin. Nevertheless, neither country could yet sustain a deep and steady stream of fundamental science. Most contributions from Russia and America were such as depended upon the situation: geographical and geological explorations, meteorological and astronomical information, studies of local flora and fauna.

All the foregoing concerns the public history of science. Its private history must be told rather in relation to nature than to society. And the secular movement of science *per se* in our period will appear most boldly in reviewing the deepening grasp and widening reach over phenomena encompassed by the two chief devices for reducing descriptions of the world to statements of exact quantity—mathematics and experiment. On the one hand, science moved from the eighteenth century into the nineteenth amid a golden glow of confidence in classical analysis. On the other hand, experiment now became, not simply the talisman of a Boyle, a Lavoisier or a Priestley, but a systematic, regularised procedure conducted in established laboratories from which reproducible results were reported in specialised periodicals. This was more than a change of scale. For until this development occurred, experiment was rather the characteristic instrument of a Baconian, classificatory science than it was the complement to mathematics in an abstract, quantifying science. And if a central theme were to be found for these decades, it would be the encroachment of exact and quantitative science upon 'natural history', that old sympathetic vein of collecting and ticketing characteristic samples of all the objects and wonders of the world.

It was the golden age of analysis. The task of the eighteenth century had been to translate Newtonian mechanics from geometric to algebraic terms, and to define quantities to suit the latter language. Science would describe the laws by which bodies move as inertial masses subject to radial forces, attractive or repulsive. Sun and planets offered the gross model of a mechanical system. And the *Mécanique céleste* of Laplace stands as the monument to this ideal of science. Between 1808 and 1823 that great work assembled in five volumes the perfected memoirs in which Laplace had demonstrated that every apparent exception to the Newtonian theory of gravity is in fact an instance of its validity. Therein he resolved one after another all the discrepancies between prediction and observation, showed that seeming anomalies were expressions of mutual gravitation among the planets themselves, and calculated the corrected theories of the heavenly bodies. Indeed, the phrase 'Newtonian World-Machine' is a misnomer. The actual world-machine was computed by Laplace.

The *System of the World*, a fine essay in responsible popularisation, expresses Laplace's faith in a deterministic and universal science of matter in motion in service to Newton's laws. Even the historical development of the solar system from some original nebula into the present congeries of masses might be embraced in such a conception. Nor was Laplace's other great work, mathematically his far more original work, the *Analytical Theory of Probabilities*, unrelated to his high determinism. A mind of infinite capacity informed by senses of an infinitesimal refinement might know the position and velocity of every particle of matter in the world, and thereby foretell the future with perfect accuracy. But there is no such mind. There are no such senses. It is the limitation of our capacity, the inevitability of our errors, and not some imperfection in the scheme of things, which throws science back upon probabilities as upon a crutch. This is the branch of analysis which estimates and hence reduces the role of error and mitigates the play of ignorance. A similar association between the perfection of stellar motion and the imperfection of observation appears in the lonelier work of Gauss. The first of the asteroids, Ceres, was picked up by Piazzi at the Observatory of Palermo on the very first evening of the nineteenth century. Calculating her course from a very few elements led Gauss to devise a new and more general method of computing celestial orbits. And Gauss formulated also the Law of Error, the method of least squares for taking the most probable value among a series of varying observations, or (what was geometrically the same problem) of finding the bullseye amid the dispersion pattern of shots on a target.

But though this, the analytical vindication of Newton in the heavens, was the most dramatic conquest of this science, it was Lagrange's abstract formalisation of mechanics in general, from macro to micro, from comet to mass-point, which stood in all algebraic austerity before this generation as the examplar of tact and taste in mathematical physics. Published in 1788, *Mécanique analytique* announced the policy by which the analytical school of Paris would press into the new domains of experimental fact—into heat, light, electricity and chemistry. No geometry nor any graphs or pictures sullied the pure pages of Lagrange. There equations marched without interruption from the principle of virtual velocities through the whole field of statics, and from d'Alembert's principle right through dynamics.

Even so would Joseph Fourier in *The Analytical Theory of Heat* in 1822 simply eschew the question which agitated more concrete minds, whether heat is a weightless fluid substance or a manifestation of motion in the particles of matter. 'Of the nature of heat,' he writes, 'uncertain hypotheses only could be formed, but the knowledge of the mathematical laws to which its effects are subject is independent of all hypothesis; it requires only an attentive examination of the chief facts which common observations have indicated, and which have been confirmed by exact experiments.' 'The effects of heat' he explains 'are subject to constant laws which cannot be discovered without the aid of mathematical analysis. The object of the theory which we are about to explain is to demonstrate these laws; it reduces all physical researches on the propagation of heat, to problems of the integral calculus whose elements are given by experiment.' Elsewhere he says, 'These considerations present a singular example of the relations which exist between the abstract science of numbers and natural causes.' And it is an instructive instance of those relations that it was this analysis of a physical problem which led Fourier to devise the series for expanding functions by sines and cosines of multiple arcs. 'Profound study of nature,' he says, 'is the most fertile source of mathematical discoveries.'[1] It was magnificent, this ferocious abstraction from all models in Lagrange and Fourier. But perhaps it was excessive. It never led on to a science of energy, as did the more naïve debate between heat as substance and heat as motion. But it was eminently in the spirit of a purely rational mechanics.

Physics had two characteristics. Its model of order was astronomical, and its technique was analytical. Thus Newton's law of gravity served as exemplar of a force law, to be adapted to other realms, and physicists would strive to express their findings in the formalism of the differential calculus. They would write equations of which the elements were point-masses under the influence of forces that diminished in intensity as the square of the distance between any two in question. Already in the 1780's Coulomb had demonstrated with a torsional balance that the inverse square relationship governs the interaction between

---

[1] Joseph Fourier, *The Analytical Theory of Heat*, trans. A. Freeman (Cambridge, 1878). The passages quoted will be found on pp. 26, 14, 24, and 7, respectively.

magnetic and electrostatic charges, here considered as masses. As with Newtonian gravity, only this essentially geometrical relationship obtained between centres of force. Theory contemplated no physical connection, no mechanical linkages, across the intervening space. In 1791 Galvani made the first artificial electrical current flow around a circuit including as fundamental elements the nerves of a frog's leg and a metallic couple. Beginning in 1800, Volta learned to sustain the current by means of his 'piles' composed of coupled discs of silver and zinc, each pair separated by a layer of moist felt. From 1806, Humphry Davy turned the wet cell to chemical account in the isolation of new elements. And then in 1820 Hans Christian Oersted reaped the reward of his idealistic belief in the ultimate identity of all the forces of nature, and found that an electric current in a wire affects a magnetic needle. Word of this effect reached Paris, whereupon Ampère immediately established the mutually attractive and repulsive effects of currents on each other. Ampère was a polytechnician. True to his training, he named the new subject electrodynamics, and set about to embrace electromagnetic induction in the formalism of corpuscular mechanics. This task required great virtuosity. For Ampère had to treat the elements of each current infinitesimally and to suppose that the force is radial which operates between any two electrical point-masses in motion. For himself, he said explicitly, scientific explanation consisted in resolving phenomena into statements of the quantity of equal and opposite forces acting and reacting between pairs of particles. Ampère brought great clarification. He abolished the distinction in kind between static and dynamic electricity, and assimilated the difference to the categories of mechanics. The term which appears as height in gravitational equations becomes statical potential in electrical ones.

Meanwhile, the laboratory was bringing quantification to the physical sciences in another vein throughout these years, not in this imperious abstraction, but concretely by measurement and simple, systematic numeration. Chemistry now completed its revolution into the status of an exact science by taking decisive advantage of Lavoisier's principle of conservation of mass and his conception of oxidation and reaction. Fundamental though that work of theory had been, Lavoisier still organised the science by classification and nomenclature, by principles of language rather than of measure. And the atomic hypothesis ultimately attached numbers of general significance to the individual substances of the chemical population. This was no simple tale. John Dalton was thinking along channels that ran straight back through the Newtonian and corpuscular philosophy of the seventeenth century, and beyond that all the way to antiquity and the Epicurean policy which made change in nature a rearrangement of the parts rather than an alteration of qualities. He was at first concerned with the physical behaviour of gases, in diffusion and in solution. That led him to the question of the relative weights of particles, and from this physical question he moved on to the chemical thought that the percentage composition of compounds must be in proportion to the weights of the constituent atoms. If so, then the intimate structure of compounds must be discrete atom-to-atom linkages. What was novel here was the combined notion of the atom, first as distinguished chemically by the physical attribute of weight (rather than shape), and secondly as specific to the chemical element (rather than being the last point of physical division).

Nor was Dalton himself perfectly clear that his advantage lay in exploiting the strategy of weight as the chemist's metric. What pleased him more was the naked (and mistaken) numerical notion that atoms always combine in the simplest ratios—one-to-one in the case of elements that combined to form only one compound, one-to-two or two-to-one for the next higher order in cases (like nitrogen and oxygen) which form a series of compounds in differing proportions. Thus, for Dalton, water was HO. Nor did he prove the two empirical laws of definite and multiple proportions. He simply assumed the invariability of chemical composition, and then offered the atomic hypothesis as an explanation. And such was his pleasure in his simplest ratios that he failed to see confirmation of the atomic model itself in a beautiful discovery of Gay-Lussac in his laboratory at *Polytechnique*. In 1809 Gay-Lussac established that volumes of gases which react chemically do so in some ratio of small whole numbers. But not necessarily the simplest ratio—thus, one volume of oxygen combines with two (not one) of hydrogen to give two of water. That equal volumes of gases contain equal *numbers* of particles was the obvious explanation. This was reconcilable with Dalton's *gravimetric* ratios through the suggestion, proposed independently by Ampère and Avogadro, that molecules may be polyatomic.

Moreover, cross-currents in the torrent of discovery obscured the clarity of these relations and brought more information than the atomic hypothesis might organise. Electrolysis was a cornucopia of new metals, opened by Humphry Davy—potassium, sodium, barium, strontium, calcium and magnesium. In Paris Gay-Lussac identified gaseous elements at the opposite electrode—chlorine and iodine. The greatest chemist of the period was Berzelius. He designated the elements with the symbols they still bear, and built up a table of their combining weights based on oxygen as 100. Because of the contrary polarity of metals and (say) the oxygen, chlorine, or iodine with which they combine, he considered the chemical bond to be the attraction between positively and negatively charged atoms. For this reason, he made dualistic classification of the elements according to their electrical properties—and refused to admit the polyatomic molecule. These and other fruitful confusions led the atomic hypothesis a chequered career. Nevertheless, it did now exist as a scientific hypothesis and not simply as an ontological policy. And this subjection of the science of combining matter to the rule of number was what made chemistry an exact and no longer a mere descriptive science, continuous with physics now rather than with natural history.

To return for a moment to physics, the partnership of experiment and theory in nineteenth-century science nowhere appears more characteristically than in the work which created the first faint cloud in classical corpuscular mechanics. The nineteenth-century wave-theory of light was the joint work of Thomas Young and Augustin Fresnel. Young was a self-taught prodigy, ingenious in the English way and unskilled in mathematics. In 1802 and 1804 he published experiments which displayed interference phenomena in a fashion that argued the periodicity of light. Fresnel was a polytechnician whose brief career lay mainly in the 1820's. Ignorant at first of Young's work, he expressed the same results in partial differential equations of the second order. They struck a discordant note in the physics of the day since they described the motion of the wave in a medium instead of the particle in a void. Moreover, Fresnel postulated of the medium, the aether, just that paradoxical elasticity and permeability which would later make it the seat of the continuous field not yet conceived in Faraday's mind.

Biology was the coming science in the nineteenth century, favoured by positivists and romantics alike. Comparative anatomy dominated in the first third of the century. At the same time, however, the great technical specialties were forming in the laboratories—histology, embryology and physiology together with foreshadowings of cytology and pathology. These were the studies in which by mid-century biology would transcend the superficiality of natural history and the dependence on medicine. Intellectually, the problem of biology was one of scientific self-knowledge. The character, nature and object of the science needed to be defined. In over-simplified accounts, mechanism and vitalism are presented as the alternatives. Might phenomena of life be reduced to laws of physical nature, i.e. to mechanics? Or is life different? Perhaps ineffable? The boundary intruded even into chemistry where the inappropriate distinction between organic and inorganic compounds preserves its memory. One might have thought the question settled in principle by Wöhler's synthesis of urea in 1828. But it was not, for the real issue was deeper and more complex than vitalism, a vague position at best. What kind of science was biology to be? Not mathematical, evidently. What then? What model of order was it to contemplate? The organismic? If so, the organism was the ultimate object of inquiry, the whole rather than the parts. Or the physical? If so, its object will be the order and arrangement of the parts, as in physics, rather than some superior wisdom of the whole. And it makes an instructive lesson in the difference between what scientists say and what they do, that different answers were given to these questions of scope and method by each of the four leading biologists of these decades, and that nevertheless their works chimed harmoniously together. Lamarck and Cuvier, firm in their disagreement over theory, together established by comparative anatomy the fundamental classifications of systematic biology. Bichat and Magendie, on the other hand, the one regarding himself as a student of life and the other of living machinery, succeeded one another at the head of the great, deep-cutting tradition of experimental biology in the nineteenth century.

The founder of histology, Xavier Bichat, may be considered a prototype of the professional biologist. Bichat took life to be the object of his science, and defined it in a famous formula as the 'ensemble of functions that resist death'. He has, on this score, often been called a vitalist. Nevertheless, Bichat was not one to regard biology as a refuge from determinism, or as lacking in the rigour of physics. His intellectual method was the strictest application to organisms of the analytical technique. He would resolve the study of organisms into the knowledge of their elements. These he found in the tissues, each type with a specific function. That is the principle of his *Anatomie générale* of 1801: 'All animals are assemblies of diverse organs which, each performing its own function, co-operate in conserving the whole. They are so many particular machines in the general machine which constitutes the individual. But these particular machines are themselves formed of several tissues of very different types which form the true elements of the organs. Chemistry has its simple bodies ... Anatomy has its simple tissues which, by their combinations ... form the organs'.[1] Bichat was less fortunate in his doctrine of the two lives, animal and vegetable, situated respectively in the symmetrical and unsymmetrical organs. The forward thrust of his analysis was sharpened by his passion for dissections, practiced in the wards and morgues of the Hotel-Dieu of Paris, in which fetid corners he caught a fever and died in 1802 at the age of thirty-one, brilliant and barely under way, and the inspiration of all who knew him.

The practice of experimental biology was extended and consolidated in the career of François Magendie of the *Collège de France*, where he installed the first laboratory. Severe and mechanistic, Magendie held that organisms were complex problems in chemistry and physics. He published a corrected edition of Bichat, in which he as editor skips in footnotes along the bottoms of the pages pointing up to the beauty of his teacher's findings and the error of his views. Since Magendie

---

[1] *Anatomie générale* (1812 edition, Paris), vol. i, p. lxxix.

severely renounced all general views, he himself left a collection of fine discoveries, especially in neuro-physiology, but no body of thought. Even more important, perhaps, was the example he set of experimental discipline and fidelity to fact. Claude Bernard was his great pupil, in whose work experiment would truly rival mathematics in precision, fertility and sophistication. And already the process by which French rationality took on body in German thoroughness was bringing sobriety and realism to German science, and foreshadowing a symbiosis between the science of biology and the culture of Germany. In 1824 Prévost and J. B. Dumas established the role of spermatozoa in the fertilisation of frogs' eggs, and observed the differentiation that ensued. In 1827 Karl von Baer identified the ovum itself in the ovary of a bitch. The discovery announced the imminence both of cytology and embryology.

This experimental motif prepared the future of biology as an exact science. In its contemporary state, however, the humbler instrument of taxonomy still seemed the way to order things all across the living front of nature. Lamarck's *Natural History of Invertebrates* was published between 1815 and 1822. Cuvier's *Animal Kingdom* appeared in 1817 in four volumes, followed by *Researches on Fossil Bones* in seven volumes from 1821 to 1824. In this painstaking detail natural history passed over from Aristotelian classifications to those of modern zoology. The newer science linked old nature with living in palaeontology. It established relationships between species in space and time by the rigorous techniques of comparative anatomy. The regulative principle was Cuvier's, the principle of correlation of parts. 'Every organic being,' he laid down, 'forms an ensemble, a unique closed system, of which all the parts mutually correspond, and co-operate in any definitive act through reciprocal relations. No one of these parts may change without the others changing also, and consequently each of them, taken separately, indicates and gives all the others'.[1] Thus, confronted with a tooth, Cuvier could predict what the hoof would be, or the digestive tract; and by this means he related the creature's organisation to its way of life.

Lamarck applied Cuvier's technique to the classification of invertebrates, a task which he discharged with acumen and skill. But although the actual work of Cuvier and Lamarck was complementary, their thinking presupposed very different models of biological order, the one naturalistic and metamorphic, the other theological and providential. Lamarck published his *Philosophie zoologique* in 1809. The argument has since become famous as anticipating the theory of evolution and offering a humane and idealistic alternative to the mechanistic tenour of natural selection. Lamarck's views were in fact derived from the organismic and romantic philosophy of nature started by Diderot, and

---

[1] Georges Cuvier, *Recherches sur les ossemens fossiles* (nouvelle ed., 5 vols. in 6; Paris, 1821–4), vol. I, p. xlv.

charged with power by Goethe. His theory of evolution was an application to taxonomy of this outlook, and it is famous only since Darwin. In his own generation Lamarck's speculations about transformation of species were regarded by his colleagues as the embarrassing aberrations of a gifted observer, to be passed over in silence. Living nature, in Lamarck's zoological philosophy, is a plastic force, forever forming all manner of animals from the simplest to the most complex by the progressive differentiation and perfection of their organisation. But the innate tendency to complication and specialisation is not the only factor at work. Over against it, constraining it into shapes which we mistakenly think of as immutable species, works the influence of the physical environment. Changes in environment lead to changes in needs. Changes in needs produce changes in behaviour. Changes in behaviour become habits, which ultimately alter individual organs and even the whole organism. Thus, the environment is a shifting set of circumstance and opportunity to which the organism responds creatively.

Cuvier's was by far the more characteristic, conservative and persuasive explanation of biological adaptation, that striking fact in the relation of organisms to the economy of their lives, of form to function. This was simply the old argument from design. It had been respectable ever since the time of Aristotle, the master classifier, and had long been the mainstay of Christian natural theology. In this perspective all nature is a divine artifact, and every effect is a device for carrying out the purposes of the creator. Cuvier's conception of his science was conservative and Aristotelian in yet another way, a way most important for the value which his work would hold for Darwin. He was a naturalist rather than a biologist. He distinguished in science between 'physique générale' and 'physique particulière', or natural history. And Cuvier would agree with the argument of the present chapter that quantification and experiment make the difference. 'Physique générale,' comprising mechanics, dynamics and chemistry, admits quantification and employs experiment. Not so natural history, which studies the particular object and may not aspire to abstract theories. Experiment is impossible in natural history, thought Cuvier, since to dissect a living whole is to destroy the object under study. Comparison must take the place of experiment, and thus the naturalist may only discern by observation and shrewd judgment the operation in his realm of laws which the physicist has discovered in his.

Despite his own belief in fixed species, the comparisons of Cuvier's natural history rather than the speculations of Lamarck were what readied the scene for evolutionary biology. Already in Cuvier, the creature's organisation is a function of its way of life. Darwin will only have to turn the argument from design on its head to explain adaptation naturalistically instead of theologically. He will have to transfer the problem of arrangement of discrete populations into that of historic phyla and to ask for pedigrees as well as to make comparisons. Cuvier himself raised the question of succession in the populations of the globe. Palaeontology was the great development of his later years, a new science of archaic forms. And thus if biology joined on to chemistry and physics on the one side through its growing mastery of experiment, on the other it merged through natural history into geology and description of the world.

Thanks to the key offered in palaeontology, the early nineteenth century was the heroic age for geology, when it first mastered its materials. Until the 1790's, the study of the earth was little more than an indeterminate blend of mineralogical lore with speculations about the origins of the globe. In 1795 James Hutton's *Theory of the Earth* did assert the principle of uniformity of nature in historical terms. Hutton would restrict geologists to inductive analogies from the effects of natural forces currently in operation. He required a near infinity of time ('no vestige of a beginning—no prospect of an end'), and the 'Vulcanist' school he inspired argued for the igneous origin of the fundamental formations. Their views were opposed, violently at times, by 'Neptunists', followers in the early 1800's of Abraham Gottlob Werner, of the Mine school of Freiberg-im-Sachsen, who fought fire with water, and whose followers held to the aqueous deposition of all strata in a series of vasty inundations. These disputes would have remained quite unsettled had it not been for discovery of the technique of fossil stratigraphy. The pioneer was William Smith, an English drainage engineer who between 1810 and 1820 identified successive formations from East Anglia and the Channel across to the coal measures of Wales by reference to their characteristic populations of fossils embedded in the rock. And in the more recent layers of the Paris basin, Cuvier and Brongniart employed similar palaeontological indices for geological classification.

Cuvier, together with most of his English colleagues in the 1820's, saw the evidence in the light of the doctrine of geological catastrophes, and they still placed it in a time-scale reduced to the dimensions of human history. No doubt theological presuppositions disposed their minds in favour of the flood. But this was no simple question of the Bible, true or false. It was a deeper issue of the relation of God to nature. Geology was the first science to touch on the history as well as the structure of nature, and the first, therefore, to contemplate God as governor and not simply as creator. Nor did science here speak with determinate authority. In traversing the front of early nineteenth-century science, we left the realm of the exact and quantitative for the merely descriptive when we moved across the divide marked by Cuvier in biology between the new experimental disciplines and the old practice of natural history. By ranging the forms of life in the secular order of the geological succession, from the simpler to the more complex, palaeontology prepared the evidence for ordering science in historic time by means of evolutionary theory. But not yet, not quite yet.

When the scene shifts from theory to practice, from science to industry, Britain rather than France appears the technical pacemaker and schoolmaster of Europe. The progress of the steam engine—there was the truly revolutionary element in the process of industrialisation. Increments of power now began waxing exponentially along a curve bound to rise infinitely above what could be pulleyed, levered, geared and screwed out of the actions of man or animal, wind or falling water. After Watt's retirement in 1800, Trevithick developed engines toward the employment of higher pressures, double-action pistons, and reduction in the beams. Horizontal cylinders began to appear only after 1825. And engines found application, no longer just in pumping or blowing the blast, but in locomotion and in powering factories in place of water-wheels. Fulton ran his steamboat from New York to Albany in 1807. Trevithick built a locomotive in 1805, and Stephenson a better one in 1813 for use in Killingworth colliery. In 1830 Stephenson's first train ran from Liverpool to Manchester. But what impressed contemporaries even more notably was the application of steam to cotton, first for spinning, then for weaving. The change from water to steam shifted industry from rural streamsides into centres of population, and scarred the face of many a Midland city with the hideous factories of the early industrial age. By 1830 the cotton mills of Manchester had reached enormity as well as immensity. But, except here and there in France, none of this had gone beyond the stage of pilot plants outside of Britain.

This most important sector of industrial technique bore little relation to science—unless it be that James Watt named the linkage a 'sun-and-planet-gear' by which he converted the reciprocating action of a piston to the rotary motion of a wheel. Indeed, it is somewhat puzzling to know precisely what credence to give the common belief in science as the fructifying seed in technology. Their intimacy produced offspring only within the last hundred years or so. Nevertheless, the prophecies of Francis Bacon had shaped belief long before, and never more confidently than on the early nineteenth-century eve of their fulfilment. Theoretical science still had very little to offer to industry. But if the concept of a scientific movement be enlarged so as to include, not merely ordered knowledge of nature, but systematic patterns of rationality, empiricism, and coercion of opportunity throughout the whole realm of technics, then the behaviour of the engineers and industrialists resonates with that of men of science.

Rationality—the encyclopedic movement had left the extravagances of Diderot far behind and expressed itself prosaically now, in two great compilations, the *Encyclopédie méthodique* and the *Encyclopedia Britannica*, and in many lesser technical dictionaries. Nor was this in principle different from the taxonomies of systematic biology. It is to be seen as the application of descriptive science to industry, publicising and thus standardising, not some novelty suggested by theory, but the best method used in practice. Publicity was a condition of the awards offered to inventors by the societies for the stimulation of industry, the Royal Society of Arts in England and the *Société d'encouragement* of Napoleonic France. Similarly, patents must ultimately come into the public domain. Continental patent legislation dates from the Revolution. Hence, too, stemmed the systematic interchange through societies and publications of agricultural information among 'improving' landowners, not only in England now, but also in Prussia and even Austria. Agronomy attempted to supersede the ignorant routine of centuries in a descriptive science of farming, the same for all producers. Lore gave way to method, secrecy to publicity, craftsmanship to mechanisation and division of labour. In many sectors reason thus marched into industry and analysed procedures into elements. Eli Whitney of New Haven, Connecticut, was the apostle if not the inventor of interchangeable parts. Is it fanciful to describe this movement as the importation into machinery of the very possibility of rationality created by the scientist's assumptions of uniformity in nature? Thenceforth the student of machines could analyse structures with the same expectations of generality as an anatomist. Henry Maudslay pivoted his engineering practice upon the cutting of uniform screws. His lathe equipped with a slide rest for assuring plane surfaces was the fundamental machine tool, and precise machine tools are the guardians of the republic of engineering. Maudslay's micrometer of 1829 reduced tolerances to the vanishing. And writing of the quality of his influence, his contemporary biographer and disciple, James Nasmyth, tells of 'the innate love of truth and accuracy which distinguished Mr Maudslay'.[1]

The nature of materials and the empirical knowledge of their properties determines within limits what the most rational technology can make of them. The chemical industry, though not the greatest in drama or scale, was the most novel in point of product and possibility. Nor did its innovations depend upon theory. The atomic hypothesis was no help in a dye works or sulphuric acid plant. Even Lavoisier's reorientation of the science around the theory of combustion was irrelevant to the requirement of the manufacturer. What profited the industrialist was rather the increasing volume of detailed experience in

[1] Quoted in Friedrich Klemm, *A History of Western Technology* (New York, 1959), p. 285.

the handling and behaviour of diverse chemicals. Commercial soda and sulphuric acid were the fundamental heavy chemicals. Effective and economical methods for the production of both were in operation by the 1830's. James Muspratt of Liverpool put the Leblanc process for extracting soda from sea-salt into profitable operation in 1823. He did not understand the reactions involved. No one did until the 1890's, by which time the method was being superseded. The Leblanc process converted sodium sulphate to soda by fusion with charcoal and limestone. A quite fallacious analogy with smelting ore was what had suggested it to Leblanc himself. That was long before. He took out his patent in Paris in 1791, and the factors that then impeded his own exploitation were political, personal and economic, not theoretical. Throughout the industry, indeed, chance and fortune governed within the boundaries of technical possibility. The lead-chamber process for sulphuric acid depended on the imperviousness of lead, and thus freed producers from the limitations in scale imposed by the use of glass vessels. Scotland was in the business from the mid-eighteenth century, and England a little later. What induced its expansion in the 1830's was the market created by the soda trade. So it was in all the chemical industry. Every novel outlet and every cut in price created a pull felt throughout the whole nexus of connections between acids, alkalis, fertilisers, bleaches, dyes, glass, soap and gunpowder, and all redounded to economic growth.

Perhaps the important themes in the evolution of technology are to be understood in Lamarckian rather than Darwinian terms. For industry requires the coercion of opportunity. Technology is art, not nature, and is goal-directed. Acquired characteristics of machines are inherited. And only some evolutionary formula will contain the growth of the iron industry. The most fundamental material changeover in industrialisation was the substitution of iron for wood and stone as the basic structural substance. The nineteenth century was literally the iron age. But this was not the result of some crucial invention. Substitution of coke for charcoal permitted rather than caused expansion. Only in Britain was coke generally the fuel by the end of the Napoleonic wars. Foundries altered in design to accommodate the new fuel, and grew in scale to serve the market. Cast and puddled iron had still to do the work awaiting steel. Furnaces rose higher when steam blew the blast, straining upwards for advantage like Lamarckian giraffes. And the evolutionary metaphor does impose itself in thinking about the stages of the major components of technology. In transport, for example, the system of canals and turnpikes was suited to a highly specialised and temporary set of circumstances and elicited by a rapid expansion of demand for cheap and certain haulage. Our brief period almost contains the canal age, however, and one may imagine it represented on one of those diagrams where phyla vary in width along the ages, a ribbon of possibility waxing into fatness in some certain time of swamps, only to attenuate and continue as a thread after a slight change in circumstance. After 1830 canals gave place to railways as rapidly as they had appeared.

Occasional voices might be raised across the divide that still separated science and industry in practice. Humphry Davy designed the miners' safety lamp upon appeal from humanitarians. Joseph Fraunhofer, an optician by trade, identified the absorption lines in the solar spectrum. Machine tools benefited from the skills developed in the manufacture of precision instruments to the exacting specifications of scientific clients. New elements found unexpected uses. A great chemist, Berthollet, developed the technique of bleaching by chlorine, and applied himself to the rationalisation of dye-stuffs. Adventurers filled balloons with hydrogen, and the aerial observation of artillery fire began at the battle of Fleurus in 1794. Fresnel earned his living as an engineer for the French highway and harbour administration, and designed the lenticular light-house beacon to replace the feeble torches and lanterns for which ship-captains had anxiously had to peer. In 1799 London's Royal Institution was founded to brighten the life of the poor by instruction in science. The patron, Benjamin Thompson, Count Rumford, an ingenious Yankee turned renegade and ennobled by the Elector of Bavaria, was also the experimental originator of a mechanical view of heat, a designer of flues, and the husband for a time of Lavoisier's widow. In the 1820's Mechanics' Institutes carried on the movement for the scientific improvement of the working men themselves. And in 1831 the British Association for the Advancement of Science, modelled after ephemeral German societies, prepared to carry science to more influential segments of the population, and to permeate the nation with its spirit in the interests of progress.

Among these random voices, two contributed deeper statements. Sadi Carnot published *Reflections on the Motive Power of Heat* in 1824. Michael Faraday announced the induction of an electrical current in a magnetic field in 1831. The two findings were quite unrelated. They started, indeed, the two new subjects, thermodynamics and field physics, in which physics would ultimately transcend its classical Newtonian heritage. And—what may seem even more significant—they opened the dialogue, since become incessant, between basic science and rational technology. Technology for its part poses problems worthy of the theorist's steel. Science replies by arming technology with powers, so enhancing its capacities that the employment decides the fate of men and nations, and the combination is thus become the arbiter of civilisation.

Carnot's was an extremely abstract memoir. The reasoning is all about steam engines, however, and this no doubt was what inspired a famous remark by L. J. Henderson to the effect that science owes more to the steam engine than does the steam engine to science. What are the optimum conditions for converting (as does a steam engine) heat to motion? That is the question which Carnot put, or which the analytical spirit of *Polytechnique* put in his mouth. And to answer it, he imagined the reversible heat cycle in an ideal engine. Two reservoirs contain heat, one at a higher and the other at a lower temperature. Flowing from the former, heat expands the gas in a cylinder, pushing the piston first at constant temperature, then at constant pressure. Reversing these steps successively, the piston then compresses the gas and casts the heat down to the second reservoir. In place of an actual engine, full of friction, leaking heat, its piston slamming to and fro quite irreversibly, Carnot substituted this ideal engine, departing from and returning to an initial state. The finding is that the motive power of heat depends only on the absolute temperature-differential across which it is employed. And the reasoning founded the science of thermodynamics, abstracted from the hiss of the steam to the general case of 'all imaginable heat engines'.

Faraday's discovery reciprocated knowledge-out-of-power with power-out-of-knowledge. His scrupulous conscience about facts might also be taken as a decisive instance of the degree to which experiment had become capable of the precisions more traditionally reserved to mathematics. The inductive current came to him as the reward of a shrewd, patient series of experiments in which he sought to produce the reverse of Oersted's effect and to get electricity from a magnetic field. Frustration greeted his first attempts. No current could be made to stir in the circuit except at the moment of presenting or withdrawing the coil or magnet. But it was the signet of Faraday's genius to exploit his disappointments rather than to wilt in discouragement. And he found that the secret of sustaining current precisely was to cut continuously through the lines of force (as he later called them). He had, in a word, come upon the principle of the dynamo. He himself was a scientist, interested in nature rather than advantage, in reputation rather than profit. Nevertheless, the ensuing development of the electrical industry was in all the long history of science the first truly portentous application of a major piece of basic research (and not just of rational method) to the occasions of industry. Electrical power poured from the dynamo to augment the capacities of steam. Not only so, but (to look far ahead) critical analysis of spatial relations involved in electromagnetic 'lines of force' was at the bottom of relativity and its prediction of the convertibility of matter into energy, whether by fusion or by fission.

Power out of knowledge, in hardest fact.

CHAPTER VI

RELIGION: CHURCH AND STATE IN EUROPE AND THE AMERICAS

Cross and Tricolour had become opposing symbols for millions of Europeans by the end of 1793. In France, the fatal split between Church and Revolution, opened wide by the Civil Constitution of the Clergy, now seemed unbridgeable (see Vol. VIII, Chapter XXIV). In 1790 it had seemed self-evident to the Constituent Assembly that the Gallican Church should be reorganised and brought into line with the democratic institutions of the new France, that her officers should be elected by the people, and be independent of alien control. But this had raised the crucial question of competence and authority. What right had even a national assembly so drastically to reorganise a branch of a Catholic Church? Tragically, the first principle of the Revolution, the sovereignty of the people, was pitted against the basic conceptions of catholicity and tradition which Rome considered fundamental to the very essence of the Church as a spiritual society. Belatedly, Pius VI condemned the Civil Constitution. The clergy who refused the oath to it were proscribed, driven into exile, or to a clandestine ministry, and often into furtive and provocative counter-revolution. In their turn too, the 'patriotic clergy', the Constitutionals who took the oath, fell foul of the Revolution, especially after it swung to the left on 10 August 1792. Many resented the relentless demands made on their conscience: the introduction of the *état civil*, the encouragement of clerical marriage, the execution of the king. On the other hand, the revolutionary leaders grew more disillusioned with the results of the Civil Constitution, which had disrupted the patriotic cause and issued in schism and public disorder. Breaking point came in 1793. In March came news of the part played by non-juring priests in the Vendée risings: in July many Constitutionals were involved in the federalist revolt. So in Jacobin eyes the clergy as a whole seemed discredited as plotters, actual or potential, against the patriotic cause. In the hysteria of civil war and foreign invasion, fear of non-juring priests broadened into a general suspicion of the priesthood, and in places into an attack on Christianity itself.

The causes of the deliberate de-christianisation which began in the autumn of 1793 are complex. It was not so much a single movement as a series of movements, or of incidents, often set off by an explosive local situation or by individual caprice. Reversing the usual sequence of political events, the first systematic campaign began, not in Paris but in the provinces, where a pattern for violent iconoclasm was set by the representatives on mission, most notably Fouché in the Nièvre. Helped by troops and local patriots, the representatives stopped the mass, desecrated churches, executed captive non-jurors, and browbeat priests into apostasy or the semi-apostasy of enforced marriage. Christian worship was replaced by a Cult of Reason and the Republic. After the famous Feast of Reason in Notre Dame de Paris (9 November 1793) the campaign was taken up by the Paris sections, with prompting from the bourgeois anti-clericals of the Commune. As sensational as the violent dechristianisation of the Commune was the legislative dechristianisation of the Convention. The ancient clerical monopoly of education was swept away, and in October 1793 France deliberately broke with her religious past when the Convention voted the most anti-Christian act of the Revolution, the replacement of the ancient Gregorian calendar, woven intricately into the whole cycle of national life, by the new calendar of the Revolution (Appendix, pp. 691–2).

To Catholic historians, dechristianisation has appeared largely as a work of sheer destruction. Certainly, its negative side was uppermost in the grim horseplay of Paris *sansculottes*, parading before the bar of the Convention in looted vestments; in the ribaldry of Hébert's journal *Père Duchesne* which encouraged them; in some of the proconsular iconoclasm of the representatives, among them ex-priests who destroyed with the joyful ferocity of the apostate. But even in its destructive aspects, dechristianisation was more than a simple Saturnalia of impiety. Its roots lay deep in the group psychology of revolutionary patriotism, in the siege mentality of France hemmed in by foreign armies and distracted by fear of internal treachery. Aulard has described the early dechristianisation as an 'expedient of national defence'.[1] A good deal of the destruction was the work of troops moving along the great military routes to the front, or of detachments of the irregular 'revolutionary armies', trying to overawe a hostile rural population by sudden, dramatic acts of terrorism. Here dechristianisation was not so much a rationalistic attack on Christian symbolism and dogma as a drastic effort to restore public order and counter the propaganda of dissident refractory priests. Again, behind some of the sacrilege lay the military and economic crisis. Church ornaments were stripped away as 'baubles of fanaticism', but also as treasure for the mint. Church bells were cut down to be melted as gun-metal in the foundries, and it was in search of them that patriots in the summer of 1793 clashed with outraged worshippers and lost their awe for the sanctuary.

Beside the destructive aim of dechristianisation lay also a positive purpose. The Jacobin leaders sought not only to destroy Christianity, but to replace it by a cult more congruous to the needs of the beleaguered

[1] A. Aulard, *Christianity and the French Revolution*, Eng. trans. (London, 1927), p. 122.

Revolution. Since the work of Mathiez there has been a deeper understanding of the succession of revolutionary cults which, as substitutes for Catholicism, continued to the Concordat.[1] Through them all ran a common purpose, the provision of a solemn focus for patriotism. Like the men of the old regime, so the Revolutionaries believed in the necessity of a system of national morale, to preserve unity and prevent a glissade into immorality. The cults were to some extent artificial creations. Yet, claimed Mathiez, their basis was none the less religious if one accepted (with Durkheim) that society, as well as God, could be the object of a truly religious adoration. Their concern was not the transcendental religion of Christianity, but a new social ideology of justice and fraternity to be realised on earth, the dream of eighteenth-century philosophers which the Revolution sought to transform into political reality. The cults were attempts—somewhat improvised—to replace Catholicism, with its super-natural frame of reference, by a secular religion of humanity which, in various forms, runs through the subsequent history of Europe. Since the Federations of 1790 there had arisen a spontaneous patriotic cult, at first side by side with the old faith, then in opposition to it. It had its credo in the Declaration of the Rights of Man, its priesthood in the lawgivers, its baptismal ceremonies in the civic oaths administered at 'altars of the *patrie*', its symbols in the cockade, tricolour and cap of liberty, its hymns, processions and calendar. From its various festivals evolved the revolutionary cults of 1793–1802, organised after the eclipse of the Constitutional Church. In the Cult of Reason (November 1793 to spring 1794) worship of the revolutionary Republic was primary; philosophical rationalism and the worship of nature and reason were secondary. If frivolity marked the beginning of the cults in Paris, in the provinces they were often celebrated with gravity. It was in no spirit of mockery that bourgeois maidens officiated as goddesses of reason, or the Besançon Jacobins despatched twelve apostles to propagate the new Gospel. The brief Cult of the Supreme Being inaugurated by Robespierre's report of 18 Floréal an II (7 May 1794) marked a reaction from the aridity of the Cult of Reason and the violent methods of some of its initiators, but did not differ essentially from it. Robespierre intended to create a more unified, aesthetically satisfying form of worship which could rally disheartened patriots, and provide a bridge between theists, Catholic and non-Catholic, in which 'without constraint, without persecution, all sects can coalesce in the universal Religion of Nature'. While the Supreme Being worshipped in the spectacular festivals of 20 Prairial resembled the god of Rousseau's *vicaire savoyard*, in the eyes of his new pontiff he was also the sanction for revolutionary justice, civic morale and patriotic obligation. Atheism, Robespierre declared, was 'aristo-

[1] A. Mathiez, *Les Origines des Cultes révolutionnaires* (Paris, 1904).

cratic'; worship of the Supreme Being was 'social' and 'republican'. Only men believing in Providence and immortality could be nerved to 'greater devotion to the *patrie*, greater daring in braving tyranny'.

The patriotic religion continued after Thermidor in the official cult of the *Décadi*. But as the fires of patriotism burned lower, enthusiasm faded. The devotees of the cults had been largely drawn from a minority group of enlightened bourgeois and officials. Here and there the *petit peuple* fused the old religion and the new in a martyr cult, like that of Perrine Dugué of the Sarthe, a Republican martyr seen rising to heaven on tricoloured wings, or in the more organised cult of the trinity of Republican martyrs, Marat, Chalier and Lepeletier. But for the uneducated the rationalism of the national cults was too cold, their didactic sermons and classical symbolism too abstract. Only the occasional pomp of orations, festivals and processions stirred the popular imagination. But if dechristianisation failed to provide an organised alternative to the old religion, it had dealt it a cruel blow. Religious indifference spread in parishes bereft of priests to celebrate mass and educate the children. To peasant communities, the dislocation of traditional habits was probably more disturbing than the impact of new ideas. Open disbelief, previously confined to aristocracy and bourgeoisie, took deep root among the lower classes. The suspension of recruitment to the priesthood was a grave handicap from which the French Church was slow to recover.

After Thermidor, governmental hostility to Christianity did not cease. But pressure from public opinion allowed a widespread thaw, and religious life revived in many parishes. In the west, generals and representatives on mission trying to pacify the rebels were forced locally to sanction religious liberty, thus creating a precedent which could be extended to France as a whole. In a series of decrees between September 1794 and September 1795 the Convention brought about the separation of Church and State in France. The State was no longer to pay for any cult; freedom of worship was to be maintained, though severely controlled; churches not already alienated (while remaining the property of the Communes) might be used by associations of private citizens for public worship; ministers of religion were to take an oath of submission to the laws of the Republic. In uneasy rotation, churches might now be shared by Constitutionals, by officials celebrating the cult of the *Décadi*, by those Catholics willing to take the new oath or by devotees of small eclectic cults like Theophilanthropy.

The Separation of 1794–1802 marked an interesting experiment in European church-state relations. It invites comparison with the more permanent system created a few years earlier in the United States, where article VI of the Constitution had prohibited religious tests for federal office, and the First Amendment provided that 'Congress shall make no laws respecting an establishment of religion or prohibiting the free exercise thereof'. Both systems were influenced, to some extent, by the incompatibility of religious intolerance with a natural rights philosophy of freedom and equality, and by the problem of maintaining dogmatic uniformity in a pluralist society. But the differences between the two systems are perhaps more striking than the similarities, and show how flexible is the term 'separation of church and state'. In the United States separation rested on mutual trust between government and the Christian denominations, and was in fact consonant with a good deal of benevolent recognition of religion by state and federal governments: in the provision of public funds for army chaplains, for instance; in tax-exemption for property used for religious purposes; or in various state laws against blasphemy. But in France the attitude of Thermidorians and Directory was generally one of ill-concealed hostility. Separation was not inspired primarily by a precocious enthusiasm for *laicité*, the idea cherished by many nineteenth-century liberals of the strict neutrality of the state to all religious faiths. France had in fact made strides towards *laicité* since 1789, notably with the introduction in 1792 of civil marriage and divorce, setting against the sacramental Catholic conception of marriage as a perpetual union the secular idea of marriage as a revocable civil contract. But in general the revolutionary leaders remained men of their century, absorbed by the old idea of a national cult and the omnipotence of the state in religious affairs. Separation was a counsel of despair, 'a policy of resignation', summed up in the phrase of one of its architects, 'keep an eye on what you cannot prevent.'[1] Since Catholicism could be neither revolutionised (by the Civil Constitution), nor eradicated (by dechristianisation), then it must be tolerated, yet tolerated so grudgingly that it would not regain its old dominance, but could be slowly eliminated from the conscience of the nation. In the eyes of the civil law the denominations possessed no corporate existence: they were unable to receive endowments, and hindered from forming a properly articulated national organisation. Harsh laws against the non-jurors remained on the statute book, though often laxly applied, particularly when the Directory, in its 'see-saw policy', felt the need for support from the right. But in 1797 the *coup d'état* of Fructidor unleashed a persecution which has been compared to that of the Terror. Thereafter, a determined attempt was made to revive the languishing cult of the *Décadi*. The *Décadi* (tenth day) was enforced as a day of rest, and its glacial ceremonies were declared compulsory for teachers and schoolchildren, and for municipal officials, who marched to them in uniform, often accompanied by a band. But the campaign proved hard to carry out (especially in the country) and brought the Directory into conflict with the Constitutionals,

[1] A. Mathiez, *La Réaction Thermidorienne* (Paris, 1929), p. 181.

unwilling to abandon *Monsieur Dimanche* in his battle with *Citoyen Décadi*.

If the Directory was reluctant to carry out separation in a spirit of calm neutrality, so were many of the clergy. A majority of the non-jurors—their ranks swelled by thousands of exiles returning when persecution slackened before Fructidor—refused to regard it as a viable system. Many preached blatant counter-revolution, praying for the royal family, anathematising owners of *biens nationaux*, and in some rural areas fomenting a virtual White Terror. A minority group, how-ever, led by the saintly Monsieur Emery, superior-general of St Sulpice, tried to disentangle the cause of Catholicism from that of the Bourbons. Between the two sections of the Catholic clergy a deep rift appeared (similar to that over *Ralliement* a century later) as they faced up to the thorny problem of obedience to a revolutionary and non-Christian government. Naturally, the argument revolved round the successive oaths of allegiance demanded of the clergy. While the oath to the Civil Constitution had been solemnly and officially condemned by Rome, this was not the case with the subsequent oaths. The intransigents, or *insoumissionnaires*, taking orders from their *émigré* bishops, refused all the oaths. How could they countenance usurpers, or give inclusive obedience to a political system which maintained laws profoundly hostile to Catholic teaching? Better organise France as a *pays de mission*, better maintain a clandestine cult, than share altars publicly with infidels and schismatics. On the other hand the *soumissionnaires* accepted most of the later oaths (though many held back from the oath of 'hatred to royalty' exacted after Fructidor). How else could the Catholic religion be kept alive, and the Roman priesthood compete with the Constitutional, save by claiming the right to celebrate mass publicly by taking the oath? Emery distinguished between active and passive obedience, between approbation of laws and a mere submission, limited, in so far as it concerned religion, to a promise not to disturb the public order. Until the eve of the Concordat, the polemic between the two Catholic parties approached the verge of schism. The old Gallican Church was fragmented into not two but three hostile groups.

Before 1795 the Revolution had threatened the existence of the Roman Church in France and Belgium. When it spilled over into the Italian peninsula it threatened to engulf the heart of Catholicism itself. In February 1797, under the Treaty of Tolentino, France detached the Legations from the Papal States: the murder of General Duphot in Rome in December led to the occupation of the city by General Berthier in February 1798, and to the proclamation of a Roman Republic. In 1799 'citizen pope', Pius VI, was removed to captivity in France, where his death at Valence seemed to portend the dissolution of the Papacy.

Yet within two years, to the astonishment of Europe, Revolution compounded with Papacy in the signing of the French Concordat on 15 July 1801. How had this come about? The way had been cleared by the advent to power of two new leaders in Paris and Rome: Bonaparte, who became first consul in 1799, and Cardinal Chiaramonti, elected as Pope Pius VII on 14 March 1800 by the Conclave of Venice. As Bishop of Imola, Chiaramonti had shown himself prepared to cooperate with the Cisalpine Republic, and in a famous 'Jacobin' homily at Christmas 1797 had told his flock 'be good Christians and you will be good democrats': as Pope, his appointment of Cardinal Consalvi as secretary of state portended a new and more liberal regime. But the initiative for the *rapprochement* came from Bonaparte. Though no *dévot*—'his whole credo,' wrote Frédéric Masson, 'was confined to a fatalist spiritualism in which his star took the place of Providence'—as a political realist he appreciated the hold of the traditional religion on the masses, and its value as a guarantee of social order, reconciling men to inequality, and inclining them to obey the worldly regiment.[1] Napoleon's task of pacification and reconciliation required a religious peace, to heal the bitter divisions among the French clergy, to ease the incorporation into the French frontiers of Rhenish Catholics and fiercely Ultramontane Belgians and to prepare the path for French hegemony in Italy. The history of the previous decade showed luridly the failure of attempting to solve the religious question unilaterally, without consulting the Papacy. For diplomatic purposes Napoleon might threaten to follow the example of Henry VIII of England. But he could not create a Protestant France, and saw little gain in reestablishing the Constitutional Church, which was weak in popular influence and in any case subordinate to his control. He could continue the Separation—but this would do little to resolve the quarrels among the clergy, and did not accord with his authoritarian spirit. France remained basically Catholic. But if Catholicism was indestructible, so too were the permanent gains of the Revolution. The French clergy must therefore be compelled to recognise the loss of their privileged position under the old order, to concede the inexorable advances made by the *état laique*, such as divorce, civil marriage and religious equality: they must accept the inalienability of the secularised church property: above all they must be detached from the Bourbons. In a crisp, military appreciation of the situation Napoleon remarked 'A religion is necessary for the people. This religion must be in the hands of the government. Fifty *émigré* bishops in the pay of England lead the French clergy today. We must destroy their influence. The authority of the Pope is necessary for that'.[2]

[1] Quoted in J. Leflon, *La Crise Révolutionnaire* (Paris, 1949), p. 175.
[2] Boulay de la Meurthe, *Documents sur la Négociation du Concordat* (Paris, 1891–7), vol. III, p. 50.

Within days of the victory of Marengo, which gave him the political security he needed, Napoleon opened negotiations with the Curia. The new Pope was prepared for many sacrifices to restore the freedom of Catholic altars in France, 'eldest daughter' of the Church. Yet there were months of hard bargaining, several diplomatic crises and many draft projects before the Concordat was signed. In several ways the new Concordat resembled its predecessor of 1516. But Rome had negotiated the Concordat of 1516 with a Catholic monarch at the head of a solidly confessional state: the new Concordat was the result of barter between two strange powers linked by no real spiritual bond. The Curia did not seek to consecrate the Revolution but to limit its results. The medieval church-state was gone. This emerged most clearly in the article dealing with the status of Catholicism in France. Rome fought hard for recognition of her Church as the 'dominant' religion of the State (which implied the legal inferiority of other creeds). But she was compelled to accept the mere recognition of Catholicism as 'the religion of the majority of Frenchmen'. She renounced her claims for the restitution of alienated Church property, accepting reluctantly in return the payment of bishops and some of the clergy by state salary instead of by the endowment which would have restored a measure of their old financial independence. Freedom of worship was guaranteed—but subjected (in a dangerously vague clause) to police regulations. For his part, Napoleon gained the old regalian prerogative of nominating bishops, whose canonical institution was reserved to the Pope; the diocesan map of France was redrawn; the clergy were ordered to pray for the government and take an oath of obedience and fidelity to it. The bishops were to nominate the *curés*, subject to government approval, and both were to be salaried by the state. To allow the reconstruction of the Church, a *tabula rasa* was made of both episcopates, Catholic and Constitutional. Gently but firmly, the papal bull *Tam Multa* demanded the resignation of the Catholic bishops. A majority submitted—but a substantial minority refused, and their sees were declared by Rome to be vacant. This was a terrible blow to the Gallican tradition that bishops held their sees by divine right from Christ, not as revocable offices held by grace from an absolute Pope. The wholesale deprivation of an episcopate had no historical precedent. An act of Papal sovereignty, it marked an important step towards the triumphant Ultramontanism of the Vatican Council of 1870.

The law of 18 Germinal an X (8 April 1802) which promulgated the Concordat, also contained a number of Organic Articles, a detailed code of regulation which severely limited the freedom of the Church. By it, Napoleon hoped to check Ultramontane encroachment and to reassert the political Gallicanism of the old regime. Communication between the French clergy and Rome was restricted, and a chain of control was forged which ran from the government through the episcopate to the lower clergy, many of whom were now removable from their posts at the will of their bishop. Organic Articles were also issued for the Reformed and Lutheran churches, controlled, established and (for the most part) subsidised on a basis of parity with the Roman, and transformed from their traditional role of persecuted opposition into docile supporters of the government. The religious equality proclaimed by the Revolution was thus maintained, not (as after Thermidor) by separating all confessions from the state, but by the contrary method of affording to the major confessions a similar state establishment. The belief that ecclesiastical uniformity was essential for the political stability of a state was openly abandoned. Speaking to the *Corps Législatif*, Portalis, Napoleon's spokesman on religious affairs, cheerfully accepted the death of the old confessional state. Provided (and it was an all important proviso) the different churches were strictly subordinated to governmental control, the existence of diverse confessions encouraged a healthy rivalry in the national service. 'The essential for public order and morality is not that all men should have the same religion, but that every man should be attached to his own.'[1]

Beneath the keen eye of the minister of ecclesiastical affairs (*des Cultes*), the churches of France lay down together in unprecedented tranquillity. The fusion of former non-jurors and Constitutionals went on apace, and as minister Portalis did his best to achieve a fair partition of parishes between the two groups and to prevent the victimisation of the old 'patriotic clergy'. To Rome's dismay, twelve former Constitutionals were among the sixty bishops nominated to the new dioceses, several of them very tardy in formally disavowing the schism of the Civil Constitution. But the bishops were soon absorbed in the urgent tasks of diocesan reconstruction. With a dutifulness that earned them the nickname of 'prefects in violet', they accepted their role as pillars of the Napoleonic system. They extolled the 'new Cyrus', the 'second Constantine' who had brought order out of chaos and restored the altars. In 1806 they accepted, with little hesitation, both a new Imperial Catechism urging obedience to the emperor in exaggerated terms, and a new saint's day, the festival of St Napoleon, a more than shadowy martyr of Diocletian's persecution, celebrated on 15 August, birthday of the emperor and Feast of the Assumption.

While restoration continued in France, the Catholic Church in Germany—perhaps the richest of all in 1789—suffered huge losses. By the Recess of the Diet of Ratisbon in 1803 the secular princes dispossessed by France of territory on the left bank of the Rhine were compensated, largely at the expense of the ecclesiastical states of the Empire. In the secularisation that followed, the ancient prince-

[1] Boulay de la Meurthe, *op. cit.*, vol. v, p. 387.

bishoprics and a multitude of convents and abbeys lost their independence, engulfed largely by Protestant states, although Catholic Austria and Bavaria shared in the spoils. Not only was territory secularised. While parish churches were spared, the goods of religious houses were widely sequestrated, and with them vanished many of the schools they supported. Of the fifteen Catholic universities existing in 1789, only five Catholic theological faculties still remained in 1815. Austria refrained from this kind of spoliation, but not Bavaria, where monastic libraries were sold by paper-weight as cheese paper and the cathedral of Freising was auctioned for a time to a local butcher. 1803 marked an epoch in church-state relations in Germany. Firstly, as the clergy of the old Church States fell suddenly under the yoke of the civil power, and found themselves regimented by authoritarian Protestant princes, or by Josephist officials in Austria and Bavaria, they began to turn, like the Gallicans of France, to Rome for protection and guidance. 'Febronianism,' the German version of episcopal Gallicanism, began to give ground to Ultramontanism. Secondly, the simplification of German political geography between 1803 and 1815 further undermined the crumbling principle of *cuius regio eius religio*. States once predominantly Protestant, like Baden, Württemberg, Nassau and Hesse, became confessionally mixed, as did Bavaria in absorbing many Protestants, who numbered now a quarter of her population. Under these conditions it became impossible to maintain the old confessional state. Here, as previously in Prussia, religious pluralism probably proved a stronger incentive to religious liberty than liberal political theories. The old debate over the toleration of dissenters gave way to the struggle for parity between the confessions. In theory—though not always in practice—the principle of religious equality gained increasing acceptance.

The immense upheaval in Germany called out for a settlement with Rome. But attempts to frame an inclusive German Concordat failed, as did later plans for a Concordat for the Confederation of the Rhine. In Northern Italy the restoration of religious peace at first went more smoothly. In 1803 a Concordat was signed between Rome and the Italian Republic, on the broad lines of the French Concordat, though, to Consalvi's joy, more favourable to Catholicism. But if Napoleon had set the pattern for agreements with the Curia, he had also created a precedent for their evasion. When the text of the Concordat was published, it was accompanied by the Melzi Decrees, a more stringent version of the Organic Articles, some of them in flat contradiction to the terms of the agreement.

The officiation of the Pope at Napoleon's magnificent imperial coronation in Notre Dame (2 December 1804) seemed to seal the *entente* between Rome and Paris. Not since the eighth century was there any precedent for this spectacular blessing bestowed on a political regime: even Charlemagne had travelled to Rome to be crowned. But the *entente* was more fragile than it appeared. Pius VII had accepted the invitation to Paris with much hesitation and in the hope of bargaining for some of the urgent aims of curial diplomacy: repeal of the Organic Articles and Melzi Decrees, restoration of the Legations, and of Catholicism as the dominant religion of France. But months of strenuous negotiation had brought little reward. While the Curia felt outmanoeuvred and frustrated, Napoleon's dazzling diplomatic *coup* encouraged his dangerous optimism about the pliancy of the Pope.

Within a few months, the precarious concord was shattered. In October 1805 French troops occupied the papal port of Ancona. It was an abrupt move. The Pope's choleric letter of complaint—reaching Napoleon shortly before Austerlitz—threatened to break off diplomatic relations, and its apparently sudden change of tone was interpreted by Napoleon as an unscrupulous attempt to make capital out of his military difficulties. A sharp diplomatic exchange followed. In February 1806 Napoleon demanded the closure of the Papal ports to enemies of France, and the expulsion of their citizens from Rome. The Pope refused. Diplomatic attitudes stiffened on both sides. When much of Italy was parcelled out into fiefs of the Grand Empire in the spring of 1806, the political position of the Papal States grew precarious, but not until after Tilsit was Napoleon bold enough to dismember them, and then only piecemeal. Rome was occupied in February 1808; the Marches were then annexed; in May 1809 the Papal States were assimilated to the Empire, and on 10 June the Papal flag was hauled down from the St Angelo, and the tricolour run up. 'We see plainly that the French have a mind to force us to speak Latin,' remarked the Pope grimly to Pacca, 'and speak Latin we will.' The papal bull *Quum Memoranda* pronounced major excommunication on all who had dared to commit sacrilege against the Patrimony of Peter. On 6 July a storming party under General Radet broke down the doors of the Quirinal with hatchets and, bundling the Pope into a carriage, rushed him off towards captivity at Savona.

Napoleon represented the conflict as a disagreement over temporalities which had no organic connection with the spiritual headship of the Pope. Seen from Paris, this interpretation was convincing enough. The Italian peninsula—the mistress with whom, Napoleon said, he alone intended to sleep—was vital to him, not only for his grand strategy in the Mediterranean and Orient, but for his immediate military security in the war against the Third Coalition, for his flank could be turned by Austrian armies on the Venetian plain, or by British naval landings along the coast.[1] The neutrality of the Papal States threatened the French

---

[1] See A. Latreille, *Napoléon et le Saint-Siège, 1801–1808* (Paris, 1935).

defensive system: they could bar the transit of troops to the south, their long and ill-defended coastline invited naval attack, and their capital harboured enemy agents. Therefore they must submit to protection by the Emperor's Catholic armies against heretic Britons, schismatic Russians, and infidel Turks. 'Your holiness' insisted Napoleon 'should have the same respect for me in the temporal sphere that I have for you in the spiritual. . . . Your holiness is Sovereign of Rome, but I am its Emperor. All my enemies must be yours.' If the Pope allowed his kingdom to become a French protectorate, no conflict need arise.

But the Pope's view was radically different. What Napoleon saw as political readjustment, Rome saw as sacrilege. Napoleon's case rested on a sharp delimitation of the temporal from the spiritual aspects of the Papal government: Pius VII's was based on an adamant belief in their inseparability. Like his successors, Pius VII insisted that the temporal power had a spiritual function. As he put it in *Quum Memoranda*, 'the liberty of the apostolic see . . . is bound up with the liberty and immunities of the universal church.' The territorial integrity of the Papal monarchy was a guarantee of her spiritual freedom, and her political neutrality a symbol of her spiritual universality. The head of a Church with a supra-national mission could never be subject to a single nation, nor a Catholic Church be contained within a single empire, even a so-called Empire of the West. Renaissance popes had warred like secular princes, but Pius VII took seriously his claim to represent on earth the God of Peace. To join the French confederation would compromise the communications of the Holy See with millions of Catholics in lands ranged against France. Furthermore, Napoleon himself, by his quasi-historical claims to be the inheritor of Charlemagne, the 'Emperor of Rome' from whom the Pope held his lands as a sort of revocable fief, had at an early stage raised the whole debate from the level of temporary military necessity to high levels of principle. Rome for her part could not ignore the religious innovations which followed in the wake of French political expansion in Italy—extension of the Concordat, and with it the *Code Civil* and religious liberty for dissidents, even civil marriage and divorce. What was deplorable in France, cradle of the Revolution, seemed intolerable in Italy, special preserve of the Papacy.

With the abduction of the Pope, the conflict entered a new phase as Napoleon made an improvised attempt to turn Paris into the spiritual as well as the temporal capital of his Empire. Almost all the Sacred College was transported to Paris, many cardinals were installed in hotels on the Left Bank, and offered a pension which most accepted: after them followed stacks of the pontifical archives, laboriously hauled over the Mont Cenis pass in winter. A large sum was earmarked for the erection of a Papal palace near Notre Dame. But the Pope obstinately refused to accept the role intended for him as imperial chaplain.

The weapons at his disposal were few, but far from negligible, and Napoleon seriously miscalculated the disparity between the political feebleness of the Papal States, with their antiquated administration of elderly cardinals, and the immense moral influence commanded by the Holy See. The Pope's Latin had at first disappointingly little effect on the emperor, for, as Gallican lawyers and prelates pointed out, the excommunication did not mention him by name. But the imprisoned Pope had a more effective weapon: he could refuse to grant bulls of institution to the bishops nominated by the emperor, and so paralyse the Concordats. In 1806 he began to apply this sanction in Italy, in 1808 it was extended to France, by 1811 twenty-seven Imperial sees lacked bishops, and a new form of Investiture Controversy shook the fabric of the Imperial Church. The cost in ecclesiastical disorder was considerable, and most visible in the vulnerable extremities of the Empire. Hundreds of Italian priests were exiled for refusing the oaths of obedience to the emperor, Spanish clergy leavened the *guerrilla* movement (particularly after Joseph Bonaparte dissolved the mendicant and regular orders in 1809), and the Belgians proved so fractious that one gloomy prefect suggested that two-thirds of their priests be transported and replaced by tractable Frenchmen from the Midi.

Over the French hierarchy, however, Napoleon kept a remarkable hold. The vital years of peace between the Concordat and the Pope's imprisonment had brought their reward. While Ultramontane ideas, fanned by secret societies, began to percolate among the lower clergy, the bishops were unwilling, by open opposition, to undo their patient work of diocesan reconstruction. Yet post-revolutionary Gallicanism was moderate and conditional, characterised by a deep sense of the role of the papacy as the bond of Catholic unity and by dread of any return to a schism like that of the Civil Constitution. This emerged clearly when in 1809 and 1811 Napoleon consulted two small Ecclesiastical Councils on problems raised by his quarrel with the Pope. They gave qualified support to Napoleon's interpretation of the conflict. The Pope had declared no canonical reasons for withholding institution from bishops irreproachable in their conduct and doctrines. The loss of the temporal power constituted no cause in itself, for the slow accretion of the Papal States had been of human institution, and what man had given man could take away. If the Pope continued to desolate the sees of the Imperial Church, the law of necessity might permit a reversion to the tradition of former ages—including the Pragmatic Sanction of 1438— by which confirmation of an election was conferred not by papal bull but by the Metropolitan or by a provincial council. But the Councils expressed quite firmly their perplexity at the conflict of allegiance which they faced, stressing their devotion to the Holy See, and beseeching that the Holy Father be set at liberty.

By the summer of 1810 Napoleon still faced his unresolved dilemma: should he leave his sees bereft of bishops, or fill them with pastors lacking canonical jurisdiction? If the latter, how could it be done without schism? Provisionally he might—like Louis XIV in his battle over the *régale*—prevail on diocesan chapters to instal his episcopal nominees as vicars capitular of their sees. This gave them an administrative authority, though not the power to confirm and ordain. There was dramatic resistance to Napoleon's move in the important sees of Paris and Florence, stiffened by clandestine papal briefs, though soon crushed. The emperor's ecclesiastical advisers had suggested the addition to the Concordat of a clause by which, after a delay of six months by the Pope, institution might be conferred by the Metropolitan or eldest suffragan. But how could the Pope be induced to agree? A display of Gallican solidarity, appealing to the historic theory of the authority of councils, might perhaps overawe him. On 17 June 1811 a grandiose National Council attended at its opening by ninety-five 'Fathers' of the Imperial Church, mostly French and Italian, assembled in Notre Dame de Paris. But in conclave the bishops showed a collective bravery that sadly disappointed the emperor's plans. The opening sermon from the Bishop of Troyes spoke feelingly of the Council's attachment to the Holy See, severed from which the episcopate would be a withered branch cut off from the trunk of catholicity. Led by Cardinal Fesch, the emperor's uncle, the members took an oath of obedience to the imprisoned Pope. To Napoleon's fury, the Committee delegated to study the question of episcopal institution declared the Council incompetent to regulate the matter without recourse to the Pope. The Council was dissolved, and the leaders of the obstinate Committee imprisoned at Vincennes. Separately, however, the imperial bishops were not so daring. As Cardinal Maury pleasantly observed, wine that was not good in cask might be better in bottle. Pressed individually, most of the bishops recognised the competence of the Council to transfer the right of institution after six months' delay. Reassembled in August to register this decree, the Council did so, but with the proviso that it be submitted to the approval of the Pope.

So Napoleon was driven back to his second method of dealing with Pius VII. Weakened, or, as Napoleon nicely put it, 'ripened' by captivity and isolation from his counsellors, the Pope might be argued and bullied into submission or at least into compromise. Spied on by his doctor, possibly drugged on occasion, kept carefully ill-informed of affairs in the world outside, he was harassed by a succession of diplomatic missions in which plaintive prelates harped on the chaos into which he was plunging the Church. But the monastic training of Pius VII made him less vulnerable to imprisonment than the emperor hoped, and at Savona he reverted easily to the simple routine of his early life as 'the poor monk Chiaramonti', celebrating mass, meditating, mending his clothes and washing the snuff off his dressing-gown. Beyond the question of the Temporal Power and the 'six months clause' he sensed the magnitude of the issue at stake: the right of the Church to a free existence as a *societas perfecta*, obeying ends, governed by laws, which were spiritual and distinct from those of the secular regiment. At times he weakened dangerously, debilitated by illness and uncertainty. In May 1811 he agreed to certain outline concessions, which he immediately retracted; in September, pressed by a 'holy caravan' of prelates from the National Council, he signed concessions which Napoleon recklessly rejected; in 1813, at Fontainebleau, after an extraordinary *tête-à-tête* with Napoleon—to whose magnetism he was curiously susceptible—he agreed to a so-called Concordat, which he soon repudiated. But when Pius was almost at the end of his tether, Napoleon's military defeat released him from his lonely ordeal. From the long drawn-out, personal clash of wills the Pope's obstinate Ultramontanism emerged unconquered by the emperor's determined Caesaropapism.

There were signs by 1815 of a religious awakening in many parts of Europe. Doctrinally, most of the religious reaction flowed in strongly traditional channels. Yet there were several important attempts to reinterpret Christianity to the European intellectual élite, which had largely lapsed from the faith. Old methods of apologetic had made little impression. The main problem, as Chateaubriand remarked, was no longer that of meeting deviations from orthodoxy, but challenging sceptical indifference. Traditional conceptions of revelation—on which most earlier apologetic had rested—seemed widely discredited by the Enlightenment. The revelation of the Bible was widely held to be the disclosure of what was actually or potentially knowable by reason: a republication, more or less useful, of natural religion. Miracles, once pointed to as convincing 'evidences' of Christianity, now appeared as difficulties needing explanation, incompatible with the uniformity of nature increasingly revealed by science. Meanwhile, old 'proofs' of God's existence, like the ontological proof, or that from design, were compromised by Hume, and still more fundamentally by Kant. New lines of defence were clearly necessary, even fresh interpretations of the working of revelation. Dissimilar as Chateaubriand, Schleiermacher and Lamennais were in their method of approach, each tried to apply to theology the vocabulary of Romanticism, to present his faith in a fresh light that would strike the imagination, and to show the educated classes that they had rejected Christianity because they had misunderstood its nature or its value. They would force the indifferent 'to examine seriously what they have hitherto despised in ignorance. That is all we ask of them. We do not say to them *believe* but *examine*'.[1] A new

---

[1] F. de Lamennais, *Essai Sur L'Indifférence* (Paris, 1817–23). Introduction.

generation of defenders, influenced by the discovery of the sense of history and development, or by ideas of divine immanence made prominent by Schelling and Hegel, sought to show the Church not as a defunct relic of barbarism, but as a living organism; religion not as antiquated superstition, but as an expression of life, integral to man's individual psyche or to his social well-being; doctrine not as a static, timeless set of propositions declared once and for all in the Protestant's Bible, or the Catholic's tradition, but as a progressive, developing revelation in history.

Through Romanticism the Roman Church found new defenders in a realm which for a century or more had been usually hostile, the world of literature and the arts. Strikingly, her chief apologists (with some great exceptions like Lamennais and Möhler) were not her priests but laymen, often converts from scepticism or Protestantism: a novelist like Manzoni, a political writer like de Maistre, a journalist like Joseph Görres, artists like the colony of German 'Nazarenes' at Rome, who spurned the classical, heathen imagery of the Rococo and Baroque for the religious symbolism of the medieval masters. In Catholicism many Romantics found symbols for the imagination, and an outlet for emotions starved by the Enlightenment and stirred by the catastrophes of the Revolution. Chateaubriand's *Génie du Christianisme* (1802) heralded an aesthetic approach to religion which, despite its superficiality, bridged the gap between a sentimental Deism and a sentimental Catholicism, and directed the man of feeling away from Rousseau to Rome, from a vague heart-religion towards the dogmatic structure of the Catholic Church. His conversion from Stoic scepticism had been a matter of emotion not of ratiocination: 'I wept and I believed.' His apologetic aim was to reveal Catholicism not as a cold official cult, but as a living religion of mystery, beauty, pathos and poetry, the matrix of European civilisation and art. Elsewhere, particularly in the school of German Romanticism which followed Novalis, the longing for social unity led to an idealisation of the Middle Ages as an epoch of simple faith and spiritual unity, with a flourishing corporate social structure of guilds, orders and Estates, under the benign guidance of Church and Empire. The traditionalists—like Bonald, de Maistre and Lamennais —were also concerned (in different ways) to show the value rather than the truth of religion. Catholicism was declared to be necessary to society. Touching man's inner will while secular authority affected only his external conduct, it provided a basis for moral and political obligation in a society terribly fragmented by the individualism of the Enlightenment and the anarchy of the Revolution. Bonald remained a Gallican, but de Maistre and Lamennais united their traditionalism with a new Ultramontanism, resting not so much on doctrinal proofs as on the need for social order and unity. Episcopal Gallicanism, they argued, with its theory that the ultimate authority of the Church lay in an aristocratic General Council of bishops, bred schism and disunity. In *Du Pape* (1819) de Maistre stressed by analogy the absolute necessity of sovereignty in the spiritual as in the temporal sphere: it was as dangerous to concede the supremacy of a Council over a Pope as to permit a States-General to control a King. Lamennais argued that political Gallicanism with its demand for the separation of temporal government from spiritual guidance, removed princes from the restraint of divine law, and hence led to despotism. In a time which produced several wistful projects for a European federation that might preserve peace and order, the new Ultramontanes could show the Pope as the key-stone of a Christian polity which could resolve the antithesis between liberty and order. He was the rightful and necessary arbiter of Christendom. 'Without the Pope' ran Lamennais's famous aphorism, 'no Church; without the Church no Christianity, without Christianity . . . no society.'

Catholic theological studies were at a low ebb by 1815. The Revolution had disrupted much seminary life; the old scholasticism was in decline; the new Cartesian apologetic, though popular, seemed limited by its effort to meet rationalism on its own ground. Lamennais opened up one fruitful avenue of thought by the application of traditionalist ideas to theology in his *Essai sur l'Indifférence* (1817–23). He derided the claim that the individual reason could arrive at religious certitude: only in the authoritative general reason of mankind, the *sensus communis* which transmitted from generation to generation, through tradition, the primal revelation of God to society, could certitude be found. Developed theologically by followers such as Bautain, the philosophy of the *sensus communis* encouraged a type of Fideism, a depreciation of the role of reason in religion, which earned the rebuke of Rome. Here, as in much romantic Catholicism, the violent reaction against the Enlightenment went too far: the exaggeration of traditionalism led to a flight from reason, as romantic medievalism led often to a flight from a puzzling present to an idealised past. It was in Germany, where the challenge of Protestant scholarship and idealist philosophy had to be met, that bolder attempts at theological reconstruction were made. In contrast to the traditionalists, Professor Georg Hermes of Bonn (1775–1831), influenced by Kant and Fichte, tried to provide a more stable intellectual basis for the Roman faith. But 'Hermesianism' made 'positive doubt' the starting point for religious enquiry, and assent to the truths of faith the necessary conclusion of a purely rational demonstration. It was condemned by Rome as semi-rationalism in 1835. More orthodox were the circles of Catholic Romanticism in Münster, in Landshut, and at the University of Munich which by 1830 boasted Görres in its chair of History, Baader in the chair of Speculative Theology, and the young Döllinger in that of Canon Law and Church History. Perhaps most influential for the future trend of Roman theology was the faculty of Catholic theology at Tübingen, where, influenced by Schelling's philosophy, J. S. Drey and J. A. Möhler, the author of *Symbolism* (1832), formulated a theory of disciplinary and doctrinal development which heralded that of Newman. The Tübingen Catholic school conceived of their Church not in static but in dynamic, biological terms, as a living organism, developing, adapting itself to new historical circumstances, yet ever preserving through its traditions the essence of the original Christian revelation.

Among Protestants, too, the prolonged European wars, with their national humiliations and triumphs, excited at least temporarily a moral fervour and a sense of spiritual need. Patriotic and religious revivals could support each other: repentance and regeneration were concepts shared by their vocabulary. The disaster of Jena stirred Prussian clergy to fervent support of the national revival under Stein. The War of Liberation was widely preached as a crusade and its battlefields resounded with Protestant chorales. Military disaster was interpreted as the refining fire through which peoples were brought to reformation, and victory as divine judgement on a righteous cause. The upheavals of the age seemed to foreshadow the apocalypse, and encouraged strange visionaries: the English prophet Richard Brothers; Madame Krüdener, confidante of Tsar Alexander; Jung-Stilling, whose predictions encouraged an exodus of Württemberg millenarians to await the Second Coming of Christ between the Caspian and the Black Sea.

In the early nineteenth century the Christian rationalism which had long percolated among most Protestant churches was often checked and forced to give ground, usually by various forms of evangelical pietism. The sharp antagonism between pietism and theological liberalism, and the divorce which it often entailed between depth of piety and depth of learning, between the traditionally orthodox and those who sought (often bravely, but sometimes precipitately) to harmonise their faith with contemporary culture and advancing knowledge, constituted one of the tragedies of the age. 'Rational Christianity' still found many exponents, and covered a wide spectrum of belief. But there were many Protestants who felt that the spiritual life had dimensions unfilled by a religion of mere commonsense, and unexplained by abstract conceptions of nature and reason. Traditional forms of piety revived. One powerful element in Protestant revival was a conservative neo-confessionalism, which looked back nostalgically (sometimes through spectacles tinted by Romanticism) to the heroic days of the Reformation, and to the authority of the old doctrinal formulae which the eighteenth century had ignored, reinterpreted or pushed aside. The tercentenary of the Reformation in 1817, and of the Augsburg Confession in 1830, reminded the Lutheran churches of Germany and Scandinavia that they were parts of a larger whole, and inheritors of a great religious tradition. An appeal to the moderate Calvinism in the Thirty Nine Articles had long been a staple of Anglican Evangelical apologetic: in 1801 it was systematically set out in John Overton's *True Churchmen Ascertained* which claimed, provocatively, that the Evangelicals alone held to the title-deeds of the Church of England.

This confessionalism was often intertwined with types of pietism. The comparative history of the many evangelical or pietistic revivals of the nineteenth century remains to be written, and will be a formidable task. It is not easy to generalise about types of Protestant spirituality which—despite a common denominator—varied from quiet mysticism to lurid hell-fire preaching. Some revivals were safely corralled within a State Church: others, like the Swedish 'New Readers', some congregations in the Genevan *Réveil,* or the Christian Reformed Church in Holland, hived off into separatism, despairing of a Laodicean establishment or a rationalistic clergy. At times a revival could sound a clear note of social protest, as in Norway, where the rural lay-preachers who followed Hans Nielsen Hauge were to form the heart of the farmer opposition bloc against the government officials in the *Storting.* Elsewhere it could be aristocratic and conservative, as among the earnest, bible-reading circles of Junkers whom young Bismarck met in Pomerania, and from whom he drew his bride; or, in its more sectarian and ascetic forms, politically quietist, channelling its energies into the intense spiritual life of the self-contained group. Through most revivals, however, ran a similar stress on the Pauline antinomies of sin and grace, Law and Gospel; on the necessity of individual conversion through faith in the atoning blood of Christ; on sanctification by the Holy Spirit; on the literal interpretation of the word of God in Scripture. They had seldom any deep interest in formulating comprehensive metaphysical systems, but were usually as conspicuously non-intellectual as they were anti-rationalist. Where revivalism flourished, its emphasis on heart-religion and on evangelism tended to erode not only the dogmatism but also the definiteness of systematic theology. In particular, strict Calvinism was steadily moderated and softened. The pessimistic Calvinist doctrine that only the predestined elect were redeemed was hardly compatible with the revivalist's confident offer of salvation to all mankind. Among the Reformed Churches of Europe and North America there were a number of fresh attempts to reconcile the doctrine of God's absolute sovereignty with the idea of man's responsibility, divine predestination with man's free agency in accepting or rejecting saving grace.

A prominent characteristic of the Protestant revivals was a concern for 'practical piety', expressed in a huge network of voluntary societies, often interdenominational and sometimes international in scope. Bible

Societies (whose British parent body James Stephen described as 'the great Protestant *propaganda*') spread translations of the Scriptures from Russia to the South Seas. Colporteurs of tract societies distributed millions of pamphlets, which penetrated not only into cottages and tenements, but into some polite drawing-rooms, closed to calf-bound sermons, but receptive to genteel homilies like Hannah More's *Thoughts on the Manners of the Great*. In England, in a host of philanthropic causes, from the City of London Truss Society for the Relief of the Ruptured Poor to the campaign for the emancipation of the slaves, Evangelicals lured many middle-class people and a sprinkling of peers into the service of moral reform and 'vital Christianity'. After the foundation of the Baptist Missionary Society (1792) a cluster of societies were formed in Europe and North America for the conversion of the heathen. While they laid the foundation for a world-wide extension of Protestantism in the nineteenth century, they were probably as yet more successful in stirring up piety at home than in creating it overseas. Missionary and philanthropic societies provided a romantic cause which could enlist idealism and harness vague feelings of benevolence to religious ends. They joined churches, locally and nationally, in communal effort. Among the French Reformed Churches, for example, the itinerant missionaries of the Continental Society spread the pietistic doctrines of the *Réveil*, while agents of tract and Bible societies linked together scattered congregations, coaxing them out of the 'moral Ghetto' in which they had been enclosed by over a century of persecution.[1]

It was in the English-speaking world that pietistic evangelicalism probably shaped society most significantly. The English Nonconformist denominations (particularly the Methodists) generally adapted themselves more easily to conditions in the new industrial cities than the established Church, whose ancient parish system was often swamped by great agglomerations of population. Anglicans encountered many legal difficulties in building new churches in old parishes, but Dissenters could quickly build little brick chapels in teeming streets, and penetrate, through their cadres of lay helpers, into recesses unvisited by parson and curate. Small craftsmen and artisans in the depersonalised industrial towns, small farmers and farm labourers, fishermen and miners, those on the fringes of organised culture, found in the fraternal life of the chapel a sense of community; in the emotional outpouring of revival and prayer-meeting a release for fettered feeling and psychological stress. Yet the drawing-power of Nonconformity on the industrial masses must not be exaggerated. Well before 1830 the major denominations, including the Wesleyans, were becoming manifestly more respectable and middle-class. In many chapels, pew-rents segregated the more prosperous who

<hr>

[1] D. Robert, *Les Églises Réformées en France, 1800–1830* (Paris, 1961), pp. 345–6.

paid for their sittings from the poor who sat on their free seats in the darker, less comfortable corners. The Religious Census of 1851 revealed how little direct impact religion now made on the labouring masses.

In the last years of the eighteenth century the revivalist tradition in North America blazed up into another Great Awakening. Some of its first major outbreaks took place in the colleges of the Eastern seaboard, notably at Yale, whose president, Timothy Dwight, like his follower Lyman Beecher, saw in revivalism a means to preserve the established New England order from the inroads of Jeffersonian 'Jacobinism' and the Unitarianism to which Harvard men seemed unfortunately prone. The Eastern awakenings were decorous and controlled compared with those which swept the West after 1800. As the thrust of population beyond the Alleghanies became almost a stampede, the Eastern churches grew deeply concerned with the problem of Christianising the unchurched multitudes of the frontier and preserving the cultural unity of the nation, threatened by the centrifugal force of westward migration. It was not, however, the educated Presbyterian or Congregationalist missionary from the East who followed the frontiersman's trail most successfully, but preachers from less sophisticated denominations: Baptist farmer-preachers, who shared the primitive working life of their flocks, or Methodist circuit-riders posting from one isolated settlement to another, Bible and hymn-book in their saddle-bags. Wesley's circuit system with its itinerant preaching was superbly fitted for the frontier, and by 1844 the Methodists had grown to become the largest Protestant denomination in the United States. Environment inclined frontier religion to be emotional, crude, democratic and unsacerdotal, and its revivals were given to a good deal of hysteria, especially at the great camp meetings, which drew settlers from wide areas and provided a welcome solace from the tedium of cabin life. By 1830 something of the Western fervour was relayed to the East in the magnetic person of Charles G. Finney, the greatest revivalist (save perhaps Moody) of the century. Finney's methods showed how self-conscious and efficient revivalism was becoming. A century earlier Jonathan Edwards had seen revivals as a 'surprising work of God', to be prayed and preached for, yet awaited as a mysterious shower of rain from heaven. Finney's celebrated *Lectures on Revivals* (1835) confidently set out the human means by which revivals could be worked up. His new measures—such as the 'anxious seat', in which the repentant, tended by 'holy bands', were isolated from the congregation at a crucial moment—showed an appreciation of the techniques of psychological manipulation, and marked an important stage in the development of modern mass evangelism.

But for many Christian intellectuals, dogmatic attachment to the

Bible or to the letter of old confessions proved increasingly difficult. Narrow conceptions of Biblical inspiration and infallibility were being steadily undermined. Christian apologists had delighted to point out the ethical value of the Bible: increasingly, this claim was countered by bold spirits like Tom Paine, who drew attention to the cruelty and immorality of many Old Testament stories, or expressed moral revulsion at some cardinal Christian doctrines, like that of a substitutionary atonement. At the same time, as scientific knowledge advanced and the world could be interpreted more and more from within in terms of its own mechanistic laws, miraculous breaks in the natural order (like the Biblical miracles) seemed less probable. It appeared decreasingly necessary to postulate a God who intervened immediately in His Creation through a special Providence. As geology progressed, a more figurative interpretation of Genesis became obligatory for the self-respecting scientist. The rocks suggested that the earth was not a mere 6000 years old, but of immense antiquity, and the Creation not accomplished in six days but over a vast time-scale.

And like the rocks, so too the Bible had its different strata, whose uncovering shook faith in the unerring historicity of Scripture. For centuries the Bible had been generally regarded as the direct revelation of the word of God. Be its inspiration literal or plenary, it was divinely inspired and unerring, the repository of an organic body of dogma, history and spiritual instruction, from which any text could be quoted as authoritative. But as new methods of analysis—already applied to other ancient literatures—were turned upon it, and its discrepancies were probed into, attention began to focus also upon the human elements in its composition, on the complexities of its authorship, on its components of legend, myth, sacred history and primitive poetry. Following the footsteps of Semler, German 'higher critics' like Eichhorn at Göttingen and De Wette at Halle uncovered some of the separate strands of the Pentateuch, separating and dating them by comparison of their style, vocabulary and content. Similar work was begun on Isaiah, and on the 'prophecy' of Daniel. It was with greater reluctance that critics approached the New Testament, though some advance was made towards the unravelling of the Synoptic Problem, the close similarities of the first three Gospels, which are in some ways as puzzling as their discrepancies. Eichhorn suggested that the three Evangelists had used a common document, an Aramaic *Urevangelium*: other critics, like Eckermann and Gieseler, put forward the claim that the Gospels derived from oral traditions, written down at the end of the first century. The riddle of the Fourth Gospel also drew fresh attention, and Bretschneider's *Probabilia* (1820) expressed current doubts about its historicity and its Johannine authorship. Meanwhile, the search continued for the historical Jesus who stood behind the Christ of theology. In the hands of rationalist scholars like Paulus, it was still restricted largely to ingenious attempts to explain the miracles by natural causes which the Evangelists had misunderstood.

Yet Protestant orthodoxy still often spoke as if the truth of Christianity stood or fell by the literal veracity of the Bible. This was especially the case in England, where the German higher criticism was regarded with great distrust. In 1825 Connop Thirlwall remarked 'it would almost seem as if at Oxford the knowledge of German subjected a divine to the same suspicion of heterodoxy which . . . was attached some centuries back to the knowledge of Greek'.[1] Already, however, there were some who tried to set their creed on bases less vulnerable than an 'infallible' Bible. The work of the higher critics had not been merely destructive: from it emerged a vision of revelation not as a static body of dogma, whose truths were timeless and complete, but as a slow and evolutionary process accommodated to the successive stages of man's development. Revelation, said Lessing, was God's progressive education of the human race. The restrictive gloss on the terms 'inspiration' and 'revelation' was slowly broken down, as a distinction came to be drawn between revelation and the documents that recorded it. The biblical books, it was argued, were not in themselves the word of God, though they contained that word. Objection to the letter of Scripture did not destroy its validity, for its truth was inward and spiritual. A conception of biblical truth as symbolic and moral, rather than literal and historical, gained support from the German idealist philosophers whose influence on speculative theology from Kant's *Critiques* to the death of Hegel in 1831 was varied and profound. In the successive idealist systems, all avowedly religious, hopeful theologians saw materials for a constructive theism which might set Christianity on foundations beyond the reach of an encroaching materialism, and resolve the enmity between philosophy and religion. The progress of science did not perturb Kant's conception of true religion since it did not affect the practical reason, or invalidate the inner moral consciousness which he saw as the basis for faith as he conceived it. Hegel's grandiose system portrayed Christianity as the positive religion which most clearly revealed the Absolute, unfolding itself in history and human consciousness, and treated cardinal Christian doctrines—such as the Incarnation and the Trinity—as symbolic representations of philosophical truth.

It was in the theology of Schleiermacher (1768–1834), Hegel's colleague and rival at the University of Berlin, that Protestantism made its most powerful effort to push through to fresh intellectual foundations. His *On Religion: Addresses to Cultured Despisers* (1799), though very

[1] C. Thirlwall, translation of F. D. Schleiermacher, *Critical Essay On The Gospel of St Luke* (London, 1825), Introduction, p. ix.

much the product of Romanticism, marked a new epoch in theology. The development of his ideas into systematic form in his *Christian Faith* (1821-2) showed him to be the greatest Protestant theologian since the sixteenth century. He began by a simple but radical definition of religion. It was not, he claimed, a set of dogmatic propositions or an ethical code, but an inward experience, direct, intuitive, existing in its own right as a central part of human life, true to its own intrinsic authority. His appeal was not to the old external evidences—Bible, prophecies, miracles—but to the living religious consciousness. The heart of religion, and its standard of interpretation, was the feeling of utter dependence on a power beyond ourselves, 'the immediate consciousness of the universal existence of all finite things in and through the Infinite.' The religious consciousness found a multiplicity of expressions, in art, science, in the great positive religions of the world, but its highest and most comprehensive formulation lay in the Christian religion, with its experience of redemption through the person of Christ. The Christian doctrines, like the Christian Scriptures, were a crystallised expression—though they could never be a complete expression—of the corporate experience of the believing community. The experience, not the dogma or the letter, was primary. If Schleiermacher's redefinition was accepted, many stumbling blocks between educated men and faith were revealed as imaginary. 'Miracles', 'revelation', 'inspiration', 'grace', 'prophecy': these were all, in their way, formulations of a fundamental, intuitive awareness of God, and of man's need for Him.

By 1815 it was widely held in governmental circles that the forces of religion should be used in the work of social restoration. Napoleon himself had set a precedent: his Concordat had been an impressive tribute to the need of secular government for the support of the Church, and of monarchy for its sacramental blessing. On a diplomatic level the Holy Alliance of Christian princes as projected by the Tsar remained an eccentric gesture, but within individual states a holy alliance of throne and altar was preached with enthusiasm. It was not necessary to read Bonald or de Maistre to see a connection between the religious and political innovation of the Revolution. By attacking Church and monarchy simultaneously, the Jacobins had emphasised the solidarity of those twin pillars of the old order. Even aristocratic sceptics now saw the value of the Church as a bulwark against future revolutions, while exile and tribulation brought to some a penitential reaction from incredulity to belief. Before 1789, in the heyday of Voltairean scepticism, the devoutly religious man had not been a common phenomenon in the forefront of politics. Things had changed: the Tsar of all the Russias was for a time a convert to biblical mysticism; Charles X of France a dedicated *dévot*; Frederick William III of Prussia the first of his line for a century to present an edifying picture of Christian family life. In France there was the powerful politico-religious secret society of the *Chevaliers de la Foi*, borrowing its organisation in part from the freemasons, but its ideals from the military and chivalric orders of the Middle Ages. Pietism flourished among Prussian Junkers and Wilberforce's parliamentary 'Saints'.

The needs of the Churches played a considerable part in the work of political restoration after 1815. After clever lobbying by Consalvi at the Congress of Vienna, the temporal power was restored to Pius VII almost in its entirety, though the concern for 'legitimacy' did not extend to the restoration of the German ecclesiastical principalities. States recently aggrandised, or in which there had been secularisations, stood in need of some form of diplomatic agreement with the Curia to restore administrative order or draw up a new delimitation of dioceses. In Germany the plight of the Roman Church was acute, for only six bishops remained alive, of whom five were septuagenarians. In a remarkable series of agreements, the Catholic Church was re-established through much of Europe. Thus Concordats or bulls of circumscription were negotiated for Bavaria (1817), Naples (1818), Russian Poland (1818), Prussia (1821), the United Netherlands (concluded in 1827 but not executed), the Upper Rhenish Church Province of Baden, Württemberg, Nassau and the Hesses (1821 and 1827), and Switzerland (1828). The bonds of Church and State, often loosened by war and revolution, were drawn closer together again, as parochial and diocesan life resumed its normal course. In the work of reconstruction the Society of Jesus (restored by Pius VII in 1814) played an important part.

In parts of Europe the confessional state re-appeared in much of its old rigour. The Inquisition returned to Spain; Sardinia declared fasting and Easter Communion compulsory once more; in the Papal States the Jews were re-enclosed in the Ghetto, and vaccination and street lighting swept away as dangerous relics of French innovation. Yet outside the Italian and Iberian peninsulas the ecclesiastical restorations, like many of the political, were characterised by some form of compromise with liberalism. Even when restoring Catholicism as the State religion, the Concordats usually reflected the advance of secularism made since 1789. Napoleon's Concordat had been once regarded by the Curia as an exceptional concession to circumstance: by 1815 it had become a much-imitated model, through which the domain of the Catholic Church, once inextricably entwined in the life of the State, was confined and carefully delimited. The ancient exemptions of the clergy from civil jurisdiction, their powers of censorship, of prosecuting for heresy, their educational monopoly, had faded.[1] An *église salariée*

---

[1] A. Latreille, *L'Église Catholique et la Révolution Française* (Paris, 1946–50), vol. II, pp. 260 ff.

lacked the protection from an encroaching Leviathan which the huge endowments of the pre-revolutionary era had provided. The comparative poverty of some churches after the secularisations helped to make the Church less attractive to a worldly nobility, and to provide a career open to talent, but it also curtailed their corporate independence. Above all, Rome observed with dismay the spread of indifferentism and tolerantism in States still predominantly Catholic. In 1824 Leo XII protested at the way in which, in France 'heterodox cults have been set on the same level as the Catholic religion', and similar protest was levelled against the Fundamental Law governing Belgium and the Bavarian Religious Edict of 1818, both of which granted equality of civil rights to non-Catholics. If it was permissible to tolerate heretics, Rome told the Belgian bishops in 1816, it was never permissible to take an engagement to protect heretical sects or their errors.

Rome continued to put her trust in princes. Under Consalvi's influence Pius VII wisely refused, when pressed, to join the Congress System. Having escaped from Napleon's confederation, he did not want to enter Metternich's. But the cause of 'legitimacy' found energetic support at Rome. The sympathies of the papal monarchy were firmly with the 'family of sovereigns' and her influence pitted against the rising tide of constitutionalism and democracy. Democracy had meant invasion and pillage by the armies of the Directory, and now meant the cabalistic plottings of the Carbonari and the secret societies, who kept the Legations in a state of simmering rebelliousness. And how could the doctrine of popular sovereignty, or even the practice of parliamentarism, be conceded within the Papal States? Was not the absolute sovereignty claimed by the Pope *in spiritualibus* incompatible with his temporal subjection to a lay, elective Italian assembly? The universal, spiritual aspect of the temporal power, which forced Pius VII to resist Napoleon, helped inspire his successors to resist the strongest political currents of their time, and to tie them to the chariot wheels of reaction. After the death of Pius VII in 1823 and the subsequent fall of Consalvi, the influence of the *zelanti* was uppermost. Leo XII issued the first of the series of doctrinal condemnations of political liberalism, soon strengthened by Gregory XVI's *Mirari Vos* (1832), which denounced the ideal of liberty of conscience as 'absurd', freedom of the press as 'execrable', and likened those who encouraged subjects to rebel against their rulers to 'sons of Belial'. Yet, beyond Rome, Catholics lay and even clerical were often driven into attitudes which conflicted with those of the Papacy; into mass political action, outright support of liberalism, or even rebellion.

In South America at least, the revolutions against the Spanish government had seldom taken an anti-Catholic or even a properly anticlerical form. The Spanish-born bishops were mostly strong royalists, but many of the American-born lower clergy had supported the revolutions. In Mexico, the Viceroy Venegas invoked the *Virgen de los Remedios* as *generala* of the royalist troops, but the rebel priest Hidalgo proclaimed the Virgin of Guadalupe as patroness of the revolt. The revolutionary leaders professed themselves good Catholics, and the constitutions of the new republics, like that of monarchist Brazil, still preserved Catholicism as the exclusive state religion, and denied the right of public worship to other confessions. But the Latin American revolutions presented the Curia with a delicate problem. The flight or death of many bishops (by 1829 there was not a single bishop in Mexico) led rebel governments to press urgently for recognition by Rome and to claim the patronage rights exercised by the Spanish crown. Yet for Rome to institute bishops for rebel South America was an affront to the prerogatives of the Most Catholic King of Spain, and to the principle of legitimacy. But to refuse institution might lead to schism, and, in Consalvi's opinion, open the way to proselytising 'Methodists, Presbyterians and even sun worshippers'. Rome hesitated long. In 1816 and 1824 encyclicals urged the clergy of the rebellious colonies to support their lawful monarch in Madrid. But by 1827 Leo XII had taken the important step of preconising proprietary bishops for some South American sees, a policy extended by Gregory XVI.

In Europe too, a number of Catholic leaders were forced to question the principle of throne and altar. It seemed hazardous in an age of revolutions to bind the Church to particular dynasties. Did this not drive the enemies of political reaction into enmity to the Church? The fall of an unpopular regime, like that of Ferdinand of Spain in 1820, or Charles X of France in 1830, discredited the clergy who had helped to prop it up. If the close association of Church and State had been accepted tacitly and naturally before 1789, the continuum had been broken by the Revolution, and its restoration in 1815, after decades of spreading secularism, appeared as a self-conscious and deliberate tactic of political reaction. Moreover, the price exacted by legitimist rulers for the protection of the Church often seemed exorbitant. What Josephist, Gallican or heretic princes construed as legitimate State protection of the Church could be regarded by Catholics as interference with her inner spiritual life. Unattractive clauses of the Concordats had a habit of being evaded by the State: promised endowments were not always forthcoming, and the liberties of the Church could be curtailed by police regulations modelled on the Organic Articles. In dealing with such problems, Rome preferred top-level negotiation between Curia and Chancellery, and her traditional methods of subtle and resourceful diplomacy. She remained in general distrustful of direct political action by Catholics, particularly priests, for religious purposes. Yet the advent of forms of constitutional government allowed Catholics to mobilise themselves within a parliamentary framework. If anti-clericals were politically organised, why not Catholics? Before 1830, when Lamennais' newspaper *L'Avenir* broadcast the ideas of liberal Catholicism, there had already been several successful attempts at Catholic political action led by men who accepted, whether for tactical reasons or with ideological conviction, the presuppositions of political liberalism: freedom of the press, of debate, of worship, even the separation of Church and State. These, it was argued, could be used for Catholic ends. Under present conditions the Church had often more to gain from a liberal regime of freedom than from the trammels of princely despotism.

The movement away from the politics of throne and altar was noticeable where the altars were Catholic but the thrones were occupied by princes who were not only heretics but aliens: Ireland, Belgium, the Prussian Rhineland, Russian Poland. Here a struggle for national independence or local autonomy could also become a struggle for confessional liberty or parity. The Irish campaign for Catholic Emancipation provided an early example. O'Connell's movement to relieve Catholics from their civil disabilities was also a demonstration of nationalism against English rule. His Catholic Association, founded in 1823, was in some ways a portent of future Catholic political action in Europe, by its use of mass meetings, petitions, press and pulpit, and its appeal to liberal principles of civil and religious freedom. Years before Lamennais, O'Connell showed himself both a Catholic and a liberal, whose liberalism rested on conviction. In 1811 he declared 'the principle on which I have been . . . the advocate of Catholic emancipation is not confined to Ireland. . . . It embraces the causes of Dissenters in England, and of the Protestants in the Spanish and Portuguese territories. . . . I hate the Inquisition as much as I do the Orange and Purple system'.[1]

Catholic leaders in Belgium, however, were driven—reluctantly—towards political liberalism for reasons that were opportunist and not ideological. The fusion in 1815 of Catholic Belgium with Protestant Holland under the Calvinist King William had aroused religious as well as political tensions (Chapter XVII (A)). Led by the choleric Bishop of Ghent, the Belgian hierarchy had bitterly attacked the obnoxious liberalism of the Fundamental Law of 1815, because it guaranteed religious equality to all religions, and thus put error on the same legal level as Catholic truth. Yet by 1828 Catholic political leaders had made a remarkable about-turn. Disgusted by William's Josephist treatment of the Church—particularly his extension of State control over Catholic schools and seminaries—they decided to join

[1] *The Life and Speeches of Daniel O'Connell, M.P.*, ed. J. O'Connell (Dublin, 1846), vol. I, p. 109.

forces with their anti-clerical liberal opponents, and to demand from the government a properly parliamentary regime, with freedom for the press and for education. Despotism was a graver threat than liberalism. Hesitantly, each party swallowed its suspicion of the other's good intentions and agreed to continue their struggle within the framework of a liberal constitution, not by the old methods of coercion, but by an appeal to the force of argument and to public opinion. The Belgian Catholics joined the huge petitioning campaign against the government: the lower clergy (though not their bishops) brought mass support for the Revolution in 1830. The lasting fruit of the Union was the Belgian Constitution of 1831, by which the Churches enjoyed a freedom much envied throughout Europe. Church and State were not separated entirely, since the State paid the clergy of the three main Churches. But Catholics at last had freedom to run their own schools, form religious orders, nominate to bishoprics, and communicate undisturbed with the Holy See. Yet the whole sequence of events had been observed with dismay at Rome. Cardinal Albani described the Union as 'monstrous', and the nuncio at Paris, the future Cardinal Lambruschini, growled at the irresponsibility of priests who helped to dethrone a lawful monarch and prepare the way for an 'atheist' constitution.

The problem facing Frederick William III in the Rhineland resembled in some ways that which the Dutch king encountered in Belgium: how to assimilate to a mainly Protestant State a Catholic population with strong local traditions. The tension between the new western provinces of Prussia, largely Catholic, with growing industries and a long contact with French liberalism, and the older provinces of the east, mainly Protestant, agrarian and conservative, did not lead to revolution. The Rhineland did not become the 'Prussian Ireland'. But by the 1840's the rumbles of approaching *Kulturkampf* were clearly audible. Prussian officials in the Rhineland were apt to be authoritarian and heavy-handed (one censored the advertisement for a translation of Dante's *Divina Commedia* on the grounds that divine things could not be comic), and the attempts made from Berlin to integrate Catholicism into the Prussian state system helped to fuse the cause of Rhenish particularism with that of Rhenish Catholicism, in a common defensive front. Though 80 per cent of the Rhineland was Catholic, the principle of confessional parity was violated by the preference given to Protestants in civil and military posts. In many parishes the *Bürgermeister* was the only Protestant. Berlin was apprehensive at the control of Prussian consciences by Rome, and tried to support Catholic opponents of Ultramontanism. Thus the sees of Cologne and Trier were filled by the two 'Febronian' prelates Spiegel and Hommer, and the rationalistic Professor Hermes was set over the Catholic theological faculty at Bonn. But it was marriage legislation that was to prove most provocative. From 1803 Prussian children of mixed marriages had to be educated in their father's religion. This ruling, extended in 1825 to the Rhineland, not only contradicted Catholic practice but seemed an attempt at proselytism, for many such marriages were between Protestant officials and daughters of the local bourgeoisie. In 1837 these grievances exploded in the celebrated 'Cologne affair', a head-on collision between the government and the new, uncompromising Archbishop of Cologne, Droste-Vischering, who refused to yield over mixed marriages and put the 'Hermesians' under a ban, so successfully that they soon lectured to empty benches. Droste-Vischering's imprisonment led to huge and noisy demonstrations of Catholic solidarity, to riots, cavalry charges, and a pamphlet war which marked the prelude to the growth of German political Catholicism.

Nowhere, perhaps, were the politics of throne and altar more provocatively proclaimed than in France, where legitimism and Catholicism seemed inextricably bound up. 'I see,' a sceptic remarked, 'that God died on a gibbet eighteen hundred years ago on behalf of the Bourbon family.' The Church gained many favours from the Ultras (Chapter VII). Yet the ecclesiastical restoration remained an obvious compromise between the norms of the old order and the achievements of the Revolution. The attitude of the Most Christian King towards the Church was ambivalent: his Constitution proclaimed Catholicism the religion of the State—yet guaranteed religious liberty. Protestant churches remained subsidised by the *budget des cultes*. Efforts to undo the work of the Revolution came to little. The attempt to replace Napoleon's Concordat, with its unhappy associations for many *émigré* clergy, failed. Another Napoleonic masterpiece, the *Université*, symbolic of the secular control of secondary education brought about by the Revolution, continued to exist, though put under a clerical grand master. The ferocious sacrilege law remained a dead-letter. Little was done to restore freedom to the religious orders. Furthermore, the attitude of Restoration governments remained firmly Gallican, and the Organic Articles not only remained on the statute book but were applied. In disgust, Lamennais and his Ultramontane followers declared that successive royalist governments had so compromised with the satanic Revolution that France was no longer a Catholic, but a secular, indifferentist, 'atheist' state. Disillusioned with the so-called Union of Throne and Altar, Lamennais began to move towards the Liberal Catholicism of which he was to be the greatest publicist. His *Des Progrès de la Révolution* (1829) called on the Church to cut loose from political entanglements, and to 'isolate herself completely from a politically atheist society'. She must close her ranks, and draw tighter the links which bound her to the centre of all her spiritual authority, the Holy See. Now that political and religious society were no longer organically bound together, the old theocratic order was no longer possible. The Church must accept her position in the indifferentist State, and use boldly for her own advantage the liberal freedoms which the Constitution professed to guarantee (Vol. X, p. 77).

In States predominantly Protestant, one could see most of the main varieties of Church–State relations. At one extreme Sweden, Denmark and Norway, overwhelmingly Lutheran, remained confessional States in which separation from the national Church was illegal. At the other extreme stood the United States where, under the system of Separation, the divisions of religious life were not those of Church and sect, as often in Europe, but those between a multiplicity of denominations, free and equal in the eyes of the federal government. Nothing, however, prevented individual States from regulating their internal affairs on very different principles. Religious tests for office survived in some States (particularly in the South) long into the nineteenth century. And though Separation was widely accepted at State level by 1800, forms of State establishment remained in Connecticut till 1818, and in Massachusetts till 1833. But many opponents of Separation came to agree, like Lyman Beecher, that its results stirred the disestablished clergy into new activity: 'by voluntary efforts, societies, missions, and revivals, they exert a deeper influence than ever they could by queues, and shoe-buckles, and cocked hats and gold-headed canes.'[1] To many Europeans, dissenters warring against an arrogant establishment, or members of a State Church fretting at Erastianism, the American system seemed to provide a working model of religious freedom. It was a paradox, much pondered by travellers like Tocqueville or Harriet Martineau, that religion appeared to flourish more under voluntarism in North America than it did in Europe, where it was protected and established; that Christianity and democracy, often dangerously opposed in the Old World, were strangely conjoined in the New.

By contrast, Erastianism still flourished in Germany. In Prussia, the direction of both Protestant Churches was brought increasingly under unified control by the government. To administrative centralisation was added an attempt at ecclesiastical fusion. In 1817, tercentenary of the Reformation, Frederick William III called for a voluntary union of Lutheran and Reformed into one united Evangelical Christian Church. In many ways the time seemed ripe for union. The old doctrinal barriers (if sometimes reinforced by the neo-confessional revival) had been largely submerged by the torrent of eighteenth-century rationalism, and did not weigh heavily on many pietists, or on clergy influenced by Schleiermacher or the idealist philosophers. But what form should union take? A

[1] L. Beecher, *Autobiography, Correspondence Etc.*, ed. C. Beecher (London, 1864–5), vol. 1, p. 344.

doctrinal 'consensus-union', based on the residuum of beliefs held in common? Or an external union in worship and organisation? And how should it be achieved? By the initiative of the Churches themselves, freed at last from the grip of bureaucracy; or by royal prerogative and cabinet order? Controversy broke out when the king applied his ecclesiological zeal to produce a new liturgy or *Agenda*, to be used by both Churches. Though it met with considerable opposition—particularly because of its similarities to the mass and its relegation of hymns and sermon to the background of worship—in modified form it was gradually extended through Prussia, though often only by crude administrative pressure. As Schleiermacher jested bitterly, honours like the Order of the Red Eagle were handed out to unworthy recipients *non propter acta sed propter Agenda.* Opposition in the Rhineland and Westphalia was largely overcome by 1835, but the obstinacy of conservative Silesian Lutherans was met by force, and led to tragic schism and mass emigrations to the United States. The union, copied elsewhere in Germany, sometimes more happily, remained in Prussia a confederation between the confessions, which preserved their doctrinal identity, though bound in worship and government.

By 1830 the dominant position of the Church of England had been much eroded. During and after the Napoleonic wars, our 'happy constitution in Church and State' was widely regarded as the Ark in which we had ridden out the deluge which had engulfed less fortunate lands. To the utilitarian arguments for the alliance of Church and State, put forward by Warburton and Paley, had been added Burke's eloquent though old-fashioned claim that this was still a Christian Commonwealth in which Church and State were 'one and the same thing, being different integral parts of the same whole'. Politicians, Whig and Tory, agreed with Croker's view of Westminster Abbey as 'part of the British Constitution'. In a time of political disorder, the prudential argument for a national religious establishment seemed stronger than ever, and in 1818 Parliament granted a million pounds, and in 1824 half a million, to build new churches in populous areas. But the anomalies of the Anglican claim to be the Church of the Nation —plain since 1689—became increasingly blatant. For in Britain, as elsewhere, mere toleration was no longer enough, and the demand for religious equality became harder to withstand. Catholic Emancipation in 1829 struck a blow at the notion of the 'Protestant Constitution' of Britain. Meanwhile, as Protestant Dissenters became more numerous, they became more vociferous about the grievances of their second-class citizenship. They were strong enough in 1811, by formidable lobbying, to scotch Sidmouth's attempt to curb the freedom of their itinerant preachers, the 'tailors, pig-drovers, chimney-sweeps etc.' whose rude homilies disturbed the slumber of Anglican parishes. In 1828 Nonconformists gained the repeal of the Test and Corporation Acts, but their campaign for parity did not stop while they were still virtually excluded from Oxford and Cambridge, buried and married by the parson, and forced to pay church rates. Increasingly, education became the battlefield between Churchman and Dissenter. Anglicans held that the Church of the Nation must be the educator of the nation. But the parish schools supported by the Anglicans' National Society were challenged by those of the British and Foreign Society, heavily supported by Nonconformists, which taught a carefully generalised version of Christianity on an undenominational basis. The Anglican monopoly of English university education sprang a small but significant leak when the secular London University was opened in 1828, with support from Dissenters and agnostics. The mounting attack on the establishment seemed to have reached a climax in 1831, when the Bishop of Bristol's palace was burned in the Reform Bill riots. Ironically, though pastoral standards had risen sharply—'whenever you meet a clergyman my age', said the elderly Sydney Smith to young Gladstone in about 1835, 'you may be quite sure he is a bad clergyman'—the clergy were less popular now than in the slumberous days of the eighteenth century. In the 'thirties a formidable, if heterogeneous, army stood ranged against the establishment: disgruntled Dissenters; Chartists calling for 'more pigs and fewer parsons'; Irish Catholics unwilling to pay tithes to an alien Church; Utilitarians inveighing against the misuse of Church property which, said J. S. Mill, was originally intended for 'the cultivation of learning, the diffusion of religious instruction, and the education of youth'. In a famous aphorism Thomas Arnold cried 'the Church as it now stands no human power can save'. In a sense he was right. But the administrative overhaul begun by Peel and Blomfield, the spiritual revival of the Oxford Movement, and Arnold's own type of Liberal Anglicanism, which adjusted churchmen to some of the shocks of German scholarship, were soon to provide the Church of England with fresh resilience.

CHAPTER VII

EDUCATION, AND PUBLIC OPINION

PUBLIC opinion first became a major force in Europe in the period of the French Revolution and of the Restoration. First of all the revolutionaries carried their gospel all over Europe. Later the opponents of French hegemony carried on the war against Napoleon through the press as well as on the battlefield. When peace returned again to Europe in 1814–15 the traditional rulers found that the tempest could not be stilled. Through the press and through the societies open and secret the struggle between the old and the new worlds went on. The old world was powerful and resourceful, but it could never strangle the demon of change. The ferment was European. Philhellenism, which appealed to the classical background of educated Europeans, aimed at aiding the Greek patriots; it also aroused the question why the fight against the oppressor should be limited to the shores of the Aegean. Daniel O'Connell's Catholic Association won the vote for Catholic Ireland from Protestant England; it was admired and copied by Catholic Belgium for use against Protestant Holland. The press became more and more the vehicle of political and of economic change, and the chief means of expression of a middle class avid for political and for economic power.

As opinion in all European countries grew more confident and more vocal, so did the activity of government in controlling it increase. Napoleon saw the importance of this; so did Metternich. Even in liberal countries like England and Restoration France governments showed great activity. For if this was the period of revolution and of the clamant popular will, it was also the period of growing state power. What the Enlightenment had promoted, the Revolution established. Unified state power was the chief beneficiary from revolution and change. If governments took care to control the way in which opinion was expressed, they took even greater care to control the way in which it was formed. Education, which in its origins had been the concern of the Church, was becoming more and more the concern of the State. This process had gone a long way already before 1789. Under the Napoleonic and Restoration regimes it was to gain steady momentum. The State's interest in education was primarily directed to training its own future servants and to creating an ethos favourable to the continuation of its own power. It might construe these duties liberally, as on the whole it did in the German States where state advantage included a broad view of national culture. It might construe them narrowly as in France when Napoleon formed his educational institutions on a more definitely utilitarian basis. In either case the underlying reality was the same, and every government saw its educational system as one of the main bulwarks of its own power.

'Educational system' in that context means the universities and the grammar schools where a learned education was given and the lawyers, the clerics, the bureaucrats of the future were trained. There was still the great problem of the education of the people. In England the state as yet took no official part. In France the revolutionaries had been generous in words but nothing was really done until after the Bourbon Restoration. It was only in the German countries that real strides had been made during this period, to a great extent under the influence of the Swiss theorist Johann Heinrich Pestalozzi. Even here danger threatened. On religious, on humanitarian, on practical grounds it was desirable that the poor should be educated. What if they used their knowledge to claim a higher place for themselves than the divine order had decreed? The dilemma extended a good deal beyond popular education. All educational institutions in the countries of the European continent were falling more under state control and aiming at fulfilling ends selected for them by the State. Yet the human mind refuses to heed the bounds set for it by its well-intentioned shepherds and friends. The knowledge which may make a man a good minor bureaucrat or a competent non-commissioned officer also enables him to read criticisms in the newspapers, whether printed legally or not. So if state power was advancing, the power of public opinion was advancing too. A clash between them could not be avoided. It became even more serious when complicated by national or religious rivalries, as in Belgium, in Italy, in the lands of the Austrian Empire or in Poland. The story of such clashes is told under the history of some of the countries concerned but they left their mark also on educational systems, and on the social organisation of opinion.

In this period the press became the most important expression of the public opinion which was everywhere growing up. It had reached its most advanced stage in England, though even there newspapers were still comparatively small and poor and venal, and were becoming only towards the end of the period the great organs of the public mind which they were to be in the middle of the nineteenth century. Although in the eighteenth century the press had been freer in England than in other countries, it was still very much at the mercy of the government. Fox's Libel Act of 1792 protected newspapers by enabling the jury to decide on the criminality of the alleged libel as well as on the fact of publication, but its passage coincided with the beginning of the struggle with revolutionary France, and of a period when government took an active part in suppressing newspapers. Eldon boasted in 1795 that 'there had been more prosecutions for libel within the last two years than there had been for twenty years before'.[1] These facts show not only that government was very active but that newspapers were becoming increasingly important as mouthpieces of public opinion. Acts of 1798 and 1799, to prevent the printing and dissemination of seditious literature, required that the names and addresses of the printer and publisher of all sorts of newspapers, books and papers should be registered. A more insidious but equally effective method of control was found by increasing the duties on newspapers and advertisements. In 1789 the newspaper stamp-duty was raised to 2d; in 1815 it had reached 4d. In 1811 duty was paid on 24,422,000 newspapers, but this number had altered very little by 1821. The number was high but was not substantially rising. In 1821 *The Times* was paying slightly less in stamp-duty than its chief rivals, the *Morning Chronicle* and the *Courier* combined. As a result of the trial of Queen Caroline (1820) its sale went up from 7000 to more than 15,000. The duties made it difficult for the circulation of newspapers to grow or for advertising revenue to provide a really stable basis for their finances. But despite all these measures and despite the extensive powers of the Attorney-General under the libel laws, there was no censorship during the war years.

At the beginning of the period the true censorship lay in the fact that the newspapers had not yet reached financial independence. The tradition was that newspapers depended on the administration or on the parties. The Treasury found money to start new journals. Journalists asked for fees to suppress gossip paragraphs or to contradict them if they had been published. In the early years of the French Revolution the government was spending nearly £5000 a year on the press; *The Times*, for instance, had a subsidy of £300 a year from 1789 to 1799. The paper most closely connected with the Tory governments of 1807–30 was the *Courier*. Canning said that one of its proprietors, T. G. Street, was paid £2000 to support the Perceval Ministry. In the 1820's Government tended to confine its advertisements to friendly newspapers, to purchase large numbers of copies of papers to give them away, and to circulate its own pamphlets.

Slowly a new tradition of press independence was growing. Here a newspaper of consequence was the *Morning Chronicle*, bought by James Perry in 1789, which became the leading political journal for a long time, really until the end of the war. *The Times*, founded in 1785, was not of great consequence until the second John Walter took charge of it in 1803. The paper had been connected with the Addingtons but after 1806 Walter maintained its independence from political groups. He strengthened its economic position and adopted in 1814 the Koenig

[1] H. R. Fox Bourne, *English newspapers: Chapters in the History of Journalism* (London, 1887), vol. I, p. 244.

steam press. He employed a more scrupulous type of journalist. He secured a better and quicker news service by attacking the Post Office monopoly of the foreign mails maintained in the private interest of the Post Office clerks. The higher standards of independent criticism which were being followed in *The Times* were represented in periodical literature by John and Leigh Hunt's *Examiner* (1808) and by the two great quarterlies, the Whig *Edinburgh* (1802) and the Tory *Quarterly* (1809).

With the new century the tradition of radical criticism which had been suppressed in the early years of the war began to revive again. In 1802 the greatest of Radical journalists, William Cobbett, founded the *Weekly Political Register* and used it to criticise government measures. In 1809 he was sent to prison for two years for criticising the flogging of some militiamen. The Hunts, too, had made reform and liberal measures an important part of their programme. They were several times in danger and finally in February 1813 were each fined £500 and each sent to prison for two years for an attack on the prince regent. In 1816 Cobbett issued a cheap edition of his *Register* for 2*d*; he fled to the United States the following year when Habeas Corpus was suspended. In the harsh years of reaction after the war the government took severe measures against Radical journalists and pamphleteers; for instance the Publications Act of 1819 made cheap weeklies newspapers within the terms of the Newspaper Act of 1798 and of the Stamp-Duty Acts and required publishers and printers of periodicals to enter into recognisances. Both government and private societies prosecuted Radicals like the parodist William Hone and particularly the deist and republican Richard Carlile, a fanatic for press freedom in the cause of which he suffered a long imprisonment. The brunt of the struggle for free expression was borne by the pamphleteers rather than by the newspapers which were more prosperous and had more to lose. Carlile was finally released in 1825 and Peel, who had gone to the Home Office in 1822, saw that no good was done by prosecutions; from 1822 to 1829 there were hardly any for libel.

Carlile and Hone were radical extremists; the emergence of a serious reforming political journalism was particularly connected with the growth of *The Times* and the work of its first great editor Thomas Barnes who succeeded to the chair in 1817. Under him the paper sought to identify itself with the substantial middle classes. It became celebrated for the excellence of its home intelligence and the accuracy with which it reflected public opinion. As Denis le Marchant, secretary to Lord Brougham, 1830–4, wrote later of Barnes: 'he had correspondents in all the populous parts of England from whom he endeavoured to learn the state of public opinion and whether he guided or followed it was much the same to him so that his paper enjoyed the credit which he always claimed of being the guardian of it.'[1] *The Times* attacked Peterloo and opposed the Six Acts. It supported the queen and canalised the great movement of public opinion which her trial produced. It supported Catholic Emancipation in 1829. It criticised King George IV after his death. In the movement for parliamentary and administrative reform the press took a very important part, through the work of journalists like James Black of the *Morning Chronicle* and Albany Fonblanque of the *Examiner*. The provincial press, which had earlier been politically insignificant, had prominent advocates of reform in the *Leeds Mercury* and the *Manchester Guardian* (founded in 1821). Benthamite opinions were expressed in the *Westminster Review* (1823) and R. S. Rintoul's *Spectator* (1828). The collapse of Toryism during the 1820's is shown by the poor quality of the Tory journalism of the time. The ultra Tory *Morning Journal* (1828) was prosecuted by Wellington's government in 1829 for its attacks on him. 'The whole press have united on this occasion,' Greville wrote, 'and in some very powerful articles have spread to every corner of the country the strongest condemnation of the whole proceeding.'[2] J. W. Croker thought at about the same time that the control of the press should be in the hands of a cabinet minister, for the days had gone by when 'statesmen might safely despise the journals, or only treat them as inferior engines'.[3] All governments felt that it was vital to control the press yet impossible to do so. The press had certainly made great strides in England since 1789. When Fonblanque wrote in the *Examiner* that Wellington's fall in 1830 was 'a warning to statesmen of the controlling genius of the age and the power of opinion',[4] the press could claim most of the credit for the change.

In France the power of the press had been one of the new forces unleashed by the revolutionary impulse of 1789, and, once its potentialities had become apparent, it had played a great part in the hands of journalists like Desmoulins, Marat and Hébert in precipitating the fall of the monarchy. The freedom of the press had been one of the common demands of the *cahiers des doléances*; it was mentioned in the Declaration of the Rights of Man and of the Citizen; it was guaranteed by the Constitutions of 1791 and of 1793. However the press fell into the hands of the Revolutionary Tribunal like all other organs of opinion, and later under the gradually strengthened control of the Directory. Bonaparte maintained the same tradition with greater force and efficiency. He was highly conscious of the power of the press and

[1] *The History of* The Times: *'The Thunderer' in the Making, 1785–1841* (London, 1935), pp. 458–9.
[2] C. Greville, *A Journal of the Reigns of King George IV and King William IV*, ed. H. Reeve, 4th edn. (London, 1875), vol. I, p. 259.
[3] A. Aspinall, *Politics and the Press, c. 1780–1850* (London, 1949), p. 233.
[4] H. R. Fox Bourne, *op. cit.*, vol. II, pp. 32–3.

appreciated the great strides which it had made as the mouthpiece of public opinion since 1789; 'four hostile newspapers', he remarked, 'did more harm than 100,000 men in the open field.' He was anxious to prevent the dissemination of news hostile to the regime and to ensure that he had at his command newspapers which would promulgate the official version of events and pour ridicule on everything else. He followed, in fact, both a negative and a positive press policy. During the campaign of 1796 he kept in close touch with journalists in Paris and made use of press propaganda to establish his position both in France and in Italy. In 1800 the official press made him out as the hero of Marengo, a victory for which he could in fact claim little credit. On many later occasions the true purpose of French policy or the correct movements of French armies were concealed behind a smokescreen of inaccurate and misleading information put out by the official press deriving originally from the *Moniteur officiel*. Immediately after the *coup d'état* of Brumaire 1799 severe measures were taken. A decree of January 1800 suppressed all political papers in the department of the Seine except thirteen, and these were subjected to a harsh censorship. The permitted papers were very closely watched by a press bureau established in the Ministry of Police, and the police kept a careful eye on printers and booksellers.

By this time, moreover, French ideas and the French appeal to the opinion and will of the peoples had spread over much of Europe. The old governments had done their best to prevent the extension of the new spirit. In so far as they recognised the role of the press at all, they interpreted that role as being merely to report facts without any comment on them. Both in Austria and in Prussia government tightened up their regulations under the French threat. It was sometimes suggested that the governments should themselves make use of the press as the French were doing, but they had at first no positive policy and the press seemed a dangerous weapon. Nor did newspapers seem in Germany a real necessity of civilised living. When in 1798 Cotta established the *Allgemeine Zeitung*, the first great German political daily, he was warned by a correspondent that, whereas daily papers were an advantage in London or Paris where thousands of men wanted to read them, they would seem a superfluity in Germany where the post went only twice a week. Nevertheless at the end of the century the importance of the press was growing in Germany and the demand for freedom of opinion which had originally been personal and individual was becoming identified more completely with the demand for a free press.

In many countries which the French overran their armies seemed to bring with them a new dawn of freedom. But, so far as the open expression of opinion was concerned, the dawn was false. Both in Switzerland and in Italy the coming of the French invaders brought the breaking of old bonds, a new interest in the press by the people, and an onrush of journalistic activity. In Switzerland the constitution of the new Helvetic Republic guaranteed the freedom of the press, and there was great activity among both supporters and opponents of the regime. However the dawn of freedom was transitory and under the Napoleonic regime strict control returned. Similarly the Italian campaign of 1796 brought with it active French press propaganda, and papers with revolutionary sympathies appeared in towns like Venice and Genoa as they were occupied. New activity and wider freedom of speech was evident and the newspaper-reading habit spread, though again the Napoleonic Kingdom of Italy had a strict press law and the bonds of State control were drawn tightly again as they had been before 1796.

In France itself a press regime which had been illiberal from the time of Brumaire grew steadily more severe. The Constitution of the Year VIII did not affirm the liberty of the press and, although a commission on the freedom of the press existed under the Empire, it provided a quite illusory guarantee. The most important of the French papers was the *Journal des Débats* of the brothers Bertin which had existed since 1789. It had ten to twelve thousand subscribers. Government control over it was gradually tightened. In 1805 a special censor was appointed for it and it was renamed *Journal de l'Empire*. The emperor himself appointed an editor and took over part of the profits for pensions to men of letters, until in 1811 the whole property of the paper was confiscated by the state. Napoleon both kept a rigid control over any hostile comment and himself sought to provide news and opinions favourable to his own cause; in 1810 he wrote to Fouché instructing him to warn the editor of the *Publiciste* against an article which seemed to favour the Spanish monks and asked him to commission articles pointing out their positive stupidity and ignorance. The provincial press was ordered in 1807 to take its political news exclusively from the official *Moniteur*. In 1809 only one political paper was allowed to survive per department, a rule which was extended throughout the French Empire, and in 1811 the Paris papers were limited to four, the *Moniteur, Journal de l'Empire, Gazette de France, Journal de Paris*. In 1810 the number of printers was limited by law and a general book-censorship was organised; the attitude of the government to the expression of critical opinion in books was shown by the ban on the printing of Madame de Staël's *De l'Allemagne* and the order that she should leave France. As the situation got worse, Napoleon's press policy became even stricter.

Of all the vassals of Napoleonic France the yoke probably lay heaviest on Germany. In the areas annexed by France on the left bank of the Rhine French control was strict despite the expectations of freedom which the Revolution had aroused, and in the days of the Empire the same regime was maintained in the states of the Confederation of the

Rhine. Cotta's *Allgemeine Zeitung* moved into Bavaria, first to Ulm (1803) and then to Augsburg (1810). It came under French control after 1805 and repeated the French directives as they were issued; for instance the troop preparations of 1811 for the Russian campaign were described as designed to protect the German coasts against an English attack. Similarly in Saxony the *Leipziger Zeitung* was instructed by the Saxon government to avoid anything which might be offensive to the French imperial court, or the publication of any news harmful or unpleasant to the French unless it had already been reported in the *Moniteur*. In 1811 the German newspapers were allowed to publish political news only from the *Moniteur*.

In the surviving states like Austria and Prussia the Napoleonic domination plunged governments into a very difficult dilemma. Their whole tradition was to avoid any kind of open press discussion of controversial issues; on the other hand the example of the Napoleonic propaganda suggested to them that they too needed a positive press policy. The two points of view were hard to reconcile. In Prussia an edict of King Frederick William III (1798) ordered newspapers to avoid anything which might give offence to foreign courts or states or which might promote revolutionary ideas and sympathies. In 1809 the publicist Adam Müller produced a plan for an official newspaper to lead and direct public opinion, but nothing came of the scheme. The Prussian minister Hardenberg in fact favoured very strict control because he did not want to arouse the suspicion of the French; thus the poet Kleist's *Berliner Abendblätter* (1810–11) was soon forbidden to publish political articles. In Austria there had been no political discussion and therefore no independent press, though Metternich from his experience as ambassador in Paris saw the importance of newspapers and wished to use them as supporters of the interests of the regime. His main agent in controlling the press was Friedrich von Gentz, who suggested to Metternich the foundation of a political paper. The *Oesterreichische Beobachter*, which had existed since 1810, was taken over, and Gentz wrote the most important articles in it; although it was supposed to have a certain amount of independence, it was in fact under very close government control.

None of the German papers of the war years achieved any real importance politically, though the periodicals fought out the literary quarrels of the Romantics and their opponents. Some faint notes of nationalism and Germanism were already to be heard from men like R. Z. Becker, who published the *National-Zeitung der Deutschen* in Gotha, and Joseph Görres, originally a supporter of the Revolution, who had turned as early as 1798–9 to criticism of the French regime and whose publications were suppressed in consequence. The press first won its right to speak for German opinion during the War of Liberation, though with only a bare and brief toleration from governments. The Berlin papers were allowed by their own authorities to publish nothing about the war. The new spirit of resistance to the French was represented there by the *Preussische Korrespondent* (1813–14), directed by Schleiermacher, Niebuhr and Achim von Arnim, for which permission was indeed granted, though there was considerable fear of the result of adding to the number of papers published in Berlin since it was difficult enough to control those which already existed. The most important mouthpiece of German opinion in the years of Napoleon's fall was Görres's *Rheinische Merkur*, published in 1814 at Coblenz. His attacks on Napoleon made a profound impression. After the peace treaties had been made he demanded a strong Germany, denounced the settlement of German destinies exclusively by the princes, and demanded that the constitution of Prussia should rest on the people. His attacks on the anti-national attitude of Bavaria and Württemberg led to his paper being banned in those states, and finally in January 1816 the Prussian government suppressed the paper which now came under their Rhineland jurisdiction.

A German scholar makes the point that gradually, as the press developed, its freedom became thought of in Germany less as the individual right of the author or the reader and more as a collective freedom belonging to the whole people, a natural expression of their corporate personality.[1] The guarantee of freedom appears again in the post-war constitutions as it had done in the Declaration of the Rights of Man of 1789. The Norwegian Constitution of 1814 established the freedom of the press among the general guarantees of life and property. The right was secured in the Dutch Constitution of 1815 and in the Constitution granted to the new Kingdom of Poland by Tsar Alexander I. In Germany and Italy the hand of reactionary governments lay heavy on all expressions of public opinion. In France the problem of public opinion, as expressed in the press and in pamphlet literature, was one of the primary internal problems of the Restoration period and is linked very closely with allied questions such as those of the claims of the Church, the rights of the religious congregations and the place of the Papacy in the government of the Church. The Charter of 1814 had granted freedom to publish and print opinions 'in conformity with the laws which may repress abuses of this liberty'. The qualifications here implied were interpreted with differing degrees of strictness at different times, but the law never seriously managed to restrain the great debate on political principles which is central to French history under the Restoration and which provided the primary training of the French people in the practice of representative government. At the core of the

---

[1] O. Groth, *Die Geschichte der Deutschen Zeitungswissenschaft: Probleme und Methoden* (Munich, 1948), pp. 110–11.

debate lay the Revolution of 1789; its challenge could not be evaded: was the system which the Revolution had established to be maintained or was it to be overthrown? These questions were argued in the Chambers; they were reported in the press. As the crisis of 1830 grew nearer, the Liberals claimed that the Charter was the culmination of the Revolution, that it meant that the Revolution had triumphed. The Royalists believed that this was a conspiracy and a crime and feared that another outbreak was drawing near. Though there were shades of opinion on both sides, the essential issue was a simple one. 1789 had to be approved or rejected, and the press was at the very heart of the great debate.

In the early years of the Restoration the law was hostile to any free expression of opinion. In October 1814 a law had been passed which decreed that no newspapers or other publications were to appear without royal sanction and that no one should be a printer or a bookseller without authorisation. After the Hundred Days a law on seditious writings was passed by the Ultra-Royalist *Chambre introuvable* which severely affected left-wing newspapers. Although the press legislation was maintained and offending journalists were punished, criticism gradually made itself heard more and more. In 1817 Guizot and Royer-Collard founded the *Archives philosophiques* which demanded freedom of the press and trial by jury for press offences; and other periodicals, like the liberal *Minerve*, were produced which escaped the censorship by not appearing at regular intervals. In 1819 more liberal press laws were passed, which required owners of newspapers to pay a considerable sum in caution money but abolished the censorship and provided a jury trial for press offences. This interlude of comparative Liberalism was brief. In the royalist reaction after the death of the Duc de Berry, the censorship was temporarily restored (1820) and in 1822 the courts were given power to prohibit or suspend papers of a dangerous tendency, the definition of press offences was extended and press cases were taken out of the hands of the jury. The Villèle ministry was exceptionally active in bringing newspapers and periodicals before the courts; it embarked on a scheme to buy up opposition newspapers and bring them under ministerial control; it even restored the censorship, though this was abolished by Charles X on his accession (1824), having lasted for only a few weeks.

The French newspapers, like the English, were expensive and burdened with a heavy stamp-duty. They did exercise great influence on the small politically conscious class, and by the middle twenties the opposition journals, like the *Constitutionnel* and the *Journal des Débats*, which Chateaubriand had carried into opposition when he was dismissed from the government in 1824, were predominant. In 1826 they each accounted for about 20,000 of the 65,000 subscribers to the political papers of Paris. The ministerial press totalled a mere 14,000. In the reign of Charles X the great issue before press and public was clericalism. The Liberals, excluded from the government after 1820, turned their attention more and more to the religious question and endeavoured to crack the alliance of throne and altar, their attack being concentrated particularly on the Jesuits and on Ultramontanism. In 1825 the *Constitutionnel* was charged with 'outrages against the religion of the state'; it was acquitted and the court decided that no abuse was caused by opposition to associations not authorised by the law. In 1826 the famous pamphlet of the Gallican aristocrat, the Comte de Montlosier: *Mémoire à consulter sur un système religieux et politique tendant à renverser la religion, la société et le trône* was only the most prominent among a crowd of pamphlets attacking the Jesuits and the growth of clerical influence.

One of the principal counter-measures taken by Villèle was the so-called 'law of justice and love' which increased the stamp duty and enlarged the responsibility of printers and publishers. This raised intense opposition and was withdrawn when the Chamber of Peers seemed likely to reject it. In 1827 the censorship was re-imposed but was abolished the next year by the Martignac ministry. Under his successor Polignac, Thiers, Mignet and Carrel founded the *National* which aimed at overthrowing the dynasty (January 1830); in February the *Globe* was transformed into a political daily and actively attacked the king's policy. The July Ordinances again submitted papers to a ministerial authorisation. Thiers and the Liberal journalists protested, and it was the attempt of the government to seize the presses of the *Globe*, the *Temps* and the *National* which sparked off the July Revolution.

In France and other countries alike both liberals and reactionaries formed societies, shading over from the entirely law-abiding to the secret organisations of which this was the great age. On the Catholic and Royalist side were the Chevaliers de la Foi and the Congrégation de la Vierge in France, the Society of the Exterminating Angel in Spain, the San Fedists of the Papal States. Among the public Liberal societies one of the most successful and important was Daniel O'Connell's Catholic Association. In France the restoration of the press censorship in 1827 produced a 'Society of Friends of the Liberty of the Press' of which Chateaubriand was president; and very soon afterwards was established the society 'Aid thyself and heaven will aid thee', which contemplated passive resistance and refusal to pay taxes and which was supported by constitutionalists like Guizot and Broglie. Rather earlier, the secret society known as the Charbonnerie, related to the Carbonari of Italy, had been formed with the object of overthrowing the dynasty. It had connexions with prominent Liberal intellectuals and deputies, and branches in many departments, but insurrectionary outbreaks which it had created in 1822 were suppressed without difficulty. The line between peaceful agitation and revolutionary conspiracy was easy to cross. In Germany the Burschenschaften and Turnvereine—the student societies and gymnastic clubs—were in their origin peaceful, but they aroused deep fears in the governments, and an easy sequence of events led from the Wartburgfest of 1817 to the murder of Kotzebue by the student Karl Sand and the Carlsbad decrees of 1819. The Carbonari were most powerful in Italy, the masonic lodges lay behind the Revolution of 1820 in Spain. The new tendencies spread even to the Russian Empire. At the Polish University of Vilna student societies had grown up advocating both nationalism and romanticism, the most important of them being the Philomathians whose membership included the great Polish poet Adam Mickiewicz. In 1823 the leaders of the Philomathians were arrested and banished to Russia. These Polish societies had been influenced by the Burschenschaften. It was the influence of western ideas in the Russian army too which produced secret groups like the 'Union of Welfare' whose ideas led to the Decembrist Revolution of 1825, the first revolutionary movement of modern Russia. If liberal and revolutionary opinion was becoming more highly organised in this way, so were the secret police of the absolute governments. The State after 1815 had a far more acute idea than its eighteenth-century predecessors about what was going on, and much more efficient means of suppressing agitations it disliked and feared.

The story of the press in Germany and Italy after 1815 is part of the general story of unrest and repression in those countries. The Carlsbad Decrees of 1819 enforced preliminary censorship on all publications of less than twenty sheets and provided that all printed materials should bear the name of the publisher, while the States had to inform the Bundestag of the measures which they had taken to carry out the decrees. In Austria there was so little freedom that the decrees probably made little difference. In Prussia the government did discuss more liberal measures after 1815, but these came to nothing and in 1819 a more rigid censorship edict was adopted. In the same year the *Allgemeine Preussische Staatszeitung* was founded as an official paper, but it achieved little importance. The *Allgemeine Zeitung* remained the greatest of German papers but it was under the direct influence of Metternich and was severely censored, with the result that articles sometimes appeared only after considerable delay. Cotta had great difficulties with the Bavarian censorship and his complaints received little sympathy. In the early years after the war the greatest freedom was to be found in some of the smaller States like Weimar. There the *Oppositionsblatt* (1817) discussed constitutional and economic problems, defended the universities and students after Kotzebue's death and criticised the repression in Prussia, though the paper, like other similar journals, soon came to an end. In the 1820's the German press was in a miserable state. Newspapers were too small and weak to be very profitable. In 1816 the Leipzig publisher Brockhaus wrote to Oken that Cotta kept the *Allgemeine* going because of his prestige, not because it paid him to do so. In 1824 the paper had 3602 subscribers. Though able journalists had appeared in Germany, there was little scope for them, and men like Börne and Heine had to go abroad. Papers were crudely composed of bits and pieces, and foreign news was often lifted bodily from foreign journals. The editor's task was made no easier by the fact that the governments often made strict provisions that no foreign news should be given which would be unpleasing to some foreign government which they wished to conciliate. Nevertheless the papers were slowly gaining ground despite all hindrances. As trade and industrial freedom grew, advertisements became more important. News began to travel more quickly, and in Berlin a daily post to and from western Germany, Holland and France was organised. This made it possible for the two Berlin papers the *Vossische Zeitung* and the *Spenersche Zeitung* to go over in 1824 to daily publication; as the editor of the *Vossische* wrote to the king, the public took a greater share in political events, and trade and commerce were promoted through daily advertisements. In 1823 the *Spenersche* introduced the first steam press into Berlin. The collective circulation of papers in Prussia according to the stamp returns was 35,516 in 1823; in 1830 it had risen to 41,049.

In many other European countries the position was no better than it was in Germany. In Italy only literary journalism was possible. In 1818 a group at Milan who believed in a strong and united Italy founded the *Conciliatore*, but this had to be given up under the pressure of the Austrian government in the following year, though many of its ideas were revived in the *Annali Universali di Statistica*. Very important also was the *Antologia*, founded in Florence in 1821, which lasted until 1833. In all these and similar reviews the need for a reformed economic and cultural organisation of Italy was stressed; among the contributors to the *Antologia* and to other periodicals was the young Mazzini. In other countries in which repressive influences were less powerful the press played an important part in the triumph of liberal ideas. In Switzerland rigid control was maintained after 1815, and in 1823 Basel even forbade newspapers altogether. In the late 'twenties, however, the press helped greatly in directing the rising tide of liberalism through papers such as the *Appenzeller Zeitung* (1828) and the *Neue Zürcher Zeitung* (1821). In the northern countries too conflicts took place. Though the Dutch Constitution guaranteed the freedom of the press, this right was limited by government decree and the Dutch government punished the Belgian journalists who expressed the discontent of the southern provinces. The situation worsened when the Belgian Liberals, led by an able journalist, Louis de Potter, coalesced with the Catholics. In 1828 the Belgian deputy Charles de Brouckère failed to get the decree of 1815 on the press rescinded and in the same year Potter was fined and imprisoned for an article in the *Courrier des Pays Bas*. In the next year there was active petitioning in the southern provinces of the Kingdom, freedom of the press being one of the petitioners' demands. Potter was still actively attacking the government and in April 1830 he was banished after a newspaper article advocating an association to assist those who resisted the government. Press attacks on Dutch domination and prosecutions by the government went on until revolution finally broke out in August 1830. In Sweden too the government had been given in 1812 the power to suspend offensive journals and this power was freely used. However the opposition papers like *Anmärkaren* (1816–20) and *Argus* (1820–36) grew in importance and advocated a liberal programme, the reform of the four-chamber Riksdag and the achievement of parliamentary government.

Political Liberalism was one of the main currents of thought, now rushing, now eddying, through the channels of European thought and action. After 1815 the Liberal exiles wove an international bond of sympathy and idealism between the peoples of many countries, as in a very different way had the French *émigrés* of an earlier generation. Liberalism was not the only international movement. Bible Societies for extending the circulation of the Scriptures spread from England, where the British and Foreign Bible Society was founded in 1804, to many other countries, and were warmly encouraged for a time by Tsar Alexander I. In literary and cultural circles this was the age of the triumphs of Romanticism. Its political sympathies were on the whole Conservative, its ideal lay in the harmonious and hierarchic order of the medieval past. It affected all European countries but its real centre was Germany and its triumph placed Germany in the very centre of European thought. This was the great age too of the Idealist philosophy. From Kant the succession had passed to Fichte, to Hegel, to Schelling. Both Romanticism and Idealism were creeds of the group. Man was considered not as an isolated rational individual but as a member of a traditional folk-group, of a nation with a heritage as much emotional as rational. To the philosopher true individuality lay not in isolation but in the acceptance and fulfilment of man's place in a moral universe, identified by Hegel with the secular state. The eighteenth century was an age of great individuals, the nineteenth century an age of corporate and national effort. For the mass of mankind greater freedom and more equal privileges might be demanded, but they were seen within a social context, historical, political or cultural. The veneration for the past is to be seen in a more reverent examination of its records. In France the *École des Chartes* dates from 1821; the great German source-collection *Monumenta Germaniae Historica* began to appear in 1826. In the contemporary world, opinion was recognised as a great social force; politically its most important expression, as we have seen, was through the press; socially and culturally men saw the school and the university as the keys to a new world based on a more profound appreciation of human personality.

One vital thread is that of freedom and moral spontaneity. It must be the duty of the society and of the school not to drill the child into dead and sterile knowledge, but to release the power of independent life and power within him. The idea is primarily Rousseau's, though he had applied it principally to the development of the individual. The task of the nineteenth century was to apply his ideas not only to the favoured few but to the whole mass of the people. Freiherr vom Stein in his *Nassauer Denkschrift* of 1807 speaks of elevating the people so that they may take a real part in the work of the state. The Prussian reformers found the means to their hand in the work of Johann Heinrich Pestalozzi (1746–1827). After early failures, he first achieved success in teaching a group of children at Stanz who had been orphaned during the disturbances connected with the Revolution of 1798 in Switzerland. He later ran several schools and, as his fame grew, especially in Germany, pupils came to him from all over Europe. He was a practical man, not a philosopher, and his fundamental idea was that education should start with the child himself and not with some abstract theory of what the child might eventually be expected to become. The fundamental approach was by sense-impression; once the wheel is set going the children will help themselves because the vital part of all education is self-development. 'All instruction of man,' he wrote, 'is then only the Art of helping Nature to develop in her own way; and this Art rests essentially on the relation and harmony between the impressions received by the child and the exact degree of his developed powers.'[1] Whereas Rousseau in *Émile* had been discussing an individual situation, Pestalozzi is concerned for the ordinary people and for raising the general level of their life. His idea of education is a profoundly social one. The human race needs the same as the single child needs, and the poor man's child needs better instruction than the rich man's.

Pestalozzi's ideas were adopted by Fichte in his *Addresses to the German Nation*; they influenced Prussian officials who were concerned with educational policy and teachers who had to administer it. They provided the fundamental inspiration for the belief that it is the duty

[1] J. H. Pestalozzi, *How Gertrude teaches her children*, trans. L. E. Holland and F. C. Turner, ed. E. Cooke, 4th edn. (London, 1907), p. 26.

of the state to teach its people to read and write, not only for utilitarian reasons but also—and far more important—because it is the duty of the state to release new power in its citizens, power to become more complete and developed human beings than they were before. Pestalozzi's work was known in England (a translation of some of his early letters was published in 1827), but even when no direct connexion of cause and effect can be proved, the same idea of freedom, spontaneity and the release of power also ran through the English thinkers of the same period. Bentham's ideas about education are more strictly practical than Pestalozzi's, but in the Utilitarian school the same sense of freedom and self-activity is to be found, particularly in James Mill. No class ought to be excluded from education, he says, because it exists to communicate the art of happiness. Though knowledge, morality and happiness may not be exactly conjoined in any one individual, they certainly are so conjoined in classes and nations. The same note is struck in the most important of the English educational thinkers of this period, Robert Owen. Convinced of the truth of the eighteenth-century tradition that men's characters are formed by their environment, he believed that the best governed state would be that which had devoted the most care to the education of its citizens. Such education must, he thought, teach them to become rational beings, a task which existing systems of popular education had hardly attempted. The problem was a practical one: 'Train any population rationally and they will be rational. Furnish honest and useful employments to those so trained, and such employments they will greatly prefer to dishonest or injurious occupations.'[1] But such honest and useful employments do not lie at once to hand for poor and ignorant men. The State must take the chief hand in the work. Sir James Kay-Shuttleworth, one of the founders of the English system of popular education, came to the same conclusion; he saw education as an important remedy for the misery of the Manchester workers in 1832: 'The ignorant are, therefore, properly the care of the State.'[2]

The search for freedom and self-development was for Pestalozzi and for Owen primarily concerned with the education of the people. In secondary and higher education the same goal was pursued by German thinkers, particularly Wilhelm von Humboldt. The traditions of German higher education in the eighteenth century were mainly practical; the universities existed to prepare men for state service. In the early years of the new century men like Fichte and the theologian Schleiermacher began to plan a new university in Berlin which should be devoted not to producing bureaucrats but to the higher culture of the

[1] R. Owen, *A New View of Society*, 3rd edn. (London, 1817), p. 65.
[2] Sir James Kay-Shuttleworth, *Four Periods of Public Education as reviewed in 1832–1839–1846–1862* (London, 1862), p. 60.

mind. The defeat of Jena must have seemed disastrous to their plans; in fact it made Prussians think much more deeply of the future of their State. Clearly new resources had to be created; some of them would be material but others were to be spiritual. The State must tap new spiritual reserves; it must make up in spiritual force what it had lost in material. These ideas were not peculiar to Wilhelm von Humboldt, who was head of the Department of Religion and Education in the Ministry of the Interior, 1809-10, but he exemplified them more fully than any other of his contemporaries. He was himself devoted to personal development and freedom and he believed that education must be based at every stage on the fullest development of individuality possible. The great force in his mind, and in the minds of his great contemporaries in the German literary world like Herder, Goethe and Schiller, was that of the Greek. It was in the study of the Greek world, not merely the word-splitting and pedantry of 'classical education' in the narrow sense, but in the appreciation of its language, history, culture, art as a whole, that men like the great philologist F. A. Wolf found the key to full self-development. This was the way to complete harmony, to realisation of the fact that man is valuable not for what he knows or can do, but for what he is. The ideal of the New Humanism, originally that of an aristocratic minority, was brought by Humboldt into the main stream of higher and secondary education. His direct responsibility in an official post was of very short duration; the effect of his work was permanent.

Education to him and to those who thought like him was the key to the moral resources of the nation. The new university of Berlin, inaugurated in October 1810, was designed to spread Prussian influence throughout Germany and to develop the spirit of the whole German nation. Although it was a state institution, the traditional corporate organisation of the faculties was maintained and some autonomy was preserved. Academically the standard of Berlin was high from the first. In other States many of the ancient universities were reformed at much the same time. Heidelberg was reorganised in 1802-3 by the government of Baden. In Bavaria King Ludwig I established in 1826 a university at Munich which became a counterpart to Berlin in the Catholic South. In their newly acquired western provinces the Prussian government founded the University of Bonn in 1818. In these and other German universities modern standards of university study and research were worked out. The professors were savants devoted to the pursuit of knowledge for its own sake. The emphasis lay on independent study and research instead of mechanical learning by rote. In every department of scholarship—in classical philology and history, in Germanic studies, in law, in philosophy, in history and in science— the Germans stood pre-eminent. Among the many students who came from other lands were Edward Everett and George Ticknor, who arrived at Göttingen in 1815—the first of the great succession of American scholars.

The intellectual stimulus which had revitalised the German universities also profoundly affected the secondary schools. New Humanism was again the predominant influence, and it was the philologists who really set the tone. Out of the old Latin schools gradually developed the gymnasia, the secondary schools, which had the right to prepare students for the university. In Prussia a teachers' examination for secondary schools was adopted in 1810; gradually an independent teaching profession separate from the clergy came into existence. In 1812 the final school-leaving examination which dated originally from 1788 was reorganised, and in the same year a standard plan of gymnasium studies was adopted, based on a ten-year course of Latin, Greek, German and Mathematics, designed to provide an all-round education. In 1817 a separate Ministry of Education was set up and in 1825 the local educational administration was separated from the religious consistories. The development was not entirely harmonious—a project for a general school law covering primary and secondary education came to nothing in 1819; but by the death of King Frederick William III in 1840, the Minister, von Altenstein, and his assistant Johannes Schulze had perfected and completed the organisation of the Prussian gymnasium in its studies and personnel. With local variations—for instance the Bavarian curricula under the influence of Friedrich Thiersch were more purely classical in inspiration than the Prussian—development of the same sort happened in the other German states.

In a period of reaction such as that between 1815 and 1830 governments were naturally very suspicious of academic free thought or free speech. The effects of the reforms made in Prussia and the other German states had been to increase their power over the universities and schools. Humboldt and others of his generation had been genuinely devoted to self-expression and personal freedom, though they had seen the activity of the State as the only way of achieving those objectives. Under their successors the balance tipped away from personal freedom and towards state control. Humboldt had wished the University of Berlin to have its own independent revenues. His successor, von Schuckmann, opposed this because it reduced the State's control over the University and caused the idea to be set aside. von Altenstein declared that the universities were not states within a state and that they were to have nothing to do with matters affecting the general political situation. In the 1820's a number of edicts were issued in Prussia regulating the private reading of schoolboys, ordering them to study 'true' and not 'superficial' philosophy and decreeing that class teachers should supervise the activities of their pupils and make a report on them which was passed on after they had left school. It is not surprising that the activities of the state, though in one sense assisting and developing educational provision, were in another cramping and deadening.

German writers of the revolutionary period had seen the role of the nation in a literary or a cosmopolitan context, with Germany playing its part among the nations in an international activity of culture and good will. Such ideas lie behind Fichte's *Addresses to the German Nation* (1807), one of the main literary documents of rising German nationalism. Fichte believed that the way to rebuild the nation lay through the adoption of a national system of education which would affect not merely the cultured class but the whole people. The way to achieve this he believed he had found in the ideas of Pestalozzi. The approach to it and the business of carrying it out was the duty of the State, which had got into its present position through its neglect of religion and morality. Opposition there might be, but in taking this course the State would be introducing nothing more radical than the system of compulsory military service which was already in force. The comparison is an interesting one. In fact the duty of the citizen to go to school is closely related to his duty to serve in the army and to pay his taxes. The contradiction is unavoidable between a genuine belief in personal and creative activity and an equally profound conviction that the educational system must produce a fixed and unalterable type in morals and behaviour, the type which has independently been defined as the correct or valid one. Much of the academic opinion of Germany after 1815 was Liberal, not only among students but among professors too; in 1819 the Berlin professor de Wette was dismissed after the death of Kotzebue because of his connexions with the family of Sand, Kotzebue's murderer. Early Liberal leaders were professors like Rotteck of Freiburg and Dahlmann of Kiel, Göttingen and Bonn. Yet there was a persistent tradition among German intellectuals that the free creative spirit was above the everyday concerns of common politics. 'I do not trouble myself about political matters,' wrote Humboldt to Goethe in 1798,[1] and the tradition persisted. Madame de Staël acutely pointed out the activity of German thinkers in intellectual affairs and their sluggishness in political ones. The genius of the nation in philosophical matters has been pushed to the furthest limit, but as a result there is no real object for men 'who do not rise to the elevation of the most rash conceptions. In Germany, a man who is not occupied with the comprehension of the whole universe, has really nothing to do'.[2] Into the gap so left the State could march in unresisted and take full possession.

[1] F. Meinecke, *Weltbürgertum und Nationalstaat* (Munich and Berlin, 1908), p. 52.
[2] Mme de Staël, *Germany*. Eng. trans., 3 vols. (London, 1813), vol. I, p. 172.

The most logical development of state activity in the educational field is to be seen however in Napoleonic France. Both the thinkers of the eighteenth century and the statesmen of the Revolution had seen education as a major function of the State, though the revolutionary assemblies had produced little more than a series of interesting projects. Education came naturally under the care of the First Consul who was restoring the institutions of France. He found himself in a revolutionary situation when everything was in flux, master of a growing empire without imperial institutions. He wanted the schools to train the creators of a new type of society. The spirit he wished to inculcate was that of order and devotion to his regime. He could hardly expect this to be universally accepted among his contemporaries, but he might hope to direct the minds of their sons. In achieving his aims he was very ready to make use of the Catholic religion, but entirely on his own terms. He was always to be the master. His aims were clear. What was needed was a teaching body with fixed principles. Without such principles the State could never form a nation and would be subject to continual disorder and change. A way must be found to direct political and moral opinion.

His plans took some time to work out. The first step was the Law of 11 Floréal, an X (1 May 1802) which created a *lycée* at the seat of each court of appeal. These were to be chiefly boarding schools and were to give a large number of scholarships to the sons of soldiers and officials. These took the place of the *écoles centrales*, and were similar in form to the *Prytanée*, a central boarding institution in Paris which had also been established by the Directory. In addition, either the communes or private individuals might set up secondary schools, though private people needed authorisation to do so. Primary education was practically ignored; there was little interest and no money. If the schools were to fulfil their purpose in the Napoleonic scheme of things they needed a national organisation which would depend entirely on the State. The idea went back to pre-revolutionary thinkers like Turgot and the parliamentarian Rolland. It represented in a laicised form the idea of the Jesuits which certainly influenced Napoleon, though the men's teaching congregations were in general uncongenial to him because of their dependence on an external authority in Rome. Napoleon appears first to have formulated the idea of such a teaching corporation in February 1805. The formation of the University was decreed in 1806 and it was set up in 1808. The University was a lay teaching corporation with a hierarchic organisation and a strict discipline. At its head and dependent on the Emperor stood the Grand Master and the Council. Beneath this central organisation France was divided into 'Academies' each presided over by a Rector. The Grand Master and Council laid down methods of instruction and the teacher might teach only what the government programmes included. Private education was not suppressed, it was incorporated in the great institution which was planned to link all higher and secondary teachers together so that they should all feel themselves to be members of one body and bound together in a chain stretching from the lowliest position in the school to the highest in the State. The basis of the teaching, according to the decree of 1808, was to be the precepts of the Catholic faith, fidelity to the emperor and the imperial dynasty, and obedience to the university statutes which aimed at producing citizens 'attached to their religion, to their prince, to their fatherland and to their family'.

The spirit of the new institutions was in fact Catholic and Conservative. Fourcroy, having been concerned with education since 1801, but having had a revolutionary past, was not appointed Grand Master. That post went to the Catholic-minded Fontanes, and the atmosphere of the Council was strongly anti-revolutionary. It was natural therefore that Catholic influence was strong in the schools and that much effort was devoted to maintaining religious orthodoxy. However the private schools, which were generally Catholic schools, suffered a good deal under the regime. They were forced to pay a proportion of their fees into the funds of the University, and they were required, at least in theory, to send their pupils to attend courses in the *lycées* and *collèges* (the communal secondary schools). Stricter rules regulating private schools were made in 1811, and measures were adopted then to control the '*petits séminaires*', the schools preparatory to the diocesan seminaries for priests, which in fact received many pupils who were not going to be ordained.

In higher education Napoleon preserved the professional schools which had been set up during the Revolution. The *École Normale* which had existed briefly in 1795 to train men for the higher posts in secondary education was re-established in 1808. Apart from these schools higher education was in the hands of the faculties of theology, law, medicine, science, and letters, the purpose of which was entirely practical—to train men for state service and to ensure that officials were ready when needed. A similar purpose lay behind the institution in 1808 of the *baccalauréat*, a school examination designed to open the way to civil functions. It is interesting to note that at the time when university education in Germany was being broadened and expanded, it was in France primarily directed to purely utilitarian ends. The Napoleonic government did indeed display real interest in the sciences. During the early decades of the century France was in fact in the lead of scientific thought in Europe (Chapter V). The curricula of the *écoles centrales* set up by the Directory had been strongly scientific. But in these matters Napoleon took a middle course between the newer ideas and the classicism of the old order, and the teaching programmes tended to favour the ancient languages. They were oriented too to maintain the security of the regime. The emperor's hatred of critical thought showed itself, for instance, in the suppression in 1803 of the class of moral sciences in the *Institut de France* founded in 1795.

The same system of state control survived the upheavals of 1814–15 and was continued by the revived Bourbon monarchy. The main problems of this later period were connected with religion and personal freedom, and are most easily considered under that head. Even more rigid state control was to be found in the countries of eastern and southern Europe. In Italy the French administration had reformed the University of Naples and established a normal school for teachers at Pisa. After 1815 these reforms were undone and the normal school closed. In the Austrian Empire a particularly close control over teachers and syllabuses was maintained. The emperor told the professors of the gymnasium at Laibach in 1821 that 'there are now new ideas going about, which I never can nor will approve. Avoid them and keep to what is positive. For I need no savants, but worthy citizens. To form the youth into such citizens is your task. He who serves me must teach what I order. He who cannot do so, or who comes with new ideas, can go, or I shall remove him'.[1] As the reign of Alexander I drew to its close, similar ideas were becoming more and more powerful in the Russian Empire. At the beginning of his reign much had been done for education. The funds available were greatly increased, a department of education was set up, new universities created at Kharkov and Kazan, and an institute of pedagogy founded at St Petersburg which became a university in 1819. In 1804 a university statute was promulgated which gave the universities considerable autonomy and placed them each at the head of one of the educational districts into which the country was divided. A generous policy was also followed in the Kingdom of Poland. A Chamber of Education had already been founded in the new French-controlled Duchy of Warsaw in 1807, which did much for primary and secondary schools, and in 1816–17 a new university was established at Warsaw. However the growing stringency of reaction after 1815 undid much of this good work. The censorship was tightened up, the Ministry of Education was combined with the office of the Holy Synod, the universities were carefully watched and some of their professors were dismissed. The universities of both Vilna and Warsaw were closed after the Polish rising of 1830–1. The ideas of the new Tsar Nicholas I are shown by a statute of 1828 which separated the district schools from the gymnasia, and decreed that the latter were to be open only to the children of nobles and officials. Education might become dangerous if class distinctions were not maintained, a point which must be expanded later.

[1] R. W. Seton-Watson, *A History of the Czechs and Slovaks* (London, 1943), p. 165.

In contrast to all these countries stood England and the United States, still culturally an English colony. In both alike education had been left to private initiative and to philanthropic activity. The New England States of the Union had an old tradition of concern for these matters, but progress in developing a primary school system throughout the republic was necessarily slow. The colleges—Harvard, Yale and their younger sisters—were still limited in their resources and aims. The only important leader of the new nation who had both thought deeply about educational subjects and taken a practical interest in them was Thomas Jefferson. Throughout his career he had hoped to create a comprehensive structure in Virginia leading from the primary schools through the higher schools to the university. He was the father of the University of Virginia, incorporated by the State legislature in 1819. He planned its lay-out; he went to great pains to recruit able professors, often from overseas; he was anxious that the university should be run on the most liberal lines and the students were given a freedom in choosing their courses which was unknown in America at that time. By 1830, however, the distinctive traditions of American education were only beginning to form (Vol. X, pp. 116-7).

In England the State had failed to exert any real control over its educational institutions under the Stuarts. After 1688 it had given up the attempt. Englishmen believed in leaving the task either to ancient independent corporations or to the efforts of private individuals. In the first category came the Universities of Oxford and Cambridge and the ancient grammar schools. All alike had many weaknesses, though before 1830 the great nineteenth-century reforms were already being foreshadowed. At Oxford a new examination statute had been adopted in 1800, and at Cambridge the high standard of the Mathematical Tripos did create an exacting though narrow road to honours. Criticism was becoming heard, more especially from the advocates of the Scottish universities, which were both cheap and efficient. In the schools the pioneers of the great generation of public school headmasters were already at work. Samuel Butler went to Shrewsbury in 1798 and Thomas Arnold to Rugby in 1828. The old universities and grammar schools were Anglican in religion, and the existence of the religious tests was one important reason for the creation of the non-sectarian 'London University' in 1828, the foundation college of the modern University of London. The State too was beginning to exercise a greater influence. The Utilitarians worked in that direction, for education, as Bentham held, 'is only government acting by means of the domestic magistrate'. The Select Committee of 1816 on the education of the poor uncovered many abuses in the management of charitable trusts and led to later legislation for more effective control. In 1827 a commission was issued for visiting the Scottish universities and, although no action was taken on its report until 1858, it prefigured the later enquiries into Oxford and Cambridge. In elementary education a general system of parochial schools had been proposed by Whitbread in 1807 and, although in England the State took no direct action to assist primary education before 1830, in Ireland, often a laboratory for trying out new forms of state activity, state grants in aid to the Kildare Place Society go back to 1815. It was clear to Englishmen by the early years of the nineteenth century that the education of the people was an enormous problem. If the State was not to take on the work itself, the only other agencies powerful enough to do so were the churches.

The traditional connexion between the Church and education was very strong, in England as in other countries, and it had not been eroded away, as in eighteenth-century Germany, by the growing power of the State. The classic English type of organisation by private individuals, combining central organisation with local initiative, went back in the educational field to the Society for Promoting Christian Knowledge, founded in 1698, which in its early years was very active in establishing charity schools. Sunday schools, also founded by private effort, had started to develop in the 1780's. All nineteenth-century Englishmen with very few exceptions agreed that education should be religious at its core. Some important thinkers like Owen and Bentham were secularists, but secularist ideas had very little influence on the majority of the nation. But, if most people agreed that religion was to be the basis of education, there were many different opinions as to its content. The sharpest division was between Church and Dissent, and in this period the influence of Dissent was growing. In 1828, with the repeal of the Test and Corporation Acts, Dissenters finally achieved political and social equality. The religious question in English elementary education is too often reduced to a simple pattern— 'Church *v.* Dissent': the division between the strictly denominational and the laxer undenominational viewpoint does not exactly coincide with the division between Churchman and Dissenter. It is certainly true, however, that the two societies, the National Society (1811), inspired by the Anglican clergyman Andrew Bell, and the British and Foreign Society (1814), inspired by the Quaker Joseph Lancaster, did stand, the one for a more strictly doctrinal, the other for a more undenominational attitude to the education of the people. It is true also that, as the societies gathered way, the divisions between them tended to become sharper, and the issue of denominational rivalry more exacerbated. Lancaster's plans, Mrs Trimmer wrote to Bell in 1805, were an organised attempt to '*educate the whole body of the common people, without any regard to the religion of the nation*'.[1] The foundation of the National

---

[1] R. and C. C. Southey, *Life of the Rev. Andrew Bell* (London, 1844), vol. II, p. 136.

Society itself was precipitated by a charity sermon at St Paul's, warning churchmen that they must stand together to promote the welfare of the Establishment. The two societies had by 1830 made a considerable impact on the mass of illiteracy which existed in the country, though there was still a vast amount left to do. How much the progress of primary education in England was held up by religious rivalries it is very difficult to assess. It is certain that, at a time when the State was not itself likely to take any active part, without the societies nothing would have been done at all.

In England religious rivalries were fought out by the churches themselves with the state in the background as the arbiter. In some other countries of Europe the conflict involved the state itself in its relations with the church, and so illustrated one facet of the struggle between individuals or groups and a state organisation growing constantly more powerful. In Napoleonic France the Catholic religion had been defined as one of the fundamental bases of teaching, but there was really little understanding between the state and the religious point of view. Despite attempts to catholicise the schools, the Catholic bourgeoisie tended to regard the state schools as irreligious, and the *lycées* were filled with the sons of civil and military officials who had grown up in an anti-clerical atmosphere and had little use for religion. Under the Restoration the general attitude of Catholic opinion was not to demand the end of the state monopoly and the right to run Catholic schools independently of the state, but to endeavour to bring the existing system under closer Catholic control. In fact the question of state monopoly and educational liberty aroused comparatively little interest until the very last years of the Bourbon regime.

The great issue confronting opinion in France between 1815 and 1830 was, as has been seen in another context, much less liberty than clericalism. It was in the schools that the Catholic reaction enjoyed some of its main triumphs. In 1822 the office of Grand Master was re-established and given to Mgr Frayssinous, Bishop of Hermopolis, who became minister of ecclesiastical affairs (to which public instruction was attached) in 1824. The *École Normale* was suppressed in 1822 and Guizot and Victor Cousin suspended from their professorial chairs. In 1824 primary education, in which the Restoration showed far greater interest than Napoleon had done, was put under the control of the bishops. The *petits séminaires* were growing in number and popularity, and the Jesuits were filtering back into teaching posts. When the Villèle government was replaced by that of Martignac, the Ordinances of 1828 severely limited the pretensions of the Church in educational matters. The bishops lost a great part of their control over the primary schools. Teaching by members of unauthorised congregations, which really meant by the Jesuits, was forbidden. Restrictions were placed on the *petits séminaires*. If the State would not support the claims of the Church, what attitude were Catholics to take? In general they moved towards demanding educational freedom which would enable them to train their children in schools which to them seemed suitable. The interests of the Church, as the Catholic thinker Lamennais now claimed, demanded liberty of education, of conscience and of the press. Liberals might have been expected to share the same point of view. In fact they were too frightened of the influence of the clergy, especially of the Jesuits, to be entirely consistent in their Liberalism.

In the United Netherlands the problem was further complicated by the conflict between the Catholic Church and a Protestant government, between the Dutch and the French languages, and between the national feelings of the Dutch and the Belgians. The government of the Batavian Republic had adopted in 1806 a very comprehensive and effective law on primary education, which included religious instruction of a very broad and undogmatic kind in the spirit of the eighteenth-century Enlightenment. Though the Dutch government after 1815 did not at once introduce this law into the Catholic Belgian provinces, it did take great interest in elementary education there, with resulting difficulties about school books and about the language to be used in the class-room. The official policy of introducing Dutch as the state language in the Flemish provinces of the south was also very unpopular. King William I was very anxious to control both the Catholic and Protestant Churches in the interest of state unity, and his ecclesiastical policy was really Napoleonic in inspiration. The Dutch government was generally hostile to Catholicism and had a good deal of trouble with the hierarchy. One obvious area of friction lay in the education of the clergy, which the government wished to control. In 1825 the closing of the *petits séminaires*—as in France, the clerical schools preparatory to the diocesan seminaries—was decreed. Candidates for the priesthood were to attend the state schools and then go on to a *collegium philosophicum* at Louvain, from which they were to proceed to the seminaries proper. It was further decreed that no priest educated abroad was to hold an ecclesiastical post in the kingdom. As feeling rose in Belgium against the Dutch connexion in the later twenties, the educational question was an important source of the trouble. Freedom of education as well as freedom of the press was one of the demands of the petitioners in the southern provinces in 1829. In 1828 the Belgian Catholics and Liberals made a concordat for common action. The Liberals were encouraged by the fall of the Villèle ministry in France. The Catholics were influenced by the example of O'Connell in Ireland and by the new turn in the ideas of Lamennais. The attacks in the Belgian press on Dutch policy in 1828–30 have already been sketched. In 1830 the government gave up the *collegium philosophicum* and made concessions over the schools and the use of the French language, but these came too late to save the tie between North and South (Chapter XVII. A).

It would of course be an exaggeration to suggest that Church and State were bitter rivals everywhere. In Scandinavia, in Austria and the German States they worked very closely together. Victor Cousin, in his report on German education (1833)[1] speaks of the strength of confessional influences in Germany and, though he considered that in Prussia the clerical spirit was weaker and the governmental spirit more powerful than in the other States, the idea of state authority itself was strongly imbued with religious sanctions. Prussian thinkers saw God and Fatherland as correlative powers and tended to equate orthodoxy with obedience. Cousin's report shows that the Prussian clergy co-operated actively in primary education, and he considered this to be one of the chief reasons for the prosperous condition of the Prussian primary schools. Among other reasons for this he cited the collaboration between the state and the local authorities in school management, and the principle of compulsory attendance, reiterated in the *Allgemeines Landrecht* of 1794, which had also made liberal arrangements in religious matters, ruling that children of a different faith were not to be obliged to accept the religious instruction provided. One especially important instrument in improving the educational standard both of teachers and of pupils was the foundation of numerous teachers' training colleges. Between 1808 and 1826 seventeen new colleges were established, and these were really the spearheads of advance. According to the statistics of 1831 the primary schools of the kingdom contained 99 per cent of the estimated number (some two million) of children aged seven to fourteen. In Austria the standard reached was much lower than in many of the German States, but school ordinances had been made by Maria Theresa, by Joseph II, and by Francis II (Constitution of the German Schools, 1805), and in the Austrian crown lands a considerable proportion of the children received at least some education.

Two other countries in which the government intervened with vigour and success were Holland and Denmark. In the former considerable efforts had been made through private initiative to improve the education of the people in the years before 1789. In 1798 a department of education was set up in the new Batavian Republic. The law on primary education already mentioned formed the permanent basis of the Dutch system. No one was allowed to teach unless he could produce a certificate of competence and a call to a particular school. Each district had a superintendent and all the superintendents formed the provincial board of public instruction. The general code for the

---

[1] V. Cousin, *De l'instruction publique dans quelques pays de l'Allemagne et particulièrement en Prusse*, 3rd ed. (Paris, 1840).

schools was issued by the Ministry of the Interior. When the French scientist Cuvier visited Holland in 1811, he found that almost all children were in schools (though education was not compulsory), that the masters were excellent and well-paid, and that the system of inspection was highly efficient. The creation of a national system in Denmark was originally an offshoot of the reforming impulse which had reorganised Danish rural society. The Great School Commission, which sat from 1789 to 1814, drew up a system for rural schools which was put into effect for the island dioceses in 1806 and for the whole kingdom in 1814. Attendance at the primary schools was made compulsory from the age of seven to confirmation—usually at fourteen (Chapter XVII. B).

England's main contributions to the educational practice of the time were infant schools, in which Owen was a pioneer, and the mutual or Lancasterian system. This system, after the end of the Napoleonic wars, had a great though short-lived influence in Denmark. Alexander I of Russia was interested in it, it was employed in Switzerland by the Dominican educationalist, Father Girard of Fribourg, and it spread widely in the United States. The mutual system had probably been adopted independently by both Bell and Lancaster, though there was much controversy as to its true originator. Bell, when a chaplain at Madras, had become superintendent of a childrens' asylum. Since he found the masters incompetent, he gradually began to get the more advanced boys to teach the others. Once the idea had caught on, the master could, by the use of the senior boys or monitors for passing on his questions, checking the answers, examining the other boys and so on, supervise a very large number of pupils at once. Joseph Lancaster claimed for the system that 'on this plan, *any boy who can read, can teach*; and the inferior boys may do the work usually done by the teachers, in the common mode: for a boy who can read, can teach, *although he knows nothing about it*'.[1] The advantage of the method was, of course, that it was extremely cheap and made possible the beginnings of a general school system with very small resources. Its great drawbacks were that it was rigid and artificial— and so in opposition to the great movement of educational freedom represented by Pestalozzi—and that it did not really recognise the importance and complexity of the work of the teacher. It is not surprising that, when Bell visited Pestalozzi, although he admired him personally he thought that he should dismiss four-fifths of his masters.

The Lancasterian system was a blind alley and was ultimately abandoned everywhere. It did however help to promote interest in primary education in France. The *Société pour l'amélioration de l'enseignement élémentaire*, founded in 1815, which showed great activity

[1] *The Practical Parts of Lancaster's 'Improvements' and Bell's 'Experiment'*, ed. D. Salmon (Cambridge, 1932), p. 33.

in founding schools, favoured it; in 1821 the society's report showed that it was used in over 1500 schools, though after this the number declined. The system was not used in the schools run by the religious congregations, the most famous of which was the Brethren of the Christian Schools. The government showed considerable interest in elementary education in general. In 1816 an appropriation of 50,000 francs was granted, which rose to 100,000 in 1829 and to 300,000 francs in 1830. By that date about half the communes in France had some sort of school, and in 1833 a general primary school law was enacted.

By that date the shadow of industrialism was already moving over Europe, though it had lengthened as yet only over Britain. The Bell–Lancaster methods bore already some of the marks of an industrial civilisation. The mutual system itself was a sort of educational mass production. The connection between division of labour and mechanisation of plant both in industry and in education was in fact stressed a great deal at the time. Bell said of his method that 'like the steam engine, or spinning machinery, it diminishes labour and multiplies work'.[1] Bentham, whose ideas on educational matters were closely affected by Lancaster and Bell, wrote in *Chrestomathia* of 'profit maximised, expense minimised'.[2] Owen's very different ideas were seen in the first theory of education designed for the conditions of an industrial society. He saw that, if education was to be effective, it must not end with the child, and he wanted to provide further instruction for adults through evening lectures. The same idea lay behind the Mechanics' Institutes which grew up in Great Britain in the 1820's, and the Society for the Promotion of Useful Knowledge, founded in 1827 under the inspiration of Henry Brougham, for the dissemination of useful literature. But here literacy might run very close to politics. If men could read, they might criticise, and the official view in England as everywhere in Europe was, as Lord Kenyon said, that any criticism was likely '*to make the people discontented with the Constitution* under which they live'.[3] A correspondent wrote to Bell in 1809 about the danger that popular education which was not based on fixed tenets might 'give birth to the most latitudinarian principles, both in religion and government'.[4] It is noteworthy that Bentham himself had found it necessary in *Chrestomathia* to deny that better education of the people would lead to the breakdown of social distinctions and had cited both Scotland and Germany as examples to the contrary.

The Germans were less sure of their own immunity, having their own fears on the subject. von Altenstein, the Prussian minister of education,

---

[1] *The Practical Parts of Lancaster's 'Improvements' and. . . . Bell's 'Experiment'*, p. 69.
[2] *Works*, ed. J. Bowring (Edinburgh, 1843), vol. VIII, p. 25.
[3] W. H. Wickwar, *The Struggle for the Freedom of the Press, 1819–32* (London, 1928), p. 26.
[4] R. and C. C. Southey, *Andrew Bell*, vol. II, pp. 599–600.

did not believe that a system of primary education which gave the common people more than the bare necessaries of knowledge would raise them out of their proper sphere. His sovereign Frederick William III admitted that he himself was quite confused. Had popular education its proper limits or not? If so, what were the limits to be? If not, then there could be no restraint at all. The problem with which the king was struggling affected the whole of European society and extended far beyond the bounds within which the king formulated it. It was the problem of a society on the move, loosed from its moorings, moving through troubled waters to an unknown destination. Liberals and reactionaries, romantics and classicists, clericals and secularists—the adversaries clashed in schools and universities, in societies and salons, in the press and the parliaments. The State had tried to educate for its own purposes and to form opinion on its own lines. The peoples of Europe were stirring uneasily under its tutelage, and demanding a greater control of their own destiny.

CHAPTER VIII

SOME ASPECTS OF THE ARTS IN EUROPE

A. THE VISUAL ARTS

ALTHOUGH this period was one of the most brilliant and productive in the history of European art, its achievements do not appear as the expression of a single religious or philosophical principle. No period seems so full of contradictions in its aims, its personalities and its modes of expression; these contradictions are at once apparent from a comparison between the work of David and Prud'hon, Turner and Constable or Delacroix and Ingres. In architecture a similar gulf appears between the supreme urbanity of Carlton House or Malmaison and the cyclopean fantasies of Boullée or Ledoux. Anomalies multiply as the period develops; in ten years Jacques-Louis David progressed from the role of official painter under the Convention to that of *premier peintre de l'Empereur*. Ingres, denounced at first as 'Gothic' and as a *barbu*, came to be regarded as the archpriest of academic convention, while the erudite and aristocratic Delacroix became the pre-eminent exponent of colour, violence and exoticism.

At the opening of the period these complexities are not fully apparent. The outstanding artistic event of the last quarter of the eighteenth century was the appearance of David's *Oath of the Horatii* (shown in Paris, 1785). In this picture the severely monumental style which had died with Nicholas Poussin was so powerfully revived that it dominated French art for a whole generation. Its subject—exemplary civic virtue and disdain of private misfortune—foretells David's personal role as a revolutionary. Its grave, simplified manner, its extreme clarity of space and the calculated grouping of its major figures in superimposed lateral planes, terminated the rococo taste which had survived three generations. Only the sensuous group of lamenting women at the right of the picture recalls David's youthful contact with Boucher, and the subdued fire of his coarse-grained execution his lifelong regard for Rubens.

The significance of the *Horatii* is not diminished by the fact that David had his precursors. Theorists such as Winckelmann had already advocated a return to calm and simplicity, and had set forth principles of composition similar to David's. His disciple Raphael Mengs (1728–79) had tried to interpret these on canvas, though his rather pedestrian figure groups merely re-animate forms surviving from Italian baroque classicism. Diderot had insisted that moral values should precede sensuous pleasure and praised David's master Vien for his *savante simplicité* and *pureté ingénue*. Such artists and theoreticians had merely begun a gentle diversion towards neo-classicism; David's masterpiece gave the movement sufficient momentum to dominate official taste for half a century.

Though this achievement alone would rank David as a great master, it does not explain the esteem of Géricault, nor Delacroix's description of him, made in 1860, as 'father of the whole modern school of painting and sculpture'. His full range first appears in the *St Roch begging the Virgin to intercede for the plague-stricken* (1780), in which the dramatic arrangement on opposed diagonals, as well as the fiery brushwork of the years preceding the *Horatii*, clearly point to the influence of Rubens. A further aspect of David's art appears in the unflinching presentation of the erupting sores of the plague victims. Only this merging of scientific realism with baroque principles can explain Géricault's regard for David. This realism reaches its zenith in the *Dead Marat* of 1793 (Brussels). Meanwhile in his largest State paintings scenes of current political history appear on an heroic scale previously reserved for religious and allegorical subjects. These works are painted with exact documentation which itself reflects a new scientific outlook and was introduced by the American painter J. S. Copley. Among them the *Tennis Court Oath*, commissioned in 1791 by the Constituent Assembly, for which only an elaborate study was executed, was the prototype of a succession of Napoleonic and later state paintings by David and his many disciples.

The period 1795 to 1814 brought no significant innovations in David's work; under Directorate and Napoleonic patronage it acquired a certain grace and delicacy of contour—perhaps the result of a study of Hellenistic sculpture not found in the revolutionary years. As he and his school absorbed an increasing share of state patronage, he came to be regarded as the defender of a sterile classicism. This view—still not quite extinct—can be justly applied to those pupils of David who reiterated his formal devices and replaced his powerful handling by flaccid modelling and mechanical contours. On the other hand, the diversity of power disclosed by David's more talented pupils is a reflection of the many-sided character of David's own gifts, whose components, isolated and explored by individuals, were to nourish two (and probably three) distinct lines of development in French painting. These are still most conveniently defined as 'classical', 'romantic' and 'realist', and their elements—more than one of which may appear in the work of a single artist—are of paramount importance for the whole of French nineteenth-century painting.

Among the major intermediaries between David and the generation of Delacroix was Antoine-Jean Gros (1771–1835). Though devoted to the classical principles of his master, he was swept to success as a painter of Napoleon's campaigns, beginning in Italy at the age of twenty-five. His first (and most romantic) portrait of Bonaparte, now at Versailles, records his crossing of the bridge at Arcola. Gros, like his master, admired Rubens whose turbulent spirit animates the neo-classic framework of his work. The full importance of Gros's position in the transition from Davidian to romantic art can best be seen in his *Napoleon visiting the plague victims at Jaffa* (1804; Louvre). Here the subject is one of the ancillary horrors of war; it also emphasises the supernatural curative (and self-preservative) powers of the emperor, who replaces the traditional saint. The Islamic setting moreover foretells the exoticism of the later romantics; and though Gros draws on Hellenistic and late Michelangelesque forms in some of the figures, a realism surpassing that of David's *St Roch* gives credibility to a supernaturally heroic theme. This mixing of classical, renaissance, Islamic and realist elements provides a valuable key to the complexities of the period.

The battlepieces which brought Gros so many honours cannot now be discussed, nor the portraits which range from a sensitive and fluent one of himself at the age of twenty (Toulouse) to that of the ageing Mme Recamier (*c.* 1824–5; Zagreb).

While Gros was mainly concerned with the external aspect and the personalities of Napoleonic history, his fellow-pupil Anne-Louis Girodet (1757–1824) adapted the forms of neo-classicism to imaginative and legendary subjects. His *Sleep of Endymion* (1792; Louvre) demonstrates the compatibility of classical forms and a romantic mood. Girodet's principal devices—irrational light and shadow, and a precise, delicate and elongated contour enclosing soft but bloodless modelling—suggest the contrivances of the theatre. Nevertheless, his *Ossian receiving Napoleon's generals* (commissioned in 1801 for Malmaison) reflects a taste for romantic fantasy shared by Napoleon himself, while the mood of the *Burial of Atala* looks forward to the religious revival of the restoration.

Girodet's achievements in this field are overshadowed by the work of a more profound and original artist, Pierre-Paul Prud'hon (1758–1823) who in the course of his education was to absorb the teaching of the Church and that of J-J. Rousseau as well. He studied at Dijon under Devosge, and in 1784 won the *prix de Rome*, having already entered on a disastrous marriage. In Italy he studied the paintings of Leonardo, Raphael, Correggio and Pietro da Cortona, whose Barberini Palace ceiling he was commissioned to copy. After his return he was compelled to work at book-illustration, which he did with a charm and delicacy foretelling the soft *chiaroscuro* which was to appear in much of his painting and evoke comparison with Correggio. David, against whose triumph Prud'hon (and the ageing Greuze) stood almost alone, compared him in respectful tolerance to Watteau and Boucher. Though Prud'hon was always supported by a small but very devoted circle, he gained little official notice until the turn of the century. By 1796 however, in the *Georges Anthony* (Dijon) and *Mme Anthony and her Children* (Lyon) he had produced two of the finest portraits of the romantic era, while his free and lyrical treatment of classical and erotic subjects was also gaining attention. In 1799 his public career began with a commission to paint a ceiling at St-Cloud, *Truth led by Wisdom descending from the Skies* (Louvre). His Italian training gave him the power to handle great allegories with a universality and conviction hardly excelled since the sixteenth century, and in these works the charming decorator appears as a powerful manipulator of figures in action. His masterpiece is perhaps the *Justice and Divine Vengeance pursuing Crime*, completed in 1808 for the Palais de Justice, in which Prud'hon characteristically adapts the biblical theme of Cain and Abel as a basis for a secular work, and this, together with the intensely dramatic quality of his design, raises it far above the empty abstraction of much state allegorical painting. This work was copied by Géricault, whose simplification of form by strong light and shade is often foreshadowed by Prud'hon. A favourite of the Bonaparte family, Prud'hon painted the portrait of the Empress Josephine (Louvre), and became drawing master to Marie-Louise, who in 1810 commissioned the *Venus and Adonis* (Wallace Collection). These associations may have deprived him of important religious commissions at the Restoration; it was however a religious work, the great *Crucifixion* of 1822 (Louvre), which closed his somewhat tragic career.

Théodore Géricault (1791–1824) was one of those artists born with an easy command of the innovations of their predecessors. Everything that the Napoleonic and revolutionary schools could teach, he amplified with his creative imagination, the power of his hand and his habit of factual observation. Given a normal lifetime, he would probably have achieved a synthesis of the heroic mould of David's neo-classicism, the passion of romantic art, and the new scientific outlook of realism; without him these were to pursue for the most part separate courses, though their meeting-points were often of special significance in nineteenth-century art. Like his first master Carle Vernet, he was a devotee of horse-racing and of anglomania. In 1810 he joined the atelier of Guérin, one of the most academic of David's pupils; but among these Gros was clearly his real exemplar. Géricault's large *Officer of the Guard* (Salon of 1812; now Louvre) is close in many ways to Gros's *Murat on Horseback*, though the twisting movement of Géricault's horseman, and the wildness of his mount and of the battle-field are the result of a more imaginative study of Rubens than Gros ever made. *The Wounded Cuirassier* (1814; Louvre) takes a more personal view of battle; the incident it depicts is passive, while its new mood of introspection is of the essence of romanticism. In 1816 Géricault went to Rome, and at a time when most students of antiquity looked at its vases, cameos and reliefs in linear terms, Géricault studied late antique horse-tamer groups and casts of the Parthenon friezes as a sculptor in terms of mass broken by strong shadow. Like Goethe he was fascinated by the annual race of wild stallions down the Corso, and it is character-istic that a large series of studies of this scene is the chief memorial of his stay in Rome. He preferred Michelangelo to Raphael, studying closely all the frescoes of the Sistine Chapel, and he was impressed (as was David) by Caravaggio's naturalism. All these influences, with the habit of exact documentation, were to play a part in the two years' work which now led to the *Raft of the Medusa*, a painting of anonymous heroism inspired by Gros's *Plague Victims at Jaffa*. The subject in-volved Géricault in precise studies of the dead, the dying and the insane, all of them landmarks of realist painting. Intended as a protest against official incompetence following a disaster at sea, it introduces such romantic attributes as a negro who shares the chance of survival and—expressive of man's impotence against nature—the sea itself. The finished work, a failure at the Salon of 1819, was sent on tour to Great Britain where Géricault followed it in 1820, establishing one of the Anglo-French artistic links which are of such importance in the first decades of the century. Here he painted dynamic instantaneous pictures of racing at Epsom, and made his lithographs and drawings of life in London, such as the *Coal Cart*, the *Adelphi Vaults* and *Capital Punishment*.

Of the three years left to him after returning to Paris, the most impressive works are the portraits of inmates of the Salpetrière, depict-ing various states of insanity (1821–4). Far from emphasising the horror of these subjects, his attitude is both scientific and humane. He died as the result of a jumping accident in 1824, full of ambition and conscious that his work had hardly begun.

Eugène Delacroix (1798–1863) who entered Guérin's studio in 1816, became Géricault's intimate companion and was to some extent his spiritual heir. With him French romantic painting reaches limits which it could not have passed without employing symbolism and abstraction; but of his forty years' activity only the first ten are within the scope of this chapter. Delacroix, who came of a high bourgeois family and was a reputed son of Talleyrand, began his training at a moment when the order of the First Empire had collapsed and given place to a new era of faith and dogma. His complex personality, best understood from his journals, is easier to comprehend if this ambience of political reaction—the aftermath of a world convulsion—is remembered. With his classical erudition, he was always to retain a respect for the order and clarity of French tradition. He was also conversant not only with Byron, Scott and Goethe, but with Dante, Shakespeare and Tasso, in all of whose works he was to find subjects.

Delacroix's first appearance at the Salon was made in 1822 with *Dante and Vergil in the Infernal Regions*; its subject, though taking its origin in medieval Christianity, draws contemporary interest from the physical and psychological reaction of its human protagonists to the dark and supernatural scene, and from the unprecedented luminosity of the colouring. The eclecticism of this picture shows how his powerful personality was nevertheless guided by familiarity with the masterpieces collected at the Louvre after the great campaigns. Though the influence of Rubens is visible throughout the picture, the swimming figures of the damned are clearly taken from the *Last Judgment* of Michelangelo. In his later work Delacroix shows an understanding of Venetian colouring; while among English painters who played an important part in his artistic make-up, Bonington and Constable are outstanding. The story of Delacroix's repainting of parts of his *Massacre of Chios* (Salon, 1824) after seeing Constable's *Hay Wain* exhibited with a group of the Englishman's works in that year, is one of the best-known anecdotes of nineteenth-century painting. This work not only adds to the romantic iconography of anonymous heroism, but expresses the artist's personal sympathy with the aspirations and tragedy of the Greeks. His exotic portrayal of Turkish riders and their captives derives strongly from Byron, and here Delacroix first employs small strokes of pure colour—yellows, pinks and greens—in such a way as to merge at a short distance into the flesh tints of the living or dying victims. This technique was to make him memorable to later generations of painters. Delacroix visited England in 1825, meeting Bonington, Etty, Wilkie and Lawrence. Both in England and in France he studied medieval and Byzantine jewelry, bookbindings, mosaics, tombs and armour; such material appears in the *Death of Sardanapalus* (1827), which displays animals, jewels, rich fabrics, slaves, women and violent death; while the *Pandects of Justinian*, commissioned in 1826 for the Conseil d'État, reveals his fascination for the last phases of the ancient world. Like Géricault, he adopted the new medium of lithography; in his nineteen prints of *Faust* (1828) the velvety *chiaroscuro* of the medium is brilliantly exploited.

At the close of our period, when Delacroix, at thirty-two, was leader of the French romantic school, academic painting had come to be dominated by Jean-Auguste-Dominique Ingres (1780–1867). Entering the academy of Toulouse at the age of twelve, he there developed an unshakeable taste for Raphael. He went to Paris in 1796, entering the atelier of David who, recognising his gift for design, employed him on his portrait of Mme Récamier. Ingres however became associated with a group of students led by Maurice Quai and known as *barbus* or *primitifs*, for whose archaising tastes David's own revolution did not go far enough. Their inspiration came from descriptive volumes of antiquities—cameos, vases and reliefs—newly excavated in southern Europe and engraved in such a way as to emphasise and harden their linear character. The literary preferences of this group were for Homer, Ossian and the Bible, and to their influence on the young Ingres was added that of Flaxman, whose engravings for Homer, Aeschylus and Dante were well-known in France. This striving after archaism and abstract purity bears no relation to David's moralist–classical purge of rococo forms; Ingres pursued linear purity as such with fanatical zeal, though in his *prix de Rome* picture, *Achilles receiving the Ambassadors of Agamemnon* (1801), this purity is somewhat muted. His *Jupiter and Thetis*, of which the first version probably dates from 1805, though an early work, shows this linear abstraction in a form as accomplished as it ever reached in a career notable for a kind of progressive crystallisation. Ingres's tonal key, like that of several innovators of this period, is extremely high.

In a group of early portraits, hardly excelled at any later date, Ingres made brilliant use of the same principles, for instance in three portraits of members of the Rivière family (1805; Louvre) and in that of Ingres's colleague Granet (Aix-en-Provence), painted in Rome in 1807. Notable too were his extraordinarily accomplished portrait drawings, mainly done during his stay of no less than eighteen years in Italy. As a southerner he was more at home in Rome than in Paris, where his work was at first received without enthusiasm. His output of superb portraits continued during this period, and he produced some masterly figure paintings, among them the Valpinçon *Bather* of 1808 and the *Grande Odalisque* of 1814 (both in the Louvre). Constant reference to Raphael and to the monumental art of Italy brought about a weakening of his mastery of linear design. This departure from his early archaistic style may explain the popular success of his feebly Raphaelesque *Vow of Louis XIII*; he returned in triumph to Paris, was elected to the *Institut* and opened an important teaching studio. In this capacity he came to rank as *chef d'école* of the academic painters and as a crusader against the example of Delacroix. That Ingres, whose own departure from the principles of David took a fundamentally romantic (i.e. primitivist) direction, should find himself leader of the resistance against romanticism was ironical; it is possible that with fewer inhibitions and a humane education his talent might have developed in unsuspected directions. But it was to Ingres and his undeviating formal abstraction that painters returned after the realist experiment of the 1860's and 1870's had surfeited itself.

Though Gainsborough died in 1788 and Sir Joshua Reynolds in 1792, the English tradition of portraiture, deriving from Titian and Van Dyck but modified by the naturalism and humanity of the eighteenth century, seemed unchallenged. Though the first British master of landscape, Richard Wilson, had died in 1782, and history painting had claimed some attention from most leading painters, almost every artist of repute in 1790 was first and foremost a portrait painter. William Beechey (1753–1839), and later John Hoppner (1758–1810), remained close to the manner of Reynolds. George Romney (1734–98) continued to paint, while John Opie (1761–1807) and Sir Henry Raeburn (1756–1823), the former powerful and subdued, the latter brilliantly endowed but lacking in penetration, were both established. Reynolds's most gifted successor, Sir Thomas Lawrence (1769–1830), had made a brilliant *début* at the Royal Academy in 1789 with a full-length portrait of Queen Charlotte (National Gallery), in which an aristocratic simplicity inherited from Reynolds is enhanced by a romantic light which, grafted to the native tradition of portraiture, was to be the key to his extraordinary success. Lawrence's full-length portraits of the 1790's were not excelled by any later work on this scale, though some later ones reveal astonishing penetration; for instance the *John Julius Angerstein* (Royal Academy, 1816). Lawrence's portraits show how by the end of the eighteenth century English society, though more anxious than ever to appear in aristocratic guise, was composed increasingly of the financiers and professional leaders who frequently sat for him; conversely, one of his finest royal portraits (1822; Wallace Collection) shows George IV himself as a man of affairs, wearing black and pausing to look up from his papers.

While the painters of London society were acquiring celebrity in a world where the principles of Newtonian science and mathematics, now applied to industry and commerce, opened unlimited prospects of material wealth, the solitary genius of William Blake, poet, engraver, visionary and thinker, was evolving the challenge to scientific materialism expressed in his early lyric verses and his later symbolic and prophetic books. The art of Blake (1757–1827) embodied almost all of the primary characteristics of romanticism. His *Songs of Innocence* (1789) and their illustrations express a deeply felt, naïve lyricism, comparable in its importance to David's far more spectacular return in 1785 to another kind of simplicity. It is characteristic that Blake, a working engraver, should have evolved an experimental technique exactly matching the spontaneity of his early verse, in the printing of which text and illustration are merged into an organic whole, as if in protest against the mechanical constriction of Augustan type-setting and make-up. Blake's progressive disillusion with rationalism (even with the rationalist element in French revolutionary thought), and his deepening realisation of the wrongs of suppressing creative energy and the capacities of the senses, led him to produce an encyclopaedic system of symbolism, peopled by the personified evils of a materialist world. To give visual expression to these concepts Blake drew not only on a vivid imagination but on a varied and unorthodox store of visual material. Gothic tomb-sculpture, engravings after Michelangelo's early and late frescoes, certain neo-classical forms and the contemporary work of Mortimer and Fuseli, were absorbed and merged. A highly irrational sense of space and scale, a dramatic *chiaroscuro* and a system of broken, flame-like colour mark out Blake's symbolic illustrations from his early lyrical ones. These characteristics, emerging in his famous design *The Ancient of Days* (1794), are seen even more effectively in *Pity* (Tate Gallery) and in the illustrations to the *Prophetic Books* begun in 1797. Blake had now perfected a complex technique in which offset printing for large colour masses is used in conjunction with an impression (often relief-etched) from a copper plate, with hand-colouring as a final stage. This can be studied in the terrifying *Nebuchadnezzar* (1795; Tate Gallery).

After a relatively tranquil period at Felpham in Sussex (1800–3), Blake returned to London and devoted much of the next seventeen years to reflection on the subject of man's redemption and of the sacrifice of Christ on the Cross; many of his designs now relate to the Passion, among these being *Albion before the crucified Christ* and the *Soul embraced by God* (c. 1818) illustrating his *Jerusalem*. In 1821 appeared the seventeen wood-engravings for Vergil's *Eclogues*, which though tiny in scale express an exalted elegiac mood which was to pervade the work of Blake's followers Samuel Palmer, Edward Calvert and George Richmond. Perhaps Blake's most important late work is the series of designs for the *Book of Job* (1823); the disturbed and poignant series illustrating the *Divina Commedia* of Dante was unfinished at his death. As an artist Blake, in spite of Rossetti's admiration, was to remain for a century almost unknown.

Though Blake made no impact on the supremacy of the principles of Sir Joshua Reynolds, another Londoner of no less obscure birth was shortly to establish within the Royal Academy an art which defied almost all its canons. Born in 1775, Joseph Mallord William Turner worked as a topographical artist while studying at the antique school of the Royal Academy (and from such drawings and prints as he could borrow). In the mid-1790's he was employed with Thomas Girtin (1775–1802) in copying and completing watercolours by J. R. Cozens. Turner responded powerfully to the scale and nervous imagination displayed in these drawings, while Cozens's methods—elision of the fore-ground, sweeping atmospheric perspective and exaggerated scale—recur through all Turner's work. Already a Royal Academician in 1802, he did not begin to show his full power as a colourist until his visit to Paris and the Alps in that year. Intensive study at the Louvre of Italian masters (above all of Titian) underlies the science which now came to the aid of his penetrating eye. His originality, unlike Blake's, did not deprive him of official success. His claim for English landscape as the equal of any class of subject in any school was obdurately pressed until his supremacy was assured, his large Academy pieces being frequently painted in the mould of some unchallengeable earlier school. Between 1801 and 1805 appeared large sea-pieces emulating—and in some respects excelling—the styles of Jacob Ruisdael, Backhuysen, Van de Velde and C-J. Vernet; while about 1815 he embarked on a grandiose series intended to rival Claude. Meanwhile, he continued to produce works like the *Thames* panels (*c.* 1807; Tate Gallery), indicating more clearly his private interests—an exquisite balance of hot and cold colour, and complexities of form and distance within a high, limited tonal key. Larger pictures in this manner include *Somer Hill* (1811; National Gallery of Scotland) and *A Frosty Morning* (1813; National Gallery). He continued to publish and by 1814 had arranged for engravings after his watercolours to be sold by subscription; thus ensuring the independence which enabled him later to defy his critics.

In 1819, at the central point of his career, Turner visited Italy. In Rome and Naples he studied the old masters and antique sculptures as assiduously as a young student; and Venice, superseding Rome as a centre for fashionable tourism, became for him a primary source of material. Many large oils of the 1820's are of Mediterranean subjects, though many were less successful than the masterly drawings for publications such as the *Rivers of England* (1821–7) and *Harbours of England* (1826–8). At the end of the 1820's important changes occur in Turner's style. His true imaginative fire reappears in *Ulysses Deriding Polyphemus* (1829; National Gallery); while the brilliant watercolours made on blue paper at Petworth House (*c.* 1830; British Museum) mark an important simplification and flattening of Turner's colour-masses, which helped him to achieve the condensation and grandeur of alpine and other later watercolours. Turner now ceased to emulate earlier masters and brought to bear the expressive potentialities of fire, air and water, atmospheric conditions, rain, clouds, mountains and waves. Ruskin saw that Turner, by exploiting the anatomy of all nature, was challenging those who regarded the human body as the supreme organ of expression in art; and from 1830 to the end of his career Turner produced the masterpieces which justify this. Among the finest are *Fingal's Cave* (1832), *The Burning of the Houses of Parliament*

(1835), *Slavers* (1840), *Steamboat off a Harbour's Mouth* (1842),
Norham Castle (*c*. 1840) and the group of seascapes of the 1840's
(National and Tate Galleries) in which Turner abandons the formal
conventions he had acquired so painstakingly and, using a more
brilliant tonal key than ever, bases his pictorial effects, both static and
violent, entirely on atmospheric and colour perspective. In these
Turner appears as the supreme romantic painter; but they are challenged
by many water-colours—particularly of alpine subjects—in which he
was unhampered by the competitive conditions of the Royal Academy.

Turner died in 1851, having enriched himself and the national collections, with the full support of a generation of academicians brought
up to regard landscape as an inferior branch of painting. John
Constable (1776–1837), who lacked both the virtuosity of Turner and his
skill in worldly affairs, met with a slow response to his less sophisticated
talent. A miller's son, accustomed to observe the wind and sky, he
attracted the interest of the connoisseur Sir George Beaumont at
an early age, and so came to know works by both Claude and Girtin.
Constable did not study at the Royal Academy Schools until he was
twenty-three; but was soon copying works by Annibale Carracci,
Gaspard Poussin, Jacob Ruysdael and Wilson. At the same time he
was sensibly advised by Benjamin West that 'light and shade never
stand still'; while exact topography and an affection for Gainsborough's
early woodland subjects laid the foundation of a love for the local and
particular contrasting strongly with Turner's remoteness and diffusion.
Constable began to exhibit at the Academy in 1802, when he painted
a small view of Dedham which, though based in method on Claude,
already has the immediacy which is the essence of his own charm.
Stoke-by-Nayland (1807; National Gallery) shows this quality too:
it reveals Constable's pleasure not in a picturesque site but in a familiar
spot suddenly transformed by sunlight. This faculty of transforming the
familiar by dew or sunlight or cloud-shadow was Constable's peculiar
contribution to romantic art. After 1810 his canvases become more
ambitious in scale and content, perhaps as a result of his study of the
great *Château de Steen* of Rubens, acquired a few years before by Sir
George Beaumont. The influence of Rubens's technique appears in
Dedham Vale (1811; Elton Hall, Northamptonshire); but it is clear
from Constable's small oil sketches of this date that he was aiming at a
new immediacy of time as well as of place. The history of his next
fifteen years' work is that of a struggle to present a particular scene at a
particular moment, on the scale of a six-foot canvas—this scale being
chosen not for its suitability for such a task, but for the sake of establishing landscape as a reputable medium. Though Turner had achieved
this long before, his carefully chosen types of heroic landscape, in the
mould of earlier masters, were far more acceptable than Constable's

raw pastorals, whose vivid sap-green met with the hostility often reserved for unexpected truths. His ambition was first realised in the *White Horse* (1819; Frick Collection, U.S.A.). This was followed by *Stratford Mill* (1820) and by the justly famous *Hay Wain* (1821; National Gallery) equalled only by *The Leaping Horse* (Royal Academy, 1825). In these last two works Constable's extraordinarily difficult problem was triumphantly solved. Such works cannot be repeated, and it is remarkable that so many of Constable's large canvases of the 1820's are successful; his small sketches, many on paper or card, are among the most delightful works of the whole century.

The first important German painter of the period, Asmus Jakob Carstens (1754–98), was born in Schleswig. After studying at the Copenhagen Academy and at Lübeck he travelled in 1783 to Italy; unable to reach Rome, he visited Milan and Mantua, where the turbulent art of Giulio Romano stirred his proud and somewhat aggressive spirit. After returning to Berlin and teaching at the Academy he went in 1792 to Rome, remaining until his death. Though his forms are in the neo-classic mould, the darkness and melancholy which pervade his designs, and his tragic personal history, mark him out as a forerunner of romanticism.

Among his followers, Eberhard Wächter (1762–1862) and Gottlieb Schick (1776–1812) had, before coming under his influence, absorbed in France the teaching of David, and their work, particularly the portraits of Schick, possesses something of French breadth and humanity. Joseph Anton Koch (1768–1839) though known chiefly as a leading exponent of landscape in the neo-classic manner, was, after reaching Rome in 1795, influenced by Carstens, whose work, he claimed, helped him shake off the inhibitions of his academic training. His landscapes, though treated with a neo-classical clarity and order, are frequently of alpine and mountain subjects and often depict the forests, mists and waterfalls which make up a large part of romantic topography in the early nineteenth century.

By far the greatest of the German romantic landscape painters was Caspar David Friedrich (1774–1840), who, born on the Baltic coast, studied at the Copenhagen Academy (1794–8) and lived mainly in Dresden. His exaggeration of scale and distance, which has some affinity with that of Turner and J. R. Cozens, was heightened by effects of light and silhouette to create a sense of infinite stillness and vastness; his figures, always tiny, usually gaze introspectively into the depths of the picture. Friedrich's *Cathedral in the Mountains* (Düsseldorf), *Moon Rising over the Sea* (1823; Berlin) and *Graveyard under Snow* (1819) exemplify his highly individual manner. Among his followers should be mentioned Johann Christian Dahl (1788–1857), a Norwegian by birth, whose landscapes, loosened and humanised by contact with Dutch (and possibly English) art are an important contribution to early *plein-air* painting. While Dahl's oil sketches of the Bay of Naples have affinities with Corot, his studies of cloud formations, like those of Constable, disclose an interest, shared by Goethe, in the classification of meteorological phenomena.

The art of Philip Otto Runge (1777–1810), the most ambitious of the German romantics, is heavily weighted by the elaboration and complexity of his pictorial schemes. Steeped in the mysticism of Jakob Böhme and in the ideas of Wackenrode, Novalis, Tieck and Hölderlin, his fundamentally neo-classical pictorial method, with its fierce contours and harsh tonality, was hardly adapted to a pantheistic expression of the infinite. In his well-known portraits, however, such as that of his parents and children (1806; Hamburg) his talent as an observer and craftsman is brought to bear with more success.

The failure of the so-called Nazarenes to achieve more than academic importance in the history of European art also results from their attempt to express a sincere and newly-found spirituality in an idiom best suited to a materialist and documentary presentation of anecdotic subject-matter.

Francisco José de Goya y Lucientes (1746–1828) was born before David and worked far from the artistic metropolis of his time. In spite of this he not only belongs unquestionably to the first rank among painters; he was at least the equal of David as a moralist; his realism is equalled only by that of Géricault, while his exploration of the remoter layers of the imagination has no parallel except in literature until comparatively recent times. He was born at Fuentetodos in Aragon and studied in Saragossa and Madrid before visiting Parma and Rome in 1771. Returning to Spain in that year he carried out religious paintings in oil and fresco, and from 1775 worked for seventeen years for the royal tapestry workshops, whose director was the German neo-classical painter Raphael Mengs. In his painted designs for this medium, mostly of rococo genre subjects, his powers began at length to be revealed, and in 1778, having access to the royal palace, he discovered the art of Velazquez, which contributed greatly to the superb directness and simplicity of his portraits. By 1780 he was one of the king's painters, and though in portraiture as in other fields his development was slow, he now became a wealthy and sought-after member of the Madrid society which he depicted. Even his royal portraits (Charles II, 1806; Madrid) could be merciless in their realism; but all his portraits display a universality and simplicity reminiscent of the greatest painters of the Venetian and earlier Spanish schools. In 1793 Goya, after a serious illness, became deaf; moreover, freed by his wealth from slavery to commissions, he began to paint subjects in which, as he said, fantasy and invention were given play. His palette also began to employ the sombre greys which distinguish some of his finest work, while in 1799 appeared the *Caprichos*, the first of this great series of etchings. In 1808 the outbreak of war against Napoleon brought a new crisis; the society which had nourished him collapsed and, once a supporter of French reformism, he now witnessed the scenes of horror which led to some of his most terrifying conceptions (*Desastres de la Guerra*, 1808–15). Further illness in 1819 and revulsion at the French re-occupation of Spain in 1823 heightened the distress of the ageing artist; his nightmare etchings of the *Proverbios* (*Disparates*) were executed before 1820. He now produced some fine and highly unconventional portraits, and religious paintings such as the *Garden of Olives* (1819). Some of his finest genre paintings date from his voluntary exile in Bordeaux, which lasted from 1824 until his death.

Among the neo-classic sculptors John Flaxman (1755–1826), known in England for his exquisitely-contoured reliefs and soft modelling, influenced European art at the turn of the century by his designs illustrating Dante and Aeschylus. Antonio Canova (1757–1822) made large figure sculptures of the leaders of Napoleonic Europe in a rigidly antique mould, but certain funerary monuments and also his maquettes and drawings reveal a dynamism and drama of baroque derivation. Bertel Thorwaldsen (1770–1844), like Canova, having reached a cold perfection and immense fame, failed to achieve lasting influence on European art. Influenced by early classical Greek rather than Hellenistic sculpture, his figures none the less betray a rather superficial aspect of the romanticism of their age.

The comparatively sterile neo-classic phase in European sculpture was succeeded in France by one of great dramatic force tempered by a new realism. Indeed, though his output as a sculptor was small, Théodore Géricault was a founder of this school. François Rude (1784–1855) executed the splendid relief of the *Departure of 1792* on the Arc de Triomphe de l'Etoile in Paris, though this and the more profound *Awakening of Napoleon* (Fixin, near Dijon) were completed outside the period of this review. Antoine-Louis Barye (1796–1875) was by 1830 producing his masterly bronze animal groups, and the splendid caricature models of Daumier date from immediately after 1830. David d'Angers (1788–1856) and Jean-Jacques Pradier (1790–1852) were among the most successful romantic sculptors and are attracting renewed critical attention.

This period is of special importance for the history of architecture, and marks the beginning of a revolution still far from complete. A fundamental break in stylistic continuity was accompanied by a series of radical changes in the function and scale of buildings and in the science of building itself, constantly accelerated by the new pressures of population, commerce, industry and financial credit. The finest buildings of the period include Soane's Bank of England, and in France the markets and the Bourse.

Most of these manifestations take their origin, not so much in the rise of the romantic movement, as in the application of scientific method. The exact documentation of historical styles which led at last to the collapse of inherited tradition began in the seventeenth century with the *Édifices antiques de Rome* (1682) of Desgodetz, whose main purpose was the correction of inconsistencies in the measurements of Palladio, Serlio and many others. There followed throughout the eighteenth century a succession of exact publications, first of Roman antiquities and later of monuments in Naples, Sicily, Dalmatia, Greece, Egypt and the Near East. Such works not only lent authority to departures from the Vitruvian canon; through them architects learned of the subtle gravity of the Doric order, the astylar masses of Egyptian architecture, and the spatial (rather than sculptural) architecture of late antiquity.

In France this revived historical science was matched by an interest in structural engineering of profound importance for architecture. The *Corps des Ponts et Chaussées*, formed at the beginning of the eighteenth century, and its school, founded in 1750, were increasingly respected by the architects and theorists who preached a return to structural fundamentals. Among these were the Abbé Laugier, whose *Essai sur l'architecture* (1753) urges the reduction of architectural elements to those of a primitive hut, and ridicules the use of features whose structural purpose has been forgotten. The theorists Algarotti and Milizia adopted a similar rationalism, and several architects adopted these principles, reinforcing them with a scientific study of structures and materials. Notable among these were J. R. Perronet (1708–94), head of the *École des Ponts et Chaussées*, and J. G. Soufflot (1713–80), architect of what is now the Panthéon and one of the first students of Gothic structural techniques. The great theorists of structure, Rondelet (1743–1829) and Durand (1760–1834), are the heirs of these pioneers.

The Revolution delayed the fruition of this alliance between structural science and a widened stylistic vocabulary until the turn of the century, and the first years of the period are remarkable mainly for the designs of C. L. Ledoux (1736–1806) and E. L. Boullée (1728–99). Ledoux, in his thirty-five gatehouses built round Paris for the tax-farmers just before the Revolution, had shown a mastery both of pure form and of the new vocabulary of neo-classicism. In his plan for a town at the salt-mines of Arc-et-Senans (Doubs) he combines this with the inherited tradition of baroque planning; certain buildings (perhaps inspired by Laugier) foretell the blend of cyclopean and geometric solids which appear in the designs he produced when imprisoned during the Revolution. Though his work was published in 1804, that of his follower Boullée was until recently unknown. One of his most remarkable designs is that of a vast barrel-vaulted and coffered royal library, while his plans for a museum and amphitheatre foretell the mass scale of nineteenth-century public architecture. Most are characterised by block-like forms and exaggerated, unbroken horizontals. Boullée used every device to enhance the scale of his works, while light and shadow were deliberately employed for emotional effect. None of the vast symbolic designs of these two architects was executed, but their effect is hinted at by the colossal astylar mass of the Arc de Triomphe de l'Etoile, begun in 1806 to the design of their contemporary J. F. Chalgrin (1739–1811), one of the beneficiaries of the cautious patronage of Napoleon I. An admirer of the *Corps des Ponts et Chaussées*, Napoleon gave precedence over works of architecture to a vast programme of public works, roads, water mains, bridges, quays and markets. The bulk of his patronage fell at length to a single partnership, that of Pierre-François Léonard Fontaine (1762–1853) and Charles Percier (1764–1838). Their work at Malmaison (after 1799), and the designs published by Percier, are a compendium of the decorative style of the First Empire, with its heavy rectilinear forms, its malachite and rosewood, and its overlay of Greco-Roman and Egyptian motifs. Percier and Fontaine showed their full powers in their share in the completion of the Louvre and in the highly-wrought Arc de Triomphe du Carrousel; Fontaine, gaining the patronage of the restored Bourbons, achieved his masterpiece in the diminutive and wistful Chapelle Expiatoire (1816–21), in the form of a Greek cross and approached by a raised and cloistered *camposanto*.

The utilitarian buildings erected under Napoleon gave scope, surprisingly, to the brilliant and versatile François Joseph Bélanger (1745–1818) who in 1779 had designed the miniature palace of Bagatelle, as well as many later buildings in the style of the Empire. His cast-iron dome for the Halle aux Blés (1813), now demolished, was based on a design he had prepared in 1782—an indication of the swift assimilation by French architects of current technology. The Bourse (1826), by Alexandre-Théodore Brongniart, was originally a severe rectangular block, its giant Corinthian peristyle surmounted by a plain parapet; its interior was an aisled hall, each bay being covered by a cupola. The church of the Madeleine, begun in 1764, was redesigned at Napoleon's wish by Pierre-Alexandre Vignon as a temple to the *Grande Armée*, work being re-started in 1807. This gigantic and unloved building, with its Corinthian peristyle, top lighting and hemicycle, was finally consecrated in 1842.

At the Restoration church-building was resumed without at first producing any outstanding work apart from the Chapelle Expiatoire and the scholarly church of Notre Dame de Lorette (1823–36) by Hippolyte Lebas. The greatest architects of the post-Napoleonic period, Jacques Hittorff and Henri Labrouste, did not produce important works before 1830; but Hittorff's publications enriched the corpus of antique architecture. The appearance in 1823 of the first part of the *Édifices de Rome Moderne* of P. M. Letarouilly (1795–1855), a pupil of Percier, marks a revival of interest in the architecture of the High Renaissance, and adds formidably to the available repertoire of styles. If, however, the legacy of eighteenth-century science in its encyclopaedic aspect was to overwhelm the architect with stylistic alternatives until they became a mere addendum to his structural core, other branches of applied science (again an eighteenth-century product) were to make available structural techniques which revealed the falsity of this additive conception of style.

While French architects derived from the State not only active patronage but encouragement in keeping abreast of technology and theory, patronage in England remained largely in the hands of private landlords and urban speculators. Even the Regent was able to carry out his ambitious planning schemes only by adopting some of the devices of the speculators. Technically English architects were outclassed by English civil engineers; the most ambitious private building of the period—the 'Abbey' begun in 1795 at Fonthill by James Wyatt for the millionaire Beckford—collapsed soon after its completion. Two royal palaces of the period were soon wholly or partly demolished, while fire destroyed not only the Houses of Parliament, which included much work of this period, but also the most notable theatres.

While French architectural theory derived much from the experimental attitude of the eighteenth century and from a Rousseauesque primitivism, English architects owed much to the theorists of the so-called 'picturesque', among them Richard Payne Knight and Uvedale Price, whose views were first formulated in the 1790's and given practical application by Humphrey Repton (1752–1812), a fashionable landscape gardener who about 1795 became a partner of the still unknown architect John Nash (1752–1835). Nash had been trained under Taylor, and frequently retained Palladian elements in his individual buildings, but he is much more important for his adaptation of the visual devices of his partner. Repton favoured elegant informality, broken skylines, surfaces which broke up the light, and curving paths promising hidden prospects. Irregular planting ensured that no vista was ever fully revealed. Nash at first designed cottages and ancillary buildings to embellish Repton's schemes, and in this work he drew freely on whatever style of architecture suited him. Before 1800 he began to work for the Prince of Wales and the court, and was thus soon able to turn his methods to the building of country houses in various styles—castellated, Tuscan, Italianate, Gothic, Palladian and (in the case of the enlarged royal pavilion at Brighton) Chinese. Such buildings, notable for their charm and as signs of a break in stylistic continuity, reveal little of the talent for speculative improvisation seen in the development of Regent's Park and its magnificent links with Carlton House and St James's. This peculiar talent, in which business acumen and a gambler's flair are combined with a sophisticated aesthetic, enabled Nash to do what has never been done before or since in imposing on London an urban scheme worth comparing with those of Napoleon I. This was achieved not only without the massive powers wielded by the state in France, but in the face of a parliament more jealous than ever of royal expenditure. The scheme for Regent's Park, published in 1812, came at a time of rapid metropolitan expansion, and harnessed the principles of Repton to an elaborate scheme of suburban development. Nash's layout included a great double circus, a royal pavilion (never built) on the axis of Portland Place, and the magnificent flanking terraces which survive. Subordinate to these were two 'picturesque' villages, a ring road, markets and a canal. While these works continued into the fifth decade of the century, Parliament in 1813 sanctioned the building of Regent Street itself, continuing the line of Portland Place and curving like one of Repton's garden paths to join the axis of Carlton House. This curve, punctuated by Piccadilly and Oxford Circuses, and at the junction with Portland Place by Nash's round-porticoed church of All Souls, marked a victory for picturesque principles over axial planning in the tradition of Louis XIV. Later additions included Carlton House Terrace, Trafalgar Square, improvements in the West Strand area, the Haymarket Theatre, the disastrous first scheme for Buckingham Palace, and the new British Museum and National Gallery.

Nash's extrovert manner is in strong contrast to the withdrawn and sensitive qualities of his contemporary Sir John Soane (1753–1837). While Nash is remembered particularly for his magnificent stuccoed facades and perspectives, the name of Soane suggests enclosed space of labyrinthine subtlety. The son of a Berkshire builder, he was in Italy from 1778 to 1780 after studying under George Dance the elder, famous for his Newgate Prison of 1769, and under the fastidious Henry Holland, who designed Carlton House and Brooks's Club. Soane visited not only Rome but Paestum, Sicily and Malta; his admiration for certain sixteenth-century architects, notably Peruzzi, shows his catholicity. His career, after a difficult start, was finally launched in 1788 when he was made surveyor to the Bank of England. Nothing could have better suited his genius than this building, which by reason of its site could be developed only as a series of loosely related halls and courts enclosed by a blind wall of defensive aspect. His first sketches for the Bank Stock Office of 1792, done in collaboration with Dance, show how, in their studies of the palaces, thermae and tombs of antiquity, the most original architects of the later eighteenth century were concerned with the use made by the ancients of interior space. The published works of Piranesi, themselves an illustration of this, must also have played their part in stirring Soane's imagination. Soane is distinguished by a severe modelling of internal space, by his elision of cornices at the springing of vaults, and by his fastidious moulding of surfaces by grooves and recessed panels. His mastery of concealed lighting by lanterns and high lunettes places him among the few romantic architects of high rank. It is clear however, that his principles derive not only from antiquity and from English exemplars and that, unlike his contemporaries, he was inspired by the primitivist theories initiated in France by Abbé Laugier.[1] This primitivism appears in the detailing of the gallery and mausoleum at Dulwich (1811–14), built aggressively in plain brick. Here the familiar components of the orders are simplified, displaced, eliminated or reduced to a rudiment. Such a building, in a style evolved simply from the demands of construction and function, is highly significant in an age when style in the accepted sense had become little more than an outer garment. Soane's originality can be studied in microcosm in the private house and museum which he began to build for himself in Lincoln's Inn Fields in 1812.

If we are content to study English architecture of this period in terms of its personalities, Nash and Soane are by far the most important. If the period is considered in terms of neo-classical or Gothic styles it will be found that almost every leading architect appears in both sections. Gothic architecture had now developed beyond the rococo of Strawberry Hill without achieving the scientific 'correctness' which followed the appearance of Rickman's textbook (1817) and A. C. Pugin's *Specimens of Gothic Architecture* (1821–3). Without the charm of eighteenth-century Gothic, it still lacks the conviction of the work of Augustus Welby Pugin and William Butterfield. Its best manifestations are probably the churches of St Mary, Bathwick (Pinch) and St Luke, Chelsea, a product (by Savage) of the important Church Building Act of 1818.

The revival of Greek styles found a more fertile soil in Scotland than in England, and a school founded by A. Elliott, T. Hamilton, designer of Edinburgh High School, and later W. H. Playfair, sustained its vigour (especially in Glasgow) to the middle years of the century. In England its best product was probably St Pancras Church (1818–22)

---

[1] M.-A. L[augier], *Essai sur l'architecture* (Paris, 1753; English translation 1755). The work was well known to Soane, who possessed five copies at his death.

by William and Henry William Inwood. Its major practitioners, William Wilkins (1778–1839) and Robert Smirke (1781–1867), were not men of genius. Their buildings and those of their more gifted juniors Charles Robert Cockerell (1788–1863) and Sir Charles Barry (1795–1860) show characteristics of scale and function easily overlooked if studied for their style alone. Buildings like Wilkins's National Gallery (begun 1833) and Smirke's General Post Office (1824–9), now demolished, though part of a stylistic evolution having roots in eighteenth-century classical studies, are new in function; equally foreign to the tradition of the preceding century is the gigantic scale of Smirke's British Museum (1823–47). The conjunction of previously unknown types of building with a mass scale—clubs, banks, museums and, soon after, industrial and commercial buildings with their attendant problems, is a characteristic of the new architecture which, far more than the stylistic dress chosen by the architect, gives it the authentic stamp of the nineteenth century. In France the technical training of architects enabled them in the first half of the century to deal effectively with these new problems by the use of new structural materials and the techniques appropriate to them. In England, where the training of architects paid little regard to the new technology, purely structural problems fell increasingly into the hands of engineers, some of whose works are recognised as among the finest monuments of the period.

B. MUSIC

Between the years 1790 and 1830 the art of music experienced a significant shift of emphasis from the disciplined forms of the Age of Reason to patterns of considerably greater freedom and individuality, even eccentricity. The limited scope of carefully controlled early symphonies gave way, by stages, to the seductive call of Romanticism. The development was stimulated by the social emancipation of the composer, whose status advanced from that of household retainer to independent artist.

The musician of 1790 was still principally an artisan. Prince Esterhazy, often graciously described as Haydn's patron, was in reality his employer. Like the pastry cook whose products must satisfy the princely palate, Haydn had his duties as a member of the domestic staff, including the composition of suitable music for various functions. Mozart, in his rebellion against this sort of relationship, and his determination to be his own master, brought upon himself poverty, overwork, and ultimately an early death. A few years later Beethoven could support himself without any permanent attachment. This was partly due to the growing interest of the bourgeoisie, for their active support not only augmented the income from public concerts but also increased the demand for printed music and so helped to establish the artist's independent rank. At the same time, respect for the musician's role in society had reached a stage where the Viennese nobles now tolerated Beethoven's forthright behaviour which, at times, could only be described as boorish. The acceptance of the artist on his own terms was accompanied by a growing self-consciousness on the part of composers concerning their art and, as a result, many felt inclined to air their views on music and aesthetics. Schumann, Berlioz and Wagner have each left behind extensive critical writings which are still being read for their intrinsic interest. Their journalistic approach was in direct contrast to earlier writings by composers whose intention was purely pedagogical. By 1830 the Romantic philosophy of music was firmly in command.

The rise of the public concert in England and France has been sketched in earlier volumes of this history.[1] In the period here under discussion certain tendencies became more pronounced, and two of these were of prime significance. There was an inclination to get away from seasonal restrictions, such as favouring the Lenten season for concerts because then the opera houses were closed; and there developed a demand for more permanent auditoriums that would be serviceable throughout the year, in place of the coffee houses and public gardens where outdoor concerts were frequently held. The following list of concert societies founded in the late eighteenth and early nineteenth centuries names those that had some importance in the history of music.

1771	Vienna	Tonkünstler-Societät
1776	London	Concerts of Ancient Music
1781	Leipzig	Gewandhaus-Konzerte
1791	Berlin	Singakademie
1812	Vienna	Gesellschaft der Musikfreunde
1813	London	Royal Philharmonic Society
1826	Berlin	Philharmonische Gesellschaft
1828	Paris	Société des Concerts du Conservatoire

With the exception of the London Concerts (1776–1848) and the Vienna Societät (1771–1871) these institutions are still in existence today. The leadership of the German-speaking countries in instrumental music in the nineteenth century is indicated by the prominence of Vienna, Berlin and Leipzig, whereas the lack of Italian cities reflects the domination of opera in the musical life of that country. An attitude of historicism is noticeable in the aims of several of the societies. The most noteworthy event in the existence of the Berlin Singakademie was the

[1] Volume VI, Chapter IV, description of the Whitefriars Concerts (founded 1672) and the Concert Spirituel (founded 1725), with bibliographical references concerning public concerts from the eighteenth century to the present. Volume VIII, Chapter IV, contains a discussion of the Lenten concerts offered by Handel in the early part of the eighteenth century and by Mozart in the second half.

revival of Bach's *St Matthew Passion* under Mendelssohn in 1829. The Concerts du Conservatoire under Habeneck were probably more important than any other in establishing the French and thereby the European position of Beethoven thirty years after he had settled in Vienna. Moreover, the London Concerts of Ancient Music stipulated that works to be performed must be at least twenty years old. Printed concert programmes were not in general use before 1800, though Reichardt had introduced them in Berlin in 1784. The modern solo recital became a popular form of entertainment after 1830, largely owing to the virtuosity and international acclaim of Paganini and Liszt.

The turning-point in Haydn's life came toward the end of 1790 with the death of Prince Nicholas Esterhazy. While his years of service with the Esterhazy family were scarcely a drudgery, Haydn's position there as a hired hand contradicted the respect and renown he commanded in the world outside. Now the accession of Prince Anton, who was without his father's musical interests, gave Haydn (while nominally retaining his post as Kapellmeister) a new freedom, of which he took full advantage. In December 1790 he agreed to a proposal of Johann Peter Salomon, the London violinist and impresario, that he visit England (Vol. VIII, Chapter IV). To this visit of 1791–2 and the second which followed in 1794–5 we owe Haydn's last twelve symphonies and, less directly, the two great choral works, *The Creation* and *The Seasons*. The symphonies were intended for public performance in London and, with the single exception of No. 99, which was written in Vienna between his two visits, all were actually composed in England. It is clear, moreover, that in composing these symphonies Haydn attempted to suit the musical taste of London whose resources as a metropolitan centre dwarfed the orchestral facilities of Vienna and the Esterhazy court. Concerning symphony No. 91, composed in 1788, he remarked in a letter to a friend that 'a great deal must be altered to suit the English taste'. This necessity to please a public that might easily become bored by an unchanging routine, one whose entertainment had included the latest instrumental effects and innovations, probably accounts for the brilliance and variety of the London symphonies. The now famous nicknamed movements such as the 'Clock' from No. 101, the 'Surprise' from No. 94, the 'Military' from No. 100, were obviously intended as novelties for a large audience. A similar endeavour to gratify his audience may be discerned behind the choice of melodies. They are truly popular without being cheap. This character of the tunes, reminiscent of folk-song and dance, made Haydn the most popular instrumental composer of the early nineteenth century, a century that was dominated by the taste of large audiences rather than connoisseurs.

The brilliance of these works was by no means superficial. In his sixties Haydn had not lost the vigour and inventiveness which he displayed in his Esterhazy works some twenty years earlier. An engaging freshness is ever present; but the quality of the London symphonies could not have been achieved without the maturity that decades of experience had yielded. They were, in fact, the culmination of the *genre* in the eighteenth century both in construction and in sonority. The slow introduction to the first movement, with which the young Haydn had occasionally experimented, had now become a regular feature. Thus a salient characteristic of Lully's French Overture of the old regime was preserved; it is a frequent ingredient of the symphonic works of the nineteenth century from Beethoven to César Franck. Unlike Lully, the old Haydn and his successors frequently integrated the introduction by means of some thematic procedure with the body of the movement.

In constructing the main body of his first movements Haydn eventually decided upon the type of sonata form that had been favoured by Christian Bach[1] and Mozart, in which a graceful cantabile melody functioned as the 'second' theme, thus providing a clearly discernible contrast to the more vigorous and masculine opening theme. In Haydn's earlier works this contrast was often merely one of key, the second theme being a modified transposition of the first. But in the London symphonies the duality of key is supplemented by a duality of melody, and melodies, since time immemorial, are readily recognised and remembered. Haydn's decision to use contrasting themes gave his works a plastic clarity which served to increase their popularity more than ever. It was through Haydn's influence that Mozart's model became the standard form, the one which Beethoven followed in all of his nine symphonies. Haydn's willingness to learn from the short-lived Mozart is also shown in his orchestral scoring. The inclusion of clarinets in the symphony orchestra, long practised in Paris, was not an international vogue. Mozart yielded to the sonorous potentialities of this instrument in his last works, and the successful results of the innovation undoubtedly tempted Haydn. In consequence, the clarinet plays an increasingly important role in the instrumentation of the London symphonies. But Haydn did not merely copy; the spaciousness of his scoring and patterning reveals that the larger orchestra at his disposal inspired him not only to larger but also to greater music.

If London proved to be the culmination of Haydn's symphonic career, the effects of these visits endured long after he returned to Vienna. Among his varied experiences the English national anthem, *God save the King*, with its simple dignity had made a great impression. As a result, he was moved to write for Austria what is probably his most widely known composition, the 'Emperor's Hymn', *Gott erhalte*

[1] Sebastian Bach's youngest son, born 1735, the 'London' Bach who, jointly with Abel, conducted London's fashionable Bach–Abel concerts from 1765 until 1782.

Franz den Kaiser! But most of all, Haydn gained in England a true enthusiasm for Handel's music, particularly for the oratorios.

Baron van Swieten (Vol. VIII, Chapter IV) had come to know some of these oratorios during his service as Ambassador in Berlin (he was responsible to Kaunitz for negotiations with Frederick the Great concerning the Polish partition). On his return to Vienna in 1777 he endeavoured to promote a wider knowledge of Handel's music by organising performances of the oratorios, for some of which Mozart wrote additional orchestral parts. Haydn undoubtedly heard some of these performances. When, therefore, he discovered in England a popular tradition and widespread enthusiasm for Handel's works his imagination took fire and induced him to create works of his own in this style.

The libretto of *The Creation*, which is traditionally supposed to have been written for Handel (who either rejected it or died before he could compose it) was taken back from London by Haydn. Its author is not known for certain, and the supposition that it was written by Thomas Linley must remain suspect. A more likely candidate would seem to be Newburgh Hamilton who had written the texts for Handel's *Samson* and *Alexander's Feast*. Returned to Vienna, Haydn set to music a German version, written by van Swieten, who also made suggestions for some of the purely musical effects.

Van Swieten's taste for pictorial imagery was largely responsible for the naïve musical descriptions which lend *The Creation* so much charm, for Haydn's imaginative treatment of the libretto gave to the music a spontaneous freshness. The opening of the oratorio, the 'Representation of Chaos', is a sustained portrayal, not of the turmoil which the title suggests, but of a dark and empty void. The pictures throughout the work are drawn with simplicity and effectiveness, nowhere more so than in the sudden brightness of C major on 'Light', in the opening narrative.

Van Swieten also wrote the libretto for *The Seasons*, which he adapted from James Thomson's popular poem. A general interest in English literature at this time was having its effect on writers of the Romantic period in Germany and accounts for the English pedigree of Haydn's two oratorio libretti. Van Swieten played an even greater role in *The Seasons* than in *The Creation*. His manuscript copy contains abundant suggestions for musical ideas, most of which Haydn was prepared to adopt. It was a fortunate circumstance that this patron of the arts had keen musical sensibilities, as the quality of many of these marginal notes reveals.[1] *The Seasons* makes little pretence at being dramatic; it is a series of tableaux of village life, rather in the manner

---

[1] *Proceedings* of the Royal Musical Association, vol. 89 (London, 1962–63), pp. 63–74, particularly p. 71.

of a Brueghel painting. Whether he depicts a hunting scene or a convivial evening around the fire, Haydn imbues them with a colour and vividness one would scarcely expect of an old man.

As far as public performances go, *The Creation* and *The Seasons* are the most important compositions of the last decade of Haydn's life, though this is not to deny the artistic perfection of the last masses and string quartets. The popularity of Haydn's two oratorios and the continuing enthusiasm for Handel's works were supplemented in the early nineteenth century by a revival of Sebastian Bach's *Passions*. Together, the choral works of these three composers constituted a vigorous inducement throughout England and Europe for the foundation of oratorio and choral societies. At a time when an enjoyment of the arts tended to become increasingly passive, these organisations played the important role of offering an opportunity for active participation, a function that is even truer today than it was in the early nineteenth century.

The presence of Haydn in Vienna undoubtedly impelled Ludwig van Beethoven to move there. His intention was to study with the great composer. Beethoven was born in Bonn in 1770 but lived in Vienna continuously from 1792 until his death in 1827 (Vol. VIII, Chapter IV). For this reason he is generally thought of as a Viennese composer. The lessons with Haydn were not a great success and ceased altogether when Haydn left for London in 1794; nevertheless, there was much to occupy the young Beethoven in the Austrian capital.

Contemporary Vienna was a musical city that enjoyed the patronage of music-loving nobles, among them the Princes Lobkowitz, Lichnowsky and Kinsky and Baron van Swieten. In 1803 the Archduke Rudolph, son of Emperor Leopold II, became a pupil of Beethoven and also took his place with the others as patron. In Beethoven's case the financial support of the aristocracy was a substantial addition to the income he received from concerts and publications. In 1808 Jerome Bonaparte, as King of Westphalia, offered Beethoven a court appointment at Kassel. But his presence in Vienna was so valued that a consortium of nobles, headed by the Archduke, offered Beethoven an annual income of 4000 florins (Gulden). Here was a striking instance of support for an independent artist who was under no obligation as a private employee.[1] The homes of the aristocracy gladly admitted promising young musicians, and we read of Beethoven playing fugues from the *Wohltemperiertes Klavier* at the home of van Swieten. This is an instance, too, among many, of the reviving interest in J. S. Bach's music. Beethoven's skill as a performer opened many doors, and his improvisations became renowned. It was inevitable that his earliest

---

[1] The devaluation of the Gulden in the Finanz-Patent of 1811 (p. 402) was a matter of much chagrin to Beethoven. Cf. E. Anderson, ed., *Letters of Beethoven*, 3 vols. (London, 1961), vol. I, p. xlviii.

compositions should reflect the style of his two great predecessors, Haydn and Mozart. Yet his reputation as a composer grew and by 1800 he had written several piano sonatas, the first two concertos for piano, the six string quartets (Opus 18) and the first symphony, this last work appropriately dedicated to van Swieten. In 1804 the full size and nature of Beethoven's genius came to flower in the *Eroica* symphony.

On its completion Beethoven wrote to Breitkopf and Haertel in Leipzig offering the publishers a 'Grand new symphony' which was 'really entitled Bonaparte'. Louis XIV of France and Charles II of England could boast that their patronages were of direct consequence for some of the greatest works of music commissioned in their time. But Napoleon was never prominent as a patron of music. In the intellectual currents of the early 1800's he became a convenient symbol of the dissatisfaction with absolutism. And the disillusionment experienced later by his republican admirers can hardly have a better illustration in the history of music than the change in the dedication of Beethoven's *Eroica* symphony: the version finally published in Vienna in 1806 forbears to mention the name of Napoleon Bonaparte and instead 'celebrates the memory of a great man'. The symphony is then dedicated to one of the Viennese nobles, Prince Lobkowitz.

This symphony in E flat begins a new era in the music of Beethoven and, indeed, in the history of the symphony as a whole. Its length alone was enough to arouse comment, and was no doubt one of the reasons why Breitkopf and Haertel refused to publish the work. This is understandable, for the magnitude of the symphony exceeds any composed by Haydn or Mozart. The first movement is, of itself, a huge and complex structure. Its themes are remarkable, not for their intrinsic melodic aptness but for their suitability for development. The opening notes generate one of the composer's most tautly constructed movements, where the introduction of a new melody in the development section is actually part of the organic growth of the movement and not a mere episodic digression. The coda, too, assumes greater significance in this work. What had been merely a consolidation of the final cadence in the early symphony now became a second development section, with further expansion and evolution before the music finally settles down to its home key. The remaining movements, too, have strength and originality: the funeral march as a slow movement, the scherzo-and-trio with its romantic horn calls, and the variations of the last movement. These variations, based on a simple theme and its equally simple counterpoint from Beethoven's own ballet, *Prometheus*, might easily degenerate into triviality but for the skilful workmanship to which the material is subjected.

The propulsive force and rhythmic drive that characterise the *Eroica* distinguish most of Beethoven's work. The impetus is still more strongly felt in the fifth symphony, completed in 1808. To maintain that the whole of the first movement is evolved from the first four notes would be an overstatement; nevertheless it is true that the rhythm of the opening bars permeates the movement and, moreover, is perceived throughout the symphony. The first movement exemplifies Beethoven's capacity for concentration of his thematic material. The second subject grows out of a variant of the opening bars, and this variant is developed to an ultimate degree during the course of the movement. It was usual for Beethoven to reduce his material to its basic elements, and in the development section of this movement he takes the practice to its limit. By reducing the motive note by note there remains finally a single note which, because of its preparation, still retains a thematic significance. The more lyrical tone of the slow movement is succeeded by the sombre scherzo which leads without a break into the last movement. The passage which connects these last two movements is one of the most dramatically striking portions to appear in any of Beethoven's works; it was inserted by him at a relatively late stage in composition. The growing tension in fifty bars of music, *pianissimo* almost throughout and supported by an inexorable drumbeat, becomes well-nigh unbearable when it is suddenly released into the triumphant C major of the finale.

In Beethoven's fifth and seventh symphonies the primary importance of rhythm is again clearly manifest. In fact, the almost demoniacal impetus of the seventh caused some contemporary critics to question the composer's sanity. Tovey suggests that many of Beethoven's themes are recognisable from their rhythmic shape alone. An extreme degree of rhythmic domination is to be found in the string quartet Opus 59 No. 1 (the first quartet dedicated to Count Razumovsky) where the second movement begins with a measured throbbing on one note. It is this rhythmic, rather than a lyrical, foundation that gives Beethoven's music its momentum and its directness of expression even to the least sophisticated listener. The finale of the fifth symphony has none of the melodic beauty of Mozart or Schubert; it has no subtlety of harmony or delicacy in scoring. But it has simplicity of expression with strong rhythmic impulses to make an immediate appeal to any audience.

The ninth symphony has been the subject of controversy since its first performance in 1824. The mysterious opening clearly heralds a work of spacious proportions and, indeed, the symphony's length of over an hour (almost twice as long as any Haydn symphony) caused some bewilderment among Beethoven's contemporaries. The dynamic quality of the first main theme sets the tone for two movements; the opening *allegro* is succeeded by a *scherzo* (instead of the customary slow movement), so that, except for some momentary bucolic relaxation in its trio-section, the tension is maintained until the *adagio* of the third movement. This beautiful slow movement (a free variation on two themes) is in itself a contradiction of the popular myth that Beethoven had lost interest in the sheer beauty of sound because of the deafness which had afflicted him since his late twenties and was now complete.

While the greatness of the first three movements of the ninth symphony is scarcely disputed, the choral finale even now remains open to discussion. Does it represent the peak of Beethoven's achievement in the symphonic form or must it be put down as a magnificent failure? Certainly, the demands made on the human voice are difficult of fulfilment, even for professional choirs; and the main melody, when compared with the finale of the first symphony by Brahms, which is derived from it, is lacking both in sophistication and harmonic interest. It is known that for some time Beethoven had entertained the thought of composing a setting for Schiller's '*Ode an die Freude*' (Ode to Joy). After much deliberation he decided to incorporate the poem into the ninth symphony in place of a purely instrumental finale. An extended orchestral opening precedes the choral singing. The material of the previous three movements is explored as if in search of an appropriate melody to accompany the chorus. Each attempt is rejected by the cellos and basses in a recitative as eloquent as though it were said in words. Finally, the 'joy' melody is enthusiastically accepted, and the movement may proceed. Even so, there are three orchestral variations of the theme, followed by the furious pandemonium with which the movement opened, which the chorus interrupts, 'O Freunde, nicht diese Töne! sondern lasst uns angenehmere anstimmen, und freudenvollere.' ('O friends, not these sounds! but let us give tongue to others, more pleasing and joyful.')

Of the many comments this movement provoked (as well as the tune on which it is built) we may quote two by Wagner since they reveal so clearly the double edge of Beethoven's style. Wagner observed that 'the musician felt the necessity to throw himself into the arms of the poet to bring about the creation of the true, unfailingly effective and redeeming melody'; and at another time, 'the most elevated art has never produced anything artistically more simple than this tune whose childlike simplicity induces in us a sacred awe. The tune becomes, in the course of composition, the *cantus firmus*, the chorale of a new congregation, around which—like a sacred chorale of Sebastian Bach—the additional voices group themselves in a contrapuntal manner'.[1] It is true that the tune in its uttermost simplicity represents the universal melody for which Rousseau had clamoured and which Haydn at times achieved. This universality of musical language, equally intelligible among nations, as well as among various layers of society, contradicts

[1] *Gesammelte Schriften*, 9 vols. (Leipzig, 1871–83), vol. III, p. 385; vol. IX, p. 123.

the facile generalisation that the music of the late Beethoven was thoroughly Romantic. On the other hand, Wagner's idea of a newly-emerged congregation listening to this quasi-chorale in 'sacred awe' sets forth an attitude that was very marked in composers of Romantic music. It was, in fact, anticipated in Beethoven to some extent: that is to say, the notion of a composer who no longer aims to amuse or even to enlighten his audience, but one who sees in himself a high-priest of society, who looks upon his audience as a congregation, and his music as part of a ritual. In Beethoven we have a fusion of the rationality of the Enlightenment and the conceits of Romanticism to an even greater degree than in either Mozart or Haydn.

The words of the finale of the Ninth Symphony proclaim the idealism of their time, the brotherhood of mankind: 'all men are becoming brothers'. This Utopian dream served the cult of the freemasons well and brought into their ranks such eminent persons as Haydn and Mozart, Wieland and Goethe. So perfectly did Beethoven's finale apprehend the current mood that the melody became widely known through its appearance in masonic song-books.

Schiller's 'Ode an die Freude' was but one instance of Beethoven's devotion to this poet's ideals. As a historian Schiller had written on the early struggle of the Netherlands to free themselves from Spanish rule. This subject came to symbolise early nineteenth-century aspirations toward political freedom. In consequence, a great impact was made on contemporary Germany through Goethe's tragedy Egmont, for which Beethoven wrote incidental music. Though temperamentally not compatible, these two men each had a perspicacious sense of the other's greatness. Few original documents exist concerning their actual intercourse, and they speak for themselves. In April, 1811, Beethoven entrusted the amateur musician, von Oliva, with a letter to Goethe:

Shortly you will receive the music for Egmont from Leipzig ... this wonderful Egmont which I have thought, felt and expressed in music as warmly as I have read it. I wish very much to know your judgment of it, even adverse criticism will benefit me and my art.

The letter as a whole is full of humility. Goethe's reply was cordial; he planned to perform the music in the Weimar theatre and he felt certain of the great delight such a performance would offer both to himself and to Beethoven's many admirers in the region. Considering his usually guarded mode of expression, the terms in which Goethe expressed his judgment of the Egmont score were forceful and unusually plain-spoken:

The vision [of Klaerchen] disappears when the drums of the guards are sounded to accompany Egmont to his death. This is indeed an occasion that calls for music, and Beethoven has followed my intentions with miraculous genius (bewunderns-wertes Genie).

Another comment states:

The compositions of songs frequently furnish only a *quid pro quo*: rarely does the poet feel [that all he has offered has really] penetrated, and usually we learn only about the art and temperament of the composer . . . . Here Beethoven has done miracles.

Beethoven's only opera, *Fidelio*, is similar to *Egmont* in theme though different in time and setting. The search for a libretto persisted for years, for Beethoven looked upon his mission with magisterial serious-ness, and he would not consider a trivial subject. The story of Leonora's enduring love for Florestan in the face of extreme danger finally met his exacting demands, and, after many vicissitudes, *Fidelio* took the form in which we know it today. Though unique among Beethoven's works, the opera shares many characteristics with contemporary French operas and, in fact, can be properly understood only in the context of French operatic history in the age of Napoleon.

With the exception of Mozart's *Entführung aus dem Serail* and *Die Zauberflöte* there were few German works of significant artistic stature. Gluck's prolonged activity as a composer of Italian opera is apt to obscure the fact that in the last years of his active life he was, to all intents, a French composer. Gluck's spirit lived on in French music long after his death. The French versions of *Orfeo* and *Alceste* and the two *Iphigenia* operas had captured the French stage, with the result that Gluck held a position in France similar to that of Handel in England. The effect was that a Gluckian style dominated French opera. At the same time, the social and political upheaval of the Revolution had a profound effect on France's musical life. The uncertainties of everyday existence were reflected in a heightening of dramatic exigencies and in the popularity of the 'rescue opera' of which Grétry's *Richard Coeur de Lion* of 1784 was a prototype. Horror scenes in which dungeons and graves played a prominent part, with the rescue of hero or heroine in the nick of time, became the accepted dramatic formula. The more popular of these works, *Lodoisca* (1791), *Elisa* (1794), *Médée* (1797) and *Les Deux Journées* (1800) could boast international success. They were composed by the Florentine Cherubini who followed in the foot-steps of Lully and Gluck in becoming France's leading musician despite his foreign birth. More important, perhaps, he achieved eminence not-withstanding his failure to win the favour of Napoleon, and he con-solidated his national and international reputation as director of the Paris Conservatoire from 1822 to 1842. As in the case of his dis-tinguished predecessors, Cherubini's method of composition also differed from that of the conventional Italian opera composer in that he extended the role of both orchestra and chorus (Vol. VI, Chapter IV). The effect of the Revolution in focusing attention on the masses was evident in the common sight of crowds taking part in Republican hymns, written for special events. Occasional commissions of this sort from the revolutionary authorities provided Cherubini with an opportunity to develop his own choral and orchestral style. With their broad intelligibility and musical scores for large resources, such works have been described as '*al fresco*'. During his residence in Vienna (1805-6) Cherubini supervised the performance of some of his rescue operas and thereby gained the esteem of both Haydn and Beethoven. It is obvious, furthermore, that the topical subject matter of these operas and Cherubini's musical treatment of them were of cardinal importance for Beethoven's *Fidelio*.

The '*al fresco*' technique was to become increasingly important in a century that experienced the construction of large opera houses and concert halls. The works of Cherubini and his rival Spontini (*La Vestale*, 1807; *Fernand Cortez*, 1809) may be regarded as the ancestors of the grand opera of Meyerbeer and early Wagner as well as the compositions of Berlioz which demanded such extraordinarily large performing forces.

Among the currently popular operas Beethoven felt that Cherubini's *Deux Journées* and Spontini's *Vestale* had the best libretti. It is not surprising, therefore, that *Fidelio* is derived from a French libretto, namely a German version of *Léonore, ou l'amour conjugal* by Jean Nicolas Bouilly, the author of *Les Deux Journées*. Thus, for subject matter *Fidelio* belongs to the genre of post-revolutionary French opera, with its rescue, dungeon-scene, grave-digging, and sermons on political freedom.

Despite Beethoven's impelling desire to write an opera, he lacked the instinctive sense of the theatre which Mozart possessed. The first version was withdrawn after three performances in 1805, and the second, which was carefully pruned, including the reorganisation of the material into two acts instead of three, failed again a year later. In 1814 the work was once more revised, the libretto rewritten by G. F. Treitschke, a man of wide experience in adapting French rescue operas to Viennese taste (including the aforementioned *Médée* and *Les Deux Journées*). Only, then, nine years after its initial appearance, did *Fidelio* meet with success. The early failures may be attributed in part to the fact that performances took place during the difficult times of the French occupation of Vienna, but it is certainly true that some revision was necessary in order to make the work effective.

In its final form *Fidelio* has successfully held the operatic stage for a century and a half. Nevertheless, as the work of one whose claim to immortality rests on the creation of absolute music, *Fidelio* has been widely criticised for its profusion of symphonic elements at the expense of dramatic integrity. The famous canonic quartet in Act I is usually cited to support this criticism although, when taken on its own terms, the quartet is appropriate in the context. But, paradoxically enough, by employing for his dramatic expression the forms mainly associated with absolute music (such as canon and sonata form) and by integrating these forms into the framework of the opera as a whole, Beethoven anticipated the future course of music. For in the Romantic and neo-Romantic works of the nineteenth and twentieth centuries the amalgamation of dramatic and programmatic intentions with the formal patterns of instrumental music is a conspicuous feature. The passage in the second act of *Fidelio* where speaking voice and orchestra are combined is particularly poignant. It derives from Rousseau and Mozart (Vol. VIII, Chapter IV) and points the way to Weber and Wagner.

In spite of its ultimate success *Fidelio* never challenged the supremacy of Italian and French opera in Vienna. Italy's most successful representative in the early nineteenth century was Rossini (1792–1868). The success of *Tancredi* (Venice, 1813) placed its composer in the leadership of Italian opera all over Europe. *Tancredi* was followed by the *Barbiere di Siviglia* (Rome, 1816), and from 1815 to 1823 Rossini was under contract to write two operas yearly for La Scala at Milan and for the Italian Opera at Vienna. When he arrived in that city in 1822 his popularity approached a veritable craze. He met both Beethoven and Schubert and was complimented by Beethoven on his 'excellent opera' (*Il Barbiere*). No professional musician could deny Rossini's obvious assets; his infectious melodies, his thorough grasp of the operatic metier and its potentialities, and his sense of humour, so indispensable for the success of an *opera buffa*. At the invitation of the manager of the King's Theatre Rossini arrived in London in 1823, met with flattering attention from the court, and found himself in possession of £7000 when he left England five months later. He then settled in Paris as manager of the *Théâtre Italien* and was appointed *premier compositeur du Roi* in 1826. His last memorable success was *Guillaume Tell* (Paris, 1829), in which he successfully transferred the qualities of the French revolutionary opera to a remote age and, at the same time, infused it with the vitality of his own Italianate melodies. Then, at the early age of thirty-seven, Rossini went into virtually complete retirement, for reasons which have never been satisfactorily explained. That his action was not due to the falling off of his musical powers is proved by the few works which appeared later, such as the *Stabat Mater* of 1842 and the *Petite Messe Solennelle* of 1863, the latter strangely prophetic of Verdi's *Requiem*.

That the robust appeal of Rossini's music would overshadow Beethoven's popularity is understandable enough in terms of a general public. But it is more difficult to explain why German opera, in spite of courtly and municipal patronage, evolved so slowly from its infancy compared with the operatic developments in Italy and France. The efforts of Emperor Joseph II to establish a national tradition in Vienna failed in spite of Mozart's *Entführung aus dem Serail*; and it must be admitted moreover that both the later *Zauberflöte* and *Fidelio* occupy their positions in the history of German opera as individual masterpieces rather than as currents in the main stream of operatic development. The incentive for a national development was eventually supplied by Carl Maria von Weber's *Der Freischütz*. This opera was first performed in the Berlin Schauspielhaus in 1821. (The Lindenhaus, where opera was usually performed, was occupied at the time by an Italian troupe under the management of Spontini, a composer favoured by Napoleon and the Prussian King Frederick William III.)

It was not only Weber's preference for folklore traditions and superstitions that assured the success of the *Freischütz*, for German operas on romantic subjects had been appearing with increasing frequency. But Weber's bold imagination, coupled with superior technical musical equipment to carry out his ideas, captured the public's attention in the same way as the German literary writers had for some years past. *Der Freischütz* contains all the ingredients of a successful romantic opera: it is concerned with village characters rather than historical or mythological figures; it has a pure heroine who confronts a hero who is human in his weaknesses; the villain is thoroughly black. There are supernatural scenes of a frighteningly effective nature and the rustic scenes are written in the folk-idiom of the shorter songs while the choruses are in an unsophisticated, popular style. (The Bridesmaids' chorus in act III is actually entitled 'Volkslied'.) The climax of the opera occurs in act II in the Wolf's Glen scene where the Devil, disguised as the black ranger (with a speaking part harking back to the tradition of melodrama) is engaged in casting the magic bullets. The strength of this scene, reminiscent of the pact between Faust and the Devil, lies in the manipulation of the orchestra which carries the burden of increasing the tension and portraying the demonic atmosphere. In contrast to operatic scenes of the eighteenth century, particularly in Italian opera, few words are spoken or sung in this underworld scene. In order to establish a diabolical and haunted atmosphere, Weber explores the different ranges of such instruments as the clarinets and flutes, and he never neglects the horns. This role of the orchestra as prime mover of his drama was in the Romantic vein and German opera was well on its way, in contrast to the Italian style where arias continued to dominate. Later in the century this suggestive treatment of the orchestra led to the striking success of Wagner.

Weber's *Euryanthe* was an attempt to write a more 'serious' work, without spoken dialogue. *Euryanthe* has never had any real success, however. In his last opera, *Oberon*, written for London in 1826, Weber carried his Romantic notions concerning the role of the orchestra a step further. About the same time the precocious Mendelssohn made an equally original and imaginative use of the wind section of the orchestra in his Overture to *Midsummer Night's Dream*. (Mendelssohn's subsequent career as a composer belongs to a later period.) Both the overture to *Oberon* and the opera proper are dominated by the well-known French horn call. In viewing the transition from eighteenth-century Enlightenment to nineteenth-century Romanticism it is obvious that the leading melody instrument of the earlier period was the violin with its sharp, clear tone. The sound of the French horn, on the other hand, with its overtones of vague yearning, was more suitable to the new attitudes and the pre-occupation with new subject-matters. What is remarkable in the case of Weber's *Oberon* is the fact that the theme itself is of such simplicity that its interest resides less in its melodic properties than in its sonority.

The classification of composers (and poets) at the turn of the eighteenth and nineteenth centuries is extremely delicate and depends on the character of the works of art produced rather than the chronology of birth. Weber is, by common consent, a Romantic composer, yet he was only sixteen years Beethoven's junior and died before the older man, in 1826. The best known works of Beethoven's last period, the *Missa Solemnis*, the Ninth Symphony, the last quartets, were all composed after Weber's *Freischütz*. In literature, on the other hand, such poets as Schlegel and Tieck were writing works of a pronouncedly Romantic character in the 1810's and 1820's.

The antithesis between Romantic and Classic was a favourite topic in the artistic controversies raging during the age of Beethoven and Goethe. The term 'Classic' has its severe limitations; yet a descriptive term is needed to serve as a contrast to the Romantic attitude. Elements of this attitude are perceptible in Beethoven's mature works: the intensely personal and individual expression, the considerable length in time which these works occupy, and the occasional programmatic whisperings. Because of these qualities later composers venerated Beethoven and, in order to justify their views, magnified his Romantic leanings out of proportion. They regarded him not as the master of formal structures but as the man who had sublimated music through his personal emotions. They saw in the Fifth Symphony not the logical construction but the fury that lay behind the notes. To account for the enormous vogue of the symphonic poem in the nineteenth century, the programme of Beethoven's Pastoral Symphony (Sixth) was often quoted as an ancestor. But whereas the slow movement of this symphony perfectly captures the atmosphere of a rural scene, the music itself conforms to the discipline of symphonic form. Indeed, strict self-discipline is never absent from Beethoven's music, whereas the Romantic attitude decrees absolute freedom for the composer. Even in his most personal passages Beethoven speaks a universal language, his idiom is that of the successor to Haydn and a contemporary of Goethe. The tendency towards individualism and delight in the singular (and, at times, even the freakish) belongs to a school which Beethoven influenced profoundly but of which he was never wholly part.

In his last works Beethoven confined himself to the intimacy of the string quartet. As early as 1798–1800 he had written a set of six quartets, Opus 18. In many ways these works are characteristic of eighteenth-century practices. They are, like most of the works of Haydn in this genre, published as a group, not as single compositions. Indeed, Haydn was largely the model of the methods of composition which Beethoven employed. In 1806–7 Beethoven wrote Opus 59, a set of three quartets which he dedicated to the Russian ambassador in Vienna, Count Andrey Kyrillovich Razumovsky, who resided in Vienna from 1793 until his death in 1836. From 1808 to 1816 the Count maintained the celebrated Razumovsky Quartet, in which he himself played second violin. This group later became the Schuppanzigh Quartet (with Sina as second violinist). Among the early professional string quartets, the Schuppanzigh ensemble is probably the most important, because its excellence as well as its close association with Beethoven destined it to establish a tradition of chamber music for public performance which still flourishes today. A similarly influential professional group was founded in Berlin by Karl Möser, who played in the private string quartet of the Prussian King Frederick William II from 1792 to 1796. Eventually Möser founded his own ensemble which proceeded to give regular public performances in Berlin in 1813. Today Möser is primarily remembered as an early champion of Beethoven, and it is characteristic of the social changes taking place during this period that Beethoven, as well as the Möser and Schuppanzigh quartets, experienced the transition from royal or aristocratic patronage to reliance on the general public for support.

The three Razumovsky quartets by Beethoven may be termed the 'Eroica' of Beethoven's chamber music in that he succeeded in developing his own language for that medium. The increasing refinement and sophistication was, alas, accompanied by an attendant loss of popularity in the later works culminating in the so-called 'last' quartets, written from 1824 onwards. At the time of their composition Beethoven's admirers found them completely incomprehensible and concluded that their composer had crossed the line between unruly eccentricity and insanity. It is worth noting that, whereas Haydn's popularity increased with the appearance of each new work, Mozart and Beethoven both wrote with a sovereign disregard of the expectations of the public. The attitude of the later nineteenth century with its neglect of Haydn and its deification of the demonic Mozart and of Beethoven may be traced directly to the respective attitudes of the three composers towards their public. The fact that Haydn was the oldest of the three is certainly relevant. Even so, the last quartets of Beethoven are not uniformly abstruse or difficult, rather they are remarkable for their wide range of expression. The *Alla Danza Tedesca* of Opus 130 is of great simplicity, suggesting the style of the eighteenth century. The same is true of the *Alla Marcia* of Opus 132. This simple march follows an intimate and unusual movement entitled 'Thanksgiving from one recovering from an illness, to the Deity, in the Lydian Mode'. It was written after Beethoven's recovery from a serious illness in 1825. In this movement the employment of one of the old church modes, as well as the treatment of the melody in contrapuntal fashion, lends to the music an ethereal quality; at the same time this procedure marks a tendency which became increasingly prominent as the nineteenth century progressed and which may be summed up in the term historicism. The fascination of Palestrina's sixteenth-century contrapuntal technique for composers of the early nineteenth century was combined with a yearning for purity in an age that considered itself to be decadent and sullied. A similar attraction lay in the Gregorian chant and its modes; here a direct line of descent may be perceived from Beethoven's Lydian Thanksgiving movement to Berlioz' quotation of the *Dies Irae* and to the employment of the Phrygian mode in Brahms's Fourth Symphony. These musical phenomena are cognate to the fascination of Gothic architecture in the early nineteenth century. It is well to remember the efforts of Boisserée and Goethe to raise funds for the restoration of Cologne Cathedral. Again, it should be emphasised that this enchantment with the past, which was to become so compelling in scholarship as well as art, is an element in Beethoven's Quartet, Opus 132, but does not by any means constitute the dominant feature. Another aspect of these last quartets is the scope they offered in fugal technique. Fugal passages occur as well in other works of Beethoven, notably in the Third and Ninth Symphonies. Beethoven's interest in the fugue, like that of Haydn and Mozart, was based on the familiarity he had gained with Bach's works at the house of Baron van Swieten. The increase of fugal passages and even entire movements in fugue after 1815 is very marked. The cello sonata, Opus 102, led to the piano sonata, Opus 110. The climax was reached in the quartets, Opus 131 and Opus 133. It is as if Beethoven wished to encircle the force of his expression by an ancient and almost impersonal technique of composition. The results, though abstruse to most of his contemporaries, have elicited wholehearted admiration from nineteenth- and twentieth-century listeners. When Beethoven died in 1827 Europe as a whole recognised that it had lost the greatest musician of its time. Schubert's death, only a year later, was scarcely noticed.

The development of modern art song is beholden to German leadership in the same way that the history of opera is the glory of Italy. The new secular non-operatic songs, performed by professionals in a concert hall, for the benefit of a paying public, constituted a quite different category from the folk and love songs of an immemorial age. The new genre required a serious, dedicated approach on the part of the audience; a training, not restricted to opera, on the part of the singer; and a pianist capable of executing a demanding accompaniment which, in its complexities, resembled a modern symphony rather than the strumming of a guitar. These were some of the social and technical prerequisites of Romantic songs, but the new German *lied* still required a composer of genius to give it wing. He emerged in the person of a Viennese school-teacher, Franz Schubert (1797–1828). Schubert's *'Erlkönig'* of 1815 is as incredible as Monteverdi's *Orfeo* of 1607, for the one inaugurated art song as authoritatively as the other initiated opera. And thanks to Schubert and his successors, Schumann, Brahms and Wolf, a song recital without German *lieder* has become as untypical as an operatic recital without Italian arias.

The developments that led to Schubert's mode of composition were brief. The early publications of the so-called first Berlin song school appeared in the 1750's. With the sole exception of Emanuel Bach, these composers were soon forgotten, although their innovations remained to influence a later generation. By turning away from operatic arias, minuets and other dances to which fashionable verses might be fitted, and by directing attention to folk-song or quasi-folk-song, in harmony with the ideals of Rousseau, the first Berlin song school created the thoughtful and soulful kind of song we know today.

The significant publications of the second Berlin school appeared approximately between 1790 and 1810. J. A. P. Schulz, J. F. Reichardt, K. F. Zelter and others had profited from the experiments of Emanuel Bach and proceeded to write melodies that would be suitable for the new poetry of Germany, of which Goethe and Schiller were the protagonists. Still, the very term 'melody' indicates musical limitations. For one thing, the piano accompaniment was frequently relegated to an optional, if not altogether a subordinate role:

The melodies of songs in which anyone who has ears and a throat can join, must be able to stand on their own, independent of all accompaniment, and must ... so catch the mood of the song that after a single hearing one can no longer imagine the melody without the words or the words without the melody. ... Such a melody ... will therefore neither require nor indeed permit any accompanying harmony.[1]

[1] J. F. Reichardt, 1781. The entire excerpt is quoted by A. Einstein, *Schubert* (London, 1951), p. 28.

Another restriction lay in the nature of strophic poetry. Following the rule in folk-song Goethe and Schiller felt strongly that the same melody should accompany each stanza of a poem. Adjustments of tempo and dynamics were deemed sufficient to convey the necessary nuances of feeling. These intellectual and poetic foundations were duly respected by the composers of the second Berlin song school.

Schubert venerated Goethe's poetry but could not accept the poet's restrictions. He continued to write full-blooded music which developed as the mood or the action of the poem developed. As a result, the songs that do Schubert honour are either free, that is, non-strophic, or settings of poems which consist of only one stanza and consequently do not shackle the composer's inspiration. Of Schubert's 660 songs about one-tenth were settings of the poetry of Goethe. Schubert was eighteen years old when he composed the '*Erlkönig*' in 1815. The most remarkable portion of the song is the poignant dissonance expressing the cry of pain of the child. Schubert intensified his effect by sequencing the phrase a semitone higher each time it appears in successive stanzas. This means of creating a cumulative impact would not have been possible in the strophic procedure of Schubert's predecessors.[1]

The '*Erlkönig*' was offered to the famous Leipzig publishing house of Breitkopf and Haertel by friends of the composer two years after its composition. The publishers submitted it, for an opinion, to the German composer Franz Schubert of Dresden. This unfortunate namesake, whose only claim to immortality resides in this episode, was emphatic 'that this cantata was never written by me'. He continued that he was eager to investigate 'who it was that had the discourtesy to send you such trash and also to discover the fellow who has thus misused my name'. The song was finally published by Cappi and Diabelli of Vienna in 1821. But the *contretemps* of 1817 throws light on the new type of composer which Romanticism had spawned, Bohemian by nature, and a misunderstood genius. Friction between conservative publishers and critics and composers whose music sounded either too old or too new was certainly not restricted to the works of Schubert; the unpopularity of Bach's fugues and Beethoven's last quartets immediately comes to mind. But these earlier composers had incomes substantial enough (and also a sufficient number of acceptable compositions to their credit) to permit them to risk a certain amount of experimentation. With Schubert's generation there began the tradition of the artist as a social misfit in a philistine, bourgeois environment. This tradition is epitomised in Mahler's dictum 'I compose for posterity' and in the popular images of Schubert, Chopin and Liszt conveyed by novels, musicals and screen-plays.

[1] Concerning Goethe's opposition to this free treatment of strophic texts, cf. Einstein, *op. cit.*, p. 45; also *Musical Quarterly*, vol. xxxv (New York, 1949), pp. 511–27.

The setting of Goethe's '*Ueber allen Gipfeln ist Ruh*', composed in 1822, is Schubert's most successful composition of a single stanza. Schubert matches the brevity of the poetic model in a new conciseness of musical expression, the irregularity of length of Goethe's lines by the freedom of musical phrases; and to these achievements adds the poignant contrary motion between the vocal line and the piano accompaniment.

Lastly, a word must be said about Schubert's settings of the poetry of the Schlegel brothers, composed in 1818–19. The text of '*Vom Mitleiden Mariae*' exemplifies the religious attitude postulated by the Mediaevalism of the nineteenth century, while its chromaticism is reminiscent of Sebastian Bach and anticipates, *sit venia verbo*, Hindemith. There are, besides, the three settings of sonnets by Petrarch, in the German translation of A. W. Schlegel. Schubert's fascination with these literary 'soundpieces' distinguishes his work from that of the Berlin song school to the same degree that the craze for sonnets became a hallmark of the Romantic poets in their rebellion against the old regime. Now the sonnet, so harshly criticised by Molière and Boileau, was rediscovered and imitated by Wordsworth and A. W. Schlegel. It is one more facet of the general European tendency toward irrational sound patterns. Schubert's novel attitude as a composer was to be emulated by Mendelssohn and Liszt.

Although Schubert wrote exquisite songs at a surprisingly early age, time was needed before he found his own idiom in instrumental music. The early symphonies were written in the shadow of Schubert's great predecessors and, in fact, his gift as a song writer seems to have hindered him in the composition of his symphonies and string quartets. The regularity of metre, the repetition of melodies weakened the structure of absolute music. A change of style is noticeable around 1820; between that year and Schubert's death in 1828, that is, between the ages of twenty-three and thirty-one, he wrote his significant works, eschewing the style of the eighteenth century and attaining an individuality of full stature that had been merely hinted at earlier. It is characteristic of nineteenth-century Romanticism that the titles and nicknames of Schubert's most successful works, the 'Unfinished Symphony' of 1822 and the C Major Symphony 'of the heavenly length' of 1828 are contradictions in terms.

Schumann first talked of the heavenly length of the great C Major Symphony. It goes without saying that length, once the listener becomes aware of it, is inevitably a disadvantage in an art whose dimension is in time. The extending of the time dimension to unreasonable and unheard-of proportions was eventually to bring forth tetralogies of operas and symphonies of gigantic length and resources. It is also characteristic of the Romantic attitude that Schubert should have allowed his 'Unfinished Symphony' to stand as such, in two movements. The reasons for his not completing the work have never been clear. But unfinished as the symphony may have been in a formal sense, it has proved entirely satisfactory to romantically disposed audiences. Another seemingly self-contradictory feature permeates both these symphonies as well as many other works of Schubert, namely, the interfusion of the symphonic and lyrical genres. The relentless reduction of thematic material to groups of three and two notes, even one note, seems alien to the lyrical temperament. Yet, nowhere have singing themes been integrated into a genuinely symphonic form so successfully as in the last works of Schubert. Moreover, these themes, once stated, were lavishly repeated in their original melodic shape.

The ceaseless repetitions that would be tiresome in a composer of lesser stature, and the very expanse of time in Schubert's works, are mitigated by his novel use of colour. He achieves new colour by restating his melodies, either in a different key or in another scoring, and sometimes both key and scoring are altered. The variety of hues which the composer could extract from his scheme of tonality and from the available sonorities of the orchestra yielded a distension that was unique both in the genre of the symphony and in that of chamber music. It was also characteristic of the period which Schubert initiated that the darker and softer colours should be preferred. His method of presenting his second subject-group more than once, arousing in the audience an ever-new interest in the progress of tonality and sonority, has hardly ever been rivalled.

No other tune depicts this preoccupation with colour for its own sake and with sound for the sake of a sound better than the horn melody which opens, unaccompanied, Schubert's last symphony in C. major. In this extensive and prominent passage the abdication of the role which violins had occupied in the eighteenth century is even more pronounced than in Weber's *Oberon* or Mendelssohn's *Midsummer Night's Dream* Overture. It was only natural that the Romantic fascination with sheer sound should reach its crowning effect in the art of music. Yet, the attitude behind this ardour was not restricted to musicians. It had, in fact, been articulated by poets decades earlier. In 1778, with the publication of the second volume of his *History of English Poetry*, Thomas Warton translated an excerpt from the medieval French *Lai du Corn*. The English version speaks of the magic horn 'where were hanging an hundred little bells . . . if any gently struck the horn with his finger, the hundred bells sounded so sweetly that neither harp nor viol nor the sports of a virgin nor the sirens of the sea could ever give such music'. The passage made a deep impression on the German Romanticists as, indeed, did Warton's enthusiasm for the art of the past altogether. When Arnim and Brentano were to publish their important folksong collection *Des Knaben Wunderhorn* in 1805, Warton's description of the magic horn provided them with the very title and also the title-plate of their collection. Thus scholars and poets had been praising the magic sonority of the horn for some time, but it was left to the orchestral arts of Weber and Schubert to suggest and interpret it in the actual sound of the modern symphony orchestra.

The author wishes to acknowledge his indebtedness to Mr Edward Olleson (Christ Church, Oxford), for his assistance in the preparation of this survey.

CHAPTER IX

THE BALANCE OF POWER DURING THE WARS, 1793–1814

THE successive coalitions organised to resist French expansion during the period of the Revolution and the Empire followed a general pattern and policy which had well-established precedents in European diplomacy. Since the close of the Middle Ages any dynasty or state that threatened to achieve a dominant position on the continent had been checked by a coalition of its neighbours. This traditional response, often described as the policy of maintaining a balance of power, operated in an intermittent fashion. It was not a consistent policy but rather a collective response to a recurrent danger. During the intervals when the states of Europe existed in an uneasy equilibrium the balance of power as a principle attracted little attention. Only when some powerful and militant state, by a dynamic expansion of its influence and territory, created a manifest *imbalance* in the European system, did the remaining states compose their differences sufficiently to co-operate in restoring a balance. How unstable such coalitions might prove, and how vulnerable they were to dissolution after a defeat or a victory, the vicissitudes of the revolutionary and Napoleonic wars repeatedly demonstrated.

Throughout most of the eighteenth century the European system remained fairly stable. From the early years of that century, when the War of the Spanish Succession finally checked the ascendancy France had gained under Louis XIV, until the final decade when the victories of the revolutionary armies again made France a threat, the balance of power in Europe was not seriously disturbed. It is true that the naval, commercial and colonial successes won by Great Britain made the eighteenth century a period of British ascendancy. But British colonial acquisitions on other continents did not unsettle the balance of power within Europe itself; on the contrary British interests demanded the preservation of that balance. There can be no question, however, that to the governments of Europe the British triumphs in the Seven Years War appeared excessive. When the thirteen American colonies revolted in 1776, and Britain failed to crush the rebellion promptly, France, Spain and the Dutch Republic sought revenge for the colonies the British had taken from them by helping to disrupt the British Empire. Furthermore, six other European states associated themselves in a 'League of Armed Neutrality' to resist the arbitrary use the British made of their superior sea power. The War of American Independence represented a reverse for Great Britain and in that sense a reaffirmation of the ideal of equilibrium.

Yet so delicately established, so sensitive, was the equipoise, that any diminution of power or prestige in one area invited further displacements. With Britain temporarily humiliated, and France progressively weakened by maladministration, bankruptcy, and (after 1789) internal revolution, the three remaining great powers, Austria, Russia and Prussia, became more enterprising. All three had gained territory through the First Partition of Poland, negotiated in 1772. In 1774 Russia advanced its frontiers at the expense of the Ottoman Empire. In 1779 Austria and Prussia agreed on some mutual gains in the Germanies. In 1783 Russia annexed the Crimea, and in 1792 Russian forces drove the Turks as far as the Dniester River. As it had long been an article of French foreign policy to support Poland and Turkey, these events demonstrated the extent to which French influence in Europe had declined.

This apparent weakness of France was the more surprising because France possessed greater resources for war than any other contemporary European power. In the absence of dependable statistics it is not possible to fix the population totals toward the close of the eighteenth century with any exactitude. But it is certain that France, with twenty to twenty-five million inhabitants, enjoyed singular advantages. Numerically, it is true, the Holy Roman Empire and the Russian Empire probably had a small lead, for in each the population may have reached twenty-five to thirty million. But the Holy Roman Empire was not a unified state and Russia suffered from a retarded economy. Spain, with some ten million people, had become a second class power. Italy, with fifteen million, remained weak and divided. Only Great Britain could match France in the vigour, enlightenment and relative homogeneity of its people, but her total population was less than ten million in 1789—less, that is, than half the population of France. With Ireland included, the British Isles then held about fourteen million inhabitants, approximately two-thirds of the number ruled by the King of France.

Neither the French foreign office nor French military science could be fairly blamed for the ineffectiveness of French policy on the eve of the Revolution. Extravagance at court, waste and inefficiency in fiscal matters, lack of vigour and direction in the royal councils, all these combined to weaken French power and prestige. But as a number of historians, including Albert Sorel and Frédéric Masson, have emphasised, the Department of Foreign Affairs was the best served, best informed and most industrious branch of the French bureaucracy at the close of the old regime. Its traditions and part of its personnel were carried into the revolutionary and Napoleonic periods. A similar tribute should be paid to the French military thinkers of the later eighteenth century. The most significant advance made in the military art on the eve of the Revolution was the improvement of artillery and in this France took the lead after 1776 under the energetic direction of Jean Baptiste de Gribeauval. Other military critics, notably the Comte de Guibert, urged the advantages of raising a popular army and encouraging a spirit of individual initiative in the soldiers. He also stressed the need to seek great mobility by splitting armies into divisions and reducing their interminable baggage trains. Roman legions, he pointed out, lived off the countries they invaded and made campaigns pay for themselves in booty and indemnities. Here in essence could be found most of the new principles of improved morale and rapid marches and manoeuvres that were to distinguish the French revolutionary armies.

If the French had been ruled by a less apathetic monarch than Louis XVI, if the ministers had been less distracted by the domestic crisis, France might have secured reciprocal compensations for the gains made by Russia, Prussia and Austria in the 1780's. After 1789 the mounting disorders, the weakening of the royal authority, and the flight of the *émigrés* (including many army officers) reduced French prestige still further. Austria, meanwhile, which had been disorganised by the precipitate reforms of Joseph II, recovered swiftly after Joseph died in January 1790. Within six months his successor Leopold II achieved a minor diplomatic revolution by reaching an accord with the Prussians. To embarrass Austria, Prussia had made an alliance with the Turks and had encouraged the Hungarians and the people of the Austrian Netherlands (Belgium) to defy the government at Vienna. Freed from Prussian intrigues, Leopold speedily reconciled the Hungarian nobles and repressed the Belgian revolt. By 1791 he also made peace with the Turks, a move for which the British government had been pressing because a successful Austro-Russian war against the Ottoman Empire might have threatened Constantinople.

The recovery of Austria in 1790-1 was paralleled by the increasing disorder in France. The National Assembly dissolved itself in September, 1791, with the announcement that the Revolution was over, and the Legislative Assembly, duly elected under the new constitution, took its place. In reality, the Revolution was still gathering momentum, and within six months the Legislative Assembly voted to declare war on the Austrian emperor. The ostensible grievances were less significant than the hidden motives. Some German princes who also held lands in Alsace denied the power of a French assembly to abolish their feudal privileges there. Pope Pius VI protested against the confiscation of Church property in France and the annexation of Avignon. The revolutionaries at Paris, for their part, had a growing list of counter-charges against Leopold II. He allowed *émigrés* to organise armed bands on the borders of France. On 6 July 1791, he invited the powers to join him in putting an end to the dangerous extremes of the Revolution, and on 27 August Austria and Prussia announced in the joint declaration of Pillnitz that they regarded the situation of Louis XVI as a matter of interest to all European sovereigns.

These diplomatic warnings were largely a bluster by which Leopold hoped to intimidate the revolutionary leaders and protect his sister Marie Antoinette and her husband Louis XVI. The royal pair had appealed to him for aid, offering their gratitude as compensation, but gratitude was not enough. French royalists, who hoped to see the Revolution crushed by foreign troops, likewise lacked a fulcrum powerful enough to move armies. By the close of 1791, however, many members of the French Legislative Assembly had likewise come to favour a war, though for opposite reasons. 'It may be,' Georges Couthon wrote to his constituents in December, 'that as a matter of sound and wise policy the Revolution has need of a war to consolidate it.'[1] In the spring of 1792 the war fever in Paris rose rapidly, and despite the sudden death of Leopold II on 1 March, the Assembly voted for war on 20 April with only seven dissenting voices. So, through mixed motives and contradictory calculations, began a conflict that was to plague Europe for twenty-three years.

Prussia supported Austria, and their joint forces pushed into France in the summer of 1792. The *émigrés*, living in a world of illusions, assured the invaders they would be welcomed as liberators; instead the French peasants received them with sullen hostility. By September their slow advance had carried the allied forces as far as Valmy, a hundred miles east of Paris. There an artillery duel fought in a heavy fog discouraged the commanders and the invasion was called off for that year. The cabinets at Vienna and Berlin judged that the French problem could wait until increasing disorganisation made France more vulnerable. For the moment they turned their attention to the Polish question which appeared to them more critical and more urgent.

Sobered by the First Partition of 1772 the Poles attempted to organise and defend the reduced territory that remained to them, but the Russians were unwilling to permit a Polish revival. In 1792 Russian armies assailed the truncated Polish state and the need to limit the Russian advance became a matter of urgent concern, not only in Vienna and Berlin, but in London, Stockholm and Constantinople. At St Petersburg, the Tsarina Catherine measured the stiffening opposition and decided to compromise. Ignoring Austria, she bought Prussian assistance by offering a share of the spoils. The Second Partition of Poland, arranged by the two powers in January 1793, left one-third of

---

[1] *Correspondance de G. A. Couthon*, ed. Francisque Mège (Paris, 1872), p. 57.

the realm independent. For the Poles the respite was to be brief and valueless, but for the French the distraction provided by the Polish crisis was providential.

The French 'victory' at Valmy coincided with the opening session of a new, hastily-elected National Convention at Paris. A revolutionary mob had already overturned the throne (August 1792). The Convention proclaimed France a republic, offered French aid to all peoples who wished to overthrow their oppressors, and condemned Louis XVI to the guillotine (January 1793). A sudden change in the military situation partly explains these acts of reckless defiance. Following the withdrawal of the allied forces after Valmy, the French became invaders in their turn. Within three months they occupied Mainz, Speier and Brussels and annexed Savoy and Nice. Intoxicated by these triumphs, and angered by the wave of protests that greeted the execution of Louis, the regicide Convention declared war against Great Britain and the Dutch Republic in February 1793, and against Spain in March. British diplomacy, naval pressure and subsidies rapidly extended the list of allies. Portugal, Piedmont-Sardinia, the Papal States and the Kingdom of Naples joined the circle. Prussia, Austria, Baden, Württemberg, Bavaria, and lesser German states negotiated conventions with London. Russia cancelled its trade treaty with France, and Catherine promised the British she would not come to terms with the French nor recognise their conquests, but her price was British silence on the fate of Poland.

The multiple assault unleashed by the allies forced the French back from the Rhine and expelled them from the Austrian Netherlands. But the allied armies lacked unity of direction and within France the defences held. By September 1793, as the Republic began its second year, the revolutionary generals resumed the offensive and the 'victories of the Year Two' cleared France of invaders. Counter-revolutionary opposition in the Vendée smouldered on, but by the summer of 1794 the extremity that had appeared to justify the Reign of Terror passed. Robespierre was overthrown (27 July 1794) and the Committee of Public Safety was stripped of its despotic powers. But the titanic defence effort militarised the Revolution. The prestige of the legislators declined while that of the successful generals rose. After 1794 the political trimmers in Paris became increasingly dependent on the support of the republican army and on the tribute wrung from 'liberated' provinces. French troops lived off the areas they invaded and when Belgians, Dutch, Germans and Italians in the border regions protested at the cost of French occupation they were told it was impossible to buy liberty too dearly.

As soon as it became apparent that France could not easily be dismembered or loaded with indemnities the First Coalition crumbled.

The Prussians, fearing that Catherine would win what remained of Poland, made peace in March 1795, conceding France the left bank of the Rhine. Three months later Spain came to terms, yielding Santo Domingo to the French. Confronted by the French successes, Russia, Prussia and Austria had already secured compensation elsewhere. The Third Partition of Poland (January 1795) divided the remaining fragment of that country among its three neighbours. At the same time these three eastern powers concluded secret agreements of wider import. If Austria failed to recover its Belgian provinces from France it might receive Bavaria as compensation, or the territories of the Venetian Republic. Furthermore, Austria and Russia reaffirmed their intention, when conditions proved favourable, of dividing the sultan's European possessions on the lines proposed by Catherine and Joseph II in 1782.

It was significant that the agreements of 1795 tacitly conceded the aggrandisement of France while envisaging a restoration of equilibrium by reciprocal compensations for the other continental powers. But the accommodations possessed two defects. The recompense promised Austria (aside from its Polish gains) lay in the future, while Britain was offered no *quid pro quo*, either for the French conquest of the Belgian provinces or for the Polish areas assimilated by the three eastern powers. Britain and Austria, therefore, had reasons for continuing the war against France. By the close of 1795 these reasons gained added weight because the French, having defeated the Dutch Republic, reorganised it as the Batavian Republic in close alliance with France. This consolidated the French hold on the Belgian provinces. The British retaliated by seizing Dutch possessions overseas. Ceylon and Cape Town passed under their control (1795–6), but these distant gains seemed inadequate when matched against the aggrandisement of the European powers.

After 1795 the French directed their military efforts against the two powers that still refused to recognise their gains. They could not attack Britain directly so they turned on Austria. In 1796 Bonaparte opened his first Italian campaign, forcing the Kingdom of Piedmont-Sardinia to make peace and to recognise the French annexation of Nice and Savoy. The pope was obliged to yield the Romagna, Bologna and Ferrara. French domination replaced the Austrian ascendancy in the Italian Peninsula, and Bonaparte's inspired generalship defeated the Austrians repeatedly, until, in April 1797, they agreed to a truce. By the Peace of Campo Formio, concluded the following October, Austria gained Venice, Istria and Dalmatia, and a promise that France would use its influence to help the emperor also obtain Salzburg and part of Bavaria. In return the Austrians abandoned the Belgian provinces and the left bank of the Rhine to France, and recognised the Cisalpine and Ligurian republics established under French influence in northern Italy.

The First Coalition had now dissolved entirely, but the British still refused to make peace. France, under the government of the Directory since 1795, expected its most successful general to bring Britain to terms. An invasion across the Channel seemed to Bonaparte too hazardous (French expeditions to support rebellions in Ireland had failed repeatedly). Instead he embarked 35,000 men at Toulon (May 1798) for an invasion of Egypt. Evading the British Mediterranean squadron, and capturing Malta on the way, he landed at Alexandria in July. Nelson promptly stranded him there by destroying his ships (Battle of the Nile, 1 August 1798).

The position of France, when Bonaparte sailed for Egypt, appeared secure. The republic had achieved what Louis XIV failed to accomplish, advancing the French frontiers to their 'natural' limits, the Rhine, the Alps and the Pyrenees. Furthermore, to make these frontiers stronger, the revolutionary government had transformed the Dutch Netherlands into a client state, the Batavian Republic. In the south the annexation of Nice and the creation of another client state, the Ligurian Republic (Genoa), gave French armies control of the coast route into Italy, where the Ligurian border touched that of the Cisalpine Republic dominating the Po valley. These dispositions not only isolated Piedmont and Parma, they limited Austrian influence to the area north of the Adige river. The keys to the Italian Peninsula were in French hands, and the profits that might be obtained by 'liberating' central and southern Italy made such a course an almost irresistible temptation to the republican generals.

In February 1798, the French entered Rome where they made Pius VI a prisoner and proclaimed a republic. In April they occupied Switzerland. By the close of the year they had seized Piedmont, and early in 1799 they changed the Neapolitan kingdom into the Parthenopean Republic and drove the Grand Duke of Tuscany from Florence. The advance of the French into southern Italy, the fact that they held the Ionian Islands and Malta, and that Bonaparte was advancing into Syria, made French domination of the Levant a possibility. For the first time the successes of the revolutionary armies threatened an area for which the Russians felt an acute concern. Paul I, who had succeeded his mother Catherine in 1796, welcomed suggestions from London that he take the lead in organising a Second Coalition against France.

The proposals that Pitt dispatched to St Petersburg in November 1798 provided the programme for a Second Coalition and invited Tsar Paul to take the lead in promoting it. More than that, they proved remarkably prophetic in their anticipation of the settlement hammered out at the Vienna Congress sixteen years later. France, Pitt suggested, should be reduced to its pre-revolutionary frontiers. The Dutch Republic must be restored to independence and might be strengthened against future French aggression by uniting it with the Belgian provinces. Switzerland must likewise regain its territory and independence. As compensation for the loss of the Belgian provinces, Austria would receive Italian territory, while Prussia (as an inducement to join the Coalition) would be offered compensation in the Germanies. To guard the passes from France to Italy, the Kingdom of Piedmont-Sardinia should be restored and strengthened by the recovery of Savoy. Unfortunately for Pitt's hopes, Prussia did not join the Second Coalition; and Russia, Austria and Britain did not exchange the pledges he proposed, namely, that they bind themselves not to make peace separately.

The three powers drafted plans to drive the French from German territory, from the Netherlands, from Italy and from Switzerland. By the summer of 1799 the French were forced across the Rhine and suffered severe defeats in Italy and Switzerland. The Russians under Suvorov and Korsakov carried a heavy share of the fighting in the Italian and Swiss campaigns and grew increasingly dissatisfied with their British and Austrian allies. In October the French resistance stiffened. Masséna forced the Russians out of Switzerland while Brune defeated and expelled an Anglo-Russian army that attempted to invade Holland. Stung by the reverses and the suffering of his troops, Tsar Paul decided to withdraw Russia from the coalition (22 October 1799). The same week Bonaparte reappeared in Paris, having left his marooned forces in Egypt. On 9 November the *coup d'état* of Brumaire ended the discredited Directory and established the provisional Consulate. By the close of the year 1799 Bonaparte had consolidated his authority as first consul and head of the French Republic.

The French nation, after ten years of revolution, desired a re-establishment of order and stability. But the governments of the other powers, after eight years of war and shifting alliances, wanted reciprocal compensation for the gains made by the French republic. Had Bonaparte been content to consolidate France within the 'natural frontiers' it had attained, while allowing the other powers comparable annexations, it is possible the fifteen years of war that followed might have been averted. But to secure the conquests of the Revolution he insisted on transcending them, while denying the other powers adequate advantages. In other words, he sought to confirm and augment the ascendancy of France, and this meant keeping Europe in a state of disequilibrium.

On Bonaparte, therefore, must rest the heaviest share of responsibility for the 'Napoleonic Wars'. Yet a survey of the diplomatic projects under consideration in other capitals during the period 1800–13 helps to explain why Britain, Russia, Prussia and Austria failed for thirteen years to unite in a quadruple alliance against France. Of these four powers, Britain alone remained firm in its opposition to the French expansion. Russia, Prussia and Austria each revealed a willingness to ally itself with France if offered a sufficient territorial inducement. The jealousy and suspicion which the four governments entertained toward one another gave Napoleon plentiful opportunities to profit by their antagonisms. His foreign policy, insofar as he may be said to have had any consistent foreign policy, was to keep at least one of the great powers as an ally while coping with the others. For this role of collaborator he chose in turn first Prussia, then Russia, and finally Austria. But to none did he concede the full inducements he had promised, and each in turn found its co-operation with France a humiliation and a disillusionment. To the last, however, Napoleon cherished the belief that every government had its price and that he could lure any of the powers (except Great Britain) back to his side if he offered a sufficiently tempting bribe.

How successfully Bonaparte could divide his foes he demonstrated in the negotiations of 1800 and 1801. As Russia had withdrawn from the Second Coalition at the close of 1799, the opportunity to secure the good will of the erratic Tsar Paul could not be neglected. The French held 7000 Russian prisoners and neither Austria nor Britain would make a sacrifice to obtain their release. Bonaparte shamed Paul's late allies by returning the prisoners, fully equipped, without compensation, a shrewd move because the Tsar had a fatherly affection for his soldiers. Following this overture came a proposal from the first consul that Paul, recently elected Grand Master of the Knights of Malta, should take the island under Russian protection. The French forces which had seized Malta in 1798 were blockaded in Valetta and on the point of surrender (they capitulated to the British 5 September 1800). Britain had promised Malta to Russia in 1798, but now, as Bonaparte had correctly anticipated, the cabinet at London declined to entrust its new conquest to the tsar's keeping. Paul reacted by reviving the Armed Neutrality of the North to oppose British sea power and made plans to dispatch an army against the British in India.

How unscrupulously Bonaparte worked on Paul's vanity and inflated his expectations may be gathered from a project the Russian chancellor, Count Feodor Rostopchin, drafted for his master on 1 October 1800. He proposed a dismemberment of the Ottoman Empire that would assign Moldavia, Bulgaria, and probably Roumelia and Constantinople to Russia. France could keep Egypt, while Austria would be placated with Bosnia, Serbia and Wallachia. As Prussia did not covet Ottoman territory, its consent could be purchased by allowing it to annex Hanover, Münster and Paderborn. Britain must be compelled to agree (without compensation for the loss of Hanover) by the (revived) League of Armed Neutrality which France and Spain would join.

These grandiose plans collapsed, along with the Franco-Russian *rapprochement*, when Paul was strangled (11 March 1801) by a group of palace conspirators, who proclaimed his son tsar as Alexander I. It is not surprising that Bonaparte chose to believe a stroke so opportune in easing British anxiety had been inspired from London.

At the Viennese court, hopes of Habsburg aggrandisement alternated with despair in 1800 and 1801. Like Russia and Prussia, Austria was willing to seek Bonaparte's friendship if the results promised an advantage. But Paul's desertion of the Second Coalition left Austria more dependent on British support and the British were not ready to yield. Baron Thugut, to whom the Emperor Francis II had entrusted the conduct of foreign affairs since 1793, played a tortuous game. Whether he was involved in the murder of two French delegates, when they were leaving the abortive congress on German affairs at Rastatt in 1799, is uncertain. But his lack of scruples, his plebeian birth, and his devious diplomacy made him unpopular. From Britain he obtained an additional subsidy of two million pounds (20 June 1800) on the condition that Austria would not conclude a separate peace with France before 28 February 1801. Napoleon's victory at Marengo the same week, however, once again destroyed the Austrian ascendancy in Italy and brought a temporary truce. In September Thugut resigned, and Prince Colloredo as chancellor and Count Louis Cobenzl as vice-chancellor sought terms from Napoleon. The latter decided to reopen hostilities, and Moreau's victory over the Austrians at Hohenlinden (3 December 1800) ended the war. Austria accepted the Peace of Lunéville, signed 9 February 1801.

The terms of the Lunéville treaty are often described as a recapitulation of those concluded at Campo Formio four years earlier. In actuality they were more extensive and more humiliating for Austria. Its influence in Italy was again halted at the Adige river; its protégé, the Grand Duke of Tuscany, lost his dominions; and Francis II had to accept the peace terms as a commitment affecting the entire Germanic empire. By these conditions Bonaparte not only reaffirmed the French ascendancy in the Italian Peninsula; he involved Austria in his plans for a rearrangement of the Germanies. The larger states there had long sought to annex their smaller neighbours, some three hundred ecclesiastical holdings, free towns, and minor hereditary domains. Austria, pursuing a policy of divide and rule, had supported the multiple divisions of the Germanies. With Austrian power weakened, ambitious German princes turned to Paris. Their 'gifts' to the French minister for foreign affairs, the astute but venal Talleyrand, laid the basis of his private fortune. A process of amalgamation commenced that was to reduce three hundred German states to less than forty.

Bonaparte explained his evolving plans for the Germanies in a private note to Talleyrand dated 3 April 1802:

I desire to pursue three separate negotiations: one with Russia, in the form of a gentlemanly discussion, designed to commit that power as deeply as possible to arrangements that serve our aims; the second with the Court of Berlin to adjust affairs which concern it, such as those of the Prince of Orange, the Elector of Bavaria and the Elector of Baden; the third with Austria, in order to conclude with her the arrangements relative to the Grand Duke of Tuscany. By these means the German Empire will find itself in reality divided in two, for its affairs will be directed from two different centres. Assuming these arrangements successful, would the constitution of Germany still exist? Yes and no; yes, because it would not have been abolished; no, because its affairs would no longer be ordered as a whole and there would be more opposition than ever between Berlin and Vienna. Time and other considerations would then decide our policy.[1]

In his diplomatic as in his military campaigns Bonaparte sought to constrict an opponent's area of operations while preserving his own freedom of action. He took the position that each of the other powers had a limited sphere of interest and that when changes were made outside its sphere a power need not be consulted. By his reasoning the interior of Europe lay outside the British sphere of interest. For France, however, he endeavoured to assert a universal claim and the right to concern himself with all areas and all issues. This arrogant attitude was strikingly demonstrated in the secret negotiations he conducted with Spain. By a preliminary accord reached at San Ildefonso (1 October 1800) and confirmed in the convention of Aranjuez (21 March 1801), Spain retroceded Louisiana to France and in return Bonaparte established the 'Kingdom of Etruria' in Italy for a daughter and son-in-law of the Spanish king, Charles IV. He also obtained Spanish aid in bringing Portugal to terms. That smaller Iberian kingdom had been at war with France since 1793 and depended on British aid and trade. In the spring of 1801 the realisation that he could not hold Egypt against the British moved Bonaparte to strike back at them through their ally, Portugal. On the advance of Spanish and French forces, the Portuguese yielded, ceding part of their territory to Spain, and a segment of Portuguese Guiana to France (6 June 1801).

French threats to annex the whole of Portugal hastened the negotiations for peace between Britain and France. The British cabinet, headed by the younger Pitt, resigned (5 February 1801) when George III refused his assent to a measure for removing the disabilities imposed on Roman Catholics. It is possible that Pitt, and the foreign secretary William Grenville, foreseeing that a peace would be concluded, preferred to avoid the responsibility for concessions they judged unsound. Certainly the Addington cabinet that took office some weeks later had

---

[1] *Correspondance de Napoléon Ier*, 32 Volumes (Paris, 1858–70), vol. VII, No. 6019.

less ability and less resolution. To Lord Hawkesbury, who succeeded Lord Grenville at the foreign office, fell the arduous task of matching wits with the first consul. A preliminary convention (1 October 1801) provided that all colonies captured by the British (except Trinidad, wrested from Spain, and Ceylon, taken from the Dutch) would be restored. Malta was to be evacuated.

The definitive treaty of Amiens (27 March 1802) was negotiated by Joseph Bonaparte and the Marquis Cornwallis. It confirmed the preliminaries, stipulating further that the British would withdraw from Malta within three months after ratification and the island would be restored to the Knights of Malta under a guarantee of all the great powers. The rights and territories of the Ottoman Empire and of Portugal were to be respected save that France kept Portuguese Guiana. Prisoners of war were to be exchanged and there was henceforth to be peace and friendship between Great Britain and the French Republic.

In reality the Peace of Amiens could hardly be considered more than a truce for it omitted the most critical questions that divided Britain and France. While admitting the right of the British to concern themselves with the affairs of some maritime states (Spain, Portugal, the Batavian Republic) Bonaparte refused to discuss with them the fate of the Belgian Provinces, Savoy, or Switzerland. In both London and Paris the prospect of peace after a decade of conflict excited joyful popular demonstrations, but in Britain the enthusiasm cooled rapidly. When the terms of the definitive treaty became known in the spring of 1802 the comments, in Parliament and out, held a note of scepticism and disappointment that boded ill for the duration of the peace. Three developments that gathered momentum during 1802 hardened the British determination to resume hostilities.

One consequence of the peace that shocked and sobered British opinion was the revelation of Bonaparte's colonial ambitions. With Louisiana to control the mouth of the Mississippi and French Guiana expanded to the mouth of the Amazon, he could control the two greatest rivers of the Americas and held the potential bases for a Caribbean empire. France had obtained the Spanish half of Haiti in 1795, regained Louisiana in 1800, and Tobago at Amiens. In November 1801, taking prompt advantage of the maritime truce, Bonaparte dispatched an expedition under General Leclerc to suppress the Negro insurrection in Haiti. Leclerc and most of his troops succumbed to yellow fever, and the ill-success of the Haitian project cooled Bonaparte's interest in New World conquests. But he pressed other ventures equally alarming to the British government. The recovery of the French posts in India provided him with an excuse to send troops and ships there, and the force that sailed appeared more formidable than the circumstances warranted. In April 1802, a French expedition explored the southern coast of Australia, claiming it as *Terre Napoléon*. At the same time Bonaparte indicated that he had not abandoned his interest in the Ottoman Empire. He dispatched an able and observant officer, François Sebastiani, to promote trade while surveying the local defences from Tripoli to Syria. General Brune, appointed French ambassador at Constantinople, received instructions (18 October 1802) to reassert by every means the leading position France had maintained at that capital since the sixteenth century.

For British manufacturers and merchants the suspension of hostilities provided more grievances than it alleviated. Their hope that peace would bring a renewal of the commercial treaty of 1786 was unrealistic —this Eden Treaty had been favourable to Britain but injurious to French industrialists. The fact that Bonaparte declined to discuss trade relations in the treaty should have modified British optimism. Yet even a statesman as well-informed as the Earl of Minto ventured to predict that 'Our commerce will penetrate deep into France itself and flourish at Paris'.[1] Instead of expanding with the return of peace, however, British foreign trade declined. During eight years of conflict, from 1792 to 1800, its value almost doubled; but when peace ended the naval blockade the ships of France and her client states renewed contacts with their restored colonies. That Bonaparte should seek to protect French manufacturers from the competition of the more advanced British factories was understandable, but it exasperated the British to find that high tariffs virtually excluded their wares from Holland, Spain and Italy also. By 1801, the last year of war, the total tonnage of ships leaving the United Kingdom had reached nearly two million tons. In 1802, the first year of peace, the total declined, and in 1803 it declined again.

The disappointment felt in British business circles sharpened to apprehension as Bonaparte made it clear that the general peace would bring, not a cessation, but an acceleration of French expansion in Europe. In Talleyrand's judgment, Bonaparte's moves after Amiens revealed for the first time an immoderation that increased with each of his subsequent successes. Even before the treaty was signed he 'accepted' the post of President of the Italian Republic (26 January 1802). Before the end of the year he annexed Piedmont to France and re-occupied Switzerland with his troops.[2] Following a secret understanding with Russia (10 October 1801) he encouraged a radical reassignment of German territories. The nominal excuse was the need to compensate with lands beyond the Rhine some of the German princes dispossessed by the French acquisition of the left bank. The principal beneficiaries were Prussia and such secondary German states as Bavaria, Baden, Württemberg, and Hesse-Darmstadt. Over one hundred lesser

---

[1] *Life and Letters of Lord Minto*, vol. III, p. 209.
[2] See note on p. 274.

units, including forty-five free cities and all but one of the ecclesiastical territories, were absorbed by more powerful neighbours. Representatives of the German states, meeting in the Diet of Ratisbon, accepted the changes, and Austria, yielding under pressure, granted its consent (26 December 1802).

The mounting dissatisfaction in London, and the chagrin and humiliation felt at Vienna, strained the newly established peace, but Bonaparte saw no reason to check his course. His achievement of a successful peace, and his conclusion of a Concordat with the Papacy (promulgated on Easter Day, 18 April 1802), had raised his popularity in France to a new peak. A second plebiscite (2 August 1802) made him consul for life; a third, two years later, was to make him emperor. Such success might well have corrupted the sanest of mortals. It helps to account for his peremptory attitude in 1803 and 1804, which hastened the collapse of the precarious peace.

Malicious and scandalous attacks by the British press on Bonaparte and his family provoked his ire, and the frosty reserve of Lord Whitworth, British ambassador to France, did little to soothe it. When Whitworth protested against the continued expansion of the French frontiers, Bonaparte dismissed Piedmont and Switzerland as '*bagatelles*'. The British, he pointed out, had violated the treaty by refusing to evacuate Malta and Alexandria as stipulated. At a diplomatic reception, 13 March 1803, he upbraided Whitworth violently, declaring that the English wanted war; and on 2 May Whitworth asked for his passports. Despite the efforts of Talleyrand and Joseph Bonaparte, who sought to prolong the negotiations, Whitworth left Paris ten days later and crossed the Channel on 17 May. The following day the British government issued a declaration of war. It is still a matter of debate whether Bonaparte or the Addington cabinet should bear the heavier responsibility for the rupture.

If the British had delayed another year or longer they would almost certainly have been forced to resume hostilities under graver handicaps. With the Netherlands, Spain and northern Italy subordinate to his wishes, Bonaparte planned to raise his naval forces to equality with those of England. Whether a prolongation of the peace would have enabled him to do so is questionable, but it seems clear that the resumption of war came sooner than he anticipated. On 6 March 1803 he allowed an expedition under General Decaen to sail for India from Brest, with instructions that did not seriously envisage renewed hostilities before September 1804. Ten days later a swift ship followed to warn Decaen to seek Mauritius instead. The precipitate sale of Louisiana to the United States suggested a similar unanticipated urgency, for the negotiations were completed in three weeks (12 April–2 May 1803). Whatever hopes Bonaparte may have nursed that he might come in time to match the British at sea, he could not ignore the fact that they held a two-to-one superiority in 1803, and this sufficed to strangle his colonial projects. Thenceforth, Bonaparte's sphere of operations was restricted to Europe, a limitation of portentous significance for world history. 'Viewed from the standpoint of racial expansion,' John Holland Rose concluded, 'the renewal of war in 1803 is the greatest event of the century.'[1]

The conclusion that British recalcitrance disrupted Bonaparte's plans is strengthened by the fury of his retaliation. On 22 May he ordered that all Englishmen between eighteen and sixty found in France should be arrested as prisoners of war. This savage reprisal against civilians flouted accepted practice, the more so as the British ambassadors to Turkey and Denmark were among the unfortunate victims. The arrest of Sir George Rumbold at Hamburg further violated the principle of diplomatic immunity and roused even the hesitant Frederick William III of Prussia to forward a vigorous protest to Paris. The increasing bitterness of Anglo-French relations was also advertised by the treatment accorded to the British scientist and explorer, Matthew Flinders, when (unaware the peace had ended) he put in at Mauritius late in 1803. Four years earlier, in the midst of hostilities, the British had permitted and even aided a French scientific expedition to the south Pacific, but Flinders' passport from the French government was disregarded by the authorities at Mauritius, who impounded his records and detained him for seven years.

The arrest and execution of the Duc d'Enghien in March 1804 so far overshadowed all other examples of Bonaparte's ruthlessness that it merits more detailed consideration. Fear of royalist conspiracies had become a mania in France at the height of the Revolution; the death penalty was invoked against *émigrés* who returned secretly and even against those who sheltered them. Under the Consulate several royalist plots were formed to do away with Bonaparte. One of them failed by the narrowest margin when an 'infernal machine' exploded as his carriage passed (24 December 1800). Although the outrage was promptly blamed on Jacobin terrorists and many were seized and deported, further investigation traced it to royalist agents. The renewal of war in 1803 inspired fresh conspiracies in which royalist and Jacobin plotters joined forces and subordinate officials of the British government aided them. These machinations, reported to Bonaparte by his secret police, must be taken into account in judging the d'Enghien affair. By the close of 1803 he had conclusive evidence that British diplomatic representatives, including the envoys to Bavaria and Württemberg, were involved in a far-ranging plot to overthrow him.

---

[1] J. Holland Rose, *The Life of Napoleon I*, 6th Edn. (London, 1913), vol. 1, p. 429.

Between January and March 1804, leading conspirators were rounded up. The republican general, Charles Pichegru, had returned to France secretly in August 1803, and tried to enlist Moreau in the plot: both were arrested in February 1804. The redoubtable Breton, Georges Cadoudal, was discovered and overpowered early in March. But a major figure apparently remained to be apprehended, for some of the prisoners asserted that a French prince was to arrive at an opportune moment and join them. At first the police surmised, erroneously, that they might expect the Comte d'Artois; then misleading reports from French agents on the Rhine focused Bonaparte's attention on the Duc d'Enghien. This young relative of the Bourbons was living quietly at Ettenheim in Baden.

In the night of 15 March 1804 French soldiers and gendarmes crossed into Baden, surrounded d'Enghien's residence, and carried him back to France. No evidence could be found to associate him with the plot, with which he had no connection. Nevertheless, Bonaparte had him brought before a specially convoked military court at Vincennes. He was convicted on the charge of being an *émigré* who had borne arms against France, and was shot (21 March 1804).

At most European courts the news of d'Enghien's death excited expressions of horror but no positive reactions. His arrest on neutral territory, the rapidity and secrecy of the trial, and the hasty execution, left no doubt that Bonaparte had resorted to a deliberate act of terror and reprisal to check further plots and intimidate the Bourbons and their adherents. He had also climbed the final steps to a throne. Two months later (18 May 1804) the obsequious Senate offered an imperial crown to the new Caesar. Georges Cadoudal, about to die, saluted him. 'We have done better than we intended,' the defiant prisoner is reported to have said. 'We came to give France a king and we have given her an emperor.'

The same week in May that Bonaparte assumed the title Napoleon I, William Pitt returned to power in Britain at the head of a makeshift cabinet. At once, with Lord Harrowby as foreign secretary, he began the task of planning a Third Coalition. Unfortunately, the release of documents in Paris, inculpating British diplomats in the recent plot against Napoleon, had damaged British prestige; no one believed the feeble denials the discredited Addington cabinet had offered. Pitt could draw some comfort, however, from the attitude of Tsar Alexander —a Russian protest over the d'Enghien affair so angered Napoleon that he recalled the French ambassador from St Petersburg. Alexander, in turn, refused to recognise Napoleon's imperial title, although Prussia and Austria did so. The tsar distrusted Napoleon's meddling in the Levant, and Prince Adam Czartoryski, who directed Russian foreign policy after January 1804, favoured a new league against France.

Pitt's return to office pleased the Russians, and the prompt offer of British subsidies encouraged negotiations. In November Alexander dispatched Nicolai Novosiltsev to London with full power to conclude an alliance, but an agreement was not completed and signed until 11 April 1805. Austria, allied with Russia by a secret defensive pact since the previous November, joined the crystallising coalition and obtained a British subsidy on 9 August 1805.

The internal defects of the Third Coalition stemmed from the disparate ambitions of the three allies. Prince Czartoryski dreamed of reuniting his native Poland under Russian protection, while his master hoped in addition to obtain Constantinople and the Dardanelles. Austria wanted to reclaim its lost ascendancy in Italian and German affairs. The British government desired the defeat of France and its reduction to its former frontiers. Pitt distrusted the protestations of Alexander and his envoys that Russia sought only to liberate oppressed nations from Napoleon's yoke, but he welcomed the opportunity to deflect French attention by a new war on the continent.

Napoleon, for his part, wished to delay a breach with Austria until autumn. He still hoped, in the summer of 1805, that his navy could gain control of the Channel long enough for the divisions stationed at Boulogne to invade England. In the first week of August he joined them. But his naval plans miscarried, and before the end of the month he ordered his waiting forces to the Germanies. On 20 October he forced an Austrian army to capitulate at Ulm and on 13 November the French entered Vienna. Ten days earlier the Russian and British diplomats at Berlin had drawn Frederick William to the side of the Coalition. The Prussian foreign minister, Count von Haugwitz, carried an ultimatum to Napoleon at Brunn (28 November) but softened the terms to an offer of mediation. On 2 December (the anniversary of his coronation) Napoleon defeated the Austro-Prussian armies at Austerlitz. When Haugwitz next talked with the emperor of the French in Vienna (14 December) he offered congratulations. Napoleon was not deceived, but next day he granted Hanover to Prussia to keep Prussia and Britain apart (Treaty of Schönbrunn).

Austerlitz did more than keep Prussia neutral: it wrecked the Third Coalition. The thunderous events that crowded one upon another at the close of 1805 marked a turning point in the Napoleonic drama. On 21 October, in his Ninth Bulletin to the *Grande Armée*, Napoleon urged the Austrians to cease fighting England's battles and to co-operate with him. 'I want peace on the Continent,' he insisted. 'What I desire is ships, colonies, commerce, and that is as advantageous to you as it is to us.'[1] The hope that, with Britain humbled, he could expand French influence beyond the seas still lured him: he had spent nearly

[1] *Correspondance de Napoléon Ier*, vol. XI, No. 9408.

five hundred million francs on naval construction since 1803. But the same day that this Ninth Bulletin appeared, Nelson attacked thirty-three French and Spanish ships off Cape Trafalgar, and sank or captured twenty-two without losing a single British warship. The battle of Trafalgar left Napoleon no choice but to confine his energies to Europe.

The severe terms imposed on Austria at Pressburg (26 December 1805) excluded the Habsburgs from Italy and reduced their influence and territories in the Germanies. Francis II agreed to recognise Napoleon as head of an Italian kingdom and to admit the Electors of Bavaria and Württemberg to the rank of kings. Austria also had to pay an indemnity of forty million gold francs, but as a small compensation Napoleon permitted it to incorporate Salzburg and Berchtesgaden.

The reconstruction of the Germanies, in progress since the changes of 1802–3, received a vigorous impulsion in 1805–6. Bavaria, Württemberg and Baden became sovereign states allied with France. Together with a dozen lesser German states, they renounced all ties that had bound them to the House of Habsburg and the Holy Roman Empire, and were organised as the Confederation of the Rhine with Napoleon as Protector (12 July 1806). Many minor principalities and knightly domains, enclaves within the area of the Confederation, were absorbed by the larger states, which pledged themselves in return to support France with 88,000 men in case of war. On Napoleon's announcement that he no longer recognised the Holy Roman Empire (*empire germanique*), Francis II resigned an elective title that had become a diplomatic fiction and styled himself Francis I, Emperor of Austria.

By 1806 Napoleon had secured the 'natural' frontiers of France and the territory beyond them. Spain was his subservient ally. French influence extended throughout the Italian Peninsula, for Joseph Bonaparte replaced the Bourbon king Ferdinand IV at Naples in February of that year. In June Louis Bonaparte became king of the Dutch Netherlands. The German states bordering the Rhine from Holland to Switzerland were allied with France and so was Switzerland itself. The policy of creating a cordon of vassal states beyond the Rhine, the Alps and the Pyrenees had been realised in full.

Throughout the summer of 1806 Napoleon negotiated with Britain and Russia, the two great powers that still refused to recognise his imperial title or his conquests. Tsar Alexander had withdrawn his forces to Poland after Austerlitz. In London the death of Pitt in January 1806 led to a reconstructed ministry. Lord Grenville formed a cabinet with Charles James Fox directing foreign affairs, but Fox was already ailing and he died in September. Both Britain and Russia rejected Napoleon's proposals before the summer ended.

Meanwhile, at Berlin, Haugwitz as foreign minister negotiated with France while Prince Hardenberg and the war party sought Russian aid. Ten years of neutrality (1795–1805) had gained little for Prussia save Hanover. In August 1806, the court at Berlin learned from its ambassador at Paris that Napoleon had secretly offered to restore Hanover to George III. Without waiting for Russian military support the Prussians dispatched an ultimatum to Napoleon (September 1806) and he struck back with appalling speed. In the twin battles of Auerstadt and Jena (14 October) the French won crushing victories. Prussian resistance collapsed and two weeks later Napoleon was in Berlin.

French historians count the victory over Prussia in 1806 as the defeat of a fourth coalition. In reality no new coalition had been organised and in this chapter the term 'Fourth Coalition' will be reserved for the alliances formed in 1813. With Prussia prostrate, Napoleon pushed across the Vistula to settle with the Russians. A battle fought at Eylau, near Königsberg (8 February 1807), proved costly and indecisive. For the first time he found himself at war without a single great power as an active or tacit ally. He proposed to the court at Vienna the restoration of Silesia as the price of an Austro-French alliance: the overture was rejected. Turning to the Prussians he offered to re-establish the Prussian kingdom in return for co-operation: Frederick William's reply was to contract a closer accord with Alexander. When spring came, Napoleon put his forces in motion and again sought the Russians near Königsberg; the battle of Friedland (14 June 1807) was a victory for the French; and Alexander agreed to a truce. Napoleon decided to see if he could substitute Russia for Prussia or Austria as his partner in the control of Europe.

The Peace of Tilsit changed France and Russia from enemies to allies and divided Europe between them. Out of deference to the tsar's wishes Napoleon allowed Frederick William to remain on the throne of a reduced Prussian state. In secret provisions Napoleon agreed to help Russia 'liberate' most of European Turkey, while Alexander promised, if the British refused his mediation, to declare war on them. Sweden, Denmark and Portugal were to be summoned to follow the same course. By sealing the entire European coastline to British trade the prosperity of Britain would be destroyed.

The concept of a continental blockade or 'Continental System' to exclude British trade had been considered earlier. After Tilsit the possibility that it might succeed lured Napoleon into attempting the gamble in earnest. Because it failed in its aim and drove him to measures that hastened his downfall the system has often been described as an impracticable scheme that demonstrated Napoleon's ignorance of economics. On the other hand, François Crouzet, in the most recent and most exhaustive examination of the evidence yet attempted, concluded that it is an error to insist that the blockade was unworkable. Its failure resulted, not from a defect in the grand concept itself, but from the fact that it was never applied long enough and consistently enough to prove its effectiveness. The resiliency and ingenuity of the British merchants enabled them to exploit alternative markets overseas, and unanticipated events in Europe partly reopened the continental markets at critical intervals so that Britain never suffered the full penalties of the system for more than two consecutive years.[1]

In London the death of Fox brought George Canning into a reconstructed cabinet as minister for foreign affairs. Learning by mid-July 1807 that Napoleon and Alexander were discussing an agreement, Canning acted with ruthless promptitude. The Danish navy, though small, could help France and Russia to close the Baltic. When the Danes refused to lease their fleet to Britain, a British naval and military force invested Copenhagen (16 August) and carried off the Danish warships two weeks later. The Swedes, from fear of Russia, remained in alliance with the British, and the Russian navy was not strong enough by itself to close the Baltic Sea. The British continued to obtain pitch, timber and other naval supplies there, and at need they purchased further stores from the United States. Although Alexander fulfilled the Tilsit agreement and declared war on Britain (November 1807) he did not press it. The British seized the small Danish island of Heligoland as a depot and continued to land goods on the Scandinavian and north German coasts.

At the opposite end of Europe the Iberian Peninsula provided another long coastline difficult to seal. To bring it under stricter control Napoleon demanded (July 1807) that Portugal break with Britain: when the government at Lisbon refused, a French military force invaded Portugal and the royal family escaped to Brazil. Spain, though it had been an ally of France for a decade, suffered equally harsh treatment. Summoning Charles IV and his son Ferdinand to Bayonne, Napoleon coerced them into an abdication (5 May 1808) and declared his brother Joseph king of Spain. The Spanish people resisted with unexpected energy, the British aided them, and from 1808 until his downfall in 1814 Napoleon found his resources drained by 'the Spanish ulcer'.

Hitherto Napoleon had fought governments: after 1807 he found himself fighting nations. The Prussians and Austrians, their temper toughened by defeat, began to train for a war of liberation, but as in 1805–6 they failed to concert their efforts. Napoleon did not believe that either would dare to attack him if Alexander warned them sternly enough. He sought a conference with the tsar at Erfurt (27 September–

[1] François Crouzet, *L'Économie britannique et le blocus continental, 1806–1813*, 2 volumes (Paris, 1958), vol. II, pp. 854–5.

14 October 1808) but despite cordial expressions of friendship the results proved inconclusive. Napoleon hastened to Spain to crush the resistance there, but before he could do so events recalled him to Paris in January. The Austrians were preparing for war and (though Napoleon could only surmise this) they had a private assurance from Alexander that he would not intervene. By April 1809, the armies were in contact. Defeated in Bavaria the Austrians fell back and by 13 May Napoleon entered Vienna. But the Archduke Charles had learned something from successive reverses; a costly battle at Aspern placed the French in jeopardy until Napoleon called up reinforcements. His victory at Wagram (5 July) ended the conflict. Count Stadion, who had headed the Austrian ministry since 1805, yielded his place to Metternich who conducted the peace negotiations for Austria.

The war in 1809 intensified the spirit of anger and resistance that Napoleon's high-handed methods excited among German patriots. Three years earlier a French military court had condemned to death the Nuremberg bookseller Palm for distributing anti-French pamphlets. In 1809 a Thuringian youth who sought to free Germany by assassinating Napoleon was executed, and in 1810 the brave Tyrolese leader Andreas Hofer met the same fate. Napoleon's demand that Prussia surrender the Baron vom Stein, its minister of foreign affairs, for conspiring against France, might have cost Stein his life if he had not escaped to Russia. This treatment of German patriots as if they committed treason when they dared to criticise or oppose the emperor of the French made all thoughtful Germans ponder where their first loyalty lay.

The premature Austrian attempt to lead a war of liberation in 1809 cost Austria heavily. Impatient at Metternich's efforts to prolong peace negotiations, Napoleon hastened a treaty with Francis I at Schönbrunn (14 October 1809). Francis ceded territory to the Confederation of the Rhine, to Saxony, and to the Italian kingdom. Russia, which had taken Finland from Sweden in 1809, also secured part of Austrian Poland. It is surprising to find Austria, after such humiliating concessions, seeking an alliance with France. Metternich, now Chancellor, believed that Austria must have time for recovery and reorganisation. On 9 March 1810 he signed a marriage treaty that betrothed a daughter of Francis II, the Archduchess Marie Louise, to Napoleon, who had divorced his first wife Josephine the previous December. A proxy marriage at Vienna, 11 March 1810, was confirmed on 1 April after Marie Louise reached Paris. A son, saluted with the title King of Rome, was born on 20 April 1811.

Napoleon's Austrian marriage did not please the Russians, and the pro-English faction regained its influence at the tsar's court after 1810. Alexander was learning as others had done that Napoleon could be a niggardly and suspicious friend. French arms could be spared to assure the Elector of Saxony a royal title and to carve out the Kingdom of Westphalia for Jerome Bonaparte. But the promised partition of Turkey did not progress, and the tsar's relative, the Duke of Oldenburg, found his domains annexed to France without warning. To check the smuggling ashore of British goods, Napoleon decided in 1810 to take possession of the coastline from Holland to the Baltic Sea. Alexander complained at these violations of the Treaty of Tilsit, but he also evaded the treaty himself. Though he excluded British merchant ships from Russian ports, British and colonial cargoes were landed by convoys flying neutral flags but guarded by British warships. Import duties on these wares helped the tsar's finances, and at the close of 1810 he raised the duty on French goods shipped to Russia overland. These affronts, coupled with disputes over Poland, and mistrust at St Petersburg when the French Marshal Bernadotte was nominated heir to the Swedish throne, dissolved the Franco-Russian alliance by 1811.

In the opening months of 1812 Napoleon concluded a treaty with Prussia (24 February) calling for 20,000 men, and with Austria (12 March) calling for 60,000, to fight Russia. By spring he had over 500,000 troops under arms. Alexander, on his part, made swift and realistic preparations for the approaching conflict. On 5 April 1812 he formed an offensive and defensive alliance with Sweden. On 28 May he made peace with the Turks. His secret overtures to Frederick William of Prussia brought him an assurance from the harassed monarch (31 March) that Prussia would not aid Napoleon more than necessity compelled. From Vienna Metternich sent word (25 April) that the Austrian forces opposing the Russians would fight only a sham war. In July Russia made peace and formed an alliance with Britain and also negotiated an accord with the Spanish insurgents who were harassing the French in Spain with British aid.

For the British the *rapprochement* with Russia proved a timely relief, for poor harvests and the curtailment of their trade with Europe exposed them to severe economic hardships in 1810 and 1811. In June 1812, the United States added to their difficulties by a declaration of war. As a neutral nation the Americans had both profited and suffered from Napoleon's Continental System and from the British Orders in Council adopted to cope with it. Events in Europe overshadowed the Anglo-American war of 1812–14, whose indirectly important results were not immediately obvious (Chapter XXII, pp. 598, 601, 611).

Napoleon's invasion of Russia, which commenced 24 June 1812, the capture and burning of Moscow in September, and the disastrous retreat of the Grand Army in November and December, hastened a reversal in European alignments. On 30 December 1812 General von Yorck, commanding the 20,000 Prussians in Napoleon's service, made a separate peace with the Russians. A month later Frederick William left Berlin (which still supported a French garrison) for Breslau, on the pretence of raising troops for Napoleon. Instead, he negotiated a convention with Alexander for the immediate co-operation of the Russian and Prussian armies (Treaty of Kalisch, 28 February 1813). Their plans at this juncture aimed at confining France to the left bank of the Rhine. In April, however, Viscount Castlereagh, who had become British foreign secretary a year earlier, reminded Alexander of Pitt's proposal of 1805 that France should be reduced to its pre-revolutionary frontiers. Britain, already allied with Russia since July 1812, strengthened the bond by a further pledge and subsidy of one million pounds, 15 June 1813. At the same time Britain and Prussia became allies, the Prussians receiving over six hundred thousand pounds for the year 1813. Britain had already induced Sweden to promise military assistance.

Thus by the summer of 1813 a Fourth Coalition, including Britain, Russia, Prussia, Sweden, Spain and Portugal had formed against Napoleon. Austria, however, remained, nominally at least, the ally of France. Neither Francis nor his chancellor, Metternich, considered it wise to break the alliance: instead they offered to mediate between Napoleon and his opponents. In May 1813, Napoleon took the offensive, defeating the Russians and Prussians at Lützen in Saxony on the 2nd and at Bautzen on the 20th. Russia and Prussia appealed to Austria for aid. In suggesting the contraction of the French Empire to the frontiers that bounded France in 1789, the Allied statesmen were naming terms they knew Napoleon would never consider. Metternich, as mediator, proposed a much more moderate three-point settlement. The Duchy of Warsaw, created by Napoleon in 1807, and enlarged in 1809 as the nucleus of a revived Polish state, was to be dissolved. French territorial annexations in north Germany were to be relinquished and Illyria transferred to Austria. Such minimum concessions by Napoleon did not represent the real terms the Austrians hoped to impose and bore little resemblance to the drastic demands of the Allied Powers. Napoleon knew this; but the Austrian overtures placed him in a dilemma. To reject them would make him appear wholly unreasonable even to his own subjects. To accept meant that the Allies might increase their demands with each concession he made. Playing for time, he accepted the armistice of Pleiswitz on 4 June, believing that he could strengthen his forces faster than his enemies could assemble theirs. In this he miscalculated. For the Allies knew that when the armistice expired they would have the Austrian army with them. By the Treaty of Reichenbach, signed 27 June 1813, Francis I promised to declare war on France if Napoleon did not accept conditions of peace by 20 July.

Napoleon had lost the diplomatic contest. Metternich realised this when he visited him in Dresden from 26 to 30 June and persuaded him to send delegates to a conference at Prague. The Prague discussions made no progress although the armistice was extended from 20 July to 10 August. Napoleon rejected the moderate Austrian proposals even though Metternich warned the French negotiators that, unless a favourable answer were received by 10 August, Austria would open hostilities on the 11th. If Napoleon had accepted, the Allied statesmen intended to announce that the proposals were only a *preliminary* programme, stiffening their terms in subsequent discussions. Napoleon may have guessed as much; in any case he withheld his assent. On 11 August Austria declared war.

The Allies had not only thrown on the emperor of the French the onus of rejecting what appeared to be reasonable terms, they had gained the time to strengthen their forces and concert their military plans. Nevertheless, when Russian, Austrian and Prussian armies converged on Napoleon at Dresden he hurled them back (26–27 August). But he could no longer rely on the loyalty of his German allies in the Confederation of the Rhine—on 14 October a contingent of eight thousand Bavarians deserted his standard. Two days later, at Leipzig, he withstood an Allied army that outnumbered his own. Both sides sought reinforcements; a hundred thousand Russians and Prussians arrived on the 17th; and on the 18th this 'Battle of the Nations' ended in a disastrous French defeat. A remnant of Napoleon's forces, forty thousand at most, retreated across the Rhine early in November. Over two hundred thousand, dead, wounded, or prisoners, remained in the Germanies.

When Austria entered the war in August 1813, Napoleon, for the first time, faced a Grand Coalition of four great powers. This time his enemies exchanged the pledges that Pitt had urged in vain in 1799 and 1805. The Anglo-Russian and Russo-Prussian treaties of Reichenbach, in force since the previous June, precluded separate negotiations with Napoleon. A similar provision was included in conventions signed by Austria at Teplitz with Russia (9 September) and England (9 October). On 29 January 1814 Castlereagh induced the four allied powers to agree that France should be reduced to the territorial limits it had attained under the Bourbons. The view, so frequently reiterated by the British government, that the French ascendancy must be annulled and a balance of power restored in Europe, became the official policy of the Grand Coalition.

With Napoleon's withdrawal across the Rhine at the close of 1813 his allies abandoned him and his empire collapsed. His battered divisions in Spain were already retreating across the Pyrenees pursued by the Anglo-Spanish army commanded by Wellington. In Italy Joachim Murat, whom Napoleon had made king of Naples, was negotiating with the Austrians. By the opening of 1814 the ascendancy in

Europe that the French had tried for twenty years to achieve and preserve was at an end, and the principle of equilibrium reasserted itself. The campaigns and negotiations of 1814 which led to Napoleon's abdication, and the peace settlement arranged at the Congress of Vienna in 1814–15, will therefore be reserved for a later chapter (Chapter XXIV).

Viewed in historical perspective the temporary expansion of French influence after 1793, and the creation of the Napoleonic Empire, cannot fail to appear excessive and anomalous. They contradicted a dominant political trend that had been shaping European society since the later Middle Ages, the trend toward a system of individual sovereign territorial states. By the close of the eighteenth century many of the earlier dynastic kingdoms had developed into organic national realms with definitive geographical limits. The events of the revolutionary period hastened this transformation. Where Napoleon could appeal to the frustrated national consciousness of divided and subjugated peoples, notably the Italians and the Poles, he found it possible to arouse enthusiasm and secure recruits. But his efforts to reduce all western Europe to unity under a Napoleonic dynasty ran counter to the emotions and aspirations of the leading European nations. There is an element of historical irony in the fact that his attempt to make France secure by extending French influence over Germany and Italy contributed to an opposite result. His policy of encouraging the larger German states to absorb the smaller and his appeals to Italian patriotism hastened the evolution and consolidation of Germany and Italy into first class powers pressing upon the French frontiers. Within fifty years of Napoleon's death the relative might of France declined to a level at which *La Grande Nation* offered, and could offer, no further threat to the European equilibrium.

Note on Switzerland

The Helvetic Republic, formed after the French occupation of April 1798, painfully survived two momentary withdrawals (1798 and 1802) and a sudden re-occupation (October 1802), but was dissolved by Napoleon's Act of Mediation (February 1803). This re-constituted a less unpopular but still satellite Swiss Confederation, restored to independence in 1815. (See pp. 256–7, 262, 658.)

CHAPTER X

THE INTERNAL HISTORY OF FRANCE
DURING THE WARS, 1793–1814

A<small>T</small> Valmy, on 20 September 1792, the first of the many victories of the armies of the Revolution marked for Europe the start of a twenty-year war, only interrupted from 1802 to 1804 by two years of precarious peace. For France, this meant the beginning of a new regime—the Republic. Democratic at first, then middle-class and, later, Consular, it finally turned into a military dictatorship which, from 1804, adopted the name of Empire. This new regime sprang from the big social, economic and administrative changes which had occurred since 1789. The democratic republic, in 1793 and 1794, tried to fulfil the ambitions of the Revolution by combining economic equality with the equality of civic rights that had been secured in 1789. In so doing, it was to give the world an example which would inspire future socialism. But these ideals were to be short-lived. The bourgeois republic, like the military dictatorship, was to be content with consolidating the achievements of 1789, now firmly established even against the reaction of 1814.

No doubt the administrative and social achievement of 1789–92, and the socialist experiments too, would have taken shape differently if France had not been in an almost permanent state of war which dominated internal policy during the next twenty-two years. The war, and the dangers to which France was exposed by repeated defeats during the first five months of the struggle (April to September 1792), developed in the people an exalted patriotism along with the fear of enemy invasion and of seignorial reaction. In the face of danger, the majority of the bourgeoisie, artisans and peasants united to resist, but the bourgeoisie had to make temporary concessions to the people's demands. Then again, the revolutionaries believed that they could only face the dangers at home by terrorising their opponents. Thus the war produced the Terror. The Revolution which, until 1792, had only rarely and accidentally spilt blood, was now to wallow in it; violence and murder were to become a method of government.

Violence and terror were advocated by the *sans-culottes*, not a social class as such, but a fairly mixed group of workers, humble artisans and small shop-keepers, only partially educated but ardently patriotic, quick to react in the most primitive ways. The national danger was such that the bourgeoisie, though shocked, turned a blind eye in order to save both France and the Revolution. The bourgeoisie, in power since the autumn of 1789, had temporarily to alter its attitude by admitting that it was necessary, for a while, to sacrifice individual and economic freedom. It agreed to postpone the liberties of the individual in order to improve financial and social equality. Thus, the war was to produce a new regime, ephemeral but inspiring the ideologists of social equality whose number was to grow in France and Europe. Without war there would have been no Terror, but without the Terror victory would not have been possible. And, without victory, a general could not have changed the republic into a military dictatorship nor created an empire which extended for a moment over two-thirds of Europe and left the world a changed place when, in 1814, it finally collapsed.

As the battle of Valmy was ending, the Legislative Assembly was giving way to a new one called the Convention, named after the North American assemblies because it was to give the country a new constitution.[1]

The Convention was to be chosen, no longer by the votes of property-owners only, but by nearly universal suffrage. But in the elections, held at a moment of exceptional tension in Paris, in the provinces and on the frontiers, those who did not uphold the Revolution abstained from voting so as to remain unnoticed. Only the most revolutionary fraction —less than one-tenth—went to the polls. The Convention was drawn almost entirely from the bourgeoisie—lawyers for the most part—with only two workmen among its 750 members. It was to remain in being a little over three years—until 31 October 1795. This period falls into three clearly marked phases: that of the 'Girondin Convention', ending on 2 June 1793; that of the 'Revolutionary Government', brought to an end by the fall of Robespierre on 27 July 1794; and finally that of the 'Thermidorian Reaction'.

The first act of the Convention was to abolish the state of monarchy, which had been suspended with the arrest of Louis XVI on the demand of the insurgent Commune of Paris after the storming of the Tuileries on the morning of 10 August 1792. The middle-class Convention had some difficulty in asserting itself against the Commune. It had no intention of redistributing wealth on a large scale, far less of bringing back the economic controls abolished in 1789. But some of its members, the Montagnards, considered that, in order to keep the support of the sans-culottes, who had helped them to victory, they had to make a few concessions, temporarily at least. Another group, the Girondins, was linked with the important business men of the capital, chief ports and big cities. It was suspicious of the sans-culottes, and would not hear of controls which it regarded as an unacceptable attack upon property.

---

[1] The events of the first months of the Convention (from its meeting on 21 September 1792 to the French declaration of war on England and Holland on 1 February 1793) are described in vol. VIII, ch. XXIV. Only the leading threads are picked up again here.

Between these two groups lay the majority of deputies, like a plain or swamp of indecision. There were no 'parties' in the modern sense within the Convention, still less in the country. Nevertheless, all the members were ardent patriots, determined to repel invasion and to secure a peace which would henceforth protect the new institutions from foreign intervention. At first, fortune seemed to smile on them. The invaders retreated and the revolutionary troops entered Belgium, the German Rhineland, Savoy and Nice, where votes were taken in favour of joining France. The Convention agreed and, under Girondin pressure, even declared that it would grant 'fraternity and aid to all nations who wished to regain their freedom . . .' (19 November 1792).

At the same time the Convention was divided about the fate of Louis XVI. The Moderates, and many Girondins, would have been content to keep him in prison until the end of the war; but the Montagnards, backed by the *sans-culottes*, were determined to make restoration impossible by striking at the very principle of monarchy. By a small majority, Louis was condemned to death as a traitor and guillotined on 21 January 1793. The execution shocked Europe and widened the gap between the Montagnards, most of whom had voted for death, and the Girondins who, on the whole, wanted to save the king's life. Moreover, the king's fate, and the annexationist policy of the Convention, caused the war to flare up again. A mighty alliance was formed against France. In all Europe, only Turkey, Scandinavia and Switzerland remained at peace with her (Chapter IX, p. 254).

The force built up by this alliance shook the French armies, from which many of the volunteers, enlisted for only one campaign, had gone home. Dumouriez, commander-in-chief of the Northern army and victor of Valmy, was beaten at Neerwinden, in Belgium, on 18 March 1793. He blamed the regime for his defeat, negotiated with the Austrian general, Coburg, and attempted to march on Paris with his army. But, as the men refused, he went over to the enemy, taking with him the Minister of War, Beurnonville, and four commissioners who had come to arrest him. This treason disorganised the national defence and caused a political crisis, all the greater because the economic situation had deteriorated during the winter. Through repeated heavy issues, the *assignat* had lost more than 50 per cent of its original value and, for lack of control on the price of grain, the cost of living, as a whole, kept rising. The Girondins, who had wanted the war in 1792, and the annexations of 1793, were fiercely opposed to all price controls. And the fact that the traitor, Dumouriez, was closely associated with them made them appear even more responsible for the crisis.

As in 1792, the crisis produced another crop of revolutionary institutions. Once more, there were the *comités de surveillance* (vigilance committees) and the *bataillons révolutionnaires* (irregular forces). The

Jacobin clubs, where, increasingly, the *sans-culottes* were replacing the bourgeoisie, intervened with greater frequency and efficiency in the political scene. Arrests made without government sanction increased in number. Lists of suspects were drawn up. In Paris, the Sections, controlled by the *sans-culottes* and guided by the Commune, accused the Girondins of paralysing the Convention, and the government of leading the Revolution to its downfall. Within the Convention, the struggle reached its climax when on 31 May the *sans-culottes* rose, as in August 1792, but this time against the Convention. Armed, they presented their demands: dismissal of the Girondin leaders; abolition of a twelve-man committee of enquiry set up on 8 May and conspicuously hostile to the *sans-culottes*; a purge of officials; the creation of a 'revolutionary army'; control of the price of bread; a tax on wealth; public assistance for the old, the sick and the relatives of the 'defenders of the republic'. The Convention would not give way until, surrounded on 2 June by 80,000 armed *sans-culottes*, it was forced, after a final show of resistance, to yield to their demands. Twenty-nine deputies and two Girondin ministers were arrested.

But in many departments the Girondins, who held the principal administrative posts, staged a revolt against the Parisian *sans-culottes*. This movement, called '*sectional*', or federal, was especially strong in Normandy, the Bordeaux district, Lyons, the Rhône Valley and Provence. It was all the more serious because it followed a strong uprising of three months earlier (10 March) in Vendée and the adjoining departments. The peasants of that region, whose interests were opposed to those of the bourgeoisie, had risen when the Convention had decreed a levy of 300,000 more men for the army. At the beginning of June 1793, there were more than sixty departments opposed to or openly rebelling against the Montagnard Convention. It was a struggle, not between two political conceptions, but between two social groups: the upper-middle class, backed by the royalists and frightened by the growth of the revolution it had unleashed, and the lower-middle class which had the support of the *sans-culottes* and was determined to use extreme measures to guarantee 'public safety' and defeat all enemies of France, both within and without.

Immediately after 2 June, the victorious Montagnards tried to re-assure the country and disarm rebellion by voting a constitution which would show that there was nothing alarming in their tenets. The Convention had already been discussing the new constitution, but its drafting had been delayed by the quarrels between the Girondins and the Montagnards. Once the former were out of the way, the work was quickly finished. The Constitution of 1793 was infinitely more democratic than that of 1791. It set up universal franchise for men, and the referendum; it proclaimed the freedom of nations to be masters of their own destiny, and the fraternity of free peoples everywhere. It declared, in its first clause, that the aim of society was 'the common welfare'; it affirmed the right to work, to State assistance and to education, but, against Robespierre, it maintained the right to property defined in the Declaration of Rights. Economic freedom was asserted, but also the right to rebel. The Constitution granted legislative power to an Assembly elected for one year only, and executive power to a council of ministers chosen from outside the Assembly and in effect subordinate to it. This constitution, having been approved by a referendum (with 1,800,000 in favour) but judged inapplicable at the moment, was placed in a cedar-wood 'ark' and presented to the President of the Convention—and there it remained. Nevertheless, it did play an important part in history. For the first time it officially presented to the world the problems of social democracy. It became a guide to social democrats like Babeuf, Buonarroti, and later Louis Blanc, Barbès and Jaurès, all of whom were to sing its praises.

Since the Constitution was now in abeyance, the Convention declared on 10 October that, until the end of the war, the government of France would remain 'revolutionary'—that is, abnormal. This revolutionary government was set on its feet during the summer by numerous separate measures, without any overall plan but supported by the *sans-culottes*. It was codified, up to a point, by the decree of 14 Frimaire an II (4 December 1793). In effect, the executive powers were left to two Committees of the Convention, those for Public Safety and General Security. The former had been started on 1 January 1793 under the name of the Committee for General Defence at the time when the tension between France and England was mounting. Reorganised and reduced to nine members after Dumouriez's treason, it was charged with advising the government on all subjects except finance and police. After the removal of the Girondins, the Committee underwent another reshuffle. It was in July and August 1793, when the situation at home and abroad was deteriorating and the food shortage was being seriously felt, that this committee (known also as the *Grand Comité*) took shape so as to rule dictatorially for a year and save France from invasion. It consisted of twelve members who did not, however, form a harmonious group. There were moderates like Robert Lindet, Lazare Carnot, Prieur de la Côte d'Or, specialists in military and economic problems; and, on the 'left', Robespierre, Saint-Just and Couthon in the political field. Jean Bon Saint André and Prieur de la Marne dealt with naval questions. Hand in glove with the *sans-culottes* were 'extremists' like Billaud-Varenne and Collot d'Herbois; in the centre, Barère, the eloquent man of compromise; and, on the right wing, a former member of the Parlement of Paris, Hérault de Séchelles. The Committee for General Security, as old as the Convention itself and successor to the Vigilance Committee of the Legislative, was also, from September 1793, composed of twelve members who survived in office for nine months and controlled the political police. These two committees, responsible to the Convention which could renew or overthrow them each month, formed a kind of 'parliamentary' government which had unrestricted power as long as it held the assembly's confidence.

The Committee for General Security saw to the prompt execution of its decisions by means of *représentants en mission* (members of the Convention sent to the provinces and the armies) and of 'national agents' superimposed by the government upon the local administrative officials. The revolutionary vigilance committees were legalised and entrusted locally with watching suspects; but in fact they often exceeded their powers. The part played by the Jacobin clubs was officially recognised, as a popular check upon the local authorities. Elections were deferred, and the task of renewing the administrative councils was given to the *représentants en mission* aided by the popular clubs. The 'revolutionary armies', on the other hand, which had set themselves up in many *départements* to arrest suspects, commandeer food and supply markets, were suppressed as insubordinate. The most rigid centralisation that France had ever known was replacing the extreme decentralisation initiated by the Constituent. The first result of these measures was to check the civil war in which two-thirds of the *départements* were threatening to rise against Paris. The federal insurgents of Normandy were defeated at Pacy-sur-Eure on 13 July. Most of the *départements* rallied to the Convention and the revolt was thus confined to three regions, against which regular forces were sent: Vendée; Lyon; Provence and the rebel cities of Marseilles and Toulon.

In order to smother the risings and to prevent others, the *sans-culottes*, by the demonstrations of 4 and 5 September 1793, forced the Convention to adopt extreme measures which, together, added up to the Reign of Terror. As early as March 1793, the sending of 'suspects' to prison had begun. The edict of 17 September ordered the arrest of stated categories of suspects. It is still difficult to know exactly how many Frenchmen were imprisoned as suspects, estimates varying between 300,000 and 500,000. To judge them, revolutionary tribunals were established. Already on 17 August 1792, a first, special tribunal had been formed in Paris, but the slowness of its methods had provoked the September massacres and it was suppressed on 29 November. After Dumouriez's treason, a revolutionary tribunal was again set up, divided in September into four sections, of which two worked simultaneously. Some tribunals and military courts were organised in provincial cities. At least 17,000 suspects were condemned to death; including summary executions and deaths in prison, the number of victims amounts to 35,000 or 40,000—figures as high as those of the sixteenth century, though hardly comparable with the wholesale massacres of the twentieth century in Russia, Spain and Germany. Eighty-nine per cent of the executions took place in the areas of revolt: in the west, in the Rhône Valley, and on the northern and eastern frontiers. In six *départements* there were no death-sentences; in each of thirty-one others, fewer than ten. The biggest contingents of victims came from the working men (31 per cent) and the peasants (28 per cent). Compared with the total number, casualties among the aristocracy and clergy were few, but high in relation to their number and importance.

The Reign of Terror raged from October 1793 to July 1794. It was essentially political and repressive and its aim was in no way, as has sometimes been asserted, to wipe out a social class. In essence it was a defensive measure designed to protect the country and the Revolution. The two 'Committees of Government', besides having to deal with the 'enemy within', also had to repulse foreign armies all along the frontiers, and to fight on land and sea against the European Coalition. In this struggle, France was in a position to overcome the unequal odds, providing she made use of all her man-power. With about 26 million inhabitants, France was the most highly populated state on the Continent; indeed, taking area and resources into account, she was overcrowded. The resulting mass of unemployed was easily absorbed into the army.

The setting up of the National Guard was the first step towards conscription. As early as February 1793, the Convention ordered a levy of 300,000 men which, as we have seen, sparked off the Vendée rising. Finding this measure inadequate, and under pressure from the *sans-culottes*, the Convention declared a 'general levy'. Unmarried men from 18 to 25 were required to enlist, while the rest of the population was expected to direct its activities to a single end: victory in war. A massive effort was needed to arm, feed and equip these numbers. France was the only country on the Continent where industry was sufficiently developed to provide what was needed quickly. Arms factories were multiplied, all textile mills were made to work for the army, and workshops for the manufacture of uniforms and shoes sprang up everywhere. Deficiencies were made good by requisitioning. Scientists were called upon to improve equipment and invent new war machines. The semaphore, invented by Chappe, and the use of balloons, perfected by Conté, made their first appearance in the field. A year after the invasion, in the spring of 1794, the Committee of Public Safety was able to face the enemy on all fronts with superior forces.

Financing such a war would have proved an almost insoluble problem to the old regime, but now the *assignat* gave the government almost unlimited funds: all they had to do was to print banknotes. But this produced a problem that was new, or at least unprecedented in scale: that of inflation, together with its immediate consequence—the high cost of living. This was the result, not only of easy money but also of the mobilisation which had taken active men away from the land and reduced production. It was also linked with a series of bad harvests. After the famine of 1788–9, the years 1791 to 1793 showed shortages. The markets were badly stocked for this reason and also because the peasants would not accept the *assignats* which were steadily losing value. Thus the cost of food kept rising and inflation spread to the prices of all commodities.

In such conditions, it was not surprising that those who suffered felt that the Revolution had fallen short of its aims—a view held by the *sans-culottes* in the cities, particularly in Paris. Their ideas on property differed greatly from those of the bourgeoisie. Like the peasants, bent on preserving communal customs, the *sans-culottes* would have liked property to be based on personal labour, but limited by the needs of all. On 2 September 1793, the Paris section demanded that the Convention should 'fix once and for all the price of vital commodities, wages, and profits in industry and trade'. They added: 'Doubtless, the aristocrats, the royalists, the moderates and the intriguers will say, "this is interfering with property which must remain sacred and inviolable" . . . but don't these scoundrels know that the right of property extends only to basic necessities?' In this conception of property within strict limits, they were opposed to the ideas of the revolutionary bourgeoisie, indeed of almost all members of the Convention. In short they wanted equality not only in 'rights' but also in wages and in the distribution of necessities. Their ideal was that of a society consisting of small independent producers and landowners. Their theory of government was inclined to be anarchistic. They would have liked to see it exercised directly by the people debating and voting openly in primary assemblies. Their main spokesmen were Hébert, Jacques Roux and a group called *les enragés*. But these men were not original thinkers, able to stir the masses; on the contrary, they only appeared, in their pamphlets and newspapers, as the 'sonorous echoes' of the *sans-culottes*.

To fight the rising cost of living, the Convention, very much against its own conviction, had to bring in far more thorough and strict controls over supplies than any enforced under the old regime. The *maximum général* of prices and wages was introduced, under *sans-culotte* pressure, on 29 September 1793. The 'revolutionary armies' and committees were to use the Terror as a means of forcing the peasants to supply markets and to sell within the maximum price. A law of 26 July 1793, which prescribed the death-penalty for hoarders, was rarely put into operation; but the mere threat of it, and the activities of the revolutionary institutions, were enough to improve supplies to markets and shops. In Paris and other cities ration cards were issued.

Improving food supplies was only part of the *sans-culottes*' programme. They also wanted to reduce inequality by increased taxation of the wealthy and by sharing out the land. At the same time, some of them accused even the 'constitutional' clergy (as well as the refractory priests) of *modérantisme*, thus attacking Christianity itself. As early as 1790 a 'revolutionary' cult had developed with civic demonstrations and anniversary festivals (for instance on 14 July); the *sans-culottes* were adding to these a cult of the 'martyrs of freedom' and aiming to 'dechristianise' the country. Most of the Committee of Public Safety, including Robespierre himself, were opposed to these tendencies which might alienate the masses from the Revolution and paralyse the country's defence. Although the Committee made the Convention adopt the revolutionary calendar—perhaps the most anti-Christian measure of the Revolution—it also gave a free hand to Danton and his friends, (*les indulgents*) to start a reaction. At the same time it placated the *sans-culottes* by ordering the distribution to the needy of the property belonging to suspects recognised as 'enemies of the republic' —measures which were difficult to execute and could only bear fruit over a long period. On one side, the Committee arrested the spokesmen of the *sans-culottes* for their violent attacks on its policy and for planning a new insurrection. On the other side, it arrested Danton and his friends so as to forestall a peaceful compromise and the restoration of the king. Summoned before the revolutionary tribunal in quick succession, Hébert, the *enragés* and the *indulgents* were sentenced and executed (24 March, 5 and 13 April 1794).

For four months, the Committee of Public Safety, led by Robespierre, was all powerful, but in fact it had lost the support of the people of Paris by the execution of the *sans-culotte* leaders. 'The Revolution is frozen', wrote Saint Just. The Committee wanted to achieve the final victory of the Revolution by using the Terror in the name of 'virtue'. To offset the measures against Christianity, and in the hope of rallying the masses, it tried to implant a deistic religion—the Cult of the Supreme Being. It also pursued a policy of social security by instituting, with the Register (*grand livre*) of National Welfare, unemployment benefit for the able-bodied poor, home assistance for the sick and relief for the old. At the same time, the principle of compulsory primary education without fees was adopted, and slavery in the colonies was abolished. But the application of these innovations had to be postponed for lack of funds and the prospect for them in future seemed dubious.

The Terror, the tremendous defence effort and the economic and social controls produced the anticipated results. At home the revolts were overcome. Lyons and Marseilles were recaptured on 9 and 25

October, Toulon on 18 December 1793. The Vendéens were crushed on 23 December, and although the rebellion in the west lingered on with guerrilla warfare, this *chouannerie* was more tiresome than dangerous. In the spring of 1794 the main body of the French troops were able to face the external enemy. After several local successes in attack, on 25 June they won the resounding victory of Fleurus, thus reopening the way to Belgium. With the civil war ended and invasion halted, the Reign of Terror and all its restrictions could no longer be endured.

Yet, precisely at the time of Fleurus, the Terror was intensified. In an effort at centralisation, most of the revolutionary and military tribunals in the provinces had been dispensed with, and suspects were tried in Paris. In face of new 'aristocratic plots' (indicated by attempted murders of some members of the Committee of Public Safety), Robespierre's law of 10 June changed the procedure of the revolutionary tribunal, abolishing even the scanty guarantees enjoyed by the accused and refusing them any defence. The number of executions in Paris from March 1793 to June 1794 was 1251; from 10 June to the fall of the Committee on 27 July it was 1376. This new Reign of Terror, at a time when victories seemed to make it less necessary, widened the split between the Committees of Public Safety and of General Security, and aggravated the lack of unity between the members of the former. The effect of victory also loosened the bonds which had for the past year linked the Jacobin bourgeoisie with the *sans-culottes*. The liberalism of the one clashed with the *dirigisme* of the other. The majority of Frenchmen turned against the Terror, and against Robespierre who appeared to be responsible for it. At the same time the *sans-culottes* were drifting further from the government which had executed their leaders in March. They were, moreover, irritated by the limitation of wages which the Commune of Paris first promulgated on 23 July; this in fact meant a compulsory drop in real wages, just when in spite of price-regulation the cost of living was still rising.

The 'Great Committee of Public Safety' was overthrown by the Assembly on 27 July 1794 (9 Thermidor, an II), having lost all support from the deputies and the populace alike, as a result of an alliance between the terrorists recalled from the provinces and intimidated by Robespierre, and the moderate 'Plain'. After a vain show of resistance, Robespierre and his associates were 'outlawed', arrested and beheaded the following day. With them disappeared the prospect of an egalitarian and democratic republic which they had tried to create.

The first consequence of Robespierre's fall was a quick ending to the Reign of Terror. The regulation of prices and wages was soon abolished (December 1794), and the social legislation of the Year II collapsed after no more than a first attempt to apply it. The surviving Girondins were recalled to the 'Thermidorian' Convention as it was now called.

For a year the assembly had supported Robespierre from necessity, because victory was essential to the survival of the principles of 1789; now the majority returned to its individualistic and liberal ideas. The Constitution of 1793 was considered too democratic to be enforced. The revolutionary government was kept in office but in a much more restrained form. Power was divided between three committees instead of two: much of the authority of the Committee of Public Safety passed to the Committee of Legislation. Other revolutionary committees were reduced in number and scope. Under the influence of the Moderates (while the Democrats were divided into *néo-hébertistes* and Jacobins) and owing to pressure from groups of young rebels, deserters and released suspects, the Convention gradually moved into a path of reaction. It obstructed the activities of the popular clubs and societies, and on 12 November closed the Jacobin club itself in Paris. On 24 December, it abolished the Law of the Maximum and restored economic freedom. This measure caused a steeper rise in prices, followed by huge issues of *assignats*. In May 1795, the *assignat* lost 68 per cent of its face value and in July, 97 per cent; what was later called the 'infernal cycle' had begun. Investors were ruined, workers reduced to near starvation, while the *nouveaux riches*, the *merveilleuses* and the *incroyables* ostentatiously wallowed in luxury and abandoned themselves to pleasure. The plight of the working classes was aggravated by the unemployment that followed the closing of most arms factories built the preceding year, and by the rigours of the winter of 1794–5, one of the coldest of the century (even the rivers were frozen for several weeks).

In March 1795, the people's despair changed to fury. On 1 April an unruly mob broke into the Convention and demanded the re-establishment of the 1793 Constitution and measures to control the food shortages. The National Guard from the rich quarters had no trouble in dispersing the demonstrators, twenty Montagnard deputies were arrested and the militant *sans-culottes* disarmed. But these measures, far from quelling, only excited the spirit of insurrection, already endemic in the poorer quarters of Paris. On 20 May the *sans-culottes* stormed the Convention once more and killed a deputy, but failed to impose their programme. The 'committees of government', controlled by the Moderates, organised a counter-attack. Fourteen more Montagnards were arrested and, with the help of the army (now first used by the Revolution against popular demonstrators), the Saint-Antoine district was made to surrender. Many *sans-culottes* were arrested, forty were executed, and the reaction spread through the rest of France: this was the White Terror. The popular rising was crushed and the bourgeoisie took the helm. The 1793 Constitution was declared void, and the Convention set out to draft a new one. The Royalists saw in the situation an opportunity of seizing power; but an attempted landing at Quiberon by a corps of *émigrés* (27 June–21 July) was bloodily repulsed, and a rising of the Parisian Royalists on 5 October 1795 was crushed by government troops under the command of the young general Bonaparte, who had distinguished himself at the siege of Toulon in 1793.

The political vicissitudes should not obscure the work done by the Thermidorian Convention in the spiritual and intellectual fields. In some respects, it was a remarkable achievement. To put an end to the religious crisis begun in 1790, it separated the Church from the State. This experiment did not eliminate religious conflicts but it was a forward-looking effort which was to last longer than those tried in the economic and social fields and was to have strong repercussions throughout the world. Free and compulsory primary education was not put into practice, but secondary education was rejuvenated by instituting 'central schools' which broke with tradition by putting science, art and modern languages to the fore. Higher education was improved by the creation of the *École Polytechnique* and other foundations (Chapters V, pp. 121–3, and VII, pp 198–200). The intellectuals were proud of these achievements: France appeared as *la Grande Nation*. Victories beyond the frontiers also seemed to justify the title, and with the return of peace on the Continent in 1795 (Chapter IX, p. 255) it looked as though the new regime, born of the revolution, could at last take root and consolidate itself within France.

The outgoing Convention tried to give France a stable political framework which neither the Constituent in 1791 nor the Convention itself in 1793 had succeeded in making. It now drew up a new constitution and approved it on 17 August 1795 (an III). This was endorsed by a referendum (1,000,000 in favour, 5,000 against); most of the six million voters abstained. The constitution was much less democratic than that of 1793 or even that of 1791: with a franchise based on a property qualification, the Directory has been described as a bourgeois republic. In place of the declaration of the rights of man (1789) stood a declaration of rights and duties, eliminating one of the most significant phrases—'men are born free and with equal rights.' As the deputy Lanjuinais said in debate: 'if you say that all men are equal in rights you incite to revolt against the constitution all whose exercise of civic rights has been denied or suspended for the safety of all.' The Thermidorians were content to say, cautiously, that 'equality consists in having one law for all'. The declaration did not mention the rights to education, work, public assistance or rebellion, which had all been included in 1793; but it retained the definition of the right to property as a man's 'right to enjoy and dispose of his property, income and the fruit of his labour'. Thus it unambiguously sanctioned economic freedom.

Universal suffrage, introduced with the Republic in 1792, disappeared in the Republic of 1795. Only Frenchmen who paid direct taxes could be called 'citizens' and have the right to vote. The franchise may seem wider than in 1791, when it had depended on paying taxes equal to at least three days' work; but it is not certain that there were more voters, in the country districts anyway, in 1795 than in 1791. The system of election in two stages was continued; to be nominated an elector at the second stage, a man had to be over 25 and to own property producing an income equal to 200 days' work or to rent land or a house to the value of 150–200 days' work, according to the locality. In all, there were about 30,000 electors who met in electoral assemblies.

Legislative power had been given since 1789 to a single assembly; now, for the first time in France, there were two: the Council of Five Hundred (*les Cinq-Cents*) and the Council of Elders (*les Anciens*), the latter consisting of 250 members, married or widowers, all over 40. No property qualifications were required from the deputies. One-third of the seats became vacant each year. The executive power was vested in a Directory of five—hence the name of the regime. The Directors, elected for five years by the legislative councils (one retiring each year) had powers much wider than those of the king in 1791. They appointed the ministers, who were merely their agents. They controlled the civil service, army, police and foreign affairs. Finance alone was separately administered by five treasury commissioners, and five from the exchequer (*comptabilité nationale*), who were elected in the same manner as the Directors. The administrative framework created in 1790 was preserved in the main. The *départements* were left as they were, but managed by five elected members who were in turn controlled by a central commissioner appointed by the Directory—a forerunner of the prefect of the Empire. The *districts* of 1790, which had played a great part in the revolutionary government, were abolished, but each *canton* was under a municipal body—an interesting experiment which did not outlast the Directory. On the other hand, the *communes* of less than 5,000 inhabitants lost their town council, which was replaced by an elected municipal agent and his deputy (*adjoint*). Generally speaking, centralisation was less strong than in 1792–3, but far stronger than in 1791. In particular, the Directory had power to annul administrative acts, suspend or dismiss any official and fill his place until the following year. The organisation of justice changed little. There was still one magistrate for each canton, but each *département* now had only one civil tribunal.

The new constitution attempted to reduce the activities of the popular clubs and societies. Although the press was controlled, and newspapers could by law be suspended for as much as a year, there was more freedom under the Directory than under the Convention. Church and State were separated, but attempts were still being made to establish an official cult, first the deistic theophilanthropy, then the rationalist '*décadaire*' cult, both of which were miserable failures. The authors of the constitution did all they could to prevent a return to the recent dictatorship of an assembly or committee and to forestall military rule. They separated the powers of government as much as possible, and provided for annual vacancies in elected bodies. But there were no safeguards against conflicts, always possible, between the executive and the legislative powers, nor for supporting the government in emergencies, for instance in time of war. And it was precisely in emergency that the constitution was to be swept away.

The economic situation had gone from bad to worse. The cost of living in Paris, taken as 100 in 1790, was said to be over 5000 in November 1795. The plight of the poorer classes was critical. The Democrats, whose boldest spokesman was now Babeuf, were trying to regain the support of the people by criticising the new constitution. In his periodical *Tribun du Peuple* Babeuf wrote on 6 November: 'What, in general, is a political revolution? What, in particular, is the French revolution? An open war between patricians and plebeians, between the rich and the poor.' The Royalists also were trying to exploit the situation. Although the last bands of *chouans* in the west had been defeated and their leaders shot, the Royalists had at least 200 deputies in the councils, and might win over an equal number of uncommitted Moderates. So, changing tactics, they hoped to gain power either legally by winning a majority in the legislative body, or else with the help of a general and his men. They were counting on Pichegru, commanding the army of the Rhine and Moselle. The Directory had no broad political foundations: it could only rely on that part of the well-to-do *bourgeoisie* to whom the revolution had brought some position of consequence or the opportunity to acquire confiscated lands or to gain a fortune by war-contracts: in short, the *honnêtes gens* or the *notables*. The influence which the Directory and the Legislative Councils could exert on each other was so much limited by the excessive separation of powers that the Directory took refuge in a series of *coups d'état*. The first took place on 4 September 1797 (18 Fructidor, an V) and put an end to the 'First Directory' which, for two years, had tried to govern France constitutionally.

This 'First Directory' was composed of regicide members of the Convention like Barras, Reubell, La Révellière-Lépeaux, Carnot, Letourneur. It first tried to surround itself with sincere republicans, especially the Jacobins. But Babeuf remained unapproachable. A warrant having been issued on 5 December 1795 for his arrest, he went underground and with the Italian Buonarroti and other members of the Convention he organised a plot intended to replace the Directory by a communistic regime. In so doing, Babeuf was the first politician of the Revolution who wanted to change into reality what, so far, had been considered a mere philosophical Utopia. Furthermore, he broke away from insurrectional methods so far used in France by organising a conspiracy of equality led by a small group of men on whom he thought he could rely, and who would not divulge the ultimate aims of the conspirators.

The economic crisis favoured the propaganda of Babeuf's supporters (*Babouvistes*). The *assignat*, which had dropped to zero, was replaced by the *mandat territorial* (a new version of the same thing), which lost 70 per cent of its value soon after the first issue and continued to drop very quickly. The inevitable return to a metal currency meant a sudden deflation, disastrous for the poor. Hesitating and internally divided, the Directory eventually resolved, under pressure from Carnot, to tackle the *Babouvistes*. Betrayed by double agents, their leaders were arrested on 10 May 1796. Among those summoned before the High Court, Babeuf and another were sentenced to death and executed. The Conspiracy of the *Égaux* was to have immense repercussions in the nineteenth century. At the time, it encouraged the Directory to move towards the Moderates. During the elections of spring 1797 (an V) which affected one third of the Legislative Councils, the Moderates were markedly successful; and Letourneur lost his seat as a Director to Barthélémy, a Moderate and a negotiator of the treaties of Bâle. Since the Babeuf plot, Carnot too was moving into the same camp. The Councils, where the Moderates (strongly infiltrated by Royalists) were dominant, wanted an early peace without further annexations. The Royalists hoped that peace would favour the early restoration of Louis XVIII, although the constitutional royalists and the believers in absolute monarchy were divided on the nature of the regime. But the republican Directors were in conflict with the Councils, and the Directory's policy was not exactly aimed at peace. In fact, it was influenced both by the foreign refugees and 'patriots' who wanted to 'liberate' their homeland, and by the military men who wanted war to continue, whether from a desire to spread republican propaganda or from ambition or cupidity. Out of the three main French armies, two (those of Italy under Bonaparte and of Sambre and Meuse led by Jourdan) clamoured for continuing the war. Only that of the Rhine and Moselle, once led by Pichegru and now by Moreau, was less committed.

The campaigns of 1796 and 1797 favoured the supporters of the war and strengthened the Republicans. The resounding victories of the army of Italy obscured the defeats suffered by the armies in Germany (Chapter IX, p. 255). Bonaparte emerged as the great conqueror of the coalition. And, since the taxes he raised in the conquered countries made it possible to give up paper money and were partly used to balance the budget, it was becoming more and more difficult for any party, or even the government, to oppose his political views. But at home the financial situation was still unsatisfactory. The sudden deflation caused by the return of metal coinage was further aggravated by the bumper harvests of 1796–7. The price of farm produce fell. Doubtless, the situation for the poor in the cities was improved by this, but the peasants' position was worsened, and the yield from taxes was disappointing. The royalists and moderates, who met at the Clichy club—hence their name *Clichyens*—took advantage of the situation to force the repeal of a whole series of laws against the *émigrés* and their relations and the refractory priests. They thought that the Directors, among whom they already had two allies, would accept their ideas if Barras, the fifth director, would join them. If on the other hand, Barras sided with Reubell and La Révellière, they were counting on General Pichegru, who had been elected president of the Council of Five-Hundred, to stage a *coup d'état*. As it happened, Barras had received from Bonaparte some papers seized in Italy from a Royalist agent, the Count d'Antraigues. These documents exposed Pichegru's treason. Barras joined Reubell and La Révellière, so that the majority in the Directory became definitely republican. This majority decided to outwit the Clichyens by calling upon the apparently least dangerous general—Hoche, the new commander of the Sambre and Meuse Army. Under the pretext of going to the west coast to prepare for an invasion of Britain, Hoche's troops were to pass through Paris and arrest the Clichyen leaders. The Clichyens were eliminated from the Ministry and Hoche himself became minister of war. These preparations were exposed by their opponents in the Directory who pointed out two violations of the constitution: the unauthorised entry of the Sambre and Meuse troops into the *rayon constitutionnel* (i.e. Paris and its environs) without the consent of the legislature, and the nomination of Hoche as a minister while he was under age. The Directory had to withdraw. The plot had misfired (July 1797).

The royalists and the moderates lost no time in reorganising the National Guard (weeding out the republicans) and demanding the closing of the 'constitutional clubs' authorised by the Directory. But they lacked both daring and speed. Pichegru could not bring himself to act, and once more the Directory forestalled them. Unable to call upon the *sans-culottes* suppressed since May 1795, the Directory had no choice but to approach Bonaparte. Since he had been violently attacked by the Legislative Councils about his Italian campaign, Bonaparte had despatched to Paris, through various units of his army, some addresses fulminating against the Royalists and demanding the elimination of the Clichyens. One of his subordinates, General Augereau, conveniently happened to be in Paris together with others on leave from the Italian army. So the 'triumvirate' of Barras, Reubell and La Révellière called upon them for help. On the night of 3–4 September

1797 (17–18 Fructidor, an V) the triumvirate had the Clichyen leaders and the Director Barthélémy arrested; Carnot was warned and was able to escape. At a meeting of the Councils (legally convened but with none present except republicans), the election of 198 deputies was quashed. Thirty-three of these were sentenced to deportation, together with twelve other men including Barthélémy. All the 'reactionary' laws passed since the royalist election of the previous spring were repealed and the former laws against *émigrés* and refractory priests revived. As the constitution allowed, a new law submitted the press to a year of police inspection. Neither the constitution nor the institutions were altered. The Directory, brought up to strength with two republicans, François de Neufchâteau and Merlin de Douai, was content merely to appoint republicans in place of officials suspected of 'moderate' views. But, in fact, the Directory and the Councils were no longer free to act. They were dependent on the Army of Italy and on their leader, Bonaparte, who had come to their rescue. Bonaparte at once imposed his views on foreign policy, in particular the terms of the Peace of Campo Formio with Austria. Already he would have liked to make his influence felt at home, but circumstances were not yet in his favour.

The *coup d'état* of 18 Fructidor had, in effect, united the Directory, allowing it to concentrate on the improvement of existing institutions. In this field it played a useful but little acknowledged part in heralding the work of the Consulate and Empire. Finance was its first problem. On 10 September, six days after the *coup*, Ramel, the finance minister, proposed a bill for reducing the national debt by means of virtual bankruptcy; the Directory would thus be able to free itself from the financial tutelage which bound it to the generals. The law passed on 30 September reduced the debt from 250 to 83 millions (by two-thirds). A third of each government bond, the *tiers consolidé*, remained inscribed in the great book of the public debt. The other two-thirds were refunded by means of bonds which, to a certain extent, could be used as payment for the purchase of national property. Share-holders were thus partially robbed, but the country's finances looked healthier. Revenue was increased by new taxes: a tax on doors and windows was added to the three direct taxes already brought in by the Constituent. These *quatre vieilles* were to be the foundation of the French fiscal system until 1914. Thanks to an Agency of Direct Taxation made up of civil servants, taxes were more efficiently collected, the deficit was reduced and the financial state of the country was better than it had ever been since 1778.

Another important reform concerned recruitment. The Legislative and the Convention had dealt with it by calling upon volunteers and by the 'requisition' or 'mass levy' of the men who at that time (August 1793) were between 18 and 25. But no one had been called up since then. The law on conscription, proposed by General Jourdan and the deputy Delbrel, permanently established compulsory and universal military service: 'Every Frenchman is a soldier, and the defence of his country is his duty.' At the age of twenty, all citizens had to be registered—that is to say 'conscripted'—on the army recruiting rolls. In peacetime, the length of service was to be five years; but it was possible that the government might not call on all the conscripts, in which case the selection would be done by drawing lots. Conscription has ever since remained a basic French institution.

In spite of achieving some important laws, the regime of Fructidor failed to bring political stability. With the Jacobins apparently in power again, a violent repression—the *terreur directoriale*—struck especially the *émigrés* who had returned (160 of them were shot), and the refractory priests: 263 priests were deported to Guiana whose climate, which was then a killer, was known as the 'dry guillotine'. About 1500 others were interned in the islands of Ré and Oleron. Yet the Directory consisted mostly of moderate republicans, who were as much afraid of the *sans-culottes* (now called anarchists) as of the Royalists. These 'anarchists' seemed the more redoubtable as being in league with the 'patriots' in the French occupied countries and in the new sister republics. So the 'Second Directory' soon began treating the Jacobins as suspects. But the elections of April 1798 (an VI), although carefully prepared by the government, produced a Jacobin majority. Owing, however, to schism in many of the electoral assemblies, minority candidates were also declared elected. It was up to the Legislative Councils, under a law passed in January 1798, to decide which deputies should be confirmed. By the law of 11 May, they rejected 106 of the newly elected, including 104 Jacobins, or *exclusifs*, and two Royalists. Fifty-three candidates from the minority were admitted, but 53 seats remained vacant. Many judges and other regularly elected officials were also invalidated. This was called the *coup d'état* of 22 Floréal.

Given peace abroad, the Directory could perhaps have relied on the newly formed majority. But instead of dying out, the war was flaring up again. Unable to invade England, Bonaparte and Talleyrand induced the Directory to send a military expedition to Egypt. Nearer home, French armies invaded Italy and Switzerland. France was soon confronted by a second coalition and, in the spring of 1799 (as six years earlier) was being attacked on all fronts except the Pyrenees (Chapter IX, pp. 256–7). French troops had to fall back to the Alps and the Rhine.

These defeats greatly disturbed the French patriots. The Army put the blame on the government. So did the Jacobins since the *coup* of 22 Floréal (May 1798) against them. After the elections of April 1799 (an VII), the Jacobins once more had a majority in the Legislative Councils; egged on by the generals, they pointed to the Directory as responsible for disaster. Early in June 1799, the Council of Five Hundred requested the Directory to justify its policy and declared that the election of one of its members a year earlier had been unconstitutional and was therefore void. The Directory did not reply for a fortnight, and then only evasively. The opposition, led by Napoleon's brother, Lucien Bonaparte, pronounced the text unsatisfactory and secured the resignation of the two Directors considered responsible for the *coup* of 22 Floréal. Although the whole procedure was legal, this was called the *coup d'état* of 30 Prairial, an VII (18 June 1799). The outgoing Directors were replaced by Roger Ducos and General Moulin, both unobtrusive men and reputedly Jacobins. Together with Barras, Siéyès and Gohier, they made up the 'Third Directory', choosing ministers with a Jacobin reputation, such as Fouché for the police, Robert Lindet for finance, Cambacérès for justice, Bernadotte and later Dubois-Crancé for war.

Once again the Jacobins seemed to be in control at home. They tried to bestir the country by appealing to the 'public safety', as in 1792–3. In *départements* where there were frequent political riots and murders, the local authorities were empowered in July to arrest nobles and the relatives of *émigrés* and suspected culprits as hostages. Furthermore, these hostages were made legally responsible for indemnity due to the victims and for the rewards granted to the agents of reprisal. The rich were made to contribute to a graduated loan of one hundred million, repayable in national lands, in order to provide the necessary funds for the armies without again resorting to the ill-famed paper money (August). Measures were taken for the prompt enforcement, without exemption, of the conscription law. Committees of inquiry were set up to identify those responsible for military defeats and to probe into the behaviour of some of the former directors. Control was lifted from the press and the clubs, and the Jacobins gathered once more in the *Salle du Manège*. But these measures for 'public safety', effective for a moment, soon met with strong resistance. The hostages law was unevenly applied, and the compulsory loan outraged all the rich bourgeoisie (now the ruling class), which accused the Jacobins of reviving the schemes of Robespierre and Babeuf for equality of property. Neither directors nor ministers could afford to lose the support of the bourgeoisie which had helped them to power, so on 13 August Siéyès and Fouché decided to close down the Jacobin club. Thus the government, having lost the support of the Jacobins, had to gain that of the army instead.

The coalition had been expecting large-scale risings in the south-west and west at the beginning of August. Those in the south-west, around Toulouse, were crushed in mid-August. Those in the west, being badly co-ordinated, both flared and died in September. At the same time,

French armies were winning important victories over the Austro-Russians in Zurich and over the Anglo-Russians to the north of Amsterdam. These successes gave the Directory a respite. But how could it survive without military support, having already lost that of the Jacobins? And how could it keep within the frame of the Constitution of 1795? This was constructed for peacetime and made no provision for exceptional procedures in case of war; it also engendered instability by the yearly re-election of a third of the legislative body, and incited the executive powers to *coups d'état* for long-term political schemes.

Directly after the *coup* of 18 Fructidor (September 1797), a number of politicians and intellectuals had thought of altering the constitution. But the procedure for constitutional revision required nine years at least—a delay quite incompatible with the urgency of the moment. It was therefore necessary to resort to a new *coup d'état*—now a familiar technique to the statesmen of the Directory, who had not only used it three times in France but were constantly advising the 'sister republics' to use it too. There had been repeated *coups d'état* in the Cisalpine, Ligurian, Roman, Batavian and Helvetic republics, most of them having been carried out by generals—Brune and Joubert amongst others. The bourgeoisie in power wanted to stabilise the government, revise the constitution and defeat the counter-revolution by preserving the 'conquests of 1789' without frightening the rest of their class by a return to the regime of 1792–3; inevitably it had to call upon a general. 'I am looking for a sword,' announced the Director Siéyès in the summer of 1799. It seems that Moreau was envisaged, but his record was disquieting as an associate of Pichegru, a proved traitor, and his natural irresolution made him elusive. Joubert was then approached. He was experienced in *coups d'état*, but lacked military prestige. For an opportunity of gaining it, he was put in command of the Army of Italy, but was killed during the first battle, at Novi, on 15 August 1799. There remained only Bernadotte, the Minister of War, but he was said to be involved with the Jacobins.

A dramatic turn of events now transformed the scene. Bonaparte, believed to be still in Egypt, landed unexpectedly at Fréjus on 9 October 1799. He was welcomed as a saviour. The people of France did not know of his distant defeats and still pictured him as the wondrous victor of Italy who had dictated peace to Europe two years ago. They thought that he would again give France a glorious peace. As for the planned *coup d'état*, what other general could be approached now that Bonaparte had returned? Arriving in Paris on 14 October, Bonaparte was immediately canvassed by Siéyès and his associates, and was easily persuaded. Siéyès imagined a repetition of the preceding *coups*: Bonaparte would quietly retire as soon as the new constitution was in force. Instead,

Bonaparte saw in their offer the gateway to supreme power such as he had already held in Italy and Egypt.

The *coup* was planned early in November. The Council of Ancients, most of whom were privy to it, was to allege an 'anarchist plot' and decide, as allowed by the constitution, to move the Legislative Councils from Paris to St Cloud. At the same time, it was to put Bonaparte in charge of the army of Paris. The first act was performed without difficulty on 9 November (18 Brumaire); the second nearly failed. The Councils had to be induced to alter the constitution by infringing the laws of procedure. A minority of the Ancients protested, and a strong majority in the Five Hundred showed violent hostility, some deputies even demanding that Bonaparte should be outlawed. Fortunately for him, it was his brother Lucien who was presiding in the Assembly. At the critical moment he suspended the session. Together, they called in the troops assembled round the Château of St Cloud to 'protect' the deputies. The soldiers stormed in among the Five Hundred, while the deputies escaped out of the windows. At the same time, the Directory was disrupted by the resignation of Siéyès, Roger Ducos and Barras, while the other two were kept under close watch by Moreau in the Luxembourg Palace.

Thus it became necessary to set up a provisional government. The same day, in the evening, Siéyès and Bonaparte collected a number of deputies whom they knew to be sympathetic. These decided to entrust the government to an 'executive consular committee' made up of two former directors, Siéyès and Roger Ducos—and Bonaparte. The provisional 'consulate' would be responsible for the drafting of a new constitution with the help of two legislative committees, each composed of twenty-five deputies, one from the Ancients, the other from the Five Hundred. In fact, the consulate held complete power, and, contrary to Siéyès' hopes, Bonaparte immediately assumed the leadership.

The apparently unbroken success which had marked Bonaparte's career was the key to the political stability under the Consulate—a stability which promised to bring back order at home and peace abroad. Bonaparte was only thirty then. But he was gifted with exceptional intelligence and a boundless capacity for work. His never satisfied ambitions carried him relentlessly beyond his set goals. He seemed to be the very embodiment of the Revolution. But, even more, he was a man of the eighteenth century—an enlightened despot; perhaps the most enlightened of despots: a true son of Voltaire. He did not believe in the sovereignty nor in the will of the people, nor in parliamentary discussions. But he relied on reasoning more than on reason, on 'men of talent'—especially mathematicians, jurists, statesmen (even the cynical or the venal)—more than on actual technicians. He believed that the power of an unshakable and clear-sighted will, backed by bayonets, was limitless. He despised and feared crowds, but believed it possible to mould and direct public opinion as he wished. He has been described as the most 'civilian' of generals, but he remained essentially and at all times a soldier—neither clothes nor titles could alter that fact.

The dictatorship imposed on France by Bonaparte was a military one. Its true aspect was at first disguised by the Constitution of the Year VIII—'short and obscure', drawn up by Siéyès who had the reputation of an expert in that field since the States General. For the first time since 1789, this constitution contained no declaration or guarantee of the rights of man, no mention of liberty, equality or fraternity. But it reassured the revolutionaries by expressly stating that the laws against the *émigrés* and the sale of national lands were irrevocable.

Bonaparte alone, as first consul, was invested with vast legislative and executive powers. His two colleagues were only supernumeraries with consultative powers. He alone could initiate laws and nominate ministers, generals, civil servants, magistrates and members of the Council of State. In 1799 also, his was the chief influence in the appointment of members of the three legislative assemblies—the Conservative Senate, the Legislative Body and the Tribunate. Universal suffrage was brought back, but steps were taken to render it ineffective. Siéyès had invented a system of electing 'notables' in the proportion of one-tenth of the electorate. The senate, itself recruited by cooptation, was to choose the deputies and tribunes from among these notables. But the system was never applied. In 1802, Bonaparte substituted electoral colleges composed of wealthy citizens elected for life by universal suffrage, and themselves electing the candidates for the assemblies; from these the Senate then made its choice. Of the three assemblies, the Senate alone had some independence, as its members were elected for life, and some importance as the guardian of the constitution. But it made little use of its powers, and the *sénatus-consultes* which it promulgated gave ever greater powers to the first consul. The Tribunate was to consider the bills proposed by the government. But it showed some signs of opposition; its most independent members were purged as early as 1802, its powers were reduced in 1804, and it was to disappear in 1807. The Legislative Body was to pass or reject bills, without debate; but in fact it hardly rejected any.

Like the two previous ones, the constitution was submitted to a referendum. Undoubtedly, most citizens were then in favour of it, but it should be noted that the voting lasted a month, that the government used every possible means of pressure and that the constitution was promulgated even before the final results were known. More than three million approved it, but four million abstained.

Far more important than the Constitution of the Year VIII was the Consulate's administrative work, and especially the spirit in which it was undertaken. At the top, the Council of State played a decisive role. A revival of the former King's Council, it was formed by Bonaparte from the 'men of talent' whom he particularly valued. The Council had a double task: drafting laws and dealing with administrative disputes. At first, Bonaparte often took part in its sessions and thereafter kept closely in touch. Local administration was still based on the *département*, but its subdivisions were somewhat altered. The great innovation was in putting, at the head of the *départements* and of the new *arrondissements*, men nominated by the government and subject to dismissal. These *préfets* and *sous-préfets* revived the traditions of the old *intendants*, and administrative centralisation progressed still further. The *préfet* was assisted by a *conseil de préfecture* (an administrative tribunal) and by a *conseil général*; the latter was formed of reliable men nominated for fifteen years, and did not get in the way. The *sous-préfet* had a *conseil d'arrondissement* which hampered him even less. In communes with less than 5000 inhabitants, the mayors were nominated by the prefects, and by the first consul in the rest. The municipal councils were no more to be feared than those just mentioned. Only in communes of less than 5000 were the members elected directly, and for a period of twenty years. The rest were chosen from the candidates proposed by cantonal assemblies.

The judicial system underwent considerable changes. No longer elected (except for local justices of the peace), the judges were appointed by the government but irremovable; thus their independence was secured and they became the core of the body of magistrates. A hierarchy of tribunals was restored. Above the courts of first instance —one for each *arrondissement*—were twenty-nine Courts of Appeal. In a way, these revived the old *parlements* but their duties remained strictly judicial. For criminal cases, each *département* had local courts of summary jurisdiction and an Assize Court; here, Napoleon suppressed the 'accusing jury' but reluctantly kept the jury for verdicts. The coping stone was the Supreme Court of Appeal (*Cour de Cassation*). Yet there were abnormal features in practice. Under the Consulate and Empire, the police was all powerful and omnipresent, special tribunals multiplied, arbitrary arrests were numerous, and internments in state prisons by administrative action recalled the old *lettres de cachet* and the Bastille.

The financial system was improved by creating a large number of specialist officials, including permanent state-appointed collectors of the direct taxes which had been inefficiently managed by local authorities. In obedience to the school of the *économistes*, the Constituent had abolished indirect taxes, but they were now revived and consolidated as the *droits réunis*. To compete with the British economy, Bonaparte wanted to give to French currency and credit the standards which they lacked. The law of 28 March 1803 settled the monetary charter of France for 125 years. To match the Bank of England, Bonaparte, helped by the financial backers of the *coup* of 18 Brumaire, created the *Banque de France*. This did great service by advancing money to the State in the form of bank-notes and by discounting the bills of the leading Paris merchants; but the benefits were not felt throughout France for several decades.

Teaching was transformed into a broad public service and teachers were grouped into one body, the University. Public assistance also became a state service, and hospital and charitable institutions were regulated.

The army, of course, was the favourite of the regime. Broadly speaking, it remained as the Convention and Directory had shaped it: recruiting by conscription (but allowing provision of substitutes), mixing young conscripts with veterans, and offering chances of promotion to the highest ranks. However, Napoleon smoothed the road to commissions for the bourgeoisie by creating the *École speciale militaire de Saint-Cyr* for training infantry officers, while the increasingly militarised *École Polytechnique* supplied officers for the artillery and the engineers.

This gigantic administrative reorganisation, involving state appointment to a large number of well paid posts, gave Bonaparte the opening for a work of reconciliation. The Directory owed its fall partly to the narrowness of its political foundations. Bonaparte, well aware of that fact, looked for allies on the Right as well as on the Left, and his most successful method of winning sympathy was to appoint men from all sections of the political world to the new posts which were opening. The assemblies contained some former members from all the revolutionary ones—though admittedly the tamer men. Similarly among the prefects: in the first batch were 15 *constituants*, 16 *legislateurs*, 19 *conventionnels* and 26 former members of the Directory's Councils. Some had been terrorists, others belonged to the nobility. Bonaparte opened wide the door to the *émigrés*, most of whom came home. Only the irreconcilables—the avowed Royalists and Democrats—were still harried: at first, it seemed as if there were only a few of them, but as the regime disclosed its defects, their numbers grew and repression became heavier.

Bonaparte's reconciling influence was not seen only in the satisfaction which he gave to the ambitious. He also wanted to put an end to the schisms that had been dividing France since 1790 and to give a lasting mould to the new society that he wished to create. Together with the army, magistrature, university and administration, the Civil Code and the Concordat formed the *corps intermédiaires*, the 'mass of granite', upon which Bonaparte built his regime.

Bonaparte, an enlightened despot, thought like Voltaire 'that the people needed a religion'. Circumstances happened to be favourable for an agreement with Rome. While in France, Pope Pius VI had died at Valence in 1799. His successor, Pius VII, had come to Rome in June 1800 in time to hear of Bonaparte's new victories. Negotiations started in September and ended ten months later with the signing of a Concordat (Chapter VI, pp. 153–4). Thus the schism was at last ended which had so deeply split France and poisoned the Revolution for ten years. The Protestant and Jewish Churches also came under control. Another 'mass of granite' was the Civil Code. Since Louis XIV, the monarchy had dreamed of submitting all Frenchmen to a uniform code, and every assembly since 1789 had worked towards it. But it was Bonaparte who was responsible for the decisive impetus— the 'Code Napoléon' was promulgated on 21 March 1804. It enshrined the great achievements of the Revolution: individual freedom, freedom of work, freedom of conscience and the secular character of the State. As for equality, the Code proclaimed all men equal before the law, at the same time safeguarding acquired wealth: its articles were largely devoted to defining, preserving and protecting property, especially landed property. On the other hand, it had little to say about work for wages or salaries, merely forbidding life contracts. On the pretext of giving free play to economic 'laws', it gave complete freedom to the employers. It even infringed equality of rights by stating that only the employer's testimony should be accepted in wage disputes. The code also ignored equality when it came to women. Their legal rights were extremely restricted compared with those of men, though divorce was not abolished. Finally, slavery was reintroduced in the colonies (which were then in open rebellion). Like the Concordat, the Civil Code was a compromise between the old regime and the Revolution. It strengthened the latter wherever the rift between it and the former was not too deep. A difficult task, admittedly, and carried out with surprising speed.

If these 'masses of granite' were to be firmly anchored, peace was indispensable. After great victories in Italy (Marengo, 14 June 1800) and in Germany (Hohenlinden, 3 December 1800), Bonaparte succeeded in signing peace treaties with Austria at Lunéville in February 1801 and with England at Amiens on 27 March 1802. Thus, for the first time in ten years, peace reigned in Europe. Bonaparte seemed to have kept his promise of Brumaire when he declared: 'Citizens, the Revolution is now settled in the principles which started it. It is completed.' Indeed, with the restoration of order at home and peace abroad, the Revolution and the old regime seemed to be thoroughly reconciled. Should not the hero of this prodigious achievement be given a 'token of national gratitude'? Spontaneously given, such a token would have been weighty indeed, but it was Bonaparte himself, with his friends, who instigated a law for a referendum on the following question: 'Should Napoleon Bonaparte become consul for life?' The plebiscite, held under similar conditions, gave Bonaparte an even greater majority. This display of his ambition showed that pacification was only one stage in his designs. Bonaparte and the British government did not have the same conceptions of peace. To the former, it was a means to make France even greater through peaceful methods; to the latter, it represented the most extreme concessions it could afford.

The Peace of Amiens, therefore, rested on a kind of misunderstanding and started off a dangerous economic conflict. As soon as the war was over, Bonaparte turned to encouraging industry. Cotton was reviving rapidly; imports of raw cotton had risen from 4,770,000 kg. in 1789 to 11 millions in 1803–4. Competitive awards were offered for inventors of new machines. Prefects were called upon to draw up statistical inventories for their *départements*. But, in order to protect this growing industry and to prevent an outflow of gold which could hamper the new Bank of France, Napoleon, to the great disappointment of the British, who were hoping for a return to the Eden Treaty of 1786, brought in some extremely high protective tariffs. Thus, a France which included Belgium and stretched as far as the Rhine closed its doors to British goods. The Dutch, Swiss and Cisalpine markets were almost as unapproachable. As England could no longer benefit from prizes captured at sea, peace had become less profitable for its trade than war. This economic conflict might not have been sufficient to provoke war again, had not the British Government been alarmed by Bonaparte's expansionist policy, to which there seemed to be no limit (Chapter IX, pp. 261–3).

The reopening of hostilities against England in May 1803 revived royalist activities, conspicuously with Cadoudal's Plot. Bonaparte decided to reply with a hard blow which would smother any fresh attempts. The execution of the Duc d'Enghien (Chapter IX, pp. 264–5) kindled opposition within the old aristocracy and some of the bourgeoisie, but served as an excuse to reinvigorate the police. The chief of police and former terrorist Fouché, hoping to consolidate his growing influence, began to flatter the master, pointing out that the best way to discourage future plots would be to change the Consulate for Life into a hereditary Empire. Assassination could then do nothing to change the form of government! Inspired by Fouché, the Senate sent an address to Bonaparte, suggesting a hereditary, but not mentioning an imperial, title. Bonaparte wanted more. He asked the Senate to make known its 'full intentions'. But already the well-tamed Tribunate was expressing the desire that 'Bonaparte should be proclaimed hereditary

Emperor of the French' (3 May 1804). The people were asked to express their opinion in a referendum which gave the same result as in 1802. So, once more, the constitution was altered. 'The government of the Republic,' it was stated, 'is now entrusted to an emperor. Napoleon Bonaparte, first consul, is Emperor of the French.'

The organisation of the government was scarcely changed. Napoleon's powers, however, were strengthened, the three assemblies became even less independent and the influence of the Council of State was weakened. Napoleon was quickly heading towards the setting up of a system similar to that of the old monarchies. First, he wanted to be crowned with even more ceremony than the Bourbons, by the Pope himself. Pius VII hesitated, but his anxiety about the still fragile Concordat led him finally to accept. The ceremony took place in great pomp in Notre-Dame on 2 December 1804. Like Charlemagne, the emperor took the crown from the Pope's hands and himself set it on his own head. The royalists were shocked. As for the republican veterans, they thought, like General Delmas: 'What a mummery! Nothing is missing but the hundred thousand men who sacrificed themselves in order to do away with all this. . . .' Henceforth, the Roman eagle adorned the tricolour flag and figured, with the golden bees, in the arms of the new dynasty. The decoration of the Legion of Honour, created in 1802, soon took on the appearance of the old orders of chivalry, in particular that of the Order of Saint Louis, which the medal resembled in shape and the ribbon in colour. In 1804 princely titles were revived for Napoleon's family, and in 1808 an imperial nobility was created. It included hereditary *grands feudataires* (land owners), princes, dukes, counts and barons. They could create entails for their eldest sons but, unlike the old nobility, they had no fiscal or judicial privileges. Napoleon tried to blend the old nobility with the new; but the returned *émigrés* scorned these sons of peasants, 'masquerading as lords' but keeping the language and manners of their youth.

All this alienated the republicans, without appeasing the royalists as the emperor hoped. Propaganda, a new weapon borrowed by the emperor from the Revolution, was elaborated. Censorship of the periodical press became stricter and the number of newspapers was reduced. Finally, it was decreed on 3 August 1810 that, except in the Seine, each *département* would be allowed only one periodical. No political article could be printed unless it was copied from the official *Moniteur*. The non-periodical press was also censored. On the other hand, writers in sympathy with the regime were given generous allowances. All original or personal literary thought was banned. Madame de Stael was exiled and Chateaubriand and Benjamin Constant were both harried. Naturally, the theatre was under strict supervision, companies of players and dramatic performances being subject to a kind of military discipline. Imperial propaganda penetrated the arts, education, and even the Church. Nevertheless, opposition persisted. State prisons were as full as ever: arrest would follow the slightest dig against the emperor or the regime. For this bad couplet: '*Oui, le Grand Napoléon est un grand Caméléon* . . .' the poet Desorgues was sent in 1804 to a mental institution. Sometimes, suspects were confined under police surveillance to particular districts, or to fortresses; or they might be forced to join the army, or their sons might be kept as hostages, so to speak, in lycées or military schools.

This dictatorship allowed Napoleon to fight his wars for eleven years without having to worry much about French opinion. On the Continent war was interrupted by truces (some quite long ones), but it never ceased at sea or in the colonies. War at sea brought the blockade in its wake. With the 'Continental Blockade', started in 1806, Napoleon endeavoured to close the European markets to Britain. For this purpose he made France the nucleus of a *Grand Empire* and the centre of a 'Continental System' which attempted to alter the entire European economy to French advantage.

From 1807, Napoleon thought of himself more as Charlemagne's successor than as the heir of the Revolution. He divorced his first wife, Josephine, as their marriage had been childless. In 1810 he married the Archduchess Marie-Louise of Austria, and next year the birth of a son seemed to ensure the future of the Empire.

The *Grand Empire* was conceived as a kind of federation, ruled by France, but without any notion of nationality or 'natural' frontiers. France itself included some 130 departments spreading beyond the Rhine and the Alps. In 1810 Holland was annexed to ensure the protection of the coast and, for the same reason, the coast of Northern Germany up to Lübeck was soon to form three new 'Hanseatic' departments. In the south, a third of Italy was integrated with the Empire, and at his birth Napoleon's son was given the title 'King of Rome'. In 1812, Napoleon even made a momentary decision to annex the whole of Catalonia, to be divided into four *départements*. Around the French Empire revolved the vassal states ruled by the emperor's relatives. There were his brothers: Jerome, King of Westphalia, Louis, King of Holland until 1810, and Joseph, King of Spain. Eugene, his stepson, was Viceroy of Italy, and Murat, his brother-in-law, King of Naples, while his sister Elisa, wife of the Italian Bacciochi, more modestly governed Lucca and Piombino. Less closely related to the emperor's circle, other territories also were under France's domination. There was the Helvetic confederation with Napoleon as its mediator; west of the Elbe there were the German states grouped in the Confederation of the Rhine and headed by the former Archbishop of Mayence, Charles Theodore de Dalberg; to the east, the Saxon

Duchy of Warsaw came under the Empire's influence as far as the Vistula. Prussia, surrounded by French satellite states, was rendered harmless.

Thus the map of central Europe, which had been so complicated before 1796, was much simplified. Whatever he may have said later at St Helena, Napoleon never intended to achieve the unity of Italy or Germany. Yet, by reducing the number of states, reshaping frontiers and amalgamating hitherto separated populations, he paved the way in both cases towards unity—all the more by introducing, together with new institutions, the revolutionary ideas of national freedom, sovereignty and independence. On all these countries shaped by his own hand, Napoleon imposed the main reforms of the Revolution, namely abolition of internal tolls, suppression of serfdom, more or less complete destruction of feudalism, abolition of the corporations and of most privileges, freedom of thought and worship, secularisation of Church property to help finance the new administrations and, above all, the application of the Civil Code, the *Code Napoléon*, which was a kind of synthesis of all the recent social achievements. These institutions awakened men's minds, not inspiring much attachment to the new master, but encouraging men to reflect on their past and present situation and on their future. Why could they not, like the French, become unified and independent? The consequent reaction against Napoleon's regime was aggravated by the unavoidable war vexations of taxation, requisitioning, and billeting of troops, and finally by the economic decline due to the continental blockade. For the great ports of Bordeaux, Nantes, Le Havre, Amsterdam, Bremen, Hamburg, Lübeck, Marseilles, Genoa, Venice and Naples, the blockade meant total ruin. Even industry gained little from the interruption of British competition, for Napoleon, whose power was centred in France, favoured French factories above all and channelled all available raw materials towards France. The German and Italian textile industries were working below capacity, wages were cut and there was heavy unemployment. Both employers and workers in the textile industry, and the traders in the great ports, began to lead the opposition to the Empire. Only the steel plants in the Ruhr, and also in Belgium and the Saar (then integral parts of the Empire) were making progress—because they were contributing to the war effort. As for the 'substitute industries' by which Napoleon hoped to begin replacing colonial products (sugar from sugar-beet for instance), they were still in their infancy.

Thus we can see that by 1812 the *Grand Empire*, far from being content under the emperor's rule, was an artificial entity, likely to crumble at the slightest setback to his fortunes. In 1812, although French troops were occupying three-quarters of Europe, the French language was less widespread than in 1750. Within the Empire, the coercive measures taken by Napoleon to make French compulsory in the newly annexed departments of Holland, Germany and Italy only gave greater resisting power to the vernaculars. In vassal or allied countries there was no serious attempt to implant the language, but the presence of French troops and officials, bringing French expressions with them, also provoked counter-movements for the purification and growth of national languages. As the French armies moved in, the French language receded—all the more since German and Italian literature could now rival the French in masterpieces such as they had lacked sixty years earlier. These works echoed the new genre of Romanticism which, by appealing to popular traditions and the glories of the past, brought into relief peculiar characteristics of each nation and went altogether counter to the unifying classicism of empires.

Even in France the best literary work either escaped Napoleon's ascendancy or was aimed against it. From 1803 onwards Chateaubriand was considered as suspect. Madame de Stael, still less in favour, was sent into exile. In *Corinne ou l'Italie* and in *l'Allemagne*, she stressed the peculiar characteristics of two nations arbitrarily cut to size by Napoleon and stifled in their deepest desires. The arts, like literature, also reacted against official classicism (Chapter VIII. A). David had become the regime's artist, but the younger French painters rebelled against tradition. Abroad, Goya made his protest in his scenes from the Spanish war; the Italian sculptor Canova, though loaded with honours by the Bonaparte family, denounced the removal of Italian works of art to France. Beethoven refused to dedicate his *Eroica* symphony to the emperor—a traitor to the republican ideal (Chapter VIII. B, p. 234). Although France kept the ascendancy in the field of science (Chapter V), yet even science, in principle less sensitive than literature or art to political fluctuations, also took on some national characteristics during the Revolution and Empire: scientists renounced Latin or French in order to write in their own languages.

Nowhere in those days could be found a sound apologia of the imperial system. Political and economic thinkers were either advocates of liberalism like Jean-Baptiste Say, or else partisans of an absolute monarchy refreshed by a return to its older traditions—admirers of Burke and of the theorists Joseph de Maistre and Louis de Bonald (Chapter IV, pp. 105–6). Napoleon's attempt at unifying Europe found no more support among the intellectuals than among the politicians or the people. A united Europe could not be built by one man's will, or without the wholehearted support of most of its inhabitants. The fragile construction of the *Grand Empire* came too late —or too early. It was doomed, and it must soon collapse.

It was Napoleon himself who hastened the ruin of the Empire by undertaking in 1812 a war with Russia, so as to keep her by force within the 'Continental System'. The catastrophe of the Russian campaign of 1812 galvanised resistance against him in Germany and Spain and throughout the *Grand Empire*. In the spring of 1813, he won a few victories in Germany, but after the defeat of Leipzig (16–19 October 1813) the French armies had to fall back on the Rhine. In January 1814, France was attacked on all fronts. Skilfully, the allies proclaimed that they were not fighting the French people but only the man who had refused the conditions offered in the Frankfurt declaration. During the first three months of 1814, with an army of young conscripts, known as the '*Marie-Louise*', the emperor accomplished remarkable feats of strategy, but in vain. He could neither defeat the overwhelming superiority of the allied forces nor rouse the great majority of Frenchmen from a state of sullen torpor. The Senate and the Legislative Body, once so docile, demanded peace and a return to civil and political freedom.

At last, on 9 March, the Allies signed the general treaty which they had failed so disastrously to achieve ever since 1793: they agreed not to negotiate separately but to fight on till they had defeated Napoleon. Then the Allied commanders concentrated their forces and resolutely marched on Paris. On 30 March, they were at the gates of the capital while Napoleon had moved east to attack their rear. Freed from the fear of the emperor, the authorities hastened to negotiate. The Senate set up a provisional government presided over by Talleyrand, who proclaimed the fall of the emperor and, without consulting the people, called on Louis XVI's brother, Louis XVIII, whose only firm supporter among the Allies was England. Napoleon, hurrying to Fontainebleau, was forced by his generals to abandon the struggle and to abdicate. The Allies allowed him to retire to the island of Elba between his native Corsica and the Italian coast.

The future of France was then settled by the Treaty of Paris. She retained the boundaries of 1792 to which were added the western part of Savoy, Mulhouse and Sarrebruck. Of her colonies, she recovered only Martinique, Guadeloupe, Guiana, the Senegal trading posts and the island of Bourbon.

France had been pushed back to her 1792 frontiers, but she retained the essentials of the 'conquests of the Revolution', which had been achieved precisely in 1792: abolition of the feudal system, redistribution of the land after the sale of clerical and *émigrés'* property, economic liberalism, secularisation of the civil registers, educational and administrative reorganisation. All these changes had been consolidated during the Consulate and Empire, and it was no longer possible for any regime to establish itself in France without accepting all the economic, social, administrative, religious and cultural institutions built on the 'principles of 1789'. The political regime alone could be changed. But when the monarchy, restored in constitutional form in 1814, tried in 1830 to go back on these fundamentals, the sparks of revolution, still smouldering, ignited again to destroy it. Eighteen years later, revolution again re-asserted, but more democratically, the essentials of the conquests of 1789.

CHAPTER XI

THE NAPOLEONIC ADVENTURE

THE last, but not the least of Napoleon's victories was won at St Helena. There he created the Napoleonic legend, and there he lived long enough to see his own career in perspective, and to reinterpret it in tune with the forces of liberalism and nationality which were to shape the Europe of the nineteenth century. Bonapartism was thus preserved as a living force, and the foundations of the Second Empire were laid. Though he often complained in exile that his career should have ended at Moscow, the Hundred Days and the 'martyrdom' of St Helena gave it the proportions of Greek tragedy, of hubris followed by nemesis. Like the music of Mozart's 'Don Giovanni', (which Napoleon heard shortly before the battle of Jena and, rather surprisingly, admired) his personality and career combine classical proportions with a wilder note of romantic, daemonic and unlimited ambition.

The mists of St Helena and the legend still obscure the figure of Napoleon.[1] It is the task of this chapter to present him as the product of his age and also the moulder of it, and to analyse the interaction between his personality and the forces, moral and material, at work in Europe.

Napoleon was born at Ajaccio in Corsica in 1769, the year in which the French occupied the island. His father, Carlo Buonaparte, abandoned the cause of General Paoli, the patriot leader, and rose to high office in the French administration. Through the good offices of the French governor he obtained a place for Napoleon at Brienne, from which he proceeded to the *École Militaire* in Paris. Both these royal schools were exclusive, and required proof of noble descent for entry.

Although Napoleon appeared as a somewhat solitary oddity among his school fellows, since he clung passionately to the idea that he was an alien patriot among his French conquerors, his ability in mathematics was soon noted and, in his leaving examination for the artillery corps, he was placed forty-second in the national list and commissioned as a lieutenant. Like the majority of the young officers in the artillery, who were drawn from the minor *noblesse* and better educated than the officers of the line regiments, he greeted the dawn of the Revolution with enthusiasm. In 1791 he wrote a prize essay which reflects the spirit of Rousseau. When the Constituent Assembly incorporated

[1] Professor P. Geyl's *Napoleon—For and Against* (1949) is a penetrating analysis of French historians of Napoleon. He concludes: 'The argument goes on.'

Corsica into France, he sided with the French and Jacobin faction in Corsican politics, and obtained leave from the Ministry of War to transfer from the regular army to a Corsican volunteer battalion. His first experience of war was in a bungled invasion of Sardinia in 1793. The French Convention then precipitated civil war in Corsica, and the British occupation of the island, by ordering the arrest of General Paoli.

The Buonaparte family, as leaders of the pro-French party, were forced into exile at Toulon. It was Napoleon's luck that he was at hand when the crisis of the surrender of Toulon to the British fleet gave him his first great opportunity, and he was brought in to replace the wounded officer in command of the artillery of the Jacobin army besieging the port. His plan for attacking the vital point of Fort Éguillette was sent to Paris, and formed the basis of Carnot's directive. The successful execution of this plan, and the recapture of Toulon in December 1793, won for Napoleon promotion to the rank of brigadier-general, and Augustin Robespierre described him in a letter to his brother Maximilien as 'an artillery general of transcendent merit'.

It was again his luck that brought him to Paris during the crisis of Vendémiaire, after two setbacks which nearly cut short his career. Owing to his association with Augustin Robespierre, he was arrested, but cleared after an inquiry, in the proscription which followed the fall and execution of the Robespierre faction in Thermidor (July) 1794. Then the government's suspicions of English influence in Corsica led them to transfer Corsican officers from the Army of Italy, and Napoleon was posted to the Vendéan front. On arriving in Paris he evaded this order on the plea of illness, but only a fortnight before the crisis of Vendémiaire broke out (5 October 1795) he was struck off the generals' list for refusing to report to the Army of the West. When the Paris Sections rose against the new government of the Directory, Barras was given command of the government troops. He had been a deputy on mission to the south in the Toulon affair, and he now summoned Napoleon as the artillery expert. So it was that his 'whiff of grapeshot' crushed the last threat that Paris was to offer to republican governments.

As the reward for his services, Napoleon was promoted to the rank of major-general and given the command of the Army of the Interior. It has often been alleged that his appointment to command the Army of Italy in March 1796 was Barras' wedding-gift to him when he married Barras' discarded mistress, Josephine Beauharnais. There is no reason, however, to disbelieve the statement of La Revellière, one of the directors, that it was a unanimous decision of the Directory on strictly military grounds. Since 1794 Napoleon had been urging on the government an offensive in Italy, but Carnot did not consider it feasible until Prussia and Spain dropped out of the war in 1795. When Schérer was ordered to take the offensive with the Army of Italy, he proved so hesitant that the Directory decided to replace him by the man who had planned and promised a successful offensive strategy.

In one month, by a series of battles round Montenotte and Mondovi, Napoleon knocked Piedmont out of the war and by the middle of May he entered Milan, after compelling the Austrians by the battle of Lodi to retire to the quadrilateral fortresses round Mantua. He recalled at St Helena that Lodi was a landmark in his career and his outlook. 'It was only on the evening after Lodi that I realised that I was a superior being and conceived the ambition of performing great things, which hitherto had filled my thoughts only as a fantastic dream.' At this point he forced the government of the Directory to climb down, in a tussle highly significant for the future. The Directory had no intention of conquering Lombardy; they wished only to exploit it, and exchange it for the Rhine frontier in a general peace. They now proposed to divide the command of the Army of Italy: Kellerman was to occupy Lombardy, and Napoleon was to move south to plunder Rome and Naples. This order was cancelled in the face of Napoleon's vigorous protest; already the prestige of his victories and the money which flowed from them to Paris gave him the whip hand over the government.

He now wrote to Carnot, 'Soon it is possible that I shall attack Mantua. If I capture it, nothing can prevent me penetrating into Bavaria.' But the failure of Moreau to take the offensive on the Rhine allowed the Austrians, with their interior lines of communication, to counter-attack vigorously over the Brenner Pass, and for the remainder of the year Napoleon was forced into a defensive strategy. The Austrians mounted no less than four successive counter-offensives, which were broken up and defeated, often by the narrowest margins, in the battles of Castiglione (August), Bassano (September), Arcola (November) and Rivoli (January 1797).

By March 1797 Napoleon had received reinforcements and was able to advance rapidly towards Vienna by way of Udine. At Leoben, less than a hundred miles from Vienna, he negotiated preliminaries of a peace treaty, by which France was to keep Belgium and Lombardy and Austria was to be compensated with Venetia. The political situation in Paris favoured his *fait accompli*. The threat of a moderate and royalist majority in the Legislature which might make peace with England in the negotiations at Lille and pave the way for a monarchical restoration forced the Jacobin directors, Barras and Reubell, to act with Napoleon, and Augereau was despatched to Paris to carry out the military *coup d'état* of Fructidor against the Legislature (September 1797). Napoleon's plans for Italian annexations were thus ratified in the Peace of Campo Formio (October 1797). By the end of his Italian proconsulate he hardly troubled to disguise his contempt for the Directory and his ambition to seize power in France. He remarked to his entourage, 'Do you think that I triumph in Italy in order to benefit the lawyers of the Directory?'.

With the support of Talleyrand he persuaded the Directory to switch their plans from an invasion of England to an expedition to Egypt (Chapter XIX). He condemed the invasion project as impracticable, and the threat to India offered more brilliant opportunities for immediate and dramatic action. He realised that 'In Paris nothing is remembered for long. If I remain doing nothing for long, I am lost'.

The expedition was on such a scale, including a comprehensive corps of scientists, that it may be assumed that the object was to found a permanent colony in Egypt and, if things went well, to use it as a stepping-stone to the conquest of India, where there was plenty of scope to stir up trouble for the English. In 1797 Arthur Wellesley had foreseen the danger of French contact with the native Princes. 'They would shortly discipline their numerous armies in the new order which they have adopted in Europe, than which nothing can be more formidable to the small body of fighting men of which the Company's armies in general consist.' In retrospect, Napoleon was fond of remarking that he 'had missed his destiny' at the abortive siege of Acre: but at the time he knew well that the battle of the Nile had cut short any hope of further progress in the east, and his Syrian expedition was undertaken strictly as a limited sideshow, to forestall a Turkish attack. Paradoxically the Battle of the Nile, which sealed the fate of the Egyptian expedition, also gave Napoleon his opportunity to seize power in France. He was able to put the blame for the defeat of the Nile on his admirals, and his return to France was preceded by the news of his brilliant victory over the Turks at Aboukir. The Battle of the Nile revived the coalition against France. Turkey, Naples, Prussia and Austria in turn entered the war. With the defeat of Jourdan on the Rhine at Stockach (March 1799) and of Joubert at Novi (August 1799), all Italy was lost and France appeared to be threatened once again with invasion. At the beginning of August Napoleon received French newspapers which told him of the situation in Europe, and three weeks later he sailed secretly from Alexandria. The die was now cast: he saw clearly, not only that the fate of the army in Egypt depended on victory in Europe, but that the crisis had arrived which would bring him to supreme power or to the guillotine.

On Napoleon's arrival in France, Bernadotte as Minister of War proposed that he should be court-martialled for deserting his army without orders. But the reaction of public opinion left the government helpless. On his journey from Fréjus to Paris, he was acclaimed as the one man who could restore victory and peace to the Republic. The significance of the *coup d'état* of Brumaire is analysed in Chapter X, pp. 294–5; clearly, the decisive factor throughout was Napoleon's hold on the imagination of the French people, at a moment when they felt themselves threatened by a renewal of Jacobin terror and invasion. Sieyès and the politicians thought that they could make use of his reputation and yet control him; in the event it was Napoleon who turned the tables on the politicians. But the survival of the Consulate and the Napoleonic dictatorship remained in question until the victory of Marengo, the peace-treaties of Lunéville and Amiens, and at home the Concordat, gave it overwhelming prestige.

Napoleon's Italian campaigns of 1796–7 seemed almost miraculous; twelve victories in a year, announced in bulletins which struck the world like thunderclaps. It was a revelation of a new kind of *blitzkrieg*, and it was natural to ascribe its success to the genius of the commander and the élan of the revolutionary army. To the military historian it appears as the culmination of changes in the theory and conditions of war which had been taking place since the Seven Years' War. It is clear from his early military memoranda that Napoleon as a young professional officer had absorbed the ideas of such military thinkers as Bourcet, Guibert and du Teil, who formulated the doctrine of a mobile, offensive warfare. But the realisation of these ideas required a new kind of army, in which individual initiative would replace mechanical drill and discipline. As Guibert predicted in 1772: 'It would be easy to have invincible armies in a state in which the subjects were citizens.' By 1796 the Revolution had created such an army. The wholesale emigration of regular officers in the Revolution opened the way for vigorous young leaders from the ranks of the non-commissioned officers, such as Masséna and Augereau in the Army of Italy. The fact that a shortage of professionally trained officers, capable of commanding above the divisional level, was particularly felt makes it less difficult to understand how a man with Napoleon's qualifications and background could reach high command at the incredibly early age of twenty-seven.

In his first campaign, which is the model of all his later campaigns, Napoleon thus had in his hands the instrument with which the new theories could be translated into fact. To explore the origins of Napoleonic warfare is not, however, to belittle his military genius. His own comment that 'everything is in the execution' says the last word on the difference between theory and practice in war. An exasperated French general of the First World War once exclaimed 'Napoleon was not a great general—he only had to fight coalitions'. To which Napoleon could have replied, as he did to one of his ministers 'It is evident that you were not at Wagram', where the Austrians alone were formidable opponents. Up to 1796 none of the French generals had been able to exploit the possibilities of offensive warfare on the same scale as Napoleon, and no general of his epoch succeeded in doing so.

It is alleged that Napoleon neglected tactical and technical innovation. It is true that the weapons used in the Revolutionary and Napoleonic wars were designed well before 1789. It was not until the third decade of the nineteenth century that radical changes in design began. This delay was not due to mere military conservatism; neither the revolutionary government nor Napoleon can be accused of a lack of interest in science. He was proud of being a member of the *Institut*, and had close relations with the leading French scientists, whom he frequently consulted on technical points. It is true that he dropped the military observation balloon corps which had first been used at the battle of Fleurus (1794); but in 1802 he instructed Marmont, his artillery expert, to redesign the field artillery. Renewal of war cut short this project, but in any case it could only have been a refinement of Gribeauval's excellent designs, already thirty years old. The brake on innovation was, in fact, the existing state of technology, even in England, where the technological revolution had progressed most rapidly. On the other hand, industrial expansion had gone far enough to equip large conscript armies. Valmy (1792) was the biggest artillery battle yet known, and France produced 7000 cannon in 1793. Rapid technological change in the military sphere does not favour the emergence of military genius, as the First World War showed, and a technologically stable period put the highest premium on Napoleon's generalship.

Napoleon seldom interfered in minor battle-tactics, as his job was to keep general control of the battle. But the extent of his innovation in army organisation has often been overlooked, and in this respect the most important development was the expansion of the Imperial Guard. In August 1810 he sent Bessières a lengthy memorandum on the organisation of the Guard, which was to be expanded to 100 battalions, or a total of 80,000 men. The Guard has sometimes been described as an expedient to offset the declining quality of Napoleon's troops of the line. But in 1810 he could look forward to a considerable breathing-space, with no great manpower shortage.

The significance of the Imperial Guard was that, unlike the guard formations of other armies, it was a self-contained force of all arms. Its superb artillery was commanded by the brilliant Drouot, known as *le sage de la Grande Armée*. The fighting morale and *esprit de corps* of the Guard were extremely high. But the Guard, which had been carefully built up by Napoleon and was regarded as so valuable that he refused to sacrifice it at Borodino, was almost entirely destroyed in the snows of the retreat from Moscow. It had to be rebuilt from the barest *cadres* for the campaign of 1813. Even so it was the decisive weapon in the campaigns of 1813, 1814 and 1815. In June 1813 Napoleon wrote 'In most battles the Guard artillery is the deciding factor since, having it always at hand, I can take it wherever it is needed'. Reporting the victory of Montmirail (February 1814) he wrote 'The Old Guard has exceeded all that I could expect from an élite corps. It was absolutely like the head of Medusa!' If Napoleon the statesman had not set Napoleon the general an impossible task, and if the Guard had not lost most of its veterans in Russia, he might well have remained unbeatable in the field.

In trying to analyse Napoleonic warfare, Clausewitz recognised that strategy cannot be reduced to a 'system'. Reminiscing at St Helena, Napoleon ridiculed 'maxims' of war. 'Of what use is a maxim which can never be put into practice and even if put into practice without understanding would cause the loss of the army?' It is true that a basic principle is present in his campaigns from the start—the dispersion of self-contained units of divisions in order to march, and their concentration for fighting. Hence he often writes of 're-uniting his forces'. But the application of this principle is so flexible that no two Napoleonic campaigns or battles are alike. 'Set-piece' battles such as Austerlitz, Wagram, Borodino, Waterloo were exceptions. Normally the battle would be engaged in a piece-meal, pell-mell fashion, leaving plenty of room for the appearance of fresh divisions on the battlefield to turn the scale. If Austerlitz was Napoleon's tactical masterpiece, the apogee of the Napoleonic battle is Ulm, where the capitulation of the Austrian General Mack with 50,000 men was decided in advance by the strategic approach. The most that can be said is that Napoleon favoured two kinds of strategical manoeuvre: first, the flanking threat to the enemy's rear and communications, as in the Marengo campaign, Ulm, Jena, Friedland, Smolensk (where it misfired), Montmirail; and secondly the attack on the centre of an enemy dispersed on a wide front, so as to defeat him successively in detail. This is the strategy of his first campaign in Piedmont, as it is of the last campaign of Waterloo.

The conception of the Waterloo campaign was as brilliant as ever, but it was ruined by errors in execution. In contrast with 1814, Napoleon now had a veteran army composed of released prisoners of war. Its morale was high but brittle; some of the generals were mistrusted because they had accepted the Bourbon restoration. Confidence was shaken by the desertion of General Bourmont with his staff on the eve of the fighting. Napoleon had been unable to persuade Berthier, his irreplaceable chief of staff, to return: Soult was an inadequate substitute, and inferior to Davout who had been left in Paris as minister of war. Ney was distraught by a feeling of guilt after breaking his allegiance to Louis XVIII and bringing the army over to Napoleon. Grouchy, a good cavalry commander, had no experience of independent command. Murat was in disgrace, after his treachery to Napoleon in 1814, which had ended in the fiasco of his defeat at Tolentino.

At the beginning of June 1815 the allied forces on the Belgian frontier consisted of some 90,000 Belgians, Dutch, Hanoverians and British under Wellington, and some 120,000 Prussians under Blücher. Napoleon's plan was to surprise them while they were dispersed along the frontier. By 14 June he had concentrated 120,000 men on the frontier at Charleroi before Wellington and Blücher were even aware that he was taking the offensive. He explained to his marshals that he intended to operate with two wings and a reserve, and to beat the English and Prussians separately. On the 15th, the French made contact with an isolated Prussian corps, and Blücher concentrated 90,000 men at Ligny on the 16th. Napoleon ordered Ney to contain the English at Quatre Bras, and to send every man he could spare for an attack on the Prussian right flank while he attacked their centre. Napoleon drove back the Prussians, but the decisive enveloping movement failed because d'Erlon's corps received contradictory orders from Napoleon and from Ney, and never arrived in time on either battle-field.

But for this confusion, Ligny might have been the decisive victory; and within a few hours Napoleon had lost the strategic initiative. As an English military historian points out, 'It was in these twelve hours from 9 p.m. on the 16th to 9 a.m. on the 17th that the campaign was lost.'[1] Blücher was able to disengage under cover of night, and took the bold decision to retire northwards on Wavre, instead of east towards his base. Overcome by exhaustion and over-confident that the Prussians were out of action for several days, Napoleon did not decide until noon of the 17th to join Ney and deal with Wellington, and to detach Grouchy with 33,000 men to pursue the Prussians. Ney, left without instructions, had failed to pin down Wellington at Quatre Bras by vigorous action on the morning of the 17th, and Napoleon's pursuit of Wellington, retiring to the strong defensive position of Mont St Jean, was hampered by drenching thunderstorms.

On the morning of 18 June Napoleon with 74,000 men faced Wellington with 67,000 men. The stage was set for a decisive battle, as Napoleon assumed that the Prussians were out of action or contained by Grouchy, while Wellington had received news from Blücher that at least one Prussian corps would join him by mid-day. Napoleon ignored the warnings of his generals who had been in Spain that the fire-power of the British line against massed columns was formidable. Having decided on a mass frontal attack on the centre, he left the tactical handling of the battle to Ney, whose desperate courage was not matched by his skill on this occasion. Drouot, his artillery expert, persuaded him to delay the start of the battle till noon, to let the ground dry out. At 12.30 a column approaching on his right flank was identified as Prussian. Napoleon could have broken off the battle at this point, but the campaign would have been lost, and he preferred the chance of smashing Wellington before the Prussians could intervene.

What had happened to Grouchy? In the order Napoleon dictated at

[1] A. F. Becke, *Napoleon and Waterloo* (London, 1936).

noon on 17 June, Grouchy was told to proceed to Gembloux, and to look for the Prussians in the direction of Namur and Liège. At 2 a.m. on the morning of the 18th Napoleon received a message from Grouchy, still at Gembloux, that one Prussian corps was at Wavre. Only at 10 a.m. did Soult dictate a message to Grouchy to 'direct his movements on Wavre, to draw near us, and establish communications with us'. Two subsequent messages urging him to hurry did not reach him till 4 p.m. and 7 p.m. By the time he heard the opening guns of Waterloo, Grouchy correctly judged that it was too late to cross the river Dyle and march to the sound of the guns. But if he had shown more energy and appeared in force at Wavre on the morning of the 18th instead of 4 p.m., he might well have deterred or decisively delayed the Prussian flank march from Wavre. Gneisenau was hesitant in committing the Prussians to an advance, even though he underestimated Grouchy's strength by half.

Grouchy's failure was due to a combination of his own inadequacy and Napoleon's errors; he revealed his character when he defended himself after the catastrophe by saying that, 'Inspiration in war is appropriate only to the commander-in-chief, and his lieutenants must confine themselves to executing orders.' He showed no initiative, authority or energy: he took refuge in a literal obedience to orders, and the orders he received from Napoleon were lacking in precision, and too late. Neither took seriously the possibility that Blücher would recover from Ligny in time to join Wellington. If Napoleon had done so, he would have instructed Grouchy on the morning of the 17th to make for Wavre with all speed and seize the crossings over the Dyle. In any case, it was contrary to the basic Napoleonic strategy to allow a detached wing to be out of reach for the decisive battle. Napoleon had nearly lost the battle of Marengo by taking this risk: and it was only because he had been delayed by bad roads that Desaix had been able to rejoin him in time.

Despite this error, everything could still be retrieved by routing Wellington quickly. The best chance of victory was lost when Ney made the mistake of first sending in the infantry columns unsupported by cavalry, and then the cavalry unsupported by infantry. A carefully combined assault of all arms, after Drouot's tremendous artillery preparation, would have forced the enemy to form into squares, which could then have been ripped to pieces with case-shot from the horse-artillery and divisional artillery. The appearance of the Prussians in force, which tied up 15,000 of Napoleon's reserves, and the failure of the last, diminished assault by the Guard after 7 p.m., finally broke the French army in panic and rout.

It was thus revealed in his last campaign that Napoleon no longer had the stamina to resist battle-fatigue in order to keep things moving and convey clear-cut decisions. He admitted afterwards, 'I had no longer within me the feeling of certain success.'

But while Napoleon's military genius laid the foundation of his career, it is clear that from the start he was more than a professional soldier. At an early age he had learnt to judge and handle men in the rough school of Corsican politics, and his interests were as much political and literary as military. No mere general could have mastered the politicians and established a government of national recovery and re-conciliation as Napoleon succeeded in doing after Brumaire. He could fairly claim that 'it is not as a general that I am governing France; it is because the nation believes that I possess the civil qualities of a ruler'. As First Consul he sometimes worked 18 hours in the day; it is estimated that during the fifteen years of his rule he dictated some 80,000 letters and orders—an average of fifteen a day. Roederer remarked to him that life in the Tuileries was melancholy. 'Yes,' said Napoleon, 'so is great-ness. My mistress is power, but it is as an artist that I love power. I love it as a musician loves his violin.' He himself once said, 'What will they say of me when I am gone? They will say "Ouf".' He wrote to Josephine in March 1807 'All my life I have sacrificed everything, tranquillity, interest, happiness, to my destiny'.

His legendary capacity for work seems to have been due to will-power and highly-strung nervous vitality rather than an exceptionally strong physique. In the end he had to pay the price of a premature ageing. Even before 1805 there were two occasions when he suffered a nervous crisis which simulated epilepsy. Chaptal noted that 'after his return from Moscow those who saw him noticed a great change in his physical and mental constitution'. It was difficult to recognise in this ageing and corpulent man, often drowsy, the slim, taut, energetic figure of the First Consul. At critical moments in the 1812 and 1813 campaigns his energy and judgment were impaired by bodily ailments.

One of his ministers, Mollien, affirms that 'in the midst of his camp and during military operations, he wished not only to govern, but to administer France by himself, and he succeeded'. His ministers were allowed no collective responsibility, and their work was co-ordinated through Maret, the Secretary of State. Only Talleyrand and Fouché were capable of standing up to him; and, when they lost office, Talley-rand in 1808 and Fouché in 1810, Chaptal's comment that Napoleon wanted 'only valets, not counsellors' was confirmed. Even when the Imperial court outshone the Bourbon court in magnificence and bore-dom, Napoleon's private life remained simple, laborious and even bourgeois. Murat, the dandy, told him that his clothes were un-fashionable; and his tailor complained that his account was not worth much. He would have nothing to do with the formal levées of the Bourbon court; and neither Josephine nor Marie-Louise nor any of his mistresses were allowed any political influence. His rough treatment of Madame de Staël was due to his fear and dislike of her pretentions as a *femme politique*. He told Madame de Rémusat that 'he would have no women ruling at his court; they had injured Henry IV and Louis XIV'. Napoleon frequently lectured his brothers on the art of ruling. He told Louis, King of Holland, that 'a prince who in the first year of his reign is considered to be kind, is a prince who is mocked at in his second year'. 'Abroad and at home I reign only through the fear I inspire.' He told Bourrienne, the friend of his youth 'Friendship is only a word: I care for nobody'. He confided to Fain, his Secretary, that his anger was often simulated, in order to inspire fear. 'Otherwise they would come and bite me in the hand.'

This image of the inhuman tyrant is far from being the whole truth about Napoleon. He was by origin and temperament a man of the Mediterranean, of warm and violent feelings, and vivid imagination; gregarious, voluble, intensely interested in people and ideas. He knew how to be fascinating as well as formidable. Caulaincourt, his close companion for ten years as Master of the Horse and Foreign Minister, records that 'the emperor's feelings were expressed through every pore. When he chose, nobody could be more fascinating'. His superb intellect was matched by a striking physical presence, despite his large head and relatively small stature, no more than five feet six inches. The idealised portraits of David and the rest of Napoleon's immense pictorial propaganda-machine may be suspect, but the death-mask of Napoleon reveals features of classic beauty. Madame de Rémusat, a waspish critic of Napoleon after his fall, describes his appearance: 'His forehead, the setting of his eye, the line of his nose are all beautiful, and remind one of an antique medallion.'

On the military mind, the impact of Napoleon's personality was irresistible. He said at St Helena that 'the most important quality in a general is to know the character of his soldiers and to gain their confidence'. 'The military are a Freemasonry, and I am their Grand Master.' He played on the emotions of military glory, emulation and comradeship with unprecedented virtuosity, and not even disaster and slaughter could break the bond between them. Even in the appalling retreat from Moscow, there was less grumbling in this army than in Wellington's army which was at the same time retreating from Burgos. Wellington reckoned that the moral effect of Napoleon's presence with his army was the equivalent of 40,000 men. This was due not merely to his professional skill and the prestige of victory. Marmont explains that it 'was by familiarities that the emperor made the soldiers adore him, but it was a means only available to a commander whom frequent victories had made illustrious; any other general would have injured his reputation by it'. Marshal Lannes used to complain that he 'ought to be pitied for having conceived an unfortunate passion for this harlot'. When Napoleon boarded the *Bellerophon* in 1815, fat, middle-aged and totally defeated, he captivated the officers and men within a couple of days, to such an extent that the Admiralty were alarmed. 'Damn the fellow!' exclaimed Admiral Lord Keith, 'if he had obtained an interview with His Royal Highness, in half an hour they would have been the best friends in England.'

Napoleon's personality presented a dazzling combination of intelligence and imagination. He was a product of the revolutionary age, a time when the crust of social custom had been broken, and nothing seemed impossible of achievement to men with clear minds and strong wills. He was moulded by the two powerful influences which inspired the Revolution, the scientific rationalist spirit of the Enlightenment, and the romantic sensibility of Rousseau. The romanticism of his youthful writings is soon soured by a colossal egoism: just as the style of his writing changes from a turgid imitation of Rousseau. But the romantic element in his character was not extinguished: it was rather transformed into a romantic ambition—romantic because it was unlimited, feeding on dreams of a career surpassing anything in history. The carefully calculated and limited ambition of a Frederick the Great was no longer enough for Napoleon. He wrote to his brother Joseph in 1804 'I believe I am destined to change the face of the world'. 'If I had succeeded, I should have been the greatest man known to history.' Molé, who began his career as one of Napoleon's *auditeurs*, thought that 'he was much less concerned to leave behind him a "race", a dynasty, than a name which should have no equal and glory that could not be surpassed'. His passion for the poetry of Corneille and the mediocre Ossian was due to their themes of heroic glory. His prodigious rise had been due to the exquisite balance between his imagination and his intelligence. But what would happen if this balance was upset—if the imagination became uncontrolled and the realistic appraisal of the facts obscured? Moscow and St Helena, as well as Austerlitz and the Empire, seem to be implicit in his nature.

His experience of the Revolution had given him a horror of the mob and of 'ideology'. It is significant that his confidence and his moral courage wavered on two occasions—when he was faced with the hostile assemblies at St Cloud in Brumaire, and with royalist mobs in Provence on his way to Elba. In the *Conseil d'État*, the main instrument of government of the Consulate, he aimed to gather the ablest men of all parties, irrespective of their past. Chaptal said that 'Bonaparte conceived the idea of uniting and amalgamating everything. He put in the same committee, side by side, men who had been opposed in character nd opinions for the last ten years, men who detested each other, men who had proscribed each other. It was in this way that Bonaparte assembled all the talents in every sphere and fused all the factions. The history of the Revolution became as remote for us as that of the Greeks and Romans'. In 1803 he created the post of *auditeurs* to the *Conseil d'État*. These were young men attached to the Ministries and sitting in on the meetings of the *Conseil* for training as higher civil servants. Often they were sent on special missions and reported directly to Napoleon. By 1813, three hundred *auditeurs* had been appointed, and Napoleon gave them every encouragement. He boasted that 'there is no conquest which I could not undertake because with the help of my soldiers and my *auditeurs* I could conquer and rule the whole world'. In this bold and imaginative conception Napoleon was at least half a century ahead of his time. He claimed to have created the 'most compact government with the most rapid circulation and the most energetic movement that ever existed'. 'I wish to govern men as they want to be governed.' In the main institutions of the Consulate—the Civil Code, the Concordat, the Legion of Honour, the Bank of France—there was much that was sound and enduring, because they were in accord with the interests and the aspirations of the dominant classes in the Revolution, the bourgeoisie and the peasant proprietors.

In spite of his lucid intelligence and his passion for facts, there were fatal limits to Napoleon's political insight, and contradictions in his policy which he was unable to see or unwilling to resolve. He remained the prisoner of his heredity and his environment. He had finished with Corsica by 1794, but his relations with his family and his followers show a persisting Corsican feeling of clan, which seriously hampered his policy. His reactions in the Enghien affair betray an element of the Corsican concept of the vendetta. 'They have not the right to murder me' he exclaimed, when he learned of the Comte d'Artois' complicity in the Cadoudal plot. If the Bourbons chose to assassinate him, despite the fact that he had no part in the execution of Louis XVI, he had the right to kill a member of the opposing clan. A curious example of this thinking occurs in his will, when he left a bequest to a man who had tried to assassinate Wellington, whom Napoleon held responsible for the execution of Marshal Ney. He was meticulous in remembering the friends of his youth. Des Mazis, his closest friend as a cadet and subaltern, was given a palace appointment as Keeper of the Wardrobe, as soon as he returned from exile as an *émigré*. Maréchal de Ségur, the veteran royalist, who had signed his first commission as Lieutenant, was received at the Tuileries with the highest honours. His old nurse was brought from Corsica to be present at his coronation.

Still less was he able to resist the demands of the Bonaparte family, though it was his Beauharnais relations who gave him the greater affection and loyalty. His stepson Eugene Beauharnais was a loyal and efficient viceroy in Italy: but Napoleon never dared to adopt him as his heir to the imperial crown, as it would be too great an affront to his Bonaparte relatives. In 1804 Fouché condemned the 'revolting incapacity' of Napoleon's brothers; but, if they lacked his ability, they were liberally endowed with self-will and ambition; and neither they nor their sisters were overawed by their illustrious brother. Their grumblings, their sulks and their pretensions so exasperated him that he complained 'From the way they talk, one would think that I had mismanaged our father's inheritance'. 'With the Queen of Naples I have always to fight a pitched battle.' Yielding to his sense of family obligation, he committed the political error of organising his Empire by giving thrones to his relatives. Joseph, first made King of Naples and then of Spain, Louis, King of Holland, and Jerome, King of Westphalia, did not merit their promotion. If Napoleon expected them to obey his orders, he was quickly disillusioned when they expected to be treated as independent monarchs. Lucien refused to break up his second marriage, which Napoleon considered to be a *mésalliance*, and quarrelled with him after 1802. At the end of 1807 Napoleon hoped to arrange a marriage-alliance between Charlotte, Lucien's daughter, and Ferdinand, heir to the Spanish throne: but Lucien refused to be readmitted to the imperial family on Napoleon's terms.

Still more extraordinary was Napoleon's treatment of Murat and Bernadotte, who rewarded him with the most cynical treachery. He knew that Murat, a superb cavalry leader, was politically worthless: but he was given the throne of Naples, because he was married to Napoleon's sister, Caroline. Bernadotte was a political general, who was lucky to have escaped arrest for treason in 1804. Napoleon wrote of him in 1809 'Bernadotte is an intriguer whom I cannot trust. He nearly lost me the battle of Jena, he was mediocre at Wagram, and he did not do what he might have done at Austerlitz'. Yet Napoleon made him marshal and prince, and acquiesced in his becoming Crown Prince of Sweden, simply because his wife Désirée Clary was the girl Napoleon had first thought of marrying, and was Joseph's sister-in-law.

Napoleon was a shrewd judge of the qualities of his generals. He thought that Desaix would have been 'the first general of France' if he had not been killed at Marengo: Lannes might have become so, if he had not been killed at Essling. Ney and Murat were incomparable leaders of men on the battlefield but no more. Berthier was a superb chief of staff, but a muddler if left to himself. Only Masséna, Davout, and possibly Soult were capable of independent command of large armies. It was, therefore, against his better judgment that he gave Junot the command of the Army of Portugal in 1808, and appointed Marmont to command against Wellington in 1811, because they had been his friends and aides-de-camp in his youth. It was similarly a costly mistake to give his brother Jerome command of a corps in the Russian campaign of 1812: and to leave Murat in command of the Grand Army in the final stages of the retreat from Moscow, when his nerve had obviously gone.

Napoleon was successful in keeping his generals out of politics, but only at the cost of loading them with honours and wealth. The establishment of an imperial nobility in 1808 with hereditary titles and landed estates was a flagrant breach of the revolutionary principle of equality. Napoleon defended it on the ground that 'I do not hurt the principle of equality by giving titles to certain men without respect of birth, which is now an exploded notion'; and that it was necessary to efface the prestige of the *noblesse* of the old regime. He told Joseph in 1808 that 'my intention is to make the generals so rich that I shall never hear of them dishonouring by cupidity the most noble profession, or attracting the contempt of the soldier'. But the extravagance which he encouraged among his marshals was morally corrupting, and in·the final débâcle of the Empire, they thought more of preserving their lives and their fortunes than of fighting to the last gasp for their benefactor. Ironically it was Lefebvre, the first to be created a hereditary duke by Napoleon, who blurted out the truth when the marshals forced Napoleon's abdication at Fontainebleau in 1814: 'Did he believe that when we have titles, honours, and lands, we would kill ourselves for his sake?'.

The ex-Jacobin Thibaudeau warned Napoleon against the attempt to revive hereditary monarchy: but Napoleon saw no reason why a 'fourth dynasty of France' should not be established on the basis of the social changes brought about by the Revolution. After the coronation in 1804, and still more after the Austrian marriage and the birth of the King of Rome, he hoped that his dynasty had acquired the sanction of legitimacy. Having married a niece of Marie Antoinette, he even took to the ridiculous habit of referring to Louis XVI as 'mon oncle'. He found it difficult to believe, until it was too late, that the Emperor Francis would join in the destruction of his son-in-law and his grandson. Henri Beyle (the author Stendhal), who, as an *auditeur*, was sometimes in close contact with him, observes that 'Napoleon made the mistake of all parvenus—that of estimating too highly the class into which he had risen'. He had not realised that in France the monarchical principle had died with Louis XVI. The bourgeoisie might be prepared to accept a temporary Napoleonic dictatorship, but sooner or later they would demand a share in the government. The Malet conspiracy in October 1812, in which the government was nearly overthrown by the simple announcement that Napoleon had been killed in Russia and none of his officials thought of proclaiming his son as Napoleon II, came as a severe shock to him. The climate of opinion which he found in Paris on his return from Elba in 1815 shocked him even more. He was obliged to accept a liberal constitution devised by the 'ideologist' Benjamin Constant, the friend of Madame de Staël, as an *Acte Additionnel aux Constitutions de l'Empire*. At the ceremony of the Champ de Mai which promulgated the new constitution, Napoleon appeared in the costume which he had worn at his coronation, of elaborate pseudo-Renaissance design which jarred with his own personality and with the spirit of the age.

Napoleon's appreciation of the political importance of religion may well have begun with his experience of Corsican politics, and of the Federalist civil war in France in 1793. In 1793–4 he was in close touch with Augustin Robespierre, one of the ablest of the Jacobin *représentants en mission*, who frequently warned his brother Maximilien of the danger that militant Jacobin atheism would multiply the Vendéan revolt in the provinces. In Italy he was aware of the danger to his small army of provoking clerical and peasant fanaticism: and this was reflected in his careful treatment of the Pope in the Treaty of Tolentino (February 1797). It was rumoured when he was in Egypt that he had adopted the Moslem faith. The Concordat with the Pope in 1801 was conspicuously the personal policy of Napoleon. 'In religion, I do not see the mystery of the Incarnation, but the mystery of the social order.' 'The people need a religion; this religion must be in the hands of the government.' Despite the declaration, in his will at St Helena, that 'I die in the Catholic, Apostolic, and Roman faith in which I was born more than fifty years ago', it can hardly be doubted that Napoleon remained an agnostic in the tradition of Voltaire and the enlightenment. He told General Bertrand at St Helena that 'it bothered him that he was unable to believe'.

Having driven a hard bargain with the Pope in the Concordat, he intended to make the Pope and the bishops instruments of his policy, his 'moral prefects'. Had not the enlightened monarchs of the eighteenth century treated the Popes with scant consideration? He was enraged by the Pope's insistence on the independence of the Temporal Power: it was incompatible with Napoleon's growing conception of an Empire of the West. At St Helena he said: 'I should have controlled the religious as well as the political world, and summoned Church Councils like Constantine.' In 1806 he wrote to the Pope: 'Your Holiness is sovereign of Rome, but I am its emperor. My enemies must also be yours.' When the Pope refused to enforce the continental blockade, he occupied the Papal States in February 1808; and in 1809, during the Wagram campaign, he proclaimed the annexation of Rome to the French Empire. The arrest of the Pope in the Vatican probably went beyond his instructions, which were to arrest Cardinal Pacca. But Napoleon hoped that confinement and isolation of the Pope in Savona and later in Fontainebleau would wear down his resistance. In 1815 he admitted 'I was blind. I always believed the Pope to be a man of very weak character'. But his attitude to the Pope was already as out of date as the enlightenment; Catholicism was no longer on the defensive. A religious revival, allied with the romantic movement and a counter-revolutionary political philosophy, which was to reach its zenith under the Bourbon restoration, was already heralded by the writings of Maistre, Bonald, Chateaubriand and Fontanes. The Concordat itself had encouraged this movement. It is easy, however, to exaggerate the political effects of Napoleon's quarrel with the Pope. The religious fanaticism of Calabria, Spain and the Tyrol would have broken out, whatever the state of Napoleon's relations with the Pope. Even after the arrest of the Pope, Catholic opinion in the Rhineland, the Low Countries, Poland and even in the Vendée does not seem to have been greatly stirred.

In his dealings with England, Napoleon also fell a victim to the 'ideology' of the Revolution which he so much despised. To him, as to the Convention, England stood for a ruthless commercial 'oligarchy' holding down a population ripe for the principles of the Revolution. He was shocked by the barbarous methods of discipline which still prevailed in the English armed forces; and being an abstemious man himself, he was fascinated by the alcoholic consumption of the English upper classes. The 'drunkenness' of English officers was a theme on which he harped at St Helena. He was exasperated by the excesses of the English press, especially when a paper like the *Morning Post* could refer to him as 'an indefinable being, half-African, half-European, a mediterranean mulatto'. The wild inflation caused by the paper-money of the Revolution, the *assignats*, was associated in his mind with the privations of his youth; and it had left him with a deep distrust of financiers. Looking at England's vast national debt and her resort to paper-money since 1797, he assumed that her wealth was fragile and vulnerable.

The weapon of economic warfare, which he inherited from the Convention and developed into the Continental System after Trafalgar, was based on this assumption. By the Treaty of Amiens Napoleon intended to exclude the English both politically and commercially from the Continent; and it was the dashing of English hopes of a commercial treaty with France, and Napoleon's cold-war encroachments on the Continent, that precipitated the rupture of the treaty. On his failure to preserve the peace, a French historian comments, 'It is impossible to say if the task was beyond his genius; it was certainly beyond the capacity of his character.'[1]

[1] A. Vandal, *L'Avènement de Bonaparte* (Paris, 1905).

In 1798 Napoleon had reported to the Directory pessimistically on the prospects of an invasion of England. 'With all our efforts we shall not for many years obtain command of the sea. . . . The suitable moment to prepare for this undertaking is perhaps gone for ever.' But his ignorance of the technicalities of naval warfare made him unable to grasp or unwilling to admit that English naval superiority could not be challenged. At St Helena he complained that 'there is a specialisation in this profession which blocked all my ideas. They always returned to the point that one could not be a good seaman unless one was brought up to it from the cradle'. Unlike the unfortunate Admiral Villeneuve, Napoleon was not aware of the immense divergence that had developed since the Revolution between the English and French navies in standards of seamanship and gunnery. In the American War of Independence they had fought more or less on equal terms. But the Revolution had deprived the French navy of most of its experienced officers, disbanded its corps of seamen gunners and ruined discipline. The English strategy of close, continuous blockade of the French ports deprived the French navy of adequate training: while hard and continuous experience at sea brought the English standards of seamanship, signalling and gunnery to a pitch of perfection. The tactics of breaking the line, instead of fighting in line ahead, first used by Rodney in the Battle of the Saints in 1782, could now be developed by Nelson into a battle of annihilation, which was the naval counterpart of the Napoleonic battle on land. Shortly before Trafalgar, Villeneuve wrote, 'We have obsolete naval tactics; we only know how to manoeuvre in line, which is what the enemy wants'.

In view of the immense preparations (Chapter III. B, p. 80) it can hardly be doubted that Napoleon really meant to invade England between 1803 and 1805. At the same time the 'Army of England' had the advantage of enabling him to concentrate and train, in a time of peace on the Continent, the finest army he was ever to command. If he ever seriously considered a crossing by the barge-flotillas without temporary command of the Channel by the battle-fleet, the idea was soon dropped, when it became evident that only a proportion of the flotillas could leave the ports at each tide. In the spring of 1804, Napoleon issued detailed instructions to Admiral Latouche-Tréville, commander of the Toulon squadron, for a combined operation of the fleet with the flotilla. He was to elude Nelson's blockade in the Mediterranean, join Villeneuve's Rochefort squadron, and enter the Channel. 'Let us be masters of the Straits for six hours, and we shall be masters of the world.' Latouche-Tréville, the best of the French admirals, died in August 1804, and for some months the plan was shelved.

The entry of Spain into the war against England in December 1804 altered the prospects. The French ambassador in Madrid reported optimistically that Spain could have thirty ships of the line ready in a few months. Napoleon now conceived his 'grand design' by which Villeneuve, now in command at Toulon, should sail for Martinique, after picking up a Spanish squadron, and there meet Ganteaume with the combined Brest, Rochefort, and Ferrol squadrons. Having thus forced the English fleet to disperse in defence of the West Indies, Villeneuve would return with temporary command of the Channel to cover the crossing of the flotilla. Villeneuve sailed at the end of March 1805, and succeeded in eluding Nelson, who was obsessed by the threat to Sicily, Malta and Egypt. He did not know for certain till 18 April that Villeneuve had passed through the Straits of Gibraltar. By the middle of May Villeneuve was at Martinique, with Nelson hard on his heels, favoured by a fast passage. Ganteaume had failed to break the blockade, and Villeneuve was now instructed to return to Ferrol if Ganteaume had not joined him within forty days. Nelson was able to send a fast ship to warn the Admiralty of Villeneuve's departure from the West Indies. Calder's squadron off Ushant was ordered to intercept and prevent Villeneuve from entering Ferrol. After an indecisive clash with Calder, Villeneuve took refuge in Corunna. By 18 July, Nelson was back at Gibraltar, and finding that Villeneuve had not re-entered the Mediterranean, moved north to join Calder.

Napoleon's plan had started well, but he had failed to disperse the English fleet. Lord Barham, now First Lord of the Admiralty in place of Dundas, had followed imperturbably the principle of concentration of force. Napoleon assumed that Nelson had returned to the Mediterranean. On 16 July he instructed Villeneuve to join Ganteaume at Brest, but gave him discretion to retire to Cadiz 'in case of an unforeseen event'. By 14 August, Villeneuve was at sea again, but on sighting five ships of the line he turned south to Cadiz. By the irony of fate, these were not the vanguard of the English fleet, but Allemand's Rochefort squadron. Napoleon had been waiting at Boulogne since 3 August, ready to embark the army. As late as 23 August he wrote to Talleyrand 'There is still time—I am master of England'. But Admiral Decrès, his minister of marine, who had never believed in the possibility of dispersing the English fleet, begged him not to order Villeneuve north to certain destruction. On 24 August, Napoleon dictated to Berthier the orders for the Grand Army to break up the Boulogne camp and march to the Danube.

Once the English fleets were concentrated, it was fatal for Villeneuve to allow himself to be blockaded in Cadiz; he should have made for Toulon as soon as possible. By the end of September Nelson was off Cadiz with thirty ships of the line against the Franco-Spanish fleet of thirty-three; his only fear was that Villeneuve would not be tempted to come out, and he kept his main force well out to sea to conceal his strength. Villeneuve was in a desperate state of mind, acutely conscious of the inferior quality of his fleet, and knowing that he was about to be superseded in his command. Finally he received orders from Napoleon to sail for Naples 'at all costs' to counter the Anglo-Russian expeditionary force which was threatening the flank of the Grand Army. When Villeneuve emerged from Cadiz on 20 October, the result was never in doubt. Nelson had thought out his battle-tactic before he left Portsmouth, and thoroughly explained it in conferences with his captains. 'Rodney broke the line in one point: I shall break it in two.' With further reinforcements he would have used a three-column attack. Nelson and Collingwood led the two columns which broke the enemy line, and crushed the centre and rear. 'I shan't be satisfied with less than twenty ships.' Nelson died knowing that eighteen enemy ships had sunk or struck; in the event only ten of Villeneuve's fleet got back to Cadiz, and of these only three could be made fit for action.

Trafalgar disposed of any threat to English command of the sea for many years; but Napoleon did not admit that the decision was final. The lure of Spain in 1808 was partly the hope of 'regenerating' the Spanish navy. Canning's decision to seize the Danish fleet in 1807 and the Walcheren expedition of 1809 show that English governments took seriously a revival of the challenge to English naval superiority. Reduced to 35 ships of the line in 1807, Napoleon hoped to have 102 by 1812. But by this time the English naval lead was overwhelming; in 1813 Napoleon could only count on 71 ships of the line, against England's total of 235.

If Trafalgar had indefinitely postponed a direct naval and military attack on England, the weapon of economic warfare might yet bring her to her knees. With the collapse of Prussia after Jena and the Tilsit agreement with Russia in 1807, Napoleon was in control of the whole northern coastline of Europe through which passed the bulk of English trade with Europe. In November 1806 he issued the Berlin Decree which declared that the 'British Isles are in a state of blockade'; all commerce with them was prohibited, and all goods belonging to, or coming from, Great Britain and her colonies were to be seized. The Continental System thus inaugurated was aimed at exports, not imports: it was, in fact, a boycott, not a blockade. Napoleon told his brother Louis, King of Holland, 'I mean to conquer the sea by the land'. In August 1807 he predicted the plight of England with 'her vessels laden with useless wealth wandering around the high seas, where they claim to rule as sole masters, seeking in vain from the Sound to the Hellespont for a port to open and receive them'. Given his conception of England's financial structure, Napoleon was optimistic about the speedy effect of this boycott. If her exports were stifled, her delicate balance of payments would be upset: she would be unable to subsidise continental allies with her sovereigns, the 'Chevaliers de St George', and then unemployment would produce either a revolutionary upheaval or at least a public clamour which would force the government to make peace.

English opinion at first greeted the Berlin Decree with derision; caricatures showed Boney blockading the moon. The coast system which had been in operation since 1803 had proved quite ineffective; and English trade continued to flow through Holland and the North German ports. Moreover world markets were an expanding alternative to Europe. In the years 1803–5, Europe took only 33 per cent of English exports and the United States took 27 per cent, while 40 per cent went to the rest of the world, principally the colonies and South America. Contraband trade with South America was considerable, and in 1806 great hopes were raised by the capture of Buenos Aires and Montevideo. But after Tilsit the pressure began to be felt. In his Grand Army Bulletin of July 1807 Napoleon threatened that 'It is probable that the Continental System will not be an empty word'. In July 1807 there was fear in England of war with the United States when the U.S. frigate *Chesapeake* was boarded by the Royal Navy in search of deserters. A simultaneous closing of Northern Europe and the United States to English trade would be extremely serious, as together they accounted for 60 per cent of English exports. Moreover Napoleon's discrimination against English merchant shipping might divert the profitable colonial trade to neutrals. The English government replied to the Berlin Decree with the Orders in Council of November and December 1807, requiring neutral ships to be furnished with a licence in an English port. Napoleon in turn intensified the pressure on neutrals by the Fontainebleau and Milan Decrees of October and December 1807 which declared that neutral ships complying with the Orders in Council would be treated as English ships. President Jefferson hoped by his Embargo Act of December 1807 to force the belligerents to relax their controls, but in practice it caused only harm to American interests, and was repealed in March 1809.

Though the total volume of English exports for the year 1807 was satisfactory, the figures conceal the fact that there was a serious drop in the second half of the year, and this continued through the first half of 1808. Exports to Europe sank to 15 millions as compared with 19½ millions for the corresponding period in 1807. This menacing situation was unexpectedly relieved by the opening of the Peninsular War. The flight of the Portuguese royal family, and the refusal of the Spanish colonies to acknowledge King Joseph, meant that English trade with South America was now open and official. The Spanish rising, and the French defeat at Baylen (July 1808) in turn encouraged Austria to attack

Napoleon, and during the Wagram campaign of 1809 Napoleon lost his grip on Northern Europe. English exports in 1809 reached a record height. As early as March 1809, Napoleon began to waver in his policy of strict prohibition. The success of the 'smogglers' was such that he preferred to authorise limited trade with England in colonial produce, subject to high tariffs, in exchange for French wines and silks. The licence-system was regularised by the Trianon Decree of 1810 but it never accounted for more than a fraction of English exports.

After Wagram Napoleon was in a position to tighten his grip on Europe. Holland, the Hanseatic towns and the Duchy of Oldenburg were annexed to the French Empire. The ruthless Davout was put in command of North Germany. The Fontainebleau Decrees of October 1810 ordered the seizure and burning of English manufactured goods, and the establishment of special tribunals to strike at the contraband trade. These measures hit the English economy when it was already running into a combination of difficulties. The Peninsular and Walcheren campaigns put a heavy strain on the gold-reserves and balance of payments. The capacity of the South American markets was wildly over-estimated. The colonial and New World markets might compensate for the loss of European markets but in the long run these markets could only pay in colonial products, of which Europe was substantially the sole consumer. In 1810 a glut of colonial produce was piling up in English ports. By September 1810 a wave of bankruptcies heralded a severe economic crisis. Unemployment and distress were aggravated by the bad harvests of 1808 and 1809, and the government was forced to import wheat. Moreover Napoleon had succeeded in embroiling England with the United States. He offered to revoke the Milan decrees if the Orders in Council were also abolished. In February 1811 President Madison, failing to persuade the English government to revoke the Orders, reimposed the embargo. Napoleon saw signs that the expected crisis in England's economy was at hand, and encouraged the import of wheat from France and Holland for payment in gold. Would he have done better to withhold these exports and so intensify the high prices and scarcity which provoked the Luddite disturbances of 1811? But it is unlikely that continental imports of wheat could have been decisive, as they were only a quarter of the total wheat imports in 1810, and a reasonable harvest in 1810 brought relief. The year 1811 was the worst of all for English exports, and the outlook remained gloomy until Napoleon's retreat from Moscow. Meanwhile the United States had declared war on England in June 1812, in the very month that the obnoxious Orders in Council were finally revoked.

It appears from this fluctuation on the economic front that the Continental System could exert severe pressure on England, when it was rigorously applied. To be decisive, it had to be so applied over a fairly long period: in fact it was only properly in force from mid-1807 to mid-1808 and from mid-1810 to mid-1812. The most dangerous threat to England was a conjunction of the Continental System with a rupture with the United States. In 1812, Napoleon was not far wrong in thinking that victory in Russia would also settle the fate of England. But he considerably underestimated the toughness and resilience of the English economy. A system of banking and credit, such as was unknown to France, had been built up since the days of Godolphin, Walpole and the Younger Pitt. Nor had Napoleon reckoned with the speed and scope of the industrial revolution in England. In 1785 England and France were comparable in economic development. But between 1785 and 1800, while France was retarded by the upheavals of the Revolution, England was experiencing one of the major technological revolutions in human history. By 1800 Boulton and Watt had built and installed hundreds of their steam-engines, particularly in the important exporting industry of textiles.

The price that Napoleon had to pay for embarking on the gamble of the Continental System was a heavy one. He intended it, not merely as a method of economic warfare, but as a decisive shifting of the axis of European trade from England to France. As in 1802, French industry at first welcomed the opportunity of exploiting European markets free from English competition. But by the beginning of 1810 the French economy was in serious difficulty. There were shortages of raw materials for industry, and the purchasing power of the Continent was reduced by the large war-indemnities and contributions exacted by France from enemy and vassal states. French overseas commerce, languishing since 1793, was completely sacrificed; the great ports like Marseilles and Bordeaux seethed with discontent and latent royalism. Napoleon's policy took the blame for the economic depression of 1810–12, despite his keen interest in industrial development and his large subsidies to manufacturers. The support which Napoleon had won from the bourgeoisie during the Consulate was irretrievably dissipated by the crisis of 1810–12. Agriculture, to which Napoleon gave priority, suffered less. It was helped by the export of surplus wines and wheat, and by the development of beet sugar and indigo as substitutes for colonial produce.

In his propaganda on behalf of the Continental System, Napoleon took the line that Europe must undergo temporary hardship in order to achieve emancipation from the English 'tyranny of the seas' and commercial domination. If he had genuinely aimed at fostering a free-trade area in Europe, he might have won more support. But the Trianon Tariff of 1810 made it obvious that France was to enjoy exemptions, denied to the rest of Europe, from the hardships of the system. In 1810 Napoleon told Eugene, his viceroy in Italy, that 'my policy is France before all'. Metternich predicted that 'this mass of ordinances and decrees which will ruin the position of merchants throughout the Continent will help the English more than it harms them'. Moreover it was impossible, despite Napoleon's efforts to develop roads and canals, for land-transport in the pre-railway age to begin to compete with the relative cheapness of sea-transport. Not only in France but in Italy, Germany and the Low Countries it was the bourgeois class that was most likely to respond to Napoleon's claim to stand for enlightenment and equality: and by the Continental System he forfeited their support. The logic of the system was an important, though not the only factor in the fatal errors of his European policy—the Spanish entanglement, the breach with the Pope, and the war with Russia.

Some historians have sought to explain the extension of Napoleon's empire in Europe as a by-product of his struggle with England, and of the Continental System. Such a view under-estimates the extent of Napoleon's ambition, and the radical nature of his European policy. As early as 1805 Talleyrand had foreseen the essential contradiction between Napoleon's conquests and his desire to be admitted into the club of legitimate European monarchs. If the 'natural frontiers' of France and the Napoleonic dynasty were to be preserved, Napoleon must acknowledge a European balance of power. Talleyrand therefore wanted a 'soft peace' with Austria after Austerlitz, and after Tilsit surreptitiously disengaged himself from Napoleon's fortunes, in his own interests and, as he believed, in the interests of France and Europe. But in his treaties and alliances Napoleon was willing to acknowledge only vassals, never equals. Such an attitude implied a claim to 'universal monarchy'. But if Napoleon could defeat the monarchies, how could he hold down the peoples? In the light of developments after 1815 it is puzzling that Napoleon as emperor paid so little heed to the force of nationalism. At St Helena he fabricated the legend which presented his career as a struggle on behalf of the peoples against the dynasties. But this was an afterthought and a travesty of the facts. The Napoleonic empire was the negation of nationality, and never more so than after 1810.

As the heir of the Enlightenment and of the Revolution, Napoleon was cosmopolitan in outlook. Nothing is more revealing than his complete inability to understand the psychology of the young Austrian patriot, Staps, who tried to assassinate him in Vienna in 1809. After talking to him for some time after his arrest, he was driven to the conclusion that he must be mad. In 1789 the French had made the 'Declaration of the Rights of Man', not merely of Frenchmen. By 1802 the decay of the old regime in Europe appeared to be leading to the emergence of a united Europe, with uniform and enlightened law, administration and citizens. Napoleon was a zealous propagandist for the *Code Napoléon*; and the code was the vessel in which the administrative and social principles of the Revolution were exported, as far as Illyria and Poland. He told Jerome, King of Westphalia, that 'in Germany, as in France, Italy and Spain, people long for equality and liberalism. The benefits of the *Code Napoléon*, legal procedure in open court, the jury, these are the points by which your monarchy must be distinguished.... Your people must enjoy a liberty, an equality unknown in the rest of Germany'.

Napoleon did not foresee, until too late, that sweeping away the lumber of the old regime would only allow the latent seeds of nationalism to sprout vigorously. He was not alone in this error, which was shared by many of his contemporaries. Up to 1805 the moral and ideological forces seemed to be on Napoleon's side. It was only in 1804 that Beethoven struck out the dedication of his *Eroica* Symphony to Napoleon: and Goethe remained an admirer of the emperor, and totally uninterested in German nationalism, until the end of his life. The statesmen of the Congress of Vienna paid no more attention to the principle of nationality than had Napoleon: with less excuse, because they could already see the writing on the wall. It must be admitted that the march of events and the evolution of ideas under the pressure and turmoil of the Revolutionary and Napoleonic wars were so rapid that men's minds could not keep pace with them.

Earlier in his career Napoleon seemed willing to encourage national aspirations in Italy. The Cisalpine Republic became in 1802 the Italian Republic, and in 1805, the Kingdom of Italy under the viceroyalty of Eugene. But in 1806 the Kingdom of the Two Sicilies was given to Joseph, and in 1808 to Murat. Various principalities were carved out of Italian territories for the benefit of the Bonaparte family and the imperial dignitaries. In 1806 the Duchies of Parma and Piacenza were annexed to the French Empire; in 1808 Tuscany also, and in 1809 the Papal States. The Illyrian provinces taken from Austria in 1809 remained directly under the control of Napoleon through a governor-general. In 1811 the title of King of Rome given to his son foreshadowed the merging of Italy into a European empire. Rome was to be the 'second city of the Empire' and plans were drawn up for a vast imperial palace to be built on the Capitoline Hill. The Napoleonic reforms in Italy, partial and inconsistent as they were, were a landmark in the development of the Risorgimento. Uniformity of law and administration, and the application of conscription, helped to break down particularism. Italian troops fought well in their own divisions; and the Napoleonic officers and civil servants were to form the spearhead of the Risorgimento after 1815. But only a handful of intellectuals like Alfieri and Foscolo openly turned against Napoleon because he had betrayed their hopes of Italian unity. When Murat tried to rouse Italian nationalism against Austria in 1815, he met with very little response. Active resistance to French rule was local, clerical and reactionary: guerrilla warfare in Calabria between 1806 and 1808 tied up considerable numbers of French troops. Napoleon seems to have ignored the political implications; as he ignored the military portent of the battle of Maida in 1806, when the firepower of the English infantry under General Stuart defeated General Reynier's columns in a few minutes.

In Germany Napoleon continued the historic policy of Richelieu and Louis XIV—that of keeping Germany divided by fortifying the particularism of the client kingdoms grouped in the Confederation of the Rhine. Up to 1806 he hoped that Prussia would remain within his system as a vassal state; he afterwards regretted that he had not taken the opportunity after Jena of eliminating Prussia altogether. The creation of the Saxon Duchy of Warsaw in 1807 appeared to be a step towards the restoration of Poland. But Napoleon was in fact interested in Poland only as a pawn in his strategy. At Tilsit he first suggested that Russia should have the whole of Poland and that Silesia should go to Jerome Bonaparte: the Duchy was a compromise solution. In 1812 he disappointed the Poles by his evasive pronouncements about Polish independence.

The origins of German nationalism are discernible in the intellectual sphere long before it affected politics. The intellectual renaissance of Germany at the end of the eighteenth century, headed by such great writers as Goethe, Kant, and Schiller, was at first cosmopolitan in outlook. At the turn of the century the romantic movement began to modify the rationalism and cosmopolitanism of the Enlightenment: its interest in history, custom and tradition, and in the language and literature of the *Volk*, pioneered by Herder, was a powerful stimulant to national consciousness. The initial enthusiasm in German intellectual circles for the French Revolution gave way to a conservative and religious reaction which condemned the anarchy and atheism of the Terror, and exalted the spiritual superiority of a distinct, unique German culture. But nationalism was still conceived as cultural, not political. Schiller wrote in 1802 that 'the greatness of Germany consists in its culture and the character of the nation, which are independent of its political fate'.

The turning-point in the intellectual evolution of cultural into political nationalism was the collapse of Prussia in 1806. The younger generation of intellectuals such as Fichte, Arndt, Kleist and Schlegel began to preach patriotic resistance to Napoleon. The collapse of the Prussian government gave a chance for the nationalists to gain control: Frederick William was forced to appoint Stein and Hardenberg as his ministers in 1807. Hardenberg wrote in his memorandum on reform (September 1807) 'The French Revolution, of which the present wars are only a continuation, has given France, in the midst of stormy and bloody scenes, an unexpected power. The force of the new principles is such that the state which refuses to accept them will be condemned to submit or perish.' Gneisenau, who had seen the American militia in action in their War of Independence, also wrote: 'The Revolution has set in motion the national energy of the entire French people. . . . If the other states wish to restore the balance of power they must open and use the same resources.' Frederick William and the Junkers feared and disliked a 'Jacobin' policy, and sabotaged much of Stein's far-reaching reforms. After his dismissal in 1808, Scharnhorst and Gneisenau succeeded, however, in carrying through an effective reform of the army. The abolition of serfdom and of degrading punishments, the exclusion of foreign mercenaries, and a drastic overhaul of the officer corps improved the army's spirit and tactics; the adoption of conscription in 1813 allowed it to be rapidly expanded (Chapter VIII).

In Austria also reform was the work of a handful of men like the Archduke Charles, Stadion and Hormayr, and was hampered by the Emperor Francis's distrust of 'Jacobinism'. The army was modernised, and a reserve *Landwehr* created in 1808. After the defeat of Wagram, the emperor was disgusted with the 'patriots' who had dragged him into a disastrous war. In April 1813, he wrote to Napoleon, 'Every prolongation of war which does not allow the sovereigns to devote themselves seriously to stamping out the Jacobin ferment which daily spreads, will soon threaten the existence of thrones.' The patriotism aroused in the war of 1809 was Austrian and Habsburg in its appeal rather than German, and the guerrilla warfare under Hofer in the Tyrol was directed more against Bavarian anti-clericalism than against the French.

Central Europe did not produce, either in 1809 or in 1813, a general guerrilla resistance such as appeared in Spain. The spirit of nationalism was hardly yet stirring beyond a comparatively small circle of intellectuals, reformers and officers. The German nationalists of the nineteenth century created a romantic legend when they christened Leipzig the 'Battle of the Nations'. The collapse of the Napoleonic Empire cannot simply be attributed to the rise of national consciousness, to the exclusion of the military and diplomatic factors, without distorting the perspective of European history.

Because Spain was the first example of large-scale resistance to Napoleon, it was hailed as a portent of a general movement in Europe. Napoleon was particularly enraged by the suggestion that two of his divisions had surrendered to Spanish partisans at Baylen (July 1808). In fact, Dupont's raw conscripts had been defeated by Spanish regular troops, and he had signed a convention for evacuation, which was subsequently broken. In his bulletin announcing the capture of Burgos (November 1808) Napoleon tried to dispel this propaganda. 'It would be a good thing if men like M. de Stein who, lacking regular troops which were unable to resist our eagles, entertain the sublime idea of arming the masses, could see the misfortunes which ensue, and the weakness of the obstacles which this resource can offer to regular troops.' It is true that the French army had little difficulty in defeating Spanish armies in the field, and that without Wellington's army organised resistance would soon have collapsed. Wellington wrote home in August 1809, 'The Spanish troops will not fight; they are undisciplined, they have no officers, no provisions, no means of any description.' And again in October 1809 he wrote, 'As to the enthusiasm, about which so much noise has been made even in our own country, I am convinced that the world has entirely mistaken its effects.' The unpredictable character of Spain is shown by the history of the French Bourbon intervention in Spain in 1823. Wellington and most observers then assumed that the French would get into the same trouble as in 1808. Nothing of the sort happened, principally because on this occasion the French were intervening on behalf of the king and the Church against a minority of liberal reformers. Spanish nationalism had very little in common with the general movement of European nationalism in the nineteenth century which sprang from the liberal middle-class.

Napoleon completely misread the temper of the Spanish people from the start. After Tilsit he was in his most dogmatic and ruthless mood. Metternich, who was then Ambassador in Paris, observed in October 1807, 'There has recently been a total change in the methods of Napoleon: he seems to think that he has reached a point where moderation is a useless obstacle.' In February 1808, Napoleon wrote to Caulaincourt: 'As for Spain, I tell you nothing but you can understand that it is necessary to shake up this power, which is useless to the general interest.' In April 1808, he wrote to Murat, his lieutenant in Spain: 'If there are movements in Spain they will resemble those we saw in Egypt.' Even when the people of Madrid rose against the French on 2 May, and had to be savagely repressed by Murat, he wrote that 'the Spaniards are like other peoples and not a class apart. They will be happy to accept the imperial institutions.' In his proclamation to the Spanish nation on 28 May he wrote, 'I wish your descendants to say "He is the regenerator of our country".'

Napoleon had an exaggerated notion of the latent resources of Spain, both naval and economic, which were being mismanaged by the incompetence of her rulers, the decadent and disreputable trio of the

Bourbon King Charles IV, his queen and the favourite, Godoy. Lured by the prospect of gaining Portugal for himself, Godoy had kept Spain in uneasy alliance with France, but during the Jena campaign he showed signs of disloyalty to it. At the end of 1806 Napoleon demanded that Spain should adhere to the Continental System and send a corps to occupy Hanover. In October 1807 he sent Junot to occupy Portugal, promising Godoy that he should have southern Portugal as a principality for himself. As Junot's army crossed Spain, he was able to infiltrate troops at strategic points. Meanwhile Ferdinand, Charles IV's heir, was afraid that Godoy intended to usurp the throne at his father's death, and negotiated with Napoleon for the overthrow of Godoy. The idea thus grew in Napoleon's mind of regenerating Spain by an efficient French administration, either by marrying Ferdinand to a Bonaparte princess, or by a deposition of the degenerate Bourbons. A revolt took place against the king and Godoy, and the king abdicated. Napoleon summoned the royal family to meet him at Bayonne, and the result of the conference was that the king and Ferdinand both abdicated their rights to the throne, and Napoleon gave it to his brother Joseph.

Up to the Bayonne meeting the Spanish people remained quiet because they thought Napoleon intended to back Ferdinand against Godoy. While the grandees of Madrid were accepting an enlightened constitution from Napoleon at Bayonne, the provinces were flaming into spontaneous revolt. Canning hastened to give support to the insurrectionary juntas, and Wellesley forced Junot to evacuate Portugal by the victory of Vimiero (August 1808). The main Spanish regular forces were easily defeated at Medina del Rio Seco (July 1808), and Dupont was ordered to march south with two divisions and occupy Cadiz. Here he was caught by 20,000 Spanish regular troops supported by guerrillas, and forced to capitulate at Baylen (July 1808). Napoleon was at last forced to recognise that he had a full-scale war on his hands, and ordered the mass of the Grand Army from Germany to Spain. At the end of 1808 he assumed command there himself, and narrowly failed to catch Moore's army in the Corunna campaign. He never appeared in Spain again and, distrusting Joseph's competence, preferred to send orders from Paris to his disobedient and quarrelsome marshals.

The turning-point of the Peninsular War came in 1810–11. Having dealt with Austria in 1809, Napoleon gave Masséna 100,000 of his best troops with orders to 'drive the English leopard into the sea'. Masséna was defeated by Wellington's defensive tactics at the lines of Torres Vedras, and by the jealousy of Soult who failed to back him up from Andalusia. Thereafter Wellington was able to take the offensive and by the victories of Salamanca (1812) and Vitoria (1813) to drive the French out of Spain.

Although there was a considerable pro-French party in Spain, Napoleon's mistake was in thinking that there was a sufficient middle class which would welcome the reforms of the *Code Napoléon*, including the secularisation of Church property. In fact Spain was predominantly a country of priest-ridden peasants, swayed by religious fanaticism and a reactionary provincial patriotism. The enlightened reforms of Charles III in the eighteenth century had been greeted with sullen hostility. Napoleon described the Peninsular War as 'a war of monks'; and it did resemble the wars of the Vendée on a large scale. The Cortes which met at Cadiz in 1810 promulgated a liberal constitution to compete with the enlightened constitution formulated under Napoleon's eye at Bayonne. But in the light of subsequent history it is difficult to believe that this is what most of the Spanish guerrillas were fighting for. When Ferdinand was restored in 1814 the people shouted 'Long live the absolute King' and 'Down with the Constitution'. It is by no means certain that French intervention in itself would have produced the explosion, especially if Napoleon had followed his original intention of backing Ferdinand. Once Napoleon was committed to keeping Joseph on the throne, he could not face until too late the loss of prestige involved in cutting his losses in Spain. In November 1813 he exclaimed, 'I have sacrificed hundreds of thousands of men to make Joseph reign in Spain. It is one of my mistakes to think my brother necessary to assure my dynasty'. The veteran troops locked up in Spain might well have turned the scale in Germany in 1813, and it was not till the beginning of 1814 that Napoleon offered to restore Ferdinand to the throne.

The conclusion to be drawn from this analysis is that Napoleon, in his mentality and his policy, had much in common with the enlightened despots of the eighteenth century. His claim to be the '*Roi des Peuples*' rests on the legend, not the reality. On the day after his coronation he made the extraordinary but perhaps prophetic remark, 'I have come too late: men are too enlightened. It is no longer possible to do great things. Compare Alexander.' Both his strength and his weakness lay in the attempt to harness explosive political forces which he could not comprehend or control.

CHAPTER XII

FRENCH POLITICS, 1814-47[1]

THE defeat and abdication of Napoleon did not automatically mean the restoration of the Bourbons. That solution had secured the more or less reluctant consent of those who could have any influence on the decisions—that is to say, the Allies on the one hand and on the other the leading figures in the government of the Empire, represented by the Senate and by the provisional government over which Talleyrand presided. But, even after that, the exact nature of the future regime was still undecided. Monarchy, no doubt, but what brand of monarchy? The pre-1789 monarchy, with the king ruling by *divine right*, his good pleasure limited only by his own conscience and by the traditional privileges of the various groups and collective bodies of State? Or the 1791 monarchy, the king ruling only with the authority delegated by the nation and as the nation's principal servant, by virtue of a contract freely entered into by both parties?

The senatorial party, including as it did the surviving members of the revolutionary assemblies, clearly hoped to secure the triumph of the second solution. They had the support of Tsar Alexander of Russia, who had announced his intention of securing a regime in France corresponding to the enlightened spirit of the age. The very day the emperor abdicated, the Senate adopted a constitution in conformity with the principle of popular sovereignty. It was stated therein that the late king's brother was *freely* called to the throne, and might reign only after swearing to observe this constitution. The condition was unacceptable to the *Prétendant*; since the death—shrouded in mystery—of his unfortunate nephew, Louis XVII, he had considered himself the only legitimate monarch, and had always shown himself inflexible where his rights and dignity were concerned. Still, the prince was intelligent enough, and sufficiently matured by his trials, to be inclined to make the necessary concessions. He manoeuvred cleverly to preserve the principle of a monarchy not deriving its authority from the will of the people. He did not hurry to leave England, where he had been living since 1807; and when he arrived in France, on 24 April, the enthusiastic welcome from the people in the north, and the manifestation of their devotion offered by the various representative bodies and by the marshals of the army, put him in a strong bargaining position.

---

[1] At the editor's request, a sketch of the developments under Louis-Philippe, not much noticed in vol. x, is included here.

At the moment of his entry into the capital he had the *Declaration of Saint-Ouen* published, the terms of which had been worked out by his representatives and those of the Senate: the senatorial constitution was put aside, on the pretext that it had been drawn up too hurriedly; the king undertook to have another framed by a commission of both Chambers; assurances were given that the constitution would be a liberal one, and the principles that it was proposed to embody in it were briefly stated, together with guarantees of a kind to reassure those who had benefited under the previous regime.

This new constitution, known as the *Constitutional Charter*, solemnly proclaimed on 4 June 1814, was to provide the framework of the French State (with a few minor changes in 1830) up to the revolution of 1848. It is essentially a work of compromise, and by this very fact shows well enough the balance of political and social forces in the country at the time.

The theory of royal power by dynastic right or by *divine right*, otherwise called the principle of legitimacy, was affirmed in a long historical preamble, in which the limits set on the old absolutism were presented as 'gracious concessions' due to the king's free-will, and consequently involving no impairment to the principle of his authority.[1] But on the other hand the chief political and social victories of the Revolution were confirmed in a great many clauses; equality of all men before the law and in respect of taxation and military service; freedom of the individual, freedom of thought and expression, freedom of religion—though with this new fact, that the Catholic religion was declared to be the State religion, no longer just the religion of the majority of Frenchmen, as it was under the regime of Napoleon's Concordat of 1801. The Civil Code of the Empire was retained *en bloc*; Church or *émigré* properties that had been sold as 'belonging to the nation' remained the property of those who had bought them. Titles, decorations, pensions and ranks granted by preceding regimes were allowed to stand, and the State recognised all its financial obligations. Finally, the rigorously centralised administrative system established under Bonaparte's Consulate also remained unchanged.

The king retained considerable power under the political mechanism set up by the Charter:

The King's Person is inviolable and sacred. . . . Executive power belongs only to the King (Art. 13). The King is the supreme head of the State, he commands the armed forces on land and sea, declares war, makes peace treaties, alliances and trade agreements, nominates to all public administrative offices, and makes the rules and ordinances necessary for the execution of the laws and the safety of the State (Art. 14).

[1] 'Nous avons volontairement, et par le libre exercice de notre autorité royale, accordé et accordons, fait concession et octroi à nos sujets . . .'

The ministers were responsible to him, not to the two Chambers. He retained part of the legislative power, since he alone could initiate laws, and not even an amendment could be made to some debated text save with his consent. National representation was assured by two Chambers: the Chamber of Peers, nominated by the king, and the Chamber of Deputies. A law was to determine the way in which deputies were to be elected, but the Charter laid down that electors must have reached 30 years of age and be paying 300 francs in direct tax, whilst to be eligible for election candidates must have reached 40 years of age and be paying tax of 1000 francs. The two Chambers were on an equal footing in the framing of laws; but the budget had to be voted first by the deputies. The Chamber of Peers would function on occasion as a High Court of Justice to judge crimes of high treason. The king was to summon the two Chambers and determine the duration of their sessions; he might dissolve the Chamber of Deputies. Judges were to be nominated by the king, but their independence was assured in that they could not be dismissed.

This regime, though inspired by the English model, cannot be called parliamentary in the present sense of the term, since the government would not depend on a parliamentary majority; and it was representative only if we are prepared to admit that fewer than 90,000 persons privileged by their wealth—for that was the number of electors paying 300 francs in tax—validly represented the nation. Even though we may feel that the constitution limited too severely the number of men who could take part in the political life of the country, we must admit that material and social conditions for the working of a truly democratic regime were far from being realised in the France of this period. More than half the French nation were illiterate, and knew of events only through talk in taverns and markets. In the provinces where religion kept its vitality, as in Brittany, the priest's opinion was law. About 75 per cent of the population lived in small villages and were absorbed in their agricultural labours. Apart from the capital, which had more than 700,000 inhabitants, only two cities—Lyons and Marseilles—had above 100,000 and not more than five had over 50,000: Bordeaux, Rouen, Nantes, Lille and Toulouse. Small provincial towns were well enough linked with one another and with the capital by the network of some 20,000 miles of royal roads maintained by the State; but many villages remained practically isolated, through lack of the means for road-building—for what could take the place of the *corvée*? As for the main highways—with their coaching stations at regular intervals—the time and money consumed by a journey put their use out of reach of the great majority, and notably restricted the circulation of goods, and of ideas too.

The periodical press, systematically stifled by Napoleon, was to go on being submitted under the Restoration to restrictions that would limit circulation. In 1826 the fourteen political newspapers in the capital together totalled only 65,000 subscribers, and there was no casual sale. Lastly, the rigorously centralised administrative system helped to choke provincial political life and to concentrate it in Paris. 'The nation,' wrote Benjamin Constant in 1812, 'exists to-day only in the capital.'

In the *pays légal*—that is to say, that minority of citizens sufficiently well off to have the right to vote—we can distinguish three social groupings. First, the big landowners: contrary to what is often alleged, this class was not wholly devoted to the conservative party; alongside the nobility that had managed to save their lands during the Revolution, it contained *nouveaux riches* who, by purchasing 'national property', had profited from the Revolution and had acquired estates. Though the former might incline towards reaction, the latter must fight hard against everything that recalled the *ancien régime*. Amongst the liberal opposition leaders we even find aristocrats, landed proprietors of the old regime, such as Lafayette and the Duc de la Rochefoucauld-Liancourt. Secondly, the industrial magnates, merchants and bankers: in contrast to the position in England, these economic activities had been closed in the past to the nobility. The rich bourgeois who by inheritance occupied these controlling positions in the economy feared a return to the old regime, with its State controls, quite as much as those who had bought 'national property' feared it; and for class reasons, too, they could put up with aristocratic pretensions less patiently. Thirdly, the leading civil servants, recruited from the two categories above, especially from the first: by definition it was they who upheld the ministry of the moment; and, if they were tempted to forget the fact, summary dismissal brought it back to mind soon enough.

The beginnings of the new regime were not happy. Less than a year after his return Louis XVIII had to flee shamefully before Napoleon. The ease with which the nation at first appeared to accept this revolution may be explained by the discontent that prevailed in a large part of public opinion. This discontent was due in good part to circumstances beyond the control of Louis XVIII's government. The loss of territories conquered twenty years previously was an inevitable consequence of Napoleon's defeat: all the same, it was bitterly felt as a national humiliation. The state of the treasury, likewise a consequence of the defeat, imposed strict economy: cessation of public works; the dismissal of many civil servants; the placing of many of the officers of the Napoleonic army on half pay, since they no longer served any useful purpose; lastly, the retaining of the unpopular *droits réunis* (excise duties), despite the rash promise to abolish them which the king's brother had made when he came back to France. Nor was it in the king's power to silence former *émigrés* who were claiming back their former properties, now in the hands of others, any more than he could silence those members of the clergy and of the aristocracy who were demanding that the old order of things be re-established, despite the royal intentions proclaimed clearly in the Charter. It remains properly a charge against Louis XVIII, and more especially against the princes of the family, that these pretensions were encouraged by the revival at court of outworn institutions, the costly re-forming of the ceremonial troops of the Royal Guard, and by the too pointed and exclusive favour shown towards former companions in exile; that memories of the revolutionary period were re-awakened by ceremonies of expiation; and finally, that a section of the nation had been disquieted by policies too openly favourable towards the Church.

However this may be, clearly these mistakes would not have sufficed to bring about a catastrophe if Napoleon had stayed quietly on his island. The miraculous ease of his return to Paris was due essentially to the military element, and does not mean that the nation as a whole wished to have imperial despotism restored. At the time of the plebiscite concerning the *Acte Additionnel*—the new constitution granted by Napoleon—and the election of the new legislative body, citizens and electors abstained *en masse*.

The conditions under which the king's second return took place were to weigh heavily on the regime's future. In the immediate aftermath of Waterloo and of Napoleon's second abdication (22 June 1815), the materials were assembled for a civil war between Frenchmen. The royalist party, which had been almost non-existent in 1814, was now large, and filled with hatred of its opponents. Whereas the year before all who served the State had rallied without any difficulty to Louis XVIII, now those who had broken their bond and had followed Napoleon found themselves compromised, with no going back. The emperor had abdicated in his son's favour only, and the army was passionately devoted to the imperial dynasty, as was a section of the ordinary folk of Paris; the Legislative Body, dominated by liberals such as Lafayette, inclined towards the Duc d'Orléans, Louis XVIII's cousin: but it also contained plenty of partisans of Napoleon II. Wellington, marching on Paris with his victorious army, was determined to do his utmost to establish the Bourbon king again; but he was to find a hundred thousand determined men facing him beneath the walls of the capital, under the command of one of Napoleon's ablest lieutenants, Marshal Davout; and the outcome of a battle fought under these circumstances was not certain. If in these conditions France managed to avoid the double scourge of continued war abroad and an outbreak of civil war at home, that fact was in large measure due to the skill of a quite unscrupulous man. Joseph Fouché, former Convention member, and former minister of police under the Empire, had been kicked out by the first Restoration as a regicide. When Napoleon came back from the island of Elba he gave him back the Ministry of Police, and Fouché had made use of it to establish his own contacts, in all parties. After the battle of Waterloo his aim seems to have been to lead the country, with the least possible damage, towards the solution which in the long run could not be avoided, as his realistic view of things told him. By serving the king in this way he hoped to safeguard his own interests, and the interests of a class that had profited from the Revolution: of which class Fouché was himself the perfect representative.

This plan required first of all that Napoleon be eliminated: and this first aim was achieved when Napoleon abdicated and left for the port of Rochefort. Fouché had a provisional commission of government nominated, and made himself president of it. He got rid of Lafayette by having him entrusted with an entirely hopeless mission to the Allied Command, and kept the Chamber occupied by inviting it to draw up a Constitution. Finally he persuaded Davout that a further battle, even if it ended in victory, would only prolong the war uselessly and add to the evils of foreign invasion. A military convention was therefore signed on 3 July, whereby the French army might withdraw behind the Loire, whilst the armies of Wellington and Blücher were to occupy the capital without bloodshed. From then on Napoleon II's partisans in Paris found themselves powerless. Fouché went in secret to Louis XVIII, who had hastened back from Belgium to France behind Wellington's armies, and met him at Saint-Denis. Despite his repugnance Louis XVIII consented to make Fouché one of his ministers. Next day Fouché calmly told his colleagues in the provisional government that their role was now over, and that all was in order for the king's return. One squad of the National Guard was enough to block the access of the deputies to the Legislative Body. They went home without putting up the least show of resistance.

Louis XVIII re-entered the Tuileries on 8 July. Everything had to be started all over again, and under conditions disastrously less favourable than in 1814. Then, the Allies had used their victory with moderation, leaving the country almost at once and imposing no monetary contributions. This time they were firmly resolved to make the incorrigible nation feel the weight of defeat, and to recover a large part of the cost of the last campaign. Until peace was concluded sixty-one French departments were going to find themselves occupied by 1,000,000 foreign soldiers, crushing the population by their requisitions and harassings. The second treaty of Paris (20 November 1815), besides some further lopping of territory, was to impose an enormous financial burden on France, and temporary occupation of the frontier provinces. As the disasters were associated with the king's return, they inevitably aroused patriotic sentiments of humiliation, directed against the Bourbons, who were exposed to the shameful charge of having 'come back in the foreigners' baggage'.

Equally serious for the future was the fact that the nation found itself sharply divided into two camps. In 1814 the Restoration came about in such a way that there were neither victors nor vanquished. This time, the exasperated royalists were to insist on reprisals against those whose treason had brought on the disasters of 1815; while the emperor's followers, marked out by their conduct during the Hundred Days, found themselves barred for ever from the roads to power—condemned, so to say, to go in fear and into opposition. And this opposition was to benefit from the unnatural but infinitely dangerous alliance between liberal revolutionary ideology and the military nationalism of the Empire.

The first year of Louis XVIII's government after his return was marked by three things that were important for the future of the regime: the white Terror, royalist differences, and the miscarriage of parliamentary government.

Popular reaction had been unleashed in the royalist provinces of the south as soon as the events in Paris were made known: some of the emperor's followers were massacred, notably in the department of Gard and at Marseilles; whilst many more had to undergo all sorts of rigours and humiliation. When Louis XVIII returned, he had announced his intention of limiting sanctions to those chief army officers and leading civil servants whose participation had been decisive in March 1815; shortly afterwards a list of fifty-seven names was published. The best guarantee of moderation on the part of the government lay in the composition of the ministry itself; almost all who sat beside Talleyrand and Fouché were men who had formerly served Napoleon. But this ministry was not to survive the assembly of a new Chamber of Deputies. Because the Chambers of the first Restoration had not found time to vote the electoral law prescribed in the Charter, the king had wanted, for the elections that took place at the end of August 1815, to enlarge the Napoleonic electoral colleges by lowering the minimum age for electors from 30 to 21 years and that of candidates from 40 to 25, whilst the number of deputies was raised from 262 to 402. The result was a surprise to the government: the majority turned out to be made up of relatively young and zealous royalists, who were soon dubbed 'ultra-royalists'. It was, as Louis XVIII put it, a *Chambre introuvable*.

Even before the opening of the session the deputies let it be known that they declined to collaborate with a government that included Fouché the regicide. Talleyrand sacrificed his old accomplice, appointing him the king's representative at Dresden, then himself retired (22 September). Louis XVIII replaced him by the Duc Armand-Emmanuel de Richelieu, a *grand seigneur* whose generous and disinterested character commanded respect. Whilst an *émigré* in Russia, he had served Alexander I as governor of the southern province recently won from the Turks. The friendship shown him by the tsar had given hope that he would secure better peace conditions than Talleyrand, who was compromised by his anti-Russian dealings at the Congress of Vienna. Next to the president of the council the most important figure in the new ministry was Élie Decazes, a young magistrate and a native of the Bordeaux region, whom Fouché had been unwise enough to make prefect of the Paris police. This led on to his becoming minister in charge of the police of the whole country. Gifted with great flexibility, with rare charm and also rare talent for intrigue, and totally devoid of scruple, Decazes had succeeded in winning the affection of the old king, who soon made him his favourite and called him his 'dear son'.

Under pressure from the *Chambre introuvable* the ministry drew up and carried repressive measures permitting the imprisonment of suspects without trial, severe punishment of the authors of writings or manifestations hostile to the regime, the creation of *cours prévotales* intended to punish attempted rebellion by court martial procedure, and the exiling of those former regicides who had supported Napoleon during the Hundred Days. A few of those chiefly responsible were tried and condemned to death—amongst others Marshal Ney, whose trial before the peers stirred great emotion; the execution of this gallant soldier was to be an ineffaceable stain on the Bourbon regime. Royalist reaction showed itself, too, in systematic purgings in the administration and the army that deprived at least a quarter of the civil servants and army officers of their jobs.

In the early weeks of 1816 the government tried to put a brake on the reactionaries, and it was then that a division between ultra-royalists and moderate, or ministerial, royalists appeared for the first time in the Chamber of Deputies. The moderates proved to be in the minority; the government did not succeed in getting an electoral law voted, and had the greatest difficulty in getting the budget voted before the close of the session (29 April 1816).

It was clear that when parliament reassembled the ministry would find itself unable to govern, so lively was the hostility of the majority towards the favourite Decazes. By resigning he would have established the principle that was being upheld in the Chamber by the ultra-royalists' spokesmen, whereby the king was obliged to choose ministers acceptable to the majority; it would have amounted to setting up the practice of a parliamentary regime within the framework of the Charter. Louis XVIII, encouraged by the pressing advice of the Allies, decided to dissolve the *Chambre introuvable* (5 September 1816) and by this act affirmed the preponderance of the crown over national representation;

by a strange irony of circumstances this gesture was applauded by the very men who posed as the defenders of liberal principles.

The elections carefully prepared by Decazes took place with the same electoral colleges, but the number of deputies was put back to 262, and their age was increased to 40 as laid down in the Charter. This made it possible to oust a good many of the ultra-royalist deputies, and in the new Chamber the ministerial party proved to be in a majority. From then on, as the three powers—king, ministry and chambers—were in agreement, Louis XVIII was able to experiment with a middle-of-the-road government, aiming on the one hand at barring the pretensions of the ultra-royalists, and on the other at rallying to the monarchy those who in one way or another clung to the Revolution. It was to succeed on the first point, but on the second it was to fail; for all efforts made to conciliate the liberals were to end merely by strengthening the parties that were hostile to the monarchy, and putting the regime itself in danger. This second point has often not been sufficiently underlined.

During the four years that this experiment lasted—from 1816 to 1820—the political forces in the country, as in parliament, were divided among three tendencies.

The ultra-royalists—as their opponents called them, for they preferred to call themselves 'true royalists' or simply 'royalists'—would not allow any attempt to found a monarchical regime on concessions to the principles or the men of the Revolution. Some, such as the philosopher Louis de Bonald, considered Louis XVIII's Charter 'a work of folly and of darkness'. Others, such as Chateaubriand, were disposed to accept it and to derive from it an order of things at once monarchical and consistent with the tendencies of the century. They rejected the ideology of the eighteenth-century *philosophes*, whence the Revolution had sprung, and sought to restore the Church's influence in society. Lamennais at that time was the most fervent defender of this ideal of the union of altar and throne. *La Quotidienne* was the paper that stood for this ultra-clerical tendency; the *Journal des Débats*, perhaps the most influential paper of the time, took Chateaubriand's line. The *Conservateur*, a review edited by Chateaubriand, and appearing at irregular intervals from October 1818 to March 1820, brilliantly defended the party's ideas. The ultra-royalists were supported by the heir-apparent (the king's brother, Comte d'Artois) and in general by the royal family and the court; and, most powerfully, by the clergy also. Party directives were spread through the country by the secret organisation called the *Chevaliers de la Foi*, a sort of Catholic and royalist counter-masonry; it had been founded at the close of the Empire, and was not without influence on the restoration of the monarchy in 1814. A unit of the organisation existed within the Chamber of Deputies, and this gave the party a discipline and cohesion which astonished outside observers.

The ministerial or constitutional party by definition supported the government's middle-of-the-road policy. The administrative machine was in its control, and it could speak through the *Moniteur*, the official State newspaper. Its ideological inspiration came from a small group of writers known as the *doctrinaires*: Royer-Collard, Guizot, the Duc de Broglie, and others. They were sincerely devoted to the monarchy and to the Bourbons, and sought, in the phrase that Decazes made popular, to bring the king closer to the nation and the nation closer to the king ('nationaliser la royauté et royaliser la nation').

The group known as the *Indépendants* brought together under this misnomer all who opposed the regime: liberals, republicans, Orleanists, Bonapartists. Benjamin Constant supplied the brains of the party, Lafayette its banner, and Laffitte, the banker, its moneybags; the king's cousin the Duc d'Orléans flirted with it, circumspectly. The masonic secret societies, and later the Charbonnerie (Carbonari, imported from Italy about 1821), made it both wide-spread and effective. The *Constitutionnel*, a paper produced under various labels, was later to be the movement's most popular organ; but in Decazes' time its views were put forward in *La Minerve*, a review well edited by Benjamin Constant, and appearing at irregular intervals. The constitutional party took advantage of its greater numbers to get passed a long-overdue electoral law: as the Charter laid down, electors had to show an assessment of 300 francs payable in direct taxes, and candidates for election an assessment of 1000 francs; elections were to take place by direct voting, all electors coming to the chief town of a department to vote (this provision was to work in favour of the liberal party, whose members were mostly townsmen); finally, one-fifth of the Chamber was to be renewed each year. A law reconstituting the army on a new basis was vigorously opposed by the right-wing royalists because it seemed weighted too much in favour of former officers of the Empire. It worried the Allied powers for this same reason. Nevertheless Richelieu managed to secure the end of foreign occupation in 1818; loans by the houses of Baring (London) and Hope (Amsterdam) had enabled the French treasury to meet all the financial obligations imposed by the 1815 treaties, and this despite a severe agricultural crisis that hit the country in 1817.

Richelieu came back at the end of 1818 from Aix-la-Chapelle, where he had negotiated so successfully, determined to re-orientate his home policy. The Allies were worried by the spread of liberal ideas in France, and wanted to see the king's government draw closer to the right-wing royalists. Since Decazes, for his part, was determined to persist in his policy of conciliation towards the Left, there was an acute crisis within the ministry. It ended in Richelieu's resignation, and in the formation of a new ministry with General Dessolles as nominal president, but with Decazes as real head (29 December 1818). Decazes consolidated his position by getting the king to create sixty new peers, who swung in his favour the majority in the Chamber of Peers. A law was passed, inspired by the Doctrinaires, giving the press a relatively liberal regime; the main innovation was that actions against journalists were to be tried by jury, thus protecting them from the arbitrary action of government.

In the elections (autumn 1819) the *Indépendants* won so much success that Decazes himself was alarmed by it, and decided to go into reverse. Some of his colleagues declined to follow him in this complete change of front, however; there was a fresh crisis, and a fresh shuffling of the government, and Decazes was unwillingly obliged to become president of the council himself (November 1819). He was busy negotiating with the Right about modifying the electoral law, when an unforeseeable accident threw him out of power. During the night of 13–14 February 1820 a fanatic assassinated the king's nephew the Duc de Berry, alone of the princes capable of ensuring the survival of the elder branch of the Bourbons. 'It was not the guiltiest hand that struck the blow' wrote Chateaubriand at the time; in effect, the royalists put the responsibility on Decazes for the state of mind capable of inspiring the crime. Louis XVIII had to resign himself to the dismissal of his 'cher fils', and call the Duc de Richelieu back to head the government. The elimination of Decazes set a seal on the dissolution of the constitutional party of the centre; its remaining members were to join themselves on to the right or left wings, retaining more or less trace of their origin under the labels 'right centre' and 'left centre'.

Without delay the press was put back again under a regime of strict censorship, and (as in 1815) the government was given authority to arrest without trial. But a new electoral law was needed, to reverse the tendency which in recent years—so it had seemed—must shortly give to the Left control over the parliamentary majority: the new law was passed at the end of June 1820 after violent debate, accompanied by disturbances in the streets of the capital. The system provided for two kinds of electoral college: on the one hand those of the *arrondissements*, containing all the electors who paid 300 francs in direct tax, and electing 258 deputies; on the other, those of the departments, the *grands collèges*, which were to choose 172 additional deputies and were to consist of one-quarter of the electors in each department, namely those paying the highest tax. As this amounted to giving two votes to those who were richest—and therefore presumed to be most conservative—this electoral law of 1820 was called the 'law of the double vote'.

Two circumstances intensified the result that had been expected from this. The first was the failure of an attempted liberal and Bonapartist *coup de force* which had Lafayette behind it, and which frightened those who genuinely wanted order. The second was the posthumous birth of a son to the Duc de Berry, a chance next to miraculous for assuring the continuity of the dynasty (29 September 1820). The elections of the month of November 1820 considerably strengthened the ultra-royalist party in the Chamber. Richelieu nevertheless intended to go on governing with the ministers whom he had inherited from Decazes, without making way for the leaders of the new majority. When the two Chambers reassembled at the end of 1821 they joined their votes to those of the left-wing opposition in condemning the government's foreign policy. Richelieu resigned (12 December 1821), as the king, weakened by age, showed no determination to support him vigorously.

The new ministry was entirely composed of members of the ultra-royalist party, acceptable to the king's brother, 'Monsieur'. And indeed it seemed as though the heir-apparent was already beginning to reign in his brother's name. The dominating personality in this new team was the Comte Joseph de Villèle, minister of finance, whose primacy was confirmed in September 1822 when he became President of the Council. Coming from the lesser gentry of the Toulouse region, Villèle had shown himself unrivalled in the Chamber of Deputies by his skill in debate and by his practical grasp of affairs. Thanks to him, the financial administration of France was to know a period of regularity and prosperity almost unique in her history. As head of government he showed himself tireless in parliamentary debate, fertile in expedients, at once tenacious and supple in his plans. But as his mind tended fundamentally to be interested in material problems, and because of his cunning and jealous nature—and his timid pacifism, too, in foreign policy—his government had a low and utilitarian stamp about it, of a sort displeasing to a nation now stirred by romantic breezes and by her memories of the Imperial epic. Nor did he dare to stand out against certain foolish demands made by his party; and by his personal animosities he made royalist divisions worse. He believed he was master of the situation because he had the king's confidence and the support of a majority of the Chamber, and he did not trouble, therefore, to conciliate opponents or manage public opinion.

When the royalist government came to power its opponents believed it would soon be discredited through incapacity. They were soon deceived, for Villèle and his colleagues scored so many successes in their uphill struggle that two years later the regime seemed to be firmly consolidated. Throughout the administration reliable and devoted men replaced any that were suspected of left-wing sympathies. Fresh conspiracies by the Carbonari were foiled by the police, with severe punishments. The press was placed under a regime that, without reviving the censorship, did seriously curtail its freedom of expression. Secondary education had been put under the supervision of the clergy by an ordinance of 27 February 1821; this seizure of education by the Church was confirmed by the creation of a Ministry of Church Affairs and Public Instruction. It was held by a bishop, Mgr Frayssinous, who in fact was an enlightened and moderate man. Nineteen archbishops and bishops became peers.

The government's position was more strongly reinforced by the success of the French intervention in the Spanish revolution than by all these measures. The intervention was determined upon in agreement with the great continental powers, and despite the furious opposition of the liberal party. Villèle himself had become resigned to it only with the gravest apprehensions, and under pressure from Chateaubriand, who had become Minister of Foreign Affairs at the end of 1822. Cruel memories of Napoleon's reverses in Spain had made the undertaking appear fraught with perils: but in fact it was carried through with complete success, at least at the military level. The army came back from it with its morale strengthened in devotion to the monarchy; the collapse of the Spanish liberals discouraged enemies at home. French liberals found themselves in disrepute because they had predicted so many disasters, and also because they seemed dejected by a success that afforded the country's pride some satisfaction. Chateaubriand could boast: 'eight years of peace have not strengthened the legitimate throne as much as have twenty days of war'. The government hastened to make political capital out of its advantage. At the end of December 1823 the Chamber was dissolved. The general elections that took place on 26 February and 6 March were an overwhelming success for the ministry: the liberal opposition was reduced from 110 to 19 seats. It was, as Louis XVIII put it, la Chambre retrouvée. The victorious party intended to give itself the leisure in which to take up quietly again the work of reaction interrupted in September 1816: one of the first things it did was to vote a law suppressing the annual renewal of a fifth of the Chamber, and it raised the duration of the parliamentary mandate to seven years.

Nevertheless, the very extent of the royalist party's parliamentary victory made for conditions threatening its cohesion. A group of extreme right-wing deputies had already appeared by 1820, accusing Villèle of being too moderate: the annihilation of the Left was to give them full liberty of action. In the Chambre retrouvée of 1824 this 'counter-opposition' was to number about seventy deputies. The president of the council was unwise enough to aggravate their quarrels by the revenge he took against right-wing personalities who criticised his policy. His worst mistake of this kind was the dismissal of Chateaubriand. The great writer's prestige and vanity, carried to their zenith by the success of the Spanish expedition, weighed upon the president of the council. In May 1824, in the Peers, Chateaubriand refused to support a project for a loan conversion that Villèle was absolutely set on, and he was dismissed in the most insulting fashion (6 June 1824). Chateaubriand at once became head of the counter-opposition, and took the *Journal des Débats* with him. The *Journal* now began to denounce the government's sins in violent tones. 'An un-adventurous administration, without glory, full of cunning, greedy for power; a political system out of sympathy with the genius of France, and contrary to the spirit of the Charter; an obscure despotism, mis-taking effrontery for strength; corruption raised to the level of a system. . . .'

The death of Louis XVIII (16 September 1824) and the accession of his brother Charles X made a temporary diversion. The fact that the new sovereign was apparently welcomed by all parties without any trouble, even gladly welcomed, emphasised the progress that had been made since 1816, when everyone, including the Allies, thought that the change of reign would bring troubles with it inside the realm. Charles X, though less intelligent than his brother, had a more attractive and more generous character. As king he was very anxious to do the job well, and to attach his subjects to him; he therefore quickly announced that he adhered to the Charter, and he suppressed the censorship which Villèle had re-established shortly before Louis XVIII died.

Moreover, there were no changes in the members of the government. After Chateaubriand's dismissal Villèle was undisputed master of the government. All the same, he was to be less able to resist the pressure from a section of his majority demanding reactionary measures; not merely because he was going to need them in order to stand up to the right-wing opposition, whose numbers were increasing dangerously, but also because the new king's views inclined him towards the ultra-royalist programme, especially in matters of religion.

The indemnity granted to *émigrés*—the first important measure voted in Charles X's reign—has often been ascribed to Charles's reactionary spirit. But in fact the initiative for this measure went back to Louis XVIII, and what was involved was quite other than the interests of a single class of Frenchmen. So long as former land-owners who had been despoiled by the Revolution did not recognise the transfers that had taken place—and how could they?—property of this kind was afflicted by a sort of moral blemish, which decreased its value and made transactions difficult; most of all, the new owners had feelings of guilt and uncertainty that prevented them from rallying to the monarchy in all sincerity. The answer was to render void the claims of former owners by making them accept an indemnity. The difficulty was to find the money, about a thousand million francs. Villèle had thought that it would be possible to provide for it by distributing the indemnity in the form of 3 per cent stock; the money needed annually to service this new item of the national debt would come from a conversion of the 5 per cent stock, the market price of which had risen at that time considerably above its nominal value. The measure was put forward in May 1824 and was defeated by the peers' opposition to it. Villèle learned by experience, and at the beginning of 1825 changed his tactics; first he got the principle passed that there should be an indemnity for *émigrés*, and then got the financial arrangements accepted that were to create the necessary resources. But in the course of the bitter debates in the two Chambers and in the press, most painful memories of the Revolution were revived. And the small investors—most of them Parisian bourgeois—suffered from the fall in the rate of interest and the general weakening of the stock market. This was still further accentuated by an economic crisis that affected all Europe. Yet, if the ministry could be accused of having sacrificed the interests of the people to the greed of the *émigrés*, at least there were no longer to be two kinds of property in France, and the problem of *biens nationaux* disappeared from political life.

At the same time the government was intensifying its policy in favour of the Catholic Church. The chief demonstration of this was the voting of a law punishing acts of sacrilege in churches by death; the conditions necessary for finding the offence proved were such that in practice the law could not be applied, but its promoters—they included Bonald— had wanted to demonstrate for the sake of principle against the secularity of the State; the opposition denounced it, also on principle, as opening the way to a theocracy, since it required the secular power to intervene in favour of a truth that was purely theological in nature. The king's coronation, which took place at Rheims on 29 May 1825 and followed the ancient ritual with barely any change, appeared to demonstrate the crown's submission to priestly authority.

In other respects the government's religious policy, which since 1820 had become more resolutely favourable to the Church, began to make its results felt. Relations between Church and State continued to be controlled within the framework of Napoleon's Concordat: negotiations entered into by Richelieu in 1816 and 1817 with a view to changing it had failed, because of the gallican prejudices of the majority of parliament, and the intransigence of the Holy See. Nevertheless thirty new dioceses had been created, and the State budget for the Church raised to twice what it was in 1815. A big effort had been made to secure the recruiting of clergy; the bishops had been allowed to open Church schools or *petits séminaires* exempt from the University's control; the number of students in the theological colleges (*grands séminaires*) had almost doubled in ten years, and in 1825, for the first time for a long while, more young priests were ordained than old ones buried. Likewise, congregations of religious were being revived, whose existence was not recognised by the then laws; the government's tolerance offset this, and in 1825 it even had a law passed giving legal status to the congregations of nuns. As for the men's congregations, save for a few exceptions they had to be content with a *de facto* existence that gave them no right to own corporate property. The Society of Jesus was amongst them: Pius VII had reconstituted the Jesuits, and in 1826 they had charge of seven secondary schools—disguised as *petits séminaires* so as to escape control by the University authorities. The University itself, as we have seen, was coming more and more under the Church. Teaching was to be the preserve of the clergy, it seemed, as it was before the Revolution. Laymen were encouraged to help the clergy in works of piety and welfare. The famous *Congrégation* founded and inspired by the Jesuits drew its members from the aristocracy of birth or position. Its members were behind a number of other activities of various kinds: amongst them the *Société de la Propagation de la Foi*, which collected money for Catholic foreign missions. Home missions, conducted with plenty of money and with an outward show intended to strike the imagination, sought to bring about the return to the faith of people dechristianised by the Revolution. Despite all these efforts the Papal nuncio in Paris, Mgr Macchi, estimated in 1826 that more than half the population was indifferent towards religion, and that in Paris barely 10,000 men used the sacraments.

In these conditions—to say nothing of the very active Protestant minority of 500,000—a policy that might perhaps have suited a 100 per cent Catholic nation, or that set out to achieve that proportion willy-nilly, could not fail to arouse hostile re-actions. And round about this time, it is true, opposition polemics seemed to concentrate on religious matters. Clerical domination, government submission to the orders of the *Congrégation*, ultramontanism, priestly obscurantism, the setting up of an Inquisition, the revival of tithes, and—above all—Jesuit intrigues (which were made into a real bogey), such were the themes broadcast in thousands of pamphlets, newspaper articles, caricatures, and songs. Whether deliberately concerted or not, these tactics gave the liberals a double advantage: they could run down the regime without directly attacking the king or the constitution; and they were able to split the royalists, quite a lot of whom remained attached to the rationalism of Voltaire or to eighteenth-century parliamentary gallicanism.

The government was weakened by the campaign, and suffered two serious parliamentary defeats. The ministry wanted to strengthen the landed aristocracy, who were the regime's chief stay, by avoiding the endless fragmentation of estates through the play of successive inheritings. With this aim in view, in 1826 it put forward a proposal for a law modifying the Napoleonic civil code in respect of inheritance; the idea was to secure preferential rights in favour of the eldest son, in families rich enough to have a 300 franc assessment of tax. The liberal opposition denounced this measure as being an attempt to restore the social order of the *ancien régime*, with its *droit d'ainesse*. The peers threw out the proposal. In the following session, in 1827, Villèle and his minister of justice, Peyronnet, alarmed at the more and more hostile current which was carrying public opinion along, tried to take counter-action by attacking what they believed to be the root of the evil: the press. As the king did not wish to have recourse to censorship in advance of publication, and as the courts showed themselves very weak in dealing with offences, the remedy seemed to be a new law considerably restricting the circulation of newspapers and printed matter in general. The bill gave rise to memorable discussions in the Chamber on the question of the freedom of the press; left-wing and right-wing oppositions joined hands in its defence. In the end, despite the fact that the deputies had finally passed the bill, the government was obliged to withdraw it in face of the peers' determined opposition.

This opposition had to be broken. Villèle persuaded the king to appoint seventy-six new peers. At the same time the Chamber of Deputies was dissolved (6 November 1827). Villèle's reasoning had been as follows: since public opinion was turning more and more against him, and since in any case partial elections must be held to replace forty deputies elevated to the upper chamber, it would be better to go straight to a general election before it was due, and so take the opposition unawares. If he managed to get a working majority again he would be master of the parliamentary situation for another seven-year period. It was a gamble—and a failure. For the elections of November 1827 proved that even then Villèle had underestimated his unpopularity with the electorate: the new Chamber was to contain only 170 to 180 government supporters, against an almost equally large opposition of liberal tendencies on the left, and a right-wing opposition of about seventy. Charles X resigned himself to changing ministers: he chose a team of secondary figures, some of whom had been in the previous administration. There was no president of the council. Martignac, a Bordeaux lawyer, was his minister of the interior: he was likeable and spoke well, and was the king's mouthpiece in the Chambers. This government soon found itself in an exceedingly uncomfortable situation; the king would have liked to continue Villèle's policy, but in order to find a majority in the Chamber the ministry was obliged to make concessions to the left: changes in administrative personnel, a new and more liberal regime for the press, safeguards against governmental despotism in establishing the electoral lists. The main concessions, however, given the particular nature of the opposition's campaigns, were to be made at the expense of the clergy. The Ministry of Public Instruction was detached from that of Church Affairs, and given to a layman; Jesuits were forbidden to teach, and restraints were imposed on the *petits séminaires* of such a kind as to keep out pupils who had no intention of becoming priests; thus the University's control over secondary education was re-established (Ordinances of June 1828). The government also sought to flatter public opinion by pursuing a more active policy than Villèle's; Villèle had been accused of submitting too readily to what Metternich or Canning wanted. French intervention in favour of Greek independence gave the nation's vanity some satisfaction but it did not improve the government's parliamentary position.

Charles X, more and more displeased with the line Martignac was following, negotiated secretly with the several right-wing royalist factions—counter-opposition, Villèlists, ministerial group—in order to form a ministry entirely to his liking. The composition of this new government, brusquely announced on 8 August 1829, was of a kind calculated to upset public opinion: Prince Jules de Polignac, Minister of Foreign Affairs and soon president of the Council, bore a name that conjured up the worst abuses of the old court: besides, he was a former *émigré*, and tool of the *Congrégation*; the Comte de La Bourdonnaye, minister of the interior, had constantly expressed the most reactionary views in the Chamber, ever since 1815; and finally General de Bourmont, minister of War, was held to have betrayed Napoleon before Waterloo, and had testified against Marshal Ney in 1815. The *Journal des Débats* summed up the general impression: 'Coblenz, Waterloo, 1815. There you have the three principles, the three personalities, of the government . . . no matter how hard you press it and squeeze it, the only drops it yields are humiliations, misfortunes, dangers.'

Just when people expected some show of strength, the government astonished and reassured its opponents by its inactivity. It limited itself to putting off summoning the Chambers as long as possible, meanwhile trying to win some prestige in the field of foreign policy: that was the object of the expedition planned against Algiers. The show of strength came at last in the month of March 1830, at the opening of the parliamentary session. In his speech from the throne Charles X declared: 'Should guilty manoeuvres ever place in the way of my government obstacles which I have no desire to foresee, I would find the power to overcome them in my resolve to maintain public order, strong in the confidence and love that Frenchmen have always shown towards their king.' The majority address in reply, voted by 221 in favour with 182 against, was a polite rebuke to the king: 'The Charter . . . confirms as of right the country's participation in discussion of the welfare of the people. That your government's political views and the wishes of your subjects should be in unity is, under the Charter, the necessary condition of the proper conduct of public affairs. Our loyalty, Sire, and our devotion, compel us to tell you that this unity does not exist'. This time the essence of the conflict was clear; was government to represent the king's will, or the will of the majority of the Chamber? In adopting the first of these interpretations Charles X could maintain that he remained faithful to the letter of the Charter; the outcome of the second must in effect be a parliamentary regime on the British model. Having prorogued the Chamber the king then dissolved it and announced new elections. They took place in the first weeks of July; despite all the efforts of the administration, and despite the king's personal intervention, the result gave 274 seats to the opposition against 143 to the ministry: the restricted electorate was disavowing the king. Nevertheless Charles X determined to maintain his prerogative; he was encouraged to do so by the successful taking of Algiers (5 July), and also by the memory of the Revolution, when his brother Louis XVI had saved nothing by making concessions.

The *Moniteur* of 26 July published four Ordinances that had been prepared in the utmost secrecy. Taking their stand on Article 14 of the Charter, which empowered the king to make any regulations and ordinances necessary to protect the State, they changed the rules governing the press and the rules for elections, which were normally the business of parliament. Periodical publications were subject to preliminary authorisation, which needed to be renewed every three months. The Chamber elected in July was dissolved without ever having met, and the new elections were to take place under a system calculated to cut out liberal voters. The announcement of this *coup d'état* was accompanied by none of the army or police precautions that any government less inept than Polignac's would have taken to meet the all too predictable movement of protest. Three days of disturbances in Paris, and the resolute conduct of the Duke of Orleans' followers, put an end to the reign of Charles X. He abdicated (2 August), and then took refuge in England.

Thus ended in pitiful failure the attempt at a regime combining the traditions of the old monarchy with the principles popularised by the Revolution. If the king had been more skilful, could he have imposed his point of view on the nation and carried off his *coup d'état* successfully? We may suppose that such a success would have remained precarious; for, all things considered, the political problem that had been the immediate cause of this new revolution was not the only problem involved. Deeper, and perhaps more basic, was the social and moral conflict between the old ruling classes—the nobles and clergy—seeking under royal protection to recover their old predominance, and the bourgeoisie determined to keep the place they had won thanks to the Revolution of 1789. These fifteen years had not been without their use

23-2

to France, however. Not only had the State recovered its stability and prosperity thanks to an excellent administration; not only had the nation risen again, well and truly, after the defeats of 1814 and 1815; besides all this it had been able to try out, within a limited framework, and for the first time, the practice of representative government.

The victors of the 'Three Glorious Days'—the men who had fired the shots on the barricades—were doubtless republicans and Bonapartists for the most part; but once Charles X was out of the way they discovered that they could not impose their will on the politicians. Lafayette was the only man well enough known to act as leader of this party; and as usual he showed himself weak and vacillating. The Orleans party, in contrast, was strong because of the support that the Paris middle classes gave it in their hatred of disorder and risk, and strong, too, because of the popularity of the deputies who had stood out against Charles X. And then, the revolution had been instigated with *Vive la Charte* as battle cry; in all logic, therefore, victory could hardly lead to a change of constitution.

The Chamber hastened all the same to touch up the Charter here and there in ways calculated to satisfy the *Hotel de Ville* party and make sure of its being interpreted in the sense of the liberal opposition to Charles X. The principle of national sovereignty was obliquely affirmed by the suppressing of the 1814 preamble, as 'seeming to grant to the French people rights which are theirs essentially'. The Catholic religion ceased to be that of the State, and once more—as under the Napoleonic regime—became that of the 'majority of Frenchmen'. The wording of Article 14 was changed in such a way as to avoid the unwarranted interpretation that Charles X had put on it; censorship and extraordinary courts of justice were abolished in perpetuity. The Chambers were granted the right to initiate laws; and, pending the voting of the new electoral law that had been announced, the age-qualifications for being an elector or a candidate were lowered to twenty-five and thirty respectively. The new monarch, who was to take the name of Louis-Philippe I, would be called 'King of the French' and no longer 'King of France'. The tricolour was to replace the white as the national emblem, and the Gallic cock would take the place of the traditional lilies. At last on 9 August the investiture ceremony took place; and the ceremonial was deliberately meant to mark the contractual nature of the new monarchy. Only after he had sworn to observe the revised Charter did the prince take his seat on the throne and receive the insignia of his office at the hands of four marshals.

In the course of the following months the features of the new regime were completed by important new organic laws. First, the organisation of the National Guard (22 March 1831). 'Instituted to defend the constitutional monarchy, the Charter, and the rights confirmed by the

Charter, to maintain obedience to the laws, to keep or to re-establish order and the public peace, and to support the fighting troops', the Guard was put under the command of elected officers and was at the disposition of the civil authorities—the mayors and prefects. In effect it consisted only of citizens who paid some direct tax and could afford the expense of the equipment. So the middle classes, but not the common people, found themselves enrolled and armed for the defence of the regime. In the course of the following years this bourgeois militia stood constantly in the breach in the struggle against popular riots. A sort of sentimental solidarity grew up between the Guard and the citizen-king, who was careful to wear its uniform; and only during the last years of the regime did this solidarity break down.

Secondly, municipal organisation (21 March 1831). The municipal authorities were elected by a restricted electoral body; besides civil servants and the members of certain middle-class professions, this consisted of a varying proportion of the highest-taxed citizens: 10 per cent in communes of less than 1000 inhabitants, 2 per cent in those of more than 15,000. Later on, an analogous system reserved to the wealthiest citizens the privilege of being represented in the departmental councils.

Thirdly, by the electoral law of 15 April 1831, the system of the double vote of 1820 was suppressed. The tax-qualification for election was lowered from 1000 to 500 francs; that for the franchise from 300 to 200 francs.

Finally, the peerage was down-graded. In August 1830 the Chamber of Peers had been mutilated by the arbitrary annulling of Charles X's new creations. Others had retired of their own free will, so as not to swear the oath of loyalty to the new king. A law of 29 December 1831 weakened the aristocratic character of the Chamber by ruling that the dignity of any new peer would no longer be hereditary.

Thus the French bourgeoisie, having a monopoly of wealth and, to a large extent, of intellectual culture also, arrogated to itself the monopoly of political power as well. In the administration it occupied every road of advancement, for the nobility had been driven out, or had voluntarily retired out of fidelity to Charles X. The resources of political power were to serve the material interests of the bourgeoisie; for example, the system of protective tariffs and prohibitions built up during the Restoration continued (despite some efforts made by Broglie and Guizot towards freer exchanges) to exclude foreign competition and to allow the survival of routine methods at home. The law forbade workers to unite in defence of their interests. In a country in which population increases faster than production, free play of the law of supply and demand ends by reducing the wages of the working classes; and so we have the contrast of increasing prosperity among middle-class business men and growing poverty amongst working people. This social *malaise* was clearly seen in November 1831 in the city of Lyons: the silk-workers had secured a ruling from the prefect prescribing a minimum wage; the factory-owners refused to apply it; the workers then rioted and occupied the public buildings; the government dismissed the prefect, and sent an army to occupy Lyons: working-class poverty should not disturb bourgeois order.

The political basis of the regime remained narrow and unsteady. It could lay claim neither to those sacred traditions that were the strength of the old monarchy, nor to that popular consent which was the basis of the republican and even, by virtue of the plebiscite, the Napoleonic system. The July monarchy was founded under the pressure of Paris in revolt, and by 219 only of the 430 deputies who should have made up the Chamber. Out of 35 million Frenchmen, the bourgeois class numbered only 3 million persons, on the most liberal count. And of these bourgeois only about 200,000 privileged persons took part in political life. Finally, within the *pays légal* itself there were to develop conflicts that still further reduced the extent to which the basis of government could be called national. Thus the political system could be shown in diagram as a pyramid balanced on its point.

Order and prosperity, the bourgeois ideals, were likewise those of the regime. Generous aspirations, and the spiritual forces of both past and future, served to strengthen the oppositions, whether of the Right or of the Left. Historians have doubtless underestimated just how dangerous at the beginning was the legitimist—also called Carlist—opposition. So long as Louis-Philippe's situation remained insecure, the legitimist party could count on a good deal of secret support inside the army and inside the administration. The ordinary folk of Paris were doubtless hostile to the fallen monarch, but so they were equally towards the new king. Half-formed alliances sprang up even between republicans and legitimists, to overthrow the *Usurper*: each hoping to profit in the event of a collapse of authority. The old dynasty could muster many partisans in the provinces—especially where the clergy's influence remained strong, as in the west, and in the south along the Mediterranean coast. The legitimist papers profited to the full from the freedom of the press, and lacked neither money nor talent; Chateaubriand, amongst others, struck some bloody blows at the expense of the new regime. Lastly the continental Powers, who had recognised Louis-Philippe without enthusiasm, were all of them ready to look with favour on a third restoration. At least two monarchs—of the Netherlands and Piedmont—gave financial aid.

All these trump cards were lost, through the ineptitude of the Princes and their advisers. The idea was to put forward the Duchesse de Berry, the young Duc de Bordeaux's mother. She had only to land at some chosen point in the realm, and to be surrounded by a number of devoted partisans: and then, so they fondly supposed, she could reconquer the throne—following Napoleon's experience in 1815—thanks to the defection of the troops that would be sent against her. Supposing this plan (like something out of Walter Scott) ever had the slightest chance of success, then it should have been attempted in the early months after the revolution, at a moment when Louis-Philippe's government seemed unable to bring anarchy under control. But the enterprise was put off several times, for futile reasons. When in the end the Duchesse de Berry did land, on 29 May 1832 close to Marseilles, the government was well consolidated and on its guard. Even so, she managed to get as far as the Vendée, but the rioting that took place on 3 June was quickly stamped out. The Duchess hid at Nantes, in the house of some devoted followers. Only in November did Louis-Philippe's police manage finally to discover her hiding-place and arrest her. She was imprisoned in Blaye fortress, near Bordeaux. But a captive princess, and romanticism at its height! Here was a situation even more embarrassing. Luckily for Louis-Philippe the Duchess, a widow since 1820, was found to be pregnant. Her dishonour once having been established by the birth of a daughter, she was restored to freedom. This ridiculous misadventure compromised all chance of a legitimist comeback. The party resigned itself to putting up a sterile opposition in the press, and in the Chamber where its spokesman was the advocate Berryer, considered the greatest orator of the time. The party tried to popularise itself by adopting a democratic-looking programme, with universal suffrage and administrative decentralisation.

The Bonapartists could have taken advantage of the incredibly swift rise of the Napoleonic legend, which the government unwisely fostered. It organised, for example, ceremonies of great pomp to mark the return to France of the emperor's remains (December 1840). But the survivors of the imperial epic had no cause to complain of the new regime, which loaded them with honours and material benefits. The premature death of Napoleon's son at Vienna (22 July 1832) had completely upset the party's plans. The new pretender, Louis-Napoleon, made a fool of himself by his two attempts at a *pronunciamiento*, at Strasbourg (1836) and at Boulogne (1840). After the first he had merely been packed off to America; after the second they locked him up in the fortress of Ham.

The Republicans were to show themselves more active and more dangerous. Their hatred for Louis-Philippe, and for the bourgeois politicians who had robbed them of their victory in July 1830, drove them to frequent acts of violence. Freedom of the press and freedom of association, which in the early days were virtually complete, enabled them to recruit a good many partisans—students, needy clerks and even, later on, the better-educated members of the working class. The society called the *Amis du Peuple* grouped together the most active members in the party. It tried to start a revolution in Paris during the funeral ceremonies of General Lamarque (June 1832), who had been a very popular figure in parliament. The insurrection set up barricades in part of the capital, and was broken only after two days of bloody fighting, in which the National Guard gave no quarter.

Another tragedy of bloodshed allowed the government to complete its defensive system. On 25 July 1835, as the king, with his sons around him, was reviewing the National Guard, a hail of machine-gun bullets raked the cortege, killing or wounding forty-one people. The attempt, which had missed the king, was the work of two republican fanatics, Morey and Fieschi, who had concealed a kind of makeshift machine-gun behind the shutters of a window. Outraged public opinion allowed the government to get the 'September Laws' passed, making the procedure for the courts of assize more efficient, and submitting the press to as strict a regime as possible without actually re-introducing a censorship. Moreover, this last measure was applied also to prints and other illustrations, which the opposition had used with great effect up till then in their attacks on the king and those in high places.

Thus armed, the government was able to stifle public propagation of revolutionary ideas, though not to prevent criminal plotting. There were further attempts on the king's life. The republican ideal enjoyed indirect support from many intellectuals: novelists, such as George Sand and Eugène Sue; poets, such as Lamartine; historians, such as Louis Blanc and Jules Michelet. Republican thought was deeply impregnated with socialism, and hence had a large working-class audience; political emancipation was looked on as the means to social emancipation. Thus the right to work, management of workshops by workers, and paying out of profits to workers, all became part of the republican programme. So powerful was the spread of socialist ideas that they worked their way into the Napoleonic party through the book that Louis-Napoleon wrote in his prison, *l'Extinction du Paupérisme*; and also into certain Catholic circles, by way of Lamennais and Buchez.

Catholicism itself, which before 1830 had paid court to authority faithfully—not to say servilely—became the parent of a new opposition. Immediately after the July revolution the government had alienated the clergy by its hostile or scornful attitude towards religion. The reply came from a little group of gifted young people, inspired by Lamennais. Their paper, *l'Avenir*, proclaimed their solidarity with the liberal movements at home in France and abroad, and their will to set the Church free from the State's degrading hold on it. When Lamennais was condemned by Rome, in 1832, his followers went on inspiring a Catholic revival amongst the bourgeoisie. The clergy having accepted the *fait accompli* of the new regime, the government treated them with greater favour. This peaceful condition was broken towards 1840, when Catholics began to claim freedom of secondary and university education, against the University's monopoly. A real Catholic party was formed, under the leadership of Charles de Montalembert, a peer of France and a wonderful orator. This party caused the government serious difficulty, and helped to turn away the moral support of Catholic believers from it.

These currents of thought that stirred society barely penetrated political life, restricted as it was by the constitution to the narrow circle of the electorate and the two Chambers. Material interests and conflicting personal ambitions made up its day to day pattern. The story has no grandeur in it; we can see three important matters only which in turn dominated the sterile play of parties and ministerial groupings. Immediately after the revolution it was the very survival of the regime, and what line it should follow, that were in question; then, by the end of 1832, when the new monarchy had survived its early crisis and had asserted its conservatism, the play of politics was dominated by the king's stubborn will to impose his own direction over the government. Finally, after 1840, when Louis-Philippe had achieved his ends, the question of reforming the regime crystallised the opposition's efforts.

The first ministerial team invested by the new king on 11 August 1830 reflected in its composition the diversity of the elements which had brought the revolution into being. One section, that of the liberal doctrinaire parliamentarians—Guizot, Molé, Broglie, Casimir Périer—wanted to see in the revolution no more than a change of sovereign, permitting a sincerer application of the system of the Charter; 'return to normalcy' was their main pre-occupation. The others—Dupont de l'Eure, Laffitte, Marshal Gérard—thought of the revolution as a point of departure towards establishing a more democratic regime: 'Evolve the consequences of July' was their watch-word. *Resistance* and *Movement* were the names soon given to these two tendencies. All that this first government could do was to gain time and set a limit to the damage, making some concessions to public opinion, and also to replace civil servants suspected of fidelity to Charles X. Louis-Philippe, taking an active part, spent a good deal of his time in receiving delegations and in making patriotic and soothing speeches.

At the end of October the men of the Resistance, declining any longer to be associated with a policy of surrender, advised the king to let the party of Movement show proof of its incapacity and misdoing. This was the starting point of Jacques Laffitte's ministry, on 28 November 1830. This important banker, weak, vain and longing for popularity, practised 'government by surrender' as Armand Carrel put it. The capital seemed to be given over daily to riot. In February 1831, acts of popular violence were directed against the clergy: the church of Saint-Germain l'Auxerrois, the palace of the Archbishop of Paris and other buildings were sacked; priests could no longer show themselves in the streets. The foreign policy of the party of Movement, giving unwise encouragement to liberal revolutions, was leading straight to war with continental Europe, and this at a time when the army had barely any organisation left.

In March 1831 public opinion was ripe for a change of policy, and Louis-Philippe gave power to Casimir Périer. He typified the monied bourgeoisie, loathing disorder, and he brought to the task of governing a force of will-power and energy that was almost wildly passionate. From his colleagues and all public servants he compelled unquestioning obedience. Even the king himself must bend before this imperious minister of his, and give up directly intervening in affairs. In the Chamber, Casimir Périer announced as his programme: 'At home, order, without calling on liberty to make any sacrifices; abroad, peace, with no cost to honour. . . . We hold that riots have no more the right to force us into war than they have the right to push us into political innovations.' The remarkable thing is that he was able to succeed in this programme, without recourse to exceptional measures, but simply by regrouping around him the forces of the Resistance, and infusing his own energy into the engine of State. And even whilst he was defending the regime against its enemies, both of the left and of the right, he was at the same time getting the fundamental laws passed that in fact shaped its structure. Périer's government did not last much more than a year, for he himself died on 16 May 1832, falling a victim to the cholera epidemic that decimated the population of Paris. But in one year he had put right a situation that had seemed past saving, had averted European war, throttled anarchy and truly set the regime on firm foundations.

Périer's death was to leave the king a free field. In many respects he was one of the most capable men who have ever occupied the throne. He was born in 1773 and had received an exceptionally good education from the famous Madame de Genlis. With a widely cultivated mind went exceedingly practical notions; he spoke four languages fluently, and he could cook a meal too if need be; and even the cleverest of business men had nothing to teach him about how to look after his wealth. At the start of the Revolution he had belonged, like his father Philippe-Egalité, to the Jacobin party. Luckily for him, his youth had prevented him from taking part in the revolutionary assemblies, and he had served the Republic as a soldier. For his own personal propaganda, the fact that he was present at the battles of Valmy and Jemappes was to prove an inexhaustible theme. Compromised with his chief Dumouriez, he too in his turn had to go into exile: and he went through hard times, for he was equally detested by the revolutionaries and by those *émigrés* who had stayed faithful to the Bourbons. A few years later he came back into favour with his cousins of the eldest branch of the family, and married a daughter of the King of Naples—Marie-Amélie, an excellent and pious woman. He had behaved with prudence under the Restoration, being respectful to the sovereigns, who treated him generously, and at the same time courting the liberal opposition, who counted on him. At the age of fifty-seven he was a man full of vigour, with features that rather called to mind Louis XIV, only with long side-whiskers that were soon to be of legendary fame. In many ways he was the incarnation of the faults and virtues of the bourgeois class who had brought him to power: a family man, happy in the midst of his many and handsome children; living modestly, and a democrat in his manners; thrifty, to the point of avarice; naturally kind and good; brave, too, in the face of physical danger. On the other hand, he always preferred wily and temporising ways to those that were bold and direct; he was a master at hiding what he thought under a flow of genial talk; yet by deceiving everybody he was bound to lose the respect and confidence of honest men. This opportunism and flexibility concealed a determination to govern France. Under the restoration, national representation had to struggle to free itself from the position of dependence in which the constitution had placed it in relation to the throne. After 1830 the situation was reversed: since the revolution had confirmed the supremacy of the people, it was the king who must struggle to secure his influence; in the framework of the revised constitution this could only be won by equivocal methods, to which the king's character was only too well adapted.

His designs were served by the ambitious rivalries of the politicians, and by the division within the great party of Resistance that Casimir Périer had welded together. The Left Centre, inspired by Adolphe Thiers, upheld the theory of parliamentary government on the English model: 'the king reigns and does not govern'. The Right Centre, with the Doctrinaires and Guizot, were content with the constitutional system of the restoration, which gave the king an active say in the government. Between these two floated a hundred or so deputies—the 'third party', whose only principle was to turn authority to their own account whilst taking credit for criticising it. Later on there also appeared a 'dynastic Left', which claimed to reconcile attachment to the king with part of the republican programme. From the death of Casimir Périer (May 1832) up to October 1840 there were no less than ten successive ministries. The most notable were those of the Duc de Broglie (March 1835–February 1836) and Comte Molé (September 1836–March 1839). The first was an unaccommodating doctrinaire, who declined merely to carry out the king's wishes and was for that reason dismissed by him. The second, by contrast, was a perfect courtier, as docile as could be, and was for that reason removed by a coalition of leaders of the Chamber.

In the end, as a result of the foreign crisis of 1840, when Thiers' lack of prudence nearly made the eastern question provoke a European war, a more lasting ministry was constituted. Marshal Soult was nominally its president, but the real head of government was Guizot: he was in fact minister of Foreign Affairs, and took the title of president of the Council only in September 1847, when the aged marshal at last retired, loaded with honours and greatly enriched. This ministry was to last as long as the monarchy itself. Three main factors seem to have contributed to its exceptional stability. First, the perfect understanding that ruled between the king and his minister: Guizot had learnt the lesson of experience, and had resigned himself once and for all to letting the king exercise that share of influence which he expected in the government; Guizot's well-known strength of character removed all taint of servility from his attitude. Secondly, the breaking up of the parties in the Chamber, which made it possible for the government to secure a majority by the granting of personal favours: Duchâtel, minister of the Interior, excelled in this, and hence was particularly entrusted with these dirty jobs. And finally, Guizot's own personality, then in its full strength of talent ripened by experience. Few statesmen of the time possessed such eminent qualifications: a magnificent mind, widely and deeply cultivated in history; a talent for oratory, characterised by a gift for raising the level of the debates; courage, and a lofty idea of his mission. By contrast, he had no notion of winning over public opinion, of which he was contemptuous; and he irritated his opponents by obstinately refusing to consider what might be of value in their aspirations. 'The duty of the government,' he declared in 1847, 'is to go slowly, and wisely; to maintain, and to set bounds.' Lamartine, the mouthpiece of the new generation, had answered him: 'Supposing that were the distinctive genius of a statesman charged with presiding over a government, then we could do without a man—a boundary stone would do.'

This narrow conservatism, encouraged and shared by the king, was to lead in the end to the downfall of the regime. At the end of the year 1846 the question of reforming the political institutions became the common platform of the various opposition groups. Their demands concerned two things: the corruption of the representative system by the presence in the Chamber of civil servants whose votes were all too manifestly controlled by the government; and the corruption of the electoral system, enabling the government, by bribes or other means, to sway as it wished the votes of an unduly restricted electorate. The electoral law of 1831, by lowering the tax-qualification from 300 to 200 francs, had increased the electorate to the figure of 166,000; and since then, by the mere fact of the growing wealth of the middle classes, the figure had reached 241,000 (in 1846). But what was that in a country of 35 million souls? One voter for every 75 male inhabitants.

A proposal put forward by Thiers and others of the opposition at the beginning of the 1847 session provided for the lowering of the tax-qualification to 100 francs, and the granting of the right to vote—without any means-test at all—to various classes of the people, simply by virtue of their professions or their jobs. The effect would have been to create about 200,000 new voters. Limited as this proposed reform was, Guizot nevertheless had it thrown out by his loyal majority, declaring that the nation wished only to live in peace and to prosper, and that it would do harm to allow such sterile political agitation to find its way down to the masses.

The opposition determined to try and shake the all too real indifference of the country. As political meetings were forbidden by law, they had the idea of falling back on a method that had been found effective in England: the political banquet. Who could prevent honourable citizens from assembling together in order to eat a little cold veal and drink a bottle or two, even if it happened that speeches were made and toasts given on such occasions? The banquet campaign started in Paris in 1847, and then spread to the chief provincial towns; Lamartine was the most sought-after speaker, also Ledru-Rollin the republican lawyer. Although at the start the Republicans were only a minority on the committees, they contrived nevertheless to turn the campaign into a veritable attack on the regime as a whole. The campaign was helped by the economic crisis that ravaged the country from the end of 1846. It hit agriculture first; following a very bad harvest, the prices of food-stuffs went up in a way that spelt catastrophe for the poorer classes. Next, industry was short of capital, and lacked orders; over-ambitious schemes for building railways had to be stopped; many industrial firms turned away their workmen; there were nearly a million men out of work.

The turning of public opinion against the government showed itself even in parliament, as soon as the Chambers reassembled in 1848. In the first debate, on the Address, one section of the conservatives voted against the government, whose majority fell to 33. Guizot seemed to be shaken. But the king, impervious to advice and blind to public opinion, refused to contemplate the least change in his system: 'There will be no reform, I do not wish it. If the Chamber of Deputies votes for it, I have the Chamber of Peers to throw it out. And just supposing the Chamber of Peers votes in favour of it, there remains my veto'. The opposition thought that the way to get the better of this obstinacy was to frighten the king by fresh agitation. So it was decided to start the banquet campaign again (it had stopped with the opening of the new parliamentary session), and to do so in Paris itself. The revolution of February 1848 was destined to spring from it.

As M. Charles Pouthas has very truly said of it, 'Never was an event more unavoidable nor yet more accidental.' *Accidental*, because none of those who instigated the movement intended or hoped that the regime would be overthrown; for in the past the government had triumphed over much more dangerously organised attempts. *Unavoidable*, because the way in which the system set up in 1830 had subsequently developed had in the end robbed it of any firm base at all in the nation; not only was political life the arbitrary preserve of a minority of privileged bourgeois, but—still worse—by cunning and corruption the king had succeeded in also robbing even that minority of any effective control of public affairs. There was too great a contradiction between the system as it actually worked and the principle of national sovereignty that lay at the basis of the regime. And finally the very success of Louis-Philippe's government contributed to its ruin; for the order and stability which it had won for the nation led men to forget those compelling reasons which had led them to accept the usurpation of 1830: fear of revolutionary anarchy, and fear of war.

CHAPTER XIII

GERMAN CONSTITUTIONAL AND SOCIAL DEVELOPMENT, 1795–1830

B Y the last decade of the eighteenth century, a national consciousness had developed among educated people in Germany, 'un-
sought and as if by accident,' as Meinecke says, owing to the recent
outstanding achievements of German poets and thinkers, but it was a
cultural, not a political, nation to which this small minority of the
population felt itself to belong. As Goethe and Schiller expressed the
feeling of the intellectuals in their satirical *Xenien* (1796):

> Germany? Where does it lie then? No map of mine seems to show it.
> Where that of culture begins, there that of politics ends.

In the century just drawing to a close, the two outstanding features
in the history of Germany outside the Habsburg territories had been the
establishment by Frederick William I and Frederick the Great of
Brandenburg-Prussia as a centre of political power of European importance, and the creation by a number of writers, mostly residing outside
Prussia, of a body of literature and philosophy that already made
nonsense of the earlier French assertion that no German could be a
man of wit, and that was to gain for Germany, after the inevitable time-
lag, a position of intellectual leadership in Europe. The way in which
these two new factors in German history, in origin almost entirely
separate, now helped and now hindered each other's further growth, and
in which the ruling classes, in general obstinately conservative, reacted
under these and other influences to the events of the Revolutionary and
Napoleonic era, must be the main topics in any account of German
constitutional and social history between the Peace of Bâle (1795) and
the French Revolution of July 1830.

The basis of German social and economic life remained in most
respects very much what it had been since the Thirty Years' War and
even earlier. Germany was an agrarian country, where 'status classes'
retained the distinctions that had grown up in the Middle Ages and were
now largely sanctified by law, and where a very large number of virtually
independent political authorities ruled territories varying greatly in
size, and treated the Holy Roman Empire, for all practical purposes, as
if it no longer existed. In the generation with which we are concerned
in this chapter, this amorphous country, with its many little centres of
culture but no single capital, began to take shape as a national state.
Vigorous as the intellectual life of the Germans undoubtedly was, their

lethargy in political and social matters was so great that it needed the invasion and occupation of much of the country by the French to rouse their desire for national independence, and the determined efforts of an able group of high officials in Prussia, stimulated by military defeat, to initiate and carry through administrative and social reforms long overdue in this most advanced of German states.

To begin with the peasantry, who made up more than three-quarters of the population, a brief description is difficult, because conditions varied so much in different geographical regions of the country, and within the same region from one small political unit to another. To English travellers at the beginning of this period, accustomed by now to compact farms and the results of at least half a century of greatly improved techniques, German agriculture seemed backward, almost medieval, because of the great predominance of open-field cultivation, with its scattered strips of holdings, its communal cropping routine, and the consequent discouragement of individual effort to imitate more advanced countries in introducing artificial grasses, improved crop rotations and so on. As travellers went from west to east, they found progressively worse cultivation and a more and more ignorant and socially depressed peasantry, bound to the soil in virtual serfdom in the eastern provinces of Prussia, and owing extensive, sometimes unlimited, services to their *Gutsherr*, the lord of the manor, who had also complete jurisdiction over his peasantry in his own court. In this originally colonised land east of the Elbe, as also in Mecklenburg in the north, estates were large and were worked mainly by the aristocratic landlord himself, partly with the labour of his peasants and partly, from an early date, with the paid labour of landless men.

In central Germany, and still more in the west and south-west, the area of greatest political fragmentation, estates too were mostly made up of small and scattered units, so that it had long been usual to commute peasants' services for money payments, but some relics of the feudal system survived almost everywhere, although frequently condemned by enlightened opinion. In response to this humanitarian pressure, to English example and to the theories of the physiocrats in France, several states of the Empire abolished serfdom before Prussia. It happened in Austria under Maria Theresa and Joseph II, in Baden under Karl Friedrich, and in the Duchies of Schleswig and Holstein, following Denmark's lead. Frederick the Great had at least protected the rights of the Prussian peasantry to their inherited holdings, preventing the enlargement at their expense of their lords' estates by the type of enclosure for which Mecklenburg was notorious. He had done this however solely in the interest of his army, which relied mainly on a healthy peasantry for its recruitment under the cantonal system. With the same military aim in view, he had refrained from interfering with the privileges of the landed nobility, who furnished him with officers and high civil servants. It was part of the understanding that had gradually been worked out between the nobility and the crown, that if they renounced many of the traditional rights of their class in relation to the central government, and entered its service, as they had gradually been compelled to do, they should at least be left complete masters of their own estates and peasantry, free from land-tax and free from government interference. Even after the French Revolution, the peasantry in the east gave very little trouble to their landlords, whereas on the Rhine they came to resent even their nominal subservience. It was not pressure from below therefore that brought about reform in Prussia, but the efforts of government officials and an enlightened monarch, backed to a small extent by landowners who had learnt from foreign experience that paid labour offered them better prospects of efficiency and profit than the existing system.

The peasants were freed on the royal domains in Prussian territory, both in Westphalia, where Freiherr vom Stein had much to do with it, and in the eastern provinces, where over 50,000 of the superior class of peasants who did service with their draft animals benefited from Frederick William III's reforming zeal before the battle of Jena, many being given the hereditary right to their holding as well as personal freedom.

Stein saw clearly, before Prussia's downfall, that the small beginnings thus made in the break-up of the old feudal order must be followed by many further reforms if the country was to hold its own in the rapidly changing world, but it was only the total defeat of 1806 that gave him his chance for decisive action. Before that, the trading and industrial class in the Prussian towns was almost as unenterprising and uncomplaining as the peasantry. Germany had been dignified by the papal court, Herder wrote in 1792, with the title of 'the land of obedience', and had well deserved it. Though private enterprise had long been encouraged by the state, which wanted a prosperous middle class that could be heavily taxed, small-scale businesses on guild lines still greatly predominated, as they did all over Germany, and there were few, even in the Prussian towns, who found anything wrong with the pre-capitalistic ideals of a subsistence economy. Nor was there any evidence of a desire for self-government in the towns. Even the so-called free towns of western and south-western Germany were thoroughly undemocratic oligarchies, while the Prussian towns submitted themselves passively to the direction of the ever-watchful Local Commissary appointed by the government. Very little was left of the old autonomy of the craft-guilds, prices being largely controlled, for instance, by the military governor in the many towns in which troops were permanently billeted, while apprentices and domestic servants seeking a new situation had to present the

'Employment Book' containing their whole history. The freedom of the merchant and manufacturer was severely restricted in the interest of the mercantilist policy inherited from Frederick's day, all goods being subject to excise when introduced into a town, and to import duties at every state boundary. But merchants, shop-keepers, master-craftsmen and their families were not, like their apprentices and the peasantry, liable to be called up for military service, it being considered their function to provide only the sinews of war.

Professional men of all kinds, civil servants, civic officials and educated people generally in Prussian towns were also exempt from military service, and from the burdens of active citizenship too, so that civic government was left entirely to professional administrators and to the selected tradesmen, shopkeepers and government nominees who served on the town council. In the free towns of the Empire outside Prussia, which were little republics, extending in most cases to a considerable area beyond their walls, the position of a town councillor was honourable and often lucrative, but he was almost always a member of one of the small number of recognised patrician families. It was only in Prussia that 'noblesse' carried the obligation to serve the state, and this tradition had only been established by the two soldier-kings. Elsewhere nobility conferred privileges without duties. The landed aristocracy still included nearly all the wealthy, though many estates were heavily mortgaged, and the careers open to younger sons were severely restricted, as in France but not in England. In most states, the higher court and civil service offices were reserved for the local nobility, but a great many chose or were obliged to seek service outside, preferably in the army or civil service of one of the greater states, where prospects were better than at home. The ecclesiastical states offered special opportunities to Catholics, and Austria to imperial knights and their sons, while Prussia was usually ready to employ men of outstanding ability and energy, whether noblemen or commoners. The chief Prussian ministers in the period of the great reforms, Stein, Hardenberg, Scharnhorst and Gneisenau, were none of them Prussian by birth. The young nobleman was made conscious of his privileged position from his earliest years, never mixing with commoners at school, like his English counterpart, but being educated privately, if he did not go to one of the 'Ritterschulen' reserved for his class. Besides being excluded from a career in trade or industry, he was marked off from the generality, even if he was a younger son, by his prefixed *von*, and usually he maintained this aloofness jealously throughout life, unless he was moved, as some eccentrics were, by the ideas of the Enlightenment and perhaps joined the Freemasons, one of whose aims was to break down such barriers. His social privileges were backed by important legal rights, for which it would have been hard to find a rational justification. One of the most highly prized was exemption from the land-tax, the commonest form of direct taxation, both in Prussia as we have seen and in most other states. For peasants, this tax, together with the associated dues, amounted in Prussia, round about 1800, to about 40 per cent of the net yield of a man's holding. No wonder that Goethe who, as the Duke of Weimar's favourite, took over for many years onerous official duties in his little state, found that 'the peasant always had to carry the sack', and compared him once to the green-fly which, when it has sucked itself full on the rose-leaves, is preyed on in its turn by ants. 'And it has gone so far now,' he added, 'that more is consumed in a day at the top than is produced in a day at the bottom.'

It is surprising to find that, in the face of social disharmonies as grave as these, there was not at least a persistent public protest on the part of the intelligent minority of the German middle class, whose education had familiarised them with the general movement of opinion in Europe in the age of reason. In France, after abuses in many respects no more intolerable had been satirised and philosophically analysed for many decades, an attempt had finally been made to sweep them away by the violent overthrow of the existing state. In Germany, Rousseau, Montesquieu, Voltaire, Diderot and the 'philosophes' had been read with passionate interest, but the resulting criticism of society had remained on the purely literary level, or had led to generalisations so obviously out of touch with reality that no one took them seriously. The 'Storm and Stress' movement in literature, beginning in the early 'seventies, had clearly been full of Rousseauistic feeling and, particularly in the drama, had pilloried the inhumanity and injustice of many features in the society of the day, but the self-indulgent courtiers of the Bishop of Bamberg in Goethe's *Götz von Berlichingen* (1773), or the inconsiderate and narrow-minded aristocratic employers of Lenz's *Private Tutor* (1776), were new and original literary subjects, presented as particular aspects of a richly varied world rather than as anachronisms calling for political and social action; and so it was with other less striking writings of the movement, the poems and ballads, for instance, in which the young Göttingen poets denounced tyranny and serfdom and idealised the simple life. Lessing, the greatest of the rationalist writers, made a much more effective protest than any of these in his *Emilia Galotti* (1772), for no one could fail to take his ostensibly Italian princelet, in this modernisation of the Virginia story, as a portrait of a petty German despot, corrupted by power and flattery; but Lessing intentionally avoided the directly political implications of his theme, keeping his tragedy on the domestic level. A long series of domestic dramas by lesser talents followed in the 'eighties and 'nineties, the general tendency of which was to bring out the virtues of the middle class in relief against the vices of the aristocracy. Schiller's early plays,

The Robbers and *Cabal and Love*, are superior versions of the same kind of thing.

The best of these writers in their maturity, aiming at a more discriminating public, which included aristocratic readers nurtured on French literature and thought, were of course less one-sided, though their sympathies were still middle-class. They continue the tradition of the European Enlightenment in their pursuit of freedom from every kind of prejudice, political, social or religious, trying always in their serious work to present what they feel to be the essential and lasting traits of humanity, the noble serenity that Winckelmann found in Greek art, the ethical striving that Herder, in his *Ideas for a Philosophy of the History of Humanity*, saw as characteristic of all the great civilisations, in spite of the unique form assumed by each in response to the particular conditions of its time and place.

Lessing's *Nathan the Wise*, Goethe's *Iphigenie*, Schiller's *Don Carlos*, products of the decade that saw the outbreak of the French Revolution, are all in their different ways inspired by the same conviction, developed from the Renaissance belief in man's ability, unaided by supernatural powers, to advance towards perfection, by the proper use of his intelligence and the conquest of his baser instincts. Reading them now, however, we find them less universal than their authors imagined, for what is most striking about these great writers is their extreme self-consciousness and preoccupation with the inward. Originally religious attitudes and emotions, often strongly influenced by pietism, have become secularised in this rationalistic age but have remained unworldly, a concern for supernatural salvation turning, for instance, into a passion for the things of the mind. In some the pursuit of *Bildung*, of personal cultivation, is more ethical, in others more philosophical or aesthetic, but at the root of it is always the conviction that the things prized by 'the world' are far less important to a man than certain states of mind, to which he can attain with a minimum of material aids.

Dilthey, summing up what seemed to him the chief characteristics of German literature and thought between Lessing and Hegel, said that a generation that felt the political and social world it lived in to be repellent but unchangeable strove to make itself independent of the world by an inward adjustment. Certainly, the German writers of the age of the French Revolution who aimed at a direct effect on society could be counted on the fingers of one hand. The most outspoken publicist, Schlözer, was a professor at Göttingen, in the virtually neutral territory of Hanover, attached to the English crown, and the Mosers, father and son, had come from Württemberg, the only state where some sort of representative assembly had survived under an absolute regime. A strict censorship, tightened up in Prussia and many other states after the outbreak of the Revolution, made free comment on politics and religion impossible for most writers in any case—even a theatre critic who seemed to Goethe persistently unfair was summarily expelled from Weimar. The hypothetical and the fanciful were accordingly the usual modes of utterance on topics that could be considered dangerous, and it was exceptional for an author to think that his words might have any effect on action.

It can readily be imagined that the news of the storming of the Bastille and of the early debates of the National Assembly, like that of the American War of Independence earlier, was greeted with enthusiasm by a great many German writers, with their vaguely progressive sympathies and openness to ideas that did not commit them personally. The courts, on the other hand, and those closely in touch with them, like Goethe, were alarmed and unsympathetic from the beginning. In Weimar, Wieland and Herder held on to their early hopes until the Terror and the execution of the king rallied almost all German opinion to the side of the princes, for the great mass of the people were devoted to their local dynasties, often with good cause. Despotism had become genuinely benevolent in many small and medium-sized states; and in Prussia, those who had liked Frederick least had to acknowledge his courage, disinterestedness and efficiency, though all now enjoyed by contrast the reduction, by his incompetent and self-indulgent successor, Frederick William II, of the pressure formerly put upon them in the interest of power.

With the accession of Frederick William III, in 1797, a positive policy following that of Joseph II in Austria, aiming at public welfare and the removal of restrictions on trade and industry, was adopted by the king and his advisers in the *Kabinett*, Beyme and Minister Heinitz, without any stimulus from public opinion. We have mentioned the chief result, the freeing of the domain peasants. The king would have liked to extend the reform to all the peasantry, but his plans had to be abandoned, first because of the resistance of nearly all the landed aristocracy, and then because the worsening international situation after 1803 gave him other things to think about. A few East Prussian landowners did however follow the king's example. In spite of his free trade ideas, now widely shared by influential officials, the king did not risk a reversal of the traditionally mercantilist policy of Prussia, in the peculiarly difficult economic situation created by the struggle between France and England, nor did the Finance Commission set up in 1798 get further than discussing the abolition of the nobility's immunity from land-tax; but the privileged classes were at least made to pay duty and excise at the new higher rates, instead of being partly exempt.

In October 1804 the king, apparently at the suggestion of Beyme, strengthened the reform party among his ministers by making Freiherr vom Stein the member of the General Directory concerned with taxation, customs and manufactures. Stein was an imperial knight from the Rhinelands, who combined the desire to maintain the Empire, with which his family had been intimately linked for hundreds of years, with unswerving loyalty to the state created by Frederick the Great, which he had served since 1780. His outstanding efficiency and energy had earned for him in 1796 the post of senior president of all the Chambers through which the province of Westphalia was administered for the Prussian crown; but in the same year in which he was promoted to the central government he had made his name known to the educated class all over Germany as the champion of the fast vanishing class of imperial knights, by an outspoken open letter to the Duke of Nassau-Usingen, who had annexed some of the Steins' ancestral possessions, as similar lands were being taken over throughout south-west Germany and the Rhinelands by the larger states, once the game of grab had started in 1803. Stein had already prudently sold most of his estates in the Rhinelands and bought extensive properties in the south of Prussia, a clear indication of his confidence in that state.

Stein was known to be a strong, even at times an intimidating personality. 'What he loathed,' says his friend Rehberg, 'was indecision, gossip and the glossing-over of unpleasant truths' yet 'he was always ready to listen to objections, and to think again'. This born administrator was also a reading man, interested in economics and history, certainly, rather than imaginative literature, but well aware of the importance for the leader of men not only of firmness, but of the capacity to take a broad, philosophical view of things, inspired by great historical examples. The author he particularly recommended to Prince Louis Ferdinand, the king's brilliant but dissolute cousin, whom he hoped to reform, was Plutarch. His best letters were written to Frau von Berg, a friend of Herder and Jean Paul, steeped in Weimar humanism; but when, after careful enquiry, he chose a wife, she was the daughter of a Hanoverian general, a natural son of George II, a lady of sound principles but also of a rank sufficiently high to satisfy the family tradition. It was action, not contemplation, he lived for, and what he most desired, he told Frau von Berg, was to remain, in spite of bitter experience, active and tolerant.

From his student days in Göttingen Stein had greatly admired England and English institutions, like his friends A. W. Rehberg and Ernst Brandes, both of them Hanoverian officials and severe critics of the French Revolution; Rehberg was the first German reviewer of Burke's *Reflections* in 1790, and Brandes a friend and admirer of Burke some years before the Revolution. All three believed in an organic society, the nation as 'an idea of continuity which extends in time as well as in numbers and in space', but they were progressive conservatives, not doctrinaire theorists like Adam Müller, the Romantic publicist. Stein was intensely practical, with a very un-German distrust of any political action based on abstractions, but with a good knowledge of French political writings and complete readiness to learn from French experience, much as he disliked what he considered to be their immorality and frivolity.

When Stein became a member of the General Directory in 1804, he carried through with great energy several administrative reforms initiated by the Finance Commission: a simplified administration of the salt monopoly, the abolition of some internal customs duties, the establishment of a statistical bureau and the unification of the excise offices with the 'war and domains chambers' in the provinces. He was most anxious to move in the direction of policy-making on all levels of government by full oral discussion. He wanted something like the English cabinet, a council of responsible ministers, instead of the existing system of personal government by the king and his intimate non-ministerial advisers, the 'Cabinet Councillors'. With Frederick the Great these councillors had been no more than secretaries, but Frederick William III, with not a tithe of Frederick's ability and energy and with a becoming diffidence, relied first on Mencken, then on Beyme, for advice in every step he took, to the disgust of ministers like Hardenberg, who remained merely departmental chiefs. As senior president of the provincial Chambers in Westphalia from 1796 to 1804, Stein had already tried to develop what little survived there of the older constitution of the provincial estates. He was influenced in this not only by Rehberg, but by the knowledge he had himself acquired at first hand of English institutions during a six-months' visit to England in 1786. In his *Nassau memorandum*, written in retirement after his dismissal by Frederick William III at the beginning of 1807, he developed these ideas on self-government, putting forward as the great goal to be aimed at 'the revival of public spirit and civic feeling, the utilisation of dormant or ill-directed efforts and uncoordinated sources of information, harmony between the spirit of the nation, its opinions and needs, and those of the civil service, and the stimulation of patriotism, independence and national honour'.

The guiding principle of Prussian policy between the Peace of Bâle and the battle of Jena was the maintenance of peace, so that the reforms of the internal administration and the army, which the country's untimely exhaustion in 1795 had proved to be necessary, might be carried through. New ways of increasing the country's man-power were considered, the cutting-down of exemptions under the cantonal system, the formation of a militia, the relaxation of the inhuman discipline in the army and the general acceptance of others than noblemen for commissions. But there was as yet no sense of urgency behind this reform movement. It was not easy to believe that Frederick's well-proved military machine had really lost its efficiency, and the king was inclined to be too kind-hearted to the veterans in command. There was still a great spirit of optimism abroad, though it was not shared by the king himself. The French attaché was told in 1799 by a high official that the wholesome revolution which the French had carried through from below would be accomplished in Prussia, by slow degrees, from above, for the king himself was a democrat after his fashion, and was ceaselessly working to reduce the privileges of the nobility, following with greater caution the methods of Joseph II. In a few years there would no longer be a privileged class in Prussia. It is true that the harm done by the disastrous reign of Frederick William II had to some extent been retrieved before Jena. The state debt had been reduced by nearly a third, and seventeen million thalers had been put back into the empty war treasury. But with taxes unchanged since Frederick's time, the emergency could not be met in spite of economies. Fortresses and equipment were not maintained at their old pitch of efficiency, and the troops were not even provided with winter greatcoats. It was becoming manifestly impossible to run an army on the old lines, in an economic and military situation that had radically changed. Staff work had least of all kept up with the times, as was to be discovered when Frederician tactics proved so hopelessly inadequate at Jena and Auerstedt against Napoleon's inspired energy in dealing with new situations.

After Prussia's defeat, a strong group of high officials was bent on immediate reforms, convinced as they were that far-reaching political and social changes would be necessary to make Prussia capable of competing with revolutionary France, where so much more of the national potential could be made available to the common cause through willing co-operation. The essential was, as Stein had realised long before the crisis, that all classes should rally round the government, but until many obvious social abuses had been swept away nothing of this kind could be expected. As in the reforms initiated before Jena, the state of the peasantry and of agriculture came in for consideration before anything else. Before Stein himself returned as first minister (October 1807), good progress had been made by the government with plans for the abolition of serfdom on private estates, hitherto strongly opposed by most landowners. The owners of large estates in East Prussia, which were well-suited to the new capitalistic methods of exploitation, did not now require very much persuasion, for many were making ever increasing use of landless labour. There had for some time been brisk dealings in agricultural estates, many had changed hands, and the older patrimonial relationship between landowner and peasantry had become correspondingly rarer. Schrötter, provincial minister of East Prussia, and Schön, Stein's colleague, like many others in Königsberg, now the seat of government, were full of the ideas of Adam Smith and believed in giving private enterprise unlimited scope. That landlords should be relieved of their obligations to their peasantry in time of need, in return for the renunciation of their claims on them, seemed to them one of the advantages of the abolition of serfdom. They even favoured a considerable measure of enclosure of peasants' land, if this step was co-ordinated with the formation of large peasant holdings, four to eight times the normal size, on an area equal to that enclosed. These were to be free from services and to be held on hereditary tenure, leasehold or freehold, with a view to the development of something like a yeoman class. Stein himself gave his approval, intending to revise the scheme in the light of experience. He boldly made the emancipation edict of 9 October 1807 apply to all the provinces left to Prussia by the Peace of Tilsit, without consulting their Estates representatives. The provision about enclosures was added in a supplement of 14 February 1808. The main decree removed all existing restrictions on the sale of land, so that landed estates hitherto reserved for the nobility could now be acquired by middle-class or peasant purchasers, and conversely, the nobility were now allowed to engage in industry and commerce. The effect of this was to remove the legal basis for the existing class system, with its sharply differentiated *Stände*, or status classes.

It was fully anticipated at the time that further decrees would follow to complete the reform, but when Stein was forced by the French to resign later in 1808, the remaining reformers were not strong enough to face the collective self-interest of the landowners. The aim of social justice, which had been at least part of the intention of those responsible for the October edict, was in the end hardly furthered at all by this measure, but the landlords were given freedom to move rapidly in the direction of capitalism, once the difficult war period was over, and provided with a new source of landless labour, through the inability of many peasants to keep up the payments now required from them for rent and so on, especially after the 'Regulating Laws' of 1816, which were made entirely in the landlords' interest. The decrees of 1807 and 1808 had indeed made the peasants on private estates, like those on the royal domains earlier, direct subjects of the king, and no longer, as hitherto, of their landlords as intermediate authorities who could restrict their freedom of movement. In this sense these peasants had been freed, but they had not been relieved, like the domain peasants, from the services with which their land was burdened. A further step was taken in 1811 (decree of 14 September), but it affected only the superior class of peasants, and by a decree of 29 May 1816 they were compelled to give up a large part of their land, in some cases one-third, in others one-half, so that in the agricultural crisis of the 1820's many found themselves so seriously impoverished that they had to become landless labourers. The provision for the encouragement of larger peasant holdings had, on the other hand, been a dead letter from the beginning. Meanwhile the nobility retained their exemption from land-tax (until 1861), their police authority (until 1872), their jurisdiction on their estates and their game rights (until 1848) and their church patronage (into the twentieth century). Credit banks were set up for them from about 1809, but the peasantry had to wait until 1849 before being given similar assistance. In every respect, therefore, this part of Stein's reforms represents a triumph for the individualistic tendencies of the time. It worked in favour of the propertied class, however much it might seem on the surface to be dictated by a humane regard for the peasantry. The officials on the domains were the first to discover that the obligations of a landlord to his peasantry had cost him far more than their services had been worth to him. Strict accountancy soon proved him, after the reforms, to be the gainer.

A second matter urgently in need of reform after Jena was the organisation of the central government, which had been discussed inconclusively before the war, and after it, at the end of 1806, had become the subject of so heated a dispute, at a time when the country was still in the greatest danger, that Stein felt himself obliged to resign, instead of becoming foreign minister as the king wished. Stein made his acceptance of the office conditional on the dismissal of Beyme, the king's all-powerful cabinet councillor. His resignation was accepted and he was heaped with reproaches by the king. When he was persuaded to return to the government, nine months later, he became first minister, with direct access to the king, but Beyme was still there, and only the queen's urgent entreaty prevented another outburst on Stein's part. He was at least allowed to allot to Beyme duties which he considered suitable for him, until finally Beyme became President of the *Kammergericht* in the following June. Meanwhile at least a provisional solution of the constitutional problem had been found.

Hardenberg had been forced by the French to resign in the summer of 1807; in September the king, then in Riga, received from him an important programme of reform, worked out with the help of Altenstein and Niebuhr. Its leading idea was that Prussia must now resolve to learn from her enemies, from revolutionary and Napoleonic France alike, how to strengthen her government by the introduction of democratic institutions, firmly controlled by the monarch. The king had promptly set up two special committees, the 'Immediate Commission', consisting mainly of former members of the General Directory like Schön, Altenstein and Niebuhr, to deal with the reform of the civil service, and the 'Military Reorganisation Commission', headed by Scharnhorst and Gneisenau. Stein returned with a complete scheme that he had sketched for the reform of the principal government departments and their procedure, and he soon obtained the king's approval of it in principle, though he had to agree to the postponement of its introduction until French evacuation of occupied Prussian territory made it financially possible.

Instead of three boards, collectively responsible in the traditional way, one for foreign affairs (the 'Cabinet Ministry'), one for Church affairs and justice, and one for general administration (the General Directory, with its mingled provincial and specialist departments), Stein wanted a logical set of five ministries, for finance, home affairs, foreign affairs, war and justice, the same five that existed in France. The work of the five ministers in charge of them was to be co-ordinated by a Council of State, on which they were to be joined by several additional privy councillors, and over which the king would preside. The ministries were duly created, though initially the first two were combined under Stein himself, but the idea of a Council of State did not meet with the king's approval, chiefly because he did not feel capable of acting as its chairman. Hardenberg, for a month or two before he departed from office, had acted as a kind of prime minister and in some measure, with the collaboration of the king and Beyme, harmonised the decisions of the various boards. Stein had to be content with a similar make-shift arrangement, and it was continued again when Hardenberg came back as his successor, until in 1810 the king accepted Hardenberg's suggestion that he should be styled 'State Chancellor' and recognised as the head of the government, representing the ministers in their relations with the king, or at any rate controlling those relations. Stein was at least able to break down the old practice of exclusively written communications between departments, by holding weekly conferences with his fellow-ministers, and the king ceased to rule in the traditional arbitrary manner from his cabinet because he recognised his personal deficiencies. When Hardenberg became state chancellor, he remained the opportunist he had always been and, on encountering opposition from the nobility, returned more and more to bureaucratic methods of government, having more confidence in his own diplomatic adroitness than in the democratic principles dear to Stein. He successfully resisted Wilhelm von Humboldt's efforts, after the Congress of Vienna, to introduce some degree of ministerial responsibility into the constitution, and retained his full authority until his death. From Humboldt's letters we gain a very similar impression of Hardenberg to that conveyed by Stein's description of him in his memoirs:

Hardenberg had the good-humoured affability found in sanguine, pleasure-loving natures, he had a quick intelligence, a capacity for work and a pleasing exterior. But his character had no moral, religious foundations, it lacked greatness, drive and firmness, his understanding lacked depth, his knowledge thoroughness. Hence his weakness, his over-confidence in prosperity, his whining in adversity, his superficiality, defects which under the influence of his sensuality, pride, and insincerity did so much harm. .... He did not aim at the great and good for its own sake, but for the glory it might bring him. He therefore misunderstood it, never attained to it, and passed away neither respected nor lamented.

Stein's views found their fullest but still only partial realisation in the Municipal Reform Edict of 19 November 1808. He was not, like Hardenberg, Schön and Altenstein, an advocate of social and economic *laisser-faire*. His decidedly idealised notion of the long-vanished provincial estates system, and the perhaps over-favourable picture that he had formed for himself of English self-government, led him to seek the natural basis of a well-organised society in a system of corporations, not in uncontrolled private enterprise. The citizen should not be ordered about and prevented from expressing his own opinion by a remote central authority, but he should have his roots in a local community and share the self-governing activities in the first place of an organised regional group which, in its turn, through a hierarchy of district and provincial bodies, might indirectly influence the central government.

The Municipal Reform Edict made each town responsible for the whole of its own general administration, instead of its having to leave the initiative and the last word in all important matters to the Local Commissary, the government representative. Only the police force and courts of justice were withdrawn from civic control, the maintenance of law and order being still regarded as one of the functions of the central government, though for convenience it might leave the control of the police in quite small towns to the town council. The active citizens in the various wards into which the town was divided were to elect a Council of Deputies, and this in its turn the Executive Town Council. A man still did not need to become an active citizen unless he wished to buy a house and land or to practise a trade in a town. If, like most residents, he rented rooms in someone else's house, he remained a 'legal citizen' (*Schutzbürger*), with neither the rights nor the duties of active citizenship, which no one particularly wanted. 'The people were commanded, not allowed, to govern themselves' (Seeley), and even the new Town Councils consisted mainly of shopkeepers and tradesmen. Of the active citizens only the poorest, those with an income below 150 (or in larger towns 200) thalers a year, the pay of an apprentice, were debarred from voting or being candidates in the election of the Council of Deputies.

Frederick the Great had tried, without very great success, to encourage individual enterprise in certain industries which seemed to suit his purpose of making Prussia less dependent on imports and increasing her taxable income; but the traditional guild form of industry still prevailed here, as in the rest of Germany, and those who wished to practise any handicraft had to join the appropriate guild, with its often fantastically elaborate regulations. It had been part of Stein's purpose to do away with this compulsion, but for the moment it was only possible to establish freer forms of business in the case of butchers and bakers, and to abolish another medieval monopoly, the compulsion resting on certain tenants to have their corn ground at particular mills, the 'milling soke' familiar to students of the English manorial system. The principle of free enterprise was however recognised in the Memorandum of 16 December 1808, and Hardenberg later followed this up with the Edict of 2 November 1810 and the Industrial Law of 7 September 1811, introducing the full French system. Anyone was now free to practise a trade who had paid a certain fee and obtained a permit (the *Gewerbeschein*) from the government, which continued to exercise supervision only over callings such as that of an apothecary (and a chimney-sweep!), where public welfare seemed to require it. The guilds persisted as voluntary associations, and in the new territory acquired by Prussia in 1815 the old industrial system was allowed to continue, as it did in most other German states. A more or less uniform system of free enterprise was not introduced even into Prussia until 1845. Stein had also wished to abolish the sharp distinction made between town and country in their economic functions and forms of administration, involving the restriction of industrial production to the towns. As a first step he would have had to do away with the excise, the tax levied on the towns exclusively, and to find a substitute for it, an impossible task at a time when money was urgently required by the government for war contributions. An experiment with an income tax on the English model in East Prussia was short-lived and was not repeated.

The provincial organs of government were reorganised by a decree of 26 December 1808, after Stein's departure, on lines approved by him. No fundamental changes were made in them, and the War and Domains Chambers, now given the name of Governments, retained most of their old functions. The principle of the separation of justice and administration was however carried through systematically here too, the administrative bodies losing the right of jurisdiction they had had where questions of state finance or police were involved. The name Government had formerly been given, in the Prussian provinces, as in most German states at that time, to the Departments of Justice. They were now called Supreme Provincial Courts, and these courts handed over to the provincial Governments their earlier administrative functions in ecclesiastical and educational matters and questions concerning sovereign rights. The work of the Governments was for the first time divided logically among specialised sections, but the principle of corporate responsibility was retained, and the President of the Government was not appointed to be a dictator, but a chairman. The extent to which *laisser-faire* ideas had replaced the old mercantilism comes out in the standing instructions provided for his guidance, with their insistence on the minimum of government interference with free enterprise. Stein's suggestion that laymen, representing various classes, should be given a share in the administration, working in committees alongside permanent officials, was given a short trial in Brandenburg and Prussia, but the practice was soon abandoned.

The abolition of so many privileges of the aristocracy had a direct effect on the Prussian army, which under the soldier kings had exactly reflected, in its social structure, that of rural Prussia, the nobility providing its officers and the peasantry most of the rank and file, so that men often found themselves, in the army, still under the control of a young squire they had known from their boyhood. When the barriers between the social classes were breached, as they were particularly by the *Städteordnung* (Municipal Reform Edict), the reform of the army then proceeding had to take account of this important new factor. Stein as First Minister supervised both the civil and the military reforms and gave his full support to the radical ideas of Scharnhorst, the regular chairman of the Military Reorganisation Commission at the vital stage.

Reform was facilitated by the resignation of many of the senior officers after the Peace of Tilsit and the drastic reduction of the army, a maximum of 42,000 men being eventually allowed by the French. The Commission's attention had been directed by the king to three points in particular, the selection of officers, the abolition of recruiting outside Prussia and the revision of the system of military punishments. Scharnhorst, who owed to his own ability his rise to high rank in the artillery, first in Hanover and then in Prussia, wanted to see commissions in the new army awarded solely on grounds of merit, to men of character and a reasonable standard of education in peace-time, and of courage and resourcefulness in war. After much discussion he had his way. No distinction of birth was now made between candidates, and all had to pass the same examination, though a good deal of discretion was left to the company commander in the degree of importance he attached to the qualities expected of a gentleman, when aspirants came before him for interview. A decree of 6 August 1808 proclaimed these new principles.

It took Scharnhorst a great deal longer to introduce the form of recruitment that he desired from the outset as the only possible basis for a national rising, namely national service after the French model, to which the king only agreed early in 1813, when he had rejected the proposal three times. The old Prussian army had been recruited partly by the cantonal system in its own territory, partly by recruiting campaigns in any of the neighbouring states that permitted them, more than half the men being found in this way. Recent political changes due to the Napoleonic war had closed the best recruiting grounds by the time the Commission began its deliberations, and the furlough system (*Krümper* system) was first devised as a remedy for the reduction in the available man-power, before a limitation of numbers was imposed by the French. In every company, men were sent home each month as reservists and replaced by others recruited in the usual way by the cantonal system, and these were succeeded after a month's training by another batch, so that the army, while retaining a solid basis of long-service men, provided a continual stream of men with a rudimentary training, though its numbers never exceeded the total permitted, when a maximum came to be fixed.

As a preparation for calling up others than the peasants and apprentices who, with foreign riff-raff, had served in the ranks of the old army, it was necessary as a first step to improve conditions of service. One of the perennial problems of the Prussian army in time of war had been to make desertion as difficult as possible. A body of men, the majority of whom were 'foreigners', persuaded to join up in a weak moment, and the rest pressed men with scarcely any motive for fighting except fear of their officers, had to be drilled into an obedient mass, and discipline had to be enforced by 'running the gauntlet' and other corporal punishments of the harshest kind. If the privileged and the under-privileged classes were to be conscripted for army service side by side, they would clearly have to be treated much more humanely, a reform that was in any case demanded by the spirit of the times. In spite of strong protest by officers of the old school, an order embodying this reform was proclaimed on 3 August 1808. In March of this year Scharnhorst had already submitted to the Commission a draft report recommending the establishment of 'provincial troops', a kind of militia, intended for the previously exempted classes, from whom he proposed to call up all fit men between the ages of 19 and 31. His ideas were strongly opposed even by some of the most patriotic among the higher officials, because of the harm that would be done, in their opinion, to the economic and cultural life of Prussia. Even apart from this, the king could not have given his assent, because of the negotiations then taking place with the French about the withdrawal of their occupation forces. A Convention agreed upon with them on 8 September 1808 expressly forbade the setting up of a militia.

French military pressure had to be relaxed at the end of 1808, because Napoleon needed his troops so badly elsewhere, but Prussia would not join Austria in an attempt at revolt in 1809, in spite of the Spanish rising and signs of resistance to Napoleon on many sides; and again Frederick William rejected a report proposing conscription, which was submitted by a special committee appointed in June 1809. In addition to Scharnhorst's earlier proposals, revised to meet some criticisms, the plan provided for special detachments of mounted volunteers from the upper classes—the germ of what were known later as the *Freikorps* in the War of Liberation, like the Lützow Chasseurs, with whom Theodore Körner served and fell. In July 1809 came the Austrian defeat at Wagram.

In the next three years a further batch of reforms was carried through, including the far-reaching overhaul of the educational system, in spite of the heavy financial burden of the war contribution, with the instalments of which Prussia was always in arrears. The First Minister was now again Hardenberg, recalled in June 1810 at Queen Luise's suggestion, just before her death, and he remained in office until his own death in 1822. In 1811 the patriotic group of generals and high officials for a third time urged the king to break with Napoleon, foreseeing that war between France and Russia was imminent, but he still cautiously refused to move without the support of both Austria and Russia, and Austria under Metternich would not risk another defeat. In the spring of 1812 Prussia had even to promise Napoleon 20,000 men for his Russian campaign. This corps, finally commanded by General Yorck, operated in the Baltic provinces and did not take part in the advance to Moscow and the disastrous retreat. It was only the catastrophe that overtook the French in Russia in the winter of 1812, and General Yorck's bold decision, without consulting his government, to conclude the Convention of Tauroggen (30 December 1812) with Russia, and to carry on with his plans even when the king rejected the Convention and relieved him of his command, that finally forced the king's hand. Stein, now political adviser to the Russian emperor, came to Königsberg as his envoy, and Yorck and he organised from there the preparation of a rising against Napoleon, supported by the nobility of East and West Prussia. They decided to raise a *Landwehr* or militia of 20,000 men by conscription and to finance it locally with this aristocratic backing.

Now at last it was possible for Scharnhorst to execute his long-cherished plans. The calling up of the *Krümper* had the effect of trebling the standing army. On 3 February 1813 an appeal was made for the formation of detachments of volunteer chasseurs. On 9 February all exemptions in the existing regulations for the cantonal system were cancelled; this meant total conscription, and 12 February was fixed as the date of mobilisation. The concession which it had been found necessary to make in the East Prussian call-up was now abolished, namely that of allowing men to provide substitutes to serve in their place, a last relic of privilege allowed even in France.

In the long story of the preparation of the finally successful rising of Prussia against Napoleon, the diplomatic and military aspects of which must here be passed over, there is nothing that can be called heroic about the actions of the king himself, though some historians have maintained that in the end his prudent policy justified itself, and that an earlier rising would have been doomed to failure. It was constitutional inability to make an irrevocable decision, especially one involving a risk to his dynasty, that lay behind the king's inactivity, for Frederick William could only think as a Prussian, while most of the patriots, including his queen, thought by now as Germans, eager out of self-respect as a nation to assert their independence, even if Prussia's individual interests might for a time be seriously endangered.

With regard to this sentiment of national self-respect, it is certain that a great change had taken place in Germany since 1795. One obvious cause is the mere fact of large-scale invasion, and the disorganisation and suffering it brought with it. But when Germany had been invaded before, or when foreign powers had used its soil as a battle-field, few if any Germans had had this sense of national outrage, because until about 1800 it was rare indeed for any of them to think of 'Germany' as a fatherland at all, rather than his own little state with its historic dynasty. The new factor, it seems, is the sense of national identity, which had come into existence, in the minds of cultivated people, through the emergence of a new culture, valued as something specifically German, not provincial. It was in the main a literary and philosophical culture, a creation in language, the unified literary language gradually fashioned for this purpose by a series of gifted writers, from the local vernaculars still used everywhere in the family circle and among intimate friends, as Swiss German is today. It is true that pride in native achievements was modified, in many of the most distinguished writers, by a continuing allegiance to humanity as the only object worthy of the highest esteem, and there is a large component of cosmopolitanism in the nationalism even of a Fichte. He and many of his Romantic contemporaries saw Germany as predestined to lead mankind in general towards the highest ideals. Inherent in this attitude, we see now, was the danger of a lack of consideration for other national cultures, occasionally evident already in an over-confident assertion of German merits. But without this inspiration of a universal ideal, it seems clear, the great reformers of Prussia, Stein and Humboldt in particular, would not have devoted themselves to their tasks as they did.

While the administrative and military reforms aimed above all at the creation of a new spirit in the Prussian people, the reform most directly calculated to have this effect was that of the educational system (Chapter VII, pp. 193–6). It was vigorously tackled, with far-reaching results, in the dark years following the defeat of Austria, in spite of acute financial and political difficulties. Before his resignation in 1808 Stein himself had recommended to the king the appointment of Wilhelm von Humboldt as head of the section in the Ministry of Home Affairs responsible for the Church and Education, a surprising choice but a very good one. Wilhelm, the elder of the two highly gifted Humboldt brothers, early came into contact with the intellectual revival, through Jewish circles in Berlin; and at 25, after marrying a like-minded and equally well-to-do wife and leaving the civil service, in order to live wholly, with her, for the full development of their inner powers, had written the essay on the limitation of the powers of the state which is one of the classics of liberalism. He had lived for a year or two in Jena, in the closest association with Schiller and Goethe, spent some years in Paris and finally obtained a virtual sinecure in the Prussian diplomatic service in Rome, for the pleasure and stimulus of living there. Of schools he knew nothing at first hand, having been privately educated, and he was so indifferent to religion that he left church affairs entirely to his assistant Nicolovius, Goethe's nephew. He had studied however at Frankfurt and Göttingen, known Heyne and Wolf and himself translated from the Greek, and was an even more ardent humanist and apostle of culture than his Weimar friends. During his brief tenure of office, from March 1809 to June 1810, he left the mark of his personality on the whole school and university system of Prussia, and later of Germany.

Fichte, in his *Addresses to the German Nation*, public lectures delivered in occupied Berlin to large audiences in the winter of 1807–8, had laid the greatest stress, in his plea for national self-renewal, on the necessity for an educational system which should produce self-reliant men of all classes, religiously devoted to their country as the only lasting reality, and he had warmly praised Pestalozzi and his work in Switzerland. Humboldt and his staff worked out plans for a compulsory elementary educational system on modified Pestalozzian lines, and for training-schools for teachers. Humboldt personally had more to do with the improvement of the grammar schools, which he naturally favoured as against the modern schools (*Realschulen*) beloved of the Enlightenment with their emphasis on useful knowledge. His *Gymnasien* were to train the minds of their pupils through the intensive study of Latin, Greek and mathematics, and to provide for general culture through a wide range of subsidiary subjects. The system was only fully worked out under Süvern, after Humboldt's departure. It proved most successful and became the model for the whole of Germany. As early as 1812 a school leaving examination was instituted, the passing of which qualified a boy (girls were not yet provided for) to enter a university.

Humboldt's finest achievement was his planning and staffing of the new university set up in Berlin, in close association with the existing Academy of Sciences, to take the place of Halle, now in occupied territory. It opened in 1810, soon after Humboldt had left Berlin to become Prussian ambassador in Vienna. Like Newman later, Humboldt held it to be the function of a university not merely to transmit knowledge, but to train and develop the intelligence, judgment and moral resources of the student, so that he should be capable of acquiring quickly the special knowledge or skill required for any profession, and approach his life's work with a philosophy behind him. In agreement with the distinguished scholars, Fichte, Schleiermacher, Niebuhr, Savigny and others, whom he selected as its first staff, he gave this model German university its characteristic emphasis on the search for new knowledge; and, though it was never possible for all professors and students to live up to these high ideals and it became increasingly difficult as time went on, great things were accomplished and a new conception of university education was introduced to the world. (Chapter V, pp. 127-8). Berlin was also, however, in spite of the 'freedom to teach and to learn' of which it boasted, almost entirely dependent financially on the state, and unlike the Academy did not enjoy autonomy in adding to its staff.

Knowing as we do now the part played by Prussia in German history since the Napoleonic Wars, we are bound to attach more importance to the social and constitutional changes that took place there during the wars than to those experienced in other parts of Germany, but for contemporaries the picture was different. The Empire itself soon proved powerless to stand up to the shocks resulting from the French Revolution and its consequences. The first attack of Custine's army in 1792 showed how helpless the small states of south-west Germany were in such a crisis, although for the moment they were saved by the armies of Prussia and Austria. Prussia was soon preoccupied with events in Poland, where Russia and Austria were bringing about a third partition, in which they aimed at relinquishing as little territory as possible to her. When Prussia hastily withdrew from the struggle with France and concluded in 1795 the Peace of Bâle, Germany north of the Main was left to enjoy an uneasy respite for a decade. It was in these years that Goethe and Schiller in Weimar and Jena produced the classical works in which they consciously aimed, as Schiller put it in 1794 (announcing their new literary periodical, *Die Horen*), at 'restoring to men their freedom of mind, and uniting the politically divided world under the banner of truth and beauty, by cultivating a general and higher interest in what is purely human and superior to contemporary influences'.

Weimar was one of the small Saxon duchies in central Germany, and Electoral Saxony too, the fourth in size of the German states before the Revolution, was chiefly important down to the end of the wars for achievements in industry and the arts. The handsome Saxon capital, Dresden, with the finest art collections outside Vienna, inspired many romantic writings; Leipzig continued to be the centre of the book-trade; the Freiberg Academy of Mining, founded in 1765, contributed more to the advancement of natural science than any German university in this period; and an Academy of Forestry, the first in Germany, was opened at Tharandt as late as 1811. The strong practical bent revealed in such institutions was also in evidence in a number of small-scale but, for that age, highly-developed industries. In a Prussian enclave in Saxony the first steam-engine in Germany was to be seen from 1785 near Merseburg, pumping water from a mine. But even in this favoured region modern forms of industry made slow progress, severely hampered by poor communications and guild controls, and until long after 1830 there were few signs of capitalism in Germany generally, except in the form of domestic industries, producing textiles in particular, in villages on the poor soil of upland districts like parts of Saxony and Silesia, where people were in special need of such part-time occupations.

After Prussia's withdrawal, Austria continued the struggle in 1795 and 1796 with some success, though Baden and Württemberg were soon compelled to abandon the Coalition and to pay tribute to France. In 1797 Austria too, after Napoleon's defeat of her forces in Italy, concluded with him the Peace of Campo Formio, in the secret clauses of which she already gave her assent to an eventual annexation by France of the left bank of the Rhine. France's demand was made openly at the Congress of Rastatt in the following year and finally accepted by the large deputation representing the Imperial Diet. A plan was already contemplated to compensate German princes for the loss of territory consequent on this annexation by the secularisation of ecclesiastical lands on the right bank of the Rhine; but, when hostilities were soon resumed, this plan could not be carried through until the Peace of Lunéville (February 1801) brought the War of the Second Coalition to an end.

Far-reaching changes in the life of south-west Germany in particular were initiated by the shameless bargaining which now took place between German princes great and small and the French Foreign Minister, Talleyrand, at the cost of the last supporters of the imperial idea, the ecclesiastical princes, the free towns and the imperial knights. It suited the strategic requirements of France, in her fear of Austria, to set up puppet states in south Germany; and Bavaria, Württemberg, Baden and Hesse-Darmstadt welcomed the opportunity thus opened to them of territorial aggrandisement. In vain an attempt was made, in the settlement agreed to by the Deputation of the Imperial Diet on 25 February 1803, to rescue parts of the old imperial constitution. When the south German states were compelled in the war of 1805 to take the French side, the Empire itself virtually ceased to exist. The last of the south German free towns, the imperial knights and a large number of counts were mediatised, and their lands swelled still further the territory of Bavaria and the other compliant states, which were now declared sovereign powers. They joined the Confederation of the Rhine on 12 July 1806, accepting French protection and renouncing imperial titles. A month later Francis II renounced his elective imperial title, and so became Francis I, Emperor of Austria. The territorial changes thus brought about, involving an enormous reduction in the number of separate states in Germany, were comparatively little affected by the peace of 1815, by which the three hundred or more separate territories that could be distinguished in the older Germany were reduced to thirty-nine states. It was the French occupation that called into being everywhere in Germany the new kind of national feeling, political and not merely cultural, of which we have described the emergence above. The desire for a unified nation began to make itself felt, in rivalry with that of each state to maintain its separate identity. The ideas of the revolutionary age moreover aroused the demand in all states for constitutions and the blurring of class privileges.

While the Confederation of the Rhine was in existence and important reforms were being carried through in Prussia, many constitutional and social changes took place in the remaining German states, but most of them proved to be temporary, while the states which retained their old boundaries, such as Saxony (now a kingdom), Mecklenburg and the north German small states, were hardly affected at all. As a result of the protracted occupation, French law and the French system of administration took root so firmly in the states on the left bank of the Rhine that their effects were felt long after 1815, the *Code Napoléon* remaining in force until 1900. In the new states created by Napoleon—Westphalia, Berg and Frankfurt—though many reforms were initiated in accordance with French ideas, few were completed and it was possible to make a fresh start after the peace. On the other hand, in the greatly expanded purely German states of the south and south-west, Bavaria and the rest, the process of expansion itself necessitated far-reaching changes in administration, because of the heterogeneous nature of the territories absorbed. Napoleonic France was taken as a model in the working out of a completely centralised and rational absolutism.

Although it was not many years before Napoleon's Empire crumbled, he not only in that time transformed the political map of Germany, but through his vassal kings and their statesmen introduced into Germany by a revolution from above the chief political and administrative practices which, in France, were the final result of a democratic mass movement from below, when an organiser of genius had so canalised popular forces that they served to bolster up his own authority. These ideas were willingly accepted by German rulers, because the French political system under Napoleon had only carried to their logical conclusion aims already pursued by Frederick the Great and other enlightened despots. Combined with them German rulers now took over other political and social ideas of a truly revolutionary novelty, ideas which were not consistent with the continuance of the hitherto unquestioned privileges of the nobility and the church. The normal conservative citizen was bewildered by these ideas, and their final result was often not decided for decades, but it soon became clear that the old regime could no more be restored in Germany than in France.

On the face of it, the governments responsible for these reforms in the south German states differed from each other greatly and had very different historical traditions and local circumstances to contend with, yet the same broad current bore them along. In Bavaria, some opposition to the dominant Catholic priesthood had been attempted since the middle of the eighteenth century by admirers of the intellectual achievements of the Protestant north. With the support of the Elector Max Joseph a Bavarian Academy of Sciences had been established in 1759, with the aim of encouraging the spread of useful knowledge in the general interests of the community, and of fighting the all too prevalent superstition and sloth. Original research was a minor aspect of its activity while Bavaria lagged so far behind the north in literacy and enlightenment. Under the pleasure-loving Karl Theodor (1777–99) the Academy suffered a setback, although it was allowed to take over the buildings of the Jesuit College in Munich when the Order was suspended in 1783. The French Revolution brought a violent reaction against enlightenment in any shape, but Elector Max Joseph II, on his accession in 1799, gave a completely free hand to his foreign minister, Maximilian von Montgelas, who had left Bavaria in 1785 to escape arrest as a member of the secret society of the Illuminati, and had been associated for years, in exile, with the future elector. Always an admirer of French radical thought, he needed no persuasion from the French to set about the task of reforming Bavaria's finances, administration and intellectual life. By harsh and sometimes ill-considered measures he attempted in great haste to subordinate the ecclesiastical to the civil power, to secularise the monasteries and to build up a modern civil service. To help in these tasks he called in leading Protestant scholars, Anselm Feuerbach to reform the law, F. H. Jacobi and F. W. Thiersch to strengthen the Academy, and Schelling, Niethammer and Savigny to set an example in the universities, while Hegel was made Rector of the Nürnberg Gymnasium.

In a similar way Sigismund von Reitzenstein in Baden combined a policy of territorial expansion, by French favour and at the expense of a large number of weaker German states, with vigorous measures on French lines to modernise the administration of the resulting amalgam. Exploiting Napoleon's wish to ensure ready access for French forces to southern Germany, Baden was able to extend her boundaries until they took in the whole bank of the upper Rhine; and the good Karl Friedrich, when he died as Grand Duke in 1811 at the age of 83, ruled over nearly ten times the area that he had inherited as Margrave in 1738. Here also much care was given to the improvement of schools and universities. Heidelberg, acquired by Baden only in 1803, in a state of extreme decline, was completely re-established and only now became one of the leading German universities and a centre of the later romantic movement.

In Württemberg Frederick I, who became Duke in 1797 as a middle-aged man, much travelled and full of confidence in his own abilities, was determined to share his late-won power with no one. A sullen, dissolute, pot-bellied tyrant, he revived the worst traditions of his grandfather Karl Eugen, his extravagance, his love of pomp and ceremony and of the mass slaughter that was called hunting, and his total disregard for the modest representative institutions and the independent church which were so dear to his Swabian subjects. The new acquisitions of 1803 were called 'New Württemberg' and treated by him like a conquered country; and, when in 1806 Napoleon made him a king, he suspended after a struggle with the Estates what was left of their old constitution and demanded unconditional obedience from all alike. The well organised Lutheran church had over the centuries won for itself a considerable measure of independence, and acquired extensive funds with which it maintained churches, schools and charities wisely and generously. As about a third of the king's subjects were now Catholics, both churches were given equal rights and both placed under the control of the Spiritual Department of the Ministry of the Interior. The property of the Lutherans was taken over by the state, which in turn undertook to carry out the tasks hitherto financed by the church. The schools also were nationalised, while the University of Tübingen lost its endowments and its autonomy. Unpopular as all these measures were, the king's subjects had to admit that he had put the finances in order and provided the country, at the cost of much suffering, with an efficient fighting force, to be used for Napoleon's purposes.

The reforms carried through in these various ways in the south German states took them a long way towards the realisation of the ideal of equality before the law, though it was only in Baden that the *Code Napoléon* was introduced in its entirety. All Christian confessions acquired equal rights; all able-bodied men were made liable to military service, though a loophole was left, as in France, for men of means to find a substitute; all subjects alike were taxed according to their capacity, without regard to the old exemptions, and in other respects too the severely curtailed privileges of the nobility were regulated by law and left open to revision. Economic reforms included the abolition of internal duties—though protective tariffs were retained where the special needs of these states seemed to require them; weights and measures were standardised; serfdom was swept away but the peasantry were not freed from dues and services, except in the rare instances when they could purchase immunity, and the landlords retained their rights of jurisdiction. For lack of reliable officials, many reforms were not carried through completely, but rapid progress was made on the whole in the administrative unification of the new states, so that even the crisis of 1813 did not undo the work of the reformers.

After 1815, most of the differences between north and south Germany that had arisen since 1806 persisted for some decades. In the southern states there was no reversal of policy, whereas the northern small states, whose boundaries had suffered few changes, felt no need for drastic reforms except, in some cases, of a reactionary kind. In both north and south the system of government remained authoritarian, for the constitutions granted in the southern states between 1814 and 1820 were not concessions to a popular demand, but measures designed, on the lines of the French *Charte* of 1814, after the restoration of the monarchy, to increase internal unification and cohesion still further. Though lip service was paid to the 'rights of man', all effective power was retained in the hands of the government, even genuine budgetary control being denied to the elected lower chambers. The rulers, while retaining full sovereignty, undertook to work in co-operation with responsible ministers, the nature of whose responsibility was left undefined. That an educated minority, middle-class people of some substance, merchants, manufacturers and professional men, were not content with this state of things, is proved by the support they gave to the Liberal movement led by Karl von Rotteck in Baden, which constantly pressed the radical claim to government by the people. It was in the struggle for representative constitutions that political parties first began to take shape in Germany.

In the north, the political, social and economic reforms carried out in Hanover, Brunswick and Electoral Hesse while the French kingdom of Westphalia lasted were summarily rescinded in 1815, and the attempt was made to return as far as possible to the old Estates constitution. Saxony, in spite of its adherence to the Confederation of the Rhine, had under King Frederick I maintained its old forms of political and social life with as few changes as possible, and it continued to do so until his death in 1827. Hanover reverted in 1814 to its former oligarchical system of government, which was little affected in essentials by the creation in 1819 of a central representative assembly of the Estates in two chambers. In Brunswick and still more in Hesse the sympathies even of the nobility were alienated by the rulers' autocratic conduct, and it was naturally in these two states that the July Revolution of 1830 in Paris led to disturbances, which were followed by the grant of constitutions more or less resembling those of the southern states. In Saxony too a popular movement of protest was elicited by the Paris news, strengthening the hands of the reform group among the ministers, so that a constitution on south German lines could now be achieved. Soon afterwards, in 1833, Hanover acquired a modern constitution. Some of the small states of central Germany, of which Weimar is the best known, had been granted constitutions by their rulers immediately after the peace. Their earlier Estates system of representation had been slightly modernised, but the old authoritarian order of things little changed.

Prussia meanwhile, in spite of Frederick William's early promises, still had no constitution and, like Austria, remained without one until 1848. Its rulers had always detested the French Revolution and everything it stood for, though important ideas had been borrowed from the French, as we have seen, for the great reforms of the army and administration, above all that of compulsory military service for all, which was made a permanent institution in Prussia in 1814. After the sufferings and deprivations of the war years, there was naturally everywhere in Germany a longing for peace and quietness, clearly reflected in the literature of the so-called *Biedermeier* period. As the economic life even of Prussia only slowly took on capitalistic forms, and its people, like the Germans in general, accepted plain living and close supervision as something inevitable, it was possible for the government, aiming ostensibly at the restoration of a better past, to resist successfully the revolutionary ideas of nationalism, self-determination and freedom of speech, the spread of which would have threatened the existence of a multi-national state. Austria was moved even more strongly by similar considerations, and the Holy Alliance concluded by the Prussian, Austrian and Russian monarchs in 1815 signed and sealed a common policy of reaction. The ideas of the romantic intellectuals were everywhere in the air, glorifying the Middle Ages as they saw them, a period when modern doubts and divisions were unknown and the Christian order of a truly organic society was guaranteed by Church and State. There was plenty of radicalism at the German universities among the young, but at the first open signs of it, Metternich concerted with the Prussian government the repressive Carlsbad Decrees; and the Germanic Confederation, dominated by Austria and Prussia, was easily persuaded to endorse them. The only concession that was made to the ideal of popular representation was the creation by Prussia in all its separate provinces of Estates Assemblies on a strictly conservative basis. The German unity which even the unpolitical Goethe declared in his last years (to Eckermann, 23 October 1828) to be bound to come in time, though he greatly hoped that it would not efface the many local centres of culture, was urged only by doctrinaire liberals in the south-western German states, while Prussia and Austria, the only powers capable of bringing it about, pursued their separate dynastic policies, united only in their resistance to change.

CHAPTER XIV

THE AUSTRIAN MONARCHY, 1792–1847[1]

IT was the remarkable destiny of the Habsburg monarchy, after passing, between 1780 and 1792, through the most changeful twelve years (in internal respects) of all its history, to pass the next fifty-six in most respects in a condition of suspended animation as near-complete as the considerable ingenuity of its rulers could contrive. The prime responsibility for this unquestionably belongs to its monarch, Francis, whom the Emperor Leopold's untimely and unexpected death on 1 March 1792 brought, at the unripe age of twenty-four, to a throne which his physical presence was to occupy for forty-three years and his ghost for thirteen more. Francis had inherited none of his father's constitutional beliefs. Like his uncle Joseph, who had had him brought to Vienna as a boy and educated there for his future duties, he was by conviction a complete absolutist. He believed that government should be the expression of the monarch's will, and that the proper vehicle for expressing it was a bureaucracy taking and executing the monarch's orders. The supreme, if not the sole civic duty of those over whom he ruled was to be good subjects to him, and the criterion of political institutions and of social conditions was their aptitude to produce this effect.

It would not, indeed, be fair to deny to his despotism at least a negative benevolence. Personally virtuous and unpretentious, and possessed of a high sense of rectitude, he held that a monarch had, in return, a duty towards his subjects to observe justice towards them and to enforce it between them, and that he must not squander their lives on an acquisitive foreign policy, nor their property on his pleasures. But it was the very opposite of enlightened. Although not at all a stupid man, any more than he was a bad one—he was shrewd above the average, and possessed of a disconcerting power to draw from any situation the conclusions which were correct on his premises—he was mentally near-sighted and unimaginative, mistrustful and timid of the unknown, lacking any trace of his uncle's social vision, imaginative power and restless impatience with the imperfect. Moreover, in contrast to Joseph's combative readiness to take on, even to provoke, opposition, Francis shrank from controversy or unpleasantness of any kind. These negative qualities excluded any possibility that he would seek to carry further Joseph's policy of reform for reform's sake, and they also made

---

[1] At the editor's request, this sketch covers the period up to 1847, since the year 1830 is no landmark in Austrian history.

him content to accept the forms, and up to a point the substance, of an absolutism less complete than Joseph's, for he was quite capable of contrasting the real pacification which Leopold had effected by his retreat with the hornet's nest which Joseph had brought about the family ears. Accordingly, however much the autocrat in him may have disapproved, common sense told him that in the dangerous situation confronting him on his accession, present safety lay in confirming Leopold's compromises and freezing the political and social conditions established by them. Later, it might perhaps be possible to move a step back towards a more complete absolutism. The Estates of almost all his provinces, for their part, asked for little more than to see the ghost of Joseph II well and truly laid. Only the Hungarians took the occasion to secure in addition the abolition of the Illyrian Chancellery and a promise of more scope for the 'national language'. On this basis, agreement was quickly reached. Francis was crowned in Buda on 6 June and in Prague on 8 August, and was then free to devote his attention to the war with France which had already broken out.

Austria was not, in the event, to know real peace again until 1815; for up to that date even the intervals in which she was not actively belligerent were mainly spent, either in patching up wounds received in the past campaign, or in preparing for the next. In the course of these years Francis's philosophy, and the 'system' of which it was the expression, took increasingly clear shape, largely, it would appear, under the impact of two events, the first of which was the execution, by the Revolutionary Tribunal of Paris, of his aunt and her consort; the second, the discovery, by his own police, in 1794, of two inter-connected 'Jacobin conspiracies', one in Vienna, the other in Hungary. The Viennese 'conspiracy' reflected real discontent with the war, which was widely unpopular, and one or two of the participants held genuinely treasonable views; but these few cases apart, it was an almost ludicrously childish affair of a few men who had done little more than sing rather tipsy catches in praise of liberty. More persons were incriminated in Hungary, and some of these had certainly indulged in fantastic talk, but the thing was hardly more serious there, and a suspicious light was thrown on the whole business by the fact that its self-confessed leader, a certain Abbé Martinovics, had himself been a police spy for Leopold. But to Francis the affairs, of which the police made the very most, were proof that no man was to be trusted. Widespread arrests were made and exemplary punishments inflicted and, from this date on, the system became predominantly one of negation and repression. This was not equivalent to lack of government; the central ministries poured out during these years an unprecedented volume of enactments, which included several important pieces of work, notably the codifications in 1803 of the criminal and in 1811 of the civil law. Nor did Francis's

Austria ever, even at its worst, know a police terror remotely comparable to that of Hitlerite Germany or Stalinist Russia.

Not without reason, Francis held secret societies to be the chief hot-beds of subversive thought, and it was really dangerous to belong to any such society; the freemasons were particularly suspect. But in general, the function of the control was prophylactic rather than punitive. Arrests on political grounds were relatively rare, and sentences were light by modern standards, with the notable exception of those of 1794 and a few others in which examples were made, especially those made in Lombardy in 1820-1. Francis himself, who took a lively interest in the police-reports and even had his private informants and encouraged denunciants to write to him direct, used the service chiefly as a source of information. Many a man whose doings and sayings were kept for years under the closest scrutiny lived out those years quite unmolested. But the control was very widespread and very minute, particularly over the professional and 'intellectual' classes, in which Francis, drawing his conclusions from the events of the French Revolution, saw the chief danger to social stability, and over the civil servants and officers, on whose loyalty the safety of the State depended. These, from the most insignificant to the highest—those most of all—lived under its shadow, and cowered under it. And if not unusually brutal, the 'system' was, even for its day, exceptionally obscurantist. Logical in this as in all things, Francis traced subversion to its root, which he found in abstract and speculative thought, and to that root he laid his axe; systematically. After the Martinovics conspiracy, the then Palatine of Hungary, the Archduke Alexander, had advised what amounted to cutting out all education of any sort, except for future bureaucrats. Francis took the more positive view that education had a function, and he had the number of schools, both primary and secondary, largely increased; later, several new technical institutions were founded. But instruction was directed strictly towards what he regarded as its proper purpose, the production of 'high-minded, religious and patriotic citizens'. It was, accordingly, entrusted chiefly to the Church, whose endowments for the purpose were considerably increased, the Church itself being at the same time kept in strict subordination to the State, for as regards relations between Church and State Francis held unbendingly to the Josephinian tradition. Another important 'anti-thought' weapon was the censor-ship. The regulations were further tightened up and the service trans-ferred to the police. It soon became impossible either to print in Austria, or to import, anything against which the lightest suspicion of un-orthodoxy or of criticism of the regime might lie. A special 're-censoring Commission' went through the works which had been sanctioned in the years of relaxation, between 1780 and 1792, and banned no less than 2500 of them.

All this work, whether constructive or repressive, was carried out in the western half of the monarchy, including Galicia and Venice in the appropriate years, by the bureaucracy, obeying orders which issued from the central ministries, and often ultimately from Francis himself. The Estates of those Lands[1] led a purely shadow existence. In this sense Francis's Austria was, after all, a reversion to that of Joseph II, particularly since the middle and lower ranks of the bureaucracy were necessarily recruited chiefly from men of middle-class or even humble origin. Aristocratic writers complained bitterly of the invasion of the country by this horde of paid scribes. According to middle-class writers, on the other hand, Austria was still a preserve of the aristocracy. The great nobles held a near-monopoly of the higher posts in the civil service itself, outside the judiciary, as in the army and even the Church, and their dominant position in the social system was not challenged. Once the Josephinian land-tax had been finally dropped, the most important social question which Leopold's death had left undecided was whether the abolition of the *robot*[2] should be made compulsory. A committee to which the question was referred reported in 1796 in favour of the retention of the *robot*, as being 'a good school of obedience and humility'. A patent issued that year accordingly confined itself to sanctioning commutation by agreement with the landlord. This was the last legislation enacted on the peasant question, outside Hungary, until 1848, except that 'robotpatents' were issued for Galicia and the Bukovina, bringing those Lands into line with the Bohemian and German-Austrian, and also that landlords in many Lands were required (at their own expense) to employ qualified lawyers to preside over the patrimonial courts. The patrimonial system itself, for lower and middle justice, was left in being, as being cheaper than a paid service.

An influential school of thought was opposed also to the further development of industry. Man-power was still in short supply, especially in the war years, and the agrarian interests wanted all available labour kept on the land; the Church and conservatives in general warned against the social dangers which might arise with the growth of an industrial proletariat, especially if allowed to concentrate in the towns. An opposing school of thought, that of the old mercantilists, took, indeed, the opposite view in the interest of Austria's balance of payments and, as the wars proceeded, sheer necessity compelled Austria to expand her own manufactures; but even in this field the freeze was, generally, not relaxed except when this was quite unavoid-

---

[1] The word Land is used here, as in German, because any rendering such as 'province' would in some cases be technically incorrect. Those parts of the monarchy which ranked as 'kingdoms' regarded the description 'province' as degrading to their status.

[2] The forced labour or corvée performed by the socage peasant on the lord's land was universally known in the monarchy, even the non-Slavonic parts, by the Slav word *robot*, meaning work.

able, so that for the first fifteen years of Francis's reign industry developed only very slowly, and chiefly in the form of small enterprises, most of them in rural districts. The Continental Blockade then brought a sudden spurt, which, however, by no means affected all industries; textiles were the chief gainers.

On the whole, Francis's 'system' tended to become more systematic, and to reflect his own ideas more accurately, as the years went by, and as he himself acquired greater experience and more taste for the business of governing, and as the appropriate institutions and services took shape under his hand. No resistance to it came from the western half of the monarchy. The Estates, whose members thoroughly approved of its conservatism, accepted the unsubstantial role assigned to them with no more than the most half-hearted of protests. The middle classes were content to find their places in the rapidly expanding bureaucracy. The peasants, who had shown considerable unrest so long as they were still hoping for further reform, had returned to the old 'humility and submissiveness'. The demonstrations of which Vienna was an occasional witness were against unpopular wars, high prices, or shortages: not against political oppression. The only serious criticisms of Francis's conduct of affairs came from his own inner circle of advisers, chief among whom, in these years, were his old tutor, Count Colloredo (who for some years presided over his *Kabinett*, or personal secretariat, and was consulted on every question), his own brothers, Charles, John and Rainer, and a few obscurer personal confidants, of whom a certain Baldacci was for years the most influential. None of these ever questioned Francis's absolute authority, but they did often criticise the effectiveness of the machinery through which he exercised it, and his choice of ministers. Francis, who was very open to suggestions when he found time to listen to them, tinkered endlessly with the machinery, and changed ministers often enough, but without ever surrendering his own personal control, so that the innumerable adjustments had little practical effect.

There was only one interlude during which he was induced to ask from his subjects anything more than passive obedience. This was in 1806, after Austria had been forced to sign the Peace of Pressburg (26 December 1805), a treaty so drastic (for its age) as to send a shock of resentment and revulsion through the monarchy; the time when, after having two years previously adopted the title of Emperor of Austria, he renounced that of Holy Roman Emperor. Foreign policy was now placed in the hands of Count Philipp Stadion, a Rhinelander, who held that the war of *revanche* for which it was his task to prepare could not succeed unless the people held it to be their own cause. He accordingly produced a programme of reform designed to awaken German national feeling (for it was still to the German people, inside and outside Austria, that he chiefly looked). Francis did not agree to any of Stadion's proposals for social or political reform, but he did sanction a propaganda campaign, which, under the patronage of his then consort, Maria Ludovica, and the Archdukes Charles and John, stirred the German Austrians, although not the other peoples of the monarchy, to considerable national enthusiasm. But this lapse into heresy was short-lived, and the parent of a return to an intensified orthodoxy. When, after the Archduke Charles had raised hopes by defeating Napoleon at Aspern, the campaign of 1809 ended, after all, as disastrously as that of 1806, and the resulting Treaty of Schönbrunn (Vienna) was even more severe than that of Pressburg, Francis dismissed Stadion, and the idea of a partnership with the people fell with its author. The Archduke Charles and, soon after, John also fell from grace. In their lieu Francis now listened chiefly to his new foreign minister, Metternich, who already shared a large proportion of the emperor's blind spots and prejudices, and soon made most of the remainder his own.

Up to this point Hungary had been treated, at least in form, differently from the rest of the monarchy. Antagonistic as he was to all constitutions, Francis had always maintained that the Hungarian was a bulwark of social and political stability and that it would be unwise to suspend or openly violate it. For their part, the Hungarian Estates had in 1792 been so thankful to find their new king ready to re-affirm the abjuration of Josephinism that they had readily accepted his plea of the imminent war with France as excuse for postponing immediate consideration of their *gravamina* (petitions). The Martinovics conspiracy shook Francis's faith in Hungarian goodwill, but the arrests made in connection with it also frightened the Hungarians, besides confirming their leaders in a conservatism as rigid as that of Francis himself. For a number of years relations between the two parties continued on a basis which was not satisfactory to either, but still not so unsatisfactory as to tempt either to risk a head-on conflict. Francis followed the constitutional procedure of asking the Diet for the recruits and supplies required by him, and for that purpose, convoked it fairly regularly (after 1792, in 1796, 1802, 1805, 1807 and 1808). He was thus forced to content himself with what he could extract from the Hungarians, and this was always less than he wanted. He did, however, always get something, and in spite of some scares, notably in 1805, never needed seriously to reckon with a threat of rebellion.

The Hungarians could flatter themselves with the spectacle of a Diet convoked almost regularly, and thanks to the tenacity in bargaining displayed by that body, Hungary's contribution to the wars, in terms both of blood and money, was relatively light. The nobles continued to enjoy their exemption from taxation, their almost unfettered rule over their peasants and their control over local affairs, exercised through the

County *Congregationes*, and in general, the hand of the regime rested less heavily on Hungary than on the western Lands. The police was less omnipresent, the censorship lighter, intellectual freedom in general greater, so that a very considerable linguistic and cultural revival was able to develop unimpeded. Moreover, the wars brought big profits to the Hungarian wheat-producers, who found ready markets for their produce at high prices.

On the other hand, Francis regularly insisted that (as the constitution allowed) each Diet should begin by considering his own *postulata* (proposals), and as regularly dissolved it as soon as the consideration of these was finished. The Hungarians' *gravamina*, as such, never reached the stage of debate in the Diet; it was only in the course of the bargaining over the *postulata* that an occasional grievance was remedied. The most important of these demands were for extension of the use of Magyar (in place of Latin) in official life and, as a preliminary to this, in secondary education (in place of German), and for remedy of the one-sided economic system which in practice compelled Hungary to cover her requirements of manufactured goods from Austria, at the manufacturer's price plus a heavy import duty, and to offer all her agricultural produce to Austria at the latter's price. Francis was quite unforthcoming on both points; under great pressure, he made a few small concessions on the language question in 1805 and 1808, but refused to yield an inch on the economic issue.

That again and again matters were somehow patched up was due almost entirely to the efforts of the Archduke Joseph, who had succeeded Alexander as palatine in 1796 after the latter had been killed in an accident, and mediated between king and nation with quite exceptional tact. Even so, tempers on both sides grew steadily more ragged. In 1807 the Hungarians gave such forcible expression to their objections to contributing to a war, the unconcealed object of which was to strengthen Austria's position in Germany, as to earn for the Diet the historic soubriquet of 'the Accursed'. If its successor of 1808 was, by contrast, nicknamed 'the Handsome', this was mainly thanks to the unexampled pressure and corruption which had been applied before it met.

After the Treaty of Schönbrunn, a crisis seemed inevitable unless the affairs of the monarchy as a whole took a turn for the better. They began, instead, by taking a further turn for the worse. Invasion, defeat and cruel territorial mutilation, each grievous in itself, had also combined to bring to a head the one internal process on which Francis had been unable to impose a standstill. For many years the government had been spending beyond its revenue, covering the gap partly by loans, partly by the issue of paper *Bankozettel* (treasury notes). It had paid its own servants (and also collected taxes) in this paper as though it were equivalent to its nominal value in silver, but in fact, as the note circulation increased, the *Bankozettel* were quoted in Augsburg at a rising discount, rising so steeply in 1810 that by 1811 the gulden was quoted at one tenth of its nominal value. Inland prices had risen on approximately the same scale. After various expedients had been tried, and all had failed, the finance minister, Count Wallis, issued a patent on 20 February 1811. All *Bankozettel*, of which 1060 million (gulden) were then in circulation, were called in, holders being given in return for every five *Bankozettel* one new *Erlösungsschein* (redemption note) of the same nominal value. The new currency was declared to be as the old had been, equal in value to its full equivalent in silver, and required so to be taken. All government payments were to be made, and all receipts collected, in it; the interest on government bonds was, however, cut by half. The government pledged itself not to increase the note circulation beyond its new figure of 212 million, which was that at which the *Bankozettel* had last been quoted at par. Repayment of private debts contracted during the inflationary period was to be made on a scale based on the quotation of the *Bankozettel* in Augsburg in the month when the debt was contracted.

Necessary as it was to stop the inflation, this drastic measure inflicted cruel hardship on many individuals, and also caused widespread dislocation. For decades thereafter the memory of the 'State bankruptcy' remained with the inhabitants of the monarchy as one of the most disastrous experiences of their own or their fathers' lives; it was indeed that memory, more than any other single factor, that touched off the revolution of 1848 in both Vienna and Hungary. Furthermore, it did not even achieve its object, except momentarily. For a couple of years prices remained stable at the 1811 level, as expressed in the new currency, but in 1812 the Government was forced to break its promise and to issue new paper money, and the inflation recommenced, making the condition of the fixed-income classes as miserable as it had been before the issue of the patent.

Moreover, the patent precipitated the threatening crisis with Hungary. The Diet which met in 1811 flatly denied the legality of the patent, as applied to Hungary. It admitted the issue of the currency to be one of the monarch's rights, but argued that the printing of uncovered paper money was an abuse of that right, and merely an indirect way of raising taxation through unauthorised channels. It therefore refused to take over the share of the new currency which had been allotted to Hungary, or to contribute towards the amortisation fund. On 18 May 1812, Francis dissolved it abruptly (not in the event to reconvoke it until thirteen years had passed) and promulgated the patent by royal decree.

In 1815, however, peace at last returned to Austria, this time to stay and wearing a face different from that which its earlier visits had shown. At last, Austria had been on the winning side. It had recovered all its old territories lost since 1792, except the Netherlands and the outlying possessions in West Germany, and practically all its acquisitions made at any time since that date, except Cracow (now a Free City). It had also acquired Lombardy. Its position in Germany could be regarded as more really influential than before the liquidation of the Holy Roman Empire, and it dominated Italy through its own possessions and its influence over the other Italian courts. It was booked to receive a war indemnity, instead of paying one.

The decade which followed was, nevertheless, still a very hard one. It opened with inflation still rampant. On 1 July 1816, the State again in effect repudiated a big fraction (this time 60 per cent) of its debt, and it was several years more before it proved possible, with the help of a newly-founded national bank, to stabilise the rate of the paper money and eventually to return to a metal currency. Order was thus superficially restored to the state finances, but the order was never more than superficial. Economies were made, especially on the army, and the annual deficit was reduced, but it was never wiped out. Year after year the State had to resort to the money-lenders, and the service of its loans, for which it usually had to pay dearly, became a very large item in its annual budget. Nobody seemed to mind this so long as the State papers were quoted at par, and successive ministers of finance managed to achieve this, with the help of their banker friends; but it was plain that a bill was mounting up which one day would cost someone dear.

Then 1815 and 1816 were black years for the poor, with harvests failing, prices soaring and actual starvation widespread. Thereafter, the deflation, the cessation of the stimulus of war and the reappearance on the market of English manufactured goods on the one hand and Russian and Roumanian wheat on the other, brought with them an acute economic crisis under which both the industries which had sprung up during the Continental Blockade and the Hungarian and Galician wheat-growers suffered very severely. There was extensive unemployment, accentuated by the demobilisation of the field armies. It was not until the late 'twenties that production began to rise again and economic conditions in general began to approach those usually associated with the word 'peace'.

Meanwhile, the fact that he had after all weathered so many years without net loss of territory and without serious internal trouble (all the successes having come after he had stopped taking his brothers' advice) was to Francis convincing proof of the rightness of his own principles of government, and he continued to apply them, if anything, more strictly than before. In this he was abetted and encouraged by Metternich, who, if not the author of the 'system', was certainly an approving accessory to it. The only important change in tone was that under the influences of Metternich and of Francis's pious fourth wife, Carolina Augusta, the alliance with the Catholic Church became more intimate. The control of the press, the universities and intellectual life in general was even intensified under the hands of Metternich and the new chief of police, Sedlnitzky, a man even less liberal than any of his predecessors. The re-acquired or newly-acquired provinces were re-organised, or organised, on the now established principle of centralised rule from above; Lombardy and Venetia were, it is true, styled a kingdom and given a viceroy (the Archduke Rainer) and certain separate institutions, with Italian as the the language of administration, justice and education, but they enjoyed no more real self-government than the rest of Francis's dominions. Only Hungary provided a partial exception. When, in 1820 and 1821, the Hungarian counties made difficulties about delivering the men and supplies which Metternich wanted for sup-pressing the threat of revolution in Italy, the government put in 'administrators', who collected what it wanted by main force; but this operation proved so difficult and expensive that in 1825 Francis found it expedient, after all, to reconvoke the Diet and to give it a sort of apology for having violated its rights and a promise to respect them in future. Even this, however, amounted to little more than an assurance that he would use legal forms for getting his own way.

And, as in the war years, so in the fifteen years which followed them, the country in general seemed no whit ahead of its rulers. In 1820 and 1821 there were stirrings in Lombardy–Venetia, themselves not so much reactions against Austrian rule as reflexes of movements elsewhere in Italy. After a relatively small number of arrests had been made, the 'Kingdom' settled down into submission. Tranquillity was complete in the Austrian and Bohemian Lands, and hardly less so in Galicia; the modest, but in its way attractive, 'Biedermeier' culture of the period is essentially one of acceptance.

Only Hungary kicked against the pricks, and the Hungarian Diet itself, as late as 1825, was looking back rather than forward: defending a medieval constitution, not looking for a new life. This was broadly true even of its successor, which Francis convoked in 1830, this time in view of the revolutionary situations in Western Europe, Russian Poland and Italy, which again seemed to Metternich to call for defensive preparations. Most of the Diet's members were as anxious as Metternich himself to keep revolutionary infection from spreading, and they voted the required supplies readily enough. At the same time, Francis had asked the Diet to crown his elder son, Ferdinand, in his own life-time. A coronation in Hungary traditionally involved a recapitulation of the nation's rights, which the monarch, having agreed the list, then swore to respect. They therefore insisted that Francis should at last give a proper hearing to their long-disregarded *gravamina*; and Francis promised to do this at a Diet to meet the next year.

The Diet in fact assembled only in 1832, after a postponement excused by the cholera which ravaged Galicia and Hungary in 1831, but really occasioned by fear of a political infection; and by that time the successes of liberalism in Western Europe had produced a wide-spread reaction throughout the monarchy. The idea of reform was suddenly everywhere in the air. As things stood, it could not without danger be voiced outside Hungary, but there the political atmosphere had been almost magically transformed by the dynamic genius of Count István Széchenyi, a young aristocrat who, on his travels in Western Europe, had been deeply shocked by the contrast between conditions there and in his own country. On his return, he had initiated a variety of practical enterprises, including the foundation of a steamship service on the Danube, and was electrifying public opinion by his writings: according to his revolutionary doctrine, the venerated Hungarian Constitution, with its sacrosanct array of noble privileges which exempted the noble from taxation, proclaimed his land inalienable and left him almost absolute master of his peasants, was much less a fortress defending her against foreign oppression than a prison confining her in poverty and backwardness.

Széchenyi made little practical headway at the Diet with his proposals; nor, indeed, did he ever succeed in giving the Hungarian reform movement the direction wished by himself, which was one of orderly movement, paternally directed from above. But he set its floods in motion, and before the Diet (which sat for four years) had ended, the system had been dealt a mortal blow by the death of Francis, on 2 March 1835. Ferdinand was a kindly simpleton, clearly incapable of ruling except in name. Francis had left a political testament, enjoining his son 'not to displace any of the foundations of the structure of the State, to rule and not to alter' and to place himself under the governance of his youngest uncle, the Archduke Ludwig, and of Metternich. Metternich's numerous enemies, however, secured the addition to this Council of Regency (as it was in practice, although the name was Staats-und-Konferenzrat) of Ferdinand's brother, Franz Karl, and of Count Franz Kolowrat, a Bohemian aristocrat who for some years past had been *de facto* in charge of the internal administration and finances of the monarchy. The Archduke was there chiefly to represent the future, in the person of his son, Francis Joseph, the heir presumptive to the throne (since Ferdinand was unlikely to become a father). But Kolowrat was Metternich's embittered rival, and, although his own liberalism was very half-hearted, he was for that reason the hope of all liberals in Vienna, as well as of all those who, for any other reason, disliked Metternich. In fact, the new regime was little more progressive than the old, especially as Ludwig, himself in any case a man of narrow views and limited abilities, tried, out of piety, to fulfil Francis's deathbed injunctions. But it was incomparably less effective, its own immobility resulting chiefly from the reciprocal neutralisation of the equal and opposite forces of Metternich and Kolowrat. It could only be a question of time before its foundations were sucked away by the waves of pent-up discontents, national, political and social, which were now surging all around it.

For in spite of everything, the monarchy of the *Vormärz* (as the years preceding the revolution of March 1848, are commonly known) was a very different place from the monarchy of the 1790's. The population had increased, with variations between and within the Lands, by something like 40 per cent. Most of the country was still agricultural, but the larger towns, headed by Vienna, were growing apace. Industrialisation, after its long setback, was making progress again, and changing its character. The use of machinery was spreading, and many industries, headed by the textile industries of Bohemia and Lower Austria, were going over from handwork to factory production. The second stage of this process was just setting in with the construction of the railways, which, besides themselves calling into being much new industry in connection with their construction and equipment, made possible, for the first time, the large-scale development of heavy industry and mining. To the class structure of the monarchy was now added, on the one hand, a powerful independent entrepreneur class, representing the new financial and industrial interests, and on the other, a not inconsiderable, although localised, industrial proletariat. The countryside itself was altering, socially and economically. Landlords, especially on the largest estates in the more advanced Lands (the great Bohemian and Moravian landlords leading the way), were going in seriously for production for profit, and this and other factors, which did not, indeed, all operate in the same direction, were altering the position of the peasants, in relation both to their landlords and to the State.

All these developments were producing a number of social problems, which affected all the Lands of the monarchy, although not in equal degree. By 1847 the villein peasants were almost everywhere in a fair way to winning their battle. The value to their landlords of *robot* unwillingly performed and of dues ingeniously sabotaged had become so patently inferior to that of free hired labour that the more progressive landlords were themselves petitioning for the 'liberation' of this class; the main big outstanding question was that of compensation for the landlords, and the chief opponent of the reform—outside those landlords who, either from the remote geographical situation of their estates or for lack of capital, still clung to a pre-capitalist economy— was the government, which declared that it could not itself finance the reform, and even objected to proposals for carrying it through by private enterprise, as calculated to compete with the government on the credit market. Far more grievous in reality than that of the peasant farmers was the position of that agrarian class, in most provinces now outnumbering the peasant-holders, which the rapid growth of the population had left with holdings below subsistence level, or altogether landless. Among these there was in the 'forties constant and increasing distress, which catastrophic harvests in 1846 and 1847 made almost unbearable; in each of these years thousands of people died of sheer starvation. Prices of foodstuffs soared again, to twice, thrice, even five times the 1844 level. In addition, the feverishly developed textile industry ran suddenly into an acute crisis of over-production. Even the pitiful wage, itself barely enough to keep them from starvation, which the exploited factory hands had received, was now lost to many of them, leaving them dependent on crudely organised public works, or on charity. There were riots and machine-wreckings, and the suburbs of Vienna, Prague and other industrial centres swarmed with starving and desperate beggars.

The tribulations of the poor did not, however, threaten the integrity of the monarchy or the stability of its regime. The national aspirations of its peoples did, except in so far as their complexity and frequent mutual antagonisms offered the possibility of using one as an ally against another. In the first years of the *Vormärz*, the strongest of these national movements was still the Hungarian, which developed with extraordinary rapidity. Széchenyi, the pioneer of 1830, was, by 1836, already being shouldered aside by the younger generation. The mouthpiece of this was the fiery and radical Louis Kossuth, an intemperate but inspiring and convincing advocate of every kind of liberal and democratic reform; unlike Széchenyi (who wished to work with Vienna), he told the nation that the first necessity was to reduce the links with Vienna to those established under the Pragmatic Sanction, both as a postulate of the nation's right to independence and as the indispensable preliminary to any further reform, political, social, economic or cultural.

The *Staatskonferenz* began by trying repression: in 1837 Kossuth and some others were arrested and imprisoned, and the country was ruled semi-dictatorially. But the flare-up of the eastern question in 1840 compelled a return to a policy of appeasement. Kossuth was released, and became the idol of the nation, which largely adopted his liberal and anti-Austrian tenets. In this situation, a group of magnates, led by Count George Apponyi and calling themselves 'progressive conservatives', came together and evolved a programme which included many of the popular desiderata in the social and economic fields; but the reforms were to be enacted from above, under elaborate safeguards and combined with strict political control and safeguards for the link with Austria. In 1843 this group persuaded Metternich to place them in charge of Hungary. The Opposition drew together in reply, and in 1847 the most level-headed among them, Francis Deák, produced for them a programme of democratic and national reform which included a responsible ministry for internal affairs, a Parliament based on an extended franchise, complete liberation of the peasants, extension of taxation to the nobles, and union with Transylvania. The 'Government Party' itself accepted many of the internal reforms, so that when the Diet met in November 1847, it was largely agreed on these points, although differing widely on the cardinal question of the link with central authority.

The Hungarian movement was, however, the work of a class which was itself almost entirely Magyar, in feeling if not in origin, and saw its Hungary in terms which, at least on the upper levels, should be a Magyar national state; and its development was now meeting with increasing opposition from the non-Magyars who formed a good half of the population. The first conflict between Magyars and non-Magyars revolved largely round the demand of the former for the extension of the use of the Magyar language in public life. In the long struggle, which had begun as early as the Leopoldian Diet, the Hungarians had at first asked for no more than the right to use what was the mother-tongue of the vast majority of those affected in communicating with the central government of their own country, and for facilities for instruction in the same language, above the elementary level. But even the former demand had brought opposition from the Croats, who would be placed at a disadvantage if the neutral Latin were replaced by Magyar; the Hungarians replied that it was unreasonable to ask them to sacrifice their convenience and national pride for the sake of the handful of Croat nobles concerned.

But soon the conflict widened, and deepened. A chauvinistic younger Magyar generation rode roughshod over the Croats' objections and also forced through legislation which left unreasonably little scope, in any field, for the non-Magyar languages of Inner Hungary; extremists wanted to turn the whole population by force into Magyars. The non-Magyar peoples, meanwhile, were experiencing their own national awakenings, and some of them were developing national ambitions which were quite incompatible with even the more restrained forms of the Hungaro-Magyar ideal. The lead was taken by the Croats, among whom French rule in Napoleon's 'Kingdom of Illyria' had powerfully stimulated national feeling. In the early 'thirties backwoods clinging of the Croat nobles to ancient forms gave way to a heady nationalism, almost pathologically anti-Magyar and dreaming of a Great Croatia, to include Dalmatia and the disputed counties of Slavonia, and to be detached from Hungary and to own allegiance only to the emperor. The ruling spirit of this new movement, the spacious-thinking Ljudevit Gaj, cherished a still wider vision, of an 'Illyria', embracing all the southern Slav peoples; with this end in view, he sought contact with the Serbs of Hungary and of the Principality. All this was viewed with pleasure in Vienna, especially by Kolowrat, who saw in the Croats a weapon which could be used against the rebellious Magyars. After a while, the government awoke, indeed, to the dangerous implications of the Illyrian doctrine, and clamped down on it, but continued to encourage Croat nationalism, which needed, indeed, no stimulus.

The Hungarian Serbs had also turned their backs on Hungary; the hearts of many of them were in Belgrade, but for the time they looked to Vienna, under whose direct orders those of them inhabiting the Military Frontier already stood, along with that half of the Croat population which was similarly placed. They developed little enthusiasm for 'Illyrianism', which they regarded as a papistical snare, but were willing enough to ally themselves with the Croats against Budapest. Some of the Slovaks looked similarly towards Prague, or even Russia, with visions of a Czecho-Slovak polity or a great Pan-Slav State, while others said that they were willing to be good Hungarians, but not Magyars. Others, indeed, with most of the Germans of Inner Hungary and the majority of its Jews, supported the Hungarians, and far from resisting Magyarisation, regarded it as a benefit and an opportunity.

The Hungarian drama was re-enacted in Transylvania, with a time-lag. After a start retarded by particularist and conservative feeling, the nobles of the Grand Principality became enthusiastic partisans of the union with Hungary. Pending this, they tried to enact legislation, on the Hungarian model, which offended the national feeling and the historic rights of the 'Saxons' and drove them, too, closer to Vienna. At the same time, the under-privileged Roumanians, who now constituted a full half of the population, agitated for social emancipation and national liberties. The ultimate ideal of many of these was unification with their brothers across the Carpathians in an independent national State; but, so long as the Danubian Principalities were under Turkish rule, they too, perforce, placed their hopes in Vienna.

In the West, the Italian provinces had become lost spiritually to the monarchy ever since the aspiration towards national unity had fairly taken hold of the Italian people as a whole. In Lombardy and Venetia themselves the national movement was more demonstrative than formidable (Venice passed for the least revolutionary of all the larger cities of Italy), but it was notorious that Charles Albert of Piedmont was only waiting his chance to prise the two provinces out of Austria's hold, and this prospect, combined with the obligation to protect Austria's other clients in Italy, made it necessary to keep a large force south of the Alps, thus denuding other danger-spots of troops.

The chief of these danger-spots, after Hungary, was for some time Galicia, but in that province the peak of the danger passed before the *Vormärz* had ended. In February 1846 the Polish National Committee in Paris, singularly miscalculating the situation, tried to launch a revolution from bases in Cracow and Galicia, where it was hoped that the peasants would join in, in return for a promise of freedom and land. The peasants, instead, used the arms issued to them to carry through a *jacquerie* against their landlords. The chief positive result of this ill-fated enterprise was that the Powers allowed Austria to annex Cracow. This fiasco left the Austrian Poles sullen and resentful, but, except for a few hotheads, convinced of the impossibility of renewing the struggle in the face of the common front formed against them by the partition-ing Powers, and the hostility of their peasants. The imperial authorities found yet another ally in the nascent national feeling of the Ruthenes of East Galicia, a backward, impoverished and almost inarticulate people who positively welcomed the tutelage of the Austrian bureaucrats in return for the protection which it gave them against the exactions of their Polish landlords.

In the heart of the monarchy, the struggle for the restoration of pro-vincial self-government, against centralised bureaucratic despotism, was led by the Estates of Bohemia, who in the 'forties began to assert them-selves with considerable vigour. This, like the Hungarian and Croat movements in their early stages, was essentially a home rule movement, and in many respects the reverse of progressive, for the document to which its supporters appealed, the *Erneuerte Landesordnung* (Revised Land Ordinance) of 1627, was, no less than the Hungarian constitution, essentially a charter of class privileges; and, although the Estates con-tained a reform party, it was, as late as 1848, in a small minority. But Bohemia and Moravia were also the scenes of a vigorous Czech national revival, which was not merely linguistic and cultural, but also, from the first, strongly political. As its immediate objective, this movement was fighting only for equal rights for the Czech language with the German in education, justice and administration, but behind this lay the vision of a Czech national state (within the monarchy) comprising not only the Lands of the Bohemian Crown, but also the Slovak areas of North Hungary. Many of the young Czech nationalists were also strongly radical in their social and political ideas. In spite of this, the Czech aristocrats patronised and fostered the Czech national movement as an ally against the mainly German bureaucracy.

The Germans of the monarchy were the most divided politically of all its component nationalities. Outside the university students, few of them were affected by the romantic nationalism which was intoxicating the Magyars, the Croats and the Czechs. Neither, outside the Tyrol, was there any very strong provincial particularism. The whole Austrian system, although as much a negation of German nationalism as of Czech or Magyar, yet rested mainly on the shoulders of a bureaucracy and Corps of Officers mostly composed of Germans by origin or adoption. And conversely, a substantial part of the German middle classes derived their livelihoods from serving the monarch. Thus, the vast majority of these classes were loyal to the monarchy, and the greater number were also supporters of the centralising character of its system; this if only because a centralised state was the best safeguard for the Germans whose positions were being threatened by the rising Czech nationalism in Bohemia and Moravia and (in a lesser degree) by a parallel, although still much weaker, Slovene nationalism in Styria and Carinthia.

On the other hand, by far the largest part of the entrepreneur and pro-fessional class of the monarchy (outside Lombardo-Venetia) was, again, German or German-speaking Jewish (the Jews at that time usually identified themselves with the Germans). It was German and German-Jewish business men and financiers who chiefly fretted against the dead hand of the bureaucracy, German and German-Jewish intellectuals who found the censorship burdensome. Consequently Vienna, in particular, became the centre of a vigorous reform movement which was highly critical of the regime from its own point of view, and thanks to the social and financial status of its members, of an importance quite dis-proportionate to its size in numbers. Its weakness lay in the impossi-bility (soon to become apparent) of reconciling the mutually conflicting claims of liberalism and nationality.

Thus by the turn of 1847–8 almost every social class and almost every nationality in the monarchy was chafing under the system and demand-ing change. A touch (such as in the event was provided by the revolu-tion in Paris) would be enough to bring the old structure down, but what would succeed it, no man could then tell.

CHAPTER XV

ITALY, 1793–1830

THE dates 1793 and 1830 are not very helpful limits. Much that was of great importance happened in Italy between them, yet they are themselves hardly significant. 1793 began with the murder of the French agent in Rome (13 January) but this is not enough to mark an epoch. Although Italy was by then already involved in the diplomatic and military struggles of Europe, the course of her history was decisively changed only in 1796. In that year, it may be said, the *Settecento* ended and the Revolution came to the peninsula; the modern history of Italy begins with the physical presence of the French army. The next great change came at the collapse of the Napoleonic system— the restorations of 1799–1800 were only an interlude—and this chapter can be roughly divided at 1814. Before that collapse the whole peninsula had gradually been subjected to common governmental and political influences for the first time in centuries; after 1814, although all the restored regimes had to take account of Austrian predominance, the peninsula was again fragmented. 1830 did not change this state of affairs.

The starting-point of this assessment must be the structure of Italy in 1793. In no sense was it then a unity and its components were to absorb the shock of the revolution in very different ways. Its fundamental divisions were topographical: within regions divided by mountains and climate there existed widely differing societies, separated from one another even by language. Political boundaries stabilised their provincialism. Italy consisted of a jumble of states of which the kingdoms of Sardinia and Naples[1], the grand-duchy of Tuscany, the lesser duchies of Massa and Carrara, Parma and Modena and the principality of Piombino were monarchical. There were the three republics of Venice, Genoa and Lucca and a tiny fourth in San Marino. In the Po valley, Austrian Lombardy embraced the old duchies of Milan and Mantua. Finally, across the middle of the peninsula sprawled the Papal States.[2] The governments of this hotch-potch had developed in very different ways in spite of superficial similarities. Several of them had been affected by 'enlightened despotism', yet, in spite of attempts at rationalisation, their structure was often scarcely more coherent than that of the peninsula as a whole. Localism, privilege and legal

---

[1] The kingdom of Sardinia consisted of Savoy, Piedmont, the county of Nice and the island of Sardinia. That of Naples included Sicily.

[2] For a fuller description of the structure of Italy before 1793, see vol. VIII, ch. XIII. B.

diversification survived the reforming rulers and their civil servants. It is impossible to select a 'typical' Italian state of 1793; they were as varied as the landscape itself.

Only in one very general way did Italy show a certain homogeneity. Conditions of life differed greatly and the organisation of property took many forms, but the economies of all the states and regions except the great seaports were dominated by agriculture. Consequently, the social structure of all of them was shaped by the overwhelming numerical preponderance of the peasants, varied as the precise meanings of that term might be. The population had risen during the century and it is likely that the peasants' standard of living had fallen; most of them were poor and many were destitute. Urban life was too deeply embedded in this rural setting and too anaemic to develop another class which could compete with the landowners for social power. Only the clergy could match the power of the nobility and as landowners the two groups often had identical interests. The social pre-conditions of the capitalist mentality were lacking; there was little large-scale industry and much to prevent its appearance in privileges, out-dated mercantilist ideas, and localism. Eighteenth-century Italy was a bundle of societies in which small privileged classes enjoying wealth and power resisted the encroachments which monarchs and bureaucrats made in the interests of general well-being. The peasants looked on and did not understand where their interest lay in the struggle. Yet this pattern was blurred and confused at a hundred points by local and temporary differences.

The first impact of the French Revolution on these societies came before the invasion. The peninsula was so open to foreign social and cultural influences that some response, even if only from the intellectuals, was inevitable. Some were enthusiastic, like the Milanese Gorani, who became a French citizen and joined the Jacobin club; others, even when excited by the possibility of general enlightenment, were more hesitant. The Lombard economist Pietro Verri thought the Italians were too immature to be worthy of the reign of virtue. Very few Italians at first saw as far as this. The revolution in France was to them simply one more change in those diplomatic variables of which Italian history had for so long been a function. (For the Papacy's special response, see Chapter VI.) Then the rulers and the nobles began to change their views under the impression of the tales of the *émigrés* and the crumbling of the monarchy. Because of this the first important effect of the revolution in Italy was the abandonment by the princes of their patronage of the reforming civil servants; now the privileged classes could counter-attack. Some intellectuals became alarmed too; Gorani abandoned the revolution in the Terror. After 1793, such changes were hurried on by the war. Its outbreak finally divided the states into two groups, the allies and the neutrals.

Among the former, the position of Sardinia was the most understandable. Her alliances with Austria and Great Britain followed logically from the French aggression which absorbed Savoy and Nice; the influence of the *émigrés* at Turin was hardly needed to bring her into the coalition. In any case, war seemed to offer her king the chance of resuming the traditional policy of aggrandisement by exploiting the rivalry of great powers. Naples became a belligerent not only because of her Austrian queen, but also because of her special interests as a maritime power—a source at once of weakness and of strength in her dealings with France and Great Britain. Lombardy, as an Austrian possession, was involved willy-nilly in the war and, to a lesser degree, so were the neutrals, Tuscany, Genoa, Venice and Modena. Genoa had declared herself neutral in 1792, deeply distrustful of Sardinia and well aware of the importance of her commercial ties with France. Venice found her position more cramped but also remained neutral. Hercules III of Modena did the same. Tuscany was forced to dismiss the French minister after some British diplomatic and naval bullying but in 1795 she resumed complete neutrality and made a treaty with France.

Below the governmental level, the attitudes of Italians were slowly crystallising under the strains of war. Some of them were frightened by the tales of the *émigrés*, but others began to look to the new republic more hopefully. The most interesting political development of these years was the sympathy for France and the principles of the revolution which gradually drew together widely separated strands of opinion whose only common feature was frustration under the existing regimes. Reformers who could no longer obtain a hearing, anti-curialists and Jansenists in the church, freemasons and *illuminati* who resented cultural backwardness and bigotry, could all find a common focus for their hopes in republicanism and the rights of man. In 1793 an address from some Italian refugees to the Convention already announced confidently 'les italiens vous attendent'. It was untrue—and, indeed, was always to remain untrue for the majority of Italians—but it was the first gesture of a renewed Italian political life.

The origins and nature of this new political dissent have been much studied. It was stimulated by the panic shown in some of the states as the revolution went on. The Austrians were less alarmed than some rulers, but even they began to look suspiciously at the reformers whom Joseph II had encouraged. Men like Pietro Verri, once employed by the government, now found themselves distrusted. Yet Lombardy produced few 'Jacobins'[1] before 1796, in spite of the assertions of refugees at the time and historians since, and it was in other states that

---

[1] This confusing term, loosely used by contemporary propagandists and subsequent historians, does not imply common positive policies nor, often, anything more than hostility to the old regime.

governments first turned frustration into sedition. In Naples, repression was swift and violent. In 1794 there were executions and exiles; things became worse when a rising took place in Sicily in the following year. In 1794 there were executions in Turin, too. Such a potential was bound to be exploited by the French agents in the peninsula. Tilly, at Genoa, and his successor Cacault (who also served at Venice and Florence) conducted propaganda and espionage and helped the discontented to take refuge in the neutral states or France. They could point to the Convention's decree of 19 November 1792, which promised 'fraternity and succour to all the peoples who want to recover their liberty'. Persecution was their best ally; the common experience of exile was decisive in bringing about the cross-fertilisation of political dissent in Italy. Refugees came to France from all the states, but above all from Sardinia and Naples. There is little evidence that they had ever enjoyed wide and popular support in Italy, yet this was not important for the subsequent shaping of the legend about them. Exile began the fusion of the republican and democratic ideas of the Revolution with a con-sciousness of Italian nationality. The refugees found common enemies in the governments which had driven them out; to some of them alliance with the French and a united Italian state quickly seemed the logical consequence. Pre-eminent among those who encouraged such views was Buonarroti, *commissaire* of the French Republic in Oneglia (which was occupied in 1794). He became the main channel by which the Italian refugees urged on the French government the wisdom of supporting revolution in Italy. Nevertheless, more than exile was required to create Italian nationalism; the next step in the process was to be supplied only by occupation and revolution.

The invasion of 1796 ended the *Guerre des Alpes* and the revolution entered Italy. Bonaparte did more than alter the diplomatic situation there: he destroyed the coalition and transformed the European scene. The battles of April forced Sardinia to accept an armistice, and a campaign which followed in the Po valley resulted quickly in the fall of Milan (15 May), the submission of Modena (17 May) and the Austrian evacuation of Lombardy. A besieged garrison stayed in Mantua. The Neapolitans hastily came to terms (and made a definitive peace in October) and the Pope obtained an armistice. An autumn campaign thwarted the Austrian attempts to relieve Mantua and recover Lombardy, and by the end of the year the coalition was in ruins. Genoa had agreed to close her ports to the British. The treaty of San Ildefonso (19 August) between France and Spain destroyed any hope of effective British action in the Italian theatre by forcing the withdrawal of the British fleet and the abandonment of Corsica. At the beginning of 1797, only Mantua stood between Bonaparte and the resumption of the offensive; when it fell, the coalition entered its final agony.

Bonaparte pressed into Carinthia and on 18 April the Preliminaries of Leoben were signed.[1]

For the first time in half a century Austria was not the dominating power in Italy. France was now her companion and rival and the way in which her preponderance would be used was not known. Because of the secret Preliminaries, the French Directory could not take the obvious course of realising its new assets by exchanging Italian territory for a frontier on the Rhine. Bonaparte's prestige and power made it impossible to do this, whatever the wishes of the Directors. Moreover, other policies had their advocates at Paris. The instructions given to Bonaparte in 1796 had been more than fulfilled. The coalition had been broken up, Genoa's subservience confirmed and the British strategical position in the Mediterranean compromised. In addition, huge territories had been conquered. Here lay the difficulty; the alternative to using them for bargaining was to organise them—but how? There were good ideological and political arguments for the creation of satellite republics, but some of the Italian refugees who followed the French army back to Italy were asking for more. They wanted a united Italy. They should have known already that the French would not stomach this: in 1795 the Directory had hopefully negotiated with the Sardinian 'tyrant' and was prepared to leave him on his throne; it had treated the conquered area around Oneglia as French territory; Bonaparte himself had announced his intention of governing his conquests directly in the immediate future. Moreover, and this the Italians did not know, even in May 1796 reports began to come to the Directory from its diplomatic agents in Italy which strengthened its unwillingness to embrace an ideologically correct or even a republican solution of the Italian problem. As the Directory told its foreign minister, the Italians, rotted by despotism, were not yet ready for liberty.

The Italian refugees' prospects of influencing French policy had been, indeed, worse than ever when the invasion began. Their association with Buonarroti had compromised them; after his arrest for complicity in the Babeuf plot he was a useless and embarrassing ally. The Directory now regarded his Italian friends as guilty by association and henceforth proceeded on the largely mistaken assumption that the Italian patriots were Babouvist social revolutionaries. It was an assumption which was to have immense and disastrous consequences for the Italians; its immediate import could be seen when the French contemptuously abandoned the little republic of Alba set up by refugees in Piedmont after the invasion and ordered the Italian revolutionaries to stop bothering the Sardinian government. Nor could the unitarists find much support for their ideas in Italy; when an essay competition was

---

[1] A note at the end of this chapter summarises the complicated territorial changes which took place from this time onwards.

held in Milan in September 1796 on the theme of the best way of organising Italy, only one-third of the Italian entrants advocated unification.

It was the views of Bonaparte which mattered most at this juncture. He could indulge them because of his government's financial and military dependence on him. In Italy, the essence of the peace of Campo Formio (17 October 1797) was concession to Austria to secure her acquiescence in the continued existence of his creations, the Italian satellite republics. These had already begun to appear in 1796. At first it had suited the convenience of the French army to hand over Lombardy to a body of Italians termed a 'Central Administration'. Revolutions at Reggio and Modena had followed; Bonaparte indulged the rebels and, ignoring the wishes of his government, allowed the formation of the Cispadane Republic from Modena and the Legations of Bologna and Ferrara (October 1796). In June 1797 the future of Genoa was settled by the creation of the Ligurian Republic. On 15 July, the Cispadane was united with Lombardy to form the Cisalpine Republic. When it had been enlarged by the former Venetian territory west of the Adige and the Valtelline, the Cisalpine stood complete as the first great essay in Italian consolidation. Bonaparte had justified his boast to the Cisalpine National Guard that 'it is the soldier who founds republics'. (He had gone on to warn them that 'it is the soldier who maintains them'.)

The Directory unwillingly ratified the treaty of Campo Formio and soon afterwards appointed Bonaparte to the command of the Army of England, a post in which a vaulting ambition might easily o'er-leap itself. But the major achievements of his proconsulate in Italy remained as political facts: the extinction of the Republic of Venice and the consolidation of North Italy in a republican form. There also remained the presence of the French army. The effects of the revolution, therefore, did not end with the removal of Bonaparte. The experience of French domination which followed it was just as decisive in shaping the views of Italians. They were now to suffer from the Directory's uncertainty about its real aims in Italy, from its repeated changes of its commanders and its inability to control them, and from the evidence which soon began to appear that Campo Formio was not to be a final settlement and that war might begin again.

The most important signs of danger were a new and harsh treaty of alliance which bound the Cisalpine more tightly than ever to France, and the appearance of the Roman Republic as a new satellite in February 1798. Its creation was a clear breach of the Campo Formio settlement; so was the absorption of Piedmont into France in December 1798. Together with the foundation of the Parthenopaean Republic at Naples in January 1799, this completed the subjection of almost the whole of

Italy to republican institutions; even oligarchic Lucca had been purged and reformed on democratic lines (2–4 February 1799). The constitutions of the new republics, allowing for local differences of detail and nomenclature, were roughly that of France under the constitution of the year III.[1] Nearly all of them began with a declaration of rights and included specific guarantees of property. Qualifications for citizenship varied but sovereignty was said to reside in the general will of the citizen body. This sovereignty sustained a bi-cameral legislature which in turn elected what was in effect an Executive Directory (although its members were called consuls in Rome and archons in Naples). Local administration was organised in departments which were divided into cantons or districts; these were then further divided into communes. The policies of these republics varied scarcely more than their structure; much was said about revolutionary legislation but not very much was done. The abolition of nobility and of legal institutions such as entails (*fideicommessi*) which supported it, the secularisation of ecclesiastical property and guarantees to its purchasers, the removal of the ecclesiastical monopoly of education and the introduction of the republican calendar were all ideologically acceptable, but were neither intended to carry a social revolution very far nor had time to do so. In some parts of Italy such innovations had been anticipated by the rule of the enlightened absolutists.

Moreover, the new states lacked power. In most of them the social foundations of republicanism were too narrow for real innovation; the Cisalpine probably achieved the widest acceptance if not allegiance, but Madame de Staël remarked that at Rome only the statues were republican. The loyalty of the peasants and *lazzaroni* to the Neapolitan Bourbons is notorious but nowhere did the masses support the new regimes. Lack of popular support explains the feebleness with which the republics resisted their overthrow in 1799. This lack sprang from their ambiguous relations with the French; ultimately the republics depended upon French military protection for their survival, yet the protecting power used them as its instruments for the exploitation of their subjects. The new states brought only taxation and a calendar which was incomprehensible and offensive to the superstitious; the protection of inventions by patent legislation or the award of bonuses to the fathers of ten children was mere tinkering with the latent demands of Italian society.[2] The republicans offered nothing to the illiterate peasant masses; Jacobin propaganda could never move the countryman so much as the sermons of his parish priest. The true republicans were always an unrepresentative minority of Italians. Even more untypical

[1] Eight are printed in *Le costituzioni italiane*, ed. A. Aquarone, M. d'Addio, G. Negri (Milan, 1958).
[2] E.g. the Neapolitan Constitution, Art. 401; and the Ligurian, Art. 379.

were those who became unitarists under the influence of republican institutions or French exploitation. When the Italian republicans enjoyed office it was without real power. They were not allowed independence in any important matter, they were checked and thwarted by French generals and diplomatic agents who intrigued against them with other Italians and, if necessary, brought them to heel by a *coup d'état*. The Directory in Paris sometimes disapproved of particular acts by its agents but was quite firm about their general function; it urged its ambassadors in Italy to consider themselves as the overseers of the actions of the governments to which they were accredited. Thus hampered, the Italians had to levy contributions for the French army, and therefore to incur the odium of the tax-gatherer for the benefit of the *Grande Nation*. Unable to remedy the financial and economic weakness of their own states, they could do nothing to win the confidence of the French; their conquerors picked and chose nervously among them, only too willing to mistake independence and integrity for anti-French or unitarist feeling. Almost from the start, the republics were doomed.

The French were, it is true, unnecessarily nervous. Their correspondence for these years contains more and more references to the *unitaire* danger, and the Cisalpine certainly contained many anti-French patriots, because refugees had been drawn to Milan from all over Italy, and especially from Venetia whose abandonment to the Austrians had been bitterly resented. Yet in the last resort the Italian revolutionaries could not afford to desert their oppressive patrons. The French were, after all, the representatives of the great Republic which was the champion of the Revolution against the powers of the old regime. When the French occupation at last collapsed in 1799 only one of the unitarists, the Cisalpine general La Hoz, could bring himself to join the allies against the French. The other Italian 'Jacobins', though they might be bitter and might belong to secret organisations like the *Raggi*, stood by the republican cause represented by the French army. The mobs which attacked the retreating French were led by priests and nobles, not by the Italian Jacobins.

When the last satellite republic, the Parthenopaean, appeared, the Second Coalition had already taken shape. The Neapolitan government, despite British misgivings but under the influence of British successes at Aboukir and Port Mahon, had invaded the Roman Republic after allying itself secretly to Austria (and subsequently to Great Britain and Russia). After the attack on Rome the French declared war, and General Championnet entered Naples on 23 January. The royal family fled to Sicily, and Championnet sought to emulate Bonaparte by founding the new republic. After this promising start to the War of the Second Coalition the French position in Italy soon crumbled. Moreau had to abandon Milan to Suvorov at the end of

April. Turin fell and Masséna threw himself into Genoa at the beginning of 1800. The French had quickly abandoned the south, and in their absence the Parthenopaean Republic came to a tragic end at the hands of the peasant army of Cardinal Ruffo. By October 1799, when Bonaparte landed at Fréjus, the French armies were divided or bottled up, the Italians had at Arezzo and Cortona shown themselves utterly hostile to their former conquerors and all the satellite republics had collapsed. The short-lived annexation of Piedmont had provoked a rising there against the French. Now a new period of exile began for the Italians who were able to escape.

Consolidation among the exiles and a reluctant acceptance of their dependence on France were the most important consequences of the restoration of 1799–1800. The occupying allied armies were soon as unpopular as the French had been, but there is little evidence that any-one wanted the satellite republics restored. It does not seem that many Italians thought more about the change of regime than was necessary. The reactions of the Italian people during these years can rarely be observed except when they were goaded to resistance by military and fiscal exactions or incited to turn on their republican fellow-countrymen by their priests. In any case the restoration was no more than an episode. In May 1800, the First Consul joined his army at Dijon and crossed the Great St Bernard. Soon he was in Milan and on 14 June the battle of Marengo re-established French supremacy in the Po valley. An armistice of five months was agreed upon and the Austrians fell back beyond the Mincio. To the disillusionment of many Italian patriots, Bonaparte set up puppet commissions of government in Milan and Turin and put Lombardy and Piedmont firmly under the control of French generals. What his policy for Italy really was, or even whether he had a policy, are questions much discussed. The circumstances in which he later talked of his plans for Italy make scepticism permissible. It is safest to look at what he actually did.

Military victory was soon followed by financial impositions and diplomatic re-organisation. Peace was finally made with the Austrians at Lunéville (9 February 1801), roughly on the same terms as at Campo Formio. Except at Rome, where Bonaparte was careful not to disturb the new Pope Pius VII, and at Naples, too remote for immediate intervention, new puppet regimes were set up. The core of the new system of French domination was the big Italian Republic in the north and the absorption of Piedmont—the entrance to the peninsula—into France itself. Subsequent territorial changes only accentuated this direct domination by France.

The war began again in 1803. In the following year came the founda-tion of the Empire. The Italian Republic became the Kingdom of Italy and on 26 May 1805 Napoleon was crowned at Milan, uttering the traditional formula 'God has given it to me, woe to him who touches it' (*Dio mi l'ha data, guai a chi la tocca*). Eugene Beauharnais was installed as viceroy in the new kingdom and Melzi d'Eril, the Lombard nobleman who had been the vice-president of the Republic and hitherto the foremost coadjutor of Bonaparte, went into retirement. The War of the Third Coalition brought more changes and by 1811 all Italy had been re-organised.

The whole peninsula was either a part of the Empire ruled directly by the emperor or his viceroy, or else a quasi-independent satrapy. Geographically the re-organisation extended as far as Illyria. Only in the island of Sicily (where the Bourbons hatched schemes of recovery) and in that of Sardinia did governments of the old regime survive. In this re-organisation it is hard to discern anything but opportunism. Had Napoleon cherished a special policy for Italy, he could have carried it out. He enjoyed a virtually complete freedom to order the peninsula as he wished. Had he wanted to do so, he could have united it; instead, its fate was decided by the conflicting pressures of strategy, family ambition, cupidity, megalomania, and the interest of France.

These years, nevertheless, were a revolutionary irruption into Italian history and their significance has been much debated. 'Our political history only begins in 1802' wrote one Napoleonic civil servant many years later; undoubtedly the importance of the period in government was enormous. The most lasting impressions may have been in the territory of the Kingdom of Italy, the biggest state diffusing common assumptions and institutions yet to appear in the peninsula. But throughout Italy, in the kingdoms and the provinces of the Empire alike, the institutions of the French Revolution enjoyed a few years' unchecked operation. In one way, the period was a restoration of enlightened despotism; Napoleonic administration provided a congenial field of activity for the reforming intellectuals of the *Settecento*. Zurlo, Murat's minister of the Interior, had been minister of finance under the Bourbons; Prina, the finance minister of the Kingdom of Italy, had been a Piedmontese bureaucrat. Romagnosi, the legal reformer, was employed as an adviser on legal and judicial matters by the government of Beauharnais. There were many others. Members of the administrations of the revolutionary republics also worked for Napoleon, though not if they had been unitarists.

Another governmental consequence of the Napoleonic re-organisation was the introduction of the Codes. With them came the re-organisation of the judicial system on French lines. Feudalism officially came to an end in Naples in 1806 and Italy began to acquire new administrative and legal forms derived from the French departmental and bureaucratic system which became the model of modernity and efficiency for many Italians. Conscription, a far less popular institution, is often said to have been important in creating a sense of Italian nationality; it may well be so, but the scholarly examination of the subject has been neglected by historians. A more obviously admirable innovation was the conduct of statistical enquiries like those mounted in France during the Consulate. They reflected a revived concern with material progress which again recalled the reformers of the previous century. The Kingdom of Italy began one in 1807 and Murat started one in 1811. The cadastral survey (*Catasto*) which had been so long delayed under the Bourbon government was begun at last in 1807.

In one way or another it is certain that thousands of Italians gained between 1801 and 1814 experience of civil and military functions which was deeply to colour their views after the restoration (below, p. 431). Many of the Napoleonic officials were to continue in administration after 1815. Meanwhile, their practical day-to-day activity did something to mitigate a dictatorship implied by the government of Italy from Paris or the emperor's campaign tent. Napoleon's control was always close; the constitutions of the Republic and the Kingdom of Italy had given only derisory powers to the representative bodies. In Naples, Murat enjoyed a greater degree of independence only because he was further away.

It is sometimes said that economic history is the best illustration of the deliberate subordination of Italian to French interests. It is true that by 1814 economic life in Italy was at low ebb, but it is not easy to assess the precise responsibility of Napoleonic government for this. Economic development had been throttled in the eighteenth century by political divisions, dependence on small local markets, customs-charges on goods in transit, currency differences, poor credit facilities and the survivals of privilege and special interest. The invasion of 1796 had severely damaged such industry as existed. *A priori*, therefore, the sort of changes Napoleon made might be expected to have beneficial effects. One of his most important steps was the consolidation of a single market of six and a half million people in the Kingdom of Italy. Beyond its boundaries, the presence of similar legal institutions, the commercial codes, the decimal currency and better communications all helped to quicken economic life. Some economic developments had important social consequences, especially in Lombardy where the land-sales of the revolutionary era led to an increase in the numbers of small and middling properties. It has been alleged that a new bourgeoisie began to consolidate its position at this time, benefiting from the damage done to the existing class-structure by the inflation of the revolutionary wars. The precise facts about this are still hard to discover, but there is, for example, some evidence in Piedmont of the breaking-up of large properties because nobles were forced to sell land to meet the French impositions. Both this land and that taken from crown and church may have gone to men with money which had been drawn from other sources. It may be significant that Napoleon allocated one of the three electoral colleges of the Republic of Italy to the merchants (the other two were respectively for land-owners and members of the professions), and at Naples twenty of the hundred seats in the new legislative body were reserved to them. On the other hand, in spite of these hints of awareness to new social demands, it is hard to believe that merchants or manufacturers were either very numerous or very important. Incomplete figures suggest that in 1811 commerce occupied about $3\frac{1}{2}$ per cent of the population of the Kingdom of Italy. Now this was in the most industrially and commercially advanced region of Italy. In default of more precise statistical evidence, it is difficult to believe that so small an occupational group could support a middle class of any significance. A similar inference may be drawn from the dependence of taxation on agriculture. In Naples, where this was most marked, it is not easy to see that land changed hands to any appreciable degree; Murat was soon complaining that the abolition of feudalism there had only led to yet further concentration of land in the hands of *ex-baroni*.

It seems likely, then, that Napoleon's admirers exaggerated the quickening of the economic life of the peninsula under his rule, though their admiration is understandable, especially under the restoration. Some obvious qualifications can safely be made. In the first place, although the re-organisation of the peninsula overcame some disruptive forces, it introduced some new ones. The annexation of Piedmont by France cut off the Lombard silk-workers from the spinners who had previously supplied them. Parma was separated from the Reggio wine-trade and its traditional transit traffic from Lombardy was diverted. Re-organisation could have unhappy effects even when far away from Italy; when the Hanse towns were swallowed in 1810, they too were closed to Lombard goods. The blockade was damaging; Italy lost, because of it, not only the British imports which had flowed in during the eighteenth century, but also a big market for raw silk. The effects of this have been most closely studied in the Kingdom of Italy whose commercial and industrial life was regulated not only in the interests of French economic warfare with Great Britain but also by Napoleon's desire to help French industrialists. Imports of machinery were discouraged so that Italy might fit into the French system not as a competing manufacturer but as a supplier of raw agricultural produce. In reverse, manufactured goods were not to be admitted to the Kingdom of Italy unless they came from the Empire. A commercial treaty in 1808 promised to Empire and Kingdom alike a 50 per cent preference in the operation of their tariffs and this suited French manufacturers. Their products gradually replaced the British—though never completely, thanks to Malta.

The distortions of economic life which were brought about by these policies were made worse by direct French impositions. There were, for example, charges for the upkeep of French troops in the peninsula as well as the load of armaments that Naples and Milan were expected to support for themselves. The Kingdom of Italy had also to make a regular contribution of two and a half million lire a month to the Empire, and such charges were another load on an over-burdened economy. Other factors—conscription, sudden and arbitrary changes of customs operations—could be added to the list of imponderable disadvantages drawn by Italy from her French connexion.

The evidence of high interest rates seems to show that uncertainty and imposition made it difficult to get capital for industrial and commercial development. Precise quantitative evidence is harder to find. Some good signs existed; the Kingdom of Italy had favourable balances of trade in 1810 and 1812, but a rise in agricultural exports was the main support of this. Some of the other figures point to different conclusions. After 1808 the number of workers in silk declined; that the wool-makers did not decrease does not count for much because their industry had never been predominantly an exporting one. The arms industry of Brescia, certainly, benefited slightly from official demand. But it was significant that when by 1812 Venetian merchants were looking for somewhere to invest the money they could no longer employ in trade, they chose land, almost the only sector of the Italian economy where good profits resulted from Napoleonic policy. The ports had declined catastrophically. Genoa, ruined by early invasions and the British blockade, received a death-blow when the imperial customs system cut it off from Lombardy. After 1809 Leghorn was rubbing along on coastal trade with France. When, in 1808, Ancona and Macerata were joined to the Kingdom of Italy, their trade with Trieste at once declined; that port was incorporated in the Empire. Their Levant and Balkan business was interrupted by the blockade. Naples suffered from this, too; but she could still enjoy her eighteenth-century export trade in agricultural produce for France. Only between 1811 and 1813 was the balance of this trade unfavourable to her.

There were also deeper-rooted obstacles to Italian economic advance which the Napoleonic period did little to overcome. Italy remained technically too backward to embark on industrialisation if she could not import machines and men to teach their use from abroad. In 1811 the flying shuttle was still unknown in the factories of Salerno. Nor, even without the blockade, is it clear that there was either the capital or the entrepreneurial imagination available for big industrial investment. Finally, a catastrophic wave of bankruptcies in Milan in 1813 was one of the most damaging effects of the Napoleonic period on the Italian economy. As the war was now being fought again in Italy itself, protests could make themselves heard. On 11 November Murat swept away all existing protective legislation and replaced it by a light tariff. At Milan the *consiglio generale di commercio* could only protest to Eugene about economic policy, but this was at least a beginning. At the end of the Napoleonic era the Italian economy was enfeebled and retarded, there was no sign of gathering momentum for take-off into industrial growth, commerce was stagnant and only agriculture had profited from the effects of Napoleonic strategy and government.

The ideological impact of the Napoleonic regime has already been touched on by implication. In any assessment of it the relations of Napoleon with the Church must be examined briefly. He remembered the hostility of the priest-led peasantry in 1796 and 1799. In 1800 Napoleon's intentions were shown by a *Te Deum* in Milan cathedral to celebrate the liberation of Italy from heretics and infidels; he was going to allow no repetition of the priest-baiting of the first Cisalpine. He was always ready to make large concessions to the Papacy in Italy if he could have what he wanted in France; and he acquiesced in the abrogation of Leopold's reforms in Tuscany. When the question of the Concordat between the Italian Republic and Rome was under discussion, his vice-president, Melzi d'Eril, found himself forced to make concessions which, as a good child of the enlightenment, he found dangerous. Later, when quarrels with the Papacy again led to the abduction of the Pope, Napoleon only reluctantly abandoned the policy of treating the Church gently.[1] This has a bearing on the popularity of the regime. The peasants in 1814 showed once more that they remained indifferent or near-indifferent to changes of government; none of them sprang to the defence of the crumbling regime but, except in the central and southern regions which were infested by brigands, neither did they ever react so violently against the French after 1801 as they had done before. There were a few attacks on the retreating French and that was all. The policy of clerical conciliation may have been successful. The lack of opposition by the traditional governing classes to the Napoleonic regime is more difficult to explain. Individual interest, local circumstances and real idealism certainly counted for more than class solidarity. All Italians, it may be presumed, found the expense and the physical cost of continual warfare unjustifiable, and the officials and bureaucrats, aware of the subordination of their views to Paris, may have felt this more than most groups. Yet they served, and they accepted Napoleonic titles.

It is very hard to assess briefly the contribution of the years between 1793 and 1814 to the later history of Italy and the *risorgimento*. Because the political structure under Napoleon was relatively stable, there may have been time for new habits of mind to harden in a way impossible

[1] Napoleon revoked the temporal power on 17 May 1809. When the bull *Quum Memoranda* excommunicated the despoilers of the Church, the annexation of the papal states followed.

before 1799. The army, officialdom and the new legal codes were regulating factors which operated all over Italy. The radicals of the 'nineties, with some exceptions and after some early episodes which had shown Napoleon's determination to hold them in check, gradually integrated themselves with the regime. Yet the French were still disliked as the predominant power, and the roots of this went back to the disillusionments of 1797 and 1798. Some men still hankered after unity, although 1814 showed how insignificant they were. The later myth that the *risorgimento* was rooted in a national consciousness already evolved before 1814 has little substance. There was some, but not much, nationalist literature; Cuoco's book on the Neapolitan revolution of 1799 was its major achievement. There were also secret societies, looking back to the unitarists of 1798–9, but often limited by an attitude of simple opposition to the French and incapable of organising a positive nationalist programme.

Only two areas lay outside the common experiences of these years: Sicily and Sardinia. The latter was really an untouched survival from the *ancien régime* and showed it by its hostility to the Piedmontese servants of Charles Emmanuel. The experience of Sicily was different, and important for its later history. Always separatist in tendency, the island's feeling of independence was accentuated after 1806 by the presence of a court in exile. This encouraged the constitutional obstreperousness of the Sicilian grandees, who still remembered the attempts of Neapolitan viceroys to curb their privileges in the previous century. The result was that the Neapolitan court became obsessed by Maria Carolina's suspicions of plots between the British and the parliamentary party of the barons. These men were moved by a mixture of local patriotism, class interest, superficial constitutional and liberal ideas, and taste for intrigue; the presence of the British brought them together and made them look like a nationalist movement. For their part, the British soldiers on the spot thoroughly distrusted Maria Carolina, and things became worse when Bentinck was sent out to advise the Bourbons in 1811. The British government simply wanted a Sicily quiescent enough to serve as a base for operations. Bentinck was therefore instructed to warn the court that it could not hope for British support against the Sicilian population if it unwisely persisted in refusing constitutional reform. He was also given control of the subsidy paid to the court and had as a last resort the power to theaten the withdrawal of the British garrison. Maria Carolina's trouble-making at last drove Bentinck into using his powers to force her withdrawal from the island. The king had by this time granted a constitution drafted on English lines along with some features of the Spanish constitution of 1812; it was hoped that this would provide settled government. Unfortunately the constitutional movement now disintegrated and

426

Bentinck became virtually a dictator, thus, ironically, inheriting the role of the eighteenth-century viceroys.

The constitutional ferment and the propaganda in favour of reform conducted in Sicily by the British made it seem in 1813 that there was a chance of launching from the island a movement of Italian liberation; Bentinck hoped to do this. Unfortunately the game was already out of his hands by the beginning of 1814. After the failure of the Moscow campaign, Eugene had led the army back across the Elbe and had then returned to Italy. He rejected a suggestion from Murat that they should together try to come to terms with the allies and instead made ready to defend the peninsula. After Leipzig Austria could deploy large forces in Italy and by February 1814 Eugene had been forced back across the Mincio. Murat had meanwhile come to an understanding with his enemies. Yet at this time it still seemed possible that Italy might survive the collapse of the Napoleonic Empire, preserving its new institutions and independent of further foreign intervention. It was even possible that Eugene himself might become the king of a new north Italian State based on the Napoleonic kingdom. At least until Murat threw himself into the war on their side, the Austrians did not exclude this possibility. But when Murat at last turned on him Eugene had to come to terms in the armistice of Schiarino Rizzino (16 April). One of its provisions was that an Italian deputation should be sent to Paris to present its views on the future of the kingdom. Disastrously, the Lombard liberals led by Confalonieri chose this moment to make the grave and compromising mistake of supporting a rising in Milan. The exact origins of the riot which followed are obscure, but one of Eugene's ministers was lynched and he himself withdrew to Bavaria. Certainly some of those who took part wanted to put Murat on the throne and others were deluded by hopes of British support. What they did, in spite of the brief appearance of a provisional government at Milan, was to put the game firmly in the hands of the Austrians. Milan was occupied and when Confalonieri and his friends reached Paris they were told that Lombardy was to be Austrian.

The Milanese liberals had not been alone in mis-judging the situation; some of them had been egged on by Bentinck, who hoped they would play a part in his schemes for Italy. As soon as he landed at Leghorn (9 March), he advocated an independent constitutional state for Italy, quarrelled violently with Murat, who had occupied Tuscany, and proclaimed the re-establishment of the Genoese Republic although his instructions were to occupy it in the name of the King of Sardinia. 'Be Italians,' he urged, and his words alarmed his government. 'He seems bent on throwing all Italy loose' wrote Castlereagh; this disapproval meant that Bentinck was bound to fail and that his Italian friends would be left without support. British policy towards liberal and national movements was cooling quickly in the spring of 1814. Frightened by what he heard from Italy and acting in what he believed to be the interests of European order, Castlereagh was fully prepared to support Austrian action in Italy and was not going to go beyond this, whatever Bentinck might say. The Austrians, who had been jolted by the Milan rising out of an earlier moderation in which they had only envisaged recovering lands east of the Mincio, were thus left free to deal as they liked with Murat.

Murat had come to terms with them in January. In return for attacking Eugene he was guaranteed his crown and an accession of territory containing nearly half a million people from the former papal states. This agreement had been the basis of his actions in March and April, and he had performed his part of the contract. But he had done so hesitatingly and half-heartedly. Also, during the advance into the northern half of the peninsula, he had allowed his officers to try to whip up support for a nationalist programme. With his troops in possession of half Italy his position seemed strong; even Castlereagh was prepared to acquiesce in the agreement with the Austrians if some decent compensation could be found for the Neapolitan Bourbons. Unfortunately, Murat did not believe that this was British policy; he could only see the actions of Bentinck, which seemed to be as much directed against himself as against Eugene. He therefore dallied and intrigued again with Eugene and this weakened his position when, at Vienna, the newly restored Bourbons of France began to remember the Neapolitan branch of the family. At the Congress, Murat's emissaries could not obtain a hearing. He was, in fact, solely dependent upon the good-will of Austria since the British would not oppose Austrian policy in Italy. Even then, he might have kept his throne had he not gone back on his undertakings when Napoleon escaped from Elba. Seeking a quick success, Murat invaded the papal states and turned out the Grand Duke of Tuscany. On 30 March 1815 he issued at Rimini the famous proclamation whose summons to defend the cause of Italian liberty met with so little response. It was not enough. He could not cross the Po, turned south again and was finally defeated in May. After this Austria had no further obligations towards him. He left Italy on 19 May and with him went the last chance of an Italian solution to the Italian problem.

The pattern of the restoration was determined by these failures. Its basis was a reinforced Austrian predominance in the peninsula. The keystone of this supremacy was the new Kingdom of Lombardy and Venetia. This left Austria in a stronger strategical position than ever before. Within her provinces a pedantic but dependable bureaucracy, smaller than the Napoleonic, governed the country with the support of the army. Many of the Napoleonic officials were dismissed. Austrian judicial procedure was re-introduced but the French commercial code remained substantially intact and all alienations of property carried out under the fallen regime were at once given legal recognition (11 May 1815). The provinces enjoyed as little autonomy as had Lombardy under Joseph II, and a customs-barrier separated them at the Mincio. The viceroy rarely heeded the major tax-payers who formed the provincial and communal administration. He carried out a policy made in Vienna which included tariffs in favour of Austria and heavier taxation to pay for an elaborate police and censorship.

The Austrian predominance was expressed elsewhere in the peninsula by Austrian garrisons and dynastic connexion. Two states were directly ruled by Habsburgs. In Parma Marie-Louise was installed, with her paramour, Neipperg, as counsellor. At her death the duchy was to revert to the Parmesan Bourbons. Tuscany was ruled by Ferdinand III and he was also to have the reversion of Lucca when the Bourbons left it to go back to Parma. Tiny San Marino was the only republic to survive. The Papal States were restored and the Kingdom of Naples re-appeared as the Kingdom of the Two Sicilies. The Kingdom of Sardinia swallowed Genoa and the rest of the former Ligurian Republic, and regained Nice, Savoy and Piedmont. In Modena, Francis IV was put back and it was arranged that Massa-Carrara should be added to his territories when its ruler, his mother, died.

It is not easy to generalise about these regimes. Each reflected the interplay of local factors, the strength or weakness of Napoleonic achievements, the lessons or the bitterness of exile. No two were exactly alike, and all of them were carefully watched by an Austrian government as anxious to avoid provoking opposition as to crush it when provoked. Although none of them could progress freely towards reform, each could choose for itself how far it would go back towards the old regime, and few did not find some part of the Napoleonic structure to preserve. In the Kingdom of the Two Sicilies Metternich had in 1815 made stipulations to Ferdinand I about the nature of the restoration. There were to be no extreme measures of repression, no repudiation of the public debt, no cancellation of Murat's pension and titles, and a secret treaty provided that there should be no constitutional change without Austrian approval. Since there was a great fund of popular loyalism at Naples and little support for Murat, the restored regime succeeded at first in being sensible and moderate. The Napoleonic Codes were maintained, feudalism was not restored. Napoleonic personnel stayed in office and the independence of Sicily was respected. A change came after Murat's unsuccessful attempt to invade the kingdom and his execution in October 1815. Canosa, the minister of police, launched a series of measures against liberals and adherents of Murat. In December 1816 the two kingdoms were again united and all independent Sicilian institutions destroyed; the British presence had encouraged the Sicilian constitutionalists to over-play their hand but the British garrison had been withdrawn in 1815. One of the most striking confirmations of the government's anti-liberal tendency was the Concordat of 1818 which made concessions to the Papacy inconceivable in eighteenth-century Naples. But a new Code of 1819 kept the Napoleonic legal reforms.

In the Papal States, Cardinal Consalvi had hoped that the return of the Legations and the Marches would make possible some reform of the governmental structure. His aims were centralisation and the introduction of more laymen into government. Although the restored regime was not harsh and the *Motu Proprio* of 6 July 1816 did not sweep away all Napoleonic innovations, these hopes were thwarted. Tuscany was different, a liberal oasis. Under Ferdinand III, the laws of Leopold I were re-introduced and they had been as enlightened and efficient as the Napoleonic. Free trade retained official favour in Tuscany at a time when it was elsewhere distrusted as political liberalism. Tuscany was the only state not to admit within its borders the revived society of Jesus, and in Florence there began to appear a liberal intellectual élite which was to contribute importantly to the later *risorgimento*. Parma, too, avoided retrogression and retained the Codes and administrative practice of the Napoleonic period. In Modena, although Francis IV quickly established an unenviable reputation as a miserly reactionary and repealed many French innovations, there was no restoration of feudal law or *fideicommessi*. In the Kingdom of Sardinia the reaction was formally complete; the king and court re-entered Turin in the pig-tails and tricorns of the previous century. Government was restored to the hands of the 'pure', remarked Balbo later, and the 'pure' were those who had done nothing for fifteen years. Mediocrity was now firmly in the saddle and those who had shown ability under Napoleon were shunned as moral lepers. But because the monarchy was popular and could rely on local patriotism it did not need to be harsh. Nor can Sardinia really be thought of as a purely Italian state; the cultural influence of France was bound to be felt there under any regime. After a moment's hesitation, the Napoleonic currency was maintained, though the Codes were not. Moreover, Victor Emmanuel distrusted Austrian designs on Piedmontese territory. His was the one state free or almost free from Austrian influence at the restoration.

Such divergencies make it difficult to generalise about the restorations. Nowhere was there a complete reaction and nowhere was there any violent resistance; the presumption must be that few Italians were much disturbed. Particularism and mercantilism were again in fashion. Yet, although restoration was accomplished without much difficulty, evidence of discontent soon began to appear. Some connexions have been traced between the liberal movements of the restoration and such anti-French movements of the revolutionary era as the Raggi. These had been followed under Napoleon by other secret societies of which the most famous is the Carbonari. This organisation, beginning in Naples as an anti-Bourbon movement, had become anti-Muratist at the change of regime and had then reverted to anti-Bourbon activity at the restoration. During the suppression of brigandage it had spread all over the south and in 1814 Murat's invasion had taken it into the Romagna. It was to dominate the Italian conspiracies of the restoration and had led to the creation of such other societies as the Piedmontese Federati. The aims and social composition of its lodges varied from place to place. In Naples it was increasingly drawn from the fairly well-off. In the Papal States it was secular and anti-theocratic. In Piedmont the conspirators envisaged working through a member of the Piedmontese royal house. The lodges lent themselves to varied uses; blackmail, intimidation and 'protection' were common in Naples. The story of the secret societies is still very obscure; much remains to be discovered about them. The operation of such anti-liberal secret societies as the Calderari complicates the picture still further.

Other impulses to disaffection arose, not from secret societies with years of plotting behind them, but from simple disappointment with the restoration. This was above all true in Lombardy where the group of young men about Confalonieri and his newspaper, the *Conciliatore*, linked the constitutional aspirations of liberals to plans for educational and economic improvement; Confalonieri himself dabbled with Lancastrian schools and sponsored the first steamboat to appear on the Po while at the same time plotting with the Carbonari. The newspaper, founded in 1817, survived barely a year, yet in that time it provided a focus for literary and intellectual opposition to Austrian rule. Elsewhere there were other special and local reasons for discontent. In the Papal States, the Romagna felt the contrast between the rule of the returned Papal legates and that of the Napoleonic administrators. In the south, Sicilian separatism was revived by the destruction of the 1814 constitutional settlement. All over Italy there were soldiers who were discontented with enforced idleness. And there was also growing up a new generation which had grasped the idea of the *carrière ouverte aux talents*, the Julien Sorels of Italy. No safety valves were available to these pressures. The Austrians suppressed the *Conciliatore*, and Canosa held down the Kingdom of Naples. Because no institutions existed through which discontent could be expressed, great symbolic importance came to be attached to the Spanish constitution of 1812. In 1820 there broke a wave of disturbances to which many of these elements powerfully contributed.

The revolution in Naples had military leadership. Although their interests had been safeguarded in 1815, many of Murat's officers felt that they were being unjustly discriminated against in promotion. The rivalry of Carbonari and Calderari had led almost to civil war in some regions and this focused the soldiers' sense of grievance. The lodges of the Carbonari formed a link between them and the middling landowners who ran most of the lodges. In so far as they were defined, the aims of the Carbonari were limited monarchy, administrative reform, the continuation of the assault on feudalism and the abandonment of mercantilism. Occasionally there were hints of a more active Carbonarist interest in land-reform. In 1820 the soldiers and Carbonari suddenly came together because of circumstance; in the long run this was a source of weakness but it produced the Neapolitan revolution.

In Naples the repressive measures of the regime reached a climax in May and June 1820. In Spain there had been a successful revolution in January and for the moment it did not look as if the powers were going to intervene there; perhaps, then, there was reason to think they would not intervene if a rising took place in Naples. Spain was also connected with Naples through Ferdinand. He had a claim to the inheritance of the Spanish throne; to maintain his rights there he had taken an oath to maintain the 1812 constitution and, if he could do this in Spain, why could he not also swear to uphold a Neapolitan constitution? On 2 July there was a mutiny in the garrison at Nola, and the local Carbonari supported it. The garrison at Capua joined in the next day and General Pepe assumed the leadership of the rebels. The government soon gave in and promised a constitution on the Spanish model. A new ministry, consisting of former sympathisers with Murat, was set up, but contained no members of the Carbonari; this was important, for the lodges were the only effective popular or semi-popular support available to liberals. Pepe was the only real link between the ministry and the Carbonari.

It was not surprising that the Neapolitan revolution should have been followed a week later by a Sicilian separatist rising. Its disorders soon alarmed the possessing classes in the island, which was paralysed during the summer while the revolution was contained by the aristocracy and members of the corporations. The rebels were weakened by the rivalry of Palermo (where the original outbreak had taken place) with Messina, and they finally capitulated in September. When, on 1 October, the new parliament met at Naples it contained no Sicilian deputies. It supported a Carbonarist ministry deluded by the belief that Great Britain would, if necessary, intervene to protect Neapolitan constitutionalism and by confidence in Ferdinand's word.

Unfortunately the attitude of Great Britain towards intervention was that it was not objectionable if Austria acted alone. After the preliminary protocol of Troppau (Chapter XXV, pp. 676–7), Ferdinand lied himself into being allowed to present the Neapolitan case to the allies and, as soon as he was safely at Genoa on a British cruiser, disavowed all his concessions. He asked formally for assistance at Laibach. The Neapolitan government had been much weakened militarily by the absence of many of their soldiers in Sicily, and morally by the split which now divided the Muratist officers from the Carbonarist politicians. General Pepe was defeated by an Austrian army which on 23 March entered the capital. The restoration had been accomplished quickly and not very bloodily. Afterwards only two liberals were executed although many went into exile. In May an amnesty was offered to all except the original mutineers. The revolution had failed because of the divisions among the revolutionaries themselves, because of the distraction of the Sicilian revolt (which gave its last kick at Messina in March 1821), because of its lack of agreed aims, because of Ferdinand's duplicity, but above all because the powers acquiesced in the use of the Austrian army against it. Had the revolution succeeded, it might have blocked the way to unification by creating a constitutional state with a particular interest in survival. By failing, it contributed powerfully to the mythology of the *risorgimento* and to the growing number of exiles. Above all, it clearly associated Austria with the preservation not merely of a divided Italy but of anti-liberal governments. The Austrian army remained at Naples until 1827.

In 1821 there was also a revolution in Piedmont which had a strongly military character. Its leaders were officers and members of the court circles; it was a *pronunciamiento* rather than a popular rising. There was an attempt to co-operate with the *Federati*—as at Naples, the secret societies offered the only access to wider support—and this gave the revolution a general bias towards liberal constitutionalism whether or not the plotters were agreed in their particular aims. The Neapolitan revolution and the Austrian intervention brought the movement to a head and gave it a patriotic and anti-Austrian colour; this meant that the attitude of the crown was uncertain. One member of the royal family, Charles Albert, Prince of Carignano, knew about the conspiracy: even if active royal support was not forthcoming, it was hoped that he would mediate between the king and the plotters.

In January, agitation among students in Turin led to reprisals which intensified the demand for constitutional reform. On 10 March, after two or three days of ambiguous discussions between Charles Albert and the plotters, the outbreak came. Officers of the garrison seized control of Alessandria. In Turin that evening the royal council was ready to concede constitutional reforms when news arrived from Laibach of the decisions of the Congress. A few days later the citadel at Turin was seized by revolutionaries and Victor Emmanuel, unable to bring himself to crush the rebellion, abdicated. The heir apparent, Charles Felix, was in Modena; Charles Albert regarded himself as empowered to act as regent and swore loyalty to the Spanish constitution (15 March), with the aim, he later said, of maintaining order. On 20 March Charles Felix ordered him to Novara, where he was arrested. The intervention of the Austrian army followed and the rising was over. Again, the decisive force had been Austrian and the revolutionaries had suffered from internal divisions and uncertainty about their ultimate aims. As at Naples, the movement suffered from a fundamental lack of popular support; Balbo wrote that public opinion was neither for nor against it. Metternich was not far wrong; the rebellion was 'une terrible confusion'. The idea of mutiny was in itself offensive to the traditions of the Piedmontese army.

The long-term results of this failure were not serious for Piedmont's future. An Austrian occupation meant a growth in anti-Austrian feeling although for some time Charles Felix felt more inclined than before to trust his neighbours across the Ticino. The eclipse of Charles Albert and the foundation of his reputation for unreliability were by-products important for the later history of Italy. The administration and police were purged. But probably the mythical and personal legacy of the movement was its most important effect. Mazzini became a patriot when he saw the Piedmontese exiles of 1821 on their way out through Genoa.

The events in Piedmont and Naples encouraged repression elsewhere. In the Papal States, although the Legations were a hotbed of secret organisations, there had been no outbreaks—a tribute, perhaps, to Consalvi's wisdom—and not much was done until the death of Pius VII and the accession of the fiercely reactionary Leo XII in 1823. Some of the changes which followed were tragic, as when the Jews were deprived of many of their civil rights; some were ludicrous, for instance the dissolution of the board supervising vaccination. Consalvi was replaced as Secretary of State; Cardinal Rivarola was sent to the Legations to tame them and stamp out the secret societies. An attempt was made on his life in 1825; executions followed but things had not improved when Pius VIII, another zealot, succeeded to the Papal throne in 1829. Meanwhile, in the Two Sicilies Francis I had become king in 1825 and, although the Austrian government succeeded in obtaining the dismissal of Canosa, trials and investigations went on relentlessly. The secret societies survived in spite of them.

Elsewhere, governments were milder, although in Lombardy the revolutionary crisis had brought to light the connexions of liberals with movements outside the province. A series of important political trials began. First, eight death sentences were pronounced on men discovered to be connected with the Carbonari. None was carried out but the conditions of imprisonment of the condemned men became more rigorous after the outbreak of the revolution at Naples. Then came the trial of a group which included Silvio Pellico, the former editor of the *Conciliatore*. More arrests and interrogations followed. Finally, after the Piedmontese revolution there was another trial in which Confalonieri himself was among those in the dock; he had hoped to support the Piedmontese with a rising in Lombardy. One of the prisoners under interrogation also gave away the connexion of the Lombard conspirators with a movement at Genoa. These trials effectively finished conspiracy and secret organisation in Lombardy for some years. They are interesting because the social position of noblemen like Confalonieri and Arrivabene shows how quickly disillusionment with Austrian rule had come to the Lombard upper class. The prisoners became national martyrs. Their sentences, which seemed cruelly heavy, were to be major contributions to the mythology of the *risorgimento* in the poems of Berchet and in Pellico's *Le Mie Prigioni*. But in spite of this living evidence of tyranny, the repression gradually ebbed elsewhere. In 1824 Charles Albert was re-admitted to his rights of succession in Piedmont. In Parma there had been a few trials to please Metternich, but Marie-Louise either pardoned everyone or reduced their sentences. Even the badly shaken Francis IV of Modena did not carry out any of the forty death sentences his courts pronounced. Tuscany after the succession of Leopold II in 1824 became milder than ever and Metternich was continually protesting about the toleration of liberals there. One of the symbols of that toleration was the publication of Vieusseux's *Antologia* which had begun in 1820 to provide a focus for literary and academic patriotism; the first publication of Cattaneo appeared in its pages and almost the last of Romagnosi.

The artificiality of the dates 1793 and 1830 and the diversity which still marked the peninsula at its end make it hard to characterise the general significance of the period in Italian history. Economic change had been unspectacular. The industrial pattern had hardly begun to change since 1815; only in 1817 did Biella get its first power looms. For most Italians, economic life still meant agriculture; its forms had only been slightly modified by Napoleonic legislation and sales of land. The rudimentary communications of the peninsula in 1830 still strangled it; grain in Naples could cost thirty lire a hectolitre while in the Basilicata it could not be sold for eight. Rural poverty was still untouched and the evidence of mendicity figures in Naples shows it was getting worse. In the north, too, Pugliese's great study of the Vercellese[1] has detected the beginnings of the decline in peasant well-being which was to characterise the Italian nineteenth century. There was little to offset this growing incubus of rural poverty. There was, certainly, interest in new economic forms and ideas—already in 1816 there had appeared the last

---

[1] S. Pugliese, *Due secoli di vita agricola* (Turin, 1908).

of the fifty volumes of Custodi's *Economisti classici italiani*—but this was not yet changing the structure of society. The founding of insurance companies and savings banks was a beginning, and the concern with new agricultural techniques was striking, but no new directing class had yet emerged and the traditional rulers still held the reins. In spite of a slight change in the pattern of land-owning, the nobles were still dominant. They had been forced to accommodate themselves to a new Napoleonic nobility which had grown up beside them, its position consolidated by the institution of new entails; but other classes hardly counted. The masses did not share such national and political consciousness as existed and, although the expansion of the literate administrative class between 1793 and 1830 may have been important, this class tended to take up employment in the restored regimes and adapt itself to them.

Speculation about the effect of the political and legal changes of these years brings us back to the question which has preoccupied Italian historians: 'what is the relation of these years to the *risorgimento*?'. The question still has some importance because of the link between politics and historical mythology in Italy. Recent work on the later phases of the *risorgimento*, with its emphasis on the play of Piedmontese ambition and diplomatic circumstance, makes it seem that the contribution of the earlier period was above all ideological, the growing self-consciousness of some Italians *vis-à-vis* different sorts of foreigner being its central feature. There is political evidence enough of this, beginning with Buonarroti and his cronies and going on to the feeling against Austria after 1815. But such a nationalist reading of the purely political evidence must leave out a great deal. There is, for example, a strong tradition of local grievance which is entirely irrelevant to the national liberal interest; Sicily is the glaring example. There is also the willing service of many Italians to the foreign regimes. They stood in a tradition of cosmopolitan allegiance to efficient government which goes back to the eighteenth-century reformers. Men like Melzi and Prina were among the most enlightened and progressive in Italian society and they had little doubt where the true interest of their countrymen lay.

Yet the evidence of opposition to the foreigner cannot just be argued away; a mythology quickly grew up around it and itself became one of the social and political realities shaping the outlook of the first generation of the *risorgimento*. This mythology—whose essence was the identification of national with liberal aspirations—drew upon such diverse sources as Jacobin propaganda, Napoleonic administration, the poetry of Berchet and Foscolo and the schemes of economic improvement of Gioia and Confalonieri. It is true that only a minority was aware of it and that the greatest Italian writer of the age, Manzoni, in spite of his personal and political sympathies for the Lombard liberals, limited his own political activity to writing the *Proclama di Rimini* after Murat's abortive attempt in 1815 and *Il cinque Maggio* after hearing of Napoleon's death. It was also true that he was so much a Milanese that he only visited Tuscany long after he had gone to Paris and that he never went south of Florence at all. Nevertheless even he was not immune to the prevailing ideological trends; it can plausibly be argued that he contributed as powerfully to Italian nationality, in his generalisation of Tuscan usage in Italian speech and writing, as any Carbonarist conspirator.

The ideological importance of the period was connected also with its length. After it, the generation of eighteenth-century reformers had almost disappeared. A man who had been twenty in 1793 was nearly sixty in 1830. Those who grew up under the French were to be the first leaders of the *risorgimento*. Some of them survived from the Napoleonic to the restored bureaucracies. By 1820 there were many men of '92 and '93 who were cautious conservatives. Others were not: Santorre di Santarosa, the hero of the Piedmontese revolution, had been an imperial *sous-préfet* and Pepe a Napoleonic brigadier. Among those younger still, Balbo, born in 1789, had begun as a Napoleonic civil servant and Carlo Alberto had been commissioned as a French cavalry officer.

If the imponderable influences of ideology and mythology are discounted, then clearly the objective conditions of nationality were not present in the Italy of 1830. The most diverse observers were in agreement about this. It is simply not true that 'the people was no longer a confused and passive crowd, but rather an organic body, with aspirations and desires which would soon become demands'.[1] The absence of the masses from the stage was to be marked throughout the *risorgimento*; they certainly did not participate in a national movement before 1830. Brigandage in the south, mobs attacking French soldiers in 1799 or 1814, or the lynching of Prina, do not make a national movement though for some men they focused national issues. 1830 marks no epoch in Italian history; it divides the nineteenth century in Italy as arbitrarily as 1793 divides the eighteenth. All that can be said of it is that because it meant something in French history, it gave Italian liberals the hope that they could again look to France to be the *Grande Nation* of the international revolution. A new generation was young enough to have forgotten the disappointment which followed the first invasion. Pepe was in 1830 in touch with Lafayette, and in Modena Ciro Menotti was able to involve Francis IV in his plot by playing on the monarch's fears of what the French might now do. Their hopes showed what changes the revolutionary decades had brought, but also how far Italy had yet to go before she generated an autonomous national movement.

[1] Prof. Segré, in the *Cambridge Modern History* (1907), vol. x, p. 104.

A NOTE ON THE MAIN TERRITORIAL CHANGES IN ITALY, 1793–1814

At the Preliminaries of Leoben (18 April 1797) it was agreed openly that the Austrian Netherlands should pass to France and secretly that the emperor should also give up Lombardy. This, together with the former Venetian territories between the Oglio and the Adda, became the nucleus of the Cisalpine Republic. The emperor received Dalmatia, Istria and some of the Venetian *Terrafirma*. The Venetians were temporarily awarded the Papal Legations, surrendered to France at the Peace of Tolentino (19 February 1797) but the emperor received the remainder of the Venetian Republic east of the Adige at the Peace of Campo Formio (17 October 1797). The foundation and collapse of the satellite republics followed. At the Peace of Lunéville (9 February 1801) the Campo Formio terms were virtually repeated. The Austrians recognised the revived Cisalpine Republic which was soon turned into the Italian Republic. The Ligurian Republic and that of Lucca were revived. Tuscany was given to the son of the Duke of Parma as the Kingdom of Etruria and was enlarged by the acquisition of the tiny *Stato dei Presidi* (28 July 1801). Under the Treaty of Aranjuez, Parma was occupied by the French at Ferdinand's death. After the foundation of the Empire, Genoa, Parma and Piacenza were taken into the Empire, and Elisa Bacciochi, Napoleon's sister, was installed in Lucca. By the Treaty of Pressburg (26 December 1805) Austria surrendered her Venetian lands. The Kingdom of Italy was extended to the Isonzo and later acquired the Trentino. Dalmatia and Istria became part of the Empire. Joseph Bonaparte was placed on the throne of Naples where he was replaced by Murat in 1808. In 1807 the Kingdom of Etruria was turned into a grand-duchy for Elisa. In April 1808 the Papal March of Ancona was absorbed into the Kingdom of Italy and the annexation of the Papal States followed in 1809. For the changes in 1814–15, see Chapter XXIV, pp. 657–8.

CHAPTER XVI

SPAIN AND PORTUGAL, 1793 to *c*. 1840

CONFRONTED with the problem of regenerating society in decline, Iberian liberalism professed two conflicting ideals: reform by an enlightened minority within the traditional constitution, and radical revolution, deriving its political theory from the sovereignty of the people. The origins of these programmes must be sought in the later eighteenth century, when foreign influences were grafted on to the traditions of earlier diagnosticians of decline. The Iberian Enlightenment, although it revivified intellectual life, was, by European standards, a derivative and second-rate affair: its significance lies in its influence on the reforming civil servants who controlled the Spanish monarchy in the later years of Charles III; whether they drew on outmoded mercantilism, on more modern physiocratic influences or, later, on the ideas of Adam Smith, they were committed to the proposition that civil society was not an unalterable, sacrosanct structure, but susceptible of rational improvement by legislation based on political economy. Since their aim was the increased prosperity of the state, their emphasis was on useful arts, practical reform, and the elimination of useless classes, useless scholastic education and economically harmful charity. Compared with the Spanish reformers, Pombal's tightening of effective state control in the interests of increased revenue, effected by the exertions of an over-worked sole minister, was an old-fashioned programme, inspired by Colbert. Nevertheless, to the Portuguese liberals this suspicious autocrat became the picture of the enlightened reformer.

The reform programme was to be spread all over Spain by government-sponsored Patriotic Societies. Their activities were often puerile, a naive parade of scraps of scientific knowledge picked up in foreign journals. Nevertheless, these government servants and their local supporters staked out a programme: the recasting of university education on lines inspired by the regalian claims of the state; the promotion of public works, by which some provincial capitals were transformed; a network of roads from Madrid; the rationalisation of administrative divisions and the removal of obstructions to efficient government caused by municipal sloth and corruption and by provincial privilege. Apart from a few deists they were not heterodox, least of all were they revolutionaries. The monarchy was their instrument, 'the principal nerve of reform', its historical powers unchallenged as long as its utility was unquestioned. By 1809 this had changed. The feebleness of the

439

monarchy and the traditional institutions in the crisis of 1808 produced a widespread, though imprecise, demand for a constitution. Even more dangerous were the beginnings of a radical tradition, in spite of Floridablanca's (and in Portugal Manique's) efforts to hinder intellectual intercourse with France.[1] We can detect these beginnings in the haphazard and unco-ordinated activities of small groups of radicals in the university of Salamanca, in Picornell's republican conspiracy in Madrid (1795), in odd pamphlets picked up by the Inquisition in provincial towns. The war produced a peace party in which Godoy found the origins of later liberalism and which could greet the French ambassador with cries of 'Vive la Liberté'. In 1800 Southey found unpaid Portuguese sailors rioting for liberty and Bonaparte. These radicals were to turn a vague demand for reform into the precise liberal programme of the Cortes of Cadiz in Spain (1810) and the events of 1820 in Portugal.

What elements of a modern society, on the pattern of the Enlightenment and later liberalism, existed in Spain and Portugal? The Spanish aristocracy appeared a declining class. Its economic position was under attack, its political influence in eclipse and its scale of values challenged. Apart from court office, the higher aristocracy had lost political power, in Portugal through Pombal's violent onslaught on the old families, in Spain by laziness and disdain which left the chores of administration to legally trained civil servants coming from the ranks of lower nobility. Unlike the French monarchy, the Spanish Bourbons resisted all attempts to reverse this process.[2] Though aristocrats were prominent in the intellectual revival, its climate was hostile to the aristocratic values and interests. Violent literary attacks on a useless aristocracy were the echo of French polemics or the work of the bureaucrats of the lower nobility rather than the onslaught of an excluded bourgeoisie. Entail was attacked as an economic 'hindrance' rather than as a class privilege. Political economists argued that entail was the greatest single deterrent to prosperous agriculture since by starving the market of land it made profitable investment in agriculture impossible. The nobles' hold on municipal government, the jurisdictional powers of their *señorios*, were attacked as administrative inconveniences, and in Valencia and Aragon, where feudal payments were onerous, as social injustices. There was no clearly defined estate to protect noble interests: in the north the conception of nobility was diffuse, including nearly the total population of the Basque Provinces.[3] With the weakening of the diffused conception of nobility the titled aristocracy was afforced in the nineteenth century by the soldiers, bankers and lawyers of the liberal world. These accre-

---

[1] R. Herr, *The Eighteenth Century Revolution in Spain* (Princeton, 1958), pp. 239–376.
[2] V. Rodríguez Casado, *Política interior de Carlos III* (Valladolid, 1950), pp. 24–36.
[3] A. Domínguez Ortiz, *La sociedad española en el siglo XVIII* (Madrid, 1955), pp. 77–123.

tions revived and strengthened the social and political influence of the aristocracy. Thus, whereas a House of Lords was inconceivable in the atmosphere of 1809, a second chamber, including a hereditary aristocracy, was a constant feature of later conservative-liberal constitutions.

'The real power in Spain', wrote Wellington, 'is the clergy.' This power was deserved. The Spanish Church was a democratic institution: a primate was the son of a charcoal burner, the episcopate respectable and charitable. As a charitable institution and as an employer of labour, it had a direct hold on the poorer classes: but its profound influence derived from its intimate connection with all forms of social life. This popularity weakened in the larger towns as the anti-clerical riots and church burnings of the 1820's and 1834–6, unthinkable twenty years before, reveal. To Oliveira Martins, Portugal had been forced by generations of Jesuit education into superstition and hypocrisy, sharpened into hysteria by economic distress: Pombal's attack on the Jesuits strengthened rather than weakened popular faith which fed the 'white demagogy' of Miguelism. It was the attack on the Church as a political institution in the interests of the crown which produced Spanish 'Jansenism', the regalian controversy, which touched schism in 1800, and the attack on the Church's hold over education; it was the Church's position as an economic institution that led to attacks on mortmain, 'sterile' monks and convent soup. Nevertheless, the conflict between the liberals and the Church was not merely a product of economic reform. It was forced on the liberals by the violence of the Church's reaction to new ideas; nothing new could be absorbed by a moribund scholastic system; all must be rejected. If liberals wanted any kind of progressive society they could not refrain from defensive action; even Jovellanos, a pious Catholic, was embittered by the Inquisition's attempt to ruin his educational reforms. A minority of radicals in Spain and Portugal relished the battle, indeed the Portuguese democrats of 1822 openly appealed to the example of Revolutionary France. Most liberals, whether from conviction or from fear of condemning liberalism to a minority programme, strove to avoid open battle by historical disguises: the attack on the Inquisition in the Cortes of Cadiz was presented as a revival of Visigothic Law when it was the minimal liberal demand for a free press. It is on such issues that we see the liberals diverging from the eighteenth-century civil servants: liberals realised the programme of regalians but they fought, not in the cause of the rights of the crown, but for a liberal society.

To the reformers it was the practice of bourgeois virtue that would enrich the country and enlarge the revenues of the state. The Spanish bourgeoisie was only gradually fitting itself for this mission: the professional classes, except for the higher ranges of the civil service, were miserably paid and held in low esteem—the prestige of lawyers was entirely a nineteenth-century phenomenon. The commercial classes were often conservative; the typical Castilian town remained the centre of a local market, an administrative capital in economic decline. It was on the periphery of Spain that an economic revival was beginning, stimulated by a population-rise, small on European standards but remarkable given the demographic stagnation of Spain, by the opening of the American markets to the whole of Spain (1768) and by a gap between wages and prices which favoured investment and expansion. The fact that this revival was most marked in Valencia, the Basque Provinces and Catalonia created a new balance of force that was to have profound political effects in the nineteenth century.[1] Catalonia was the centre of a real industrial revolution, based on cotton; by 1805 the industry employed 10,000 workers. Catalan cork and brandy boomed. Catalans spread a new commercial outlook into Spain. In Portugal Pombal and his successors were faced by the loss of Brazilian prosperity of which the great palace of Mafra is the symbol. His methods were the old fashioned recipes of commercial monopolies and royal factories. Much Portuguese trade remained in foreign hands, although there are unmistakable signs of a native revival. By the 1820's the Lisbon merchants sought to force on the liberal Constituent Assembly their plan for the future of a truly national economy.[2]

Thus in neither country could liberalism draw its strength from a strong industrial and merchant class, but the absence of such a class has been made to explain too readily the weaknesses of Iberian liberalism. The Spanish middle class was numerous and strong, but it differed in composition from that of other countries in western Europe. It included the middling urban land-owners who were to be the beneficiaries of liberal land-legislation—the expropriation of civil and ecclesiastical entail and the municipal commons—and to give liberalism its electoral machinery in the local influence of the *cacique*. Above all it included the officer corps who were to give it its peculiar strength.

Agriculture remained the fundamental pursuit of the Iberian peoples. Its diversity precludes any generalisation. Broadly speaking, areas of peasant proprietorship were Catholic and conservative: Carlism and Miguelism were rooted in the Basque provinces and in northern Portugal: in 1822 the Portuguese reactionaries sought to mobilise the north against the liberal south. This agricultural system, if it failed to respond to the gospel of improvement propagated by the Patriotic Societies, was neither as stable nor as technically backward as has been

---

[1] P. Vilar, 'Dans Barcelone au XVIIIe siècle', in *Estudios históricos de los archivos de Protocolos* II (Barcelona, 1950).

[2] F. Piteira Santos, 'A burguesia comercial de Lisboa,' in *Revista de Economia IV* (Lisbon, 1951), pp. 22–5

imagined. Starved of capital, the traditional system could nevertheless shift its emphasis between sheep, wheat and olives, or even produce new crops like madder, in response to market conditions. Thus both Portugal and Spain in the early nineteenth century showed a truly remarkable increase in the production of the basic food crop—wheat.[1] Again, movement and increased production, resulting from drainage and irrigation, were most noticeable in the Mediterranean periphery.

The agrarian problem of Spain lay in the wretched conditions of the landless labourers on the latifundia of the south and west and in the grinding poverty of the smaller peasants and tenant farmers of the centre. In the year 1760 the government displayed interest in agrarian reform which would marry surplus labour to surplus land. One school of reformers advocated state-supported peasant holdings and rent restriction. Liberals rejected this solution in favour of sale of the Church lands and the municipal commons on the open market to be improved by new owners—the solution so powerfully advocated in Jovellanos' *Informe*. This policy of free sale inevitably benefited the economically powerful, and those who advocated it were certainly ignorant of the social consequences of free trade in land on the marginal peasant.

For the feebleness of Spanish and Portuguese foreign policy 1789–1808, the blame has been laid on the return in Portugal to the system of court piety, and in Spain on the rule of the queen's favourite, Godoy. In fact both countries were second-rate powers unable to relieve, by neutrality, the intolerable stresses imposed by the French wars on their traditional structure of alliances. The war of 1793–5 made evident Spain's weakness. Godoy had no alternative but to revert to the French alliance, seeking in it a security against his enemies at court and the prospect of a principality in Portugal should his enemies triumph on the death of Charles IV. His attempt to reverse his system, when Napoleon no longer underwrote his position and when French troops were pouring into Spain, came too late and precipitated his fall. Godoy, an inexperienced Guards officer in his twenties, was a patron of literature, mildly progressive in educational matters and a radical reformer in his attack on Church lands (a policy which made the Church look with favour on a constitution which limited the monarchy). His cardinal weakness was his subordination of policy to the shifting world of court favour; the scandalous origin of his power and his use of patronage created enemies. His fall was engineered by the partisans of the heir apparent, Ferdinand, in alliance with the hatred of a court aristocracy for a favourite who was a minor provincial noble. Ferdinand's agents organised the riot of Aranjuez (March 1808) which forced the panic-stricken Charles IV to abdicate. The crown had surrendered to the

[1] A. Moreau de Jonnés, *Statistique de l'Espagne* (Paris, 1834), pp. 106–9. A. Gilbert, *Revista de Economia* VI (Lisbon, 1953), pp. 65–80.

mob. The plot had entailed a consistent attempt by the heir apparent to discredit his mother's name and his father's minister, in alliance with a vague aristocratic constitutionalism and perhaps, though the evidence is scanty, with a nation-wide 'liberal' conspiracy against the 'Caliph' Godoy.[1] Above all, Ferdinand VII was counting on the French alliance at the very moment when Godoy, at last, saw its dangers, particularly to the Spanish Empire in America. The prince's party had been angling for French support since 1806, and Ferdinand hoped to rule as the recognised protégé of France. Thus Ferdinand was the first *Afrancesado* and it was only his rejection by Napoleon at Bayonne which turned him into a symbol of the national resistance to France.

In this resistance, as significant in the creation of Spanish nationalism as the war of liberation was in Germany, official Spain hesitated, uncertain of success against French troops and fearful of the consequences of revolutionary action against a government to which Ferdinand had legally transferred his sovereignty. To contest the rights of Joseph Bonaparte entailed appeal to doctrines that sovereignty did not lie in the crown but in the nation. The Council of Castile and the Junta, left by Ferdinand in Madrid, had no other instructions but to conciliate the French; unable to contemplate resistance to a capital garrisoned by French troops, their sole concern was the maintenance of order and the avoidance of any formal, legal rejection of Ferdinand's rights.[2] In Catalonia the authorities co-operated with the French generals: the French could only be resisted by an appeal to what a French officer called 'l'immense canaille de Barcelone'. How could the seventy-year-old captain general, Ezpeleta, be expected to make such an appeal? Official co-operation in the initial stages of occupation misled the French.

Resistance was forced on the constituted authorities from below; if the time-honoured phrase 'the people arose' conceals the activities of the organisers of the revolution, it rightly consecrates its popular nature. The Madrid rising on 2 May 1808 was the outcome of xenophobia exacerbated by friction with occupying troops. In the middle of May the movement swept over the provinces: murder and popular pressure forced captains-general and local authorities to arm the people and to accept self-constituted local Juntas. The movement was not solely directed against French butchery in Madrid: it was the last convulsive struggle against Godoy, who was protected by the French. The Juntas that were set up all over Spain represented the acceptance of the revolution by the local notables. Embarrassed by their revolutionary

[1] C. Corona, *Revolución y reacción en el Reinado de Carlos IV* (Madrid, 1957), pp. 312–88.
[2] Cp. Azanza y O'Farril, *Memoria Justificativa* (*Biblioteca de Autores Españoles*, XCVII, Madrid, 1957), vol. I, p. 288. D. du Dezert, *Revue Hispanique*, XVII (Paris, 1907), pp. 66–378. J. R. Mercader, *Barcelona durante la ocupación Francesa* (Madrid, 1949).

origins which brought constant conflict with officials of the old regime, often guilty of selfish provincialism, sometimes reduced to mere shadow authorities without even ink and paper, slack in taxing and conscripting their own districts, they included enough responsible patriots to push through the formation of the Central Junta, a clumsy body of delegates forming the government of Spain. Its position as a sovereign body, legitimate representative of a nation which had re-assumed its constituent powers, was contested by the claim of the Council of Castile that the old legality still obtained, while local Juntas accused it of conservatism. By 1811 the Juntas had been brought by a series of provincial *Brumaires* under the control of generals. Generals had no time for civilians and found in their ineptitude and failure to supply the armies a convenient explanation of a series of military disasters.[1] Romana ejected the Asturian Junta with fifty grenadiers; generals, in alliance with conservatives, intrigued against the central authorities in Cadiz. These primitive *pronunciamientos* were evil portents for the fate of liberal civilian government.

The calling of the Cortes legitimised the sovereignty of the people which could alone provide a political theory to invalidate the legal claims of Joseph. The conservative view that the old laws were still in force could not accommodate the facts of the revolution of 1808; the failure of the institutions of the old regime, from the king down, destroyed the old 'constitution' of the monarchy, and popular resistance had restored to the nation the rights it had transferred to the king. Neither the notion of popular sovereignty itself, nor the general desire for reform, need have resulted in the Constitution of 1812 with its extreme limitation of executive power. The king was locked up 'like a constitutional wild beast'; thus the fate of liberalism in the early nineteenth century was attached to a sacrosanct, unalterable constitution which made effective parliamentary government impossible and which no king could accept. The liberals attempted to conceal the rigid deduction from the principles of popular sovereignty by presenting their handi-work as the revival of the traditional constitution obscured by Habsburg despotism, a sophism exposed when Argüelles admitted that an 'inherited' constitution which no longer 'embodied the first principles of national felicity' could not limit the constituent rights of the nation.

While the political theory of the Cadiz liberals would have been anathema to the government reformers of the eighteenth century, much of the liberal programme was their legacy, invigorated and widened by the imported vision of a society based on class, property and freedom of contract, a vision that went beyond the administrative and financial convenience of the crown. The federal structure of

---

[1] For the discontents and ambitions of the Aragon command see the *Memorias* of the Marqués de Ayerbe (*Biblioteca de Autores Españoles*, xcvii, pp. 258–66).

revolutionary Spain has concealed the ideal—a unified, uniform nation of citizens equal before the law—which inspired the Cadiz legislators: no guilds, no enclaves of local jurisdiction, no remnants of an estates society in the form of seignorial jurisdictions, were to stand in the way of the liberal nation state of equal laws and proportional taxation. In their economic legislation the liberals were concerned, not with a socially desirable redistribution of the land, but with the establishment of clear and absolute property rights as against the confused notions of the old system: hence the freedom to enclose against the grazing rights of the *Mesta*: hence the abolition of *señorios*, a measure intended to establish property rights on an acceptable contractual basis, not to relieve an overburdened peasantry: hence the transfer of municipal commons to individual ownership and the absence of an agrarian reform which would imply an interference with property rights. Thus was sketched out, though the war prevented its implementation, the programme of nineteenth-century liberation.

Against their political interests the liberals were drawn into an attack on the Church, which, if aided by the arguments of regalianism, went far beyond it. In the attack on the Inquisition, the debate between a progressive and a traditional Spain took its modern form. The abolition of clerical jurisdictions, the proposed attack on mortmain as a means of paying the national debt, above all the acceptance of Joseph's suppression of the monasteries, produced a division between conservatives and liberals, and committed the Regular Orders to a counter-crusade against liberalism. Thus it was the threatened Church which led the reaction the nobility were too weak to organise; the electioneering activities of the priests helped to produce the more conservative ordinary Cortes of 1813–14.[1]

How are we to estimate Spain's military contribution to her own delivery? The regular army went from defeat to defeat. After 1809 Spanish resistance centred in the guerrillas. Numbering, probably, about thirty thousand, their partisan tactics could produce no splendid feat of arms. They did produce a powerful myth, inherited by both Carlists and the extremist Left. Guerrilla resistance became an element in the patriot creed, in the rhetorical nationalism evident in 1822: it romanticised revolution, the spontaneous rising of the locality against a corrupt central government. The most confusing legacy of the war to liberalism was the problem of the collaborators, the *Afrancesados*. Many, in both Spain and Portugal, served the French from lazy self-interest and love of office, or were political adventurers like Casanova, who made a fortune out of running the police in Barcelona. The genuine *Afrancesados* were those who served France from conviction. Their central position was that the independence of Spain as a separate king-

---

[1] M. Artola, *Los origines de la España contemporánea* (Madrid, 1959), pp. 610–15.

dom could best be preserved by the Josephine monarchy; that patriot resistance must bring military conquest that would end political independence. Moreover, since Ferdinand's abdication gave no legal grounds for resistance, patriotism implied an appeal to 'republican' doctrines which the crown itself could not accept. Popular committees, radical Cortes, ragged and revolutionary armies represented anarchy. The tragedy of the *Afrancesados* was that they backed the wrong horse, and that Napoleon's military demands for the Ebro provinces and his indifference to his brother's policy of gaining hearts destroyed their *raison d'être*. But they were not low traitors and collaborationists: they were often the progressive elements in Spanish society, liberal-minded civil servants who saw in Joseph's monarchy the hope of a reformed Spain.

In Portugal the liberal revolt of 1808 had come to nothing; in Spain the liberal experiment ended with Ferdinand VII's return in 1814. Ferdinand's hesitations about overthrowing the constitution ended once he was assured of military backing and when the right-wing 'Deputation of the Persians' revealed the strength of the anti-Jacobin feeling in the Cortes, now in Madrid. Recently much has been made of the Persian programme of a traditional monarchy, affording a *via media* between doctrinal liberalism and eighteenth-century ministerial despotism, both considered foreign importations.[1] Anachronistic, institutionally imprecise and unworkable, the Persian programme was to serve only as an excuse to overthrow liberalism and all its enactments (4 May 1814) and to return to ministerial despotism, the only system that the Bourbon and Braganza monarchs understood and could work. Popular royalism was a pretext for Don Carlos; only Dom Miguel, later, understood it as a demagogic and peasant movement. Reaction in Portugal and Spain was inefficient, insecure and arbitrary, constantly threatened by army revolt, secret societies and the hostility of exiled liberals. Tentative moves towards a more moderate administration (inspired by Ferdinand's need of the financial competence of men like Garay and Ballesteros who had liberal connections), were met by revolt and reaction towards the old system. At their best, liberal demands reflect the poet Quintana's proposition that no one who has lived in a free society can imagine an unfree society; at their worst they prove that political life was a battle for a limited supply of patronage; the liberal *pretendientes* could only make a take-over bid for a patronage system too small to be shared out. This situation was a presupposition of military liberalism.

Ferdinand's regime and the Regency in Portugal could only be saved by solvency and prosperity; this meant the recovery of the American empire and the restoration of the eighteenth-century trade relationship

[1] E.g. F. Suarez Verdeguer, *La Crisis política del antiguo régimen, 1800–40* (Madrid, 1950).

447

with Brazil, both beyond the resources of what were called 'les cours secondaires'. Spain refused concession or British mediation, 'as unbending as if Europe was at its feet'; English diplomacy showed little tact in handling the susceptibilities of declining imperialism, and her trade interests in South America poisoned relations with Spain. The last gamble was the attempt to go it alone, that refusal to concede to the inevitable which transfuses Spanish policy with a kind of mad glory. Fernandine Spain could not produce the army to stave off American defeat: the Andalusian expeditionary force defeated, not American rebels, but the monarchy itself. The Regency in Portugal and Ferdinand VII both took enormous risks in alienating sections of army opinion. In Portugal this was the result of Beresford's rule and English monopoly of high rank. In Spain enforced economy and fear of residual liberal sentiment led the government to pension off with minor posts the new officer caste flung up in the war. These officers, to their opponents upstarts deluded by rapid war promotions into dreams of a Spanish *Brumaire*, revolted. Compared to later generations of generals, who regarded revolution as a business enterprise, they were noble idealists who deserved their place in liberal martyrology.

The instruments of liberal revolution in Spain and Portugal were the secret societies (whose successful activities from 1815 to 1820 account for the obsessive concern of Iberian clericals with freemasonry) and the *pronunciamiento*, an officers' revolt based on the crude political theory that the general will of the nation, when vitiated by a monarch's evil counsellors or corrupt parliamentary institutions, was to be sought in the officer corps. The *pronunciamiento* was to develop a rigid form, with a consistent weakness: fear of discovery of elaborate negotiations meant that most *pronunciamientos* went off at half cock. This was balanced by the inefficiency of government detection and detention: Quiroga, the chosen leader in 1820, was allowed complete freedom to conspire from prison. A ramshackle despotism encouraged revolutionary irresponsibility.[1] The early *pronunciamientos* in Spain and Portugal merely produced martyrs, Gomes Freire d'Andrade in Portugal and Lacy, the symbol of Catalan liberalism. Civilian support was limited though increasing, and the rank and file were indifferent to their officers' liberalism. If there was a vast masonic, civil conspiracy in 1817, it came to nothing. Why did the Cadiz revolution of 1820 succeed, led, as it was, by young officers and inexperienced civil hotheads after the higher officers and the notables of Cadiz masonry had been frightened by O'Donnell's betrayal of the 'respectable' conspiracy of 1819? What gave the revolution its strength was 'the repugnance of the rank and file against embarking for America', which, for the first

---

[1] J. L. Comellas, *Los primeros pronunciamientos en España* (Madrid, 1958). R. Carr, in *Soldiers and Governments*, ed. M. Howard (1957), pp. 135–48.

time, gave sergeants and soldiers a direct interest in revolution. The British consul believed that revolt 'would die a natural death'; it triumphed through the feebleness of a government which could not collect a force to fight it.[1] In March the revolution spread to the great towns of Saragossa, Coruña and Barcelona. General Ballesteros and O'Donnell deserted to the revolution; the king was forced to accept the constitution of 1812 (which Riego had adopted on the spur of the moment), not by the force of public opinion expressed in demonstrations in Madrid but because he had lost control of the army.

The revolution of 1820–3 set the programme and procedures of Iberian liberalism and that of its enemies. In Spain, 1812 had been a dress rehearsal in exceptional circumstances; in Portugal, the revolution of 1808 had failed to materialise. The new party groupings of the 1820 revolution were permanent. Liberalism both in Spain and Portugal was divided into moderate and exalted wings.

The strength of the *Exaltados* lay in the provincial extremism of the Juntas, which ruled Spain until June–July, and in the revolutionary army of Riego. Thus emerged the mechanism of revolution: on its military side the army *coup*; on its civilian side, the take-over by local Juntas whose extreme claims, particularly in Galicia and the south, constituted a federal structure where sovereign Juntas, controlling the new Urban Militia, communicated directly with each other. Though these enthusiasts had made the revolution, they did not share the definitive distribution of higher patronage. The government, composed of men of 1812, regarded the new revolutionaries as 'poor folk'. In the capital the *Exaltados* could produce mob pressure which may be seen less as the emergence of an underworld terror depicted by Galdós than as the ebullience of the *fiesta*. From the ministry's endeavour to regain control of the army and from the use of the Madrid mob by the *Exaltados* in defence of Riego's army dates the split in patriot unity that was to paralyse the revolution (September 1821). The *Exaltados* were weak in a capital of satisfied job-seekers: the government impotent in the provinces. This dualism was to define revolutionary politics until 1874.

The exiles of the ministry of 'gaol birds' (March 1820) sought to control the committee stage of the revolution, enshrined in the Juntas and the clubs, and to satisfy the king by a conservative revision of the constitution of 1812. In exile, men like Martínez de la Rosa had been converted to a belief in a limited franchise, a second chamber and a strong executive. The amnestied *Afrancesados*, the ablest single group in politics, would have been their natural allies but for the doubtfully patriotic past which cut them off from office, leaving them the professional critics of the regime. The moderate programme could only

[1] P.R.O., F.O. 73 (*Spain*). Wellesley's dispatches: January–March 1820.

succeed with the loyal support of the king: instead the court plotted against any constitution to the point of allying itself with the *Exaltados*. The great weakness of the revolution was that the constitution could not do without a king whose sole aim was to destroy it.

The king's hostility flung ministers into alliance with the 'victims of September'; this alliance with the *Exaltados* was temporary, and in the summer of 1821 a more moderate ministry was confronted by a renewal in the provinces of radical revolution: whole areas of Spain were withdrawn from the control of the central government. Urban radicalism was fed by unemployment and continued taxation, the abolition of which was 'the thermometer of liberty'. In Cadiz, extremists threatened a Hanse Republic, in Coruña *Exaltados* announced their 'refusal to obey the orders of a detested ministry'. The government controlled the capital; defeating Riego's supporters in the comic opera battle of the Platerías (September 1821) it won over the 'plain' in the Cortes. The new ministry of Martínez de la Rosa now had strong foreign backing for constitutional revision. These hopes crashed with the treason of the king, who consistently failed to comprehend the possibilities for a recovery of royal power in a revised constitution backed by moderate liberals.[1] His inept intrigues produced the *journées* of July 1822, watershed of the revolution. The militia and the artillery rallied against the revolt of the Guards Regiments, some of whose officers were right-wing constitutionalists, others absolutists. Not only did the king break with the revolution—radicals now talked of a regency—but he failed his royalist allies. Their 'rage at the behaviour of the king' was the origin of Carlism. With palace counter-revolution discredited, the hopes of royalism lay in the countryside.

The royalist reaction was a renewal of the guerrilla tradition by the extreme right: small bands put isolated areas under contribution, and a regency in the name of the captive king was set up at Seo de Urgel (August 1822). Recent historians have exaggerated the strength of this native royalism;[2] Seo was captured, and the 'modern Caligula', Mina, crushed royalism in Catalonia. Once Baron Eroles, the only important soldier on the royalist side, had failed to subvert the liberal army, counter-revolution could only succeed with French arms, a lesson borne out by the subsequent history of Carlism. Most of the royalists were prepared to accept French conditions: a moderate royalist constitution. With victory the 'pure' royalist could forget these pledges. The government, now in the hands of the patriots of the 1820 lodges, after deposing the king, did nothing to resist the advance of Angoulême's troops and the revolution ended as it had begun, by the defection of the army. The generals tried to negotiate a settlement, which would save

---

[1] P.R.O., F.O. 73 (*Spain*). Hervey's report, 10 March 1822.
[2] E.g. J. L. Comellas, *Los realistas en el trienio constitucional* (Pamplona, 1958).

their 'jobs and honours and enable them to come out on top in one system as in another'.[1] Civilians hoped to survive by the sacrifice of the sacred codex. This was of no avail. The king rejected Angoulême's conciliatory advice, and Villèle, prophesying civil war, abandoned French hopes of a constitutional settlement. The first civil war ended with proscriptions, committees of purification and local reprisals, modified only by the presence of French occupying troops.

The revolution had been defeated by foreign arms, but by 1823 it had become the dictatorship of a deeply unpopular clique: the moderates and *Afrancesados* had withdrawn from politics in July 1822. A revolution, whose social content was the 1812 programme of abolishing entails, selling the commons and church property, had few attractions for the lower classes, apart from the excitement of revolutionary anarchy. Moreover, the revolution had come into conflict with the Church. In early days, the patriots emphasised the constitutional establishment of Catholicism as the sole religion, and the hierarchy preached acceptance; its neutrality weakened as the government failed to control press attacks on the familiar eighteenth-century lines and developed its attack on the property of the Regular Orders. In its final agonies the revolution turned persecutor. In 1823 the Spanish Church could count its martyrs.[2]

In the spring of 1820, de Lesseps, French consul in Lisbon, was convinced that the Spanish example would set off a revolution in Portugal; but specific discontents (an absentee king, the dominance of the English faction) gave the Portuguese revolution its own brand of patriotism, imitating the France of the Great Revolution as much as the Spain of Riego.[3] The expected 'gentle revolution' (de Lesseps) came with the revolt of the Oporto garrison and the lower officers in Lisbon: the government had neither moral nor physical force with which to combat the radical euphoria of 1820. As in Spain, the revolution divided against itself and hopes of a moderate constitutional settlement foundered: to the democrats the efforts of moderates to draw up a constitution acceptable to the king and the country at large were regarded as evidence of reactionary designs. The king possessed 'passions that must necessarily turn him into a despot' and was treated accordingly. John VI disliked the constitution but he was unwilling to support an absolutist reaction, captained by his queen and his second son, Dom Miguel, drawing its force from demagogic appeal. His final solution, never applied, was the aristocratic constitutionalism, associated with Palmella, embodied in a *constitution octroyée*. The revolution in

[1] M. J. Quintana, *Biblioteca de Autores Españoles*, vol. XIX (Madrid, 1946), p. 581.
[2] J. Carrera Pujal, *Historia política de Cataluña en el siglo XIX* (Barcelona, 1957), vol. II, pp. 115 ff.
[3] Archives du Ministère des Affaires Étrangères, Paris. *Correspondance Politique, Portugal*. de Lesseps' reports.

Portugal left a chastened radical tradition and the hostility of those classes threatened by revolutionary legislation: the Church, the civil service and the local nobility. Against these classes Saldanha saw that the Charter which Pedro, John VI's elder son, granted in 1826 must be imposed by force. As in Spain, the issue would not be fought out by two or more parties within a constitution: it concerned the existence of a constitution as such, which absolutists could not accept. Such conflicts can only be resolved in war.

The 'ominous decade' in Spain (1823–33) was not a period of unrelieved reaction: a debased version of ministerial despotism, associated with Calomarde, confronted popular 'pure' royalism which had emerged in 1823 and the persistence of a moderate reformist group. Ferdinand VII alone could arbitrate between the court factions and stave off civil war; it was this that sustained his popularity and gave the ailing despot what Miraflores calls 'moral force'. To the monarchy, the attraction of popular royalism lay in its hostility to the revolution and all its works: its danger lay in its determination to impose its terms on the monarchy, if necessary by rebellion. These terms, set out by the Catalan rebels of 1827, were the essential programme of Carlism, without the foral issue; the dissolution of the liberal army and civil service, the abolition of police and education, the restoration of the Inquisition, a patriarchal monarchy stripped of modern inventions.[1] Their strength lay in the Church and the Royalist Volunteers. We know little of this militia of reaction. To Addington, a supporter of Don Carlos's claims, it was an 'odious rabble' which could only prejudice his chances by driving the regular army to support Isabella.[2] Uncontrolled by either the War Office or the Treasury, its persecutions created the black legend of these years. The volunteers represented mass royalism, 'a royalist democracy,' wrote Balmes, 'a true citizen army, in its way an emblem of popular sovereignty.' This force lies at the origins of militant Carlism. Fortunately for the liberal cause it had been dissolved before the Carlist War began.

After the 1827 revolt Ferdinand VII set out to capture the support of 'intelligence', a policy which was strengthened by the new queen, Maria Christina, whose child would have to contend against court Carlism. One of the strands of *Cristino* liberalism was the group of civil servants and court aristocrats which this policy brought to the fore. To a bankrupt crown they held out promise of breaking the bankers' strike by which the London and Paris money market penalised Ferdinand's repudiation of the liberal loans of 1820–3. Characteristic

[1] A Pirala, *Historia de la guerra civil* (Madrid, 1889), vol. I, p. 57. The foral issue concerned the rights of self government (*fueros*) possessed by the Basques, and by extension the term was used to describe the privileges of Catalonia.

[2] P.R.O., F.O. 73 (*Spain*). Addington, 17 November 1832.

of the aristocrats was Miraflores; of the civil servants, Ballesteros and Xavier de Burgos. Ballesteros (Finance Minister, 1823–33), a minor Galician nobleman, was a treasury technician who forced through modern accounting methods and was considered a liberal through his patronage of the notables of the *Afrancesado* party. No doubt his liberalism has been exaggerated: it is nevertheless a remarkable commentary on the ominous decade that he could cling to office throughout it. Burgos represents in its purest form the provenance of one brand of moderate reform. He was an *Afrancesado* with an enduring admiration for the eighteenth-century reformers and French administrative techniques. He argued that the 'bankers' league' would only grant credit if a change of system and an amnesty prevented the exiles from 'poisoning the springs of credit'. Like most *Afrancesados* who had wanted a moderate constitution in 1820 he now believed administrative reform under an enlightened crown would satisfy liberal aspirations: a modern Ministry of the Interior, replacing the old cumbrous Council of Castile, could by a mere fiat 'bring the Lower Ebro to prosperity'. The whole of these later years is marked by the presence of penitent *Afrancesados* who hoped to work their passage as servants of a reforming monarchy. Lista, the poet, worked as a propagandist for 'strong legitimate government' which would build roads, free industry and patronise the useful arts.[1]

To liberal exiles, suffering in Somerstown and Paris, the Iberian issue was re-opened by the death of John VI of Portugal (1826), the struggle between Don Carlos and the queen's party at court and the French Revolution of July 1830. Liberalism and reaction, as in 1820, became Iberian phenomena. The Portuguese succession dominated Spanish politics, and over against the reactionary concord of Dom Miguel and Don Carlos stood the radical vision of Iberian union. Saldanha, the Portuguese liberal, was ready to join a descent on Andalusia, Mina to help Portuguese patriots. These attempts served only to reveal the petty division of exiles and to turn Ferdinand away from the queen's party and the advocates of moderation.

Dom Pedro, Emperor of Brazil, hoped to solve the Portuguese succession by the marriage of his daughter, the future Maria II, with Dom Miguel on condition that the latter would accept the Constitutional Charter of 1826. This settlement collapsed when Dom Miguel was declared absolute king. While Palmella sought compromise solutions with the help of foreign intervention, Saldanha saw that only force would make the conservative Portuguese accept a constitution, the work of an emperor who had 'stolen' Brazil. Only the liberalism of the Minho province provided the basis for a liberal revolution. This collapsed in 1828, unleashing a terror in Lisbon, a terror which alienated European

[1] H. Juretschke, *Vida, obra y pensamiento de Alberto Lista* (Madrid, 1951).

sympathy, weakening the originally strong international position of the Miguelite cause.

Dom Pedro's hesitations, the despair of the liberal Left, were ended by the loss of his Brazilian throne; he now saw himself as the chivalrous, disinterested champion of his daughter's rights, the leader who would unify Portuguese liberalism. A contradictory character, he was capable of heroic decision. With a mercenary army financed by a loan floated by the Spanish liberal Mendizábal, he endured the siege of Oporto, captured Lisbon after Napier's astonishing naval victory and, with the help of a Spanish corps, forced Dom Miguel to renounce his claims by the Treaty of Evora Montes (May 1834).

Although this victory was never reversed, liberal Portugal was always insolvent, always unstable. As in Spain, liberals could fight together only to save the succession. Party divisions were personalised. Palmella, the diplomat without faith in the liberal revolution, originally favoured an aristocratic constitution on the English model, imposed if need be by foreign influence. His rival Saldanha, theatrical but a brave soldier loved by his troops, whose dogma was the Charter and nothing but the Charter, was ready to ally with radicals (Passos Manuel with his 'throne of Maria II and the principles of '91'). The minority nature of Portuguese liberalism, the appearance of rhetorical parliamentarianism covering a spoils system, has no doubt been exaggerated. Nevertheless Miguelism was the popular creed, and Dom Miguel was loved as a Dom Sebastian whose reappearance was announced by choirs of angels in the Lisbon sky. He appealed to rural Portugal, to the Lisbon mob, to that 'fanatic, violent, apathetic, intriguing low and weak' Portugal of the Jesuits so bitterly described by Oliveira Martins. The philosophy of exile, the notion of a people groaning under tyranny and welcoming its deliverers, evaporated in the moral isolation of the liberal army. 'Do not make me use force in order to liberate you' (Dom Pedro's Proclamation on landing, August 1832). But it was only force that could impose liberalism. Mousinho, a Benthamite anti-Jacobin, sought to create by decree a liberal society that would sustain liberal institutions. Not constitutions, in his view, but developing wealth, commerce freed from antique restriction, land freed from the burden of tithes, would make liberalism viable. Domestic prosperity could not thus be created; Portugal, once the wealth of Brazil was gone, could not escape an acute deficit in its balance of payments. Liberalism was thus condemned to an insoluble debt problem, a dependence on foreign loans negotiated at disastrous rates, and to the hostility of those attacked in principles and pockets.

In Spain, a decisive choice was forced on the crown by the crystallisation of political forces at court brought about by the 'Events of La Granja' (September 1832). María Christina had succeeded in getting public recognition of her daughter's claims by the publication of the Pragmatic Sanction. This exclusion of Don Carlos was of doubtful legal validity; his supporters at court, during the illness of the king, forced the revocation of the Sanction when the queen was isolated from the ministry at the summer palace of La Granja.[1] The queen, rallying round her the moderate liberals of the capital and thus creating the nucleus of a *Cristino* party, re-established the Sanction, replacing the existing ministers by a semi-liberal ministry under the diplomat Cea Bermúdez. Carlism could no longer count on a court revolution in its favour; its only chance lay in the revolt which the pretender's legalism had eschewed and open appeal to the deep rooted loyalties to church and king, the particularism of the northern provinces and the hatred of the country for the town.

The first step in the alliance with liberalism was very cautious. Cea represented old-fashioned, administrative reform, but his ministry strengthened liberal forces: the Royalist Volunteers were dissolved, captains-general purged provincial administration (the spoils system preceded the machinery of parliamentary democracy), a limited amnesty was granted, the universities opened and the liberal panacea for prosperity, a Ministry of the Interior, was set up. Cea nevertheless obstinately supported Dom Miguel and set his face against the constitutionalism implicit in the recognition of Isabella's claim by a Cortes. Administrative reform was enough; any form of constitution would merely provoke Carlism.

The death of the king (September 1833) and the outbreak of the Carlist revolt made Cea's restricted programme impossible. On the day after the king died, Miraflores recommended strengthening the *Cristino* cause by summoning the Cortes on a narrow property basis and conceding a complete amnesty. Opposition to Cea spread from a court circle gathered in the Regency Council to a liberal opinion, vocal for the first time since 1823. Xavier de Burgos and others who had been opposed to any structural reform saw that the war demanded the support of what Addington called 'the moderate men of the country' at the price of some sort of Cortes. This was a decisive step. The crown allied with parliamentary liberalism in its most conservative form. This contract the crown could never break nor could the immediate beneficiaries maintain the permanent exclusion of the heirs of the radicals of 1820. Unable to move Cea, in October the opponents of the minister called in the generals. Llauder had been building up his army in Catalonia and had commanded the support of the Barcelona bourgeoisie, for the first time a factor in politics, in his struggle with the Royalist Volunteers. When he and General Quesada demanded Cea's dismissal

---

[1] The details of the liberal version of these events have been recently criticised by F. Suarez, *Los sucesos de la Granja* (Madrid, 1953), but their political import remains the same.

and a Cortes based on 'ancient legislation of the Kingdom', the full mechanism of the politics of conservative liberalism stood revealed. Unable to achieve political ends by civilian means, a party appealed to the arbitration of the army.

Cea's fall brought into power a liberal ministry under Martínez de la Rosa which made minimal concessions to liberalism in the Royal Statute of 1834—a conservative *constitution octroyée* suitably dressed up as the historic constitution of Spain. The opposition refused to accept the statute and sought to force parliamentary control of the ministry, bitterly attacked for its conduct of the war in the north, where the genius of Zumalcárregui defeated every general sent against him. When French aid was refused, the government had not the force to deal with the creeping anarchy of the south. The progressives were carried to power, not by parliamentary victory, but by provincial revolution, which swept over Catalonia and the south in the summer of 1835. Spain was effectively ruled by Juntas, varying from town to town and whose programme included a change in the ministry, the constitution of 1812, the creation of jobs for patriots and the abolition of taxes, the dissolution of the monasteries and a free press. On Villiers' advice the queen mother bowed before the storm and called on Mendizábal to form a government.

It was Mendizábal who, now and after the revolution of August 1836, put into effect the programme which the revolution of 1820 had inherited from the Cortes of Cadiz: financial necessity forced a decisive attack on Church lands although the debates reveal undercurrents of anti-clericalism characteristic of left-wing liberalism:[1] the law of 1820 abolishing civil entail was confirmed. Throughout the nineteenth century the 'liberation' of the land to the fructifying influence of capital was regarded as the historic achievement of liberalism. A series of Acts from 1813 to 1855 conveyed the cultivable parts of the national and municipal commons to private ownership, and by 1844 over half the Church lands had been sold, largely to holders of government bonds, while entailed land of at least an equal value passed, probably from the lower reaches of the nobility, to new owners. This large transfer of land increased agricultural productivity, as reformers had claimed, but it did not solve the social aspects of the agrarian problem. Although liberal legislation contained clauses intended to protect the small cultivator, there can be little doubt that the sale of common lands worsened the lot of the agrarian poor, while other sales strengthened the hold of the larger landowners and, as has been recently established, the position of the most prosperous peasants.[2]

---

[1] *Diario de las Cortes*, May 1837.
[2] E.g. Jimenez de Gregorio, 'La población en la Jara Toledano', in *Estudios Geográficos* (1954), vol. XIV, p. 214.

In the struggle against this new wave of radicalism emerged the two groups—the conservative-liberal Moderates and the radical Progressives —which were to share the spoils of political life. Their opposition crystallised around their respective constitutional doctrines: the historical 'internal constitution' of the joint sovereignty of the king and Cortes embodied in the moderate Constitutions of 1834 and 1845, and the sovereignty of the people of the Progressive Constitution of 1837.

The Moderates were a party of notables: distinguished ex-radicals, now repentant; the bureaucratic aristocracy which had replaced the old nobility as a political force; the well-to-do bourgeoisie of Catalonia, alarmed at mob violence; the landowners of Biscay fearing the claims of the merchants of San Sebastian. Spiritually akin to the French doctrinaires, their political theory justified their class claims to power: the 'sovereignty of intelligence' and the rejection of radical 'abstract metaphysics' in favour of constitutional structures tailored to the 'balance of forces in society'. Believers in strong government, they supported and were supported by the crown. This alliance was to ruin the crown and the Moderates alike by turning the crown into a Moderate institution and the party into an exclusive oligarchy. Given the permanent loan of the crown's prerogatives of appointing ministers and dissolving the Cortes, the Moderates could count on permanent power provided they could control local government and elections. The defeat of the Moderates' local government law was thus a life and death matter to the Progressives.

Against the 'exclusiveness' of the Moderates, the Progressives represented the claims of the urban radicalism that had inspired the *exaltado* tradition. The denial of the support of the prerogatives of the crown left the Progressives with no alternative but to force the closet by revolution; they were so installed in 1835–6, 1840, 1854 and 1868. In each case they were borne to office by a combination of provincial revolution set off by economic hardship (the corn prices of 1836–7 were the highest of the century except for 1867) and by support, more or less in each case, from the army. The provincial revolution was taken over by local Progressive notables by the formation of a Junta and sanctioned finally by a change of government in Madrid. This final stage produced a breach between the Madrid leaders and the provincial activists which was the most serious weakness of the Progressive party. The central tenet of Progressive constitutional doctrine—the sovereignty of the people—was therefore an expression of their need of a revolution, which to the Moderates threatened rule 'by cobblers in municipal office and bakers in the militia'.[1] There was, in Mina's phrase, a 'legal right to revolt' against a government which tampered with a constitution, like that of 1837, made in a Constituent Cortes;

[1] Cp. J. de Burgos, *Anales del reinado de Isabel II* (Madrid, 1850).

this was the Progressives' justification of revolution against the Moderates' attempt to reform the local government laws in 1840.

When the queen regent jettisoned Mendizábal the Progressive leaders were saved by provincial extremists. Undermined by opposition agents, the army could not resist a wave of Andalusian and Catalan urban revolution. In Madrid the government held, but in August 1836 at La Granja, a sergeants' revolt forced the constitution of 1812 and a radical ministry on the queen mother, accompanied by threats and insults to her husband which were to alienate the queen mother from Progressive politicians for the rest of her life: the ultimate consequence was the revolution of 1868 by which her daughter lost her throne.

With the Moderates and the queen chastened, this crisis gave Carlism its great political chance which the pretender's advisers rejected. On the other side, the Progressives' Constitution of 1837, without the unicameralism and hostility to the prerogatives of the crown which had inspired the constitution of 1812, created the possibility of a liberal union at the price of the rejection of the *exaltado* tradition by the 'legal' Progressives. The Moderates' greatest political blunder was the rejection of any compromise: they used the power of the crown in order to modify the 1837 constitution by the restoration of crown control over the municipalities. The liberal political system was exhausted; the way lay open for the rule of generals, the significant development of the later years of the Carlist war. In September 1840 the Progressives were again restored to power by a slow-firing mixture of a provincial revolution and a military *coup*. Whereas in 1836 the Progressives relied on sergeants, in 1840 they could count on a general.

Generals became involved in politics when politicians could not supply them with money to pay their troops and when the politicians accused generals of keeping the pay in their own pockets, an accusation which set off the mutinies in the summer of 1837. Only through a war minister, sympathetic to the demands of a given corps, could its commander maintain military efficiency. Rather than the product of a military appetite for power, rule by generals was the result of the weakness of the civil power and the party needs of the politicians. Politicians hoped that soldiers' victories would redound to their sponsor's credit, and each party wanted the prestige of ending the war. It was not merely that the army was the home of liberalism, standing between it and destruction by the Carlists: it was the only solid institution in the liberal state. The political factions sensed their weakness after 1837, realising that they could only impose their will on their opponents and the country by appealing to the army. Espartero became the 'sword' of the Progressives, Narváez of the Moderates. Civilian demand thus produced the new race of soldier politicians who were to dominate Spanish politics until Cánovas restored civilian politics in 1875. The longevity of the system is explicable only if we realise that the distinction between military and civil life was not as clear-cut as in the rest of Europe; the officer corps was a part of the underpaid clerical class, with bureaucratic interests, rather than a military caste. Army bureaucrats could look on military revolt as civilians might look on a change of ministers —the supporters of the successful general were automatically promoted a rank. Interference in politics became a habit, formalised in the rigid routine of the *pronunciamiento*, from the initial soundings of barrack opinion to the final flash of rhetoric, the *grito*. Civilian politicians, though they might threaten to strangle generals in their own sashes, could scarcely conceive of a political order without generals. Generals never acted without civilian support in spite of their professed contempt for corrupt politicians and courtiers. There is a great difference between military dictatorship and this symbiotic system where military revolution was accepted as part of the political machine, a legitimate way to oust a governing group whose hold over the crown's confidence and the electoral machine made normal party alternation impossible.

The coincidence of military ambition and party politics is demonstrated in the career of Espartero, the Duke of Victory who had forced the Carlists to terms at Vergara (August 1839). He hid his ambition behind the military political theory that it was the function of the army and the officer corps to embody the general will of the nation; he excused his hesitations by the difficulties of elucidating that will. Although he told an English admirer in 1837 that the time had come to 'over-rule an effete and corrupt form of Parliamentary Government', he hesitated before assuming the role of Cromwell. From 1838 to 1840 every ministry consulted his wishes while he appeared to be waiting for the highest bidder.[1] Once he had decided to support the Progressives, the demonstrations of the radical mob of Barcelona forced the queen regent to dismiss her feeble Moderate ministry. This was the height of Espartero's career as an embodiment of the national will: his rule as sole Regent (1840–3) lost him the support of most Progressive politicians and of Barcelona, revealing him as the *caudillo* of a military clique and a handful of civilian 'unconditionals'. Both Espartero and his victorious rival, Narváez, could only act as party leaders. Once they were mere generals they fell.

Divided and bankrupt as it was, liberalism defeated Carlism and Miguelism. Not the ultimate failure but the early triumphs of Carlism are astonishing. These were the work of Zumalacárregui, a retired colonel with a genius for leadership: starting with a few hundred men, favoured by the topography of the Basque Provinces, he built up an

---

[1] Archives du Ministère des Affaires Etrangères, Paris. *Correspondance Politique* (*Espagne*). Rumigny's report, 28 March 1840, shows how little the politicians knew of Espartero's political intentions.

army of 30,000 veterans, with an artillery corps equipped with captured guns and melted down kettles, an engineer's school and arms factories. The discipline learned in small engagements allowed it to risk battle with the liberal armies and lay siege to Bilbao.[1] This promising start was ruined by division and discord. 'The Carlists needed a man and that was denied them.' Don Carlos was a pious, uninspiring civilian, who could not master a court split between responsible leaders and the *exaltados* of Carlism, the 'brutes' of the *Apostólico* or Navarrese party. The final faction fight between Maroto and the Navarrese generals led to the peace of Vergara which left militant Carlism to a hopeless last stand in the mountains of Catalonia and Aragon.

Faction only kills a dying cause: the deep reasons for the failure of the extreme clerical right in Spain are to be found in its failure to expand beyond the homeland of the Basque provinces and Navarre, which could not support a regular war once the liberals had solved the problems of recruiting and supplying a large army. The expedition of Don Carlos which reached the gates of Madrid was a costly failure; the raid of Gomez across the whole of Spain aroused neither resistance nor support. Carlism was more than the desire of the northern provinces to preserve their independence and their *fueros* against liberal dogmatic centralism. Carlism fed on primitive royalism, on religious fanaticism, on the economic discontents of the stagnant small towns of Aragon, on the peasants' distrust of urban civilisation (thus it was the conquest of the local capital and its administrative machinery that appealed to the men of the valleys, the victory over a complicated and hostile world). This primitive programme, whatever may be said of later Carlism, made the movement as inexpandable socially as it was geographically.[2] Thus it could never attract the conservative aristocracy or the generals, and the notables of Basque Carlism deserted the cause for a peace which safeguarded the *fueros* on which their local dominance was based. After Vergara, Carlism survived as a sacred family tradition, a faith nobly kept in sterile and self-imposed isolation from constitutional Spain.

Portuguese liberalism followed Spanish precedent. The victorious liberals split into a radical wing which looked back to the glories of 1822 and found its fighting force in urban demagogy, and a conservative wing which relied on the court and diplomatic sympathy. Both factions looked to generals for decisive support; the conservatives to Terceira and later to Saldanha, who, after a period as arbiter, was led by his support of the Charter into the role of conservative dignitary and company director, abandoning his defence of Progressives to another

---

[1] A good account of Zumalacárregui as a soldier is contained in C. F. Henningsen, *A twelvemonths campaign with Zumalacarregui* (London, 1836).

[2] C. Seco, 'Semblanza de un rey Carlista', in *Revista de la Universidad de Madrid*, vol. xix, p. 339; and J. Múgica, *Carlistas, moderados y progresistas* (Madrid, 1950).

'sword', that of Sá. As in Spain, the hold of the conservative-liberal *Cartistas*, backed by the queen, could only be broken by a revolution which left revolutionary politicians to face the claims of extremist allies. The Septembrist revolt (1836), an imitation of the revolution of 1836 in Spain, gave way to the conservative *Cartistas* under Costa Cabral who refused, like the Moderates, to work within the compromise constitution of 1838, in spite of indirect election and hereditary peers. Costa Cabral was an ex-radical who hoped to establish his brand of conservative liberalism by a brilliant policy of economic development, financed by Portuguese capital, a curious legacy from his patriot past. As in Spain, the consistent support of the crown for the conservative politicians drove the opposition further to the left than its ideas and origins demanded.

The constitutional monarchy in Spain and in Portugal seemed to hostile critics a new sort of feudalism in the hands of professional politicians and local bosses. With all its faults, it was the framework of a modern society. Traditional society had exhausted its capacity to evolve: it could only appeal to the past, and all attempts— and there have been many—to present Carlism as the vital creed in nineteenth-century Spain cannot hide its purely reactionary nature. Changes in Spanish society itself made its revival impossible. Liberal legislation had destroyed the juridical and economic foundations of the old regime in the countryside; in Catalonia a modern capitalist industrial society was emerging, committed to liberalism. The commercial classes throughout Spain connected absolutism with bad trade.[1] But the fears of the notables, inspired by the social revolution they detected in urban radicalism, had already divided the liberal camp.

[1] R. Ortega Canandell, 'La crisis política española en 1832–33', in *Estudios de historica moderna*, vol. v (Barcelona, 1955), pp. 351–84; and J. Vicens i Vives, *Els Catalans en el segle XIX* (Barcelona, 1958), pp. 48–52, 227–43.

CHAPTER XVII

THE LOW COUNTRIES AND SCANDINAVIA

A. THE LOW COUNTRIES

THE Low Countries did not remain unperturbed by the political unrest which affected Europe at the end of the eighteenth century. Both halves of them were involved in the 1780's in reform movements, some aspects of which were forerunners of the French revolutionary ideas.

Dutch intervention in the American War of Independence (1780–4) had only brought the United Provinces economic losses and a feeling of impotence. The naval reverses they suffered were imputed to the stadholder William V's neglect, and gave new impetus to the opposition against the hereditary stadholderate, restored in 1747. At the same time, certain quarters, inspired by the ideology of Enlightenment, criticised also with increased vigour the inefficiency of the selfish urban oligarchies, upon which the whole system of provincial and federal representative assemblies was based, and demanded actual elections by the substantial citizens instead of *de facto* co-option of magistrates. Thus, at the very beginning, the 'Patriot' movement was split into two wings: a conservative one whose sole aim it was to count the stadholder out and revest the plenitude of authority in the patrician oligarchy, and a democratic one which intended a limited progressive reform of power. The latter was the more active. It even organised militias to resist, if need be, the stadholder's standing troops. The Conservatives used them at first for their own purpose as a pressure group against the stadholder. However, their unnatural alliance could not last. It broke down after the Democrats had seized power in Utrecht in 1785 and increased elsewhere their influence so as to counterbalance the Conservatives. This made the latter feel that the stadholder was a lesser danger to them than were their fellow-opponents, and led them to pursue a *rapprochement* with him. As usual, the small people also stood with William. An Orangist party took shape, and civil war between it and the democratic Patriots drew nearer. Eventually, Prussia, instigated by the British government, sent troops, who crossed the frontier on 13 September 1787. An appeal by the Democrats for help from France remained unanswered. With the surrender of Amsterdam (10 October), the Patriot episode was over for the time being.

Many of its supporters took refuge in the Austrian Netherlands. Here Joseph II (1780–90) had begun his reign under most favourable auspices.

Taking advantage of the prosperity brought about by the hostilities between Britain, France and the Dutch, he had been able to carry, as in his other possessions, a flow of reforms, mainly of religious character to begin with, such as granting tolerance, abolition of 'useless', i.e. contemplative, convents, and the institution of a General Seminary for the training of the clergy under government control. While these measures awoke at first remarkably little opposition, after the end of the war the fading of prosperity into a deep depression, aggravated by bad harvests and dearths, changed conditions. The emperor's ordinances of New Year's Day 1787, intended to modernise thoroughly the obsolete administrative and judicial institutions, wronged numerous people, deprived by these reforms of their jurisdiction or political influence. Their opposition first used legal means, the provincial States refusing as a protest to vote taxes; but Joseph, far from yielding to them, went on with his plans and was clearly determined to use force to ensure their execution. The 'Patriot' opposition, in fact, was double also in Belgium. Conservatives, grouping sundry privileged circles, the Church as well as the craft guilds, just wanted to undo the emperor's reforms, and first to restore the States in their original power: hence their name of Statists. On the other hand, a democratic movement, consisting mainly of professional people, represented the Enlightenment, as also did the emperor; but opposing Joseph's despotism they desired, like the French *Tiers-Etat*, a bourgeois parliamentarism.

The outbreak of revolution in France and at Liège, where the prince-bishop was driven away by a popular commotion in August 1789, encouraged a small armed force of emigrated Patriots, united in their opposition against the monarch, to leave their refuge on Dutch territory and to invade Brabant and Flanders. The Austrians had to retreat to Luxembourg. Obviously inspired by the American example, a 'Congress' of the Belgian provinces proclaimed the independence of the 'United Belgian States' (January 1790). This was short-lived. Co-operation between Conservatives and Democrats gave way at once to a bitter struggle with regard to the constitution of the new state, and the mob, worked up by the Statists, forced the Democrats to flee to France, where their ideals were triumphing. Meanwhile, Joseph's successor, the more compliant Leopold II (1790–2), had reconciled himself, by the Reichenbach convention (July 1790), with Prussia, which hitherto had fanned the Belgian disturbances in order to weaken the Habsburg power. The Austrians reoccupied the Belgian provinces by the end of the year, and also restored the prince-bishop of Liège in his powers (January 1791). Although there was no retaliation in the Austrian Netherlands, and even most of Joseph's reforms were repealed, numerous Democrats remained in France. They were joined by many revolutionaries of Liège, where the bishop pursued a policy of repression.

All set their hopes on an invasion of their respective countries by the French.

Indeed, the war broke out on 20 April 1792, and after Dumouriez' victory of Jemappes (6 November 1792), the *Belges et Liégeois réunis* acted as his advisers and auxiliaries. They aimed at establishing an independent Belgian republic, with a Girondist government; to Dumouriez' mind, this should be a first step to annexation. But Girondism was on the wane, and the Convention decided on 15 December to call in February 1793 a referendum, by which a carefully selected electorate in sympathy with Jacobinism should vote the country's immediate accession to the French Republic. Only in some parts of the bishopric of Liège did the vote of an industrial population of strong radical feelings favour the annexation. Elsewhere it was a farce. It was only just over when the Austrian victory of Neerwinden (18 March 1793) drove the French from Belgium, and operated a second restoration of the old regime both in the Austrian Netherlands and at Liège. It was of still shorter duration than the first: on 26 June 1794, the battle of Fleurus tied the fate of Belgium with that of France for the next twenty years.

This time, there was no doubt at all about the French intention to annex their conquest. However, before actualising it, the Convention wanted to exploit the country in order to relieve France's hopelessly depressed finances and supplies by imposing enormous contributions and requisitioning commodities, payable in heavily devaluated *assignats*. In addition, innumerable works of art were sent to museums in Paris or elsewhere in France. Together with their anti-religious measures, their robberies made the conquerors loathed by well-nigh the whole population. Nevertheless, it was during these ill-fated months that the country's institutions were renovated in accordance with the principles of administrative uniformity and hierarchy prevailing in France. Municipalities, districts, soon to be covered by departments, were organised, and by introducing its efficient judicial, financial, postal organisation etc., the convention brought to a conclusion the modernisation of state and society which Joseph II had failed to achieve. Also the bishopric of Liège, after eight centuries of independence, was now amalgamated for good with the former Austrian possessions. On 1 October 1795 (9 vendémiaire an IV) the Belgian departments formally became part of the Republic. Numerous laws, e.g. those suppressing feudalism, seignorial rights, nobility and the guilds were introduced at once; others gradually, e.g. the suppression of convents not dedicated to education or nursing. Eventually, French legislation as a whole was made applicable on 6 December 1796. Instead of permitting most administrative and judicial officers to be elected, as the constitution of the year III provided, the authorities appointed them, mainly in accordance with the tendency then prevailing in Paris, among moderate democrats and even, for lack of those, among moderate conservatives.

After the crushing of the Patriot movement, the United Provinces had decided, by an Act of Guarantee, upon intact continuance of their obsolete institutions under the stadholderate. The Grand Pensionary Van de Spiegel's worthy efforts to extirpate the most flagrant abuses broke down on the selfishness of provinces and individuals, and on the bungling William V's apathy, even in the case of the East India Company; only the even more moribund West India Company was suppressed in 1791, and its possessions brought under direct government administration. A more cardinal problem still was the Dutch attitude to the developments in France. Patriot emigrants had formed a Batavian legion, which took the field when the Convention in February 1793 declared war on the stadholder as a faithful ally of Britain. Its forces had soon to retreat after the defeat of Neerwinden; they came back after Fleurus. In January 1795, while Holland was threatened by occupation, the stadholder and his family fled to England. As the French advanced, the hour of the Patriots came: they were given or took over the municipal administration, and thereby were able to call the tune in the States-General. They proclaimed popular sovereignty and the Rights of Man and Citizen, abolished heredity for all dignities and offices, but otherwise confined themselves mainly to giving new names to the existing institutions. Indeed, their major care was their relation to France. Their hopes of French magnanimity proved delusive. Notably, the new 'Batavian Republic' had to pay a heavy war contribution; it was tied to France by a close alliance, which imposed on it a permanent financial burden; finally, instead of the hoped-for gain of Belgian territory, it had to cede to France Maastricht, Venlo, and the left bank of the Scheldt, on which river the restrictions on free navigation, imposed by the Munster Treaty of 1648, were lifted (Treaty of The Hague, 16 May 1795).

By the autumn of 1795, economic depression caused by British action against Dutch trade fostered impatience with the lack of profound reforms, and especially of a government really representative of the whole population. Under the pressure of radical people's clubs, an election was called for a National Assembly, which was to draft a new constitution. The franchise was nearly general, but corrected by a complex indirect voting system. A large majority of moderates were returned. The Assembly, which met on 7 March 1796, had little difficulty with the religious problem: the Catholics, whose political status had already been improved in 1787, as well as the Jews, were granted full citizens' rights, and the Reformed Church was disestablished. More thorny was the dilemma of unitarism versus federalism.

In the mind of the representatives it depended largely on the question whether it was profitable to amalgamate the debt of their old provinces. The heavily indebted provinces, mainly populous Holland, carried a unitarian majority. As for the degree of popular participation in state affairs, it was decided that voting was to remain indirect, and the franchise to be restricted to citizens of reasonable wealth. The East India Company was brought under state control, awaiting its suppression in 1798. After being adopted by the Assembly, the constitution had to be approved by plebiscite. The Orangists were excluded from it by the obligation for the voters to declare themselves against the principle of heredity, but federalist and Protestant opposition sufficed to cause the rejection of the constitution on 8 August 1797 by an overwhelming majority (108,761 against 29,755). Everything needed to be done all over again—a task set to a second National Assembly, which had been elected a month earlier. The increasing economic distress, the example of the Fructidor *coup* in Paris, and the naval disaster at Camperdown (11 October 1797) strengthened radical opinion as well as conservative opposition in the new house. Constitutional discussions made little progress until the Assembly was purged by a radical *coup* on 22 January 1798, whereupon it adopted a new constitution, strongly unitarian, and otherwise largely inspired by the French one of the Year III, with two Chambers and an executive of five members. On being submitted to the energetically purged electorate, it was approved this time (April 1798) by a majority even larger than in the adverse vote of the previous summer (153,913 against 11,597). However, the moderates were determined not to tolerate radical rule. Shortly after the Floréal *coup* in Paris, which also eliminated radical influence, a similar action was carried out at The Hague (12 June 1798) by general Daendels, an emigrant of 1787 and Batavian legionary of 1795. A third Assembly was elected and an Executive put into office by it, both of moderate opinion.

The Belgian departments were naturally still more affected by the developments in French politics. The election of Germinal, an V (March 1797), had been as conservative here as in France proper. Many people, having given up their expectative attitude or opposition on principle, helped to return nominees of the Right to the Five Hundred and to replace the officials, formerly appointed by the French administration, by even more conservative compatriots. These, anticipating the repeal of the laws on religion, reopened closed churches and connived with priests who continued their parochial functions although they had refused to take the oath of hatred of royalty, the moral admissibility of which had profoundly divided the Belgian clergy right from the beginning. Instead of the change-over they hoped for, the *coup* of 18 Fructidor (4 September) took place. Most of the newly elected officials were removed and their predecessors put in charge again. In prospect of the election of the year VI, the rolls were judiciously purged and heavy pressure was brought upon the remaining electorate. Above all, the religious situation deteriorated rapidly, the administration being very strict on taking the oath of hatred; refusers were arrested and sentenced to deportation, and the Cardinal-Archbishop of Mechlin, Frankenberg, was put over the frontier. The few parishes whose priests had taken the oath and could serve openly were boycotted by an immense majority of the believers. The sale of confiscated Church property was put through with increased impetus, which also offended strongly the deeply faithful population. At the same time, the economic situation was made disastrous by the paralysis of trade, the unemployment, bad harvests and cattle-plague. The introduction of conscription (September 1798) was the last straw. Riots broke out in the vicinity of Ghent; stirred up by British and Austrian agents, they spread like wildfire over the whole of Flanders. But both this 'Peasants' War', and the *Klüppelkrieg* which developed on similar lines in the forests of Luxembourg, lacked organisation and armaments, and achieved no other results than felling trees of liberty and destroying lists of conscripts and tax-payers. By December, it was repressed by French counter-action. Hundreds of insurgents were executed, and thousands of priests, most of whom absconded, were prosecuted.

Until the events of 1797–8 the Belgians had undergone with great equanimity their political vicissitudes. Their natural loyalty to the Habsburg dynasty had been ruined by the policy of Joseph II, so that even French conquest had been considered expectantly in some quarters. After the spoliations of 1795 had ended, still many people had thought the new regime neither better nor worse than any other. The open violation of the electoral results by the *coup* of Fructidor, the anti-religious policy of the Directory and finally the conscription disabused the Belgians for good and made their hostility to French rule nearly unanimous. At the same time, the complete failure of the revolt and the passivity of the European powers strengthened the Belgian feeling of impotence against their masters. For the remaining period of French domination, a melancholy resignation was to alternate with hopes of liberation nourished by the varying fortunes of war. About their fate in case of liberation, they felt still more vaguely. Partisans of Austrian restoration were scarce; a reunion of the Low Countries under the house of Orange, which was discussed by Belgian as well as Dutch personalities of the old regime, attracted the Belgians still less.

The Belgians' indifferent hostility appeared from their feeble participation in the plebiscites of December 1799 (to sanction Bonaparte's *coup* of Brumaire), of 1802 (to approve his life-consulate), and of 1804 (to ratify imperial heredity): every time it was considerably lower than in France proper. True, the new ruler did his best to relieve the Catholics' grievances against the former governments. Many unsworn priests could leave their shelters and reopen their churches, notwithstanding the intransigence of exiled bishops who condemned even a plain promise of fidelity to the Republic, after the oath of hatred was abolished. The Concordat did its part to ease the tension, though the renunciation by the Church of its property and rights, and still more the Organic Articles, maintained opposition among some of the clergy and gave birth to a couple of minor schisms. Napoleon's renewed quarrel with the Papacy caused the Church as a whole to turn again to opposition. On the other hand, the Emperor's efforts at organising state and society may have earned the admiration of contemporary lawyers as well as later historians. Possibly, however, to the mass of his subjects the perfection of his governmental system appeared essentially in the shape of remarkably efficient and resourceful tax-collectors. We may be thrilled by his breath-taking military successes, and so were undoubtedly many of his Belgian soldiers as well; nevertheless, the youth as a whole attempted by hiding or desertion, from which again a widespread banditry arose, to shirk the grip of conscription, becoming ever tighter with the losses of war and the monarch's growing ambitions. As elsewhere in the Empire, educated people resented the suppression of any representative government, and the ubiquitous action of the distrustful police. Only very few of them, comparatively fewer in Belgium than in France proper, were soothed by promotion to higher offices, such as that of prefect. Nevertheless, if the Belgian departments were always ruled by native Frenchmen, their subordinates, e.g. the vice-prefects or mayors of towns, were now as a rule Belgians. Even they were not always enthusiastic supporters of the regime, but many were among the resigned. Since there was no other possibility, they were prepared to accept honours and jobs from the only power which could dispense them.

Among the sincere partisans of the Empire, most were buyers of 'black', i.e. Church, property, who believed that the regime was the firmest guarantee against a restoration of the old order and the loss of their newly acquired estates. Some of them were pioneers of the industrial revolution in Belgium: indeed, during these years Belgium became the birthplace of the new industry on the continent. Based on an ancient tradition of workmanship and on abundant and cheap man-power, due to recent increase of population, Belgian manufacturers commanded the whole Empire and its satellite states as an outlet, efficiently protected against English competition. After Lievin Bauwens, of Ghent, had succeeded in 1798 in smuggling out of England new cotton-manufacturing equipment and the mechanics to operate it, his native city became the most thriving focus of that industry on the continent. From 1799 on, the Lancashire engineer William Cockerill constructed textile equipment at Verviers; after 1807 he made Liège the foremost centre of engine-building in the French sphere of economic influence. Trade was brisk and industrialists, if not the working classes, enjoyed prosperity, until in 1810 many were ruined by a slump caused by temporary saturation of the market. As for Antwerp, the British command of the sea prevented it from reaping full advantage of the freedom of the Scheldt; its improved harbour was mainly used by the navy, which also gave considerable development to shipbuilding.

While government was stabilised in Belgium since 1799, it had still to undergo several changes in Holland before reaching the same end, annexation to the French Empire. Napoleon as Consul was most interested in increased financial support from the Dutch and, in order to obtain it, favoured a reconciliation with the old merchant class and a restoration of its political preponderance. Since this patriciate still clung to traditional regionalism, a new *coup* in September 1801 largely restored their former autonomy to the provinces; a Legislative Assembly would be elected only by the well-to-do, and would appoint in turn an Executive of twelve members on a regional basis. The *rapprochement* with the older social forces was also designed by Napoleon to propitiate Britain and induce her to consent to peace. As usual, the new regime was to be sanctioned by plebiscite. Indeed, the past convulsions, however bloodless, had thoroughly tired the Dutch of politics. This had been proved already by their lack of response to the Anglo-Russian landing near Helder in 1799, and now again by the minimal participation in the plebiscite: of over 400,000 voters, only 69,000 took part, of whom three-quarters were opponents. Nevertheless, abstentions being considered by 'French arithmetic' as favourable, the new constitution was declared approved. With William V's permission, many Orangists accepted offices, now that the former oath of abhorrence of the stadholderate was abolished out of consideration for them: William seemed to have given up every hope of a restoration to his Dutch dignities and to be virtually renouncing them. The new authorities yielded to French demands for contributions in money and man-power to the war effort, but were not so servile as to neglect their country's long-term interest. Indeed, they strove for a status of neutrality which could revive trade and prosperity. After the Peace of Amiens, which cost the Dutch the possession of Ceylon, Essequibo and Demerara, Britain somewhat favoured the plan, but Napoleon was violently opposed to it, and every attempt to discuss it resulted in new demands and threats to Batavian independence.

Nevertheless, the alteration of the regime of 1801 was not caused so much by a French will to combat Dutch neutralism; it rather aimed at harmonising the satellite state's institutions with France's one-man government. After a new constitution had been once more submitted to plebiscite (but only 14,000 voters turned up out of more than 350,000, with 136 voting against), Rutger Jan Schimmelpenninck, a moderate Patriot in the 1780's and a realist throughout, who as a Dutch minister in Paris had prepared the last reform, became head of the state (29 April 1805) with the revived title of Grand Pensionary and practically dictatorial powers. These gave him the opportunity to begin with relentless energy and the help of able ministers the work of administrative and financial reform, which was to change Holland into a modern state. In his relation to France, Schimmelpenninck tried to save as much as he could of Batavian autonomy, thwarting on the Dutch coast the control by French customs over British goods. However, after Trafalgar, Napoleon decided to tie the Batavian Republic still more closely to his policy, in order to reinforce his economic warfare against Britain. On the other hand, he thought direct annexation undesirable, because it would hurt Prussian feelings too deeply. So he changed the republic into a monarchy, under his younger brother Louis Bonaparte who, after Schimmelpenninck's dignified resignation, was proclaimed 'King of Holland' in June 1806. This new turn also was accepted by the greater part of the nation with resigned indifference. The confirmation of all public servants in their offices conciliated them to the new ruler. Many Catholics hoped that the reign of a sovereign of their own confession would sweep away the discrimination of which they were still the victims in social life if not in law. Most welcoming were the Orangists: after William V's death (9 April 1806) had weakened further their legitimism, they could at least salute a monarch, if not a prince of Orange.

Rather unexpectedly, the hitherto docile Louis, otherwise a physical and psychical wreck, took his kingship seriously. While his administration proceeded with Schimmelpenninck's reforms, he tried to reconcile his loyalty towards his envied brother and suzerain with his duties towards his subjects. Thus, he was unco-operative in recruiting the troops the Emperor claimed, and in applying the Continental System. He went even so far in 1809 as to admit American vessels into Dutch ports. In the same year, inability of the Dutch to deal with the English landing on Walcheren led Napoleon to begin dismembering the kingdom. Holland had to cede that island, and soon (March 1810) its whole territory south of the Rhine, which was considered particularly difficult to secure against interlopers trading with England. French troops occupied also the remnant of the Dutch soil. Unwilling to play a mere puppet's role, Louis abdicated on 1 July 1810. On the 13th, Holland was annexed to France and a French governor-general installed at Amsterdam.

French sovereignty was at first accepted as easily as all previous forms of government in the past fifteen years. Trading people even expected economic recovery from the removal of the customs-frontier with France, a step which unfortunately was taken only in 1812, at the worst of the slump, when it could not bring great solace. However, soon the indifference of the masses turned into aversion, especially when conscription, which had been staved off by King Louis, was introduced by a decree of 3 February 1811. Frequent riots broke out, particularly after the debacle in Russia became known: of the 15,000 Dutchmen engaged, only a few hundred survived the disaster. For some time, the outcry remained limited to the popular classes, the only actual victims of the military machine. The institution of the Guards of Honour (April 1813) also afflicted the propertied people and invigorated their discontent. The tension rose with Napoleon's defeat at Leipzig. When, from 12 November on, Cossack vanguards entered the Dutch departments, when French troops left their garrisons in order to meet them and French officials prepared to withdraw, reality was overtaken by wild rumours. On 15 November, the people of Amsterdam rose in revolt, and a provisional administration, for the sole purpose of restoring order, was formed under A. R. Falck, a former high official of King Louis. However, at The Hague, where the people also rose on the 17th, events took a different course, since G. K. van Hogendorp and L. van Limburg Stirum, both Orangists who had stood entirely aloof ever since 1795, steered them resolutely into the channel of Orangism.

During the riots, from 1811 on, orange cockades had often been displayed by the populace, which had been attached before the Batavian revolution to the stadholders, and was prone to contrast its present distress with the embellished image of old times. The exceptionally stubborn legitimism of educated people like Hogendorp and Limburg Stirum had long seemed a blind-alley attitude, since William V and his son and heir William VI had concentrated their activities on their German dominions. Only after Napoleon had seized those (1806) did the new prince of Orange manifest renewed interest in Dutch affairs. In 1813, sensing the downfall of the Empire, he settled in England, ready to intervene in Holland if opportunity arose, but without even trying to organise a party there: in November Hogendorp did not even know whether to find him in Germany or in England. This did not prevent Hogendorp from sending everywhere over the country commissioners to take over powers in the name of the prince, or from trying unsuccessfully to persuade a meeting of pre-1795 notabilities of sundry trends to proclaim William. Nevertheless the Prince landed at Scheveningen on 30 November, and two days later publicly assumed the name and title of William I, Sovereign Prince of the Netherlands.

The building up of the new state was also largely due to Hogendorp. It was clear to him as well as to the prince that a policy of revenge against the former collaborators of French rule or opponents of the house of Orange could ruin it. On the other hand, most former Patriots had grown accustomed since 1806 to monarchical government, and were prepared to accept William's, if only it did not mean absolutism. It was therefore decided by a Constituent Committee, appointed by the prince, and in which Hogendorp played a major part, that the sovereign should be controlled by elected States-General, consisting, in accordance with tradition, of representatives of the nobility, the towns and the countryside, elected separately. However, Hogendorp's proposal that a Grand Pensionary should exert extensive powers next to the sovereign was defeated: the Committee feared the antagonism which had repeatedly divided the old Republic. Again contrary to his opinion, centralisation, the advantages of which had been clearly demonstrated since 1805, was preferred to regionalism. No discrimination was to exist between confessions. Thus drafted, the Constitution was submitted to 600 notables summoned by the prince, and adopted by them on 28 March 1814.

In William's as well as Hogendorp's opinion, the new state, if it was to be of some account in the future equilibrium of Europe, must be a rampart against French imperialism. This meant the necessity of an increment in territory and population. As matters stood, the only possibility of that was by union with Belgium.

In the Belgian departments, too, France's military setbacks in 1812–13 raised the first symptoms of unrest since 1798. Allied occupation, between December 1813 and May 1814, was greeted with tremendous enthusiasm, though Prussians or Russians soon proved little more likeable than Frenchmen as masters. As to the future of the country, most noblemen and clergymen, probably supported by the mass of pious believers, wanted a return to the old regime, and a restoration of Habsburg rule as a means to it. Their deputies, who conveyed their wish to allied headquarters at Chaumont (January 1814), returned disappointed: Francis I was no longer interested in Belgium. Yet the appointment by the Allies of an extremely conservative provisional administration seemed to forecast a restoration of the old social order. The progressive professional people and entrepreneurs, averse to that prospect, saw the only alternative in a union with Holland, whose new institutions appeared reasonably liberal and which could, with its colonies, compensate for the loss of France as an outlet for Belgian industry. This solution was desired not only by William but also by the British government. In June 1814, Castlereagh persuaded the Powers to support his plan to unite the Low Countries in 'the most perfect amalgam',[1] the provisional government of which was to be assumed at once by William I. Some differences arose between the prince and the London cabinet, among other things over the breakdown of the project of marriage between the young prince of Orange and the regent's daughter Charlotte as well as about a settlement concerning the colonies; these postponed William's installation at Brussels until 31 July. A fortnight later, agreement was reached about the overseas possessions: in addition to those lost under the treaty of Amiens, the Cape and Berbice were to remain in British hands.

The exact limits of William's 'increase of territory'[2] were to be decided by considerations of equilibrium and compensation. Should Belgium east of the Meuse be part of Prussia together with the whole of Saxony, and the Netherlands annex a considerable part of the northern Rhineland? Eventually, the preservation of the Saxon state caused the attribution of the German Lower Rhine to Prussia, while the Netherlands received the area on the right bank of the Meuse as far as the present eastern frontiers of Holland, Belgium (with the exception of the districts of Eupen, Malmédy and St-Vith, which the Versailles treaty of 1919 was to take back from Prussia), and Luxembourg. What remained of Luxembourg, as a former province of the Austrian Netherlands, was to constitute a grand-duchy, in personal union with the Netherlands, and to enter into the German Confederation; the fortress of Luxembourg town was to be garrisoned by Prussian troops (January 1815). At the news of Napoleon's return from Elba, William assumed the title of king of the Netherlands, and his small army fought with the allied forces at Waterloo.

The task of amalgamating Holland and Belgium was tremendous. Since the wars of religion had split the Burgundian heritage, the Dutch in their insolent prosperity and cultural bloom were apt to despise their shabby and backward southern neighbours, who in turn loathed the selfish heretics in the North. The first need was to integrate both countries, by adapting the Dutch constitution of 1814 to the new situation. A royal commission, half Belgian and half Dutch, entrusted in April 1815 with this business, had to reckon with the Eight Articles, which the Powers had imposed on the nascent Netherlands on 21 June

---

[1] The phrase used in the protocol of the Powers' agreement on 21 June 1814 ('pour opérer l'amalgame le plus parfait'). H. T. Colenbrander (ed.), *Ontstaan der Grondwet*, II (The Hague, 1909), p. 33. The Eight Articles, drafted in consequence of this agreement, said (art. 1): 'Cette réunion [viz. of Holland and Belgium] devra être intime et complette de façon que les deux Pays ne forment qu'un seul et même Etat'. G. F. de Martens (ed.), *Supplément au recueil des principaux traités*, vol. VI (Goettingen, 1818), p. 38.

[2] 'La Hollande ... recevra un *accroissement de territoire*': thus in the Treaty of Paris of 30 May 1814, G. F. Martens, *op. cit.*, vol. VI, p. 6. Already the Anglo-Russian Treaty of 1805 had provided 'de procurer à la Hollande ... des arrondissements convenables tels que les ci-devant Pays-Bas Autrichiens en tout ou en partie' (separate art. 3). F. de Martens, *Recueil des traités et conventions conclus par la Russie*, vol. II (St Petersburg, 1876), p. 433.

1814. These included the fusion of the enormous Dutch public debt with the negligible one of the Belgian provinces, and freedom of religion, violently offensive to most of the Belgian members as pious Catholics. Having to resign itself to those principles, the commission discussed mainly representation in, and the structure of, the States-General. The Belgians succeeded, against Dutch opposition, in imposing a bicameral system, with a First Chamber nominated by the king to serve as a conservative counterpoise against the elected Second Chamber. In turn, the Dutch firmly opposed a repartition of seats proportionate to population: while the Belgian provinces numbered three millions and the Dutch only two, each were to elect half of the 110 members. Thanks to its social conservatism, the constitution was accepted by the Belgian members (July 1815); but it still had to be approved also in Belgium by an assembly of notables.

Immediately, the episcopate, led by the intransigent bishop of Ghent, de Broglie, severely condemned as heretical the principles of freedom of religion, of teaching and of the press which were included in the constitution; their agitation secured the rejection of these principles by the notables (796–592). 'Dutch arithmetic' conjured a majority only by counting 280 absentees as voting in favour and by declaring void the 126 negative votes that were cast with the express statement that they were inspired by religious motives: the Eight Articles were beyond discussion. Nevertheless, the Church continued its struggle, forbidding believers to take any sort of oath referring to the constitution, and thus debarring them from most official functions. Meanwhile, moderate Catholics pursued a compromise, unwilling to leave the whole administration to Protestants. The archbishop of Mechlin, de Méan, a prelate of the old regime—he had been the last prince-bishop of Liège before the French conquest—declared in 1817 that the oath implied no dogmatic concession but only a civic protection of the various creeds. After Broglie's death in exile (1821) this interpretation was generally accepted. Another point at issue was the negotiation of a new concordat instead of Napoleon's. Naturally, the Holy See refused to let a Protestant king exert the prerogatives granted to Napoleon with reference to the choice of bishops, while William, in so many respects a belated representative of enlightened despotism, was determined to maintain them. After repeated negotiations agreement was reached in 1827. Before electing their candidates, cathedral chapters should ask the sovereign whether they were acceptable to him; in return, episcopal hierarchy, abolished in Holland since the wars of religion, was to be restored there. Dutch Protestants vehemently opposed the latter clause, and William yielded to their agitation. On the other hand, his interpretation that his rights obliged the chapters to ask him for his nominee went too far in the eyes of the Pope, and the concordat was never applied.

For some time, the king considered organising a national Catholic Church, as he had already given national constitutions to most Protestant denominations (1816), but eventually he dropped this plan also.

Another matter of conflict with the Catholics was the building up of a state system of education. While in the United Provinces before the Revolution many schools were operated by regional or town authorities, in the Austrian Netherlands they were entirely controlled by the Church. Efforts by Maria Theresa and by the Directory to found state secondary schools had met with little success, and under Napoleon religious colleges had sprung up again alongside the imperial *lycées*. As for higher education, the ancient university of Louvain had been suppressed in 1797. In William's conception, it was the task of state education not only to reduce the excessive influence of a Church whose doctrine proved incompatible with a modern state, but also to allow carefully chosen teachers to awake among the youth a Netherlands national feeling conducive to the amalgamation. Among the former high schools of the United Provinces, three were reorganised in 1815 as state universities, on the lines which had earned Humboldt so great a fame at Berlin shortly before (1809). In 1817, three were opened in the Belgian provinces too, at Ghent, Louvain and Liège, at the same time as state 'athenaeums' for classical education were instituted in all main towns. Finally, in popular education there was nothing less than an abyss between the cultural levels of Belgium and Holland. In the latter Protestant country, the addiction to Bible-reading had fostered of old a tradition of elementary knowledge without equivalent in the scarce primary schools of Belgium, for the most part run by incompetent teachers. If it was beyond the power of the state to found a system of general elementary education, at least it tried to improve the teachers by opening training-seminaries at Haarlem and at Lier (near Antwerp).

These measures appeared not to affect seriously the ecclesiastical predominance in Belgian schools. Many elementary schools were operated by brothers or nuns, and the others generally supervised by priests who also ran most of the colleges. From 1824, members of religious congregations had to apply for official permission to teach, as other schoolmasters had been obliged to do in 1822. Moreover, the opening of new secondary schools was made subject to ministerial assent and control, and nobody was allowed to teach in them without having graduated in one of the universities of the realm (1825). However, Catholic schools and parishes would only cease to instil into their pupils or flocks the spirit of opposition proper to Catholics, if the clergy itself were made tractable by direct state intervention in sacerdotal training. In 1825 a Philosophical College, clearly akin to Joseph II's General Seminary, was created at Louvain. All future priests, before studying theology in episcopal seminaries, had to attend its course of lectures, given by professors appointed by the sovereign in consultation with the archbishop of Mechlin. The Catholics were unanimous in opposing this institution, and the number of its students remained low. Its failure helped to convince William that he must negotiate with the Pope. His promise to make the college optional (1827) was not carried out before 1829, because of the breakdown of the negotiations; even then he still thought of penalising the seminarists, who had studied abroad instead of at Louvain. Once it became optional, the college proved superfluous, and was closed in January 1830.

Another conflict undermined the viability of the kingdom in addition to its struggle with the Belgian Church. Its assignment as a bulwark against France was not fulfilled, to William's mind, solely by constructing citadels on its southern border. Indeed, Frenchification had achieved more lasting results in the Flemish provinces than it had elsewhere in Europe during the heyday of this process in the age of Enlightenment. In other countries, the romantic revival of native languages had swept away the use of French. In Flanders, on the contrary, cut off from the core of the Netherlands tongue for a couple of centuries by political and religious prejudice, there was little common understanding between popular dialects, so that they could scarcely provide a substitute for French, which educated people went on speaking. It was a rock of offence to the king that Dutch remained nearly as foreign to his Flemish as to his Walloon subjects. How could the amalgamation become effective if one-half of the realm kept entirely aloof from the other's culture? French influence was to be the more combated, since so many French books and newspapers, in this age of restoration, stimulated the Belgian Catholics' spirit of ultramontanism. William therefore decided to Dutchify his Belgian provinces thoroughly. In 1819 he decreed that, by 1823 at the latest, Dutch only was to be used in Flanders for administration and justice; from 1823 on, it was also gradually imposed in secondary schools. The bourgeoisie which could not speak Dutch protested, but more vicious still was the opposition of the Church. Since hardly anybody in Flanders had sufficient knowledge of literary Dutch, it feared that many officials, judges and teachers would come from Holland, and that the true faith would be menaced by the establishment of a core of Protestants among its Catholic flock. Against this unanimous resistance of people who were far from being all clericals, hand in hand with the apostolic zeal of the clergy, the king backed out, allowing in 1829 the use of French in notarial acts and promising to reconsider the problem with reference to schools. In fact, the law had been ignored or sabotaged already whenever possible. It had been approved only by a very few scholars who were conscious that the Flemish dialects belonged to the Dutch trunk, and who were later, after the disintegration of the kingdom, instrumental in the emergence of the Flemish movement. On the other hand, it had alienated from William many people in administration or in the professions who were partisans of the Josephist tradition of a lay state and had supported his policy adverse to ecclesiastical predominance.

The king's other Belgian supporters were to be found mainly among the industrialists and entrepreneurs, who had welcomed the creation of the new state and saw their expectations materialise. The first years of reunion had been difficult, with overwhelming British competition on top of loss of the French market. Moreover, interests were clashing in the bosom of the kingdom. While the merchant interest, traditionally preponderating in Holland, wanted a return to free trade, the Belgians clung more than ever to the agricultural and industrial protection which they had enjoyed since Maria Theresa. William's compromise between those opposite tendencies left many people dissatisfied. Peasants and landlords found it difficult to resist the competition of Russian wheat, more so in Belgium than in Holland, where agriculture aimed more at cattle-breeding and dairy-produce; traders in Amsterdam and Rotterdam saw with concern that the downfall of their staple-markets, already set in during the eighteenth century, was accelerating with the progress of protectionism and the imposition, despite the Vienna treaties, of heavy duties on transport on the Rhine. Gradually, however, William leaned more and more to industrial protection, subsidising new manufactures by means of a fund drawn from part of the customs revenue. This policy led, among other results, to the beginnings of industrial revolution in Holland, where G. M. Roentgen renovated ship-building at Rotterdam (1825) and the English engineer Thomas Ainsworth was to introduce modern cotton industry in the Twente region. However, Belgian industry alone could, thanks to its earlier development, compete successfully on the world-market. Its prosperity, in turn, greatly benefited the port of Antwerp, which progressed much quicker than the harbours of Holland. Therefore, his Dutch subjects jealously accused the king of privileging the Belgians.

In any case, the economic policy was so largely due to William's personal initiative that his nickname of 'merchant-king' was fully deserved. In terms of a belated mercantilism, he considered a flourishing industry as the basis of national prosperity. A reason for inferiority, in comparison to British achievements, lay in inadequate finance. As early as 1814, he had founded the *Nederlandsche Bank* to strengthen the currency. The *Société Générale des Pays-Bas*, established at Brussels in 1822, was to provide the desirable means to industry. Indeed, this bank, the capital of which was subscribed up to four-fifths by the king personally, prefigured the Péreires' *Crédit Mobilier* of 1852, and has remained predominant on the Belgian credit market ever since. Trade organisation was equally unsatisfactory. In order to further the sale of national products, William, again with considerable personal participation, set up the *Nederlandsche Handel-Maatschappij* at Amsterdam (1824). Indeed, this corporation gradually conquered for the Belgian cotton fabrics the market of the Dutch East Indies, to which it soon limited its activity. Other companies too were called into existence with less ambitious purposes.

While the business people worked unconcerned with the trivialities of political strife, this became more acute. Hitherto, elections to the Second Chamber had aroused little interest among the limited number of voters, and debates in the States-General were rather irksome. While the Belgian Catholics were systematically in opposition, their liberal fellow-countrymen supported the government's laicism, and only criticised it occasionally for alleged prejudice in favour of Holland, just as Dutch members did the reverse. However, from 1824 on, a group of young lawyers, graduates of the University of Liège, began to champion a new liberalism. They were influenced by the teaching there of a couple of vigorous defenders of popular sovereignty as well as by the contemporary development in France of a liberal ideology, such as that of Benjamin Constant. Some of them, Lebeau, Devaux and the Rogiers, were to be among the founders of independent Belgium. They demanded direct elections instead of indirect voting, incompatibility of public offices with membership of the Chambers, effective budget control over the government and ministerial responsibility. At the same time, the king's educational policy unexpectedly converted the Belgian Catholics to the principle of freedom of education, hitherto so strongly opposed. If the older generation perhaps saw this merely as a tactical move, the younger developed a liberal catholicism, whose sincere belief that all kinds of freedom were beneficial to religion was soon to convince Lamennais. A *rapprochement* of both new trends of opinion was made easier by the example of France, where Martignac's ministry seemed to recede from clericalism. This helped the young liberals to overcome in turn their hesitations about freedom of education. From 1828 on, they united with the young Catholics in their opposition against royal despotism. Their passionate criticisms in the newspapers now for the first time aroused widespread interest in politics, not only among educated voters, but also among the popular masses, whom an economic slump made particularly accessible to anti-government propaganda. In the last months of 1828, a campaign of petitions in favour of freedom of education and of the press was started, in which the clergy particularly distinguished themselves as propagandists.

Indeed, as early as 1816 freedom of the press had been strongly restricted in connection with the conflict between State and Church, and now influential opposition journalists were being frequently prosecuted:

the conviction of the talented liberal Louis de Potter (November 1828) turned him into a national hero. Even in the Second Chamber debates gained more vivacity, and to the king's bitter indignation the decennial budget was rejected in May 1829. Much concerned about these developments, William thought some concessions to be desirable: it was at this juncture that he made the Philosophical College optional and amended his linguistic decrees; also a more liberal Press Act was carried. This encouraged rather than disarmed the opposition. A new petition was covered by 300,000 signatures. The structure of the State came under discussion: at the end of 1828 administrative separation between Belgium and Holland under a common crown was suggested in a liberal catholic newspaper[1] and persuasively advocated by de Potter in his *Lettre de Démophile au Roi*, written from prison. William balanced between further concessions, e.g. on the use of languages, and stronger repression of the press campaign. During the first half of 1830 agitation slackened, as compared with the previous year; but it subsisted, and any incident could put the spark to the tinder. Indeed, this was to happen with the French Revolution of July, giving birth to Belgian independence (Vol. X, pp. 247 ff.).

The history of the kingdom of the Netherlands, between 1815 and 1830, was essentially that of the failure to produce true amalgamation between Holland and Belgium. In the preceding paragraphs, little had to be said of the Dutch. Indeed they played virtually no part in the political dispute. In the States-General, the opposition generally comprised only a couple of particularly independent Dutch members, while a large part of the Belgian representation, and eventually all of it, usually voted against the government. In fact, the state was and remained Dutch in its core, and its Belgian subjects always felt themselves strangers in it. Apart from ultramontanist qualms about the oath on the constitution, their ignorance of literary Dutch debarred them from a multitude of offices. There could be hardly any question of posting Belgians in Holland, and the linguistic laws made them unfitted for functions even in their native country. As far as lower jobs were concerned, Dutchmen were also preferred for their superior education. In 1830, for example, among 119 generals and staff-officers in the army only 18 were Belgians. For this, King William was not chiefly to blame, though his conceit contributed to estrange his Belgian subjects; but he could not escape his own origin or that of his power. After more than two centuries of association of his house with Dutch history, he was called from exile by his partisans in Holland, while in Belgium, a territory attributed to him by the Powers, he found no equivalent clientele. Among his few supporters there, most entrepreneurs were unwilling to participate in politics and administration. Only by an

[1] *Le Catholique des Pays-Bas* (Ghent), 30 December 1828.

uncommon detachment could he have disengaged himself from these fetters of past and present. No wonder that in these circumstances the Dutchmen's sense of superiority over the Belgians was maintained and aggravated. In 1830, Ch. Rogier rightly complained that Belgium was no Dutch colony;[1] indeed it was far too often considered as such in Holland. In 1829 a Dutchman observed that one heard in Amsterdam as little of what went on in Belgium as if it had occurred in Mesopotamia.[2] Both peoples had entered their union in 1814 as foreigners to each other. When they dissolved it in 1830, they were, if possible, even more so.

B. SCANDINAVIA

In the generation before the French Revolution the two Scandinavian kingdoms and their appendages—except for Iceland, whose population fell to 40,000 after the great volcanic eruption of 1783—continued to enjoy the relative calm and prosperity which had followed the end of the Great Northern War in 1721. Copenhagen flourished as the political and economic capital of the 'twin kingdoms' of Denmark and Norway, with the duchies of Schleswig and Holstein loosely but (after 1773) completely attached to the Danish crown. Stockholm, though overshadowed by St Petersburg, was still the centre of what was probably the foremost second-class power of Europe, one which stretched eastwards across the Grand Duchy of Finland and retained a lodgment on the south shore of the Baltic, Pomerania west of the River Peene, together with the island of Rügen.

Since the death of Charles XII of Sweden neither of the Scandinavian powers had been strong enough to conduct an independent foreign policy of much importance to the rest of Europe, but they were regarded as useful assets in any major combination. Thus Catherine the Great in March 1765 concluded an alliance with Denmark which was not seriously interrupted for more than forty years, one of its original purposes being the maintenance of the free constitution of Sweden, the form of government by the four Estates which gave free play to party politics and foreign subsidies. For ten years (1762–72) Catherine held Sweden too within her 'northern system', a position in which the Swedes could continue good relations with Britain but not with France. But her distraction by the partition of Poland gave opportunity for the *coup d'état* of 19 August 1772, by which the youthful Gustavus III broke the power of the Estates. Undertaken with the support of France, this event inaugurated a period of French influence which lasted until the Revolution, while relations with Russia and Denmark continued strained.

[1] In the newspaper *Le Politique* (Liège), 24 January 1830.
[2] H. T. Colenbrander (ed.), *Gedenkstukken der algemeene geschiedenis van Nederland van 1795 tot 1840*, vol. IX (1825–30), part 2 (The Hague, 1917), p. 531, note I.

During the American revolutionary war, however, their economic interests brought the three Baltic Powers together against Britain in the Armed Neutrality of the North. This league championed principles which had been previously asserted by a Danish international lawyer, Martin Hübner, in 1759—the immunity of neutral goods in enemy ships and of enemy goods in neutral ships, except for contraband of war and the right to maintain an effective, as distinct from a paper, blockade. But the Danes had secured their own advantage by a separate treaty with Britain, made earlier in the same month as the league (July 1780), which provided that foodstuffs would not be treated as contraband. This did nothing to resolve the question of naval stores, which were of more interest to both Russia and Sweden: the former, however, was not disposed to turn strong words into strong action against Britain, and Sweden tried in vain to get an international congress called to construct a neutral code.

The league, which had recruited only four other members, ended with the Peace of Versailles in 1783. Five years later mutual distrust culminated in a Swedish attack on Russia, aimed at the capture of St Petersburg. The Russians were deeply involved in their war against Turkey, but the Swedish navy failed in its efforts to support the advance, whereupon mutinous elements in the army launched a formidable conspiracy of the nobles, known as the League of Anjala. This voiced a demand for the independence of Finland, where the Swedish landowners hoped for oligarchic self-government under Russian protection. Until Denmark as Russia's ally sent the Norwegian army to besiege Gothenburg, Gustavus's position seemed desperate. Then, with characteristic resourcefulness, he roused the feeling of the masses against the Danes; British mediation saved his second city, and Denmark not unwillingly gave up the war. The next year therefore witnessed the complete triumph of the king over the military conspirators, and although Sweden had lost nearly half her ships of the line during the fighting, it ended with an important naval victory at Svensksund (9 July 1790). Next month the Russians, hard pressed by the Turks, agreed to a peace without territorial changes, in which they tacitly abandoned any claim to use earlier treaties as a pretext for intervention in the internal politics of Sweden.

Since the main result of the war was a further change in the Swedish constitution, it is appropriate here to trace briefly the internal development of the Scandinavian countries on the eve of the revolutionary age. In Denmark the autocratic monarchy and bureaucracy had recently undergone change and counterchange. Between September 1770 and January 1772, the 1880 decrees issued by the German physician from Altona, J. F. Struensee, had brought all the most liberal ideas of the European Enlightenment to bear upon the social and economic problems of the 'twin kingdoms'. But the reorganisation of the law-courts in Copenhagen, so as to establish uniformity and equality of treatment for different classes, and a more humane poor-law system were the only important measures that survived him, though the circumstances of his execution and the banishment of the queen, a younger sister of George III, who had preferred the court doctor to her degenerate husband and was instrumental in his rise to power, gave the name of Struensee a European celebrity. A strongly nationalist reaction lasted until 1784, when Crown Prince Frederick at sixteen won an ascendancy over his now imbecile father, Christian VII, and Denmark entered upon a period of more durable reforms under A. P. Bernstorff. A Hanoverian by birth and nephew of an earlier foreign minister, he exercised a wise influence upon foreign affairs—he had been closely concerned with the administration of the Armed Neutrality in 1780—but he also championed the measures which, before the end of the century, gave Denmark a freer peasantry and a more liberal economy than any other of the continental monarchies.

Denmark being preponderantly an agricultural country, reform began with enclosure laws, the earliest dating from 1781, under which one-half of the farms were enclosed by 1807. In 1787 the new government gave tenants full legal protection against the lord of the manor, and in the following year the status of serf—the person tied to the land by the *Stavnsbaand*—was formally and finally abolished. Other measures regulated the labour-services of tenant farmers, made it easier for them to buy their land, and abolished manorial privileges, such as a monopoly of the trade in stall-fed cattle. By 1807 the crops were three times as great as they had been at mid-century, and only the landless cottar class was still being ruthlessly exploited to produce them.

A liberal policy was also applied to commerce. Copenhagen was deprived of its special privileges, which had checked the growth of provincial ports; dealings with Iceland were thrown open to all Danish subjects; and there was to be virtually free trade in corn—a matter of enormous importance to southern Norway, where the Danes had long held a profitable monopoly. By the time of Bernstorff's death in 1797 the tariff on raw materials had a maximum of 5 per cent, and it did not exceed 24 per cent even on fully manufactured products. Yet another aspect of trade in which the government showed a remarkable enlightenment was that in slaves, which was abolished in 1792 with effect from 1803. The general result of all these measures was to consolidate the position of the absolutist monarchy: grateful subjects erected the Pillar of Freedom at Copenhagen in the year when the Republic was first proclaimed at Paris.

In Sweden the reign of Gustavus III, whom their poet Tegnér calls 'the enchanter on the throne', had results which are less easily assessed.

In 1772 he had banished party strife by restoring the executive power of the crown as it had been in the great days of Gustavus Adolphus, and by making the summons of the Estates dependent upon the royal pleasure. The only definite limits left to the king's authority were that he could not continue a tax beyond a date fixed by the Estates in granting it or declare war except in defence. The sequel had been an era of brilliant cultural achievement, with French influence in the ascendant, and of considerable improvements in administration—currency reform, changes in judicial procedure, the strengthening of the navy, increased attention to the needs of Finland—which party strife had long prevented. But the nobles, who had supported the *coup*, felt themselves to be insufficiently rewarded and seized their chance, as we have seen, in 1788. The summoning of the Estates, which had met only twice in sixteen years, was one of the demands of the League of Anjala: but when they assembled in February 1789, it was the king who won the support of clergy, burgesses, and peasants against the nobles, who were forced to accept the Act of Union and Security.

By this measure noble privileges were nearly all abolished, most government offices being thrown open to the unprivileged classes and most types of land being made available on equal terms to the land-hungry peasantry, a most significant concession at that date. In return the powers of the crown were left unfettered by the intervention of the Estates. This body no longer had any right to initiate legislation, and taxes were to remain in force indefinitely pending its summons—a clause which the king in person arrogantly declared carried in the presence of the House of the Nobles and in defiance of the majority among them. Three years later he was assassinated in revenge; his son and successor was only thirteen, but the constitution was not disturbed.

Throughout Scandinavia, the direct influence of the French Revolution was slight. Gustavus III had been an ardent sympathiser with Louis XVI; as early as February 1790 he suppressed all news from France. The regency after his death courted, indeed, the favour of the Convention, but the object was to secure subsidies and a counterpoise to Russia: the so-called Swedish Jacobins were no more than a minority group of nobles, who vainly opposed the absolutist system at the next Estates in 1800. The tranquillity of Copenhagen was broken by nothing more serious than a strike of carpenters in 1794. Finnish activists looked east rather than west for inspiration. Even in Norway, where the rule of the Danish bureaucracy had always been to some extent resented, strong sympathies were roused mainly in the west coast towns, which traded extensively with France in fish. But the agitation there demanded only improvements to local government—and external measures to hinder the interference of the British navy with their lawful trade. For the conflict in Europe offered golden chances to neutrals.

The Scandinavian countries were big exporters. Sweden sent abroad about 50,000 tons of bar iron a year, half of it to England. Danish corn, the timber of the Baltic coast and southern Norway, Swedish copper, and other naval stores, such as pitch, tar, hemp, sailcloth, hides and tallow, were all increasingly profitable in time of war. So were the activities of the Scandinavian neutrals as shippers, middlemen and providers of entrepôt markets. By 1805 Denmark–Norway disposed of a mercantile marine eight times larger than they had forty years earlier, and Copenhagen had achieved a trade turnover which was not exceeded until after 1870. Some ships were built in Norway with British capital, others were French prizes sold cheap: the Far East, the West Indies and the Mediterranean, no less than home waters, offered profitable routes for sailing under neutral flags.

Politically, the result was to produce a common Scandinavian outlook which might have had lasting effects: in 1793 a Danish historian on a visit to London posed the question, 'What power on earth can endanger confederate Scandinavia?' In the first six and a half months of war Britain seized 189 Danish and Norwegian ships with little regard to the agreement made in 1780. But in March 1794 a Dano–Swedish neutrality agreement was signed, each signatory to provide eight ships of the line for trade protection, and the Baltic Sea to be claimed as neutral water. The British attitude then became less harsh, and in 1796–8, when the Royal Navy had to leave the Mediterranean, neutral shipping was encouraged to take over the trade of that region, including the importation of Spanish wool to Britain. Conversely, the French attitude became more uncompromising; this led to the start of a convoy system in January 1798, seven months before Nelson's victory at Aboukir Bay enabled Britain once again to enforce her rules more strictly.

There followed a series of small-scale conflicts, when Danish warships in charge of convoys resisted the British right of search. After the third such episode a British squadron was sent to Copenhagen, and forced the government to forego the use of convoys. But the new Tsar Paul having turned against Britain, the sequel to Denmark's humiliation in August 1800 was the signature in December of the second Armed Neutrality, in which the same three Powers made the same challenge as before. Next month all their merchantmen lying in British ports were seized; the Danish West Indies were occupied; and on 12 March Parker and Nelson sailed for Copenhagen. They acted with great promptness, so as to neutralise the Danish fleet while the Russian was still ice-bound in the Baltic. But Nelson's success was also facilitated by lack of co-operation between the other two opponents: the Danes rejected a Swedish offer to fortify the east coast of the Sound, along which the British proceeded out of range of the Danish forts, and the Swedish fleet was detained by its deficiencies (and un-favourable winds) at Karlskrona. The Swedes offered no fight when the British fleet found them there, three weeks after the battle of Copen-hagen and shortly before the admirals received belated news of the murder of Tsar Paul. Denmark and Sweden were therefore fortunate to share in the concessions made by Britain to Tsar Alexander, who had no wish to continue the conflict, including what was to them the very valuable right to conduct a port-to-port trade along the coast of a belligerent power.

They won more golden chances by the renewal of hostilities between Britain and France in May 1803, and by 1805 the maintenance of a common Scandinavian policy appeared fully feasible. For the battle of Trafalgar gave Denmark–Norway, with its big mercantile marine and vital sea communications, the strongest possible reason for not quarrelling with Britain, and only the hesitations of Prussia caused the twin kingdoms to delay in joining the coalition, to which Gustavus IV of Sweden had formally adhered in the month of Nelson's victory. His action was meant partly as a personal challenge to Napoleon, the result of a long visit to Germany and the impression made on him by the kidnapping of the Duc d'Enghien. But Gustavus was no soldier: the abortive operations in north-west Germany ended with the sur-render of 1000 Swedes to Marshal Bernadotte at the fall of Lübeck in November 1806. Pomerania, however, where Gustavus abolished serfdom and set up a constitution, might still be a valuable base for British trade. Meanwhile, to the west of the Swedish territory, Crown Prince Frederick commanded 20,000 Danes in the duchies. The demise of the Holy Roman Empire had led him to announce the inclusion of Holstein as an 'inseparable portion of the monarchy' (Patent of 9 September 1806) and to promote the use of the Danish language there, with unfortunate long-term consequences; but his immediate problem was how to avoid being drawn belatedly into the war at a very unfavourable juncture.

The Berlin Decree of December 1806 was the prelude to a year which tore the Scandinavian countries apart and has had lasting consequences. The defeat of Russia at Friedland in June would in any case have left Sweden in an unenviable position, but on 16 July 8000 British troops of the King's German Legion arrived off Rügen in time to persuade Gustavus to denounce a recent armistice with the French in order to take part in a new Allied offensive. The treaties completed at Tilsit a week before made this an impossibility and the British expedition, for reasons shortly to be explored, landed in Denmark instead. The Swedes lost both Stralsund and Rügen and with great difficulty with-drew across the Baltic. At the same time their relations with Russia began to deteriorate, as Gustavus rejected the proposal that he too should come to terms with Napoleon. But Sweden had the consolation that the British alliance both safeguarded her iron exports and focused the trade of Britain upon her west coast: imports to Gothenburg doubled in 1808, when the harbour was crowded with as many as 1200 sail awaiting entrance to the Baltic.

The plight of Denmark, driven in the opposite direction, had no such compensation. The Order in Council of 7 January 1807, which stopped the port-to-port trade in the Mediterranean, exacerbated protests against British blockade regulations, whereas the same bitterness was absent from Dano-French relations, so long as Napoleon refrained from applying the Continental System to neutrals. The belief that Danish policy was now prejudiced in favour of the French made it easier for Canning to act on insufficient evidence—a false report that the Danish fleet was being prepared for sea and dubious indications from Hamburg-Altona of an impending French move into the duchies. But it was chiefly his sense of the extreme urgency of Britain's needs at this crisis that prompted Canning's decision (18 July) to anticipate a hypothetical French move against Denmark. The Russo-French secret treaty of 7 July was not then known in London: its terms give Canning a retrospective excuse on the moral issue, but leave it an open question whether a less brusque diplomacy might not have secured Danish co-operation with Britain and avoided a not unimportant forfeiture of goodwill on the Continent. For Canning's demand to control Denmark's fleet as a pledge of her intentions rendered it virtually impossible for the crown prince to make what his minister in Paris presented as an obvious choice 'between a passing danger to our mainland possessions and the risk of terminating our existence as a sea power'. As it was, the landing of 30,000 troops (including those from Rügen) and a three-night bombardment of Copenhagen, which killed 2000 persons and destroyed the cathedral and university quarter, forced the Danes to surrender their seventeen ships of the line and naval stores worth £2,000,000. But these events also made a lasting alliance with Napoleon an affair not only of honour but of expediency: without their fleet the Danes were powerless to defend even Zealand against him.

One consequence was a Dano-Swedish war (March 1808–December 1809). A French army under Bernadotte entered Jutland with a view to a landing in Skaane; a British force of about half its size under Sir John Moore arrived at Gothenburg. Owing to distrust of the Swedish intentions, Moore never landed his troops; but the British fleet under Sir James Saumarez played a more active part, covering the Swedish coast and carrying away 7600 Spaniards from Bernadotte's command to assist the revolt of their fellow-countrymen in the Peninsula. Bernadotte's force achieved nothing except free quarters for twelve months, while the fighting on the Swedish–Norwegian frontier, which began with a small-scale invasion of east Norway, brought just enough taste of victory to the Norwegian army to stimulate pride and popularise its Danish commander, Prince Christian August of Augustenburg. No territorial changes resulted from this war; Sweden's losses were all in the east.

In February 1808 the Russian army with the goodwill of Napoleon opened its campaign for the conquest of Finland. The defenders, about 20,000 strong, withdrew northwards in the belief that the retention of Sveaborg, the powerful fortress in Helsingfors harbour, would enable them to restore the position when summer came; but Sveaborg was surrendered on 3 May without a fight. The summer, indeed, brought a partial recovery, with deeds of valour that helped the growth of Finnish nationalism, but the Russian forces grew to 58,000 men, who by the end of the year had driven the Swedish army out of the country. By March 1809 the Finns were negotiating with Russia; by May the Russians were in the Aaland Islands, poised for an attack on Stockholm. Sweden's only ally was Britain, who through Admiral Saumarez controlled the Baltic throughout the ice-free period of every year; and the British advice was to make peace. In September the treaty of Fredrikshamn ceded Finland to Russia, together with the Aaland Islands and part of the border province of West Bothnia, thus effectively ending the eastward expansion of Scandinavian power and culture which had begun with the crusades of the twelfth and thirteenth centuries.

But a sequence of events had been set in train that was to bring Sweden some compensation. Diplomatic isolation and military failure were both attributed with some justification to the king; while the war still raged he was dethroned by conspirators from the armies. The Estates were summoned to formulate a new constitution for a new king, and the throne then passed from Gustavus IV to the former regent, the younger brother of Gustavus III. Charles XIII being both old and childless, the choice of crown prince was clearly momentous. Passing over the young son of the deposed monarch, the Estates twice rejected the candidate who would have united Scandinavia, namely King Frederick VI of Denmark, his chances being ruined by his absolutist principles. Since his father's death in 1808 he had behaved more autocratically than before, introducing a strict censorship, discontinuing the meetings of ministers, and ruling mainly through his military staff. Prince Christian August was therefore chosen—partly with an eye to Norwegian sympathies—and on his sudden death in May 1810 his elder brother came into consideration as well as again King Frederick. Either of these candidates was acceptable to Napoleon, with whom Sweden had made her peace in January.

The initiative that brought Bernadotte to the steps of a throne was that of a Swedish lieutenant of noble birth, C. O. Mörner, but the controlling circumstance was the attitude of the emperor, whose approval of a French candidature—though he would have preferred Eugène de Beauharnais—was interpreted from uncertain signs as a direct mandate for the election of Bernadotte. That the choice of a French marshal would guarantee internal stability and might reverse the position regarding Finland was certainly in the mind of the Estates; they also remembered Bernadotte's tactful handling of their fellow-countrymen at Lübeck and elsewhere: but few can have foreseen that they were founding the most durable of the Napoleonic dynasties. The ailing king survived for eight more years, but Charles John (as the new crown prince must be called) was in effect regent from his arrival in Sweden in October 1810, with full responsibility for Swedish policy in relation to the international conflict, which had already cost his adopted country its hold on Finland.

In the meantime the Danes, through their enforced enmity to the supreme sea-power, were losing virtually everything. Their last ship of the line was sunk in 1808; by 1814 more than half the total tonnage of their mercantile marine—some 1560 ships to a value of £8,000,000—had been captured or destroyed; even Iceland was not too poor to fall a prey to a dissolute adventurer, 'King Jörgen', whose brief reign was terminated by the arrival of a British warship; and in January 1813 the authorities were driven to declare a formal bankruptcy. But the collapse of the old Danish economy mattered less in the long run than the effect on Denmark's relations with Norway, which had found itself suddenly cut off, not merely from its administrative centre but from one quarter of its corn supply. At first Britain enforced a strict blockade, extending eventually even to the trickle of corn from Archangel, in order to force the Norwegians to export their timber in defiance of the Continental System. Then for about two years, with King Frederick's permission, British licences were used for export and import, and trade greatly flourished. But in 1812–13, when Britain had both Russian and Swedish support and less need for Norwegian timber, the blockade was again intensified: the native crops were the worst on record, so the Norwegians lived on bark-bread or starved outright. It was some small compensation to Norwegian—and Danish—pride that their privateers took substantial toll of British shipping.

When the century opened, Norway was roughly equal to Denmark in population and wealth, had its own army, and provided the main strength in men and material for the common navy. The peasants in their lonely valleys were politically inactive for the most part, and sporadic outbursts against Danish officialdom had been quickly suppressed. But in 1796–1804 the travels of a peasant lay preacher, H. N. Hauge, a powerful evangelist who also organised profitable economic activities for the 'brethren', as he called them, began a national religious revival which in the long run did much to give the common people purpose and influence. Meanwhile the upper classes in the towns were demanding the establishment of certain national institutions, notably a bank and a university. After 1807 the circumstances of the war caused the Danes to appoint an administrative council for Norway, and eventually a Stattholder; a university charter was also conceded. But the years of *de facto* separation nourished the thought that Norway might be able to stand on its own feet, helped by its strong trade ties with Britain. Alternatively, a union of all Scandinavia had much to recommend it, especially if the popular prince Christian August had survived to become its leader. Finally, there was a small but influential group which already favoured a union with Sweden instead of Denmark.

From October 1810, when Napoleon's threats forced Sweden to declare war on Britain, her prospects for a time seemed scarcely brighter than Denmark's. Only the fact that it suited Britain to use her navy, not to attack them but to keep Gothenburg and the passage to the Baltic open for her convoys, saved the Swedes from economic disaster during the uneasy interval before Napoleon turned against Russia. But Charles John, viewing the prospect more objectively than a native Swede could have done, was already deciding that a reconquest of Finland, however gratifying to national pride, would be hazardous to attempt while Britain ruled the Baltic and, if successful, would make a lasting enemy of Russia. To take Norway from Denmark was an alternative that would give Sweden a natural frontier and could be facilitated by the offer of wide powers of self-government, which a son of the revolution might readily allow. Moreover, to Napoleon's enemies this could be represented as a reasonable forfeit which Frederick should pay for supporting him.

In January 1812 Napoleon seized Swedish Pomerania. His intention was to enforce a stricter adhesion to the Continental System, but the effect was to enrage the pro-French military circles in Sweden, making it easier for Charles John to pursue his design as the ally of Russia against his former master. In April Russia accepted a plan for a joint landing in Zealand, which was to wrest Norway from Denmark before the Swedes in return helped to create a diversion on Napoleon's flank in Germany. The plan was not carried out, but at Åbo in August Alexander gave Charles John still more advantageous terms for a similar operation to commence in September—the month of the French entry into Moscow. Thus the Swedish intervention in the war came to be delayed until after the winter, when Britain by the Treaty of Stockholm (3 March 1813) became a party to the agreement, on the basis that she would furnish large subsidies and naval assistance for the acquisition of Norway, while Sweden was to supply 30,000 men for a 'direct mainland operation against the common enemy'.

The consequence of this ambiguously worded treaty was that Charles John placed his forces in Pomerania so as to threaten Holstein, while his allies were demanding that he operate against Napoleon's armies in Germany: so far from doing this, he sentenced to death a Swedish general who defied his orders for the purpose of safeguarding the position of the Allies in Hamburg. Since no Allied troops were put at his disposal to secure Norway for him, in May he offered to accept the diocese of Trondheim (including all northern Norway) with other compensation in Germany, but King Frederick rashly refused. Eventually, however, the military situation forced Napoleon's enemies to settle their differences: Charles John was given command of an army of 160,000 men, of whom only 30,000 were Swedes, and in return undertook to operate first against the French. His defeats of Oudinot at Grossbeeren (23 August) and of Ney at Dennewitz (6 September) were skilfully conducted engagements which prepared the way for the Allied triumph at Leipzig, but on all three occasions Charles John kept his Swedes carefully in reserve. Having agreed after Leipzig to join in the advance to the Rhine, he broke off to the north instead to attack the Danes in Schleswig-Holstein. There were no major battles: with a numerical superiority of nearly four to one, and the sympathy of the German population in the Duchies, Charles John's army was assured of victory.

Nevertheless, the negotiations leading to the Treaty of Kiel (14 January 1814) were by no means trouble-free. Metternich was working to restrict the gains of Russia's friend, and Britain, while taking Heligoland from the Danes, looked very coldly upon Charles John's claims as long as he failed to move Rhinewards; only the support of Alexander, which he never afterwards forgot, enabled him to achieve his main aim. In the circumstances it is not surprising that the Norwegian dependencies of Iceland, Greenland, and the Faeroes were left in Danish hands or that the Danes were to be compensated with Pomerania and Rügen, proportionate relief for Norway's share in their national debt, and a payment towards the cost of the force they must now equip against Napoleon.

The Swedish crown prince left Kiel on the morrow of the treaty, but his army advanced no farther than Belgium during the last two months of the war, while the future of France was unsettled. Only when his hopes of preferment there came finally to nothing did he join Alexander and the other leaders in Paris, to secure the promise of a renewed British naval blockade and of military support for his acquisition of Norway, which was now challenged.

Refusing to be bound by the Treaty of Kiel, the Norwegian people had obtained a brief taste of independence. Since May 1813 their Stattholder had been Prince Christian Frederick, the youthful cousin and heir-presumptive of the king of Denmark. It was clearly not in his interest to surrender Norway, so he was readily persuaded to assume office as provisional regent, pending the election of representatives of the peasants, the towns and the Services to an assembly at Eidsvold, where the members of the official class (who were in the majority) in one month formulated a constitution. Then on 17 May the regent accepted the throne of Norway as an independent constitutional monarchy. These events aroused considerable sympathy for Norway among the Whig Opposition and the commercial classes in Britain, and Castlereagh was faced with the awkward point that international law recognised a right of resistance in the people of a ceded province. To avoid this issue, responsibility for the Norwegian uprising was attributed to Danish activity behind the scenes, and pressure was duly applied in Copenhagen. But Charles John was well aware that, the danger in Europe being apparently at an end, the powers other than Russia would welcome an excuse to deprive an upstart of a prize taken from a legitimate sovereign.

Accordingly, when the Norwegians rejected the demands of the Allied commissioners and resorted to arms, he was prompt to engage in the briefest and least bloody of all his campaigns—a week's skirmishing in south-east Norway—and then gave terms that included his acceptance of the constitution. On 4 November the king of Sweden was elected to the throne vacated by Christian Frederick, on conditions which implied the establishment of a union with a sovereign power rather than the ratification of a cession based on the Treaty of Kiel. The Congress of Vienna, then already assembled, offered no objection: there Denmark was relieved of anxiety about her retention of Holstein, long garrisoned by Russian troops, but was forced to sell Pomerania and Rügen to Prussia.

For each of the Scandinavian states, the post-war period was a time of poverty and disappointment. Denmark was hit hardest, for her corn trade had lost its hold on the Norwegian market and was shut out from the British by the law of 1815, while stricken Copenhagen had to relinquish the commercial leadership of the north to Hamburg. The staple industry of south Norway was also ruined for a generation by the preference which Britain accorded to Canadian timber; Sweden, too, lagged behind in industrial development. In each case governments had to struggle to provide for a rapidly increasing population under conditions of acute inflation and declining commerce.

Nevertheless, these were countries which stood out in an era of reaction by comparison with the oppressed condition of so many others. Denmark's reduced circumstances seemed to bring king and people closer together rather than to build up opposition to the absolutist system, which had reached logical completion as recently as

1800, the year of the formal abolition of the Icelandic Althing. Even the revolutions of 1830 caused little stir among the Danes, and it was an agitation in the Duchies with German support from outside that led to the creation of the consultative provincial Estates. The Finns, too, found themselves to be not unfavourably placed under the tsar, who in 1809 had promised them in person that his new Grand Duchy should be ruled in accordance with the Swedish constitutional provisions of 1772 and 1789. Although their Estates were not summoned again until 1863, Finland was given the Cabinet of a separate state; retained its own legal, financial, and military organisation; and had its frontiers extended by the reincorporation of the territory lost in 1721.

Sweden and Norway, however, are remarkable for their representative institutions, then new-modelled, which have survived all later upheavals. The Swedish Instrument of Government of 1809 gave the Estates absolute control of taxation, participation in the legislative power, and the right to hold the advisers of the crown legally responsible for their advice. A compromise between the historic traditions of Sweden and the ideas of Montesquieu and the Enlightenment, the system left much power to the king and the bureaucracy, especially as the Estates need only be summoned at five-year intervals and their narrow class basis was not seriously reformed until 1867. The Norwegian constitution, on the other hand, owed a special debt to the French constitution of 1791, though the ten liberal principles which were unanimously adopted as its basis also reflect a knowledge of English and American practice. Legislative and financial power was concentrated in a single chamber (working in two sections), the royal veto being effective only for the duration of two parliaments, which were to meet at not more than three-year intervals. As the franchise from the first included all peasant freeholders and five-year leaseholders, whose outlook was increasingly nationalist, the principle of popular sovereignty asserted in 1814 led on naturally to the highly democratic, separate Norwegian monarchy of 1905.

Constitutional differences were one of many factors that prevented Sweden–Norway from growing together within its natural frontiers into the substantial power for which Charles John had hoped. This was evident even in the period of reaction after the wars, when small states had reason to avoid attracting the unfavourable attention of their stronger neighbours. In 1818, the year of his accession to the two thrones, Charles John was severely taken to task by the Conference of Aix-la-Chapelle for disputing the validity of the debt payments to Denmark incurred under the Treaty of Kiel, which his Norwegian subjects declined to recognise. Accepting the inevitable, he negotiated very favourable terms for Norway, only to meet with unreasonable and ultimately dangerous delays on the part of the Norwegian Parliament.

In July 1821, when payment was at last reluctantly authorised, joint Swedish–Norwegian military manoeuvres took place in east Norway, and it is to this day uncertain whether the king's intention in ordering them had been to make the intervention of the Powers, busy that year in Italy, a little less likely—or in the last resort to enforce his will upon the Norwegians. The crisis passed, and Norway continued to grow apart from Sweden.

In conclusion, brief reference may be made to the development of the separate national cultures. Stockholm in the time of Gustavus III had figured impressively as a home of the arts, with its National Theatre (1773), Opera House (1782), and Academy (1786). The king himself contributed prose dramas that outlived their author, and a galaxy of talent adorned his court. Sweden also shared with Norway an important peasant art, of which the products decorated the churches and homes of the countryside. But with this exception Sweden was not emancipated from a dominant French influence until the Romantic movement brought in, along with German models, the direct inspiration of the Scandinavian past. The members of the famous Gothic Society and contributors to its periodical *Iduna* (1811–24) included not only Sweden's national poet, Esaias Tegnér, and her first modern historian, E. G. Geijer, but even the father of Swedish gymnastics, P. H. Ling: a mediocre versifier, he sought the rebirth of the Viking heroes in flesh and blood.

Denmark and Norway had a single literary language, and it is significant that the first—and with one exception the greatest—writer to employ it, Ludvig Holberg, though a Norwegian by birth, brought out every one of his many plays, histories, and philosophical works in Copenhagen. But after his death in 1754 the German hold upon Danish literature revived until the opening years of the new century, when the misfortunes of their country encouraged the Danish romantics, even more than their fellows in Sweden, to seek inspiration in past glories. This was the case with Adam Oehlenschläger, whom Tegnér crowned 'king of Scandinavian singers' at a ceremony at Lund in 1829, and still more with Bishop Grundtvig, who turned from his early studies of Norse mythology to earn fame as poet, hymn-writer and preacher, but above all as patriot. He has been called the Danish Carlyle, but the influence of such a sage upon the masses was far more direct in a country with a complete network of elementary schools established by law as early as 1814: for their existence made it possible later to set up the Folk High Schools, where young men (or women) of the peasant class were brought together at the most impressionable age to be taught according to Grundtvig's doctrine of the 'living word'.

However, the first Folk High Schools of 1844 and 1850 belong to the history of a later age. So does the appearance of a distinctive Norwegian literature with the first great work of Henrik Wergeland in 1830; the beginning of a separate, rather artificial, Norwegian language with Ivar Aasen's *Grammar of Common Speech* in 1847; also the more feasible purging of Icelandic from Danish usages, which began with the periodical *Fjölnir* in 1835; and, in the same year, the publication of the first of many editions of the folk-epic, *Kalevala*, which marked a significant stage in the growth of Finnish nationalism. In culture as well as in politics the peoples of Scandinavia, no less than the French of the July Revolution or the British under the Great Reform Act, were pressing forward into a new era.

CHAPTER XVIII

RUSSIA, 1798–1825[1]

THE end of the eighteenth century was an era of fulfilment in Russia even if the abuses of the regime were becoming as ingrained as its habit of success. As much of the Petrine vision had been realised as was possible through the imitation of Europe's political and social superstructure rather than through the basic transformation of Russia. The richer nobility had been entirely westernised, the diplomatic and military tools of *raison d'état* had been acquired with the narrow industrial basis which contemporary warfare demanded and with effective if wasteful methods of conscripting man-power. Even some of the cultural insignia of national greatness were apparent. With the last two partitions of Poland in 1793 and 1795, the empire had reached territorial limits in the west that were hardly to be extended until the mid-twentieth century. In the south the Black Sea coast-line had been won from the Dniester to the sea of Azov and to the northern rivers of the Caucasus. Odessa was founded by 1796, and beyond the Caucasus the Christian kingdom of Georgia was becoming a voluntary protectorate. From the Caspian sea to the frontiers of Chinese administration the nomads of Central Asia were increasingly submitting to the political influence of Russian arms, trade and even culture.

As far as can be ascertained from the periodic and unreliable census of males for fiscal and military purposes, the population in 1800 within the new frontiers was probably nearer 35 than 40 million. This population seems to have begun to surge in time with the similar phenomenon in central and western Europe, although conditions were dissimilar. In 1812, with some of Transcaucasia added, the population of the empire was not far short of 45 million; the war had set it back slightly. In 1825, with Bessarabia but still excluding Finland and the new Poland, it was nearly 55 million. Of the round 37 millions in 1800, Russian Asia, that is the vast Siberian territory, accounted for two millions at most, including natives as well as convicts, exiles and settlers. There was some industrial but virtually no agrarian serfdom beyond the Urals.[2] In European Russia over 90 per cent of the population must in 1800 have

---

[1] The editor and the author are indebted to Dr J. Frankel for some abridgement of this chapter. To convert a date from the old (Julian) into our (Gregorian) calendar, add 11 days in the eighteenth and 12 days in the nineteenth century: e.g. 16/27 November1796; 11/23 March 1801. The symbols OS (old style) and NS (new style) are often used.

[2] These figures and those which follow are arbitrary but in line with contemporaries' and recent historians' interpretations of statistics based on poll-tax liability.

been agrarian and well over half this percentage were serfs attached to the land and bodily owned by individual nobles.[1] Most of the rest were so-called state peasants attached to public or imperial family domains under various types of fiscal as distinct from the praedial discipline applied to the serfs. The Russian empire was legally a class state and the proportion between definable classes is illuminating. A compromise between contemporary estimates shows beside the peasants about a million and a half urban workers and dependants, subject like them to poll tax and conscription and mostly living in the 500 'towns' (so classified as containing 1000 inhabitants), and some quarter of a million 'merchants' and non-noble industrialists, including their families, registered in guilds and possessing free status. All these classes were defined by one contemporary statistician, Arseniev, as 'productive', the 'unproductive' ones being the hereditary nobility whom we may reckon at half a million in the first decade of the nineteenth century, the officials including life nobles amounting to a quarter of a million, the clergy, half a million, and the armed forces with their dependants at well over a million.[2]

In the first half of the eighteenth century the Russian peasantry, in spite or because of the poll tax, managed to increase the sown area of the country. Although contemporaries now started to complain that a drift to industry and the towns was damaging agriculture,[3] statistics show that this was only a marginal movement. Of more significance was the migration to the Ukraine and beyond the Volga. Nor was either movement uncontrolled. Runaway serfs were the minority. Most migrants were directed by masters to their new estates, brought in as domestics to the cities or licensed to move subject to the payment of *obrók* (body rent), virtually a ransom payable continuously in replacement of *barshchina* (week-work)[4] and arbitrarily fixed according to the serf's wages or profits—for he sometimes went into business on his own account. For other than *obrochnye* (*obrók* payers) there was no relaxation of bondage, the rigour of which may be said to have reached its peak just before classical economics and humanitarianism converged in Russia to make the case for free labour.

Even if the American example is to be the yard-stick, Russian serfs, particularly landless domestics, can quite reasonably be described as slaves—although Catherine had banned the word *rab*, a slave. The

---

[1] It should be noted that *enforced* concubinage was never legal or socially condoned, although frequently practised.

[2] A. G. Rashin, *Naselenie Rossii za 100 let* (Moscow, 1956), pp. 25, 28–9. P. A. Khromov, *Ekonomicheskoe razvitie Rossii v. XIX–XX vekakh* (U.S.S.R., 1950), pp. 79–84.

[3] P. l. Lyashchenko, *Istoriya narodnovo khozyaistva S.S.R.R.*, (1952 edition), vol. I, pp. 362, 402.

[4] Incorrectly translated as 'boon work' in the author's contribution in *N.C.M.H.*, vol. x, p. 371.

serf had no rights of redress against his master, who could at will draft him for penal deportation to Siberia, conscript him as a recruit for 25 years of military service, or put him up for public sale. The serf could not own land apart from his inalienable stake in communal tenure, and his chattels belonged legally to his master. A limit to the master's brutality was set by the law forbidding him to endanger the life of his serf, but the only sanction was denunciation by his fellow landlords, for the Empress Catherine had made the old resource of petitioning the crown with this motive punishable by deportation. Yet such a servile condition could be arbitrarily extended by the crown to state peasants of semi-free status, and this fate befell nearly a million such peasants who, with the land to which they were attached, were delivered by Catherine II and Paul I to their favourites. Moreover, despite Catherine's declaration in her celebrated *nakaz* (instruction) of 1765 that 'one must avoid making men slaves unless it is absolutely necessary . . . for reasons of state', serfdom was now fastened on the hitherto untied peasants of the Ukraine, including even some Cossack frontier colonies, and on the newly acquired Polish provinces. Paul for his part maintained the standard argument of Russian conservatives that the peasant was better off under a patriarchal serf-owner than under the soulless fisc, and he himself indeed was more successful as a landlord than as a monarch or quarter-master general.

Yet, paradoxically, serfdom was still doing more to advance than to hinder national success. Both the state peasant and the privately owned peasant provided conscript cannon-fodder and both paid poll tax (literally 'soul tax')—a few shillings a year—which nevertheless produced nearly two-fifths of the ordinary revenue in 1805. The state peasants, too, were conscripted for essential services—posts and road-making—but they were mostly subsistence farmers whose contribution to the national income did not enter the incipient exchange economy. It was mainly from the produce of serf labour on private lands—in some regions and instances already developing into *latifundia*—that the towns were fed, raw materials supplied for industry and export and the cultural transformation of the untaxed land-owning nobility financed.

Nor was industry itself yet based on free labour. In fact the metallurgical industry as established by Peter the Great still depended on peasant labour. Although non-noble proprietors could not own serfs, they could use them in their mines and iron-works which enjoyed a corporate status. Thus, in 1812, only about half the 120,000 workers recorded for 'manufacturing industries' other than metallurgy and mining were free. By then the Russian iron industry was in relative decline. The foundries, huge by contemporary standards, had been built beyond the Urals during the first three decades of the previous century, and during Catherine's reign they were less efficient than smaller plants.

Soviet historians claim that, in the latter, charcoal furnaces 10–13 metres high were more productive per unit than the new coke-furnaces in England, although new English equipment was being imported in 1800. Russian iron production was then the highest in the world—12 million *puds* or just under 100,000 tons up till 1806 when the Franco-Russian alliance cut the demand for exports to England which had taken up a half of it.[1] The absorption of the remainder in Russia is an indication of the increase in industry and internal trade in the second half of the eighteenth century. Meanwhile foreign trade rose from a turnover of some 21 million roubles at the beginning of Catherine's reign to near 110 million at the end of it. The leading export in 1796 was that of flax and hemp products at 13 million roubles, followed by iron at 5 million; among imports sugar led at about $5\frac{1}{2}$ million followed by woollen cloth at 4 million.[2] The fact that the official figures for luxury imports such as wine were comparatively low, considering what is known of the nobility's standard of living, may have been due to smuggling on a scale nullifying the ostensible trade balance.

The growth of internal and external trade hardly affected the agrarian poverty of Russia; the thin layer of beneficiaries consisted of the merchant class (*kupechestvo*), the highest of the three urban classes recognised by the legislation of 1775 and 1785, which was producing millionaires with incomes of 100,000 roubles in the 1800's, and no less the nobility. The latter took more part in trade and industry than the equivalent class in western and central Europe; they owned a large proportion of the industrial enterprises, while most of the hands employed as 'free' wage labour were in fact their serfs, paying them *obrók* for a licence to work in the factories of the *kupechestvo*. They might join the merchants' highest guild, the lucrative liquor and tobacco monopolies were usually farmed by them and above all the nobles gained as landowners from the towns' growing demand for foodstuffs.

There was by now no hereditary hierarchy among the Russian nobility; status followed rank (*chin*) in the military or civil service of which there were fourteen parallel grades; and, where the empress' private favour did not apply, place depended almost wholly, and promotion partly, upon social connexions with the court. The greater offices went to generals and state servants of long standing, lesser ones to members of rich cosmopolitan families, some of whom like the Stroganovs were recently ennobled, and a disproportionate number to Germans from the Baltic provinces annexed during the eighteenth century. This infusion was unpopular but persistent—even to 1914. Although, since the 'charter' of 1785, the local nobility had enjoyed the

---

[1] R. Portal, *L'Oural au XVIIIème siecle* (Paris, 1950), pp. 374–6.
[2] Lyashchenko, op. cit., vol. I, p. 415.

right to appoint to certain local offices, it exercised no power in the capital cities, St Petersburg and Moscow, and even in the countryside was subordinate to the centrally appointed governor and his staff. In the capitals great landed possessions (always expressed in serf units, not area) were valued as wealth, not power. At the top the nobility were completely westernised, and French had become not only their language of social intercourse but an alternative official language; it was current in the correspondence of the tsarist foreign service until 1914. This was the result of the urge to foreign travel and domestic education set in train by Peter the Great. The children of the nobility were mostly privately educated as in other countries, though less well. There were one or two fashionable private schools and the state provided cadet schools, the corps of pages and latterly the Smolny institute for girls. The university of Moscow—the only Russian one since Dorpat was German—had low standing; higher education, if any, before the routine entry to the military or state service was generally obtained in Germany.

It suited Russian liberal historians in the nineteenth century to represent the Russian nobility as gaining power at the expense of the crown by their release in 1762 from Peter the Great's imposition of service and the confirmation of their rights by Catherine the Great's charter of 1785. This was not what happened. Although the charter (paragraph 18) did confirm the right of the nobles 'to obtain release from service', paragraph 20 reminded them of their duty, when called upon by the autocracy, 'to spare neither toil nor life in the service of the state'. In fact a few years' service was to remain a condition of social respectability among educated noble families for at least another three-quarters of a century; indeed shirking service might be treated as evidence of incapacity to exercise noble privileges. Noble privileges could also be withdrawn, in spite of the charter of 1785, on the Crown's instruction; the Emperor Paul demoted a few hundred, mostly deservedly, as criminals, and a number of these received corporal punishment. Indeed, even in the period immediately following the assassination of Paul I by leading nobles and army officers, Speranskii was able to write that 'I find in Russia only two estates, the slaves of the landlords and the slaves of the Emperor'.[1]

The degree of subservience of the nobility to the crown in Catherine the Great's later years may be largely attributed, however, to her personal ascendancy. Adam Czartoryski, the young Polish noble, who came to Russia with his brother after the final partition of his country, described the awe inspired by the empress: 'As soon as the name Catherine was pronounced all faces at once took on a serious and submissive air . . . no one dared even to whisper a grievance or a reproach; it was as if . . . the most outrageous evils inflicted by her were so many

[1] M. Raeff, *Michael Speransky, Statesman of Imperial Russia* (The Hague, 1957), p. 121.

decrees of providence. . . .' But the last decade of her reign was an anti-climax so far as the political evolution of Russia was concerned. The French Revolution completed the disillusionment of the former patroness of *philosophes* which the success of Russian *raison d'état* as distinct from *salus populi* had begun, the progress of her revulsion being reflected in her correspondence with the German savant Grimm, the most constant of her academic contacts over the years. The shock of regicide in 1793 got the better of her self-confident serenity and led to demonstrative if not precautionary measures in Russia such as the banning of the word 'republic' from stage plays, the removal of effigies of politically suspect *philosophes* from the royal collection and the prohibition of some republican fashions of dress. Yet she seems to have counted on France settling its own affairs, she foresaw the advent of a 'Caesar' as early as 1791 and she was by no means active in the cause of inter-dynastic counter-revolution despite the plans for this which she optimistically drew up in 1792. She gave the *émigrés* as little cash—100,000 francs—as seemed decent, and the 18,000 men she promised to the international army at Coblenz got no further than Poland where she described the anti-Russian patriots as being Jacobins no less than the republicans of Paris.

Exactly how the revolution influenced the *causes célèbres* of the two men of letters, Novikov and Radishchev, is by no means clear. Today the long toleration of N. I. Novikov (1744–1818) seems perhaps more remarkable than his eventual condemnation. His extraordinary career as a philanthropist and publicist had begun in the 1770's, his work varying from the foundation of an orphans' school to the organisation and publicising of relief in the famine of 1787—a provocation to the regime as great as that of Tolstoy's similar campaign of 1891. But his main activity was in publishing, and the yearly output of books in the whole of Russia rose from 166, when he began to farm the Moscow university press, to 366 in the year 1791 when his own press was closed, declining in the next decade to 233. It is clear that Catherine did not want to make a martyr for political rationalism out of Novikov whose satires she had herself anonymously combated in print as a defender of benevolent despotism; but the international challenge of French anti-monarchism tipped the balance against him. In 1792 she ordered his arrest and he was sentenced to fifteen years' imprisonment for crimes intended rather than committed. She delayed the confirmation of his sentence and it was annulled by her successor Paul, who was motivated less by sympathy for the victim than by the desire to countermand his predecessor's decisions. Novikov's real offence was his connexion with freemasonry which in St Petersburg at the end of the eighteenth century was identified with a mystical sect of the Martinist movement (disciples of the contemporary French writer Saint Martin). Freemasonry became associated with non-conformist religiosity, incipient sympathy for revolution and cosmopolitanism, all of which represented a challenge to orthodoxy and autocracy, while its ritual and superstition disqualified it from privileges which a Voltairean ruler might concede to a rationalist heresy—even a republican one.

The second martyr whom the Empress Catherine supplied for the hagiology of Russian liberalism, A. N. Radishchev, had been sent abroad as a youth under the educational policy originated by Peter the Great, and brought back with him the egalitarian and republican ideas of some *philosophes* of the left, Mably and Raynal in particular. Although a somewhat audacious commentary by him on a work of Mably was published by Novikov, Radishchev drew no attention in his career as a civil servant until in 1790 he recklessly published, perforce in his own press, the *Journey from St Petersburg to Moscow* which was to become a classic of Russian literature as well as social history, together with an *Ode to Liberty*.[1] In the form of a traveller's diary, the *Journey* is a tirade against conditions in the countryside, the horrors of serfdom and the vices of the landlord class and of the government which profited by it. The empress 'read his book from cover to cover', so she wrote, and her careful comments curiously combined an acknowledgement of the detailed facts with denunciation of the conclusions and motives of the author.[2] Radishchev was sentenced to death on various counts of disturbing the peace, inciting to disaffection and insulting the empress, but Catherine commuted the sentence to Siberian exile whence Paul recalled him in the same way as Novikov. Radishchev was even taken back into the civil service in 1801, but the limitations of Alexander I's new deal disillusioned him and he committed suicide a year later.

The cases of Novikov and Radishchev were symptomatic of Russian conditions, in so many ways contradictory, at the end of Catherine's reign, but not of a political movement. Separating them from the Decembrist revolt was Alexander's entire era of abortive reform. There is only tenuous evidence to support those historians who are anxious to establish the continuity of the revolutionary tradition. Although Radishchev's book did circulate before its suppression its lessons lay dormant.

Incidents of such a kind had no bearing upon the morale of the regime. Military and diplomatic success had aroused national pride among the bureaucracy as well as the army even at humble levels; the Russian achievements in the Swedish and Turkish wars since the French Revolution, and in the final liquidation of Poland which flattered an ancient national grudge, were rightly identified with the personality of

---

[1] A. N. Radishchev, *A Journey from St Petersburg to Moscow*, ed. R. P. Thayer (Cambridge, Mass., 1961).
[2] V. A. Myakotin, *Iz istorii russkago obshchestva* (St Petersburg, 1902), p. 221.

the cosmopolitan sovereign. She was *Felitsiya*, the Russian equivalent of Gloriana, apostrophised in an ode by Derzhavin, the foremost Russian poet in the generation before Pushkin and a future minister of justice. Catherine contrived to appear as Russian as her subjects and emphasised the inheritance of Peter the Great. 'I ask myself at each instant of the day', she wrote, 'what would he forbid, what would he do if he were in my place?' Her depraved private life continued without involving any inattention to public affairs, and this was known. 'All is permitted to her,' it could be said. 'Her licentiousness was hallowed.' Indeed since Potemkin's time her favourites had less administrative control than ever. Platon Zubov held his morning levée on emerging from the empress' apartments and distributed patronage to all except the greatest officers of state, but no decisions of policy were in his hands. Catherine continued to work through her secretary of state, the first members of the *collegia* of war, marine and foreign affairs, and, more indirectly, the procurator of the Senate. The original collegiate system of committee administration was falling into disuse and was to decline further in Paul I's reign, the royal council which Catherine had remodelled as the 'council of her Majesty' rarely met, and the so-called 'directing' Senate was in fact losing all but the functions of promulgating imperial decrees and acting as a supreme appeal tribunal—one whose business was notoriously in arrear. Passive malcontents who saw the other side of the picture owing to their interests or principles included the Tsarevich Paul and his son the future Alexander I. As the son of Peter III, Paul had been excluded from the throne by his mother's *coup d'état*. The empress had isolated him from public affairs, deprived him of his children, governed in consort with her favourite, Potemkin, and so placed her morose and disagreeable son in a Hamlet-like situation. Latterly, Paul had been permitted to live in Gachina, a property near St Petersburg where he exercised the private army of 2000 troops permitted him in obsolete pseudo-Prussian drill and uniforms.

Alexander was deeply involved in these family and dynastic tensions during his boyhood, and the tragic career of his father undoubtedly had through him an indirect but powerful effect on the history of Russia. His mind was formed—or one might say divided for life—by two influences: Gachina to which the empress allowed him increasing access, and formal education by the Swiss Frederick La Harpe whom she appointed as his tutor in 1784. La Harpe belonged in his opinions to the left wing of the Enlightenment; and as a native of Vaud, resenting the overlordship of Bern, he was sympathetic to the French Revolution and the French intervention in his country. Still he held his post until the end of 1794, following Rousseau's educational principles and reading with his pupil classics of contemporary as well as ancient republicanism.

It is to the credit of both that he retained Alexander's lifelong friendship. To La Harpe's proto-romantic radicalism the corrupt regime of Catherine was not congenial. It was no more congenial, in spite of its success in war, to the militarism of the orderly room and the barrack square, rather than the battlefield, which Gachina represented and which Alexander inherited. So in 1796 at the age of eighteen the future emperor was writing to his friend the future chancellor, Viktor Kochubei, that he wanted to renounce his inheritance and live privately with his wife (Elizabeth of Baden whom he had married the previous year) 'on the banks of the Rhine'. He described by name the most powerful men at his grandmother's court as people he 'would not have as menials', and complained that 'our affairs are in incredible disorder, people steal right and left . . . and the Empire does nothing but extend its territory . . .'. This declaration marked an important stage in the development of Alexander's character and he revealed similar sentiments to Czartoryski shortly afterwards. To Czartoryski he confided his open-hearted sympathy for dismembered Poland and even revealed an enlightened respect for the motives and achievements, although not for the violence, of the French Revolution. It is from this remarkable interview that their long intimacy, and indeed Alexander's commitment to Poland, can be traced.

It is probable that Catherine had long intended to nominate Alexander rather than Paul as her successor, and a letter of Alexander to the empress in September 1796 can be interpreted as reluctant acceptance of the empress's intention.[1] But when Catherine died on 16/27 November no official steps had been taken and Alexander had already sent for his father. The succession took place without any hesitations, but it was characteristic of the regime that when the first messenger, one of the Zubovs, arrived at Gachina Paul had expected some more fatal summons and exclaimed to his wife '*nous sommes perdus*'. There was no prospect of the new tsar introducing fundamental changes and even his largely demonstrative minor ones have been exaggerated by contemporaries and by historians. Enmity towards the nobility as a caste, recurrent in the history of tsardom, was strengthened in Paul's case by jealousy of the nobility's exceptional alliance with his mother and by the isolation of his own far from aristocratic regime at Gachina. But his feud was rather with the symbols of his mother's rule than with its institutions or its secondary personnel. So the elderly Orlov as an assassin of Peter III in Catherine's interest was made to carry his victim's crown in a ceremony for reinterring Paul's putative father together with Catherine the Great, while Potemkin's tomb was broken

---

[1] N. K. Shilder, *Imperator Aleksandr I* (St Petersburg, 1904), vol. I, p. 279 (appendix). The extensive inferences and conjectures of Shilder and many other historians are quite arbitrary.

up and his remains buried in obscurity. Yet most of the great officers of state in 1796 retained their posts and even the infusion of Gachina personnel into the army, much resented as it was, did not take place at the top. Again it was the symbol, the introduction of Gachina uniforms, that counted.

That Paul at first showed some 'talent as a ruler' was admitted by one of the accessories to his murder, General Bennigsen. The German, Groeben, who found the absenteeism of the bureaucracy such that 'the vast and spacious offices of departments were frequented only by rats and mice' gave Paul credit for energising the Senate as a court of appeal so that it settled 11,000 outstanding cases in the first year of his reign. He approved, too, a new regularity in the paying of troops though he condemned the new uniforms. Less familiar uses of capricious despotism appeared in such instances as Paul's responsibility for the import of English textile machinery and his instructions that the report of a Moscow apothecary's process for producing beet sugar should be followed up—thus anticipating, if not introducing, two major lines of Russian industry. Paul's well known definition in his coronation manifesto of the serfs' labour services to their masters was, however, less effective than is commonly supposed. Although week-work on Sundays and Feast Days was categorically forbidden, its limitation to three days weekly was expressed hypothetically.[1] Apart from being ineffective, it stimulated the wildest hopes of emancipation and led to peasant disturbances which Paul ruthlessly suppressed. If this and similar prohibitions were in reality no evidence of a genuine liberalism, still less were they intended as a challenge to the rights and interests of the nobility. None of his predecessors turned so many state peasants into private serfs in so short a time and, in the same year as his edict on week-work, Paul showed his concern for the nobility by approving the foundation of a nobles' land bank to check the scandal of usurious mortgages. The fact was that his grudge against the previous regime left him with no loyalty to precedent or to the *status quo*, his conservative inhibitions were his own. So in the case of Poland he deprecated the final partition and declared that he would have made restitution if things had not gone too far. He summoned the ex-king Stanislas to his coronation, showing him royal honours but a lack of personal consideration. It was rather his mother's hostage, Czartoryski, who profited in place and favour from this respect for his country.

The tyrannical caprices which were Paul's undoing began with a ban on articles of dress reflecting French revolutionary fashion. In the same spirit, not only was the sensibly clothed Russian army given new and

---

[1] *Polnoe Sobranie Zakonov Rossiiskoi Imperii* (Collection of Laws of the Russian Empire) (S.P. 1839–43), vol. xxiv, No. 17909.

unpractical uniforms of obsolete Prussian pattern, but the pigtail and powder were reintroduced as symbols of the old regime's discipline. When the great field-marshal Suvorov criticised this, he was banished to his estate until required again for service in his famous Italian campaign of 1799. In the capital Paul's sense of insecurity and his mania for discipline put the civilian public under intolerable rules of protocol. The self-government of the nobility by their provincial corporations under the charter of 1785 was transgressed; nobles were deprived of their status to make them liable to corporal punishment, and the lower clergy as a whole was deprived of its exemption from flogging. The fear of revolution led to the closing once more of all private printing presses in Russia and eventually to the prohibition of any printed or manuscript works from abroad. But it was Paul's treatment of the officers of the army which was crucial. Transfers, demotion, the recall to service of officers in civilian and court posts, appeared not as a vast reform but as an exercise in tyranny. The garrison of the capital lived under a kind of parade-ground terror, and it became a common thing for officers to parade with their affairs wound up and with a stock of ready money lest they were sent off the square straight to Siberia.

Already in 1797 Alexander was complaining to La Harpe that 'everything has been turned upside-down and this has only increased the confusion' and he was asking 'guidance on a matter of the greatest importance, that is to give Russia the blessing of a free constitution'. Historians, following Alexander's friends and contemporaries, have tended to neglect the compromising element in this letter. When and how did Alexander envisage this fundamental reform, his father being a vigorous man of forty-three? So far as we know there was no conspiracy to which Alexander could, let alone would, have lent himself at this stage, but his ideas and words reflect perhaps the impression of impermanence belonging to Paul's psychopathic rulership. Alexander had now gathered, as he told La Harpe, a certain circle of like-minded political friends who were, as it turned out, to form or fail to form his domestic policy in the first three years of his own reign and who were individually to receive for long his intimate confidence and his friendship indefinitely. First there was Prince Adam Czartoryski, secondly Czartoryski's friend Count Paul Stroganov, the son of a rich and famous family though of comparatively recent nobility and himself a parlour Jacobin in his recent boyhood. Then there was Novosiltsev, Stroganov's cousin, and finally Count Viktor Kochubei, a nephew of the chancellor, Bezborodko, and already a man of experience in diplomacy and administration. Alexander's loyalty did not belong exclusively to this group. Parade-ground discipline of the Gachina type was represented by a man whom Paul had promoted from obscurity and who had become his son's friend too. This was A. Arakcheev, a man vilified by virtually all historians. Inhuman and obscurantist, he was nonetheless incorruptible, and efficient as an administrator although not as a soldier in the field. Alexander was to give him more frequent spells of increasing power in the course of his reign until he finally took over unofficially the whole routine work of the empire and gave his name to an era in Russian history, the brief *Arakcheevshchina*.

There are some grounds for attributing the origin of the conspiracy against Paul to the English ambassador Whitworth. The leader of the conspiracy, Count N. P. Panin, was a friend of the ambassador and supported the pro-English international policy which was reversed only late in 1799. It is plausible to suppose that Whitworth suggested a regency of the English type as a formula which might prove acceptable to the tsarevich Alexander. But relations with England deteriorated and, as Whitworth left Russia with his mission in May 1800, it is not possible to justify the Soviet textbook doctrine that English machinations were responsible for the actual assassination of Paul ten months later. In the course of this period Panin lost his post of vice-chancellor and his access to Paul, so the leadership of the plot was taken over by the military governor of Moscow, P. von der Pahlen. It is probable that the delay was due to Alexander's hesitation to give his consent. He had been approached by Panin, but how and when he agreed to enforced abdication—it is impossible to believe that he ever agreed to assassination—is unknown. As the plot developed, the two ablest men who could best work with Paul, Arakcheev and Rostopchin, and who might perhaps have saved him, were temporarily out of favour and away from the capital. So were, to the advantage of their future influence as being immune from suspicion, Alexander's three intimates Czartoryski, Novosiltsev and Kochubei. In the early months of 1801 Paul's actions and intentions became more evidently unbalanced and when Pahlen acted on the night of 11/23 March there is some (if inadequate) evidence that he forestalled measures which Paul intended against his own family, as he had become estranged from his wife and suspicious of Alexander. In form the *coup* followed the Russian pattern of action by senior officers and suborned guards. A bid for the succession by the Empress Maria Fedorovna, suspecting her son's complicity, left the household troops unmoved and was brushed aside by Bennigsen. Alexander was sent for and began his reign in tears. 'That is enough of acting like a child,' Pahlen is reported to have said. 'Now go and reign; show yourself to the troops.'

The successful conspiracy tended to perpetuate the political tradition in Russia of reform by assassination, a tradition which can be discovered again in the Decembrist mutiny and in the revolutionary terrorism of later years. According to Czartoryski, Alexander himself was permanently affected by the trauma of his accession. His responsibility for regicide, however tenuous, seems to have inclined his sensitive nature to the extremes of cynicism and mysticism. 'There is no remedy,' he told Czartoryski, 'I must suffer, this cannot change.' Moreover, the assassination re-opened that breach between the crown and the nobility which Catherine II had almost closed but which henceforward was to characterise the dynasty and to deter it from sharing its power even with the privileged classes.

The general joy at the change of regime, most marked in the capital cities and among the military and service nobility, was described by an Austrian diplomat as the normal reaction to the death of every Russian tsar, not excluding Catherine. Yet a revolution in political as distinct from national life was immediate. Alexander put administration in the hands of two of his grandmother's great officers of state, making the retired general Bekleshev procurator-general or virtual chief minister, and calling upon D. P. Troshchinskii, a former holder of that office, to be as he put it 'my guide'. The latter drafted the accession manifesto which bore no trace of the revolutionary liberalism mooted with his political friends by Alexander while tsarevich. Now he promised to 'rule the people entrusted to us by God according to the laws and spirit of our august late grandmother'. This was the policy of the conspirators and indeed Alexander kept Pahlen in office and brought back Panin, greeting him with the words: 'alas, things have not turned out as we thought.' They were both to be retained for a few months until the young emperor had found his feet and indiscretion or insolence led to their permanent banishment and disgrace. In the undoing of his father's caprices the most urgent action seems to have been remembered by Alexander himself on the night of the murder. This was the recall of an ill-found Cossack army dispatched by Paul on a desperate mission through Central Asia against India as a crazy demonstration of his united front with Napoleon against England. There was a general reversal to normalcy during the next three months. Imports and exports, from bread and liquor to books and music, were freed; frontiers re-opened to travellers; private printing re-licensed; Catherine's 'charters' to the nobility and towns renewed, and the clergy once again exempted from corporal punishment. 'Secret deportation,' a process of exile by administrative order, was nominally abolished although it was in fact to survive under a different name.

These were the achievements of the old school of administrators. Meanwhile Alexander had brought back to Russia the political friends of his minority whom Paul had dispersed: Kochubei, Czartoryski and N. N. Novosiltsev to join P. A. Stroganov who was already in St Petersburg, in the 'party of the young men' as their conservative critics began to call them. They were to meet more regularly now as a semi-official brains trust but still nominally as an 'unofficial' committee with agenda ranging from projects for a constitution and the reform of serfdom to the consideration of practical draft legislation issuing from official sources. Outside these two parties of the young and the old, Arakcheev (whom both were to loathe) had not yet been brought back into council; but Alexander was also influenced by his civil and military *aides de camp*, in particular by the ambitious and anti-Polish rival of Czartoryski, Prince P. P. Dolgorukov. Then there was La Harpe who, fresh from participation in the reform of Swiss institutions, continued to advise and admonish Alexander with impunity.

It probably accorded well with Alexander's unstable temperament to be able to work with groups which were mutually unsympathetic and indeed incompatible. As it was not his intention to resolve their disagreements, the usual outcome was indecision which lost him political devotion and intellectual respect. Nobody enjoyed his full confidence except perhaps Arakcheev whose cramped political vision Alexander came to share at the end of his reign. Though he was no 'enigma'— because there was no unresolved purpose to discover—Alexander's friends in Russia, even before his rivals in Europe, justly called him double-faced. In his politics he showed himself a cynical practitioner although his principles and emotions were those of romantic liberalism, evangelism or mysticism. In his private life, he was a neglectful and complaisant husband who, by careful dissimulation, kept up appearances and was even known as 'our angel' among his family.

The biographical approach to Alexander's reign is not a mere convention. Tolstoy decried but could not replace it. Soviet historians, with all their valuable research into the economic and social conditions of the reign, have been concerned to reveal the sporadic industrial or agrarian conflict as a cumulative development and have failed to relate it adequately to economic enterprise, still less to governmental policy. It is Alexander's individuality that probably explains the conservatives' subsequent myth of an irresponsible stimulus to revolution side by side with the liberal myth of Russia's missed opportunity to enter the main stream of western history. It was Alexander who for a time presided over the growth of Russian patriotism, the sociology of which still awaits analysis.

In the early days of the 'unofficial committee' the emperor approved its secretary Stroganov's record of his intentions. 'Reform would begin with the administration' but the committee was apparently to 'define the rights of man' and draft a constitution. The constitution was to check 'arbitrary power', and the rights of man were to be defined as liberty, property (so long as it did 'not hurt others') and equality of opportunity. No progress was ever made on these lines. Stroganov and Kochubei, the radical and the conservative, were agreed that the opposition of the emperor's official advisers was too strong, the emperor too unsystematic.[1] Nonetheless, Alexander permitted his 'unofficial committee' to debate freely and Czartoryski claimed that there was 'no useful reform during the reign which did not have its birth in these conciliabula'.

This claim was not strictly true, for Alexander's first administrative reform, the institution of a 'permanent council', took place in April 1801 before the committee was yet in being. Paul, like his predecessors, had used the 'imperial council' erratically and the object of the new reform was to diminish rather than to magnify its significance. Its function was limited to advice on legislation, and interest now focused on the Senate. The 'directing' Senate, as it was called when its executive rather than its more useful judicial functions were emphasised, nominally supervised the colleges and other administrative boards. However, the procurator-general of the Senate did not owe his authority to its power, while the emperor had his own direct links with the colleges. As office was not hereditary in Russia, the Senate was nominated largely from retired generals or leading officials, and it possessed no definable function, let alone rights. Although the oldest Russian institution, it was merely the creation of Peter the Great, who had copied foreign models. This did not prevent moderate conservatives from treating the Senate as if it were entrenched in national history and they saw in it a basis for political consolidation rather than reform. However, the so-called 'senatorial party' lacked organisation and oligarchical spirit, at any rate once the powerful personalities of Pahlen and Panin were removed. Its spokesmen were on the left of the 'party', particularly the Vorontsov brothers: Simeon, the ambassador in London, and Alexander who, soon to be made imperial chancellor, was regarded by the reformers as a bridge between their 'unofficial committee' and officialdom. The Vorontsovs were behind the drafting of a so-called 'charter to the Russian people' for Alexander to promulgate at his coronation in September 1801. Liberal and constitutionalist, combining *habeas corpus* with the entrenchment of the Senate, this 'charter' was nonetheless rejected by the 'unofficial committee' on the principle, apparently, that the good is the enemy of the better.

The emperor invited the Senate to submit proposals for its future, but before these were ready he issued his own decision on its function of resolving legislation and executive action. This was interpreted by the Senate as a right of remonstrance, and it now protested against a decree that infringed the 'charter' of 1762 by making nobles in non-commissioned ranks liable to serve the twenty-one years usual for all except officers. The protest, presented by Stroganov's father, was rejected with severity, and, ironically enough, another member of the 'unofficial committee', Novosiltsev, was sent with the autocrat's

---

[1] Note of conversation 9 May 1801. Shilder, *Aleksandr I*, vol. II, p. 343.

instructions that the Senate's task was only to resolve the conflict of existing laws. Yet despite this abject failure of the senatorial movement, the idea of noble opposition, like the alternative myth of reform from above, was long to exert a powerful political influence.

More successful than Alexander's ambiguous definition of the Senate's rights was his simultaneous decree of 8/20 September 1802, which abolished 'colleges' as departments of state and established ministries in their place. This was the work of the 'unofficial committee', its most lasting reform. Paul had already formed two such ministries—commerce and crown lands—and now there were to be in addition ministries of the interior, foreign affairs, justice, war, marine, finance and education. Like the colleges, these were to report to the Senate but, in practice, the Senate now acquired a new rival in the 'committee of ministers' set up by this same decree. The committee of ministers was attended regularly by Alexander until 1807 or 1808, and it was to remain the major administrative institution until Nicholas I began to divert its power to his personal chancery. The new ministries were generally resented by the political nobility which described them as 'vizirates' and Alexander's ideal of government as 'Turkish'.[1] Conservatives mourned the colleges, which like the Senate were the relatively recent foreign innovations of Peter, as expressions of the national genius. In reality, the nobility had only just grown into these institutions, although it is true that by chance they expressed a Russian trait—preference for collective responsibility below the dictatorship level—and that 'colleges' remained as organs within departments of state up to and even after the October Revolution of 1917.

The 'young flatterers', as the members of the 'unofficial' committee were called by one senatorial critic,[2] were blamed for the reform as a means of getting office. In fact Kochubei was already in charge of a department of state, and the others took posts only as junior ministers. The committee continued to meet and in 1803 achieved its second and last success in legislation. This was an educational reform. The programme of Catherine the Great's decree of 1776, which was intended to produce an expanding educational system at primary and secondary level in all provinces, had come to a standstill, owing to financial stringency and also to Russian rural conditions, lack of teachers and the lack of text-books in Russian. The new reform, which aimed at forty-two *gymnasia* of grammar-school type and four hundred and five other secondary schools, was hardly more successful, nor was the plan for primary schools in every parish. Of a hundred schools recorded in the Novgorod province in 1806, none were in existence two years later.

---

[1] F. F. Vigel, *Zapiski* (Moscow, 1928), vol. I, p. 298.
[2] Divov's memorandum for the Emperor, in T. Schiemann, *Geschichte Russlands unter Nikolaus I* (Berlin, 1904), vol. I, App. I.

But the new national centralising of education into university districts was promising and anticipated a Napoleonic reform in France on the same lines. New universities were founded at Kazan and Kharkov, while Czartoryski was put in charge of the university and schools of the Vilna area in which Polish was to be the main language of education.

That no reform of serfdom was undertaken through the 'unofficial committee' was not entirely due to Alexander's own sensitivity to outside opinion; the other members seem to have lost heart. Opposition was due not only to property interests but also to social and economic considerations. Although *laisser-faire* doctrines were gaining ground, even such ardent devotees of Adam Smith as the anglophile Mordvinov could not face the economic and social dislocation which could be caused by a mobile landless agrarian proletariat. Speranskii was to share these fears, and all that emerged from the revulsion of Alexander and his friends against serfdom was a decree permitting masters to emancipate their serfs through individual contract. By 1861 only some quarter of a million peasants and their dependents had benefited from this measure. The idea of peasant reform was not dropped. Even Arakcheev produced a scheme for emancipation, but the only positive measures came piecemeal in 1816 and 1817 when the German landlords in the Baltic provinces were permitted to imitate the landless emancipation which had proved profitable in neighbouring Prussia. There was not even a consistent attempt to ameliorate the established system. Alexander forbade the advertisement of serfs for sale without land and also the sale of serfs for the discharge of debt. But the penal transportation of serfs by their masters without legal process was not prohibited, although the question was raised in 1803 and again in 1811. The right of crown bailiffs to transport state peasants was expressly confirmed in 1822.

The 'unofficial committee', without being disbanded, faded away and with it the impulse to domestic reform, less as a result of the ministerial activity of its members than as a result of the emperor's growing preoccupation with foreign and military affairs which the expansion of Napoleonic France imposed. The theme which linked foreign affairs with the emperor's earlier liberal aspirations was the Polish question, and this was emphasised when in 1804 he made the Pole Czartoryski Russian foreign minister on the retirement of A. Vorontsov. Since the last partition of Poland in 1795 the greater part of the heart of the country with the capital Warsaw had been incorporated in Prussia. The Russian frontier did not run far west of what was to be the Curzon line of 1919, that is the projected ethnic frontier, or the 1945 frontier, except that what is now part of the Soviet Ukraine was then Austrian Galicia. Prussia was therefore the main enemy of the Poles, some of whom, such as Czartoryski, looked to Alexander's Russia for aid, others to France.

A Polish legion had even been formed to fight in the French republican armies. Czartoryski's position became increasingly delicate when Alexander revealed a growing sympathy for Prussia as the result of his visit to Memel and of his platonic relationship with Queen Luise. Nonetheless, Alexander insisted that Czartoryski should accept the post of foreign minister, and the latter hoped that Prussian neutrality in the War of the Third Coalition would benefit Poland: it was his enemy, Dolgorukov, who obtained Prussian concessions favourable to the Russian and Austrian allies on their way to defeat at Austerlitz. In the wake of Prussian collapse at Jena, Czartoryski proposed in vain that Alexander should proclaim himself King of Poland and so forestall Napoleon. After Friedland it was too late. During the era of Tilsit, Russian patronage seemed hopeless to the Poles, but an outspoken correspondence continued between Alexander and Czartoryski and, when in 1813 the Russian emperor emerged as the arbiter of Poland's fate, it was to his Polish friend that he turned for guidance.

The capitulation of Tilsit was regarded by almost all political opinion in Russia as an affront to the national honour. The diplomatic and economic dictation of France which followed was so obvious that people tended to ascribe acts of policy in other fields to French influence, to obedience, to sympathy or even to imitation. The war of 1808 against Sweden was rightly attributed to French temptation and pressure: patriotic officers avoided service in this and the still more unjust struggle with Finnish national resistance which followed. Then, as regards domestic policy, the imputation of cosmopolitan, indeed French, example was to reinforce the self-interest of the nobility in resisting the next set of Alexander's experiments in reform. The emperor's agent in these experiments, indeed for the most part their originator, was M. Speranskii (1772–1839), the son of a priest who was himself educated in the theological seminary at St Petersburg, and whose distinction in the ministry of the interior brought him to the Emperor Alexander's notice in 1807. As a force in Russian history Speranskii has probably been over-rated. It is true that he became a kind of one-man commission, reporting on and planning solutions for the widest range of immediate as well as fundamental problems outside the areas of war and diplomacy. But neither the quality of his voluminous papers nor his precarious authority as the emperor's virtual *chef de cabinet*, without social influence or even the highest official dignity, suggest that he brought Russia very near to a liberal revolution. His most comprehensive work, the draft constitution of 1809, was, like that prepared by Novosiltsev in 1819, never promulgated, and despite its eloquent exposition of civil rights it was silent about the emancipation of the serfs. This inconsistency was typical of Speranskii the bureaucratic thinker, who always balanced his western ideas against the realities of Russian history and society. He was a disciple of *laisser-faire* doctrine who recommended the protection of infant industry; a liberal who recommended the retention of serfdom in the early stages of reform.

Speranskii's ascendancy in Alexander's counsels followed his return from the meeting of the two emperors at Erfurt in 1808, where he impressed Napoleon as 'the only clear head in Russia'. In that year he was made responsible for the reform of ecclesiastical education and the codification of Russian law. It was in 1809 that he drafted the two decrees which did so much to make him disliked as a reformer then and praised since. The one, the '*kammerherr*' decree, attacked titular court appointments held without duties, the other made promotion in the higher grades of the civil service dependent on examination or university qualification. The decrees were not enforced owing to bitter opposition, but they made Speranskii appear as a committed antagonist of the nobility, which he was not.

In the same year he laid before Alexander his major legislative project, the abortive plan for a constitution. It was an imitation of the French consular constitution of 1799 and its influence on Russian administration proved negligible. The autocracy was to rest supreme upon three pillars, the executive, the judicial, the legislative or representative. These were to be formed in layers from the level of the *volost* (a cantonal aggregation of villages) to that of a provincial government, and then to culminate at the centre in the ministries co-operating with the directing senate as the executive, the judicial senate as the supreme and appeal court, and the *duma*, or assembly, as the representative legislature. All three powers were to be directly subject to the emperor but also to some extent subordinate to the emperor's supreme council which was to advise him. Out of all this integrated plan, the only proposal to be implemented was the reconstruction of the state council. Speranskii became its secretary and Rumyantsev its president and chancellor of the Empire. For a time the new model council seems to have gained in authority, with the emperor's attendance, but the rival institutions of the senate, the ministerial committee and the ministries themselves, soon regained their primacy in practice. Indeed Speranskii's reorganisation in 1811 of the individual ministries, which now included one for police and one for foreign religious cults, was in fact his most lasting work; the pattern lasted until the abortive revolution of 1905.

Meanwhile Speranskii had been called upon to prepare financial and legal reforms. Both his resulting plans were failures. The financial problem was one of budget deficits associated with currency inflation. Unrest throughout Europe had proved expensive, for the Tilsit system did not promise security while the war against Turkey and the continental blockade were alike exhausting national resources. The value of the paper rouble (*assignat*) had declined from 67 per cent of the silver rouble in 1806 to 25 per cent in 1810. Of Speranskii's remedies the stoppage of the issue of *assignats* could not be maintained, the receipts from his domestic loan and his sale of unoccupied public domain were disappointing, the yield of the turnover tax and the temporary and self-assessed land-tax were trifling compared to the resentment they aroused; and, as usual in Russia, only the extra burdens on the peasant of an increased poll tax and vodka monopoly profit were fiscal successes. Speranskii's reputation gained still less from his first attempt to codify the Russian law. His draft was accepted by the state council in 1812, in spite of its Napoleonic inspiration, but it too was never promulgated. His triumph over the jungle of Russian law was yet to come with his great collation, index and digest in the next reign.

For conservative or perhaps merely patriotically sensitive Russians, Speranskii's actual and projected reforms, alleged to be French in inspiration, were an aspect of the Tilsit system. It was this that brought him down, as much as high-level intrigue, indiscretion or the personal disloyalty of which the tsar accused him. Already in 1811 Karamzin's famous paper on *Ancient and Modern Russia* represented this reaction. It was written for Alexander's sister the Grand Duchess Catherine, and it was almost certainly seen by him.[1] Speranskii was the unnamed opponent, but he was rightly seen as continuing policies which Karamzin chided the emperor for patronising from the start of his reign. Karamzin idealised Catherine's absolutism and wanted to preserve and consolidate the governmental institutions of her era. At the same time, he renounced the foreign adventures which had glorified her reign and preached isolationism. His real grievance was the bureaucratisation of government which Speranskii typified; but, so long as Russia was divided between the functionless cosmopolitan nobility and the backward agrarian masses, more than half of them enslaved, Karamzin and his kind had no viable alternative to offer. The growing antipathy in Russian society to the French connexion demanded a sacrifice, and it is clear that Russian political opinion received as such the dismissal, arrest and banishment of Speranskii in March 1812. By then war was widely seen in Europe as inevitable, both sides were building up their armies and the Russians were snatching the first chance of a victorious ending to their Turkish war to release troops for a western front. It was indicative of Russia's comparative economic advancement that the immediate grounds for war were not so much ideological or even strategic as commercial. In a letter to Czartoryski of April 1812, Alexander complained that Napoleon was demanding the interruption of 'all trade with neutrals' and free entry for the 'French luxury pro-

[1] N. M. Karamzin, *Memoir on Ancient and Modern Russia*, ed. R. Pipes (Cambridge, Mass., 1959).

ducts which we have prohibited because we are not able to pay for them'. He concluded: 'As I cannot consent to such proposals, war will follow'.[1] Till the last moment the Russians were to speak the mustering invader fair, offering negotiations for a compromise even after the Russian frontiers had been crossed. And by then the confusion of nationality and liberty was so complete in the mind of the liberal emperor turned Russian patriot that he could write to the British prince regent of the defence of the serf-bound empire as 'the last struggle . . . of liberal ideas against the system of tyranny'.

Invasion intensified nationality class by class, without consolidating the nation. In the short campaign there was no unity either of experience or of confidence. The strategy of withdrawal was sophisticated and was well summarised at the outset by Rostopchin, who did much to maintain the morale of Moscow as its governor until the last moment. 'The Tsar will always be formidable in Moscow, fearsome in Kazan, invincible in Tobolsk.' The emperor's intention to command in the field was ill-received; when he left the army for St Petersburg, however, this was seen as dereliction of duty. For Moscow was the sentimental capital of Russia as well as Napoleon's obvious objective, and when the tsar visited it after the fall of Smolensk he won a brief popularity. At meetings which he summoned, the provincial nobility offered three million roubles and eighty thousand recruits, the townsmen ten millions in cash. Even the sardonic Rostopchin records that 'the Russian man for once . . . forgot that he was only a churl and roused himself at the thought that he was threatened by a foreign yoke'. Alexander shared his first commanding general Barclay de Tolly's doctrine of withdrawal but the protests of subordinate generals and public indignation forced him to replace Barclay by the elderly and tardy victor in the Turkish war, Kutuzov. The latter's reluctant stand at Borodino, which was to be for posterity the great battle honour of the war, did not alter the balance of forces, and Kutuzov abandoned Moscow. Probably less than a fifth of the population of about a quarter of a million stayed behind, but not, however, to fight; the prisons had been opened and many were down-and-outs. The burning was almost certainly Rostopchin's doing; it was an operational decision which denied Napoleon winter quarters with the hope of reinforcement.

The calamity of Moscow was received by public opinion as a humiliation and the emperor was accused in some quarters of betrayal. Yet those who suspected Alexander of vacillation or worse were probably unjust. Alexander reprimanded Kutuzov for even passing on Napoleon's offer of terms, and publicly declared 'I would go and eat potatoes with the last of my peasants rather than ratify the shame of my fatherland'.

[1] Grand Duke Nicholas Mikhailovich, *L'Empereur Alexandre I* (St Petersburg, 1912), vol. I, Appendix., p. 363.

Once the retreat began on 7/19 October, the outcome was a foregone conclusion, even if Kutuzov's inglorious methods of pursuit damped patriotic elation. The Russian regulars suffered enormous casualties, for they were hardly more used than the French to fighting in the winter. The partisans, often led by regulars like Denisov in *War and Peace*, acted a heroic part, but their numbers are not known.

With the victorious counter-offensive came a sense of pride and expectancy among the Russian public far below the level of literacy. The soldiers, praised by the emperor as the liberators of Europe, expected social rewards on their return; and in other classes too there were those who felt that the Russian state and throne would never more easily digest reform. But Alexander, the free-thinking liberal, had turned into an evangelical conservative. It was the burning of Moscow, he said afterwards, that had 'enlightened his soul'. In December 1812, he founded the Russian Bible Society on the British model; and then with Golitsyn, the head of the Holy Synod, and with Koshelev, another converted courtier, he formed a kind of devotional trio guided by a pseudo-masonic rigmarole which was gradually absorbed into the orthodoxy of the emperor's last religious phase. Even more than hitherto, Alexander was to behave as a split personality. A tough dynastic politician, he negotiated on equal terms with Metternich, Talleyrand or Castlereagh. But in time spared from diplomacy and pleasure he would wallow in the praise of such enthusiasts as Baroness Krudener or relax in the utopian internationalism of German moralists like Jung-Stilling and Baader. The tangible outcome of this mood was the Holy Alliance treaty, the text of which was prescribed in an imperial manifesto to be read in the churches.

The disappointment of the Russian public's hopes was made more bitter by the concessions which the emperor was ready to make to the Poles. Russian opinion did not grudge Finland the rights remaining to it after its annexation in 1809—its impotent Council of Notables in Helsingfors or the infrequent assemblies of its almost purely ceremonial Diet—but then the Finns unlike the Poles were not traditional enemies who had assisted Napoleon to lay waste Russian lands. However, Napoleon's Duchy of Warsaw was delivered to Russia almost intact at Vienna, and for Alexander the grant of a constitution to Poland was, understandably enough, the token discharge of one youthful commitment—perhaps, as the Russians might feel, relieving him from the pressure of others. The Polish state was to be indissolubly linked with Russia through personal union of the crowns. Although Czartoryski had helped to draft the constitution and had headed the provisional government, it was Zajączek, a veteran of the Polish resistance against Russia in the 1790's, who became first viceroy. Alexander's brother Constantine became commander-in-chief of Poland's independent army and Novosiltsev a kind of supervising high commissioner. The constitution itself was as politically liberal as any in Europe. There was a Diet (*sejm*) of two houses, although the form of representation reserved even the lower one very largely to the nobility. Ministers were nominally responsible to the *sejm*, which could petition the viceroy to initiate legislation and which could, and did, postpone measures laid before it. Religion was to be Catholic; the official language, Polish; and every official a Pole; but the Polish peasant, like the Russian, remained a serf.

The constitution of 'Congress Poland' established at Vienna, laboured in action but did not break down, and Alexander's personal appearances over the years before the *sejm* were deservedly successful. Trouble lay in national antipathy. A cycle of patriotic student movements followed by repressions led to friction between Czartoryski, the curator of Polish education, and Novosiltsev. More serious were patriotic conspiracies, involving army officers and associating Poles under Russian and Prussian sovereignty, though on a small scale. The liaison of other groups with the Russian conspirators—the future Decembrists—came to nothing, but the plots in the army produced their martyrs and maintained a continuity of resistance up to the great outbreak of 1831. On the Russian side there was jealousy of Polish civil rights, stimulated when Alexander used the occasion of opening the *sejm* in 1818 to represent the Polish constitution as an experiment which he would extend to Russia. Again, Alexander was suspected with some reason of an intention, never realised, to make a greater Poland by detaching Lithuanian provinces to it, just as he had detached to the new Finland the Finnish provinces won by Peter the Great from Sweden a century earlier. In general, the emperor's supposed preference for Baltic Germans and foreigners aggravated a long-standing grievance against the dynasty. Yet there was no truth in the allegation that Alexander 'hated Russians'. It was merely that he preferred to be advised by many individuals with disparate, even conflicting, views rather than by a close-knit, single-minded staff.

On Alexander's return to Russia Arakcheev became his closest political assistant, although he had played no part in the peace settlement. His authority and responsibility thenceforward has been magnified by the animosity of contemporaries so as to become a convention of Russian historiography. Incorrupt, brutal and reserved, he was detested by the court nobility as a parvenu bully and by liberals as a vindictive reactionary. But there is no evidence that he influenced Alexander even outside the military and diplomatic affairs which the emperor controlled in detail himself; he was simply used by Alexander and became increasingly his intermediary with his ministers.

The historical symbol of Alexander's collaboration with Arakcheev was the institution of military colonies. The Austro-Hungarian settlements on the Turkish frontier seem to have provided the example, but any Russian administrator must have had the Cossack communities in mind. The advantages of integrating regiments with villages of state peasants were set out in a defence by Speranskii in 1821. They would simplify the peasants' fiscal obligations, remove the burden of billeting, keep families together, provide labour for agriculture and secure the livelihood of veterans. The system did not so work out. The first experiment, involving a disastrous deportation of peasants, was a total failure. Then in 1817 began the amalgamation of army units with existing villages, an enterprise which at its peak involved nearly a million Russians of all ages and sexes. The villagers were subject to a military discipline that at one point even enforced annual child-bearing by fines, while the troops were liable to field labour in addition to drill and often became as embittered as the peasants. A revolt at Chuguev in 1819 had to be suppressed, a task carried through by Arakcheev with exemplary brutality. Yet Alexander retained his interest in the colonies and in the last year of his life was proposing new ones as well as improvement through the suppression of vodka-shops. The colonies were widely condemned, however, and declined during the reign of Alexander's less doctrinaire and utopian successor.

The military colonies were a parody of the kind of political reform which the paternal absolutism of the Holy Alliance seemed to promise. There were no other reforms, and the emperor's religion became increasingly clerical and sterile. Symptomatic was the decision of 1816 that Golitsyn combine the office of procurator of the Holy Synod with that of minister of education, and in 1818 Golitsyn issued an educational instruction which presaged a whole era of Russian obscurantism. That priority among the sciences should go to applied mathematics and that the greater glory of the nation be the prime aim of the humanities— these were common-places of educational thought in Peter's Russia as in many other eighteenth-century European states. Less normal, however, was Golitsyn's insistence that scientific teaching should eliminate 'vain and useless speculation about the origin and evolution of the earth'. Even more remarkable was the appointment of two notorious bureaucratic adventurers, Runich and Magnitskii, as curators at St Petersburg and Kazan Universities. Such aberrations were to exasperate the aristocratic intelligentsia and to act as a precedent for the more secular-minded repressions of Nicholas.

Seeing as he did the military establishment as a basis of general order, indeed of the national ethos, the emperor's political confidence was most profoundly shocked by the mutiny in 1820 of the Semenov guard, one of the three household infantry regiments. The affair was attributed by Russians to the misconduct of the Baltic German colonel.

It marked the rift between these two elements in the army: political disaffection was its result rather than its cause, when numbers of all ranks were re-posted to less distinguished units in some of which the future Decembrists worked on their resentment. Still, there had been agitation from outside, and this fact moved Alexander to regroup his political and religious defences against the 'empire of evil'. He had come to confuse nationalism with revolutionary liberalism and in 1822 he dismissed his Greek-minded foreign minister, Capodistrias. To Chateaubriand Alexander explained that he had seen the 'sign of Revolution' over the Peloponnese. At the same time, he was moving into his last phase of more sacerdotal religion, largely under the influence of the archimandrite Photius, a highly political priest and an associate of Arakcheev. These two were responsible for the dissolution in 1822 of all secret and quasi-religious societies (except the Bible Society, the emperor's own creation), and for the dismissal from office of his two oldest friends, Volkonskii and Golitsyn.

But in spite of his growing accommodation to the contemporary monarchical principle of 'union of throne and altar', Alexander kept a rearguard of his mind in the camp—or rather abandoned camp-site—of reform. He seems to have known since 1816 of the seditious political groups which were forming among officers and other young nobles and were to culminate in the Decembrist mutiny. However, he seems to have met evidence of the developing conspiracy by telling General Vasilchikov: 'I used to encourage such errors; it is not for me to be harsh'. And even as late as 1819 Alexander could commission Novosiltsev to draft a constitution. The result was somewhat less liberal than Speranskii's plan of ten years earlier and was remarkable mainly for a quasi-federal system of grouped provinces. Such delegation of powers was actually tried out on the administrative level in one region while the constitution as a whole was left pending. Again, the emperor was still toying with the idea of abolishing serfdom, and he not only had Arakcheev draw up plans for emancipation but also considered a scheme submitted by N. Turgeniev, the author of the influential *Theory of Taxation*.

It was not incongruous that in the same year Turgeniev should have joined a leading revolutionary society whose aristocratic members were mostly opportunist reformers as undecided in their ideology as in their strategy. The society was one of a succession of such groups which originated among the guards officers of the capital in 1816 and culminated in the united northern and southern societies responsible for the Decembrist revolt. The movement undoubtedly reflected the same contemporary taste for secret societies as did Russian freemasonry and the emperor's own private religious groups. It included members of two of the most famous Russian families, Trubetskois and Obolenskis.

Ryleev, the poet, was a member, and although Pushkin was not formally committed his politically mutinous poetry heartened the plotters.

Inspiring the movement seems to have been the fact that, as one Decembrist put it, 'all ranks from general to private' had been impressed during the war by what they had seen of freedom and progress in Europe. The criticism by one of the leaders, Bestuzhev, of conditions in Russia was representative of the right wing of the movement. He denounced the suppression of free speech, internal espionage, the restrictions on education, the corruption of justice and administration, the oppression of peasants by officials, the waste by the latter of manpower and material, the liquor monopoly and other supposed fiscal errors, the neglect of the industrial class, the illiteracy of the clergy, the futility or viciousness of the nobility except for its best element in the army and bureaucracy—an element which conditions discouraged. The right wing, roughly coinciding with the northern society, sponsored a draft constitution prepared by Nikita Muraviev. The inspiration of this was American Federalist, hardly a creative reaction to Russian conditions, although Muraviev would have asserted Russian independence from Europe in placing a new capital on the Volga. Peasants were to be legally free but landless, and so would miss political rights linked with property. The emperor was to be retained as 'supreme executive', but this derogation from republicanism was made, it seems, in the hope of bloodless revolution. Far more historically suggestive, although not in fact influential owing to the suppression of its text, was the left wing's leading document. This was composed by Paul Pestel, a young regimental colonel and son of the notorious absentee governor of Siberia. Called *Russkaya Pravda* after the oldest Russian legislative monument, it showed in fact less historical than proto-fascist character. Universal suffrage and yearly direct elections gave a pseudo-democratic framework, but the complete russification of an expanding empire, with the Poles freed on conditions and the Jews deported, the express provision of political police, the prohibition of political parties, the assimilation of the clergy to a 'branch of the administration'—all these are in the line of Russian social absolutism. He even showed a premonition of Marxism when he discerned in Russia a rising 'aristocracy of wealth which is far more pernicious than the feudal aristocracy'.

Some members of both societies had screwed themselves up to the classical Russian resource of assassinating the tsar. But the chance, as they saw it, of a transfer of power came instead with the death of Alexander on 1 December 1825 (N.S.) By then the imminence of action by the conspirators had been revealed to Alexander himself, but Arakcheev, overwhelmed by a domestic tragedy, had taken no counter-measures. So the conspirators were able to take advantage of the three weeks' interregnum which followed Alexander's death. This inter-regnum was due to his secrecy in nominating his successor. The heir apparent, Constantine, had resigned his claims after marrying a Polish commoner, and in 1823 Alexander had provisionally nominated his younger brother Nicholas, depositing his instructions to that effect with the highest civil and ecclesiastical institutions. However, when news of his death reached the capital, nobody dared to act in execution of these dispositions. The grand-duke Nicholas had no pre-arrangement with Constantine and so to be on the safe side he proclaimed the latter. Constantine, however, disavowed this step and would not leave War-saw. Finally, Nicholas decided that he should himself be proclaimed and the troops, already sworn to Constantine, resworn. This the 'young colonels' of the northern society saw as their opportunity, and on 14/26 December these 'Decembrists' brought their guardsmen on to the emperor's parade in the Admiralty square to mutiny. There they and the loyal troops faced each other futilely with hardly a shot fired (except to kill the parleying military governor of the capital) until Nicholas brought on guns to clear the square with round shot. It may have been nearer touch and go than it looks, crowds of onlookers were on the insurgents' side, the slightest wavering by the loyal troops could be expected to win the day for the Decembrists. On the other hand the independent mutiny by the southern radicals which followed was a for-lorn hope, easily suppressed, so the influence of the abortive *coup* remained only to poison Russian history.

The Decembrist revolt had not been predominantly libertarian in impulse or programme. Rather was it analogous to the twentieth-century revolts of military intelligentsias on the fringes of Western society. The appeal for national regeneration leaned towards democratic forms and to an extension of civil rights not so much for the sake of natural justice as in deference to ruling theories of economic and social efficiency. In the protest against public vices the general grievance was fundamentally the stagnation of Russia. This grievance was justified according to most European standards of life, of public morality and development. But not by all—even if one neglects the question (as the greatest of Russian intellectuals, Pushkin, did not) whether the daily lot and human dignity of a Russian serf was inferior to that of an English mill hand. For there were contemporary pilot achievements, from the literary triumph of Pushkin at one extreme, to the success of the Alexandrov machine and textile factory in St Petersburg at the other, which illustrate the perennial disparities in Russian progress. Then there was the unsurpassed military and diplomatic eminence which Russia had won in competition with the West. This the Decembrists were disposed to take for granted, all the more since they knew as soldiers how much the national glory was owed to the conscripted man-power of serfdom which they regretted, drilled by the German methods which they hated.

In fact Catherine the Great's empire had been consolidated in prestige rather than extended in territory in the last quarter of a century. In Europe, apart from the spreading of tsarist sovereignty over Finland and inner Poland, Russia had gained only Bessarabia—under the treaty of Bucharest with Turkey in 1812. In Asia the Emperor Paul's protectorate over Georgia had been replaced by annexation in 1801. The resulting encirclement by Russian jurisdiction of the martial tribes of the Caucasus provoked the beginnings of a guerrilla war which was to develop in the next reign into a great resistance campaign tying up the Russian army for a quarter of a century. South of Georgia sporadic warfare with Persia as well as Turkey during the Tilsit era brought Russia most of the petty khanates up to the Araxes frontier east of Nakhichevan and including Baku. Under the peace treaty of Gulistan of 1813 Russia obtained, moreover, control of the Caspian and a commercial position which the Treaty of Turkmanchai in 1828 was to amplify into a century-long economic and political domination of northern Persia. Within the Asian frontiers of the empire Siberia began an administrative revolution as a result of the 'revision' carried out by Speranskii. He was sent out as governor-general and inspector from 1819 to 1822 as a mark of both continued trust and continued displeasure, and his recommendations were incorporated in three decrees of 1822 which were to control Siberian destinies until 1917.

At the same time the conventional signs of economic growth were present in Russia and officially recorded.[1] Although classifications of factory labour are arbitrary, considering the overlap of rural estate workshops using serfs as well as of domestic industry, the figures are relatively significant.[2] In manufacturing (factory) industry, i.e. excluding mining and metallurgy, employment rose from about 100,000 in 1804 (82,000 in 1799) to some 210,000 in 1825. The expansion was mainly in textiles which accounted for 75 per cent of factory workers in 1814. Employment in cotton manufacture grew from 8000 in 1804 to 76,000 in 1830, in woollens from 29,000 to 67,000 and in linens (which had nothing to gain from the cessation of import during the continental blockade) from 24,000 to only 27,000. Just as the temporary exclusion of textile imports from England boosted the infant domestic industry, so did the frustration of iron and copper exports to England depress the mining and metallurgical industries. With the permanent loss of the

---

[1] E.g. The reports of the Ministries of Interior and Finance between 1804 and 1822 noted by Khromov, *Ekonomicheskoe razvitie*, p. 49, note 1, and various issues of the *Journal of Trade and Manufactures*.

[2] A recent revision is noted by J. Blum, *Lord and Peasant in Russia* (Princeton, 1961), pp. 323–4. Lenin's criticism in *Development of Capitalism in Russia* (Moscow, 1956), pp. 496 ff. applies to a later date.

English market, employment at about 120,000 hardly varied during the period.

Cotton was in all ways the most advanced industry. The proportion of freely-hired labour was highest (95 per cent in 1825), compared with a general average of about 50 per cent, although much of it consisted of peasants who were serfs but let out on *obrók* (p. 496) particularly in the Russian Manchester, Ivanovo, where some of the employers as well as most of the employees seem to have been the Sheremetiev family's serfs. Cotton too was most highly mechanised; in 1828 nine mills had 30,000 spindles between them. The Alexandrov factory at St Petersburg, with its 4000 employees, had imported English machinery in the 1790's, it introduced steam in 1805, and in 1825 used 170 out of a total national figure of some 2000 h.p. *The Journal of Trade and Manufactures* claimed in 1828 that Alexandrov 'could no doubt take its place beside the finest English factories of its kind',[1] and such pride in national industry was not exceptional. There was some influential opposition to industrialisation from archaising nationalists and commodity producers who feared the mobilisation of labour. But they faced admonitions such as those of the author of *The Russian—a complete manufacturer and factory owner*: 'Are the English lords, the English nobility less genteel than you? But they engage in trade. . . .'[2]

Official policy was progressive; for instance the influential Mordvinov maintained that agriculture depended on an expanding industry for its advancement. There was nothing like Metternich's fear of industry raising a bourgeois class with new social and political values. The government founded a commercial bank, though the Russian credit bank (accepting serfs as security) remained the preserve of the nobility; it engaged in industrial propaganda, it sponsored manufacturing and commercial associations, founded institutes of technical and commercial education, established all-Russian exhibitions of manufactures, and sponsored the imperial agricultural society of 1818 as a worthy reinforcement of Catherine the Great's 'free' economic society of 1765.

But where there was most scope for government control, in foreign trade and state revenue, expansion was not striking. The government was perhaps too concerned by the depreciation of the *assignat* which stood at 20 per cent of the silver rouble in 1814 and remained steady at approximately 25 per cent from 1816 until 1840 when the rouble was formally re-stabilised. Allowing for the fluctuation, budget revenue varied little from 1807 to the 1830's (Rs. 419 million in 1829) in spite of war, relying as it did largely on the peasants' contributions through poll tax and vodka sales. Foreign trade turnover, with (as a rule) a large

---

[1] Khromov, *op. cit.*, p. 52, note 1.
[2] From a German book, published in Moscow (1812), cited by V. Gitermann, *Geschichte Russlands*, 3 vols. (Zurich, 1944–9), vol. II, App. p. 528.

apparent balance in favour, rose on a three-year average by about a quarter (Rs. 307 million in 1814 and 384 million in 1826) during the same period; the very liberal tariff of 1819 was followed by the only apparent deficit years, and the highly protective reaction of 1822 by the intended re-adjustment.

Economic advances in the first quarter of the century, which of course only scratched the agrarian face of Russia, left the national demography virtually unchanged. The slump in ferrous mining and foundries led to the release of most of the ascribed (*pripisnye*) labour in 1807, but these workers reverted to their local state-peasant status and did not migrate. In progressive areas such as Moscow province, the mobility which eighteenth-century economists predicted began to show itself; a large increase in day labour was noted, both industrial and agricultural, and a high proportion of urban labour was registered as 'peasant' (40 per cent in Moscow in the 1830's). The incidence of strikes and factory riots increased proportionately to employment, and these have been religiously investigated by Soviet historians—as have the peasant mutinies which were almost invariably local in cause and occurrence. The plausible conclusion is that both phenomena were generically similar while the worker was, as Lenin wrote, 'getting the worst of capitalism and of the inadequate development of capitalism'. They belong in fact to agrarian history according to the Marxist scheme rather than to the prehistory of the proletariat. It is significant that the problem of industrial labour played a negligible part in the Decembrist ideology. The revolutionary and reforming intelligentsia had nothing to do with working-class agitation for another two generations, pre-occupied as they were by the serfdom of the Russian masses contrasting with their own westernisation to make their cultural schizophrenia unbearable.

CHAPTER XIX

THE NEAR EAST AND THE OTTOMAN EMPIRE, 1798–1830

THE 'Near East' is a term sometimes used to denote only the Islamic lands between the Mediterranean and the variously defined countries of the 'Middle East'. In this chapter it is used to cover all the coastlands of the eastern Mediterranean—roughly, what was known, a century and a half ago, as the Levant; and any survey of changes in European relations with these lands must include some reference to other parts of the Ottoman Empire and its immediate neighbours in Asia. The fortunes of this decaying but still tough-cored Empire were so closely linked in every part that it is difficult to separate the affairs of Egypt sharply from those of Greece, the Balkans and the lower Danube, or from those of Turkey in Asia. Penetrating all these regions were the commercial and strategical activities of the European powers—of the French and English mainly through maritime interests in the Mediterranean, of the Austrians and Russians chiefly on the landward fringes of Turkey, but with many overlapping contacts and rivalries in each direction. Finally, arising out of this penetration (perhaps even inspiring some of it) and in turn accelerating it, was the influence, both dissolving and reviving, of the technique, habits and ideas of contemporary Europeans upon the older ways of life throughout the Near East.

In this gradual process, the differences between the nations of Europe were much less important, in relation to Islam, than were their similarities. In spite of their rivalries or open enmities, the embassies at Constantinople had more in common with each other than with the intricate maze of officials at the Porte; the western consuls and merchants, there and at Smyrna, were still all 'Franks' in the eyes of Turkish pashas and even of Greek and Armenian traders; to the Mameluke beys of Egypt around 1800, the French and British armies were simply alternative brands of the same totally foreign medicine. The year 1827 was to see the spectacle of British, French and Russian warships sailing together into the Bay of Navarino, to challenge and destroy, without war, a Turco-Egyptian fleet anchored in passive defence under half-hearted commanders with some European technical advisers. In spite of the cross-currents, this spectacle was a truer mirror of the age than, say, the joint Russo-Turkish protectorate over the Ionian Islands in 1800 or the alignments of the Crimean War half a century later. Navarino (p. 549) was politically a paradox, but symbolically a pointer to the drift of the tide in the first half of the nineteenth century. The details of political and commercial conflicts among the powers should not obscure the common element in the impact of Europe on the Near East. Politically, the powers were more hostile to each other than to Islam; but, in a deeper and more lasting sense, their combined activities produced a slow revolution which led these regions, much later, to react against the political dominance of Europe from Algiers to Afghanistan, from Constantinople (now Istanbul) to Khartum, and to do so by methods and on principles partly borrowed from those of Europe.

Next, it is well to remember that very few people in Europe knew much about the Near East, and that still fewer ever visited those countries. Up to 1789, books about Turkey mostly describe a strange world, open perhaps to possible attack and liable to internal decay, but static, self-contained and not very sensitive to external influences. During and after the Napoleonic wars, similar books reflect a more confidently intrusive tone, treating Turkey as one more theatre of European war and diplomacy, as a world in which positive winds of change are blowing not only from outside but from within (Selim III, Mahmud II and Muhammad Ali). The old anecdotal descriptions persist, but mixed with more military, political and commercial speculation. In the period up to about 1830, before the age of the steamship, the railway and the telegraph, travellers for curiosity and pleasure were few, and often romantically inclined; diplomatists and military or naval men usually depended on interpreters for their understanding of people and events. Despatches, and news of all sorts, penetrated but slowly in each direction; news was often distorted on the way, and instructions or reports might be overtaken by events before any decisions on them could become effective.

It would be hard to exaggerate the long-term effects of the wars in unsettling and reshaping the Near East. It had long been common in Europe to talk about the decay of the Ottoman Empire, and chanceries were full of schemes for partitioning it—some more and some less chimerical; but these were mostly schemes for the simple annexation of provinces, with little or no idea that their way of life need be transformed or that their inhabitants, or even their local governments, might play a significant part or develop ideas of their own about their future. The literary and educational revival among prosperous Greeks (pp. 545–6) had at first no defined political aims and no reflection among the people, save perhaps in a vague hope that the Orthodox Church might some day replace the Crescent by the Cross on the domes of the mosque which had once been the great church of St Sophia at Constantinople. Perhaps that might come about by the agency of Orthodox Russia if she chose; but the main interest of Russia was necessarily in the Turkish provinces next to her own forward-creeping frontier—Armenia in Asia, and in Europe the Danubian (hardly yet 'Roumanian') Principalities and the Roumelian (hardly yet 'Bulgarian') region lying north and south of the Balkan mountain range. These provinces all touched the Black Sea; the Russians had gained control in the 1780's over its northern shores between the Kuban and the Dniester rivers and twenty years later, with the conquest of the Caucasus, over most of its eastern shores too. The new port of Odessa, founded by 1796, grew rapidly under the effective governorship (1803–14) of the *émigré* Duc de Richelieu (soon to be Louis XVIII's minister), who managed to keep its trade with Turkey prospering through most of the Russo-Turkish war (1806–12). By 1814, Odessa had a cosmopolitan population of 40,000, and the Black Sea coastlands, of which he was also governor, had been colonised by equally mixed groups of Russians, Germans, Bulgars, Greeks and Jews.[1] But much of the trade of these regions was carried on under neutral flags during the wars, and Russian naval power in the Black Sea was relatively in its infancy for many years to come.

Islam and the West understood each other very little. Moslems everywhere, like Christians, were linked by their faith, despite sectarian differences. For the Turks until very lately, as for the Arabs long ago, this had still been the faith of warriors dedicated to expanding its frontiers. The faith and its moral code, enshrined in the Koran and the Sacred Law (*Shariah*) were interpreted by the doctors of the law (*Ulemas*) under the Sheikh-ul-Islam. Turks did not think of themselves as belonging to a nation, or even to a race, they were simply Moslems who spoke Turkish; non-Moslems who did so were not Turks. Turks never used the European description 'Turkey' until the twentieth century. 'Ottoman' described a dynasty, and within the Ottoman Empire the sultan's subjects included the superior Moslem community (*millet*) and the second-class but useful and tolerated non-Moslem *millets*—Orthodox, Armenian and Jewish. A non-Moslem householder had generally to pay a capitation tax, and traditionally the tribute of a son for the sultan's service, but the tribute had been replaced by a tax before 1700. In the Empire, Islam was the established religion, which could be adopted but never abandoned. Two further principles of the Sacred Law hampered Turkish government and diplomacy in relation to the West—first, that no process of law was required in dealing with rebels, and secondly that no lands under Islamic rule could be ceded by negotiation, but only by defeat in war.

Printing-presses were known in Turkey quite early, introduced by

[1] *Imperial Russian Historical Society*, vol. 54 (St Petersburg, 1886), pp. 25–78: 'Notice sur . . . le duc de Richelieu . . . à Odessa' (by Ch. Sicard, writing in 1827 and resident at Odessa since 1804).

Jews (1493), Armenians (1567) and Orthodox (1627) for their own use; but the first press authorised to print in Turkish (1727) excluded books on religion and law, and was closed down in 1742 for forty years after producing less than twenty books. Resistance to Western ideas came chiefly from the *Ulemas*, and from the Janissaries, once the sultan's picked bodyguard, drawn as boys from his Christian subjects, but now a horde of over-privileged hereditary hangers-on with little or no military discipline. The Janissaries had secular as well as religious reasons for alarm, for eighteenth-century sultans or their ministers began to see the necessity of military reforms which were also urged on them by French advisers. Military and naval technical schools were opened and closed at intervals, but radical reform was first seriously attempted by Selim III (1789–1807), only to be set back by a reaction which led to his deposition and the death of leading reformers. Mahmud II (1808–39) had to bide his time until he felt strong enough at home finally to suppress the Janissaries (1826) and revive a reform of the army. This came too late for him to crush the Greek revolt, and much too late to reinvigorate a truly Islamic Empire. So the military and technical reforms which he desired had to be mixed after his death with a much less digestible dose of Western legislation in the age of the Reorganisation (*Tanzimat*) begun in 1839. It is unlikely, however, that success in technical reforms a century earlier could long have stemmed the tide of other Western influences after 1789. The Empire still had a medieval and feudal structure, capped by a weight of bureaucracy heavier than any medieval Western state had to bear. Inflation had added to the burden, agriculture was hampered by taxes, industry also by economic apathy and European immunities. There was never much lack of Moslem recruits from Asia and the western Balkans; but the sultans, no longer leaders in war, were prisoners of the bureaucracy. The richest men in the Empire were non-Moslems and therefore second-class subjects, whether merchants or Phanariot Greek bankers and officials in the capital. The Orthodox Church was domesticated in the Empire but not part of the family, and its clergy were traditionally almost as suspicious of the West as were the doctors of Islam.

Most of the provinces were pitifully unlike the parts of a coherent Empire. Some regions had long been detached in all but name: the sultan could react only feebly to the loss of the Crimea in 1783, and not at all to that of Algiers in 1830 (Vol. X, Chapter XVI). In the intervening period, the attachment of other regions was broken or weakened. Moslem loyalty to Islam was genuine but did not imply subordination to a central government, especially a distant one. Mahmud II did much to recover control over the governors of his still undetached provinces; but in Europe even the more Moslem districts like Albania and Bosnia were too mountainous and wild to be governed easily; and in Asia even

Anatolia, the most Turkish and most dependable region, had its own troubles. Anatolia was nearly exempt from direct European intervention, but it was disturbed by Kurdish tribesmen in the east and distantly threatened by Russian conquests in the Caucasus and Turkish Armenia. The Persians, belonging to the Shia sect of Islam, had never been on good terms with the orthodox Sunni Turks, and had often been at war with them for more political reasons. In this period, Persia was too hard pressed by Russia to be herself any danger to Turkey; defeated in two wars, she had to sacrifice much to Russia in the Treaties of Gulistan (1813) and Turkmanchai (1828). The rivalry between French and English in Persia during the Napoleonic wars was not unprofitable to the shah, who received large subsidies from both sides without ever committing himself to either; but the appearance of imposing rival missions at Tehran, pressing money and military help on the shah on condition of exclusive political alliance, pointed to a new phase of western activity in the Middle East and Central Asia (p. 532). In so far as it was anti-Russian activity, it was not unwelcome to the sultan, but in the long run it meant that even his Asiatic provinces would be dangerously near to the 'great game' of the European Powers in Asia.[1]

A French invasion of Egypt, decisive as it was to be for later history, and much as the idea had been canvassed in the past thirty years, cut right across the traditional policies of France in the Levant—diplomatic support for Turkey, protection for French merchants under the capitulations and patronage of Latin Christians, especially in Syria and Palestine. In spite of her commercial predominance, France's prestige in Turkey was low in 1789; the French were becoming sceptical about the value of their old ally and did nothing to obstruct the encroachments of Catherine II, provided that their other nominal ally, Austria, made no compensating gains.[2] French speculations about trade with the East were revived by writers like Raynal and Volney, and by the petitions (1790–) of Magallon and other Marseilles merchants in Cairo who dwelt on the prospect of overthrowing British supremacy in India by making Egypt an entrepot for French eastern trade. There were also English advocates of a forward policy to forestall the supposed designs of the French. But the activities and alarms of interested persons were damped by the indifference or hostility of their governments to any great commitment, and by the fears of both East India Companies that a short cut to India would damage their interests. A treaty with the Mameluke beys, arranged in 1794 by the British consul in Egypt, was ignored by the Foreign Office since he had already been recalled and in

---

[1] H. W. C. Davis, 'The Great Game in Asia, 1800–44', in *British Academy Proceedings* (London, 1926).

[2] M. S. Anderson, 'The Great Powers and the Russian Annexation of the Crimea', in *Slavonic and East European Review*, vol. 38 (London, 1958), pp. 17–42.

any case the Privy Council had decided in 1790 against trying to develop a trade via Suez. The revolutionary governments in Paris tried at first to maintain the old policies. In 1793 young Bonaparte's offer to go to Constantinople as an artillery expert was not pursued, but an envoy was unofficially received there, and two years later the sultan followed the Prussian example by recognising the Republic, sent an envoy to Paris and accepted some French military instructors. A few of his Turkish advisers were already pressing for a regular army and treasury and European alliances, in short for that 'new look' which took shape in the *Nizam-i-Djedid* (new ordinance) of 1801 and was to be intermittently pursued over many years to come.[1]

Bonaparte's victories in Italy (1796) led him and some of the Directory to look eastwards, both to Greece and to Egypt. Two of his future marshals, Augereau and Junot, were married to Greeks, and were present when he despatched a Corsican Greek on a mission to spread his fame among the Mainots ('Spartans'). Bonaparte praised the patriot-poet Rhigas (p. 545), and arranged to distribute a manifesto in the Peloponnese and provide arms. He also sent an agent to the cunning and ambitious Ali, Pasha of Yanina in Epirus, and very soon the French were in the neighbouring Ionian Islands (p. 535). Even if the Directory may have been glad to see Bonaparte expend his glory overseas, it was he who pressed the expedition to Egypt upon them; he was stimulated by Talleyrand who read a paper (July 1797) to the *Institut* on the advantages of new colonies, naming Egypt. On Bonaparte's return to Paris, detailed plans were set on foot in January 1798; he and Talleyrand (now foreign minister) slowly convinced the Directory. The expedition assembling at Toulon was disguised as the 'left wing of the army of England'. On 12 April Bonaparte was ordered to seize Egypt, 'assure to the Republic the free and exclusive possession of the Red Sea' and also investigate the prospect for a canal to link it with the Mediterranean.

In May the fleet sailed (at the very moment of a revolt in Ireland), but Talleyrand was wrong in suggesting that Turkey might acquiesce. It is true that, except for England, already at war, governments hesitated while the French seized Malta, Alexandria and Cairo; but the news of Nelson's victory at Aboukir Bay (1 August) stirred the sultan to allow a Russian naval squadron through the Straits into the Mediterranean, declare war on France and make treaties of alliance with Russia and England, while Russia in turn allied herself to England. Austria was drawn in (January 1799) for fear of losing her last footholds in Italy. Thus the Egyptian adventure, with its specific threats to all these interests, produced a coalition which succeeded in keeping France out of the Levant—a kind of foretaste of the events of 1840 (see Vol. X,

[1] E. O. Ciragan, *La politique ottomane pendant les guerres de Napoléon* (Aurillac, 1952).

pp. 254-8, 429). Not even the Russian alliance (1807) could save Napoleon from frustration in the East. Aboukir proved decisive; neither Napoleon nor his admiral can be blamed for this defeat, which was due to the ill-prepared state of the navy and to the initial luck and the bold genius of Nelson.[1] The Directory quickly lost interest, already within a month refusing to attempt reinforcement. It is true that, since the French army could not get home at present, the Directory suggested (4 November) that it might go on either to India or to Constantinople; but they offered no plan or help or hope of help, and there is no evidence that Napoleon had such adventures in mind when he led his army into Syria (March–June 1799) without consulting Paris. He was already before Acre when this suggestion reached him, and had given his own reasons clearly in February—namely to starve the British fleet of supplies, make Egypt secure and force the sultan to acquiesce. It was not the first or the last time that a power in Egypt has wanted to secure Syria too. Even if Acre had fallen, Napoleon knew that daydreams with maps, and mystification of his entourage, were not the same as concrete plans for undertakings within his grasp. On his return from Syria (July 1799) he defeated a Turkish fleet and army, he was busy organising Upper as well as Lower Egypt, and he did not share the Directory's desire now to cut their losses; but the general outlook was bleak—Corfu had fallen to a combined Russo-Turkish fleet in March and the French were nearly driven out of Italy. Departing secretly for Paris in August, he left orders, if no help came before May, to negotiate with Turkey (not with England) for evacuation; but the terms accepted by his dispirited successor Kléber as early as January 1800 were nullified by renewed fighting, and on Kléber's death General Menou, who had embraced Islam, had more faith in a future for Egypt as a French colony, and nursed an ill-founded belief that England might acquiesce. Meanwhile, French prospects in Europe were reviving and Napoleon, now master, agreed with Menou. He was soon busy negotiating with Russia for peace, with a radical partition of the Turkish Empire.

These negotiations hung fire for months. The unpredictable Tsar Paul I withdrew in effect from the war against France, agreed (December 1800) to an Armed Neutrality directed against England, and even set in motion the Russian contingent for an ill-considered joint Russo-French invasion of India. Even Austria seemed interested in a partition of Turkey. But Paul never agreed to let the French stay in Egypt, and all these schemes collapsed on his assassination (March 1801). Napoleon at once began to discuss peace with England too. At the same time, the British were resolved to expel the French from Egypt first, and to put Turkey under an obligation to them for doing so. Menou could not

[1] G. Douin, *La flotte de Bonaparte sur les côtes d'Égypte* (Cairo, 1922).

prevent the British landing in March and was obliged to capitulate and depart in September. Early in October England, Turkey and Russia had each come to terms with Napoleon (the first two by preliminaries not completed until March and June 1802). Egypt was to be restored to the sultan, but this did not debar him from inviting the British to help him reassert his authority and protect him from France by keeping their own army there. Meanwhile, the British commander had deeply committed himself to support the old order (or disorder) of rule by the Mameluke beys; unable either to arrange a compromise with the sultan or to sponsor an effective substitute for the French administration, the British force withdrew in March 1803, only two months before England and France were again at war. After all, neither the Turks nor the beys were able to govern, and the future of Egypt was to lie with Muhammad Ali.

The British government had shown little interest in Egypt up to 1798. The French conquest, anticipated by nobody in authority except Dundas and some of his 'London–Indian' advisers, changed all that. Immediately, Dundas gave orders to close the mouth of the Red Sea by sending an Indian force to the Island of Perim (soon moved to the less unhealthy Aden). A treaty with the local sultan (1802) was a pointer towards the later annexation of Aden as a coaling port (1838–9). In 1801 an Indian contingent arrived at Kosseir on the western side of the Red Sea, just too late to take part in driving the French out of Egypt but showing that, if India might be invaded from Egypt, the reverse could be even more true. The Navy kept watch on the Ile de France (Mauritius) until it was seized in 1810. In the Persian Gulf, the East India Company excluded the French from Oman by treaty and put a resident in Muscat. Their residency in Bagdad (since 1798) was made permanent (1802), and soon (1820) absorbed the functions of the older-established consul at Basra, with the new title of 'Political Agent in Turkish Arabia'. Malcolm's mission to Tehran (1800) secured treaties by which Persia promised, not very reliably, to admit no Frenchmen (p. 529). A regular service of mail between London and India was organised (from 1802) via Aleppo and Bagdad, a route occasionally used in the past for important despatches. In 1809 a Treaty was made with the Shah of Afghanistan. These energetic measures, combined with the defeat and death of Tipu Sultan in Mysore (May 1799), gave confidence against any French attempt on India or the approaches to India. In reality, British fears and French hopes were focused throughout not on such epic feats but on the long-term consequences of a consolidated French hold on Egypt. Thus it was the French adventure of 1798 which not only awakened Egypt out of sleep but also stimulated Englishmen to much more active and forward policies from Malta eastwards.

The activities of the French savants in Egypt were widely heralded, and later enshrined in the sumptuous volumes of the *Description de l'Égypte*.[1] These included the famous *Mémoire*[2] of the engineer Le Père about a canal, based on a hasty survey which seemed to confirm Aristotle's belief that the Red Sea level was above that of the Mediterranean, and advocating two canals with locks (Suez–Nile, Nile–Alexandria) at low cost, which would cut the distance to Pondicherry in half and the time by 25 per cent, provided the route were secured by a European colony in Egypt. At the time, the Egyptians were more impressed by the deference (unwelcome to some of his staff) which Napoleon insisted on showing to Islam, and above all by his tireless propagation of the idea that the Turks were degenerate tyrants and the Mosque of Al Azhar at Cairo the true repository of Islamic law and tradition. Here was the germ of an Egyptian nationalism which was to ripen much later. The British occupation (1801–3) had no aim more radical than that of keeping out the French during the war, and it made no appeal to the imagination. The prestige of the French was not forgotten. In the civil war which smouldered 1803–7, the French and British consuls were active, but the sole gainer was Muhammad Ali (born in Macedonia in 1769, the year of Napoleon and Wellington too), whose influence over the sultan's Albanian mercenaries enabled him, by dexterous shifts, to make himself Pasha of Cairo (May 1805) and to be recognised by the sultan as Pasha of Egypt (October 1806). The sultan's recognition (1806) of Napoleon as emperor and now apparently the master in Europe, led the British Cabinet, in fear of a French return, to re-occupy Alexandria (March 1807); but the expedition was ill-conducted, Napoleon's alliance with Russia (July) destroyed for the moment his influence at the Porte, and Muhammad Ali showed foresight in negotiating a British withdrawal (September) on terms which left room for reconciliation.

The pasha was now master of Alexandria for the first time, he knew that the British controlled the sea, and in the next few years he did good business in victualling their ships and armies in the Mediterranean, acquiring a monopoly of corn (and soon of other goods) which was highly profitable to his treasury. He expropriated or reassessed landowners and religious foundations, and built up an army which was reliable because regularly paid. Having crushed the Mameluke beys by a treacherous massacre (1811), he turned his eyes eastwards. In attacking the puritan Moslem sect of the Wahabis, who had gained control over Medina, Mecca and the Hijaz and were interrupting the

---

[1] *Description de l'Égypte* . . ., 24 vols. (Paris, 1809–22), comprising a *Préface historique*, *Antiquités* (4 vols.), *État Moderne*, (3 vols.), *Histoire Naturelle* (2 vols.), *Agriculture et Commerce* (1 vol.), *Planches* (11 vols.), *Carte topographique* (2 vols.).

[2] *État Moderne* (1809), vol. I, pp. 21–186.

annual pilgrimages, he was both obeying the order of the sultan and seeking religious and political prestige for himself. His success (with French advisers) after a savage and costly struggle (1811–18) earned for his warrior son Ibrahim the sultan's firman for a nominal lordship over the Hijaz and even Abyssinia; this meant at least that he could claim to appoint governors in some of the Red Sea ports on both sides, and collect tolls on the produce of Arabia and the Sudan for export to India. He next (1820) advanced directly from Egypt into the Sudan—in search of slaves, who proved of little use as soldiers, and of gold with disappointing results; but he maintained an uneasy grip over the Sudan, both east and west of the Nile, up to some 300 miles south of Khartum. In spite of corruption, cruelty and constant disturbances, the Sudan was spasmodically developed and began to look to Cairo as its cultural Mecca. Khartum grew from a small village in 1820 to some 50,000 in 1883 (more than two-thirds were slaves); during the British occupation it was to rise to half a million in the 1950's.

Muhammad Ali's successes were not at first unwelcome to the British, whose Indian trade in the Red Sea was disturbed by Wahabi pirates. In the opinion (1816) of Henry Salt, the consul-general, 'the pasha has become so complete a merchant that he has placed himself entirely at our mercy, his revenue now so vitally depending upon commerce...' which could be cut off at any time, by a blockade of Alexandria or his Red Sea ports. But his preference for French advisers, and his mounting ambitions, caused uneasiness in London and at Constantinople. From 1819 he had the services of the French Colonel Sève, who as Suleiman Pasha trained a new model army at Aswan, recruited at first from the Sudan and then from the hitherto unwarlike Egyptian peasants (fellahin). Already he was assembling a useful flotilla in the Red Sea, and from 1821 he began to acquire a Mediterranean squadron. For engineers, archaeologists and teachers, he also employed Frenchmen by preference, playing off France against England and both against interference by the Porte. He differed from most conquerors in his realistic sense of limits, knowing that he could not afford to break openly with the sultan or to aim at it if England were his enemy; his attempt to appease all three led him unwillingly into burning his fingers in Greece (p. 548) and later in Syria (Vol. X, p. 428), but he recovered from both setbacks and founded a dynasty which survived his death in 1849 by more than a century.

If Muhammad Ali gave a certain coherence to the story of Egypt, the fortunes of war left their mark, more capriciously, on almost every region of the Levant. When Venice, along with her northern Adriatic dependencies, was ceded to Austria at Campo Formio (1797), her much-neglected southern ones went to France, including the Ionian Islands and outposts on the mainland opposite. These had already been occupied four months earlier by a French expedition in the name of the momentarily 'liberated' Venetian Republic. Trees of liberty and French principles were planted, disturbing in different ways the Italianate Catholic nobles and the Orthodox Greek population. This first French occupation was ended in March 1799 by a strange Russo-Turkish combination, which created (March 1800) an Ionian Republic, nominally under their joint protection but actually under that of Russia alone, with a Russian garrison. An aristocratic constitution was devised and modified, operated under the eye of Mocenigo, the Russian envoy, and paying more attention than in the past to the Orthodox religion and Greek speech of the people. At Tilsit (July 1807), Alexander I handed over the Islands to Napoleon, but the smaller ones could not long be held against British sea-power and Corfu itself capitulated after Napoleon's fall. With all these changes of masters, a new Greek sentiment began to prevail in the hitherto Italianate Islands; it was the Russian occupation that directed the career of the Corfiot John Capo d'Istria (Capodistrias) into the service of the tsar (1809); in spite of his personal influence with Alexander by 1815, he failed to secure real independence for the Islands; knowing that it would be a shadowy independence at best for so small a unit, and that England would not tolerate the Russians there, he preferred a British protectorate and occupation to the Austrian one suggested at one moment by the British Cabinet. The British treatment of the Islands as virtually a crown colony soon confirmed him in his belief that Orthodox Greeks should look to the Orthodox tsar for salvation, though not for subjection. As Mocenigo's right-hand man during the Russian occupation he had learned, in preparing to defend the Islands against Ali Pasha (1807), to know some of the Greek chieftains of the Peloponnese, and he was in close touch with Ignatius, the Metropolitan bishop of Arta, an active partisan of Greek hopes and later the centre (in his retreat at Pisa) of a philhellene circle. Capodistrias's antipathy to British rule was confirmed during his visit to Corfu in 1819, and the speculation then aroused produced (probably unknown to him) a crop of Ionian enrolments in the *Philikè Hetairía* (pp. 538–9, 546–7). Unrest became endemic in the Islands until their union with Greece in 1864 (Vol. X, p. 426).

North of Corfu, the wars brought new masters, and some fighting, to the eastern shores of the Adriatic. Though Napoleon had arranged for Austria the odium of being the despoiler of proud Venice (1797), he probably regarded this as no more than a temporary expedient; after Austerlitz (December 1805), he annexed Istria and the Dalmatian coast-land, along with the isolated harbour of Cattaro which was separated from the southern tip of Dalmatia by the ancient Republic of Ragusa (now Dubrovnik) but gave an access through semi-independent Montenegro to the wild interior. Russia forestalled the French in Cattaro, but ceded it at Tilsit (July 1807) to Napoleon, who had meanwhile seized Ragusa instead—and kept it. After Wagram (1809) Austria had to cede also her inland provinces north of Bosnia; these became, with the Adriatic coastlands, the French province of Illyria and were all transferred back to Austria in 1815, stamped by Marshal Marmont with the usual marks of Napoleonic rule—sweeping administrative reforms and improvements along with grinding taxation and subordination to the conqueror's purposes. The French were not popular at the end, but the revival of the ancient name of Illyria caught the imagination of some of the South Slavs. While the Russians were in Cattaro (1806–7) there was talk of sending a force across from the lower Danube to the Adriatic, rousing the western Balkan peoples into revolt. Five years later, a similar scheme of Chichagov, Russian commander on the lower Danube, died when Russia had to make peace hastily with Turkey at Bucarest (May 1812) and bring her Danubian army north against the Grand Army of Napoleon; but it left some traces. Capodistrias believed that 'some consolation was required for the peoples whom Russia was forced to abandon for the fourth time to Turkish vengeance'; he and Chichagov pressed for increasing throughout Turkey in Europe the number of Russian consuls, whose principal aim would not be commercial but 'to prepare the spirits of the oppressed, so as to promote by their zeal the Porte's good intentions in case of an alliance or to declare openly in our favour if some day a decision is made to break the Porte's resistance'. This suggestion, though not a new one, was to bear more fruit in the coming years. A decision to 'break the Porte's resistance' could not be made in 1812, nor in 1815, nor (as the nineteenth century was to show) could it ever be made by Russia and the Balkan peoples alone. Yet Russia was so near to becoming the decisive factor that their history in this period may fairly be reviewed in this context.

The Danubian Principalities of Moldavia and Wallachia, tributary to the sultan and obliged to supply Constantinople with food, contained a large number of wealthy *boyars* (titled landowners). Their culture and that of the higher orthodox clergy, including the monasteries, had become mainly Greek since the seventeenth century, and that of the greater *boyars* was now mingled also with western influences. Most of this was centred in the capitals: Wallachian Bucharest, a city of some 70,000 which liked to be called 'the new Athens', and the much smaller Moldavian Jassy. Each had its Academy: Greek books were imported from Vienna and Leipzig, and the works of the *philosophes* were introduced by French tutors and doctors. Each had its court around the ruling hospodar (governor), usually a wealthy Phanariot Greek and often acquainted with French through service as a dragoman (interpreter) between the Porte and the European embassies.

The tenure of the hospodars was extremely precarious. In the eighteenth century, these and other lucrative offices were usually purchased by Phanariot Greeks who were the sultan's sole agents for such appointments. Greek influence was spread further by their marriages into *boyar* families. The high cost of offices made quick profits necessary during the short tenure of three or four years which suited the sultan's treasury. Without any right to conduct foreign relations, the hospodars were able in practice to seek rewards for helping or hindering the policies of Austria or Russia in the wars of both against Turkey. Each of these powers provided some stimulus for change: Austria by providing a market for grain and by the example of a better local administration in Transylvania, in 'Little Wallachia' (occupied 1718–39) and later in Bukovina (annexed 1775); Russia by her insistence on rules for the nomination or removal of hospodars and for the observance of privileges. These rules and privileges, repeatedly confirmed or extended, were often ignored with impunity, but provided treaty grounds for Russian intervention at favourable moments.[1] From 1782 Russian consuls at Bucharest and Jassy acted as watchdogs for treaty rights and soon became the focal centres of a Russophil party. During the occupation of 1806–12, the Russian commander ordered prayers to be said for the tsar as ruler, named an exarch to manage the clergy under the Patriarch of Moscow, and treated the two provinces as virtually Russian. Yet even the ruling classes, accustomed to manoeuvre between rival powers, found the occupation more burdensome than ever before and resented Russia's annexation of Bessarabia (a part of Wallachia) in 1812 when she abandoned the rest. There was growing among the *boyars* a desire for government more stable, less subject to foreign pressures and more devoted to their own local interests. For some forty years, needing more labour, they had gradually increased the real burdens of the peasants, particularly by extension of the *corvée*, in spite of the abolition of personal serfdom before 1750. They wanted to pursue unhindered the profit derived from this process of replacing customary by commercial farming.[2]

[1] Most of the European treaties with Turkey (1699–1812) are summarised in C. G. de Koch and M. S. F. Schoell, *Histoire abrégée des traités de paix depuis la paix de Westphalie* (Paris, 1818), vol. xiv, pp. 229–542; revised edition (Brussels, 1838), vol. iv, pp. 339–441. Those after 1814 will be found in Sir E. Hertslet, *Map of Europe by Treaty*, 3 vols. (London, 1875). F. Martens, *Recueil des Traités et Conventions conclus par la Russie*, 15 vols. (St Petersburg, 1874–1909), covers only Austria, Germany, England and France.

[2] A. Otetea, 'Le second asservissement des paysans roumains (1746–1821)', in *Nouvelles Études d'histoire présentées au Xe Congrès des Sciences historiques* (Bucharest, 1955), pp. 299–312.

Below the circle of the hellenised upper classes, the Slav liturgy and church books had been gradually replaced by the Roumanian vernacular, which was considered a less dangerous rival to Greek influence; the language of the people also had some literary embodiment, mainly in chronicles. But a Roumanian national sentiment as a positive force was hardly native; rather, it came from Austrian Transylvania, where Roumanian was spoken and used in schools, and where the Orthodox clergy were not supervised by the Greek Patriarch at Constantinople. Encouraged by Joseph II, they refused to be treated as Uniates under Rome, and they were eventually (1810) placed under the care of an Austrian-Serb Orthodox bishop. It was a Transylvanian, George Lazar (a peasant by origin, with a Vienna doctor's degree), who introduced a Roumanian note into his school at Bucharest, inculcating a spirit of pride in the language of the people and in the story of their Roman origins.

The fruit of this new spirit was to ripen slowly, but in the years between 1815 and 1821 the great activity of the Greek Hetairía in Bucharest was linked with that of individuals whose motives for insurrection were not Greek. The co-ordinator of the Hetairía there was employed in the Russian Consulate. He was associated with Russian officers in Bessarabia who were later prominent among the Decembrists; he was also in touch not only with Kara George and other Serbian refugees in Russia (pp. 542–3), but also with Tudor Vladimirescu, a Roumanian professional soldier who had been in Russian service and was now seeking to combine a peasant insurrection against the *boyar* landowners with a wider plan for throwing off the Turkish yoke. It seems that Tudor was not an enemy of the Hetairía, but hoped to use the coming insurrection in his own way. Some Russian army and consular officers hoped to manoeuvre the tsar into war with Turkey, which might bring changes within Russia in its train. Their activities in turn fostered the hopes of the *émigré* Serbs, the discontents of the Roumanian enemies of *boyar* privilege, and the ambitions of the ubiquitous Greeks. Most of the great *boyars* and Phanariot Greeks dreaded the consequences of an armed insurrection, but some of them were impressed by the position of Capodistrias as the tsar's adviser and by the confidence of Alexander Hypsilántes.

Hypsilántes, chosen in 1820 as leader of the Hetairía, was the son of a Russophil Greek hospodar; formerly an *aide-de-camp* to the tsar, he was popular in Russian court circles and had lost an arm in the Russian campaign of 1813. His incursion across the Pruth into Moldavia early in 1821 found so little support among the *boyars* in Jassy that he hardly dared to proceed to Bucarest, while Tudor, having started his own insurrection, seemed to be changing its character from a social movement against the *boyars* generally into an alliance with the lesser *boyars* against the Phanariots. Whatever Tudor's real intentions in Bucharest may have been, Hypsilántes' appearance there nine days later led inevitably to a breach between two men whose aims were irreconcilable.[1] Deserted by some of his captains, Tudor was arrested and put to death by Hypsilántes, who already knew that in March Capodistrias had been obliged to draft at Laibach the tsar's censure on this adventure. This killed any hope that Alexander I might be forced, even against his present will, to save Russian prestige in the Balkans by declaring immediate war on Turkey.

This ill-conceived insurrection was soon at an end, but it sparked off the less unpromising movement in the Peloponnese (p. 547). This was precisely one of its objects, and in any case the year 1821 became a landmark in Roumanian history too. The two hospodars had felt obliged to give some countenance to the insurrection after it began. The sultan at first nominated two new Greek Phanariots in their places, but soon decided to appoint native rulers who might help him against both Greeks and Russians. The result was rather different. As the Turkish armies moved in to restore order, most of the wealthiest *boyars* fled into Russia or Austria, and some hoped for rescue even by a Russian annexation. Many of the lesser *boyars* were ready at least for a permanent protectorate, but they were more hostile to Greek influence; and those of Moldavia pressed in 1822 for a native aristocratic constitution. They had to wait through the suspense of Tsar Alexander's last years for the new forward policy of Nicholas I; but this time the Russian occupation (1828–34) during and after the war was more than an interlude. The Russian governor Count Kisselev, a cultivated and intelligent man, was able to embody in the *Règlement Organique* of 1831 a fairly coherent system. The long overdue administrative reforms were mostly welcomed at the time and praised by later critics; but the political and economic settlement was an almost complete surrender to the *boyar* aristocracy, both Greek and native. The hospodar was constitutionally limited by their Assembly, but also by provisions ensuring Russian predominance. The peasant's minimum holding was reduced, his obligatory work was in effect increased, and it was almost impossible for him to move without leave. Much of this was drafted before Kisselew arrived, and he regretted that he 'could not defend the peasants against a greedy and excited oligarchy' because the *boyars* knew that the Russian government needed their support.[2] Thus the Principalities began the modern period of their history better equipped for economic exploitation than for political or social well-being.

[1] S. Stirbu, 'Tudor Vladimirescu et les mouvements de libération', in *Nouvelles Études* ... (1955), assembles evidence that Tudor was closely in touch with the Hetairía long before the insurrection, and was not opposed to its anti-Turkish aims.

[2] A. D. Xenopol, *Histoire des Roumains* (Paris, 1896), vol. II, pp. 407–19.

Nevertheless, they were irrevocably separated in effect from Turkey, and were able for a century to rely on the Western powers against a Russian monopoly of influence over them.

'Bulgaria' was hardly even a current geographical expression, but 'Roumelia' (a term used loosely) included a sturdy population of Bulgar-speaking peasants and craftsmen, whose memories of greater days were vaguely preserved in song and legend and in the exploits of the *haidouks* (mountain bandit-patriots). Here, too, changes and upheavals were at work. The military feudalism of the Turks was giving way to a growth of trade and craft industry and a greater differentiation of wealth. After each of the Russian or Austrian wars against Turkey, Bulgarian ex-soldiers either joined roving bands of robbers at home or took service with rebellious Turkish magnates. Other fighting men, and craftsmen too, escaped violence at home by emigrating into the Danubian Principalities or Habsburg territory or southern Russia (including Bessarabia after 1812). A refuge was indeed all that Russia could offer in this period; larger hopes were completely frustrated both in 1812 and again in 1829.

In spite of the almost complete hellenisation of the Church (except for a few monasteries) and of many literate townspeople, the Bulgars were never assimilated by the Greeks. Books in Bulgarian had long been circulating in manuscript, especially the popular patriotic history compiled from chronicles in 1762 (after a visit to Austria) by Paissii, a monk of Mount Athos. Western influences penetrated deviously from merchants of Ragusa and from Austrian-educated Serbs such as Jovan Rajić, who published in Vienna (1794-5) a four-volume *History of the various Slav peoples, especially Bulgars, Croats and Serbs*. No books seem to have been printed in Bulgaria before about 1840, but Bishop Sofronie, a disciple of Paissii, produced sermons in Bulgarian, settled (1803) in Bucharest and shared the simmering excitement of emigrants and others whose eyes were fixed on Russia. A pupil of his founded after 1814 some Bulgarian church schools as a weapon against Greek influence. Later, a young Ruthenian, Yuri Venelin, who had been educated at the University of Lemberg (Lvov), was confirmed in his romantic zeal for the Slavs by study in Bessarabia. Encouraged in Moscow by Aksakov and other Slavophils to study Bulgarian history, he produced in 1829 the first of several polemical works[1] which had little historical value but gave an impetus to revival of the language and led to the founding, from 1835, of a number of Bulgarian schools with more

[1] Y. I. Venelin (1802-39), *The ancient and modern Bulgarians in their political, national and religious relations with the Russians*. Vol. I (Moscow, 1829); vol. II, posthumous (1841); and other writings in Russian, all contesting the current theory of their Tartar-Turkish origins. He first visited Bulgaria in the 1830's. Article on Venelin in the *Soviet Encyclopedia* (Moscow, 1949-57).

secular and nationalist aims. But the efforts of these and other individuals hardly amounted as yet even to a literary revival.

Meanwhile, in the mountains and forests of Serbia, a not un-
prosperous society of warriors and pig-breeding farmers had been
exposed to new pressures from different sides. First, the Habsburgs
helped many families from Turkish Serbia to settle among the other
Slavs in southern Hungary (recovered in 1686); the Austrian occupation
of Belgrade (1719–39) brought the Serbs, north and south of the
Danube, still more into contact; later, Joseph II gave his South Slavs
privileges, especially in educational and ecclesiastical affairs, as an
offset against Magyar domination. This made the sultan's Serbians
turn their eyes northwards in hope. At the same time, their own once
tolerable conditions were becoming intolerable. The sultan's hope was
to detach them from Austrian leanings by promoting hellenisation
through the agency of the Patriarch at Constantinople, who was in the
eighteenth century little more than his agent. But he was also dispersing
the unruly Janissaries away from the capital into the provinces, and
allotting some of the worst of them to Serbia—a primitive region, but
prosperous enough to be harried and bullied with profit. Many
Serbs fought for Austria in her Turkish and German wars, but her
withdrawal from the war on Turkey at the Peace of Sistova in 1791 disappointed them. Others, inspired by Peter the Great's help to a rising
in Montenegro (1711), and now by Catherine II's aggressive policy,
began to look to Russia, where a number of Serbs had settled to escape
from Magyar oppression in Hungary. The reforms of Selim III benefited the Serbs in the region of Belgrade by excluding the Janissaries,
but his popular pasha there was hampered and eventually slain (1801)
by the Janissaries who returned and took revenge by beheading seventy
to eighty Serbian notables.

This was the origin of the resistance organised from 1804 by Kara
George, at first with some aid and comfort from both Austria and
Russia; but both powers were now more concerned to stiffen Turkish
resistance to France. A Serbian delegation to St Petersburg was told
that, although Russia could not aid a rebellion, she might send a consul
to Belgrade as guarantor of their autonomy. This, and some initial
successes in the field, encouraged the Serbs to raise their demands, while
they organised an Assembly (Skuptchina) to elect a senate of six under
a constitution drafted by an Austrian Serb who was now a professor at
Kharkov in Russia. The sultan insisted that, being no longer petitioners
but rebels, they must first disarm and submit. Instead, they defeated
Turkish armies coming from the west and the south (August 1806); and,
when the sultan had declared war on Russia (December), they soon
appeared as open rebels in spite of big concessions made by Turkey

(Treaty of 25 January 1807). Kara George gambled on a Russian victory and even offered to accept a Russian governor and garrison; but the news of Alexander's reconciliation with Napoleon at Tilsit led him to turn half-seriously to the Austrians, offering to incorporate an enlarged Serbia under the Habsburgs, provided it would not be treated as part of Hungary. While Kara George continued to play off Austria against Russia, the tsar wavered between two plans: listening to Napoleon's never whole-hearted talk about partition, or relying instead on hopes of extending his influence in Turkey without French help by gaining the confidence of the Serbs and other potential allies from within. In St Petersburg, Rumyantsev and Caulaincourt went on fencing about a future partition, but Serbia does not seem to have been mentioned when the tsar met Napoleon at Erfurt in October 1808. Alexander had withheld approval of the Serbian constitution, and the warmth of his agents' language seemed to vary with their need of Serbian help in their own dealings with the new Sultan Mahmud II. Kara George jumped the gun by getting his new Senate itself to declare him hereditary prince (December 1808); his further vain appeals to Napoleon, and once more to Austria, were disavowed by the Skuptchina, and early in 1810 a Russian Resident, who had left Belgrade six months earlier, returned, this time with troops, to secure Russian influence.

In December 1810 Napoleon at last acquiesced in the Russians' control over the Principalities (which they had never evacuated), while holding out hopes to Austria of control in Serbia. While the Serbs were convinced that one of the powers would eventually outbid the rest as guarantor of Serbian autonomy, the sultan was equally convinced that the jealousy of the rest would be enough to keep the Russians north of the Danube. The tsar's urgent need for peace with Turkey produced the hastily drafted Treaty of Bucharest (28 May 1812, cf. p. 536), whose interpretation was to be the subject of endless disputes over the next fifteen years. Under Article 8, the Serbians were to have an autonomous status like that of the Aegean Islanders, collecting the sultan's tribute themselves, but allowing restricted Turkish garrisons in Belgrade and other fortresses; but they were triply deceived. First, Chichagov, disliking the Treaty and dreaming of a march across Serbia to the Adriatic, concealed and even denied to the Serbians the existence of Article 8, until he was ordered (August 1812) to take his army north against Napoleon. Secondly, the sultan was expecting the Russians to be defeated and had no intention of giving effect to the Article voluntarily. Thirdly, Kara George himself refused to submit to the terms, and falsely announced that the invading Turkish armies of revenge were acting contrary to the sultan's will.

The result was the Turkish occupation of Belgrade (October 1813) and the flight into Austria of thousands of families; Kara George himself and most of the leading insurgents were removed a year later out of Austria into Russia at the tsar's personal request. Milosh Obrenovich, the one leader who had not emigrated, was encouraged by the conciliatory behaviour of the new pasha to submit and to accept headship of a district. Soon, however, a Serbian envoy was producing evidence of renewed oppression to the sovereigns at Vienna; he obtained several interviews with Capodistrias, and two with the Habsburg emperor himself. Capodistrias was probably the author of a Russian circular to the Powers (2 February 1813) in which their right to intervene was based on the novel ground that, although the Moslems were the sultan's *subjects*, the Christians were only his *tributaries*, owing him no allegiance and entitled to place themselves under the protection of any European Power. This plea for a kind of collective guarantee, not of the sultan but of the Christians in Turkey, was never submitted to the Congress, but its argument was radical and far-reaching. For the moment, after some partial successes in a renewed insurrection, Milosh accepted improved terms direct from the sultan (December 1815): Turks were to reside only in or near the fortresses; the Serbians were to collect the fixed tribute themselves, with freedom for their religion and education and for trade throughout the Empire, and the right to maintain a representative at Constantinople.

The rule of Milosh differed little in avarice and tyranny from that of many a pasha. When the Russians allowed some of the *émigrés* to slip back into Serbia, their severed heads were sent by Milosh to Constantinople. Kara George, the irreconcilable, who had lately been admitted at Jassy as a member of the Greek Hetairía, was among the victims (July 1817); nine years later, his son was cruelly mutilated for his part in Hetairist plans to mobilise the Serbians. Milosh paid little attention to Russia's interest in the Serbians in the course of her disputes (1816–21) about the Treaty of Bucharest; these disputes were interrupted by the Greek revolt. He rejected Hypsilantes' appeal for help, and kept Serbia out of the long struggle of the Greeks and the Russo-Turkish war of 1828–9, though the potential menace to the Turks of his autonomy helped the Russians indirectly at the end. His policy of conditional loyalty to the sultan was not unrewarded. At the Peace of Adrianople (September 1829) Turkey was required publicly to confirm the privileges promised to the Serbians in Article 8 of the Treaty of Bucharest, as interpreted in the Treaty of Akkerman (October 1826), and in addition to restore to Serbia six districts detached in 1813. Finally, in October 1830 Milosh obtained the long-sought recognition by the sultan of his hereditary status, which had more than once been affirmed by the Skuptchina. In pursuing his own ambitions, he had achieved a real autonomy for Serbia. Though harshly and corruptly ruled, the country was now being equipped with schools, printing presses and newspapers and with the beginnings of a regular army. All this had been achieved without exclusive reliance on Russia or any other Power, and without those impulsive offers of complete subjection which Kara George had made in turn to Austria, France and Russia. Time was to bring its revenges against the Obrenovich family, for the heroism of Kara George made a greater appeal than the cruel cunning of Milosh; but it is hard to see how a more intransigent policy towards Turkey after 1815 could have borne so much fruit for a country whose alternative fate was likely to be absorption by the Russian or the Austrian Empire.

The Greeks were differently placed. Although not influenced by direct contact with Austria or Russia across a land frontier, they were also less exposed to the calamities of war. The men of the coasts and islands were open to the sea, and so to a greater knowledge of the outer world. They were able to use their maritime skill and resources, and so eventually to interest not only Russia but the greatest sea powers, Britain and France, in a settlement of their struggle with the Turks.

In the mountains north of the Isthmus, life was mostly primitive and insecure, but trade and schools kept some regions in contact with the outer world. In the Peloponnese, the Venetian occupation from 1687 to 1715 (1699–1718 by Treaties) benefited agriculture in some ways, but it hampered the Greek Church and Greek traders by restrictions favouring Rome and Venice, and its ending was not regretted. Two-thirds of the land was owned by Moslems, who hardly exceeded one-tenth of the population. The Greeks of the Peloponnese had an exceptional degree of local autonomy, organised by election of notables and clergy; at the top, their Senate assessed the taxes, negotiated with the Turkish governor and could appeal direct to the sultan through delegates at the capital. Although this system did not exclude bribery, caprice and violence, it gave the notables political experience which could easily turn from enjoyment of local privileges into a desire for more. The islands had even more autonomy and hardly any resident Turks.

Russia made no appeal to the Balkan Christians in her war of 1737–9; in her next war, the brothers Orlov, sent by Catherine II in 1770 to organise a rising in the Peloponnese as a diversion, soon failed to persuade the Greeks that the small Russian force had serious intentions, and the only result was to bring retribution on the people, whether rebels or not. Nevertheless, Russian prestige was enhanced in Greece by the Treaties of Kutchuk Kainardji (1774) and Jassy (1792) which included ill-defined stipulations in favour of the sultan's Orthodox subjects; in 1783 also, Russia secured for Greek ships the privilege of trading under her flag. Merchants could purchase immunities by license (*berat*) from European consuls; when Selim III tried to remedy this abuse of the Capitulations by selling privileges himself, he merely created a recognised class of prosperous *beratlis*. Moreover, a merchant's son, sent abroad for study or trade, might procure the privileges of a European on his return. Greeks made full use of these chances. The wars left Greece unravaged, more populous and more prosperous than before; the island traders in particular profited as carriers and smugglers. Rich Greeks were generous founders of schools, hospitals and charities. By the combined effect of Phanariot influence at the capital and pervasive activity at all levels, the Greeks seemed capable in time of capturing much of Turkey in Europe from within. The alternative—open revolt against an Empire which had immense reserves of power in its appeal to Islam—presented a terrifying prospect and was not easily envisaged, though individual Phanariots were tempted by foreign influence to risk a combination of both methods.

The importance of the literary revival is hard to assess. Some of it had its origin inside Greece, much of it outside. For example, Vienna and Trieste each had in 1750 an Orthodox church and soon a flourishing Greek school. Between 1786 and 1820, the 'Greeks' (i.e. Orthodox) in Vienna grew from some 500 to 3000 or more, including many students at the University. Many books in Greek were printed there and at Leipzig (in addition to Venice and Trieste)—mostly concerned with education and the useful arts.[1] Literate Greeks already had a language descended from a common one (the *Koinè*) which had once been the *lingua franca* of the Byzantine world, though it had long given way to popular spoken dialects. Italian was the commercial language of the Levant, but in the eighteenth century the writing of pseudo-classical Greek became an elegant accomplishment among the families of Phanariots and prosperous merchants. But this did not imply any political design for a violent overthrow of the Turkish empire, whose loose and increasingly lax administration gave these men their opportunities. It was the French Revolution that gave a new edge to the movement. Rhigas Pheraios (*c.* 1757–98), a Vlach born at Velestino (the ancient Pherae) in Thessaly, was not exactly a Greek nationalist. After serving in the households of the Danubian *hospodars* in the 1780's, he settled in Vienna and produced a number of rousing translations and poems, such as his famous Greek adaptation of the Marseillaise, distributed through his widely-ramified Hetairía, about which little is known. He also edited a big map of Turkey in Europe. His professed aim was a reconciliation of all its inhabitants, whatever their religion or language, under the banner of the liberty and equality proclaimed by the French. He had contacts with prominent Turks and Albanians, and probably with Ali Pasha of Yanina, but most of his associates were

---

[1] E. Turczynski, *Die deutsch-griechischen Kulturbeziehungen bis zur Berufung König Ottos* (Munich, 1959). F. Valjavec, *Geschichte der deutschen Kulturbeziehungen zu Südosteuropa* (Munich, 1953).

Greeks. Later, in 1797, while the French were revolutionising the Ionian Islands, Rhigas set out for the Peloponnese, where he planned to start a rising, but he was seized at Trieste with twelve chest-loads of proclamations, convicted in Vienna and handed over with some of his associates to the pasha of Belgrade for execution.

Adamantios Koraés (1748–1833) never returned to the Levant after finally leaving his home at Smyrna at the age of thirty. After studying medicine at Montpellier, he settled in Paris in 1788, embraced the cause of the Revolution and devoted the rest of his life to an ambitious work of educating the Greek-speaking world to use a literary form which would be neither a slavish imitation of ancient Greek nor a mere adaptation of the spoken dialects. The resulting *katharévousa* (purified) form was artificial and is now less in favour; but Koraés is rightly honoured as architect of the written language generally used for a century or more and still holding its own alongside the rival demotic forms which have been enriched in imaginative literature out of the vernacular. His patriotic, republican and anti-clerical opinions were evident in the introductory dialogues to his editions of the ancient Greek classics, whose publication and distribution (1805–17) were subsidised by a wealthy merchant of Chios. Koraés declared, on the eve of the revolt, that a violent solution was premature by a generation, and perhaps eventually unnecessary; but his occasional anonymous poems and tracts were virtually calls to insurrection, and, once it had begun, he gave it countenance. A scholar, not a politician, he was apt both to under-rate the role of the Orthodox Church in Greek national life, and also to over-rate the timeliness of a republican and democratic constitution for the new Greece. His earlier respect for Capodistrias gave way to bitter and unjustified accusations of tyranny in his rule over Greece.

Koraés was part-founder of a Greek literary and patriotic periodical, published in Vienna (1811–21) and subsidised by the Danubian Hospodars. This in turn was connected with the Society of Friends of the Muses, which was patronised by the tsar and Capodistrias at Vienna in 1814–15 and became a fashionable charity whose proceeds were used for bringing young Greeks to Europe. It had no traceable connexion with the political and at first secret society *Philikè Hetairía*, whose directing spirits and travelling agents were neither fashionable nor highly educated. The three men who founded this Hetairía at Odessa in the summer of 1814 also had connexions with Ali Pasha's Epirus, a region which in turn had contacts with the French during their occupations of the Ionian Islands and of the Adriatic coast further north. The Metropolitan Ignatius (p. 535) may have been a link between the two societies.[1] A surviving register of some 550 enrolments in the

---

[1] For further details and references, see the writer's article on 'Capodistrias and the Greeks before 1821' in *Cambridge Historical Journal*, XIII, 2 (1957).

Hetairía shows that, after very slow growth till 1818, membership spread rapidly from the lower Danube into Greece, especially among men occupied in commerce or shipping. From the end of 1819, if not earlier, the register is unreliable; the trickle became a stream and soon a flood.The society's existence was hardly a secret any longer and by 1821 it was merged in the general movement. Obscure in origin, and the symptom rather than the cause of a revolutionary temper, the society attracted men both by its confident promises of Russian armed support and by its use of dramatically secret procedures borrowed from masonic clubs. The names of the leaders (the *Arché*) were unknown to the travelling agents and their recruits, who vaguely supposed that the direction was both Russian and exalted. Many believed, wrongly, that the tsar's minister Capodistrias was at its head. When he positively refused to be implicated, the direction was accepted (June 1820) by Alexander Hypsilántes (pp. 538–9), who stipulated for sole command. Neglecting advice and creating distrust by changing his plans, he was misled into making his major thrust in the Principalities, leaving other agents to stir up the Peloponnese and Islands. Without any official encouragement, Hypsilántes may have persuaded himself that Alexander I was only waiting for a spontaneous act of insurrection or at least would then be obliged to step in and save it from collapse. In the long run, he was not far wrong, but that was due, not to his own reckless enterprise, which was publicly disavowed by the tsar, but to the decisive action of some of the chieftains and clergy of the Peloponnese, to the folly of the Turks and to their preoccupation with Ali Pasha, already a declared rebel.

In April 1821 a widespread but ill co-ordinated rising in the Peloponnese began hesitantly, but soon a great number of Turks had been killed. This news, on top of Hypsilántes' adventure in the north, intensified Turkish reprisals, including the execution of the Patriarch at Constantinople. This in turn led to the departure of the Russian ambassador and a formal rupture of relations. For the next four years the other Powers did their best to prevent the revolt in Greece from becoming the occasion of a general attack by Russia upon Turkey, which might be followed by an upheaval all over Europe. At first they were successful. Capodistrias, now an embarrassment to the tsar, went into retirement at Geneva (July 1822) and for five years confined his activities, at least in public, to relief work. England, no less than Austria, was anxious to keep the tsar quiet; but, whereas Metternich hoped at first to see the revolt suppressed, Canning began to see an opportunity either of intervening alone to England's advantage or else of joining hands with the tsar in order to keep some control over the issue. In either case, the Greeks were likely to profit. In spite of personal, sectional and regional quarrels, much savage cruelty and great lack of discipline, the

Greeks had brave soldiers and skilful sailors. The failure of the Turks to reconquer the Peloponnese must be ascribed to shortage of men (owing to commitments elsewhere), jealousy between commanders and inability to secure their communications either by sea against the Greek ships under Andreas Miaoúles or by land against guerrilla harryings in the passes. During every respite, the Greek leaders quarrelled, twice to the point of civil war. An Assembly, not recognised by rival bodies, produced a little-heeded 'Constitution of Epidauros', and elected the Phanariot Alexander Mavrocordátos as president. The fighting men resented the formation of a regular government, but the 'European' Greeks had on their side the wealthy islanders, the European committees which were collecting funds (in England chiefly under Byron's influence and Benthamite management), and also most of the Philhellenes in Greece. These groups held the purse-strings, and by the end of 1824 their influence seemed to be well established.

Meanwhile, the sultan purchased the help of his nominal vassal, the Pasha of Egypt (p. 534) by allowing him to subdue and occupy Crete and by promising further rewards for the conquest of the Peloponnese. Miaoúles was no longer in a position to deny the sea passages to their combined fleets. Early in 1825, the pasha's son, Ibrahim, landed an Arab army of more than 10,000 men and soon overran a great part of the Peloponnese, without however being strong enough (or perhaps confident enough of the future) to reduce it systematically. Nauplia, the temporary Greek capital, was saved; the nearby islands of Hydra and Spezzia (the richest and most active of them all) were still unsubdued; north of the Isthmus Missolonghi held out in the west until April 1826, more than two years after Byron's death there, and in Attica the arrival of the French Philhellene Fabvier helped to postpone the surrender of the Acropolis until June 1827. At the eleventh hour, the provisional government had just agreed (April 1827) on a compromise between the factions: the 'Russian' party of Kolokotrones and other chieftains was satisfied by the election, with general consent, of Capodistrias as president for seven years; the choice of the philhellene soldier Sir Richard Church and the wayward Admiral Lord Cochrane to command the Greek forces on land and sea was a concession to the 'English' party of the islanders and some of the notables; the 'French' party of Kolettes, whose support came mainly from north of the Isthmus, was propitiated by the publication in May of the extremely democratic 'Constitution of Troezen'. By this time, the prospect of foreign intervention was at last taking shape.

The war of independence could not have been won by the Greeks without foreign intervention; but, equally, the movement could hardly have been suppressed if the Powers had held aloof. Intervention was brought about partly by the deadlock which threatened constant disturbance and piracy in the Aegean, partly by the desire to forestall Russia, and more indefinably by the interest of classically-educated Europeans (including even the critics of philhellenic sentiment) in a country which seemed familiar to them in a way that Serbia and Roumania were not. Before his death in December 1825, Tsar Alexander I had already ceased to discuss the eastern question with his continental allies, and leaned towards an actively Russian policy which his successor Nicholas I was to pursue more resolutely. Canning disliked the double prospect of Egyptian rule in the Peloponnese and Greek piracy in the Aegean, but he was hardly in a position to move alone in response to the appeal of some Greek leaders for British protection (June 1825). The upshot was the Protocol signed by the Duke of Wellington at St Petersburg on 4 April 1826. The two governments agreed to impose on both parties, by means of joint or separate negotiation, a settlement giving to the Greeks, within unspecified boundaries, an autonomous but tributary status, with compensation for Turkish proprietors. On 29 April, after the fall of Missolonghi, the Greek Assembly made a formal request for mediation on this basis, but staked out claims for inclusion of many regions which had hardly taken up arms during the revolt. Even before the Protocol was signed, the new tsar sent an ultimatum to the sultan, requiring negotiation on outstanding Russo-Turkish disputes; the resulting Convention of Akkerman (October 1826) was a diplomatic success for Russia but made no such stipulations for the Greeks as it did for the Roumanians and Serbians. The Bourbon government of France, to whom a section of the Greeks had also appealed, desired to share, not in a revolution but in a crusade. This prolonged but enlarged the negotiations.

The tripartite Treaty of London (6 July 1827), signed during Canning's brief premiership, added little to the substance of the Protocol, but an additional article provided for sending a joint fleet to Greek waters to enforce an armistice on both parties—'without however taking any part in the hostilities'. Both parties accepted the armistice, but neither fully observed it. George Canning died in August, but his cousin Stratford Canning, ambassador at Constantinople, who had met Mavrocordatos eighteen months earlier, went a little beyond his instructions by referring in a private letter to cannon-shot as the final arbiter; this was repeated by Admiral Codrington to his captains. Thus the Cabinets avoided direct responsibility for the decisive conflict in the Bay of Navarino on 20 October 1827, when the Turkish and Egyptian fleets were destroyed by the naval squadrons of England, Russia and France; Metternich might speak of a 'frightful catastrophe', and Wellington, who came into office in January 1828, of an 'untoward event'; but the three ambassadors had already left Constantinople, and England was not released from her obligations under the Treaty even if

Russia should separately pursue the quarrel to the point of war with Turkey. The Egyptians soon evacuated the Peloponnese, after a mere show of resistance to a French force which arrived in the name of the three Powers and stayed there for five years (1828–33). But the sultan would not yield. He had denounced the Treaty of Akkerman and almost invited the Russian declaration of war (April 1828); nothing but a disastrous second campaign forced him to accede to the Treaty of London as part of the peace-treaty signed at Adrianople (14 September 1829) in the presence of a Russian army.[1]

The future status and the frontiers of Greece were still undetermined. Wellington, like Metternich, thought that a small independent state under a European sovereign would be less open to Russian influence than a larger but tributary territory. As president, Capodistrias was unjustly suspected by England and France of being a tool of the tsar. His services to Greece have been under-rated in the past and perhaps overmuch idealised by Greeks more recently. It was his misfortune that in attempting a necessary period of personal rule, he had not sufficient means to enforce it and was too contemptuous of local spirit: faction culminated in his assassination (October 1831), and near-anarchy followed. Meanwhile Prince Leopold of Saxe-Coburg, soon to be the first King of the Belgians, accepted and then declined the throne of Greece (February–May 1830); it was welcomed in May 1832 by King Louis I of Bavaria, an enthusiastic philhellene, for his younger son Otho, then aged seventeen. Wellington wanted at first to liberate only the Peloponnese and the lesser islands, but the three ambassadors from Constantinople, in conference at Poros, had recommended (December 1828) a more generous settlement, and European opinion could not conceive Greece without Athens at least. The northern frontier offered to Leopold in 1830 was enlarged for Otho in 1832 by Palmerston's inclusion of Acarnania in the west. Among the islands, the ambassadors had proposed to include both Samos and Crete, but Palmerston in office could not or would not reverse the contrary decision of 1830, which he had criticised in opposition. Samos obtained, and Chios recovered, a tolerably autonomous status until their union with Greece in 1913. Crete was restored to the sultan in 1840 after fifteen years of Egyptian rule; two generations of periodical risings passed before the Turkish garrison was removed in 1898, and full union with Greece followed in 1912.

News of the Treaty of Adrianople caused a momentary panic in western chanceries, but in fact its terms were not alarming except as an omen for the future. The Russian army was exhausted, and could hardly have seized the capital, nor did the tsar desire it. He had already

---

[1] For an account of the international aspects of the Greek question, see Chapter xxv, pp. 673–4, 677–9, 685–9.

approved a report of a powerful Committee of his Council, reaffirming in effect the policy formulated by Czartoryski twenty-five years earlier, namely to avoid or postpone the crucial question of the future of Constantinople and the Straits by preserving the general framework of Turkish power while exerting continuous pressure on the sultan in furtherance of Russian interests in detail. This was not unlike the British, French or Austrian conception of the 'independence and integrity' of Turkey, with the big exception that Russia's desires to expand into Asia, to open the door to the Mediterranean and to live up to her reputation as an Orthodox Empire must inevitably erode the principle of preservation and might ultimately explode it at some great opportunity. Whatever her intention might be, Russia had not the power, in 1829 or even in 1878, to seek alone a radical solution—and in 1918 it was not under Russian pressure that the remnants of Turkey in Europe were detached. Yet the terms that Russia was able to impose at Adrianople in 1829 did mark an irreversible step in the history of not only Greece but the future Roumania. The Greek revolt and the example of Muhammad Ali also provoked the first decisive step in Turkey towards internal revival—Mahmud II's destruction of the Janissaries in June 1826, known in Turkey as the 'auspicious incident'. 'The first explosion of Greek nationalism kindled the first spark of its Turkish counterpart.'[1] But it was not until they had lost their foothold in Europe nearly a century later that the Turks appeared to others or even to themselves as a 'nation rightly struggling to be free'. To the sultan in 1830, political nationalism and its friends seemed as dangerous as they did to Metternich; in the eyes of Europe, the sultan was either an uncouth and savage tyrant, deserving no sympathy, or else an exasperatingly lethargic ally.

[1] A. J. Toynbee, *A Study of History* (abridged), p. 132.

CHAPTER XX

RELATIONS WITH SOUTH AND SOUTH-EAST ASIA

THESE were years when the boundaries of British rule were extended while its impact was intensified. New territory was acquired, both in India and outside it, while the activities of government advanced beyond the maintenance of order and the collection of revenue to economic and social policies that accorded with European ideas of utility and morality. Exaggerated fears of a revival of French power in Asia were at first associated with this territorial expansion, and the desire for a strong ally against a resurgent France was the main reason why the British allowed the Dutch to return to South-East Asia after the Napoleonic Wars. But the major concern of the English East India Company was now the establishment of its authority as the paramount power in India. Mughal supremacy had been little more than nominal after the death of Aurangzib, the last of the great emperors, in 1707, and the Maratha confederacy lacked the unity of direction and the centralised administrative system necessary for dominance over the sub-continent. Widespread disorder and devastation in central India, spreading to the borders of British territory, indicated the need for some paramount authority. Indian considerations thus brought the English Company to grips with the Marathas. Apart from arousing occasional suspicions of Russian designs, European politics were henceforth of diminishing importance in the shaping of its external policies.

European ideas, on the other hand, were of increasing importance in the development of internal policy. True, the defects that had arisen in the administrative institutions established by Lord Cornwallis in Bengal suggested that he had paid too little attention to Indian ideas and circumstances, and the reforms that were in train elsewhere made more use of local experience by modifying the rigidity of his separation of powers, by giving more responsibility to native officials, and by settling the land revenue with villages and with individual cultivators instead of with great landholders. But these new methods of settlement also accorded well with European economic notions. James Mill at the East-India House, Munro in Madras, Colebrooke in Ceylon, Van Hogendorp and Raffles in Java—all thought that they were turning custom-ridden serfs into industrious peasant-cultivators, responsive to economic rather than 'feudal' stimuli. In fact, the immediate result of the introduction of cash rents and of private property in land was often to deliver the cultivator into the hands of the moneylender. The establishment of freer trade, both external and internal, similarly tended to benefit the merchant rather than the local artisan who found it difficult to compete with the machines of Europe. But in cities like Calcutta and Bombay this same commercial class, together with the lawyers and officials nurtured by the new institutions of government, proved particularly sympathetic to European ideas and to social reforms based upon them. It was, perhaps, in social policies that European ideas had the most influence, as the British took to encouraging the diffusion of 'useful' knowledge and to discouraging customs like suttee. Also, wherever British rule was introduced, punishments such as torture and mutilation were abolished, and attempts were made to suppress bribery and corruption. There was a feeling of progress in official circles—a sense of confidence in the power of European ideas to free the people of Asia from outworn usages and superstitions. The Indian ideas that had seemed to Warren Hastings and his colleagues to be so worthy of study were now condemned as ungodly by Evangelicals or despised as inefficient by Utilitarians. The translations and researches undertaken by Sir William Jones, Charles Wilkins and the other pioneers of the Asiatic Society of Bengal now seemed to arouse more interest in Germany than in England, and Friedrich Schlegel hoped that the study of Indian literature would stimulate a second renaissance in Europe. Macaulay, on the other hand, thought that English education would engender a renaissance in India.

Among the factors governing British expansion, fear of a revival of French power in India was most apparent under Wellesley, who became governor-general in 1798. His fears were shared by Dundas, the President of the Board of Control in London, who sent reinforcements to India when he heard of Napoleon's Egyptian expedition. Wellesley was concerned not only with the possibility of a French invasion but also with the reality of French intrigues with local rulers. He knew that Tipu Sultan of Mysore had sent to Mauritius for military help, that the French governor had called for volunteers, and that some had come forward. This seemed all the more ominous in view of the threatened invasion from the north-west by Zaman Shah of Afghanistan, with whom Wellesley thought that Tipu had some understanding. Wellesley also saw danger in the many French soldiers of fortune who were still to be found in the service of different Indian rulers. He was particularly wary of the French-trained troops of the Nizam of Hyderabad, and soon persuaded him to conclude a treaty of alliance against Tipu, whereby he agreed to disband them and to accept and pay for a force of the Company's troops in their place. Tipu himself was then asked to dispense with French help, but seemed unwilling to comply. After some inconclusive correspondence, British troops entered

Mysore. The war was short and decisive. Tipu was killed in the taking of his capital, Seringapatam, and his kingdom lay at Wellesley's disposal. Part of it, including the sea coast, was kept by the Company, part was handed over to the Nizam as an ally's reward, though he had done little enough to deserve it, and the remainder was restored to the old Hindu dynasty from which Tipu's father, Haidar Ali, had taken it. At the same time, the new ruler was placed firmly under the Company's control in a subsidiary alliance: he agreed to accept a force of the Company's troops and to pay an annual subsidy for them, and he promised to have no relations with any other state without the Company's approval.

Subsidiary alliances of this type became a means of extending British control over other states and eventually of establishing British paramountcy over the whole of the Indian subcontinent. Rulers in difficulty would be offered the Company's protection against enemies abroad or rebels at home in return for the stationing of a force of the Company's troops within their territories, the payment of an annual subsidy and the renunciation of any independent foreign policy. In practice, the payment of the annual subsidy was sometimes delayed and aroused much altercation. An additional refinement was to require the cession of territory instead. These features may be seen in the subsidiary alliance concluded with the Nizam in 1800, when he was obliged to cede to the Company the territories he had so recently acquired from Mysore.

Oudh was already linked with the Company in such an alliance when the possibility of an Afghan invasion prompted Wellesley to demand an increase in the size of the subsidiary force, to meet the cost of which the Nawab had to cede extensive territories. The result of these cessions was that Oudh was surrounded by British territory—except for its border with Nepal—and therefore had no need of such an increase in the subsidiary force. Moreover, by the time that these lengthy and acrimonious negotiations were concluded, the Afghan danger no longer existed, for Sikh hostility and a lack of funds had already forced Zaman Shah to withdraw. The growth of British power in India was now a more important aim than the defence of the Company's possessions against foreign invasion.

The Maratha confederacy remained the only formidable power confronting the Company. Never tightly organised, its structure now seemed threatened by the dissensions of its leaders. The Peshwa, who had usurped the power of the Raja of Satara though still professing to be his chief minister, was losing control over the great military chiefs, such as Sindia and Holkar, who were becoming independent territorial princes. Such a situation invited British intervention. Wellesley was also encouraged by his suspicions of French influence. The forces which the military adventurer de Boigne had raised for Mahadji Sindia had been of great service in the establishment of the latter's power in Northern India, which extended to the control of Delhi, the city of the Mughal emperor. In return, extensive territories based on Agra had been assigned to de Boigne, and after his return home in 1795 his forces and territories had been entrusted to another such adventurer, one General Perron. Eight years later, Wellesley was still troubled by reports of de Boigne's influence with Napoleon. Holkar, moreover, had followed Sindia's example by engaging yet another French adventurer. If the instability of Maratha politics provided ample opportunity for British intervention, these indications of French influence provided Wellesley with ample justification for it.

That instability was accentuated by the accession of three reckless and inexperienced rulers within the same decade. Daulat Rao Sindia succeeded Mahadji on the latter's death in 1794. In 1796 a new Peshwa, Baji Rao, came to power, and quickly showed his impatience of the restraining hand of Nana Phadnis, the minister who had dominated the politics of Poona for the last quarter of the century and who himself died in 1800. Finally, the death of Tukoji Holkar in 1797 was followed by a struggle for the inheritance in which the young Jaswant Rao emerged as the ablest but also the most restless member of the family. When Mahadji Sindia had come south to gain influence at Poona, Nana had encouraged Holkar to make trouble for him in the north. Baji Rao, on the other hand, allowed the young Daulat Rao Sindia a free hand at Poona and then provoked Jaswant Rao Holkar's enmity. But Daulat Rao proved an unworthy successor to Mahadji Sindia, and was unable to protect the Peshwa from Holkar's vengeance. Baji Rao fled to Bassein in December 1802 to seek the help that Wellesley was eager to give. In return for British protection against enemies abroad and rebels at home Baji Rao promised to have no relations with other powers without the Company's knowledge and agreed to the presence of a subsidiary force, to pay for which he had to cede some territory. He was duly restored to Poona in May 1803, but Sindia was unwilling for the British to gain such influence there and was at war with them in August. It was soon apparent that the French danger had again been exaggerated. Perron offered no resistance when the British seized Aligarh, with its arsenal and treasury; then he accepted the British offer of a safe-conduct and left for France, a very rich man. His successor, Bourquin, only offered a feeble resistance when the British advanced on Delhi. With the possession of that city, the Mughal emperor passed under their protection. Such was Wellesley's opinion, though the emperor's was that the Company had now returned to their proper allegiance. Sindia also lost his control over the princes of Rajputana, who passed under British protection. Moreover, he was forced to cede extensive territories in the north and west and to dismiss his French staff. Finally, he was asked to accept a subsidiary force, but at first refused. Distrust of Holkar soon caused him to change his mind, however, and in February 1804 he accepted the protection of a subsidiary force, while promising to have no relations with 'any principal States or powers' without the Company's knowledge.[1] The British had once again been able to profit from Maratha disunity.

Meanwhile, Holkar had been preparing for a trial of strength with the Company, and appealed to Sindia to join him. Sindia duly reported this to the British, who were soon at war with Holkar. They might well have found it difficult to tackle a united Maratha confederacy. As it was, they were able to deal with their enemies one by one. Even so, Holkar proved a formidable opponent. At the same time, growing concern was being voiced in England at the successive wars in which Wellesley had involved the Company. Nor had he tried to conciliate or even to conceal his contempt for his critics. He had scarcely troubled to keep the home authorities informed of his plans. He had felt confident of the support of Dundas, the first President of the Board of Control: he understood his 'voracious appetite for lands and fortresses'.[2] But Castlereagh, who became President of the Board in 1802, proved to be less enthusiastic for territorial expansion and more conscious of its dangers. Moreover, the financial position of the Company had long aroused concern and now seemed jeopardised by Wellesley's policies. Its Indian revenues were not meeting its expenditure, and its trade was running at a loss. The exclusion of some of its European competitors as a result of the Napoleonic war had provided an opportunity for increasing its exports from India. The Court of Directors had therefore been sending Wellesley no less than one million sterling a year, but he had been spending it on his wars instead of on trade. Not only had he offended the Directors in general by ignoring their administrative authority and neglecting their commercial policy; he had also alienated the powerful shipping interest by allowing India-built ships to carry home the Company's goods. Finally, it seemed that his Maratha policy had involved the Company first in a war with Sindia and now in another with Holkar, in which British troops had already suffered serious reverses. The government could no longer withstand the Directors' pressure for Wellesley's recall. He therefore resigned in 1805 on learning that the alternative was dismissal.

In the period of peace and retrenchment that followed, some of the ground recently gained was deliberately relinquished. Conciliatory

---

[1] Treaty of Burhanpur. As a concession to his susceptibilities, the subsidiary force was to be stationed near his frontier, rather than within his territories.

[2] Wellesley to Dundas, 25 January 1800, quoted in C. H. Philips (ed.), *Correspondence of David Scott*, vol. I (Royal Historical Society, Camden Third Series, vol. LXXV), (London, 1951), p. xx.

terms were offered to Sindia as well as Holkar, and the protection that the Company had promised the Rajput states was now withdrawn. Those states were in effect abandoned to the demands of the Maratha chiefs and to the depredations of their Pindari auxiliaries—freebooters who may have had their uses in war but were the scourge of central India in peace, their numbers swelling as those of more regular armies were reduced. They were now beyond control, plundering and ravaging over long distances. If the Company were to shrink from the assertion of its power as the successor to the Mughals, there seemed to be no prospect of law and order. The land would be devastated by marauders or impoverished by the wars of petty princes. Even Ranjit Singh, who had been building up Sikh power in the Panjab, was encouraged by the Company's passivity to advance beyond the Satlej in order to intervene in the disputes of local chiefs. He could expect conciliatory treatment from the British at a time when they were suspicious of French designs upon India. But in 1809, when those suspicions had been allayed, the Company decided to assert itself, and a display of force was enough to persuade him to direct his energies elsewhere.

From the Company's point of view, the subsidiary alliance remained the most effective method of extending British influence without adding to the British territories in India. But many officials thought that states which had concluded such alliances were unlikely to prosper. Thomas Munro was of this opinion:

There are many weighty objections to the employment of a subsidiary force. It has a natural tendency to render the government of every country in which it exists, weak and oppressive; to extinguish all honourable spirit among the higher classes of society, and to degrade and impoverish the whole people. The usual remedy of a bad government in India is a quiet revolution in the palace, or a violent one by rebellion, or foreign conquests. But the presence of a British force cuts off every chance of remedy, by supporting the prince on the throne against every foreign and domestic enemy. It renders him indolent, by teaching him to trust to strangers for his security; and cruel and avaricious, by showing him that he has nothing to fear from the hatred of his subjects.[1]

Nor did rulers find it easy to bear the restraints which a subsidiary alliance imposed upon them. The Peshwa Baji Rao had been required, in the treaty of Bassein, to renounce all relations with other powers without the Company's knowledge. He was soon informed that these powers were deemed by the Company to include the other Maratha rulers, such as Sindia and Holkar, whose nominal suzerain he had been. The Company's attitude was that the Maratha confederacy had been 'dissolved' as a result of the treaty of Bassein. Another source of tension was the opportunity which the subsidiary alliance gave to the Company's residents to interfere in the internal affairs of the states to

[1] Munro to governor-general, 12 August 1817. G. R. Gleig, *Sir Thomas Munro* (London, 1831), vol. II, pp. 7–8.

which they were accredited. In the face of Baji Rao's repeated demands for the use of the subsidiary force against his overmighty subjects, the great *jagirdars* (or landholders), Mountstuart Elphinstone arranged a settlement at Pandharpur in 1812 by which they promised to serve the Peshwa according to custom provided that he in turn respected their customary rights, the British government standing as arbiter between them. The resident was in effect protecting the *jagirdars* against their own sovereign. When Baji Rao finally turned on the Company in 1817, Elphinstone was soon able to detach most of the *jagirdars* from his cause, and special consideration was accordingly shown to them after the annexation of his territories by the British in the following year.

Baji Rao had attacked at a time when the Company was involved in widespread operations against the Pindaris, whose activities were threatening the prosperity of some of its own territories. These operations required a reconsideration of the Company's relationship with the other Maratha powers, who had connived at the Pindaris' doings. They were invited to help, but Holkar followed Baji Rao's example and was quickly defeated and obliged to sign a subsidiary treaty. Sindia, in whose favour the British had, in 1805, renounced the right to make treaties with the Rajput states, was now required to release them from that pledge, besides promising them his full co-operation against the Pindaris. The Pindari menace was soon eradicated, and the Rajput states, which had suffered so much from Pindaris and Marathas alike, were joined in alliance with the Company, acknowledging its supremacy and promising to act in 'subordinate co-operation' with it at all times. The Company was clearly the paramount power in India.

Beyond India, the Company's advance had followed a similar pattern. Suspicion of French designs was again the first consideration. Indeed, towards local rulers the British were often much more circumspect than they were towards their European rivals. The British conquest of maritime Ceylon and of the other Dutch possessions in South and South-East Asia followed quickly upon the French assumption of control over Holland in 1795. Java still remained for a time in Dutch hands, but it seemed of little economic value to the English Company and the force that was eventually prepared for it was diverted to the Red Sea after the French invasion of Egypt. However, its conquest seemed the more necessary when the reforms of Marshal H. W. Daendels, that loyal servant of Napoleon, had increased its military strength and when the capture of Mauritius in 1810 had left it as the only base for French frigates and privateers in search of British shipping in Asian waters. Its occupation in the following year prompted the formulation of extensive plans for economic and social reform, under the inspiration of T. S. Raffles, as lieutenant-governor, but the British desire for a strong Dutch ally against a resurgent France led to its return to Dutch rule in 1816. Unwilling for the British to abandon their prospects in South-East Asia, Raffles established the English Company at Singapore by setting up a rival to the Sultan of Johore and securing formal permission from him. As part of a general settlement of differences in 1824, the Dutch recognised the British position in Singapore, handed over Malacca and promised not to interfere in Malaya, while the British handed over their establishments in Sumatra, and promised not to interfere south of the Straits of Singapore. From Singapore and Penang the British could dominate the Straits of Malacca and protect the sea routes to China. Commerce rather than territory was their aim in this area, but their nervous attempts to avoid entanglements with the local rulers were unsuccessful. When they acquired Penang from the Sultan of Kedah, it had been on the understanding that they would protect him against Siam, but this they proved unwilling to do: on the devastation of his country in 1821 all that he gained from them was shelter in Penang itself. But Robert Fullerton, who became Governor of Penang in 1824, found that a show of force was enough to protect Selangor and Perak from Siam when the threat came. In spite of the Calcutta Government's reluctance to assume fresh responsibilities, the Malay states gradually came to look upon the British as the paramount power, reporting to them when one ruler succeeded another and relying on them for protection in time of need. The old empire of Johore had gone the way of the Mughal Empire of India. The authority of the one sultan at Singapore was overshadowed by the British, while that of his rival at Riau was overshadowed by the Dutch.

For all the Company's reluctance to add to its territories in South-East Asia, substantial gains were made nearer its Indian borders, and in response to local pressure. In Ceylon, with the Company in possession of the coast and the Kandyan kingdom isolated from the outside world, the situation was delicate enough and there was ample provocation on both sides. As in India, intrigues with rivals to the throne seemed the most effective way to influence over the local government. British troops duly installed a puppet as king in 1802, but left only a small and supine garrison for his future support, with the result that he and they were speedily despatched. However, the legitimate ruler proved harsh enough to alienate the leading Kandyan chiefs and rash enough to provide the British with ample justification for further interference, so that in 1815 a British force, acting with the connivance of the restive chiefs, succeeded in deposing him and annexing his kingdom. The whole of Ceylon was now under British rule. (The Maritime Provinces had been transferred from Company to Crown rule in 1802.) Another mettlesome and restless neighbour faced the British across the north-east frontier of India, after the Burmese conquest of Arakan in 1785. The Burmese government was ignorant of the Company's strength but determined to pursue a spirited policy towards it. In the years that followed, relations were troubled by Burmese protests against the shelter afforded to Arakanese rebels and refugees in British territory, by successive Burmese invasions of Assam and Manipur which occasioned further flights of refugees, by Burmese threats against Cachar and by rumours of Burmese designs on Bengal. The Burmese advance was unchecked by the declaration of a British protectorate over Cachar but permanently halted by the ensuing war, which won for the British the important coastal provinces of Arakan and Tenasserim, as well as Assam.

These various conquests were, however, creating fresh problems of administration. Wellesley, and many officials in Bengal, thought that the system established there by Lord Cornwallis should be extended to the Company's other possessions. Cornwallis had, in 1793, confirmed in perpetuity the revenue settlements made by the government with the substantial landholders or *zamindars*—a term covering a variety of persons from tax-farmers to the descendants of rajas. They were all thereby made hereditary landlords at unchangeable rents. It was hoped that they would be encouraged to undertake improvements by the knowledge that any increase in productivity would benefit them rather than attract heavier government demands upon them. At the same time, security against illegal exactions was provided by a rigid separation of powers between collectors and judges. With its detailed regulations, this was intended to be a government of laws rather than of men. It was also a European government, for Indians were confined to junior and ill-paid posts. But all these features of the Cornwallis system were now under attack.

The most serious criticisms were in fact made by the officials who had been given the task of establishing that system in the Company's new territories. In the ceded and conquered provinces of Northern India, for example, they protested that not enough was known either of the resources of the land or of its proper owners for any permanent arrangements to be made. Besides, a permanent settlement would be of no benefit to the Company in the event of a rise in the productivity of the soil or a fall in the value of money. Such arguments against permanency were enough to convince the home government that future settlements must allow of periodic revision. Whether they should be made with *zamindars* was another matter of dispute. There was little to suggest that the Cornwallis system had turned them into improving landlords. On the contrary, its rigidity seemed to be making them more ruthless with their tenants rather than more efficient in their methods: they had found that, if the Company's revenue demand could not be raised, neither would it be lowered or postponed; and while some old families were displaced, others had recourse to rack-renting and sub-letting. Once land had become a saleable commodity, considerable changes of ownership seem to have taken place. Further research will have to be devoted to this matter, but it seems probable that elsewhere in India, with periodic revisions of the revenue settlement, the tendency to such changes was all the greater, and that much land must have passed into the hands of merchants, money-lenders and functionaries of the law courts and revenue offices of the new regime. Such persons would have been quick to take advantage of the strictness with which the Company's judges enforced the terms of mortgages and debtors' bonds upon which unlettered and unsuspecting landholders had placed their mark. But, although the Company's courts were too complicated and expensive to serve the needs of villagers, local agencies of justice like village headmen and arbitration tribunals were too informal and unsystematic to be fitted into the Cornwallis system. Officials with utilitarian ideas suspected that British rule was fostering the growth of a parasitic class of rent-receivers, while those who saw a meritorious simplicity and vigour in the ancient Indian village feared for the decline of its institutions in an age of reforms and regulations.

In Northern India, revenue settlements were therefore made with villages—often with a group of proprietors, sometimes with an individual headman; while in South India, under the influence of Thomas Munro, settlements were made with the individual *raiyats*, or cultivators, and more power was given to Indians, both to subordinate judges and to village headmen and tribunals. In Western India, under the influence of Mountstuart Elphinstone, more care was taken to safeguard social privilege. Unlike Munro, with his lengthy experience of settling the revenue and understanding the problems of cultivators, Elphinstone's duties as resident at Poona had brought him into close contact with the ruling classes of the Maratha Empire and had given him some insight into their difficulties on the establishment of British rule. Not only did he realise the political importance of conciliating an aristocracy which had preserved its influence among the people: he also objected on principle to the 'levelling' tendencies that he detected both in the judicial and administrative arrangements of the Cornwallis system and also in Munro's determination to make his revenue settlements with the peasants and his tendency to ignore the rights of other classes. He therefore made special provision to safeguard the feelings of the ruling classes of the old Maratha Empire. The *sardars*, or great men, were divided into three classes, each entitled to its own degree of preferential treatment in the Company's courts, while the greatest landholders (*jagirdars*) were allowed a free hand within their own estates. Care was also taken to propitiate the Brahmans in view of the privileges that they had lost with the fall of the Hindu government and the authority that they still retained over public opinion. A degree of judicial responsibility was left with the village headmen and arbitration tribunals.

Revenue settlements, too, were made with village headmen or joint proprietors where this had formerly been the custom, as in parts of Gujarat and the Konkan, though elsewhere settlement was made with the cultivators themselves. But both Munro and Elphinstone found that suitors seemed to prefer the speedy hearing offered by the Company's Indian judges to the dilatory proceedings of arbitration tribunals. Nor could the village headmen either escape the definition, and thereby the limitation, of their powers in the Company's regulations or shield their doings from the suspicious scrutiny of its collectors. In the general reaction against the Cornwallis system, with its reliance on the separation of powers, the collector had been turned into a powerful, paternalistic figure, vested with the office of magistrate and with the control of the police, as well as with the allocation of the land-revenue demand in areas which had not been permanently settled.

Even under Elphinstone, the Company's methods of government were much more systematic and impersonal than those of its predecessors. Definition and limitation of powers seemed an ominous threat to local influence and prestige; so did the sight of high office going, not to men of high caste, but to a rapidly changing succession of foreigners. When Sir John Malcolm, who succeeded Elphinstone as Governor of Bombay, received the great landholders at Poona in 1827 he found them alarmed 'at the tendency of our system of rule to destroy all those distinctions they cherish', though he thought that there was 'a better prospect of preserving a native aristocracy in this part of India than in any other quarter of our territories'.[1] But the aristocratic privileges erected in the judicial system of Bombay were only sanctioned with great reluctance by the Court of Directors, and Utilitarians like James Mill were already arguing that the Company should act as the sole landlord and appropriate the whole economic rent of the soil, to the end that a parasitic landlord class would be unable to exist. Such a principle, though never strictly enforced, was used to justify burdensome assessments equivalent to a half or even two-thirds of the estimated net produce. Attempts were also made, in the revenue settlements of the North-Western Provinces, to supersede aristocratic claims, where they existed, in favour of the village community. T. C. Robertson, who became lieutenant-governor there after serving in Bengal, was shocked at such 'a fearful experiment', which threatened so to 'flatten the whole surface of society as eventually to leave little of distinguishable eminence between the ruling power and the cultivators of the soil'.[2] But such policies did not prevent the steady transfer of land on mortgage from impecunious cultivators to prudent moneylenders. Meanwhile, the

---

[1] Minute, 16 January 1828. Bombay Judicial Consultations, 30 January 1828, p. 31.
[2] T. C. Robertson, Minute, 15 April 1842, quoted in E. T. Stokes, *The English Utilitarians and India* (Oxford, 1959), pp. 115–16.

abolition of the myriad duties on internal trade and transit went further to benefit the commercial classes. All this seemed to accord with the best economic principles.

James Mill himself claimed that under such a system 'the wants of the state are supplied really and truly without taxation', simply by transferring the rent from an idle class of landlords to the Company.[1] In fact, however, high assessment was a recurrent defect of the Company's periodic revenue settlements. Nor were the cultivators in happier circumstances in the areas under permanent *zamindari* settlement. Cornwallis, from his experience of a Bengal still recovering from the effects of a disastrous famine, had assumed that the *zamindars*, needing tenants, must treat them liberally; but this motive no longer operated as population grew along with ordered government, while customary obligations were difficult to enforce through the Company's law courts and were lightly regarded. The political economists held that the free play of economic forces elsewhere must bring increased production, benefiting the most efficient members of the community; but the merchants and moneylenders seemed to be in fact the chief beneficiaries and to be no more likely to initiate agricultural improvements than the *zamindars* had been.

In the maritime provinces of Ceylon, the establishment of British rule was soon followed by the curtailment of the privileges and authority of the chiefs and headmen. But after the conquest of Kandy, special consideration was shown to the local chiefs who had helped in that operation, until their rebellion in 1818 decided the government to restrict their authority also. Even so, the institutions of the Kandyan provinces left them a privileged position, especially in the administration of justice, but a greater uniformity was introduced after the Benthamite recommendations of the Colebrooke–Cameron Commission in 1832. A further step was taken towards equality before the law when the government renounced its right to exact forced labour from certain castes. When recommending this reform, Colebrooke had pointed to the headmen's propensity not only to divert such labour to their private purposes but also to charge for excusing individuals from their liability. A belief in economic incentives also lay behind the measure—and behind the policy of abolishing service tenures and of exacting payment of land revenue in cash rather than in kind.

There was talk of similar reforms in Java in the last painful decade of the Dutch Company's existence. Dirk van Hogendorp, who had become acquainted with the ideas behind the Cornwallis system while

---

[1] James Mill, evidence before Select Committee on Affairs of East India Company, 2 August 1831, *Parliamentary Papers, House of Commons*, 1831, v, (65), p. 292. Stokes, *op. cit.* p. 91.

serving in the Dutch factory at Patna, argued that the forced delivery of produce in kind to the Company and the policy of governing through the regents, or chiefs, left the people without the economic incentives and security from oppression that were needed for higher productivity. But the opposition was too strong. Even Daendels, who sympathised with many of the new ideas, thought that the people were too lazy for a free economy, and he extended the system of enforcing the delivery of produce, with the result that the government stores were filled with coffee that could not be exported because of the blockade. At the same time, with a truly Napoleonic desire for centralised authority, he tried to turn the regents into government officials and to impose Dutch supremacy more firmly on the princes. These centralising policies were continued by Raffles, who thought that there was a 'propensity inherent in every native authority to abuse its influence, and to render it oppressive to the population at large'.[1] But if he distrusted the 'privileged classes' he found in the peasantry the simple virtues that appealed to administrators of the Munro school. With the help of H. W. Muntinghe, a Dutch official who had been influenced by van Hogendorp, he introduced a land revenue system based at first on settlements with the village headmen and subsequently on settlements with the individual cultivators. This could be expected to forward the development of a cash economy suited more to the needs of English industrialists in search of export markets than to those of Dutch traders in search of colonial produce. Nevertheless the land-rent system was continued by the Dutch on their return to Java. But it did not prove remunerative enough to meet their financial needs, which were increased by the costs of the Java War of 1825-30—a revolt led by Dipa Nigara, a prince who thought that he had been cheated of his inheritance. Nor was Dutch trade meeting British competition, in spite of the foundation, in 1825, of a state trading corporation, the *Nederlandsche Handel-Maatschappij*. Johannes van den Bosch, who became governor-general in 1830, was therefore entrusted with the task of economic reform. If he did not think that the peasants were too lazy for freedom, neither did he think that freedom would necessarily teach them how best to employ their labour. He concluded that guidance—or compulsion—would be needed to enlighten them, and decreed that the state could require the cultivation of a specified area with a specified crop in place of the payment of rent in cash. This, the so-called 'Culture System', involved a degree of paternalistic control which had been absent from the Company's system of enforcing the delivery of produce no matter how cultivated. The co-operation of the regents was all the more necessary to its success, and much of their old authority was therefore restored. Not all of it, however: the reforms of Daendels and Raffles were not entirely

[1] Raffles, *History of Java* (2nd ed.) (London, 1830), vol. I, p. xxxvii.

obliterated. Nor was the Culture System a mere return to the policies of the old Company, though the new state trading corporation was entrusted with the resulting exports. Methods were improved, new crops were introduced, and productivity in general was increased. But guidance became control, and the government became all the more preoccupied with Java, to the neglect of the other Dutch possessions.

The English East India Company had meanwhile been fighting a losing battle for its commercial privileges. The forces behind the changing current of British trade with Asia were too strong for it. The motive underlying much of the opposition to the renewal of its charter in 1793 was no doubt the traditional fear of competition from its exports of Indian silks, muslins and cottons. But its European markets were already being invaded by English machine-made cottons, and when the renewal of its charter had again to be considered in 1813 the opposition was concerned more with the idea that its monopoly of the trade with India and China was an obstacle to the development of Asian markets for English goods. It was therefore deprived of the Indian monopoly in 1813 and of the Chinese in 1833. It soon found itself unable to compete with private traders, while Indian handicrafts proved equally helpless before English factory-made goods. But it fostered the production of raw materials, and with the help of private traders India continued to export commodities such as cotton, silk, saltpetre and indigo in considerable quantities. Penang proved a useful channel through which Indian goods flowed into South-East Asia, and its proximity to the Coromandel coast was an encouragement to the enterprise of Indian merchants. The establishment of Singapore facilitated the circulation of English piecegoods in the same area, but a steady flow of Indian trade continued. At the beginning of this period, silver was still being sent from England and Bengal to help pay for the Company's growing exports of tea from China. But the gap was soon filled by increasing amounts of Indian opium and cotton; with the result that the terms of trade had been reversed by the second decade of the nineteenth century, and it was China that had to export treasure to meet her adverse balance of payments. The cultivation of export crops also received official encouragement both in Ceylon and in Java. The conquest of Kandy in 1815 and the large-scale building of roads in the 1820's were followed by the development of coffee-growing on a plantation basis in Ceylon, while in Java the culture system enabled the Dutch to promote with vigour the production of commodities such as indigo, cotton and sugar.

While the English Company was thus losing its commercial functions, it was being forced to take a more active part in social reform. The Charter Act of 1813 which ended its Indian trade monopoly also provided for the freer entry of missionaries and for the promotion of education. The Company had hitherto been so careful to conciliate

Hindu and Muslim susceptibilities that the Baptist missionary William Carey and his colleagues had been forced to take refuge in the Danish settlement at Serampur. There were Evangelicals like Charles Grant among the directors, but they had been able to do little more than secure the appointment of like-minded clergymen to vacancies in the Company's establishment of chaplains. As proof of the need for caution their opponents had cited the Vellore Mutiny of 1806, when regulations framed to promote uniformity in attire and appearance were resented by the sepoys as an attack on their religion. But the methods that had been used with such effect in the agitation against the slave trade were again brought to bear upon the government; meetings were held and petitions were drawn up, while Wilberforce and his colleagues of the Clapham sect called upon influential persons. It was therefore provided that, if the Court of Directors rejected an application for permission to travel to India, the Board of Control could overrule them. There was little further attempt to restrain the missionaries from going wherever they wished, but the Company still tried to maintain an attitude of religious neutrality, while its officials continued to pay their traditional courtesies to the religions of the country and to levy the traditional taxes upon pilgrims. However, missionary and evangelical pressure forced the home government to issue a declaration, in 1833, to the effect that the Company must withdraw from all such connection with religion. The abolition of the pilgrim tax seems to have been followed by an increase in the number of pilgrims to Hindu shrines. This was hardly in accordance with the expectations of the missionaries who had assumed that such shrines derived prestige and popularity from their connection with the state. To disentangle the government from the management of lands and property assigned to religious purposes proved more difficult. This problem became particularly acute in the following decade in Ceylon, where a missionary campaign against the state's connection with 'idolatry' compelled the governor to relinquish such duties as the appointment of Buddhist priests and the management of the Temple of the Tooth at Kandy. The missionaries also campaigned for other objects, notably for the abolition of suttee in British India. They collected statistics, published gruesome descriptions of the ceremony and searched the sacred literature of the Hindus for texts to prove that the practice was not compulsory. The government, deterred by fear of public resentment, especially from the high caste sepoys of the Bengal army, tried at first merely to enforce the restrictions prescribed by the Hindu texts: when a suttee was announced, the Company's officials were supposed to ascertain that the widow made a voluntary and responsible decision to mount the pyre. But it was soon suggested that the presence of officials merely encouraged the practice; moreover, the opinion was growing among them too that suttee could be prohibited without political danger. Careful enquiry convinced Lord William Bentinck, the governor-general, that this was so, and in 1829 suttee was prohibited by law in the territories under the Bengal government.[1]

Much missionary labour was devoted to education, for it was widely held that the spreading of Western knowledge would weaken faith in Hinduism and thus prepare the way for Christianity as well as for further social reform. The Charter Act of 1813 provided that at least one lakh of rupees from the surplus revenues of the Company's territories should be applied each year 'to the revival and improvement of literature and the encouragement of the learned natives of India, and for the introduction and promotion of a knowledge of the sciences among the inhabitants of British India'.[2] But such phrases invited controversy. Some officials thought that the Company should promote the revival of the traditional learning of the country. This was objectionable to missionaries and evangelicals because of its associations with Hinduism or Islam, and to utilitarians because of its associations with religion as such. James Mill himself had much to do with the writing of a despatch which declared, in 1824, that the government's aim should be to teach not Hindu or Muslim learning but 'useful learning'—in other words, western knowledge.[3] The language of instruction aroused further controversy. Sanskrit, the traditional language of Hindu learning, seemed objectionable because it was a dead language, a difficult language and the sacred language of Hinduism. Persian, the language of the old Mughal government, was foreign to both rulers and ruled. The vernaculars were many and local: to translate English books into all of them would have been a long, costly and complicated operation. It seemed more economical to teach Indians to read English books. Bentinck himself considered that 'the British language' was 'the key to all improvements'. In a sarcastic minute Macaulay ridiculed the claims of Indian languages and oriental learning in general, and suggested that the result of teaching English to the people of India might well be a Renaissance there: 'what the Greek and Latin were to the contemporaries of More and Ascham, our tongue is to the people of India'.[4] The governor-general in council therefore resolved, in 1835, 'that the great object of the British Government ought to be the promotion of European literature and science among the natives of India; and that all the funds appropriated for the purpose of education would be best employed on English education alone'.[5] This was an

---

[1] The Madras and Bombay governments followed suit in 1830.
[2] 53 Geo. III c. CLV.
[3] Despatch to Bengal, 18 February 1824.
[4] Minute, 2 February 1835. H. Sharp (ed.), *Selections from Educational Records*, vol. I, pp. 107 ff.
[5] Resolution, 7 March 1835. Sharp, *op. cit.*, p. 130.

extreme position, and a degree of official support was soon restored to Indian learning. But the supremacy of English education was reinforced in the following decade by the government's decision to give preference to candidates with a knowledge of English when making appointments to the public service. English education was similarly promoted by the British government in Ceylon, in accordance with the recommendations of the Colebrooke Commission in 1832, while the promotion of Dutch education was declared in 1819 to be the fundamental policy of the Dutch government in Java.

This was a type of education suited only to a small minority—in Macaulay's words, 'a class who may be interpreters between us and the millions whom we govern—a class of persons Indian in blood and colour, but English in tastes, in opinions, in morals and in intellect'. The nucleus of such a class seemed already to be in existence in Bengal: moneyed Hindus living in Calcutta—absentee landlords, merchants, lawyers, Company officials—were showing a taste for European luxuries and ideas. Such men had taken the initiative in founding the Hindu College in Calcutta in 1817, where English was the language of instruction. As the missionaries had hoped, many orthodox Hindus found the new ideas unsettling. But comparatively few found that they pointed towards Christianity. The 1820's and 1830's were years of intellectual ferment in Calcutta: authors such as Voltaire, Hume and Tom Paine sold well in the bookshops; fresh newspapers and journals were founded, in Bengali as well as in English; literary and debating societies flourished; all things were questioned, and young men scandalised their elders by eating beef and drinking wine. But the excitement was confined to a small minority, and a movement for religious reform arose within Hinduism itself: the Bengal renaissance was to be accompanied by a Hindu reformation. Ram Mohan Roy, a Brahman and an old servant of the Company, had taken the lead in the promotion of English education. When the government proposed to establish a Sanskrit college in Calcutta he protested that the difficulty of Sanskrit had made it 'for ages a lamentable check on the diffusion of knowledge', and argued that the 'improvement' of the people would be better served by the teaching of the 'useful sciences' of Europe.[1] He was himself a student of Sanskrit, Arabic and Persian, as well as of the new learning, and compared the doctrines of Christianity with those of Hinduism and Islam. He even published with approval a selection of Christ's teachings under the title, *The Precepts of Jesus, the Guide to Peace and Happiness*. But he rejected Christian theology, and indeed converted to Unitarianism a noted Baptist missionary, the Rev. William Adam—'the second fallen Adam'. The Brahmo Samaj, or Divine Society, which was founded by Ram Mohan Roy in 1828, had

[1] Ram Mohan Roy to Amherst, 11 December 1823. Sharp, *op. cit.*, pp. 99 ff.

an influence out of all proportion to its numbers, which remained small. It provided educated Hindus with facilities for regular monotheistic worship based on selected Hindu texts. The trust deed of its first meeting-house specifically provided that there should be no 'graven image' or animal sacrifice: here was a form of Hinduism that was proof against the more obvious Protestant missionary criticisms. Moreover, it was compatible with the new ideas: its founder was a well-known social reformer, an opponent of suttee, an advocate for western education, even a correspondent of Bentham.

Meanwhile, there had been changes in the European attitude to Asia. India came to seem more interesting than China. In England, this was partly a consequence of empire: parliamentary controversy, culminating in the impeachment of Warren Hastings, had attracted public sympathy for a civilised people at the mercy of a rapacious company. More important, the Asiatic Society of Bengal had been founded in 1784, and some of the Company's servants were beginning the scholarly study of Indian learning. Wilkins's translation of the *Bhagavad Gita* and Jones's translation of Kalidasa's drama *Shakuntala* had been read with respectful attention, and the historian William Robertson made use of them when he argued that ancient India had attained a very high level of civilisation.[1] Germany then took quickly to the serious study of Indian learning. Jones's translation of *Shakuntala* was itself translated into German by Forster in 1791, and soon won the praise of Herder and Goethe. Friedrich Schlegel learnt Sanskrit from Alexander Hamilton, one of the founder members of the Asiatic Society of Bengal, who was at the time (1803–4) a prisoner on parole in France as a result of the outbreak of war with England. Friedrich's brother August Wilhelm became a professor at Bonn in 1818, and devoted himself to the study of Sanskrit literature there. Other such appointments soon followed in Germany. France was also taking account of Indian learning: Anquetil-Duperron had translated four of the Upanishads from a Persian translation in 1786, a chair of Sanskrit was established at the *Collège de France* in 1814, and the *Société Asiatique* was founded in Paris in 1821. It was over German thought, however, that Indian learning had the greatest influence. Goethe, indeed, had his reservations: he disliked, for example, what seemed to him the more grotesque aspects of Hinduism.[2] But there was much in India to fascinate the Germans of the romantic movement—especially those in search of the primitive language, poetry or religion of mankind. Perhaps India would regenerate Europe: Friedrich Schlegel suggested in 1808 that Indian literature could have as important an effect on the European mind as Greek and Latin

---

[1] Robertson, *Historical Disquisition Concerning the Knowledge which the Ancients had of India* (London, 1791).

[2] 'Keine Bestien in dem Göttersaal' (no Beasts in the Hall of the Gods).

literature had had in the fifteenth century. German idealism was also sensitive to Indian influence: philosophers from Schelling to Schopenhauer were eager to profess their approbation. The Indo-European languages were termed Indo-German by Klaproth as early as 1823, and it was sometimes suggested that such languages were purer than those derived from Latin—particularly French. These comparisons were not always limited to linguistic considerations, but extended to political, cultural and racial arguments.

Heine contrasted the German thirst for India's spiritual treasure with the Portuguese, Dutch and English appetite for India's material wealth. Under Utilitarian and Evangelical pressure, Englishmen indeed seemed to be losing some of their respect for Indian civilisation. In his influential *History of British India* (1817) James Mill criticised the oriental scholars like Jones who had praised India's cultural achievements. Instead, he laid stress upon social, moral and intellectual defects to show how badly India (and by reflection England) needed Benthamite reforms. In campaigning for the free entry of missionaries into India, the Evangelicals similarly emphasised the social and moral evils that seemed to them to be the result of Hinduism: Grant specifically attacked Robertson for his defence of Hindu institutions such as caste[1], and Wilberforce condemned the Indian 'religious system' calling it 'mean, licentious and cruel'.[2] Similar attacks on Hinduism were occasioned by campaigns for the prohibition of suttee and for the abolition of the pilgrim tax. The controversy over English education stimulated equally reckless condemnations of Indian learning. The bitterness of much of this argumentation was increased by memories of European religious disputes: in both Utilitarian and Evangelical writings comparisons were made between Hindu and Papist priestcraft and obscurantism.

Such criticisms of Indian learning and culture were echoed by some English-educated Indians. But English education never encouraged subservience, and as early as 1828 Kasinath Ghose, an old pupil of the Calcutta Hindu college, was replying to James Mill's criticisms of Indian civilisation. His arguments attracted enough attention to be published in a leading Calcutta newspaper, though they were largely unheeded. Meanwhile, there were still many English officials who fostered oriental scholarship in the older tradition. Elphinstone encouraged it in Bombay; Raffles encouraged it in Malacca and Java; the Royal Asiatic Society was founded in London in 1823, and in 1832 H. H. Wilson was chosen to be the first Professor of Sanskrit at Oxford.

[1] Grant, *Observations on the State of Society among the Asiatic Subjects of Great Britain, Particularly with Respect to Morals; and on the Means of Improving It. Parliamentary Papers,* 1812–13, X (282), pp. 31 ff.

[2] *Hansard,* XXVI, pp. 864–5.

He tried to answer Mill, but as he did so by annotating the latter's *History* as if it were a Sanskrit text his arguments also were largely unheeded. Elphinstone himself wrote a *History of India* in which the civilisation of that country was portrayed in a favourable light. But the general impression that he conveyed was one of decline, and he described the people as lacking 'veracity', 'manliness' and 'National spirit'. Such generalisations might serve not only to explain but also to justify the existence of foreign rule, and they came as readily to the pens of officials as to those of Utilitarians or Evangelicals. The tasks of government, which had originally stimulated the English interest in Indian studies, were now repressing it, for in a reforming age the English came to India to teach rather than to learn. But the corollary was that once they had fulfilled their pedagogic functions they would depart, and Elphinstone was as ready as Macaulay to concede that national independence would be the proper result of western education. Already in 1829 Bentinck was publicly inviting 'all native Gentlemen, Landholders, Merchants and others' to suggest reforms for the government to carry out. In Ceylon, Colebrooke had his commission published in Sinhalese and Tamil as well as in English, and paid due attention to the resultant petitions. Also of significance, at least for the future, was the inclusion in the Act that renewed the East India Company's Charter in 1833 of a declaration that no native would be debarred from any post by race or religion.

CHAPTER XXI

EUROPE'S ECONOMIC AND POLITICAL RELATIONS WITH TROPICAL AFRICA[1]

CURRENTS of European expansion had lapped the shores of Africa since the fifteenth century. But at the end of the eighteenth century the continent and its peoples were still little known. If anything, European knowledge of and interest in Africa had declined since the heyday of Portuguese discovery and expansion in the fifteenth and sixteenth centuries. The coastline was tolerably well known, even if its scientific survey was to be mainly the work of the early nineteenth century, and if the east coast was now little frequented by European mariners. But what knowledge of the interior the Portuguese had once gained had been but indifferently passed on to, or remembered by, the other Europeans who had now surpassed them as builders of empires overseas. Following courses set by forgotten Portuguese embassies, French merchant-explorers had sought to make the Senegal river a highway to the empires and gold-mines of the western Sudan that were known partially through some (though not always the most accurate) of the medieval Arab writers. But their ambitions had been frustrated, in part by lack of consistent commercial backing in France, in part by the hostility both of the Sudanese peoples and of British sea power. In Guinea, Europeans had been content with their trade in Negro slaves for the Americas. Slaves were readily purchasable from African merchants and rulers at the coast. Thus Europeans lacked any incentive to penetrate inland, while at the same time established African interests existed to block any such penetration. Further south, the African kingdoms of the lower Congo and Angola, and the protectorates which Portugal had once sought to establish over them, had both been largely destroyed by the concentration of Portuguese merchants on this same trade. The grand designs which the Portuguese had once entertained of making East Africa an integral part of a vast oriental trading empire had not survived the Dutch break-through into the Indian Ocean in the early seventeenth century and the subsequent revival of Arab power and trade on the east coast. With the disintegration of the Monomotapa civilisation on the Rhodesian highlands and the decline of its gold-mining, the thin line of Portuguese settlements, along the Mozambique coast and up the Zambezi to as far as Tete, had become merely a refuge for a few Portuguese cast-offs and half-castes engaging in a little

[1] At the editor's request, this topic is here pursued in some aspects into the 1870's, so as to link up with Vol. XI, chapter XXII.

planting and slaving. Although in the sixteenth century the valour of Portuguese musketeers and of Jesuit missionaries had helped to secure the survival of the Christian monarchy in Ethiopia, it was soon isolated behind a curtain of Islam. Until this was penetrated by Napier's expedition of 1868, Samuel Johnson's *Rasselas* was perhaps a better memorial than the *History* of Ludolphus (1681) or even his own translation of Lobo's *Voyage* (1735).

For the greater part of the eighteenth century, effective European interests in Africa had been reduced to two, the strategic and the commercial. Both were narrow, involving no need to know the interior or to make European power felt beyond the coastline. The strategic interest arose because Africa was a land mass lying athwart or adjacent to sea lanes of major importance to the mercantile empires of the time. British and French statesmen were obsessed with the value to the economy and power of their nations of the sugar-producing islands of the West Indies. Throughout the eighteenth century also, their soldiers were battling for mastery of the North American mainland. If the greatest significance of Africa for European enterprise in America was always as a source of labour, it was nevertheless also important that the outward-bound sailing routes upon which both West Indian trade and armies on the American continent depended passed close by the westernmost shores of Africa. Here, in 1677, the French had taken from the Dutch (the first to see the strategic importance of the site) the tiny island of Goree in the lee of the Cape Verde peninsula. The necessities of their maritime struggle with France involved the British in the occupation of the island (and often of the nearby mainland trading posts—chief among them St Louis, at the mouth of the Senegal) during each of the wars of 1756–63, 1778–83, and 1793–1815. In retrospect it is somewhat surprising that a permanent British occupation did not develop in this area. It was in fact attempted during 1763–83, when the long established British trading foothold on the Gambia was combined with the Senegalese conquests into the 'Province of Senegambia', the first British Crown Colony in Africa. But the administration of the colony was misconceived and mishandled, and its commercial purpose was thwarted by the competition of French traders from Goree, which in 1763 had been mistakenly returned to France. During the War of American Independence, although Goree was re-captured, the Senegal settlements were lost. Even supposing that it had been diplomatically possible at the peace settlement in 1783 (when Goree was again handed back to the French), there was no incentive to continue with the Senegambia colony. Indeed its principal lesson seemed to be that a crown colony government was an expensive and ineffective way of dealing with British interests in Africa. So long as Britain retained command of the sea, a strategic vantage-point like Goree could always be taken when required. For the rest, British interests were commercial, and should best be left for the merchants to manage for themselves as, for example, was the case on the Gold Coast. Here, by the close of the eighteenth century, British traders, receiving from their government nothing more than a small annual subsidy for the upkeep of their forts, had succeeded in attracting a far greater share of the local trade than was flowing to the establishments of their Dutch and Danish competitors.

Nevertheless the wartime concern with the Senegambia was eventually to help pull the British government into closer relations with West Africa. As early as the 1790's, it was even prepared to appoint a British consul to reside in the hinterland with the purpose of decoying the trade of the western Sudan from the trans-Saharan caravan routes into the hands of British merchants on the Gambia.[1] Nothing came of this scheme, but a precedent had been set for later government support for the exploration of the West African interior with a view to its being opened up to British trade. In addition, uncertainty about the political future of Goree did serve to draw attention to the advantages of the Sierra Leone river, a little further to the south, a natural anchorage of considerable potential value to the British navy.

The sailing routes to India and further Asia, the other major field for European imperial rivalry in the eighteenth century, touched upon Africa more directly than those to the West Indies and America. Initially the main focal point was South Africa. This had been largely ignored by the Portuguese. They thought its coastline treacherous and its interior unpromising. In the west, the land, lacking in rainfall, was barren and thinly peopled. In the better watered east, the Bantu tribes possessed little to attract traders and were strong enough to deter European penetration. This isolation of South Africa ended when the Dutch realised the advantages of the trade-winds south of latitude 40° for ships sailing to and from the East Indies. The ports of the East African coast, which the Portuguese had used as stepping stones to India, were now by-passed. Instead attention was turned to the southernmost limits of Africa. A port of call here would serve the dual purpose of a victualling station for ships setting out on the long open sea voyages to east and north, and of a base from which in wartime naval vessels might protect friendly shipping and bar an enemy's access to the Indian Ocean. In 1652, therefore, the Dutch East India Company planted a settlement, the future Cape Town, on Table Bay, the least unsatisfactory of the anchorages near the Cape of Good Hope. Its less powerful English and French rivals for the time being contented themselves with the use of the flanking islands of St Helena and Mauritius respectively. During the War of American Independence,

[1] C.O. 267/10. Minutes of instructions to James Willis Esqr., His Majesty's Agent and Consul General for Senegambia, December 1795.

however, Cape Town was used to advantage by the French navy. With the resumption of hostilities in 1793 and the ensuing French occupation of the Netherlands, Britain acted at the Cape. A temporary military occupation, 1795–1803, was followed by a second occupation in 1806, and ultimately in 1814 by the cession of the Cape to Britain.

The colony that thus came into British hands was now far more extensive than was warranted on strategic grounds. To provide for the effective victualling and defence of Cape Town, the Dutch company had been led to encourage European settlement. This proved all too successful, and by the time the policy was reversed, a European farming community had developed at the Cape which produced appreciably more than the Company's ships and garrison could absorb, and which was increasingly restive under the Company's economic monopoly and authoritarian government. The settlement continued to grow, through natural increase and through miscegenation with the local Hottentots and with the Malay and Bantu slaves imported by the Company in a vain attempt to keep down production costs. A growing number of the colonists turned their backs on the restrictions and limited opportunities of life at the Cape. They began to make a new life for themselves trading and cattle farming on the wide grasslands of the interior. The direction of their expansion was east and north-east towards the better watered lands that the Bantu occupied. By the time of the British arrival, a distinctive trek-Boer society was already in evidence, a community of sturdy, individualist, pioneer families, whose seventeenth-century Calvinism inspired them to regard themselves as an elect chosen by God to civilise the wilderness and to master its heathen coloured peoples. The trek-Boers had largely cut loose from the currents of contemporary European civilisation that touched at the Cape, and they were resentful of control or interference from the authorities at Cape Town. Indeed, in 1795, some of them had already proclaimed their formal independence in republics of their own. Just as significantly they were already fighting for land and cattle with the Bantu tribes along a frontier which had emerged along the Great Fish River, some five hundred miles east of Cape Town.

Until about 1825, Britain chose to regard the problems occasioned by this unwanted inheritance of involvement in the South African interior essentially in a military light. Her prime concern was the base at Cape Town. Her policy with regard to the hinterland was therefore to bring the trek-Boers under control, and to garrison the frontier—in part with troops, in part with ex-servicemen settlers of her own stock—with the idea of preventing upsets with the Bantu which might prejudice the security of Cape Town. In Boer eyes, this positive frontier policy tended to offset the disadvantages of being brought under stricter and more effective judicial and administrative control. Yet the South African situation was inherently unstable. The growing Boer community was always avid for more land, and this could now only be found at the expense of the Bantu tribes that stretched in a solid block north and north-eastwards of the Great Fish River. Only the continual advancement of the frontier and the reduction of the tribesmen to the status of serfs could really ensure the quiescence of Anglo-Boer relations. British actions in a contrary sense would naturally tend to make the Boers break away from British control in further treks into the interior. Either way Britain would be enwebbed in a Boer-Bantu conflict which might reach almost indefinitely into the hinterland, and which would certainly affect Natal, where lay the richest land and the densest Bantu settlement.

Natal was an area of some concern to Britain because at Port Natal (the modern Durban) lay potentially one of the best harbours at the southern limits of the East African coast. Towards the end of the eighteenth century, this coast had once again begun to come within the sphere of European maritime strategy. The French, losing ground to Britain in the naval struggle for mastery of the ocean lifelines of European trade and empire, had re-opened interest in the old route to Asia through the Mediterranean and the Levant. Napoleon's expedition to Egypt was frustrated by Nelson's victory at Aboukir Bay in 1798, and French plans for a canal through the isthmus of Suez were delayed for nearly seventy years (p. 533). Nevertheless French interest in the Levant remained a source of anxiety to Britain, especially since the increasing transformation of her East India Company into a territorial government was drawing attention to the advantages of the Mediterranean and Red Sea route for the speedy transit of despatches and officials to and from India. The British and East India Company governments thus engaged the French in a cold war of diplomatic intrigue and counter-intrigue, among the Arab states on the shores of the Red Sea and the Persian Gulf as well as in the Levant proper. Stategically the East African coast could never be far removed from these intrigues. In fact there were both diplomatic and commercial reasons why it must be involved. In 1798, the East India Company entered into the first British treaty with the ruler of Muscat, in southeastern Arabia at the mouth of the Persian Gulf. In the latter part of the seventeenth century, with Portuguese power weakened by the Dutch break-through into the Indian Ocean, it had been the Omani of Muscat who had taken the lead in expelling the Portuguese from the East African coast north of Mozambique. The Omani rulers still maintained a claim to suzerainty over the Arab coastal settlements north of Cape Delgado, even if this was effective only in the island of Zanzibar. But Zanzibar was significant as the place where Indian merchants, some of them now British subjects, were becoming indispensable as merchant-bankers for the Arab trade in East Africa. Furthermore, under the shelter of British sea power, an able sultan, Seyyid Said (1806–56), perceived the advantages to himself and his people of developing Muscat's African trade and of building up a navy of his own which could bring the mainland ports under his control.

Although the French were eventually worsted by the British, both in competition for the favours of the Muscat court and in the maritime struggle in the Indian Ocean, they too retained an interest in East Africa. They had developed the Mascarene Islands with sugar plantations which, like their West Indian prototypes, were dependent on Negro slave labour. This was largely drawn in the first instance from Madagascar, but the markets here were fed by Arab slavers from the mainland via the Comoro Islands. Mauritius, which alone among the Mascarenes has passable harbours, was lost to the British in 1810, but Réunion (Ile de Bourbon) remained in French hands. Its labour needs combined with the urge to resist the growing power of Britain in the Indian Ocean to draw the French not only towards Madagascar and the Comoros, but also into relations with the rulers of East Coast ports like Kilwa and Mombasa who were naturally hostile to the increase of Omani power.

Strategic interests underlay much of Europe's relations with Africa until as late as the 1860's, by which time old patterns of maritime strategy had been upset by such varied factors as the decline of the colonial economies in the West Indies, the introduction of the compound engine for steamships, and the opening of the Suez Canal. Nevertheless the prime importance of tropical Africa to Europe at the end of the eighteenth century was commercial. Towns like Liverpool and Nantes, for instance, had become among the greatest of English or French ports mainly through their connection with 'the African trade'. In practice 'the African trade' meant trade with the West African coastlands from about the mouth of the Senegal to about the mouth of the Congo. Though interest in other products had never lapsed, notably in gold (from the Gold Coast), gum (from Senegambia), and ivory,[1] yet 'the African trade' was now virtually synonymous with the trade in Negro slaves to the Americas.

Despite the interference to Atlantic navigation caused by the sea wars of 1778–83 and 1793–1815, the slave trade had continued to expand. By the end of the century at least 75,000 African slaves were being landed alive in the Americas each year. Their market value was probably of the order of £4,000,000, and the purchase of them in Africa probably involved Europe in the export of something like

---

[1] The 'Ivory Coast', between Cape Palmas and the Gold Coast, took its name from the trade, though by 1800 elephants seem to have become increasingly scarce even in this rather thinly populated region.

£2,000,000 worth of goods a year. It is true that not all of these goods were of European origin, but the most important exception was Indian cottons, probably not worth more than about £300,000 a year. It is thus evident that West Africa was by no means negligible as a market for European manufactures—wrought metals and hardware, spirits, guns and gunpowder, beads and trinkets. In Britain's case, it took some 5 per cent of her exports and, with the growth of industrialisation— especially perhaps the development of cotton manufacturing—it was to be expected that its value as a market would increase. Furthermore, the business of buying slaves in Africa and selling them in America was extremely profitable. It is true that risks were also high, especially that of losing part or even the whole of the human cargo from disease, or from a shortage of water and victuals occasioned by an unexpectedly lengthy voyage. But these risks could to some extent be offset by profits on other purchases in Africa that were marketable in Europe, and also by profits on cargoes picked up in the Americas (though in the eighteenth century the West Indian sugar crop was no longer brought to Europe in the ships of the slavers). Even without taking into account the fact that the whole of plantation production in the American and West Indian colonies—production which in the case of Britain accounted for no less than a quarter of her imports—was dependent on a regular supply of labour from Africa, the slave trade was an important national interest for the colonial and maritime powers. Thus, for example, between 100 and 150 British ships sailed for West Africa each year, some two-thirds of these from the port of Liverpool alone. Contemporary estimates exist which assert that in the new manufacturing towns like Manchester and Birmingham, the proportion of the working population engaged in the production of goods for the African trade may have been at least a fifth and sometimes, perhaps, something nearer to a half.

Historically the value of the slave trade to Britain is more significant than its value to France or to any other European state. In the first place, by the end of the eighteenth century, British merchants had secured the lion's share of the trade: at least half the slaves reaching the New World were being taken there in British ships. The French were the nearest competitors, carrying about a quarter of the trade in the 1780's, though thereafter their share suffered considerably from the effects of British command of the sea during the war years 1793–1815. The only other European nation in anything like the same class of business was Portugal, whose merchants had a distinct southern Atlantic trade of their own between Angola and Brazil. Against this background of British predominance, Britain's decision by Act of Parliament in 1807 to cease trading in slaves was of the first importance in determining the future pattern of relations between Europe and tropical Africa.

The British were neither the first nor the only nation of European stock to reach the conclusion that the slave trade was an immoral activity. The Danish slave trade had become illegal in 1804, while slaving was outlawed in the United States in 1808 and in the Netherlands in 1814. But the Dutch and Danish shares in the trade were now insignificant (around 4000 and 2000 slaves a year respectively), while the American prohibition could hardly be effective so long as an increasing number of the states of the Union were economically committed to slavery and capable of frustrating effective enforcement of the federal law. Britain, however, possessed not only a strong slave-trading interest, but also both the will and the naval strength effectively to impose her laws on it. But the significance of Britain's action was not only—or indeed mainly—that at one stroke half of the old eighteenth-century slave trade was abolished. In actual fact the volume of the trans-Atlantic slave trade grew substantially in the years immediately after 1807. The prime reason for this was the greatly increased demand for slaves in the Americas, occasioned by the growth of the plantation economy on virgin soils in Cuba and Brazil and by the remarkable expansion of cotton cultivation in the southern United States. Merchants of other nationalities hastened to fill the gap left by the British. Some of these were Europeans,[1] but for the most part, with the New World ever more independent of the Old, it was merchants from North and South America who more than made good the decline in the European supply of slaves to their expanding economies. By about 1810, the number of slaves reaching America each year is thought already to have exceeded the peak figures of the eighteenth century. Twenty years later, slave imports were running at the rate of some 125,000 a year, and it was as late as the early 1840's that the trade reached its absolute maximum, with an annual volume estimated at some 135,000 slaves.

The real significance of the abolition of the British slave trade lay elsewhere. In the first place, as a result of her eighteenth-century predominance in the trade, Britain had a greater established stake in West Africa than any other nation. She could not, as the Danes and Dutch eventually did, simply write off her West African interest. Her merchants needed new opportunities for the shipping, manpower, capital and goodwill involved in the African trade, needed in short to find new trades to take the place of that in slaves. This was not easy. Almost the whole of the existing relationship between Europeans and Africans on the west coast was conditioned by the business of exporting slaves. Europeans knew of few other African products which might offer comparable prospects of profit, while for their part the Africans

---

[1] Particularly Spaniards, for while elsewhere in Europe the forces of intellectual and social reform were tending towards anti-slave-trade legislation, in Spain the same forces occasioned the sweeping away of the old ecclesiastical prohibition of slave-trading.

were not generally organised to produce alternatives for sale at the coast in worthwhile and regular quantities. Of the four principal alternatives that were known at the beginning of the nineteenth century, only one proved capable of development to a level at all equivalent to that of the slave trade. Ivory was already becoming scarce in West Africa, and neither the exports of gum nor those of gold were capable of expansion —the one because the European demand for it was limited, and the other because output could not increase until European technologies penetrated to the Gold Coast hinterland to reinforce traditional methods of mining. Only in the case of palm oil was a steady growth in the European demand matched by an equivalent response from African producers and exporters. This was most notable in the Niger delta, then indeed known as the 'Oil Rivers'. Slave-trading continued here, but the fortunes of a number of emergent merchant city states became increasingly dependent on their efforts each to secure a monopoly of the export of palm oil from its adjacent hinterland. British imports of palm oil, negligible before 1800, were by the 1860's running as high as £1,500,000 a year, rather more than half of this coming from the Oil Rivers.

But, with this one major exception of the oil trade, the generality of African merchants found it easier and more profitable, especially in view of the growing American demand, to continue exporting slaves. The British merchants trying to develop 'legitimate' trades thus often found it difficult to make headway. This was early demonstrated by the experience of the Sierra Leone Company. This was founded in 1791 by the British promoters of the agitation against slavery and the slave trade. In 1772 they had induced the Lord Chief Justice of England, Lord Mansfield, to give his celebrated judgment that the status of slavery had no standing in the law of England. Consequently such slaves as had been brought into England by planters returning from the West Indies became free men. Some of them found it difficult to adapt themselves to free society, while comparable problems soon arose in British North America with Negroes from the thirteen colonies lost to Britain in 1783 who had fought on the British side during the war of independence. The abolitionists therefore conceived the plan of resettling some of these former slaves in Africa. Sierra Leone was chosen for the experiment and, after some early troubles, the Sierra Leone Company was formed to administer the settlement that was established at Freetown. The company looked to profits from legitimate trade from the interior as a source from which it could defray its administrative expenditure, necessarily heavy in the early years of the colony. But it was soon apparent that legitimate trade could not flourish in a region where slave-trading was still active. From 1800 onwards, the colony was enabled to continue only through the receipt of annual subsidies from the British government. Finally, following the abolition of the British slave trade, responsibility for the colony was transferred directly to the British Colonial Office.

The second respect in which the British abolition of the slave trade was significant was that, having persuaded their own government of the justice of their cause, the British abolitionists prevailed upon it to use its influence and power to extend the prohibition of the slave trade beyond its own realm. Here the inability of British legitimate trade to compete successfully with slave-trading provided a powerful material interest in support of the moral argument. Following the cessation of hostilities in the Napoleonic wars, the British government began to urge other governments to prohibit slave-trading to their subjects. By 1835 the maritime nations of western Europe and the newly independent American states had all taken legislative action against the trade, in many cases of their own free will, but sometimes as the result of direct British pressure. But, as has already been indicated, it was one thing to enact legislation against the slave trade but quite another matter to secure its effective enforcement. Of the other major slave-trading states, only France had anything like the British incentive to enforce her laws, and most in any case lacked the naval resources to secure compliance with their laws by their shipping on the high seas. While both the French and the United States navies occasionally acted against the slave trade, only Britain consistently mounted patrols whose sole purpose was the interception of slave ships. For this purpose, Freetown became an important base, and for a time the ships of the British West Africa squadron also utilised the Spanish island of Fernando Po at the other end of the Guinea coast. The weakness of other nations' naval efforts led Britain to engage in a second round of diplomatic activity, negotiating for the right to allow her warships to arrest the slave ships of other nations, and to bring them before Courts of Mixed Commission which were established alongside her own Admiralty Courts at Freetown and elsewhere.

But even in the 1830's, it was apparent that diplomatic and naval measures alone could never completely stop the export of slaves from West Africa. So long as a legal demand for slaves existed in the Americas—as it did until 1863 in the United States and until the 1880's in Cuba and Brazil, there were lawless men prepared to run the risk of interception and capture at sea. It was impracticable for any navy to maintain a complete watch over the whole coastline from which slaves might be exported. Moreover such ancient naval rivals of Britain as France and the United States could never agree to allow the British navy the full powers which the British government sought to search and arrest their merchant ships.

Inevitably, then, the British abolitionist interest had to turn its attention to Africa itself and try to prevent slaves being offered for sale on its coasts. This involved it in two principal kinds of activity. Logically enough, one of these came to be the extension to African rulers of a system of preventive treaties comparable to those negotiated with European and American governments. But before this was embarked upon to any great extent, an attempt had been initiated to create new economic and moral climates among the African peoples, with the hope of encouraging the replacement of slave-trading as a source of wealth and power by a growing legitimate trade.

The first necessity here was clearly the exploration of the African interior, hitherto concealed behind the coastal barrier erected by the slave trade. It was desirable to discover what commodities other than slaves the hinterland might offer to Europe, to what extent African communities were organised to produce and to trade such commodities, and what (if any) means of transport existed by which they could be brought down to the coast and European goods taken inland in exchange. Between 1788 and 1855, the main lines of the interior geography of West Africa were laid bare by a succession of European explorers entering either from the coast or along the traditional trans-Saharan trade routes from North Africa. Britain took a predominant part in this exploration. It was Mungo Park and the Lander brothers who were primarily responsible for charting the 3000 mile course of the great river Niger which, whether reached from the Senegal or Gambia rivers in the west, or through its own delta (the Oil Rivers) in the southeast, offered the most promising natural access to the western Sudan. The principal pioneers who disclosed to the outside world the ancient civilisation and commerce of the Sudan itself were Denham and Clapperton, René Caillié and, above all, Heinrich Barth. Of these explorers, only Caillié was acting independently of Britain; the German, Barth, like Park on his second expedition, Denham and Clapperton, and the Landers, was in the employ of the British government.

The credit for awakening official British interest in the exploration of West Africa must undoubtedly go to the Association for Promoting the Discovery of the Interior Parts of Africa, founded in London in 1788, which sponsored the early journeys of Niger exploration that led up to Park's first journey in 1795-7. It has been argued, however, that the African Association's purpose was not so closely tied to the British anti-slave-trade movement, or to the humanitarian movement generally, as has commonly been supposed, but rather that its colouring was first scientific and then commercial.[1] It would seem that it was the British government, instructing Clapperton on his second journey (1825-7) to negotiate a treaty of friendship with a Sudanese ruler which would

[1] See, for example, A. Adu Boahen, 'The African Association, 1788–1805', *Trans. Hist. Soc. Ghana*, vol. VI (Achimota, 1961), pp. 43–64.

ban the slave trade, which first put a deliberate anti-slave-trade gloss on the exploration.[1] It would seem indeed that the abolitionist cause was first projected into Africa less by the explorers than by the missionaries of the new Protestant missionary societies which were multiplying in Europe—not least in Britain—by the end of the eighteenth century. But even here the approach to the problem of the slave trade was initially indirect. The first of the new missions to Africa was that of the Moravian Brethren. As early as 1737 this society had sent out a pioneer to convert the South African Hottentots. But within a few years he had felt the hostility of the social environment at the Cape and had returned to Europe. When, two generations later, the crusade was resumed, it was due to British initiative, and the first efforts were not unnaturally directed to Sierra Leone. But the first missions of the Church Missionary Society and of the Wesleyans in Sierra Leone (1806 and 1811) were not intended to convert Africans and to create new social orders inimical to such barbarities as the trade in human beings, but essentially to minister to the needs of the freed slave community at Freetown, for which Britain was already responsible and which was already subject to European influences. The extension of missionary activity into the truly indigenous field in West Africa was largely a consequence of the official British espousal of anti-slave-trade action. In particular it arose from the activities of the British West African naval squadron.

It was these activities that were to make Sierra Leone far more significant in Europe's relations with West Africa than either of the other two coastal colonies for freed Negroes that were established in emulation of it. The independent Afro-American Republic of Liberia, proclaimed in 1847, was always handicapped by its origins (1821) as a private venture of the American Colonisation Society. It lacked both adequate finance and the political support which only an established government could provide. Libreville, established by the French on the Gaboon in 1849, did not develop as Freetown and Sierra Leone did, mainly because the French naval effort against the slave trade was nothing like as great or as consistent as the British. But in the sixty years after 1807, as many as 70,000 Negroes liberated from captive slave ships were settled at Sierra Leone. The majority of these became assimilated to European and Christian civilisation and, beside swelling the creole population of Sierra Leone itself, became an important acculturating influence elsewhere in the West African coastlands. Some of them became considerable merchants in the coastal trade. Many more found employment with British traders or missionaries, and not only at the lower levels, for the missionary foundation of Fourah Bay College in 1827 had opened up an important channel to higher education. Sierra Leone

[1] C.O. 2/16. Bathurst to Clapperton, 30 July 1825.

was soon producing, and exporting, not only clerks, but schoolteachers and priests, and eventually lawyers and doctors also. It was also training Africans from other territories. Some of the Sierra Leone creoles established themselves in business or the professions elsewhere along the coast. A notable re-emigration of former slaves who had been taken from Lagos and its hinterland afforded a significant beginning for the growth of European influence there and gave the missions their first entry into Yorubaland. To a much lesser degree, the British naval occupation of Fernando Po during 1827–34 produced similar results further east, notably in the Cameroons.

If Sierra Leone thus became a vital nursery for the extension of an informal European and Christian influence, an influence which inevitably had a British tinge, the existence of the colony also tended to bring about an increase of formal British power in the West African coastlands. The British government was committed, for the first time since 1783, to the administration of an area of West African territory. It is true that, compared with the bold Senegambia scheme, the territorial conception of Sierra Leone was limited, even though the colony did naturally tend to expand to some small extent as more liberated slaves were landed. But the British government was now dedicated to the eradication of the slave trade, and the actual and continuing presence on the coast of officials of such a government was apt to have important consequences. It was not long before a governor of Sierra Leone, Sir Charles MacCarthy, concluded that the most effective method of stopping the export of slaves from the coast was to extend direct British control over it. A number of new annexations were made, and in 1822 the administration of the British merchants' forts on the Gold Coast and Gambia was placed under his government. This brought MacCarthy into a fatal collision with the armies of Ashanti, a growing inland power which had for some time been seeking to dominate the small states of the Gold Coast littoral. In 1828 this led the British government, aware that the cost of its West African administration to the British taxpayers was steadily growing while the volume of the Atlantic slave trade was still increasing, to reverse course and to cut its direct commitments in West Africa to the minimum.

But although the traditional attitude that the British interest in West Africa was more commercial than colonial lasted into the 1870's, and was indeed given perhaps its most positive expression in the report of a Parliamentary Select Committee of 1865,[1] it proved impossible to maintain in practice. Freetown, both as the home of the creoles and as a vital naval base, could not be abandoned, and the continuance of the anti-slave-trade patrols created countless situations in which direct

[1] 1865, V (412), *Report of Select Committee on the state of the British Settlements on the West Coast of Africa.*

British governmental intervention in West Africa could scarcely be avoided. Furthermore, the activities of the British traders—and to some extent also of the missionaries—continued to draw their government into assuming greater West African responsibilities. This was first seen on the Gold Coast. Here, following the official withdrawal in 1828, the merchants had thought it desirable to create for the forts a government of their own. The agent they chose to lead this administration, George Maclean, was a forward-looking man who conceived that the British commercial interest on the Gold Coast could best be advanced through the establishment of a firm peace with Ashanti and of some degree of British jurisdiction over the weaker states between Ashanti and the sea. By 1842–4 he had extended British power so far in advance of official policy that the government thought it desirable to return to the Gold Coast and assume direct control of the informal protectorate he had erected. That its agents were generally less successful than Maclean had been in dealing either with Ashanti or with the increasingly western-influenced communities of the coastal states, in the long run served only to enmesh the Colonial Office more firmly in Gold Coast affairs. Eventually, in 1873–4, a punitive expedition was mounted against Ashanti and the Gold Coast was annexed.

Further east too, the combined activities of Britain's anti-slave-trade squadron, her merchants and missionaries, led in the same direction. In 1849 the Foreign Office thought it necessary to begin appointing consuls for the Gulf of Guinea. These had the dual purpose both of keeping a watch on the slave trade and negotiating treaties against it with African rulers, and also of protecting the interests of legitimate traders and missionaries in their dealings with the numerous African authorities. The first of these consuls, John Beecroft, came to his duties with experience of administering the freed slave community on Fernando Po and of exploring the commercial possibilities revealed by the Landers' discovery that the Oil Rivers were the Niger Delta; he quickly developed the practice of calling on the might of British warships to support the growth of British influence. The result was the occupation (1851) and finally the annexation (1861) of Lagos, hitherto a major port for the export of slaves from a Yorubaland beset by civil war, and also the growth of an informal British jurisdiction over the Delta and its competing states.

Britain's preoccupation with the fight against the slave trade and with the promotion of legitimate trade in its place, meant that by the 1870's and the eve of the European partition, she had developed a wide interest along the West African coast, and had secured positive footholds at a number of points. The only other European state with a considerable stake in West Africa was France. But the French position was a very different one. Along the coast generally, the activities of French merchants (and, for that matter of the French navy and missionaries) were spasmodic and of relatively minor significance. French interest was concentrated in her traditional sphere of the Senegal. Here, after a number of other schemes had been tried, a French soldier-administrator, General Faideherbe, had at length found a worthwhile replacement for the outmoded gum- and slave-trading interests. Between 1854 and 1865, he had engaged in the systematic conquest of the Senegal valley and the conversion of its peoples into peasant producers of groundnuts, another oil-crop valuable to the European economies and to that of France in particular. Faideherbe's conquests had been brought to a halt, on the verge of their extension to the upper Niger and to the Sudan generally, in part by the domestic misfortunes of France, in part by the stiffening resistance of the Sudanese peoples, who during the nineteenth century were experiencing a remarkable Islamic renaissance. Nevertheless it was his territorial advance rather than the infiltrative activities of the British merchants, missionaries, naval officers and consuls along the coast, that set the pattern for the future expansion of European power in West Africa.

Neither the British explorers nor the British anti-slave-trade campaigners were content with their achievements in West Africa. They ventured into other fields, notably into the interior of east and central Africa, where the growth of the power and wealth of the Omani government of Zanzibar was producing an extensive and destructive burgeoning of the combined slave and ivory trade of the Arabs. These ventures flowed in part from the established British and British–Indian connexion with Zanzibar, but they were also a consequence of developments in South Africa. Here, by the 1830's, the increasingly liberal and humanitarian trends in British society had produced an explosive situation. The British occupation occasioned a flowering of Christian missions to the Cape's non-European peoples. From about 1825 onwards, the missionaries' promptings that the colony's legal and social system was prejudicial to coloured rights and interests began to find ready ears among those responsible for the direction of British policy. The liberalisation of the Cape's constitution and laws after 1825, and the reluctance of the British government to contemplate any further costly advance of the frontiers of white settlement, combined after 1836 to induce many frontier Boers to break out from the Cape Colony in the exodus known as the Great Trek. By the 1850's, the British government had reconciled itself to the recognition of independence for Boer republics on the interior plateau, though not on the shores of the Indian Ocean, where in 1845 Natal had been annexed. But the poverty of the small and isolated trekker communities—in itself sufficient justification for the limitation of the British frontiers—inevitably led to further involvement. The continuing Boer demand for land, and to some extent also for servile labour, placed intolerable strains on African peoples whose political cohesion was necessarily menaced by the advance of European settlement. The republics were ill-equipped to deal with the inter-racial unrest and warfare which resulted. In the 1870's and 1880's the discovery that the interior was rich in both diamonds and gold began to change the economic picture, and at the same time the anti-colonial strain in British policy began to weaken. Thus the stage was set for further conflicts between Britain and the Boers, conflicts in which the interests of the non-European majority were largely forgotten.

One effect of the expansion of the racially exclusive Boer society into the South African interior was to narrow the field available for missionary enterprise beyond the borders of the Cape Colony. There were openings for missions to the Bantu tribes in British Natal and in areas like Basutoland whose density of population was such that they had been left as black islands in the flood of white settlement. But the main northward drive of the missions from the Cape into the interior became concentrated along the narrow corridor of Bechuanaland between the Boer republics and the arid Kalahari. In 1849–51, the greatest missionary pioneer of them all, David Livingstone, debouched from this corridor into the more fertile lands of the middle Zambezi. But access to this region was not easy over the 2000 miles of a tenuous line of communication northwards from the Cape. So in 1853–6 Livingstone undertook the great lateral journey across the continent which brought him first to Luanda, in Angola, and then to Quilimane in Mozambique. This journey was to have most important consequences. Livingstone had begun to disclose to the outside world the existence of the great, climatically attractive, highlands of central and eastern Africa. Their native peoples, unaffected by the discomfitures of Boer expansion, seemed a fruitful field for missionary endeavour. Much of this country was claimed by Portugal, on the ground that it lay between her long established Angolan and Mozambique colonies; but Livingstone revealed that the only effective Portuguese influence in the interior was that of half-caste traders whose expeditions in search of slaves and ivory were bringing about a steady destruction of African life. Livingstone began to argue most forcibly that this destruction must—and could best—be stayed by the injection into the highlands of a leaven of European missionaries and traders whose example would bring about the material as well as the moral regeneration of African society. His propaganda caught the public ear at home, and in 1858–64 he was commissioned by the British government to explore and develop the route into the interior from the east coast. The Zambezi did not prove to be a useful navigable waterway, and Livingstone was thus diverted northwards into the highlands of Nyasaland. But here he witnessed an even greater destruction of African society than that caused by the Portuguese traders, for in Nyasaland he was entering the southern fringes of the trading empire operated by Arab and Swahili merchants from Zanzibar. East and central Africa's need for Christianity and legitimate commerce became even more evident.

The immediate response to Livingstone's appeal for European missionaries and traders to go to central Africa to redeem it from barbarism was small and ineffective; and when in 1873 he died during the course of his third great journey of exploration, he was a lonely and a frustrated man. But the magnetism of his personality and the romance of his discoveries had drawn a flood of other explorers into the heartlands of Africa. Between 1857 and 1877, Richard Burton, J. H. Speke, James Grant, Samuel White Baker and H. M. Stanley had between them solved all the main problems of the interior drainage system of Africa that Livingstone himself had been erratically exploring during his own last journey. Lakes Nyasa, Tanganyika, Victoria Nyanza and Albert had all been placed on the map. The whole course of the great Congo river had been explored, and the age-old mystery of the sources of the Nile had been finally solved. The ground-work had therefore been laid for later European penetration. By his journey down the Congo in 1874–7, Stanley had revealed one of the principal arteries of this penetration. He was shortly to appear as one of its first agents, for when he next came to the Congo, it was as an employee of King Leopold II engaged in laying the foundations for the Congo Free State.

But a more immediate consequence of Livingstone's travels, and of the books and speeches in which he presented both them and his ideas to a European public ever more interested in Africa, was to intensify British hostility to the East African slave trade. This trade differed in a number of respects from that which Britain was fighting, and at length beginning to overcome, in West Africa. Here was no network of trade between African states, ending in African coastal merchants presenting slaves for sale to Europeans. Arabs and Arabised Africans resident at the coast operated slaving caravans which penetrated far into the interior, by the 1860's indeed as far as the upper Congo. These men were Muslims to whom slavery was a matter of course. There was the further difference that their operations were designed to produce ivory just as much as slaves. It is true that substantial numbers of slaves were exported to Muslim markets in Arabia and elsewhere in western Asia, and were also employed on the profitable clove plantations which Seyyid Said had initiated in Zanzibar and Pemba; but the first purpose of many of the slaves taken in the interior was to carry down to the coast tusks of the ivory that was so much in demand in Europe as well as in Asia. In default of other means of transport, head-porterage was the only means of taking goods into and out of the interior. It was naturally expensive, prohibitively so if the porters had to be paid as well as fed. Thus in East Africa there was at once a strong established interest in slavery and the slave trade that was difficult for any Christian power to assail, and also a major difficulty in the way of developing alternative legitimate trades. On the other hand, in East Africa Britain had the advantage that she did not have to deal with a multiplicity of European and African authorities, but essentially only with the government of Zanzibar. It was from Zanzibar that the whole trade was financed and controlled, and Britain already had established relations of friendship with its Omani government.

As early as 1822, when Said was still at Muscat, Britain, anxious to stop the importation of slaves into her Indian territories, had used her influence at Oman to secure the Moresby treaty by which Arab slave-ships became legally restricted to the coastal waters of East Africa and Arabia. This treaty had a certain advantage to Said, for it implicitly recognised his claim to suzerainty over the East African coast north of Cape Delgado, and he loyally co-operated with the British navy to secure its enforcement. The umbrella of British approval was also of service to Said when he came to take steps to enforce this suzerainty over the Arab coastal towns. There was thus little difficulty in securing a second treaty (1845) by which, to help stop the smuggling of slaves into India, the Arab slave trade was further restricted to Said's African territories.

But these treaties had no effect on the destructive activities of the slave-traders in the interior. On the contrary, the growth of power and wealth at Zanzibar made possible the organisation of ever bigger and stronger caravans, capable of penetrating ever further into the interior towards less depleted sources of ivory and slaves. It was on this aspect of the trade that attention became focused as a result of Livingstone's explorations. But to act against it involved Britain in a frontal assault on what the friendly Muslim government and community at Zanzibar could only regard as its most vital and legitimate interests. From 1869 onwards, however, Britain had at Zanzibar a consul, Sir John Kirk, who was an old associate of Livingstone. The argument was presented to the successors of Said (who had died in 1856) that the continued independence and prosperity of their government and people was so dependent on Britain's favour and protection that they could not afford to defy her. This argument had its validity. By the 1860's, Britain and British India had secured a dominant position in Zanzibar's growing legitimate trade. Moreover, in 1862 Britain had finally removed the danger of French intervention in East Africa by securing France's subscription to a joint declaration to respect the independence of the Zanzibar sultanate. (A tacit corollary was that France was to have liberty of action in Madagascar and the Comoro Islands.) But even so, it was only the threat of a British blockade of Zanzibar that finally induced Sultan Bargash in 1873 to agree that the slave trade should be outlawed throughout his realm. The treaty effectively put a stop to the importing and exporting of slaves at Zanzibar itself, but, like its predecessors, it proved to have no effect on slave-trading in the interior. The Arab merchants there, though acknowledging the ultimate sovereignty of the sultan, were operating far beyond his effective jurisdiction. The main practical effect of the treaty was twofold. First, the maintenance of the sultan's government, even in Zanzibar itself, was henceforward largely dependent on British support. Secondly, Britain had virtually committed herself to a policy of helping the sultan develop an effective political administration on the mainland.

Thus by the mid-1870's, the situation in East Africa had been brought into line with that in West Africa. Nowhere in Africa, except in the extreme south, had Europeans made any deep impression on the continent. The vast majority of Africans were still under native governments, however much the strength and purpose of these governments had been twisted or undermined by the operations of the slave trade (or, in South Africa, by the advance of European settlement). The formal advance of European power into tropical Africa was thus small. On the other hand, in both East and West Africa, and, in a different way, in South Africa also, a dominant external *influence* had been created by the advance of British merchants, missionaries, explorers and consuls. This was not to be without its significance in formulating the course for the European partition of the 1880's and 1890's.

CHAPTER XXII

THE UNITED STATES AND THE OLD WORLD, 1794–1828

W HEN on 16 August 1823 the British Foreign Secretary, with unwonted affability, suggested to the American Minister in London that the two countries might go hand in hand in disapproving French interference with the independence of Spanish America, George Canning was swallowing his distaste for republican principles in deference to the logic of British interests as interpreted by the Liberal Tories. The gesture was motivated both by the problem set by the friends of legitimacy and by a consciousness that British industrialism needed American markets and raw materials. In Washington, President Monroe's first reaction to this proposal was to follow Jefferson and Madison in encouraging a *rapprochement* with Britain which would benefit American interests in the Atlantic; but the decisive voice was that of the secretary of state. John Quincy Adams ignored Canning's offer and drafted that independent declaration warning the European Powers off the Western Hemisphere which the world came to know as the Monroe Doctrine.

the American continents, by the free and independent condition which they have assumed and maintain [ran Monroe's Message to Congress] are henceforth not to be considered as subjects for future colonization by any European powers.

And the Message went on to explain:

The political system of the allied powers is essentially different from that of America. This difference proceeds from that which exists in their respective Governments; and to the defense of our own, which has been achieved by the loss of so much blood and treasure, and matured by the wisdom of their most enlightened citizens, and under which we have enjoyed unexampled felicity, this whole nation is devoted. We owe it, therefore, to candor and to the amicable relations existing between the United States and those powers to declare that we should consider any attempt on their part to extend their system to any portion of this hemisphere as dangerous to our peace and safety.

In these phrases Adams, the son of the minister who had refused to wear court dress at St James's, assumed the correct republican posture. Experienced in diplomacy and bred in the stiff-necked puritanism of the Adams family, John Quincy was more fiercely nationalist than his colleagues, more aware of the possibilities for American freedom of action and of the need to re-define a republican isolation from the concert of European Powers. Despite the fact that its efficacy depended on the British navy, Monroe's message was not empty rhetoric. It showed the world that the American Republic, founded on revolutionary principles and developing an unique national character, could not acquiesce in the role of an appendage to the European system. Paramount among American interests was republicanism; and in successfully asserting this, the United States showed that she had found herself as a nation.

Long after independence, the possibility of achieving a republic had remained in doubt at home as well as abroad; and yet there could be no turning back from the American Revolution. The thirteen ex-colonies must either evolve a common frame of government consonant with the principles which had justified taking up arms, or fall prey to anarchy and foreign domination. And the implications of the Revolution were profound. A state grounded upon natural rights, upon a federalism which would provide sufficient unity in continental diversity, upon the principle of limited powers defined by a written constitution; a republic which separated church from state, which denied the morality of empire, of dynastic aggrandisement, of Old World nationalism, which was isolationist, if not pacifist, by instinct; a state in which citizenship was the privilege of those who chose to embrace republican principles irrespective of native nationality and ethnic origin, and where the private, material interests of the individual were exalted over all other ends of government: such were the implications faced by the generation which came to maturity at the turn of the nineteenth century. For them the unfinished portico and dome of the Capitol rising above the swampy Potomac, with fluted pillars carved with a *motif* of Indian corn, symbolised what had come to seem a noble, if still precarious, experiment in government. There was a chance that the experiment could succeed if it could be protected in its American wilderness from the European world's slow stain.

Isolationism, however, was a state of mind rather than an objective condition, and the preoccupied Americans had to feel their way towards their new synthesis of society amid the distractions of a disordered external world. Virginians, New Englanders and Pennsylvanians became conscious of enjoying a common, and peculiarly American, national character, in addition to sharing republican institutions, as a result of their common resistance to outside pressures. In 1794 the natural frontiers of the Republic had still to be established against the claims of Britain, France and Spain. Though the Jeffersonian ideal might be a republic of self-sufficient husbandmen, the United States could not exist, let alone grow, without those commercial connections overseas which enabled her to exchange her raw materials for manufactures and to attract European capital and labour for her internal development. It was in pursuit of such interests that Americans

became accustomed to rallying beneath the Union flag in western outposts and to protecting on the high seas not only their trade but that
citizenship by naturalisation which was unique to their national
character. From 1794, when Washington retired from the presidency
counselling, not the absolute isolation he knew to be impossible, but the
avoidance of permanent alliances which would draw the Republic into
the alien system of European Powers, until Canning's approach of 1823
with its recognition of a genuine American sphere of interest, the
Americans struggled to preserve an independent identity in the turbulence of international politics.

The Republic was first and foremost an idea, not a land or a people;
and its very abstraction was enhanced by the lack of definition to its
geographic boundaries and to the make-up of its population. The open
westward-shifting frontier and the recruitment of immigrants encouraged Americans to think dynamically of movement, growth and the
future, to turn their backs on the European past and to assume a
manifest western destiny to which the persistent intrusion of European
Powers was an affront. The settlement of the lands between the
Appalachians and the Mississippi was the dominant influence shaping
the fortunes of the young Republic, setting the terms for her resumed
relations with Europe, and, by creating a new great sectional interest,
profoundly altering the balance of politics.

An early, characteristic act of the Republic was the conduct in 1790
of a census. From this and its decennial successors we know that the
population more than trebled between 1790 and 1830, from 3·9 to
12·8 million, largely the result, since there was yet little immigration, of
natural increase. The older areas of the littoral became more densely
settled and people were especially attracted to the bigger ports, notably
New York which almost quadrupled its 1790 population (33,131) in the
subsequent thirty years; but they also spread south and west through the
valleys and passes of the Appalachians, out beyond State boundaries into
the country of the Ohio and Tennessee, the advance guard of a migrant
army which neither natural hazards, Indians, European Powers nor the
United States Government could ultimately discourage or control.

Nomads like Daniel Boone were followed by individuals and families
riding and waggoning along the Cumberland and Wilderness roads,
floating down the Ohio tributaries and clinging to the wooded river
bottoms, intent on settling with rifle and hatchet to a wilderness life.
The Indian menace was checked by the tiny United States Army, from
the Battle of Fallen Timbers in 1794 to the War of 1812 which finally
secured the Old Northwest, by successive treaties, more or less dis-
honoured, for the cession of Indian lands, and in 1825 by the Federal

Government's policy of removing the remaining tribes across the Mississippi. Already in 1784 the trans-Allegheny settlements had clamoured to enter the Union as the State of Franklin; and the North-west ordinance of 1787 had established the procedure whereby the western lands, ceded by the States to the Federal Government, should be administered as Territories until, as in the case of Kentucky in 1792, Tennessee in 1796 and Ohio in 1803, they should qualify by population for admission as States.

The settler's assumption of a natural right to land he had cleared frustrated a Federal land policy which favoured systematic development by moneyed interests. The Act of 1796 which attracted the speculative investor with a minimum price of $2 an acre and a lot of 640 acres was successively modified until the Act of 1820 reduced the price to $1.25 and the purchase to 80 acres, and shortly thereafter rights of pre-emption were granted. Easier conditions lured settlers to the west in land booms, in the 1790's, between 1816 and 1819 and in the mid-twenties. The territory accessible to the Ohio and lower Mississippi became thinly populated by rude communities raising a surplus of corn and salt pork, potash and timber which could be rafted down stream to New Orleans market. In the early 1820's steamboats made the entire Mississippi–Ohio into a single economic system with inland ports like Nashville, Cincinnati and St Louis and a Gulf port at New Orleans. Pioneers were settling the wooded country of Ohio, Indiana (admitted a State in 1816) and Illinois (1818); planters, the rich alluvial cotton lands of Mississippi (1817) and Alabama (1819).

By 1828 most of the best wooded country east of the Mississippi had been taken up, together with two tongues thrust west across the river into Louisiana, a State in 1812, and Missouri, a State in 1821. Save for Stephen Austin's settlement beckoning from distant Texas, further expansion seemed to most Americans problematical. The open prairies towards the Great Lakes which would grow wheat were still shunned by pioneers used to forest craft, and further to the north-west, the Territory of Michigan was described in school atlases as 'interminable swamp'. Beyond the 'Permanent Indian Frontier' established by Congress in 1825 between the Big Bend of the Missouri and the Red river stretched a formidable barrier of Indian reservations; and beyond this lay the High Plains, written off as 'the Great American Desert', unfit for habitation. Only trappers and an occasional missionary left Independence, Missouri, for the Rockies along trails blazed by fur companies and explorers such as Lewis and Clark, Pike, Long and the English botanist Thomas Nuttall. It seemed as if the Republic had reached her natural frontiers.

These frontiers were not stabilised without conflict. In the wilderness of the Wabash, on lonely Mississippi waters and in Florida swamps the

American intruder found evidence of European activity; and his rights were only established by the diplomatic and military intervention of the United States Government which took full advantage of the Powers' preoccupations during and after the Napoleonic upheaval. Although the British evacuated the military posts of the Old Northwest in 1794 under the terms of Jay's Treaty, Canadian Governors were suspected of intriguing with Indian tribes until the bloodletting of the War of 1812 reduced the temperature of Canadian–American relations. Thereafter it was possible in 1817 for Rush and Bagot in Washington to negotiate that virtual demilitarisation of the Great Lakes which was a landmark in the history of disarmament and in the following year for Rush and Gallatin in London to settle the north-west boundary between the United States and Canada along the 49th Parallel between the Lake of the Woods and the Rockies. Spain had recognised the rights of navigation on the Mississippi and granted the right of deposit at New Orleans by the Pinckney Treaty of 1795; but the continental future of the Republic was only assured as an uncovenanted benefit from Napoleonic preoccupations when in 1803 Jefferson acquired Louisiana from Napoleon for three million dollars: a bargain lot which consisted not merely of New Orleans but of the entire territory between the Mississippi and the Rockies. The seizure by the United States of West Florida in 1813 and the acquisition of East Florida by the Adams–Onis Treaty with Spain in 1819 rounded out the territorial possessions of the United States for a generation.

If the western communities were to transcend a subsistence life they must find a surplus of commodities to trade, means of transport and markets. To send the products of the forest economy, apart from maize-distilled whisky and pelts, east through the mountains was too costly; and the trade in provisions and timber products down river was limited by distance, uncertainty and lack of demand. The West needed what the old tobacco-planting South had enjoyed: a low-cost staple with a sale in European markets. By such means this undeveloped area could obtain the profits of specialisation and the benefits of integration with the advanced economies of Europe. Fortunately the opening of the lower Mississippi valley coincided with a phenomenal growth in the demand for a commercial crop peculiarly suited to it. Eli Whitney's famous invention in 1793 of the gin which permitted the use of the ubiquitous, short-staple cotton plant made possible a re-deployment of the old plantation economy based on Negro slaves in order to take advantage of the insatiable demand of Lancashire for cotton; and by the 1820's the cost advantage of the virgin soils bordering the Gulf of Mexico and the ease of river transport to

New Orleans and Mobile made Mississippi and Alabama the centre of a primary industry which was shipping sixty million pounds of raw cotton annually to Europe.

It is hardly possible to exaggerate the importance of cotton in the development of the West and of the United States as a whole. The Cotton Kingdom was an integral element in that great textile innovation which made Lancashire the power-house of the early industrial revolution; and the United States benefited from the phenomenal increases in productivity which ensued. Cotton brought about the commercial reconciliation between Britain and her one-time colonies, the cordiality of which was masked by the record of diplomatic friction. By 1820 Britain and the United States were once again each other's best customer, and cotton was the dominant factor in the equation. By 1830 raw cotton, the greater part of which went to Britain, constituted nearly 50 per cent of the value of U.S. exports, and 76 per cent of the raw cotton imported into Britain came from the Southern States; cotton manufactures represented 48 per cent of British exports in general and 33 per cent of exports to the U.S.A. The relationship, in terms of products and markets, of primary producer and manufacturer, could hardly be more complementary. By means of cotton the United States and Britain were so closely bound together that it is appropriate to speak not of two separate economies but of two sectors, one 'colonial', the other 'metropolitan', of a single Atlantic economy.

In the United States the influence of cotton was felt beyond New Orleans, Savannah and Charleston, in eastern ports and above all in New York whose commercial advantages enabled her to dominate a trade which had much to do with her ascendancy as the American terminus of the Liverpool trade. The merchant houses of Baltimore, Philadelphia and New York were linked with those of Liverpool and London in a commercial system which was coming to have as its object, not only the exchange of British textiles, hardware and other manufactures for American cotton, flour and timber products, but the long-term development of the American interior. In the late 1820's British merchant bankers were beginning to look to North America as an object of investment, not merely in those Government securities and land titles which had continued to interest a few like Alexander Baring since the 1790's, but in the means for opening up the land to markets: planters' banks, turnpikes, canals, even a railroad; and a few of the more resourceful Anglo-American houses, such as Brown Brothers of Baltimore and Liverpool, were acquiring experience as merchant bankers which was to enable them in the next decade to abandon dry goods for commercial loans and the selling of American securities to British investors. By re-investing British earnings in the American trade, the City of London protected the United States from difficulties about her balance of payment and provided funds for the further development of the Mississippi valley. As with capital, so with labour. Empty shipping space on the westward run left room for emigrants, a commodity which brought profits to ship-owners and from the mid-1820's an inexhaustible labour supply. Goods, capital and labour moved easily across the Atlantic. By 1830 the commercial relations between Britain and the United States had become something unique between two sovereign States. No wonder George Canning favoured a diplomatic *rapprochement*.

This new equilibrium, which restored the independent Republic to a position in Atlantic commerce with most of the advantages and few of the disadvantages of colonial times, had only been reached after decades of strain culminating in war.

In 1783 the Americans had still been faced with the problem of the British colonial system, except that instead of being inside gazing out they were outside gazing in; in particular, they were now denied access not to the French but to the British West Indies. The British Government, judging correctly that the Americans needed the British connection, adopted the policy, advocated by Lord Sheffield in his *Observations on American Commerce*, of denying commercial concessions to the Republic. Because British manufactures were superior and cheap and British credits generous, Americans continued to import from the United Kingdom, to the amount in 1784 of $18·5 million, whereas they were only able to send thither $3·75 million of raw materials. The resulting deficit was made good only with difficulty by earnings elsewhere.

Fortunately, though trade with western Europe proved disappointing, profitable connexions were established with Russia, the Far East and later with South America. Ships built in New England out-sailed, Yankee masters out-navigated, and Yankee supercargos out-bargained their rivals in distant seas; and with the unpromising counters of fish, rum, timber and furs, they manipulated a complex trading system which filled stores and homes with a remarkable array of imports, exotic and utilitarian, brought affluence to a score of small New England ports and provided specie and bills of exchange to balance the British account. But the situation remained precarious until the outbreak of the French Revolutionary wars disrupted normal channels and gave a providential opportunity to a neutral trader. Britain was forced to look to North America for timber, flour and, as her industrialisation proceeded, increasing quantities of cotton and other raw materials as well as for markets for her manufactures; and a large part of the carrying trade of beleagured European countries fell into American hands. Between 1790 and 1807 American exports rose from $20 to $108 million, of which re-exports jumped from practically nothing to over half, and the

American merchant marine grew to over a million tons. These prosperous years established the United States as an important maritime nation.

However, this prosperity, the artificial by-product of war, was also put in jeopardy by war. After Trafalgar, blockade and counter-blockade subjected ships flying the American flag to ever more stringent regulation; and since the British commanded the seas, it was the British system with which the Americans came most into conflict. The seizure of American ships and cargoes and the impressment at sea of British-born American citizens for the Royal Navy so affronted American opinion (though tolerated by merchants who, despite the risks involved, made money from the trade), that Jefferson's administration attempted retaliatory measures. The non-intercourse policy pursued after 1807 ruined trade and exposed American shipping to a devastating spoliation from both British and French, but was sufficiently successful in starving British industry of markets and raw materials to force a reconsideration of the Orders in Council on the eve of war in 1812.

Despite the inconclusiveness of the Treaty of Ghent (24 December 1814) which terminated the War of 1812, this lesson of the new importance of the American connection for the British economy was not altogether forgotten by either the British or the American Government. On the return of peace the United States, under John Quincy Adams, continued to pursue, now from a position of greater strength, a policy appropriate to a primary producing and trading nation, of breaking down the barriers to her overseas trade on the basis of reciprocity. As far as direct trade with the United Kingdom was concerned, discriminatory rates for goods and ships were abolished in 1815; but the full rigours of the Navigation Code remained in force against American entry to Canada and the British West Indies, and it was only after the United States retaliated by prohibiting goods from entering American ports in United Kingdom ships in 1820 that Britain began to re-consider her policy. In 1822 pressure from West Indian interests and from British manufacturers worried about their newly important American markets led Lord Liverpool and the Liberal Tories to contemplate that liberalisation of commercial policy which lay behind Canning's approach towards the United States in 1823. The negotiations for free American entry to the British West Indies were protracted; but their success in 1830 marks a triumph for free trade interests in both countries, in Britain of manufacturers, in the United States of Southern planters and the merchants of New York, Philadelphia and New England, all conscious of the potential of the Atlantic economy.

It is ironic, however, that at the moment when American economic power at last forced Britain to recognise the virtues of Atlantic free trade, other voices in the United States were advocating a conflicting policy. Within six months of his famous Message to Congress, Monroe signed a tariff bill which substantially increased the duties on imported textiles; and this was the precursor of an even more rigorously protective tariff, passed in 1828, two years before the freeing of the West Indies.

Lancashire was the key to the development of the Gulf States; for the upper Mississippi valley, however, there was no easy solution to the problem of markets. There was some sale of provisions down river to feed the plantations; but commercial farming on any scale awaited practicable transport for wheat and flour, salt pork and timber products which would enable Kentucky and Ohio to take advantage of the urban markets of the eastern seaboard. Western politicians clamoured for such 'internal improvements'. For their part, the merchants of the rival ports of Boston, New York, Philadelphia and Baltimore competed with transport schemes for the prize of annexing the West to their hinterlands. The National Road, built by the Federal Government through the Alleghenies to Wheeling on the Ohio, could not handle bulk cargoes. In the age of Brindley and Bridgewater the solution appeared to be canals to cut the watershed between the Ohio or Great Lakes and the Atlantic-flowing rivers. From the 1780's when Washington and his friends promoted a canal to link the Potomac with the Kanahwa many projects were attempted; but success came eventually to the State of New York which between 1817 and 1825 dug the Erie Canal across comparatively level country between Lake Erie and the Hudson River. This great waterway, which cut the cost of transporting a bushel of wheat between Buffalo and Albany from $108 to $7, not only opened the wheat-growing lands of western New York to immediate settlement but brought the whole Great Lakes basin and with it the fertile northern parts of Ohio, Indiana and Illinois within the economy of the Northeast. Cheap western flour on Boston market put the Vermont farmer out of business and sent him west by canal barge and ship along with European immigrants to settle in the Northwest, whose commercial future was now assured.

The Northwest's object, however, unlike that of the cotton States, was a domestic, not an overseas market. As Henry Clay, her chief spokesman, was quick to point out, the inflated demand for American flour which obtained in Europe during the decades of war was not likely to be maintained after the return of peace, a prediction confirmed by the introduction of the British Corn Law of 1815 which virtually excluded foreign grains until home-grown corn reached famine prices. Fortunately for the Northwest, however, the rapidly growing urban population of the ports and a few inland towns provided a ready and less speculative alternative. It also offered an attractive political

599

programme. The Northeast must be encouraged to grow as an industrial economy to substitute for that of Britain, providing a market for western produce and a domestic source of manufactures. Henry Clay's 'American System', with its quadruple points, cheap land, 'internal improvements' in transport, a national bank to provide credit, and a protective tariff for manufactures, was a programme designed to develop systematically a self-contained, national economy.

'The American System' depended on the feasibility of rapid industrialisation in New England. In advocating this, Clay was only building upon the foundations of economic policy conceived by his brilliant predecessor Alexander Hamilton, whose ambition it had been to make the Republic a strong mercantile country on the model of Great Britain.

The Founding Fathers had already ensured at Philadelphia that the powers of the States should be so restricted and those of the central government so strengthened as to establish one single, continental economy without internal tariff barriers, with courts enforcing contracts under a common commercial law and with a common fiscal and monetary system. As secretary of the treasury, Hamilton gave definition and force to these conditions in a bundle of radical measures. By imposing a revenue tariff, by funding Federal and State securities at par and by establishing a national bank which he justified by a novel, broad construction of the power, in the Constitution, to control commerce, he married the commercial interest to the constitution, expanded credit and invited that return of European investment into American ventures which was essential to capital development; and in forcing through Jay's Treaty he did what he could to re-establish commercial relations with Britain.

All this was in the best interests of a primary producing and mercantile country. Yet, though a reader of Adam Smith, Hamilton remained mercantilist enough to believe that to be powerful the Republic must also follow Britain in establishing a great manufacturing interest. In his *Report of Manufactures*, he had argued, against the agrarians, the virtues of industry with its increased productivity derived from the division of labour, from machinery, capital and the mobilisation of women and children, and he proposed a protective tariff behind which the new manufactures could be established. He was too sanguine; and the coalition of agrarian and overseas trading interests which defeated his tariff proposals was more realistic in its assessment of the advantages of exchanging American primary products for British low-cost manufactures. The failure of the Society for Useful Manufactures, which attempted a variety of manufactures at the falls of the Passaic river in New Jersey, demonstrated that Americans must import technology and technicians, accumulate capital on an ambitious scale, and raise tariffs against the cheap manufactures of Britain, before they could domesticate the new industries.

However, Hamilton was only a little before his time. Within a generation of his death in 1803 all three conditions had been partially achieved. Already in 1790 at Providence, Rhode Island, Samuel Slater had managed to build from memory the spinning frames he had operated for Jedediah Strutt in Derbyshire. Following him across the Atlantic travelled a clandestine but vitally important succession of weavers and spinners from the Pennines to perform, in the water-driven mills of Rhode Island, the rudimentary processes of textile manufacture. From the start American inventiveness improved on British example, as in the case of the functional Mississippi steamboat with its high-pressure engine. There were also signs of a distinctly American approach to manufacture. The shortage of skills and high cost of 'help' in a country of plentiful farm land encouraged the capital-intensive use of machinery which could be minded by unskilled hands. Oliver Evans's automatic flour mill of 1785 had halved the cost of labour; by 1800 that ingenious Connecticut Yankee Eli Whitney had perfected the technique of making muskets by assembling interchangeable parts which demanded machine tools and pointed the way to mass production; and during the war boom of 1813 Francis Lowell, cadet of the Boston merchant family, designed the first large-scale, rationalised factory in which the pinafored farm girls whom he lodged in model boarding houses performed all the processes of manufacturing coarse, standardised cottons for farm wear. Capital was painfully accumulated out of profits; but by 1830 Lowell's Boston Associates, an incorporated public company controlling not only textile factories but marketing outlets, real estate, water power and insurance companies, was a more advanced and powerful unit than any in Lancashire. Though exceptional it demonstrated that the cotton industry had become domesticated on the western shores of the Atlantic nearer its source of raw materials and its American market. 'The lords of the lash and the lords of the loom' were already in working partnership.

None of this would have come about without the almost inadvertent protection of the domestic market which resulted from the disruption of trade during the Napoleonic blockades. Jefferson's non-intercourse policy, followed by the War of 1812, ruined overseas commerce but shut out British manufactures. The resulting shortage of consumers' goods caused a boom not only in mill, cottage and foundry enterprise but in the new textile industry. Much of this mushroom growth failed to survive the flooding-in of cheap British wares after the Treaty of Ghent; but enough firms persisted in the coarser lines of manufacture in textiles, ironware and other trades to form the nucleus of a lobby demanding protection by Congress. The result was a series of tariffs in 1816, 1818, 1824 and 1829 which progressively raised *ad valorem* rates from 25 per cent to as much in some cases as 45 per cent. The 'Tariff of Abominations' of 1828 was a freak tariff but demonstrates the rise of a powerful manufacturing interest. Especially significant was the apostacy of Daniel Webster, senator for Massachusetts, once the eloquent spokesman for New England shipping interests, who, sensing a shift in the predominant interest of his State, embraced protection and ardently supported the Tariff of 1828. By 1828 Henry Clay's 'American System' was a practical programme of economic nationalism to counteract agrarian free trade in the counsels of the Republic.

The Mississippi valley radically altered the balance, and exaggerated the sectional character, of national politics. The establishment of a constitution with a strong central government had not fundamentally modified the geographic bias of politics. In the Republic's first years, before the West had to be reckoned with, the lines of political allegiance were roughly drawn between north-east and south-west, between the maritime and commercial interests and those of the frontier and planting, between Atlantic and continental, mercantile and agrarian, with cross-lines which drew northern up-country farmers and the popular element in the ports towards the south and great planters towards the merchant princes of the north. The Federalist Party under Hamilton and Adams and the Democratic-Republican Party under Jefferson and Madison provided an effective counterpoint in which all the principal voices were heard. In domestic affairs, the Federalists preached strong, central control in the interests of systematic commercial development, the Republicans State autonomy in the interests of rural self-sufficiency.

Foreign affairs, which after 1795 came to dominate national politics, sharpened the issues between the parties and underlined deep temperamental contrasts between planting and mercantile communities. Both parties remained deeply convinced of the need to isolate the Republic from European conflicts; but self-sufficient farmers and primary producers, who could sell tobacco and later cotton at the dock-side to foreign ships, could be more complacent about the disruption of commerce, more absolute in their isolationism, than overseas merchants dependent for a livelihood on the carrying trade; and the gentry of Virginia, educated in the liberal culture of the Enlightenment, were more sympathetically drawn towards the principles of the French Revolution than the more Calvinistic and Tory merchants, lawyers and clergy of the Northeast for whom, after the Terror, England was the defender of religion and morality, liberty and property against the tyranny of the mob. This taking of sides produced a bitterness which led the Federalists in 1798 to pass the Alien and Sedition Acts against the activities of allegedly seditious refugees, several of whom were Republican publicists; and when President Jefferson tried to protect American commerce from Algerian pirates with under-armed gunboats and in 1806 fell back on economic sanctions against Britain, the Federalists thought these a frivolous sacrifice of their livelihood, and were in no mood to rally patriotically in defence of the consequences. The Northeast, not the South or the West, suffered from British impressment of American seamen, but when war came in 1812 New England opposed it bitterly; and in 1815 the New England Federalists, meeting in convention at Hartford, upheld the right of States against the Federal conduct of the war by resolutions which exposed them to the charge of sedition.

The Federalist record in the War of 1812 gave the *coup de grâce* to a party which had steadily lost its hold over national politics. Under Hamilton's leadership, the Federalists had conducted themselves as a party after the English fashion, with an articulate legislative programme based on consistent principles and appealing to a coherent interest. Although the Republic was fortunate in its formative years to have its political habits given so forceful a direction, this style of politics proved inappropriate to a federal system designed to give expression to a multitude of disparate claims. Federalist acts provoked opposition throughout the continent, which Jefferson, less consistent, prismatic, luminous and sometimes devious, was temperamentally suited to galvanise into political action. The anti-Federalist coalition of Virginia planters, States'-rights men, up-country farmers, city mechanics and Clinton and Burr's benevolent Society of St Tammany in New York, which Jefferson pieced together from the time of his famous botanical excursion up the Hudson in 1791, proved, as the Democratic-Republican Party, not only able to wrest power from the Federalists in the election of 1800 but to be the first essentially American and national party commanding continent-wide support. After 1800 the Federalists were too consistently mercantile in their appeal to attract the continental support needed to capture an administration; and since the rift between Adams and Hamilton and the latter's death in a political duel with Burr in 1803, the party had been little more than a New England rump. With the return of peace ex-Federalists like John Quincy Adams looked for national expression to the Republican Party which, in absorbing them, took the name of National Republican and, under Monroe's presidency, became the only effective national party. The fact that for three administrations thereafter the Federal Government was in the hands of a single party has given the period down to 1828 the misleading name of the Era of Good Feelings. In effect the National Republican Party was little more than a holding operation until the time when the coalition of interests composing it should break apart to form a new party alignment. This alignment was to be the result of the breakaway of the new West from the old South.

Henry Clay, John C. Calhoun and Andrew Jackson had all been born to frontier families, two of them of Scots-Irish stock, living on the slope of the Southern Appalachians. All three rose to prominence as nationalists during the War of 1812, Jackson as the glorious conqueror of the British at New Orleans, Clay and Calhoun as 'War Hawks' in Congress and Clay as one of the American peace commissioners at Ghent; yet so strongly did the flood of settlement swirl through the Appalachian valleys that it carried them along to fortune and leadership in widely differing spheres. Jackson, senator from Tennessee, was the darling of the pioneer West; Clay, senator from Kentucky, the spokesman of the commercial Northwest; Calhoun, moving south-east to tidewater, senator for South Carolina and statesman of the Cotton South. Their careers epitomise the break-up of the old Southwest into three regions with distinct voices in national affairs.

The boom after the War of 1812 established cotton planting as the dominant interest in Southern politics. Whereas the older, Jeffersonian generation, pessimistic about the future of tobacco planting, had manumitted slaves in their wills and had looked to an economic future not very different from that of the mid-Atlantic States (even Calhoun voted for the Tariff of 1816), a younger generation was wholeheartedly committed to planting and slave-holding and the idiosyncratic way of life that this entailed. Leadership passed from the Virginia dynasty with their liberal and national outlook to the cotton oligarchy of Charleston, South Carolina, with a narrow, more legalistic view of its special interest. This meant protecting slavery and promoting cotton in Federal policy. By 1820 the Cotton South was in entrenched opposition to the tariff, a national bank, national roads and canals and to a cheap land policy, all of which it was felt would benefit North and West at her expense. Above all, the South was newly conscious of the need to reinforce the constitutional protection of her peculiar institution. With population in the free States outstripping that of the South, it was ever more imperative to preserve the equality of slave against free States in the Senate. A Northern proposal in 1820 to admit Missouri as a State with slavery prohibited brought about a major crisis in Congress, only resolved by a compromise whereby Maine was admitted as a free and Missouri as a slave State and slavery was excluded from the Louisiana Territory north of the line 36° 30'. This compromise held the issue uneasily in check for twenty-five years; but served notice on the nation that the South demanded special accommodation for its peculiar interest. As the aged Jefferson remarked, it was a 'firebell in the night'.

The defection of the seaboard South emphasised the arrival of the Mississippi valley as a separate interest in the nation. The westward-looking back-country communities had a few, simple claims to make in Washington: Federal protection from, and removal of, Indian tribes, the cheapest possible terms for title to the lands of the public domain, and Federal aid for transport improvements; otherwise they wished to be left alone to grow up with the country, without restraints from the eastern seaboard such as that control over credit inflation which the United States Bank was beginning to exert from Philadelphia. Yet in the booming 'twenties this old, frontier West, which sent Jackson to the Senate, was rapidly growing up. The colonisation of cotton and sugar planting in the lower Valley identified the Gulf States with the Old South as part of the planting interest; and north of the Ohio the possibilities of commercial farming were turning the Northwest towards Henry Clay and to those proposals for union with the Northeast which harmonised so well with those of the ex-Federalists of New England who would soon be called Whigs. Neither of these tendencies had yet achieved sufficient definition to detract from the power of Jackson's image as frontier hero, and he acquired a bare plurality of electoral votes over John Quincy Adams, Clay or Crawford (Calhoun was elected vice-president) in the presidential election of 1824; but he was not elected president on this occasion because Clay persuaded the Kentucky representatives in the House to vote for Adams, who became the last president of the National Republican dynasty. Before Jackson was to succeed to this office the West would come to be felt, not merely as a new section, but as an influence pervading the political system as a whole.

Hitherto, despite the magic of the Declaration of Independence, republicanism had been by no means synonymous with democracy. The Federalists who had put through the new constitution had been acting to restore the balance of interests in favour of property and oligarchy in opposition to levelling tendencies. Though few were so reactionary as the jurist James Kent and the Essex Junto, who were Tories as high as it was possible for republicans to be, most wished to keep political power in the safe hands of birth and breeding. Even Jefferson, though he differed from Hamilton in preferring land to funds as the basis for a moral Republic, equally believed that political rights must depend on property; and designed accordingly his University of Virginia, with its domed library and pilastered rooms flanked by slave quarters, for young gentlemen who might be talented rather than well-born but would be recruits for an aristocratic elite. Most States had substantial property-qualifications for office-holding, as high as £10,000 for the governorship of South Carolina, and in the very great majority of them property remained the basis of the vote. With few exceptions, notably the populistic City of New York controlled by Tammany Hall, politics were monopolised by propertied connections in an eighteenth-century style. Affairs were manipulated in caucus by gentlemen in tie wigs who knew each other's minds. It appeared an age of good feelings partly because its manners were well bred.

The Mississippi valley changed this. The Americans who moved west temperamentally rejected the constraints of an inherited life and looked to a better, freer existence over a western horizon. The often harsh conditions of the back-country gave a new, crisis quality to social relations. Squire and parson stayed east of the mountains; family connexions and letters of credit counted for less than more immediate human qualities in the chances of survival. Although the migrants carried in their baggage the Bible, Blackstone, Shakespeare and Noah Webster, and had the habits of vestry or town meeting, they were forced to improvise and adapt. Society meant the neighbourhood and, where there were few extremes of wealth yet most owned land, a sawmill or a tavern, property ceased to be a test of responsibility. In the back-country equality seemed a self-evident absolute and it was natural that new States should enter the Union with virtually manhood suffrage.

This egalitarian temper directly infected the more newly-settled regions of seaboard States such as New York which had its own West in the booming Finger Lakes district opened up by the Erie Canal, and indirectly encouraged artisans, shopkeepers and small men in general to demand the vote. The seaboard communities, and particularly the ports of Philadelphia, New York and Boston which were rapidly growing in population, began to show signs of restiveness under the policies of the oligarchs who controlled city and State affairs. For if State interests opposed Federal intervention in economic matters, the same prejudice did not extend to internal affairs which were still conducted on robustly mercantilist principles. The demand for rapid economic development, which in practice meant transport improvements, in a country with exiguous capital resources, could only be met by direct State action. From Virginia to Massachusetts turnpikes, bridges, canals and other works were built either by direct government undertakings or by chartered monopolies; and the influence of mercantile syndicates with State legislatures in acquiring such privileges came to be suspect, particularly in times of trade depression when artisans were unemployed and their efforts to combine frustrated under the common law of conspiracy by courts prejudiced in favour of property. To break the supposed hold of privilege over economic life, mechanics and small traders and 'manufacturers' outside the charmed circle of mercantile family groups on whom they depended for credit, turned to the novel weapon of the franchise. In response to popular pressure eastern States liberalised their constitutions, removing property qualifications, as in

Massachusetts in 1820 and New York in 1821, abolishing religious tests and relating constituencies more numerically to population. The Politicians had to reckon with a new, swollen electorate, democratic in temper, with a grudge against caucus politics and sanguine about the prospects of removing grievances by means of the vote. It was to this ill-instructed, populistic electorate that Jackson, a national hero, made an irresistible appeal; and his election to the presidency in 1828 by an overwhelming popular vote represented the victory, not merely of the west but of a new, democratic America which chafed at the tight controls of the old Republican regime. It was a political revolution.

The shifting interests of politics were held in balance within a constitution which commanded from its inception a remarkable loyalty but which had uncertain implications concerning the boundary of powers between the Federal Government and the States. The assertion of a strong, central authority was countered by that concern for the rights of States which had led Virginia to insist on the attachment of the Bill of Rights to the Constitution. Hamilton's broad construction of the commerce power to justify the establishment of a national bank was vigorously challenged, then and later, by those who were jealous for State authority. This conflict concerned not merely a definition of powers; but the underlying theory of sovereignty. Was the Republic an indissoluble Union created by the people of the United States as a whole, or a compact between States? This ambiguity was brought into the open whenever a State or group of States felt its fundamental interests to be threatened by Federal policy. In 1798 the Alien and Sedition Acts, which were aimed at the Republicans, were denounced in Jeffersonian States as unconstitutional. The Kentucky and Virginia Resolves protesting against them invoked the compact theory and asserted the right to States to judge infractions of the Constitution; the second Kentucky resolution claimed 'that a nullification of those sovereignties, of all unauthorised acts done under the colour of that instrument, is the rightful remedy'. Similarly in different circumstances, the Federalists at the Hartford Convention, believing the fundamental interests of New England to be threatened by the conduct of the war, asserted that 'in cases of deliberate, dangerous and palpable infractions of the Constitution affecting the sovereignty of a State and liberties of the people, it is not only the right but the duty of such a State to interpose its authority for their protection. . . .' In each case the crisis passed; but the doctrine of nullification, based on the compact theory, was to persist to justify extraordinary measures to defend the greatest of all interests, cotton, and by implication, slavery, in the crisis of 1832. Nullification was an extreme and doubtful theory; but throughout the period advocates of States' rights strongly resisted the efforts of the Federal Government to extend its authority.

This conflict centred on the claims of the Federal Supreme Court to an overriding jurisdiction extending to the power to decide whether acts of private citizens, States or the Federal Government itself were or were not in accordance with the Constitution and thereby to expound the nature of the Constitution itself. In its first decade the United States Supreme Court had performed a subordinate and largely ineffective role; but a re-organisation during their last months of office in 1801 permitted the outgoing Federalists to reinforce the power and Federalist character of the court, notably by the appointment of the Virginia Federalist and secretary of state, John Marshall, as chief justice. This highly political manoeuvring was challenged by the incoming Republicans; but though Jefferson succeeded in having Justice Chase impeached he was unable to make headway against the court itself and especially against its remarkable chief justice whose appointment left a doughty champion of central power in Washington at the moment of Federalist eclipse. Under Marshall's leadership the court assumed the central and dominant position it was ever after to hold in the constitutional framework. Though no learned jurist, Marshall during thirty years on the bench developed the doctrine of judicial review in a score of leading cases to extend the supremacy of the national government against the States and to delineate the Constitution as an indissoluble Union which derived its sovereignty from the people as a whole.

From the start the Marshallian court made categorically clear the underlying nature of the Constitution. 'The Constitution of the United States', in an opinion by Justice Story, 'was ordained and established, not by the States in their sovereign capacities, but emphatically, as the preamble of the Constitution declares, by "the people of the United States" '; and Marshall himself

That the United States form, for many and for most important purposes, a single nation, has not yet been denied. In war we are one people. In making peace we are one people. In all commercial regulations we are one and the same people. In many other respects the American people are one; and the government which is alone capable of controlling and managing their interests in all these respects is the government of the Union.

And building on these premises Marshall reinforced the authority of the Federal Government, and of the Supreme Court. He established the right of the court to judicial review in Marbury v. Madison (1803) by declaring an Act of Congress unconstitutional; and in Cohens v. Virginia (1821) when he insisted that the decisions of State courts were subject to review by the Supreme Court. In McCulloch v. Maryland (1819) he built on Hamilton's doctrine of implied powers to uphold the constitutionality of the United States Bank. In Gibbons *v.* Ogden (1824), by denying the validity of a State-chartered steamboat monopoly on the Hudson between New York and New Jersey, he revolutionised the power of Congress to regulate interstate commerce. In Fletcher *v.* Peck (1810) he upheld the right of contract even when one of the parties was a State Legislature, and in Dartmouth College *v.* Woodward (1819) he held that the College's charter was a contract which could not subsequently be impaired by the legislature, a decision fraught with significance for future business corporations. Marshall's decisions, throughout his career, were unpopular and met with protest from lawyers and politicians alike, especially from the Jeffersonian Republicans and advocates of States' rights; but in general, the judicial framework which he established was never successfully challenged.

In taking their stand on the abstract rights of Englishmen, the American Revolutionaries had been forced to resist the instinctive, quasi-tribal loyalties binding them to the British community; indeed the Revolution was in one sense an attempt to break away from European nationalism, which was identified with tyranny. The institutions of the Republic evoked a fierce pride and a belief that America represented a virtuous future, Europe a corrupt past. Engravings of State capitols, the United States Bank, the Philadelphia waterworks, the model State penitentiary at Auburn and the Erie Canal proudly represented republican equivalents to Windsor Castle, Westminster Abbey and the Tower of London; and from Philadelphia to Rochester on the New York fringe of civilisation, banks, exchanges and villas were built in that Greek Revival style which Jefferson, the architect, had introduced in preference to the English colonial and which, like the town-names Rome, Syracuse, Ithaca and Athens identified Americans with the cause of Greek independence and gave a classical *cachet* to republican principles in the New World wilderness.

However, a government of laws and not of men was an abstract object of patriotic devotion, capable of kindling emotion in the breast of a philosopher like Joseph Priestley in his Susquehanna retreat, but hardly the intimate, earthy affections of ordinary men. And so Americans gave their warmest allegiance, not to the distant and aloof Federal Government, but to State and region. Even for Jefferson 'my country' meant Virginia; and when New England congressmen, after weeks of arduous travel, reached Washington they eyed their stylish, drawling colleagues from the plantations with suspicion as foreigners.

If culture was regional it remained provincial, even colonial. New Englanders hated Britain for her politics but called England 'home' and conducted business in pounds, shillings and pence. Manners were republican; but fashions and furnishings, when they were not the spoils of a Chinese trading voyage, were Federalist, that is to say a domestic version of Empire or Regency. Although the great religious 'Awakenings' of 1800 and 1826, which swept like prairie fire through the back-country, gave a camp-meeting intensity to evangelism, the Churches followed the lead of Clapham and the English Cambridge in establishing the full apparatus of Bible, tract, temperance and peace societies on the British model of spiritual imperialism. Americans took pride in their common schooling and in their remarkable literacy of speech and writing expressed in abundant newsprint and the lexicographic standards of Noah Webster; but they read Scott, Byron, Wordsworth and Jane Austen in the pirated editions which, it seemed, were a republican privilege; and Joel Barlow's attempt at a republican epic was written in pale, derivative and outmoded heroic couplets.

Yet within twenty years of Barlow's *Columbiad*, Fenimore Cooper and Washington Irving were writing in a spirit recognisably American. This new American consciousness owed much to emanations from the land itself. Irving's evocation of the ghosts of Dutchmen on the Hudson, the upper reaches of which were depicted in a golden light by the Hudson river school of painters, and above all the forest life and American characterisation of Cooper successfully transmuted the temper of the romantic movement into American experience. With a violent climate, continental distances and hidden dangers from man and beast, nature could never be the intimate, familiar experience of the Lakeland poets; but as Americans turned inland they invested with grandeur and sublimity the mountainous wilderness of the Appalachians, and the rivers, forests and prairies beyond, and as they identified themselves with it those who went west became more self-consciously American.

The West acted in other ways to foster a national consciousness. Experience in more primitive communities simplified the habits and rounded the edges of Pennsylvanians and Virginians who came to think of themselves as Americans first and State citizens only second. Territories looked to Washington for government and when they became States the Stars and Stripes continued to stir emotions which the new, contrived State flag could not rouse. And the brash, exuberant, undisciplined temperament of the frontier lent itself to an aggressive nationalism whenever westerners found foreigners blocking their path. In particular, as settlers moved north-west towards the Great Lakes, keeping to forests and shunning the unknown open prairies, they came increasingly to resent the power of Britain in Upper Canada. Canada, which stood in the way of an American destiny, must be annexed, if necessary by force of arms.

Hatred of Britain was the earliest and the most primitive force shaping American nationalism. The inspiring memory of comradeship in arms during the long, discouraging Revolutionary War gave Americans their most highly-charged tradition, kept alive after 1783 by the existence of Britain in Canada and an uneasy conviction that there was unfinished business with the old enemy. Jay's Treaty, with its humiliating price for the evacuation of western posts, was an arrogant affront. The long years of the British continental blockade kept nerves frayed while United States merchantmen were forced into British ports and His Majesty's frigates cruised in wait within sight of Long Island; and the impressment of British-born citizens on the high seas by Royal Navy captains, in their contempt for certificates of naturalisation, defied the whole unique concept of American nationality and stirred the old revolutionary patriotism to a new intensity. The violent feeling which pushed the Republic into war with Britain in 1812 at the moment when the British were relaxing their pressure on American commerce was the expression of a new and strident nationalism which transcended the immediate issues involved. New England, which had suffered most, responded least. The clamour for war was not maritime but continental, and it was voiced in Congress by War Hawks like Calhoun, representing the South, and more especially by Henry Clay, the spokesman of a Northwest intent on annexing Canada.

The War of 1812 settled none of the specific issues which caused it, and it is doubtful who won it. But psychologically it was a triumphant experience for the American people. The humiliations, the landings of Royal Marines, the burning of the President's mansion, were expunged in American eyes by successful actions on the Great Lakes and above all by the resounding defeat of Pakenham's Peninsular veterans by Jackson's force at New Orleans in 1815. It is misleading to think of the War as the final stage in the struggle for independence; but this last bloodletting with the old enemy, fought however desultorily on a continental front stretching from the Gulf to the Great Lakes, made Americans conscious that they were not only a republic but a nation. Francis Scott Key, as he watched the Union flag at Fort McHenry survive the battering of a British bombardment, caught the new mood in verses which, set to music by an English composer, provided a republican nation with a national anthem.

CHAPTER XXIII

THE EMANCIPATION OF LATIN AMERICA

LATE in November 1807 a French army under General Junot crossed the frontiers of Portugal. Early in the morning of the 29th the prince regent, later King John VI, his demented mother, Queen Maria I, his termagant wife, Carlota Joaquina, the daughter of Charles IV of Spain, the rest of the royal family, and an immense crowd of courtiers, set sail from the Tagus to seek refuge in Brazil. The fleet, convoyed by British warships and carrying a great quantity of treasure, was dispersed by storm. Some of the vessels made Rio de Janeiro on 15 January. The prince regent himself, however, first touched Brazilian soil at Bahia six days later, and there, on the 28th, he issued the famous *Carta Régia* declaring the ports of Brazil open to the trade of all friendly nations. Once more embarking, he reached Rio de Janeiro on 7 March, to land, amid scenes of great enthusiasm, on the following day.

The effects of this royal *hegira*, of the arrival of the court, and of the opening of the ports, were immediate and profound. An impulse of fresh and vigorous life was transfused throughout the colony. 'New people, new capital, and ideas entered.'[1] A bank was founded, a printing press introduced, a royal library opened, a gazette established. Foreigners were invited to enter the country, industry was encouraged. European diplomats, English merchants, German scientists, even a colony of Chinese tea-planters arrived at Rio de Janeiro, now the British South American naval base as well as the metropolitan seat of government. And while between native-born Brazilian and Portuguese immigrant a bitter rivalry, the fruit of an old antipathy, soon became evident, Brazilians in their own eyes and in those of the world acquired a new dignity, officially recognised when, in December 1815, the colony was elevated to the status of a kingdom, co-equal with the Kingdom of Portugal.

The flight of the house of Braganza from Lisbon to Rio de Janeiro began the process which culminated, fourteen years later, in the almost bloodless secession of Brazil from Portugal. And as the Napoleonic invasion of Portugal thus led finally to the peaceful dissolution of the Portuguese Empire in America, so the Napoleonic invasion of Spain precipitated, except in the two islands of Cuba and Puerto Rico, the violent dissolution of the Spanish Empire in America.

Portugal had been caught between the sea-power of England and the

---

[1] A. K. Manchester, *British Preëminence in Brazil. Its Rise and Decline* (Chapel Hill, 1933), p. 72.

land-power of France; and Spain had abetted France. By the Treaty of Fontainebleau (27 October 1807), indeed, Charles IV and Napoleon had agreed to divide between them both Portugal and the Portuguese dominions. But, Portugal over-run, it was Spain's turn next to pass beneath the harrow. And whereas the Portuguese crown—and the Portuguese fleet—had escaped the clutches of Napoleon, the Spanish crown fell into captivity. On 19 March Charles IV abdicated in favour of his son, Ferdinand VII. Four days later a French army under Murat entered Madrid. In May both Charles and Ferdinand, lured by Napoleon to Bayonne, were forced to renounce their rights. And on 6 June, by Napoleonic decree, hurriedly ratified by an 'Assembly of Notables' convoked at Bayonne, Joseph Bonaparte was proclaimed 'King of Spain and the Indies'.

But Napoleon reckoned without the Spanish love of independence. On the famous day of 2 May 1808 the people of Madrid rose against the French troops. This was the prelude to the national uprising against the invader. In province after province juntas of resistance sprang into life. In May the Junta of Asturias, and in June the Junta of Galicia and the Junta of Seville (arrogantly assuming the title of 'Supreme Governmental Junta of Spain and the Indies') declared war on France and sent deputies to England. On 4 July peace with Spain was formally proclaimed in London, and eight days later the expedition which Sir Arthur Wellesley had been preparing at Cork for the invasion of northern South America sailed to liberate, not Spanish America from Spain, but Portugal and Spain from France. As, wrote Castlereagh on 20 June, 'by the insurrection in the Asturias, some probability of restoring the Spanish monarchy is revived . . . it is wished to suspend any measure tending to divide and therefore to weaken that monarchy.'[1] Henceforth, so far as Britain was concerned, ideas of liberation in Spanish America, like those of conquest, were officially renounced. Spain, like Portugal, had become the ally of England, united in a common cause. In the event of the subjugation of Spain, wrote Castlereagh in August, Britain 'would confine her views to forming such a connexion with the Spanish dominions in South America as might be best calculated to protect their independence and resources against the designs of the common enemy';[2] and Canning, at the Foreign Office, laid it down in September that England could countenance no designs hostile to the Spanish colonies.[3]

The news of the invasion of the mother country, of the fall of the monarchy, and of the Spanish rising *en masse* reached northern South

[1] Charles Vane, Marquess of Londonderry, *Memoirs and Correspondence of Viscount Castlereagh* (12 vols., London, 1848–53), vol. VI, p. 375.
[2] Castlereagh to Admiral Sir Sidney Smith, 4 August 1808. Public Record Office, F.O. 72/91.
[3] Canning to Strangford, 2 September 1808. F.O. 63/59.

America in July and New Spain and the Río de la Plata in August. It provoked an explosion of loyal indignation. Funds were raised to help the patriot cause. The agents of Napoleon, who soon appeared—the Marquis de Sassenay at Buenos Aires, Lieutenant Paul de Lamanon at Caracas—were coldly received and quickly expelled, Sassenay to be imprisoned at Montevideo, Lamanon to fall into the hands of the captain of the British frigate *Acasta*. The loud demands of the Princess Carlota Joaquina at Rio de Janeiro to be recognised as the legal representative of the Spanish royal house were similarly ignored. Little that was good, in Spanish American eyes, could come out of Rio de Janeiro. And though in the Río de la Plata Carlota did indeed acquire a certain following and her intrigues did more to stimulate a revolutionary spirit than to allay it, there, as everywhere else in Spanish America, from New Spain to Chile, the authority of the captive king, Ferdinand VII, was loyally proclaimed.

But Ferdinand was a king without a crown, and the royal officials in America—the peninsular bureaucracy which formed the civil service of the empire—were left without a master. In Spain itself a Central Junta was, with some difficulty, formed in the king's name at Aranjuez in September 1808, only to be forced to flee to Seville two months later. There, in January 1809, it issued a royal decree declaring that the Spanish dominions in the Indies were not colonies but an integral part of the Spanish monarchy and, as such, entitled to representation in the junta. But the junta's life was short. In January 1810, as the French armies overran Andalusia, it again took flight, this time to the island of León, and here it dissolved, leaving in its place a Regency of Five instructed to summon a Cortes which should represent both Spain and America.

Meanwhile, the structure of colonial government, already subjected to severe strain—an unanticipated effect of the Bourbon administrative reforms—during the closing decades of the eighteenth century, showed signs of collapse. While some of the royal officials, preferring any king to none, were suspected of collaborationist sympathies with the *rey intruso*, Joseph Bonaparte, Spaniards, in this crisis of authority, looked with suspicion on Spaniards, and the age-old antagonism between creoles and *peninsulares*, Spaniards born in America and Spaniards born in Spain, flared into open strife. In New Spain the *cabildo*, or town council, of Mexico City, representing the creoles, and the *audiencia*, or high court, representing the *peninsulares*, each sought to impose its will on the viceroy. In the Viceroyalty of the Río de la Plata, where the British invasions of 1806–7 had sowed the seeds of revolution and fertilized the soil, the enmity between Governor Élio of Montevideo and Viceroy Liniers at Buenos Aires, superimposed on the jealousy which each city felt for the other, led to the temporary secession of Montevideo from the rest of the viceroyalty, and Buenos Aires itself, in 1808 and 1809, was the scene of a struggle both of Spaniard against Spaniard and of Spaniard against creole. In Upper Peru the Audiencia of Charcas, long at odds with its president, who was also the Intendant of La Plata, deposed and imprisoned him in May 1809. At La Paz, in the same presidency, creoles and mestizos, in July, overthrew the local bishop and the local intendant, declaring that the time had come to 'organize a new system of government' and 'to raise the standard of liberty in these unfortunate colonies'.[1] And at Quito, in the Viceroyalty of New Granada, the creole aristocracy in August rose in revolt against its peninsular governors though warmly protesting its loyalty to the crown.

These cracks in the fabric of colonial government were, temporarily, repaired. A new viceroy, appointed by the Central Junta in Spain, arrived in the Río de la Plata, and Montevideo returned to its allegiance. A new president-intendant was sent to Charcas. Troops from Peru crushed the rebellion at La Paz. The creoles of Quito were subdued. Nor was it till the Central Junta itself collapsed that the full magnitude of the imperial constitutional crisis, and, with it, of the crisis in the relations between Spain and her colonies, was revealed.

The dominions overseas, the Central Junta had declared, in January 1809, were an integral part of the Spanish monarchy, and the deduction followed that they owed obedience to the extraordinary authorities established in Spain. But this had not been the Habsburg view of the nature of the empire. Nor was it the American view. *'Estos y esos reinos'* ('these and those kingdoms') was the famous phrase used to describe the royal possessions in Spain and the Indies. The kingdoms of the New World had never belonged to Spain. They were the patrimony of the crown of Castile, united to the kingdoms of Spain merely by a dynastic tie. The Bourbons, in their desire to rationalise, to systematise, and to centralise colonial government, had forgotten, or ignored, this Habsburg view, and so had the Spaniards. But the creoles remembered it, and, as the English colonies in the eighteenth century, victorious in their struggle with the instruments of the royal prerogative, refused to accept subordination to the sovereignty of parliament, so the Spanish colonies, once the crown had disappeared, refused to accept subordination to the people of the peninsula.

Already in 1809, at Quito and Chuquisaca, and in other parts of the empire also, the argument had been heard that Spaniards born in America were just as much the guardians, or residuary legatees, of the authority of the crown as Spaniards born in Spain and that the several regions of the Americas had just as much right to establish provisional governments of their own as had the several provinces of Spain. From

[1] Ricardo Levene, *Ensayo histórico sobre la revolución de Mayo y Mariano Moreno* (3 vols., 2nd. ed., Buenos Áires, 1925), vol. I, p. 303.

this it was no long step to the further argument that since the crown had fallen into captivity, since the legal government had ceased to exist, sovereignty had reverted to the people, though by 'the people', it is true, nothing more was meant than a small but active creole minority; and to this doctrine of 'popular sovereignty', in origin quite as much a conservative as a revolutionary doctrine, the news of the dissolution of the Central Junta in Spain and of the apparent conquest of the peninsula gave additional force. 'The monarchy dissolved and Spain lost,' wrote Camilo Torres, one of the leaders of the revolutionary movement in New Granada, 'are we not in the position of children who come of age at the death of the father of the family? Each one enters into the enjoyment of his individual rights, sets up a new hearth, and governs himself.'[1]

The insurrectionary movement that followed in South America began as a revolt of the cities, or, rather, of the cabildos, those organs of municipal government which, in some parts of the empire at least, had been stimulated to a new activity during the later years of the eighteenth century, and in which the creole aristocracy and professional class, excluded generally from the higher offices of state, enjoyed some measure of representation and authority. Semi-nationalist and semi-monarchist, as compared with the nationalist and monarchist revolt which had swept Spain two years earlier, it was essentially a movement for local autonomy, the capital cities, for the most part, taking the lead, the provinces following or resisting; and it revealed at the outset a striking unity of action. Beginning with an extraordinary meeting of the cabildo of Caracas on 19 April 1810, when the Captain-General of Venezuela was deposed, juntas and cabildos assumed the powers of viceroys, governors, and captains-general: at Buenos Aires on 25 May; in the Viceroyalty of New Granada at Cartagena early in June, and at the viceregal capital, Santa Fe de Bogotá, on 20 July; and at Santiago de Chile in September. In each case these new authorities declared their loyalty to the crown. It was not, indeed, till July 1811 that Venezuela proclaimed its independence, nor till July 1816 that the Provinces of the Río de la Plata took the same step. But the revolution of 25 May 1810 at Buenos Aires, like that of 19 April 1810 at Caracas, was in effect, if not in formal fact, a declaration of independence. It was under the legal fiction of obedience to a captive crown that a movement begun as an assertion of freedom from French control was transformed into a war of independence from Spain.

That this transformation took place was in part due to the ineptitude and bewilderment of the colonial authorities themselves. In part it was the deliberate design of a small, intelligent creole minority, re-inforced

[1] Jules Mancini, *Bolívar et l'Émancipation des Colonies Espagnoles des Origines à 1815* (Paris, 1912), p. 271.

by some mestizo blood, which was determined 'to supplant the peninsular Spaniards in government and trade, and in whose hands the ignorant classes were a ready tool for the accomplishment of their aims'.[1] But partly also it was the result of the uncompromising hostility of successive governments in Spain. For though the monarchy had collapsed, though the peninsula had been over-run, liberals and conservatives in Spain still clung to the principles of imperial monopoly and colonial subordination. The regency instituted a blockade of Venezuela. The Cortes, which met on the island of León, under the shadow of Cadiz, in September 1810, and produced the liberal constitution of 1812, declared that the Spanish dominions of both hemispheres formed a single monarchy, a single nation, and a single family, and that Americans possessed the same rights as Europeans. But the colonial demand for equality of representation within the Cortes was, inevitably, denied. The colonial petition for freedom to trade with the world at large was rejected. In all that concerned the dominions overseas, Americans and Filipinos on the one hand—at first represented by thirty of their number resident in Cadiz—and the peninsular delegates on the other were usually ranged on opposite sides. The Cortes twice rejected an offer of British mediation between mother country and colonies: it sought, indeed, not so much a reconciliation with the insurgent provinces as their 'unconditional submission by force of arms'.[2] Spain, like Britain, was unable to conceive of a Commonwealth of Nations united by allegiance to the crown. It did not need the restoration of Ferdinand and despotism, in 1814, to make the independence of Spanish America ultimately sure.

Except in Mexico (p. 634, below), the revolutions which broke out in 1810 were political revolutions. They aimed, not at the re-organisation of society, but at the redistribution of authority, from Spaniards to creoles. They looked also to the destruction of the commercial monopoly of Spain and the opening of the continent to the trade of the world. It was from Caracas and Buenos Aires, where foreign trade and foreign influence had most deeply penetrated, that the revolutionary movements in South America took their rise and drew their strength; and in so far as these movements completed the transition, begun by the illicit trade of Spain's colonial rivals, from the closed to the open door, they cradled an economic revolution. But they stopped short at the point at which they might have cradled a social revolution. They opened wider horizons to the Spaniards born in America. The mestizo, the man of mixed blood, also gained, though not the American Indian, and

[1] C. H. Haring, *The Spanish Empire in America* (New York, 1947), p. 346.
[2] Sir Henry Wellesley to Castlereagh, Cadiz, 5 July 1812. Sir Charles K. Webster, ed., *Britain and the Independence of Latin America, 1812–30. Select Documents from the Foreign Office Archives* (2 vols., London, 1938), vol. II, p. 330.

negro slavery and the slave trade were everywhere restricted or abolished. But it was a demonstration of the strength of the traditional order that, though creoles had stepped into the shoes of Spaniards, and though political institutions had been shaped anew, in most areas, but more particularly in the rural and Indian areas, the structure of colonial society at the close of the wars of independence had been little changed.

The economic organisation of Spanish America, on the other hand, like its administrative organisation, lay in ruins. The wars of independence were civil wars. Creoles fought Spaniards, but Spanish Americans also fought each other. Separatists and loyalists—the latter proportionately far more numerous than the loyalists in the mainland colonies of England during the war of North American independence—alike exploited the illiterate masses, and the struggle once begun released incalculable forces, was waged with a savage intensity, and left desolation in its train. Its consuming fires spread from one end of the continent to the other, and in parts of South America the agony endured for fifteen years. A few regions—Paraguay was one, Central America another—escaped comparatively lightly. On the waters of the Río de la Plata, Buenos Aires, like its great province of the same name, quickly responded to the new currents of foreign trade. In Chile the port of Valparaíso was revolution's child. But the Banda Oriental,[1] and some of the interior provinces of what was to become Argentina, suffered heavily. The high plateau of Upper Peru, the modern Bolivia, was constantly a battlefield. So also was Venezuela, where tens of thousands perished by the lance and by the sword. And though the extent of the damage varied from region to region, in general the economic life of Spanish America was disrupted and the prosperity which had marked the closing years of the colonial era destroyed. Trade routes were abandoned, mines deserted, crops and livestock laid waste, the labour supply was dislocated, capital put to flight.

The empire disintegrated along the lines of its major administrative and jurisdictional divisions. The thirteen mainland colonies of England became one United States. Thirteen states replaced the empires of Spain and Portugal. But, except in one area, the Río de la Plata, the early revolutionary movements, complicated and embittered by personal and regional rivalries as well as by divergencies of aims and opinions, failed; and in the Viceroyalty of the Río de la Plata itself the success obtained was precarious and the price of victory heavy.

The Viceroyalty of the Río de la Plata, the newest of the four American viceroyalties, embraced not only the present provinces of Argentina, but the modern states of Uruguay, Paraguay and Bolivia as well. Here, the events of 25 May 1810 at the viceregal capital, the deposition of the

---

[1] The name by which the territory to the north of the Río de la Plata and east of the Uruguay, later the Republic of Uruguay, was commonly known.

viceroy and the establishment of a junta, were the culmination of a movement long preparing (pp. 614, 616, above). But the revolution had been made at Buenos Aires. If it was a creole, it was also a *porteño*[1] revolution, and, as such, by no means everywhere acceptable. High up the Paraguay river, for example, the creoles of Asunción had no wish to exchange the sovereignty of Spain for that of Buenos Aires. For the *porteños*, indeed, they entertained an instinctive dislike, born of isolation, of old traditions, and of the exactions which Buenos Aires levied on Paraguayan trade. In vain the *porteños* attempted to impose their will by force of arms. Their troops, in 1811, were twice defeated, and in the same year the Intendancy of Paraguay carried out its own revolution, deposing its governor-intendant and establishing its separate junta, of which one member, Dr José Gaspar Rodríguez de Francia, a doctor both of the civil and of the sacred law, became in 1813 one of the country's two consuls and in 1814 its dictator. He remained its dictator till his death in 1840. Paraguay, under Francia's rule a state barely possible to enter and almost impossible to leave, had been for ever lost to the Provinces of the Río de la Plata.

As Paraguay repudiated the authority of Buenos Aires, so also, across the Río de la Plata, did the city's rising commercial rival, Montevideo. Resentful, like Asunción, of the monopolistic tendencies which the capital displayed, and garrisoned by Spanish troops, Montevideo adhered to the cause of the regency in Spain. It remained an outpost of Spanish power till 1814. But it stood alone. In 1811 the surrounding population of the Banda Oriental rose under the leadership of a gaucho[2] guerrilla chieftain, José Gervasio Artigas, who first fought against the royalists in Montevideo and then, late in 1813, turned against the creoles of Buenos Aires also. Montevideo, attempting at the outset to blockade Buenos Aires by sea or river and itself besieged by land, at last, in 1814, surrendered to the *porteños* and was by them abandoned to the *orientales*[3] in the following year. But this triangular struggle in the debatable land north of the Río de la Plata, for which Spain and Portugal had long contended, was an opportunity which the Portuguese crown in the neighbouring Viceroyalty of Brazil found too good to be lost. Its intervention, ostensibly on behalf of the royalists in Montevideo, was at first held in check by the restraining hand of Lord Strangford, the British ambassador at Rio de Janeiro and the peace-maker of the Río de la Plata, who sought to restrain *porteño* ambitions also. But by 1816 it could be held in check no longer. Portuguese invasion was renewed, this time with at least the connivance of the *porteños*, so deep

[1] *Porteño*, belonging to the *puerto* or port, the name customarily given to the inhabitants of Buenos Aires.

[2] The 'man on horseback', or cowboy, of Argentina and Uruguay, originally a smuggler in cattle hides.

[3] The inhabitants of the Banda Oriental.

was their hatred of Artigas; Montevideo was captured, and, once again, the frontiers of Brazil extended southwards to the waters of the Río de la Plata.

Paraguay had established its independence. The Banda Oriental had fallen to Brazil. Upper Peru was re-annexed to the old, and loyal, Viceroyalty of Peru, from which it had only been severed when the Viceroyalty of the Río de la Plata was created in 1776. A *porteño* army, marching to the liberation of these mountain provinces, reached, in 1811, the high waters of Lake Titicaca, only to be annihilated by royalist troops from Peru; and though twice again, in 1813 and 1815, an Argentine army stormed the heights, each time it struggled back defeated. Upper Peru, like Paraguay and like the Banda Oriental, had been for ever lost to the Provinces of the Río de la Plata.

For the Viceroyalty of the Río de la Plata, therefore, the revolution of May 1810 at Buenos Aires spelt dismemberment; and disruption on the periphery was accompanied by anarchy at the centre. For many years after 1810 any government at Buenos Aires was a belligerent government, engaged in warfare on two fronts, in the Río de la Plata and on the frontiers of Upper Peru, and to some extent the fortunes of administrations—juntas, triumvirates, congresses, directorates—followed the fortunes of war, as well as the rise and fall of contending groups. A constituent assembly, meeting in 1813, unified the central government in the hands of a supreme director and took every step to make Argentine independence plain to the world except that of explicitly declaring it. But it failed to formulate a constitution, and it refused to admit deputies who, representing those rural areas of the Banda Oriental which were under the control of Artigas, brought with them instructions to demand an immediate declaration of independence and the establishment of a federal system of government in which each province would retain its own autonomy.

So far the leadership in the revolution had belonged to Buenos Aires. Now that leadership was challenged. As the 'Protector of the Free Peoples', the champion of the rude democracy of the rural masses and of provincial against *porteño* interests, Artigas soon dominated not only the Banda Oriental but the adjoining provinces of Corrientes, Entre Ríos and Santa Fe as well; and while the territory of the old viceroyalty seemed about to suffer yet further dismemberment, in Buenos Aires itself the 'national' government was overthrown by rebellion and mutiny. The United Provinces had become, by 1815, no more than a league of semi-independent, imperfectly organised, and even semi-hostile states. Temporarily, however, the tide of disunity was arrested. At the instigation of the cabildo of Buenos Aires a new Congress met in the interior city of Tucumán in March 1816, and though the regions which Artigas controlled were not represented, all the other provinces sent delegates. It was this body which, restoring national government, proclaimed on 9 July 1816 the independence of the provinces of Argentina.

Time and again one or another Argentine leader had despaired of the republic and had turned his thoughts to the erection of a constitutional monarchy under a European prince. The Congress of Tucumán even contemplated the re-establishment of the dynasty of the Incas. But in the Río de la Plata the revolution had survived. It had done so nowhere else. In Chile, where, in 1810, the creole aristocracy had instituted a junta at Santiago after the manner of Buenos Aires, the movement for self-government had been brought to destruction by the divisions within the ranks of the aristocracy itself, by regional jealousies and personal rivalries, and finally by royalist invasion from Peru, long to remain the stronghold of Spanish power: the battle of Rancagua in October 1814 marked its end. In northern South America, in the Captaincy-General of Venezuela, a republican regime had twice been instituted and twice overthrown, and in the neighbouring Viceroyalty of New Granada viceregal authority, subverted in 1810, had been restored by an army of peninsular veterans six years later.

Nowhere did the early revolutionary movement have more disastrous consequences than in these two most northerly regions of South America. In Venezuela the junta established at Caracas in April 1810 had deported the chief colonial officials, sent agents abroad—among them, on a mission to London, the young Simón Bolívar, the future liberator of half a continent—and summoned a congress. The congress, in July 1811, proclaimed the independence of Venezuela and adopted, in December, a constitution modelled on the federal constitution of the United States. But creole leadership was inept, the country soon faced an economic crisis, and the royalist reaction was swift; and when, on Holy Thursday, 1812, an earthquake laid waste the patriot strongholds but left the royalist centres untouched, the forces of reaction were strengthened by the forces of nature. In the stress of emergency Francisco de Miranda, who had long sought in Europe and America to promote the independence of Spanish America, who had been a French revolutionary general as well as much else in the course of his astonishing career, and who had only recently returned to his native land, was made dictator. But Miranda, losing heart, signed a capitulation with the royalist leader. Attempting to fly the country, he was betrayed by his own officers, Bolívar among them, and perished miserably in a Spanish prison in 1816.

So ended the first Venezuelan republic. The second was as transitory as the first. Bolívar, escaping by sea to New Granada, there found a base from which to lead a liberating army back to Caracas, proclaiming 'war to the death' against the Spaniards as he marched. But his triumph was short-lived. The second republic fell before a horde of half-naked *llaneros*, the plainsmen of the Orinoco valley, who followed a barbaric Spaniard, José Tomás Boves. In July 1814 Caracas was again abandoned, its population streaming from the city in terror, and Bolívar, by the end of September, was once again a fugitive in New Granada.

But the doom of New Granada itself was already sealed. Since 1810 the *granadinos* had found their chief occupation in the drafting of constitutions. 'It was widely assumed that federalism was the perfect form of government; hence each province, and often just one section of a province, had to be a sovereign state; and each sovereign state, not to mention each confederation of sovereign states, produced one or more constitutions.'[1] Amidst this doctrinaire enthusiasm New Granada remained, till January 1815, disorganised, disunited, and in a state of intermittent civil war. Meanwhile, in July 1814, Spain had resolved on the reconquest of her colonies. An expeditionary force of 10,000 men was collected together at Cadiz under the command of General Pablo Morillo. It was originally intended for the Río de la Plata. But since the pacification of Venezuela and New Granada was considered to be even more urgent, its destination was changed. It arrived off the coast of Venezuela in April 1815, and Morillo soon moved on to New Granada. Cartagena fell first, after a siege of more than a hundred days, and after it the capital, Santa Fe de Bogotá. By the middle of 1816 the Viceroyalty of New Granada had been reconstituted and the revolution in northern South America appeared to be dead or dying. Only in the more easterly parts of Venezuela was it still flickeringly alive.

This was the critical year of the revolutionary wars. In 1816 the reaction was at its height, the cause was in the balance. But the revolution was now to be revived with redoubled force. In the south, in Mendoza, at the foot of the great mountain wall which divides Argentina from Chile, José de San Martín was quietly organising his Army of the Andes. 'Mendoza was the door to Chile; Chile was the door to Peru.'[2] And by one of the great coincidences in Spanish American history, in December, when San Martín was getting ready to move, Bolívar landed for the last time in Venezuela to renew his campaign for the liberation of his native land; and Bolívar, like San Martín, took the long and distant view. 'Yes, yes,' he told his companions, 'you shall fly with me to rich Peru. Our destinies call us to the uttermost parts of the American world.'[3]

[1] David Bushnell, *The Santander Regime in Gran Colombia* (Newark, Delaware, 1954), pp. 6–7.
[2] J. P. Otero, *Historia del Libertador Don José de San Martín* (4 vols., Buenos Aires, 1932), vol. I, p. 278.
[3] Simón Bolívar, *Obras Completas* (ed. Vicente Lecuna and Esther Barret de Nazaris, 2 vols., La Habana, Cuba, 1947), vol. I, pp. 223–4.

San Martín had been born on a remote mission station high up on the banks of the Uruguay river. Educated in Spain, he returned to Buenos Aires in 1812, a professional soldier, a strategist and a tactician. His famous design to carry the revolution to Peru by way of Chile, instead of by the long road through Upper Peru, was formulated two years later, and his organising genius was then directed to a single end, the raising and equipping of an army to invade Chile by the high Andean passes, one of them lying between the great peaks of Aconcagua and Tupungato, at a height of 12,600 feet above the level of the sea. By January 1817 all was ready. Each route had been carefully surveyed; great pains had been taken to conceal San Martín's real intentions and his true line of march; a time-table had been minutely laid down; and despite the terrible nature of the terrain, the fierce cold of the nights, mountain sickness, and skirmishes with parties of the enemy, the whole operation, conducted over a front of some five hundred miles, proceeded with clockwork precision. Early in February each of San Martín's commanders arrived exactly where he was intended to arrive and at exactly the right time. The two main columns, joining forces, took the royalists by surprise at Chacabuco on 12 February, and two days later San Martín entered Santiago. He refused to accept the reins of government himself, and the cabildo of Santiago thereupon appointed as supreme director of Chile a leader of the earlier insurgent movement, Bernardo O'Higgins, who had crossed the Andes with San Martín and whose father, an Irishman in the service of Spain, had been in turn both captain-general of Chile and viceroy of Peru.

Chacabuco was one of the great battles of South America. But it was not decisive. Nor was it till April 1818, when the royalists were again defeated at Maipú, to the south of Santiago, that the seal was set on the independence of Chile and the way prepared for the accomplishment of the second stage in San Martín's great design—the seaborne invasion of Peru. Meanwhile, O'Higgins had begun the creation of a navy. It was formed from English and American merchantmen and privateers, ex-East Indiamen, a captured Spanish frigate, and some other, smaller ships of war, and it was placed finally under the command of one of the most daring as well as one of the most incalculable of British seamen, Thomas Cochrane, the future Earl of Dundonald, who, engaged in a private war with the British Government, had been persuaded to enter the service of Chile. Officered and manned by Englishmen, Irishmen, Scotsmen, Americans and Chileans, it set sail from Valparaíso Bay with San Martín's army—San Martín had refused to obey an order to return to Buenos Aires—in August 1820. The first landings were made at Pisco, a thousand miles to the north, and from here an expeditionary force was sent into the highlands, the fleet and army then sailing to the north of Lima to blockade the capital and its port, Callao. Outnumbered by the royalist troops and pursuing a policy of watching, waiting and negotiation—much to the disgust of Cochrane, whose patience soon wore thin—San Martín was rewarded in July 1821 by the peaceful evacuation of Lima. There, on the 28th, the independence of Peru was solemnly proclaimed and, six days later, San Martín assumed the title of Protector.

As in 1817 San Martín had crossed the Andes to the south, finally to invade Peru—the fortress of Spain in South America—by sea, so in 1819, by an equally heroic march, Bolívar had crossed them to the north, ultimately to invade Peru by land. Endowed with extraordinary gifts, with talents that amounted to genius, Bolívar had been born at Caracas in 1783. As a young man he had read avidly and widely, Rousseau and Raynal, Voltaire and Montesquieu, Locke and Hobbes. In Paris he had seen and worshipped Napoleon, 'the bright star of glory, the genius of liberty,'[1] worshipped him, that is, until Napoleon assumed a crown; and when not yet twenty-two he had stood on the Monte Sacro outside Rome and there had sworn to free his country from Spanish rule. His early career as a soldier (pp. 621–2, above) had been compounded of brilliant successes and disastrous failures, ending in exile in Jamaica (May 1815) and then in Haiti. But even in his darkest hours Bolívar never lost faith in his star and his cause. 'If nature opposes our designs', he declared when the earthquake of 1812 laid Caracas in ruins, 'we shall fight against her and make her obey';[2] and the same faith burned in the famous letter which he wrote from Jamaica in 1815 when all seemed to be lost: 'The destiny of America has been settled irrevocably. The bond that held it to Spain has been sundered . . . it is less difficult to unite the continents than to reconcile the spirits of the two countries.'[3]

Disembarking at Barcelona on the Caribbean shores of Venezuela on the last day of 1816, Bolívar, three months later, took the decisive step of abandoning the coast for the interior, where the Orinoco gave him direct communications with the outside world and where his authority was gradually consolidated. Here, with his base at Angostura (Ciudad Bolívar), he began to plan the foundations of a new state: he thought of it as a 'conservative republic', embracing both Venezuela and New Granada and reproducing in some respects at least what he conceived to be the peculiar excellences of the British constitution.[4] Here also he was joined by large numbers of foreign legionaries, re-

---

[1] Bolívar's words as reported by his Irish aide-de-camp, Daniel O'Leary. *Memorias del General Daniel Florencio O'Leary. Narración* (3 vols., Caracas, 1952), vol. I, p. 61.

[2] *Obras Completas*, vol. II, p. 994.

[3] 'Contestación de un Americano Meridional a un Caballero de esta Isla,' Kingston, 6 September, 1815. *Obras Completas*, vol. I, p. 160.

[4] 'Discurso pronunciado por el Libertador ante el Congreso de Angostura,' 15 February, 1819. *Ibid.*, vol. II, pp. 1132–55.

cruited in England, Ireland and Scotland, many of them disbanded soldiers of the Napoleonic wars. And from here, finally, late in May 1819, he set out with some three thousand men on his famous march over the hot and flooded plains of the Orinoco, crossed the Andes by the bleak Páramo of Pisba, 13,000 feet above sea-level, defeated the main Spanish army at Boyacá (7 August), and, four days later, entered the capital of New Granada, Santa Fe de Bogotá, in triumph. A proclamation of the union of New Granada and Venezuela in the Republic of Colombia soon followed and a constitution for the new state, not wholly, it is true, to Bolívar's liking, was drafted at Cúcuta in 1821, Bolívar becoming the first president of the republic and Francisco de Paula Santander its vice-president in charge of the civil administration during Bolívar's absences from the seat of government.

Even after Boyacá a European army, re-inforcing the Spanish commander-in-chief, General Morillo, might still have turned the scales against Bolívar. Certainly it could have prolonged the war; and such an army was assembled at Cadiz in 1819. But once again events in Spain profoundly influenced events in Spanish America. On 1 January 1820 Colonel Rafael Riego raised the standard of revolt against the despotism of Ferdinand VII and proclaimed the restoration of the Constitution of 1812. The revolt rapidly spread; the king was forced to give way; and, instead of troops, commissioners breathing peace and reconciliation were dispatched to America. Instructed to enter into negotiations with Bolívar, Morillo concluded an armistice (November 1820) and then returned to Europe. But reconciliation, even with a constitutionalist Spain, was now impossible, and the tide of victory was flowing fast. The armistice having expired, Bolívar again crossed the Andes finally to free Venezuela from Spanish control, except for the fortress of Puerto Cabello, at the second battle of Carabobo (24 June 1821), where the British legion played a notable part, and thereafter was able to turn his attention from the eastern and central regions of what had been the old Viceroyalty of New Granada to the western and southern, to the strongly royalist province of Pasto and to the presidency of Quito.

Pasto was an integral part of New Granada. The presidency of Quito was not. It was, however, a dependency of the viceroyalty, and for this reason Bolívar regarded it as forming, quite naturally, a part of his new Republic of Colombia. Save for the port and province of Guayaquil, it had remained loyal to Spain. But Guayaquil, asserting its independence in October 1820, had asserted also its right to join whatever association might be formed in South America which should best suit its interests, to join, that is, either Peru, where San Martín had recently landed, or Colombia, whose independence Bolívar had lately proclaimed. Each of the two great liberators hoped for the incorporation of Guayaquil within the territory which he controlled;

each sent agents to the city; and it was with the aid of troops from Peru as well as from Colombia that Bolívar's greatest lieutenant, the twenty-nine-year-old Antonio José de Sucre, dispatched to Guayaquil by sea in 1821, won at Pichincha in May 1822 the decisive victory which put an end to Spanish rule in Quito. Meanwhile Bolívar had begun his own long and arduous march through Pasto to Quito, and whatever may have been the views of San Martín, Bolívar, certainly, had no intention of allowing to Guayaquil any substantial freedom of choice. Reaching Quito itself in mid-June, he hurried from the capital to the port, and from that moment self-determination, so far as the *Guayaquileños* were concerned, became an academic question. Guayaquil, like Quito, was annexed to Colombia.

Under the shadow of this seizure, for it was little less, Bolívar and San Martín met on 26 July 1822. They met as equals. But while Bolívar's star was still waxing, San Martín's had already begun to wane. Endowed with an immense vitality, enamoured of 'glory', eager for fame, Bolívar had come to Guayaquil after a series of resounding triumphs. He was the liberator of Venezuela and New Granada; he had just consolidated his position in Quito; Guayaquil had fallen into his hands. San Martín, on the other hand, was ill and weary. In Peru he had reaped little but bitterness and misunderstanding. There had been signs of disaffection within his own ranks. Cochrane had quarrelled with him and abandoned him. Above all, Peru was still not free. He had redeemed the coast, but not the highlands, and there the viceregal forces remained intact. To destroy them, he needed Bolívar's help, and he failed to obtain it. The interviews between the two men were held in private. No third person was present. But from the statements of each it is plain that they could agree neither on the future form of government in Peru—San Martín favoured a monarchy under a European prince—nor on the conduct of the war in Peru and the means of bringing it to an end. Such aid as Bolívar promised, San Martín considered inadequate, and his own offer to serve under Bolívar, Bolívar could not accept.[1]

For San Martín this was the end. He returned to Lima a bitterly disappointed man. The thought of abdication had been present in his mind even before he left Peru. Now his resolve was taken. On 20 September he resigned his protectorate to a constitutent congress newly assembled and the next day sailed to Chile. 'My promises to the countries for which I have fought are fulfilled', he declared—'to secure their independence and to leave them to select their own governments. The presence of a fortunate soldier, however disinterested he

---

[1] The evidence for this offer is disputed. See the discussion in Gerhard Masur, 'The Conference of Guayaquil', *Hispanic American Historical Review*, XXXI (1951), pp. 189–229.

may be, is dangerous to newly constituted states.'[1] From Chile he moved to Argentina and then to Europe, and there he died, more than a quarter of a century later.

It remained for Bolívar to complete the emancipation of Peru. But it was impossible that he should leave Colombia at once—his pre-occupations were too many—nor would he have been immediately welcomed in Peru; and when, in response to tardy but increasingly urgent solicitations, he did at last reach Lima, in September 1823, it was to find the country in chaos, one president in the northerly town of Trujillo, another in the capital, and an undefeated viceroy in the highlands. In February 1824, moreover, the garrison at Callao revolted and went over to the royalists, and while a despairing Congress invested Bolívar with dictatorial powers, a viceregal army, sweeping down from the mountains, re-occupied Lima. But the final stages of the war were now approaching. Rallying and recruiting his forces—he was always magnificent in adversity—Bolívar met, and defeated, his opponents at Junín in the high Andes on 6 August—so cold was the night that 'nearly all the wounded on both sides perished';[2] and this was the beginning of the end. It came at Ayacucho—Sucre's victory—on 9 December, when the last Spanish viceroy laid down his arms. A few royalist strongholds—the fortress of Callao, the island of Chiloé off the coast of Chile—held out till 1826. But what Yorktown had been to the British Empire in North America, Ayacucho was to the Spanish Empire in South America. All Peru to the Desaguadero river, the boundary between Peru and Upper Peru, or the Presidency of Charcas, was now in patriot hands. It only remained to eliminate royalist resist-ance in Upper Peru itself, the first part of the empire to rise (p. 615, above), the last to be freed, and this was soon accomplished. As Sucre advanced the country rose to greet him. He summoned an assembly, and the assembly pronounced in favour of independence. So, in August 1825, the republic of Bolivia was born. In compliment to Bolívar it took his name, offered him the executive power whenever he should visit the country, as he soon did, and invited him to draw up a constitution.

Liberator of Colombia, dictator of Peru, president of Bolivia, Bolívar, at the end of 1825, had reached the height of his power and fame. He was dreaming now of a Spanish American League of Nations, its seat at Panama, and he dreamed also of a still closer federation between the states which he had helped to found. But the waters of anarchy were rising. For Bolivia he drafted a constitution which the

[1] *Documentos del Archivo de San Martín* (12 vols., Buenos Aires, 1910–11), vol. x, p. 356.
[2] John Miller, *Memoirs of General [William] Miller in the service of the Republic of Peru* (2 vols., London, 1828), vol. II, p. 134.

other states, he hoped, would adopt. He looked upon it as the ark which would save all from drowning,[1] and it was in fact a monarchy in disguise—a republic with a life-president who would nominate his successor, a legislature far removed from popular control, and a Chamber of Censors, appointed for life, to watch over the constitution and the laws. 'I am convinced to the very marrow of my bones,' he wrote in this same year, 'that our America can only be ruled through an able despotism.'[2]

The end was tragedy. All his plans, all his hopes, collapsed. The Congress of Panama, meeting in June 1826, but attended by delegates from Peru, Colombia, Mexico and Central America only (p. 635, below), was a failure, except in so far as it afforded an inspiration for a distant future. The Andean Confederation remained a dream. Bolivia turned against Sucre, whom Bolívar had left behind as president. Peru, adopting Bolívar's constitution while he was present but repudiating it so soon as he was absent, invaded both Bolivia and Colombia, and Colombia was divided against itself. The liberator became a dictator. His life was attempted, and amidst a falling world he despaired. 'There is no good faith in America, nor among the nations of America,' he wrote in 1829. 'Treaties are papers; constitutions, books; elections, battles; freedom [is] anarchy; and life, a torment.'[3] At the last he trod the road of exile, and on that road, in December 1830, he died. It was the death both of a man and of a system. Venezuela, under the leadership of its great guerrilla soldier, José Antonio Páez, had already seceded from Colombia, and so also, under the new name of Ecuador, had the old Presidency of Quito.

So vast a state as Great Colombia, so thinly peopled, so regionally divided, never, perhaps, had much chance of survival. But throughout Spanish America, in Mexico as well as in Colombia, and in Argentina as in Peru, the problem of organising viable and stable states on the ruins of an imperial administrative system which had carefully excluded Americans native-born from the technical tasks of government proved to be formidable in the extreme. Chile, it is true, found an acceptable solution of the problem in the 1830's. There, O'Higgins (p. 623, above) had fallen in 1823, a victim to the resentments of the Chilean landed gentry, inimical quite as much to his social policies as to his personal rule; and his exile was followed by seven years of political experiment and debate—there were three constitutions between 1823 and 1829—and of increasing confusion and disorder. But the victory of the conservative forces in the civil war of 1830 put an end to this turbulence,

---

[1] Bolívar to Gutiérrez de la Fuente, 12 May 1826. *Obras Completas*, vol. I, p. 1326.
[2] Bolívar to Santander, 8 July 1826. *Ibid.*, vol. I, p. 1390.
[3] 'Una Mirada sobre la América Española,' attributed to Bolívar. *Obras Completas*, vol. II, p. 1304.

and Chile, under its aristocratic constitution of 1833, became an oasis of peace in a continent of disorder.

Argentina was less fortunate. The Congress of Tucumán (p. 620, above) had proclaimed the independence of the 'United Provinces of South America' in 1816. It had re-established a Supreme Directorate, and, moving to Buenos Aires, it had promulgated, in 1819, a constitution. This provided for a highly centralised, unitary state. It ignored provincial ideas of local autonomy and provincial fears of the economic hegemony of a single city, a single port, and a single province. It ignored also the fact that many of the provinces had fallen into the hands of military chieftains, the *caudillos* of the plains, and that men such as Estanislao López of Santa Fe and Francisco Ramírez of Entre Ríos (who was soon to drive his old ally, and indeed master, José Artigas,[1] into exile in Paraguay) were unlikely to submit tamely to orders from Buenos Aires. Finally, some at least of its authors were soon discovered to have been engaged in plans to convert the republic into a monarchy. The result was the 'anarchy of 1820'. López and Ramírez led their cowboy cavalry against the capital; congress and directorate vanished; national government disappeared, and only the shadow of a federation remained.

Amidst this national disintegration, Buenos Aires, after the first shock of confusion, quickly recovered its stability. In September 1820 a Junta of Representatives called Martín Rodríguez to the governorship of the province (1820–4). Rodríguez appointed as his Secretary of Government and Foreign Affairs a forty-one-year-old *porteño* statesman, Bernardino Rivadavia, recently returned from Europe, and within three years Rivadavia, in the opinion of the first British consul-general to Argentina, had done more for the amelioration of Buenos Aires than all his predecessors put together.[2] A representative assembly was established, a bank and a university were founded, the frontiers of the province were extended, its finances were re-organised, the police and judiciary reformed. 'Never before, and only rarely afterwards, was Buenos Aires the scene of such varied and far-reaching legislative and administrative activity.'[3] Finally, in December 1824 a constituent congress again met. This body, in January 1825, enacted a 'fundamental law' which provided that the provinces should govern themselves until a national constitution should be approved but placed the conduct of foreign affairs in the hands of the Government of Buenos Aires, and this law made possible the signing, in February, of a commercial treaty between Britain and the United Provinces. Finally, a year later, in

[1] See above, pp. 619, 620. Artigas fled to Paraguay in 1820 and died there in 1850, the same year in which San Martín died at Boulogne-sur-Mer.
[2] Woodbine Parish to Canning, 27 April 1824. P.R.O. F.O. 6/3.
[3] Miron Burgin, *The Economic Aspects of Argentine Federalism, 1820–52* (Cambridge, Mass., 1946), p. 87.

February 1826, the Congress appointed Rivadavia, who had again been absent on a mission to Europe, as president of the Republic and in December, at long last, it promulgated a constitution. But experience had taught little to the constitution-makers at Buenos Aires. Like the Constitution of 1819, the Constitution of 1826 would have created a highly centralised, unitary state, and, thus flouting federalist feeling in the country at large, it had no chance of survival. Province after province rejected it. The president resigned. The Congress dissolved itself. And on the ruins of the Rivadavian system was now to arise, not the federal organisation of the state, but the absolute rule of the greatest of the Argentine *caudillos*—Juan Manuel de Rosas.

The country, meanwhile, had gone to war with Brazil, which had invaded the Banda Oriental—the future Uruguay—in 1816 (pp. 619–20, above) and had erected it into the Estado Cisplatino in 1821. But neither the Banda nor Buenos Aires could reconcile itself to Portuguese, or Brazilian, dominion in the Río de la Plata, and in April 1825 Juan Antonio de Lavalleja, an 'Oriental' exile, launched the liberating expedition of the 'immortal thirty-three' across the Río de la Plata. The rural population of the Banda rose. An assembly meeting in the little town of La Florida pronounced in favour of union with 'the other Argentine provinces'. The Government of Buenos Aires accepted this incorporation, and war with Brazil followed. It lasted three years, with no very decisive results by land or sea but considerable damage to British trade; and it was finally ended through British mediation. As early as February 1826 Canning had suggested that 'the town and territory of Montevideo' might 'become and remain independent';[1] and when, in August 1828, after prolonged pressure from Lord Ponsonby, the British Minister first at Buenos Aires and then at Rio de Janeiro, a peace treaty was at last signed between the rival powers it recognised, and guaranteed, the existence of the independent republic of Uruguay as a buffer state between them.

The war over the Banda Oriental contributed to the downfall of Rivadavia in Argentina. It seriously impaired also the prestige of the young Dom Pedro I of Brazil. Brazil, a colony in 1807, a kingdom in 1815 (p. 612, above), had become an independent empire in 1822; and for this last transformation events in Portugal had been directly responsible. For Portugal, like Spain, had experienced a revolution in 1820. A Cortes had been summoned, meeting in January 1821, the basis of a constitution was prepared, and King John VI, as he had become in 1816, was placed in a painful dilemma. Happy in the country to which he had fled, thirteen years earlier, to escape the clutches of Napoleon, he had long resisted Portuguese, and British, pressure that he should return to Lisbon. But even he could not but realise that the

---

[1] Canning to Ponsonby, 28 Feb. 1826. Webster, *op. cit.* (on p. 617 above), vol. I, p. 138.

future of the House of Braganza was now at stake. He hesitated to stay, and perhaps to lose the Portuguese crown; he feared to go, and perhaps to lose the Brazilian. Finally, after extreme vacillation and tumultuous scenes in Rio de Janeiro, he set sail on 26 April 1821, taking with him some 3,000 Portuguese and almost the entire contents of the Bank of Brazil, and leaving behind him his twenty-four-year-old son and heir, Dom Pedro, as regent.

So far, Brazilians had embraced the constitutionalist cause with enthusiasm. They were now to be disillusioned. For the Cortes at Lisbon found no difficulty in reconciling liberalism at home with despotism abroad. Its intention to reduce Brazil to its former colonial status was all too evident. The authority of Rio de Janeiro was to be overthrown, the provinces were to be made dependent on Lisbon, and Dom Pedro was ordered home. The young, impetuous, ardent prince, with his dissolute habits and easy manners, now became the symbol of the unity of Brazil and the hope of its native aristocracy. On 9 January 1822, in response to petitions and appeals from Rio de Janeiro, São Paulo, and Minas Gerais, he gave his promise to remain. As his chief adviser he chose José Bonifácio de Andrada e Silva, a native of São Paulo, a former professor of the University of Coimbra, a mineralogist of note, and the presiding genius of Brazilian independence. In May he accepted from the Municipality of Rio de Janeiro the title of 'Perpetual Protector and Defender of Brazil'. He summoned in June a constituent assembly and, in August, undertook a visit to São Paulo. There, on 7 September, on the banks of the little stream of Ipiranga, he received dispatches from Portugal annulling all his acts. Declaring 'The hour has come! Independence or death!', he hurried back to Rio de Janeiro. On 12 October he was proclaimed Constitutional Emperor of Brazil and on 1 December was crowned. It remained to expel the Portuguese troops from the northern provinces of Bahia, Maranhão and Pará, as they had already been expelled from Rio de Janeiro; and with the aid of Lord Cochrane, who had exchanged the naval service of the republic of Chile for that of the Empire of Brazil, this was done. In the southern 'Estado Cisplatino' Portuguese soldiers in Montevideo long defied Brazilian. But by the end of 1823 the independence of Brazil was complete. Civil war had been avoided, separatist tendencies resisted, administrative continuity preserved.

But Dom Pedro had already forcibly dissolved the constituent assembly, less than seven months after it had met, angered by its high views of its powers and its marked hostility to the Portuguese elements in the country. He had broken with José Bonifácio, who, however arrogant his conduct as the Crown's chief minister, had been the real founder of the empire; and José Bonifácio and his two brothers, assuming the leadership of the anti-Portuguese party both within the assembly and outside it, had been exiled to France. Liberal by intention but despotic by nature, he had ordered, finally, a new or revised constitution to be substituted for that which the assembly had been engaged in drafting; and in March 1824, by imperial decree, this was promulgated. It turned Brazil into a highly centralised, unitary monarchy, which was to survive for sixty-five years; and, though it placed immense powers in the hands of the crown, in form, and perhaps in character, it was liberal enough. But the assembly had been dissolved. The constitution had been granted by the emperor to the nation, not given by the assembly to the crown; and Brazilians felt a grave mistrust. So great was the dissatisfaction in 1824 that Pernambuco, a centre of strong regional loyalties and the scene of a republican revolt in 1817, denounced the emperor, repudiated the constitution, and attempted to establish a new state, the 'Confederation of the Equator'; and to crush this movement Dom Pedro had, once again, to seek the aid of Lord Cochrane and to suspend also the civil rights' clauses of his constitution.

Revolt in Pernambuco in 1824 was followed by revolt in the Estado Cisplatino in 1825, resulting in a long, expensive and unpopular war with Argentina and a peace, still more unpopular, in 1828, by which the empire's most southerly province became the independent state of Uruguay (p. 630, above). Meanwhile, Dom Pedro had signed treaties both with Portugal and with Britain, herself greatly interested in the reconciliation of Dom Pedro and King John. Portugal was Britain's oldest ally. Imperial Brazil, in Canning's eyes, was a link between republican America and monarchical Europe, and in no part of South America were British commercial interests so extensive. But it was only after negotiations of extreme complexity, which needed all the skill and energy that Canning could command, that Portugal, in August 1825, was at last brought to sign a treaty of recognition with her former colony, King John assuming, *pro forma*, the title of Emperor of Brazil, and then renouncing it in favour of his son. But the treaty left open, as Brazilians duly noted, the question of the succession to the Portuguese throne, and, still worse, by an additional article, at first kept secret, Dom Pedro agreed to compensate his father for losses in Brazil and to assume responsibility for a debt contracted by Portugal in England. Two treaties with England followed. The one, a commercial treaty, signed in 1827, in effect duplicated in Brazil those special privileges which Britain had long enjoyed in her trade with Portugal. The other, a convention (November 1826) for the abolition of the slave trade by 1830, Dom Pedro was equally unable to resist. Both treaties were disliked. But the second, seeming to threaten the very foundations of Brazilian prosperity, based on slave labour and the plantation system, gave bitter offence and proved impossible to enforce. The fact that the number of slaves imported rapidly increased told its own tale.

The estrangement between the Emperor of Brazil and the Brazilians who had crowned him was now almost complete. On the death of his father in 1826, Dom Pedro had assumed and then renounced the Portuguese crown. But he had continued, as Brazilians thought, to be unduly concerned with Portuguese affairs. His autocratic tendencies had grown more pronounced, his private life more scandalous, and his reliance on his Portuguese friends and supporters more marked. His relations with his parliament—it had not been summoned till 1826—had become intolerably strained, and, to crown all, the national finances were in chaos. The end came in 1831, when the country had reached the verge of revolution and the emperor could no longer rely on his own troops. On 7 April he abdicated in favour of his infant son and embarked on board a British warship to sail for Europe. Brazil henceforth was in the hands of Brazilians.

Two other countries experimented with monarchy. These were Haiti, occupying the western third of the island of Hispaniola, and Mexico. In Haiti, the old French colony of Saint Domingue, which had become the first negro republic in the modern world in January 1804, Jean-Jacques Dessalines, a brutal savage from the Congo, was proclaimed emperor as Jacques I in the following October, to be murdered two years later, having himself contrived the murder of almost the entire white population that had survived the terrible events enacted in the French part of the island during the last decade of the eighteenth century. His empire fell, in the north, to a more remarkable leader, Henri Christophe, also an ex-slave, who was crowned as Henri I in 1811, and ruled his little kingdom with vigour, brutality and success, and, in the south, to an educated mulatto, Alexandre Pétion, who governed, more mildly but less competently, as president for life, and was succeeded by another mulatto, Jean-Pierre Boyer (1818–43). On Christophe's suicide in 1820 his kingdom was absorbed by Boyer, who then united the whole island under a single government by annexing the Spanish colony of Santo Domingo. This unhappy country, nominally ceded to France in 1795, temporarily occupied by Haitian troops in 1801, and then held for France by a small force under General Ferrand, had been restored to Spain as a result of an uprising in 1808–9 supported by British ships and Spanish troops. In November 1821 it again rose and sought, as an independent state, union with Colombia, only to fall, early in 1822, under the rule of Haiti and to remain under Haitian control for the next twenty-two years.

Santo Domingo had been lost as much by conquest as by insurrection. Spain's other insular possessions, Cuba and Puerto Rico, remained loyal to the mother country. They were relatively strongly governed and relatively prosperous. Cuba, moreover, was both a base from which operations against the mainland colonies could be conducted and a refuge for loyalists, and, despite some stirrings of discontent, neither its Spanish nor its creole population wished to risk the horrors of a slave insurrection such as had occurred in Haiti. On the North American mainland, however, the great Viceroyalty of New Spain, which had been the wealthiest of Spain's dominions at the end of the eighteenth century, and the neighbouring Captaincy-General of Guatemala, both proclaimed their independence in the 1820's, though in them revolution took a different course from that which it had followed in South America.

In New Spain, as in other parts of the empire, the events of 1808 in the peninsula had precipitated a struggle for power between Spaniards born in America and Spaniards born in Spain, a struggle fought out, for the most part, in Mexico City itself (p. 614, above). Here, however, the European Spaniards had retained control, though not without the illegal deposition of a viceroy, and creole ambitions were frustrated. Revolution in New Spain, indeed, began not in the capital but in the provinces, and less as a political than as a social movement, a revolt of the dispossessed against the possessing classes. It began on 16 September 1810, when Father Miguel Hidalgo y Costilla, the parish priest of Dolores in the Intendancy of Guanajuato, summoned his Indian congregation to arms. A member of a conspiratorial group in the neighbouring town of Querétaro, Hidalgo had been plotting a creole rebellion to take place in December when the discovery of his plans drove him to precipitate an immediate Indian rising instead. It was unpremeditated and unorganised. But, as the Audiencia of Mexico complained, it spread with the rapidity of a pestilence.[1] With a few creole officers, ex-conspirators of Querétaro, and a few trained troops, Hidalgo was soon at the head of a mob of 50,000 Indians and mestizos who attacked and sacked, with great barbarity, the provincial capital, Guanajuato, and then, their numbers still swelling, moved on to threaten Mexico City. But here the 'Captain-General of America', as he now called himself, halted; his ragged army turned back, and in January 1811, on the banks of the Lerma river at no great distance from Guadalajara, it was put to flight. Captured some six weeks later, Hidalgo was first condemned by the ecclesiastical courts, and then, abjuring the insurrection and repenting of his own part in it, in July was shot.

But the flame which he had lighted was not so easily quenched. Collapsing in the north, the insurrection revived in the south, where the mantle of Hidalgo was inherited by another priest, and a greater man, José María Morelos, who made himself the master of much of southern Mexico for nearly four years, summoned a congress and promulgated a constitution, before he also was captured and shot in 1815. Thereafter the congress did not long survive; the armed bands roaming the

[1] H. G. Ward, *Mexico in 1827* (2 vols., London, 1828), vol. I, p. 497.

countryside were gradually reduced; and by the time of the liberal revolution of 1820 in Spain only a few irreconcilables remained, notably Vicente Guerrero and his followers in the south-east, and Guadalupe Victoria (Félix Fernández), wandering hopeless and alone in the mountains and forests of Vera Cruz, but destined to become the first president of Mexico.

With the victory, though transient indeed, of liberalism in Spain in 1820, the scene in Mexico was changed. Indians and mestizos, with some creole leadership and support, had begun the revolution. Creoles and *peninsulares*, resolved to preserve New Spain from the dangerous innovations of old Spain, completed it. They found an instrument for their purpose in a young creole officer, Agustín de Iturbide. Sent by the viceroy to crush Guerrero, Iturbide made overtures to him instead, proclaiming in the so-called Plan of Iguala (February 1821), which offered some concession to almost every faction in the war-weary country, the independence of Mexico, the equality of Mexicans and Europeans, and the supremacy of the Roman Catholic faith. The plan provided also for the establishment of a monarchy, preferably under a prince of the Spanish royal house. Guerrero and the army accepted it. The viceregal authorities were compelled to acquiesce, and in September Iturbide entered Mexico City—to establish a regency and summon a congress and, in May 1822, to secure his own elevation to the throne of Mexico by the acclamation of his troops. In July, as the Emperor Agustín I, he was crowned. But though Iturbide could seize a throne, he was unable to hold it. His own ambition and incompetence, his inability to pay his troops, the jealousies of others, all precipitated his fall. In December the commandant of the port of Vera Cruz, Antonio López de Santa Anna, 'pronounced' against him, and in February 1823 he was forced to abdicate. A republic was proclaimed and in August 1824 Guadalupe Victoria was inaugurated as its first president.

These events in Mexico inevitably affected the neighbouring Captaincy-General or Kingdom of Guatemala, which, despite occasional disorders between 1811 and 1814, had so far remained loyal to Spain. In September 1821 the province of Chiapas decided to throw in its lot with Mexico, and in the same month a junta of the principal officials meeting in Guatemala City pronounced in favour of independence. But Iturbide had other views. In June 1822 a Mexican army entered the capital and for a brief period Iturbide was able to extend his rule over the whole of the ancient kingdom. On his fall, however, a 'national constitutent assembly', in July 1823, declared that the provinces of which the kingdom was composed were free and independent both of old Spain and of New Spain and that together they formed the United Provinces of Central America—a federation which survived only till 1838, then dissolving into its component parts of Guatemala, Honduras, Nicaragua, El Salvador and Costa Rica.

No outside Power came to the formal assistance of the mainland colonies of Spain in their long struggle for independence, as France and Spain had come to the aid of the mainland colonies of England. But foreign soldiers and sailors, more particularly the British and Irish soldiers who fought under Bolívar and the British and Irish seamen who sailed with Cochrane, gave invaluable help to the insurgents; and the services of British merchants and bankers were equally important. They were not, of course, disinterested services. But they provided what the insurrectionary governments needed—money, credit and supplies. In England capital looked abroad. In Spanish America British brokers and commercial agents, who had eagerly awaited the opening of the Spanish American markets with or without the permission of Spain, established themselves in one liberated area after another, their interests in part protected by the ships of the Royal Navy, whose captains transported also immense quantities of specie to England. And while the continent was flooded with British goods and the orgy of speculation in Spanish American mines in 1824–5 recalled the days of the South Sea bubble, revolutionary government after revolutionary government successfully raised loans in London. The bubble burst at the end of 1825 and the collapse of the mining schemes heralded default on the loans. But by this time more than twenty million pounds sterling of British capital had been invested one way or another in Latin America, more than three times the amount that had yet found its way to the United States.

No British statesman could ignore the interests of British trade. None would forego the trade of Spanish America. But so long as the Napoleonic wars continued, the British government, far from desiring the disintegration of the Spanish Empire, would have preferred its entire strength and resources to be concentrated against the common enemy (p. 613, above). Castlereagh was willing, even eager, to promote the reconciliation of Spain and her colonies. But he saw, perfectly clearly, that unless the mother country was prepared 'to place the inhabitants of America upon a commercial footing of corresponding advantage with the inhabitants of European Spain', and unless she realised that 'provinces of such magnitude' would no longer 'submit to be treated as mere colonies', their 'separation from the parent state' was 'inevitable and at hand'.[1] On these conditions, and no other, he was ready to mediate. But he not only refused to support Spain by force of arms, he made sure, in 1817, that the European Powers should

[1] Castlereagh to Sir Henry Wellesley, 1 April 1812. Webster, *op. cit.*, vol. II, p. 311.

not feel free to do so either;[1] and, by 1820 he was himself convinced that the recognition of the independence of large parts of Spanish America was merely a matter of time and method. It was not, however, till 1822 that Britain recognised the flags of South American vessels, an act which constituted recognition *de facto*; not till late in 1823 that she appointed consuls and commissioners of enquiry to the new Spanish American states; and not till 1825 that, by the negotiation of commercial treaties, she accorded recognition *de jure* to Mexico, Colombia and the United Provinces of the Río de la Plata.

The United States had taken earlier action, sending out commissioners to South America in 1817, signing a treaty with Spain for the cession of the Floridas in 1819, and recognising Colombia and Mexico in 1822 and Buenos Aires and Chile in 1823. John Quincy Adams, the greatest of American secretaries of state, would have been prepared, though reluctantly, to go hand in hand with England in a common policy of recognition before the Florida treaty had been signed, but Castlereagh at this time had other views; and when in 1823, after a French army had restored despotism in Spain, Canning sought the co-operation of the United States in a joint declaration of policy, a warning to Europe and France, it was Adams's turn to hold back. Adams believed, as he told the British minister, that the idea of any 'active and substantial interposition' by Europe in Spanish America was 'too absurd to be entertained'.[2] He believed also, as he told the cabinet, that it was 'more candid as well as more dignified' for the United States to avow its principles 'explicitly' than to 'come in as a cock-boat in the wake of the British man-of-war'.[3]

In 1823, therefore, the United States acted alone. President Monroe's famous message to Congress on 2 December[4] was partly a gesture of sympathy with the young republics to the south; it was designed partly in the interests of the security of the United States, and partly also to enhance the political prestige of the United States in the western hemisphere, at the expense both of Europe and of England. There could have been no clearer demonstration of the clash of interests, within the framework of a common purpose, between the two Anglo-Saxon powers. Britain and the United States were each opposed to European intervention in Spanish America, though the danger of such intervention was always remote. Each was throughout determined to uphold the right to trade freely with the Spanish American area, and, except for the duplication, or near-duplication, in Brazil of the special privileges which Britain had enjoyed in Portugal, neither of them sought

---

[1] See his circular memorandum of 20 August 1817. *Ibid.*, vol. I, p. 14; vol. II, pp. 352–8.
[2] Bradford Perkins, ed., 'The Suppressed Dispatch of H. U. Addington, Washington, 3 November, 1823', *Hispanic American Historical Review*, xxxvII (1957), p. 485.
[3] Dexter Perkins, *The Monroe Doctrine, 1823–26* (Cambridge, Mass., 1927), p. 74.
[4] See Chapter xxII, p. 591, and Chapter xxv, p. 682.

exclusive commercial advantages for itself. But the rivalry between them was only thinly veiled. Castlereagh would have been glad to see Bourbon princes at the head of the new Spanish American states. Canning regarded the preservation of the principle of monarchy in Brazil as a cardinal point in his grand design to link Latin America to Europe (p. 632, above). But to these ideas the United States was ineradicably opposed. She wished to see an American system and an American policy predominate. Each country, moreover, feared the territorial ambitions of the other. On the Spanish borderlands the expansion of the United States did indeed contribute to the collapse of Spanish rule, and Canning and Adams each suspected, though with little justification, the other's designs on Cuba. Finally, to political rivalry there was added also commercial hostility.

But the Monroe Doctrine was important not for what it did but for what it became, and Canning, for his part, was quick to undermine any temporary advantage that the United States had gained. The memorandum of his conversations in October 1823 with Prince Jules de Polignac, the French Ambassador in London—conversations in which Polignac abjured, on behalf of France, any design of interfering by force of arms in Spanish America—was widely used to show 'how early and how anxiously' Britain had 'declared against any project of bringing back the late Spanish colonies under the dominion of the mother country by foreign aid';[1] and to this riposte were added the commercial treaties of 1825—treaties, which, given the great disparity in power between Britain and the United States, inevitably meant more to the infant Spanish American republics than did recognition by the United States. In Europe also their effect was decisive. The three Eastern Powers indeed protested, but principally as a matter of form, and France as well as Britain now tried to induce Spain to come to terms with the new states. France herself recognised them in 1830. The Papacy did so in 1835. It was not, however, till 1836 that Spain began the process of recognising her former colonies and not till 1895 that she completed it.

[1] Planta to Woodbine Parish, 30 December 1823. P.R.O. F.O. 118/1.

CHAPTER XXIV

THE FINAL COALITION AND THE CONGRESS OF VIENNA, 1813–15

As Napoleon's fortunes declined, those of his enemies rose; and a coalition, destined to be finally victorious, began to emerge in the chaotic winter of 1812–13. While remnants of the *Grande Armée* stumbled westward out of Russia, Tsar Alexander I decided to pursue Napoleon beyond Russian soil and out across Europe, seeking allies as Russian arms advanced. Prussia became the first by the Treaty of Kalisch of February 1813, which provided for obvious war needs, and promised to restore Prussia to her former proportions. Austria was slower in responding to Russian advances, but Great Britain signed treaties of alliance and subsidy with both Prussia and Russia at Reichenbach in June. Following a fruitless armistice and a singularly barren 'peace' conference at Prague they resumed the struggle against Napoleon in August, this time in the Germanies and with Austria finally in the coalition. After several secondary engagements, the battle of Leipzig, 16–18 October 1813, demonstrated the impressive power of the coalition by smashing Napoleon's position in Central Europe. His last German allies deserted him, and his army of nearly 200,000 was utterly routed, two-thirds of it killed, wounded, sick or captured. Before the end of the year the French had been confined to territory west of the Rhine for the first time since their eruption in 1805.

The autumn of 1813, so successful in allied military affairs, was a singularly frustrating period for Britain's foreign secretary, Lord Castlereagh. Although his country had been constantly and actively in opposition to Napoleon for years, although she had driven the enemy from Spain, rendered his fleet useless and financed the coalition, scant attention was paid to her counsels by remote allies preoccupied with Napoleon in Central Europe. In addition, Castlereagh felt particularly thwarted when Aberdeen, ambassador to Vienna, joined Metternich in the 'Frankfurt Proposals' of November 1813, an attempt to negotiate an end to the war by offering Napoleon frontiers at the Alps, Pyrenees and Rhine. This last proposal clearly violated one of the canons of English foreign policy, and was something no British foreign secretary of sound mind could condone. Finding it clumsy to deal with inattentive allies through inadequate ambassadors, Castlereagh decided to go himself to the Continent.

His *Instructions*,[1] drawn by his own hand and approved by the

---

[1] C. K. Webster, *British Diplomacy, 1813–15* (1921), pp. 123–6; this book will henceforth be referred to as *B.D.*

Cabinet, form one of the major documents of the period of peace-making and furnish us with splendid insight into the structure of his plans. His primary aim, which was to prevent France from establishing a naval position on the Scheldt, 'especially at Antwerp', he proposed to achieve by uniting most of the Low Countries under Holland. To secure this vital point he was prepared to bargain over some of the islands England had seized during the war. He wanted also a consolidating alliance which would give sounder shape to the miscellaneous operations and agreements of the coalition. This alliance was 'not to terminate with the war', but to remain as a deterrent to 'an attack by France on the European dominions of any one of the contracting parties.' In the territorial settlement he wanted Prussia brought more to the west, and hoped for a re-establishment of Holland, Spain, Portugal, and Italy 'in security and independence', a restored Papacy and a strengthened Sardinia. His separate 'Memorandum on the Maritime Peace' of the same period called for the return of France to her old frontiers. It also called for the creation of a naval as well as a military balance of power, but here he spoke more in lip service to the equilibrist ideal; however much a balance helped her in military matters, it obviously threatened Britain's clear leadership in naval affairs. In all of these points it is evident that he drew heavily on the earlier, brilliant analysis of Pitt, whose disciple he had been and whose legacy was summarised in the 'Draft to Vorontzov' of 19 January 1805. Pitt had discussed this remarkable statement of policy with Castlereagh, and it is possible that the latter had even helped in its formulation.

As he now left a fog-bound London for a frost-bound continent, Castlereagh was a man of forty-five, a leader of courage and character rather than intellect, a person firmly in command of himself, steadfast, simple, and coldly aloof, combining an uncertain hold on the French language with a secure grasp of foreign policy. Early 1814 found him at headquarters, which had moved forward into eastern France. Here he was in almost daily communication with Tsar Alexander, Metternich, and Chancellor Hardenberg of Prussia. The latter two agreed with him on turning Antwerp over to Holland. He expounded to them his plan of bringing Prussia forward in western Germany and felt that he and Metternich were close to agreement on the desirability of restoring the Bourbons in France.

All this served as a helpful preliminary to negotiating with France at a conference which emerged from the largely useless Frankfurt Proposals. The conference convened at the picturesque and nearly-deserted village of Châtillon-sur-Seine in early February 1814, with the Allies determined to confine France to her frontiers of 1792. Napoleon was represented by Caulaincourt, his ever-loyal, much-exploited, former ambassador to Moscow. The conference was held without armistice and was subject to swift atmospheric changes as fortunes fluctuated during the military operations of February. Early in the month Napoleon had appeared hopelessly in trouble, having been recently deserted by his last ally, Murat, and having seen the Allies advance 250 miles in four weeks, overrun a third of France, thrust armies down the Marne and Seine toward Paris, and probe with Cossack patrols as far as Orleans; he had then snatched four victories in five days.

The Allies presented their terms for peace in a document known to us as the 'bases de Troyes', given to Caulaincourt on 17 February. In this, Castlereagh had been careful to see that the offer of the left bank of the Rhine was not repeated. Bonaparte might at this time have ended the war, had he been willing to accept the French frontiers of 1792, the re-birth of a balanced state system, and the loss of most of his titles. It was his last genuine chance to save his throne, but as the insecure head of a dynasty unsanctified by time he felt the ignominy of accepting a shrunken France, and allowed the offer to lapse.

In spite of the generally favourable stance of the coalition, its many disagreements were deepened by dismay over the French victories, by Alexander's unwillingness to co-operate at Châtillon, and by his bad relations with Metternich. To meet these difficulties and dissolve the bad temper, gloom and even panic at headquarters, Castlereagh brought forward his long-favoured plan for a consolidating alliance. His suggestion served admirably to re-unite the Allies and was swiftly adopted as the Treaty of Chaumont, signed 9 March and pre-dated 1 March 1814. The alliance established precise conditions for the conduct of the coalition, provided for 150,000 troops from each of the Four Powers, bound Britain to supply a subsidy of £5,000,000 for pursuit of the war, and confirmed through secret articles most of the prior agreements on the re-creation of the state system. The coalition, thus consolidated, accepted also the remarkable commitments of Articles 5–16 whereby the Four Powers agreed to defend each other against any future French attack by taking the field, each with 60,000 men (or, in the case of Great Britain, its financial equivalent), the Auxiliary Army to be under the orders of the power requiring help. Supporting arrangements were specified in some detail and the agreement was to last twenty years. The treaty embodied ideas which had been expounded by balance-of-power writers for a century but which had not previously been written into an international agreement in such practical fashion. It represented the emergence of a considerably more sophisticated form of balance-of-power statesmanship which was soon to be tested in the first years of peace.

With Napoleon's continued failure to accept the 'bases de Troyes', the congress of Châtillon disbanded on 19 March and the Allies, prodded by Alexander, undertook a direct march on Paris. They accepted the unusual risk of leaving Napoleon to their rear, but the strategy worked. A rather listless Paris fell on 30 March 1814, after Prussian and Russian troops had taken Montmartre, from whose slopes their cannon could command the city. The occupation of Paris quickly terminated the long-standing problem of the political succession in France. During the last months of the war five possible alternatives had emerged. Metternich had at various times indicated an interest in a regency under Marie-Louise for Napoleon's son, who was half-Habsburg; Metternich had also believed there would be advantages in retaining Napoleon himself on the throne, since the latter had disciplined the Revolution; Castlereagh had eagerly argued since January for a restoration of the Bourbons, provided they were sufficiently acceptable to the French; and Alexander had pressed intermittently for the accession of Bernadotte, ex-French marshal and prince-royal of Sweden, or even for a plebiscite by the French people.

From the point of view of the re-creation of a balance of power at the end of the war, the restoration of the Bourbons was easily the most desirable alternative. They had the advantage of legitimacy, their return would not give disproportionate influence to any one foreign sponsor, their conservative presence on the throne would tend to shut off the dangerous dynamism of France, and they could without loss of face accept the *anciennes limites*, since those were clearly their own former frontiers. Moreover, public support was evidenced in Bordeaux in March, and a group in Paris stood ready to establish a government on behalf of Louis XVIII. It seems reasonably clear that the major Allies were in agreement on the Bourbons several days before the occupation of Paris, a conclusion which is strongly suggested by the toast of diplomatists to the Bourbons during an exuberant gathering at Dijon on 28 March. Castlereagh, consequently, felt no need to hasten to Paris to assure the success of a policy to which he was deeply committed; both he and Metternich were content to trust the tsar to follow it.

In the city the moment belonged wholly to Alexander. He arrived on 31 March in the triumphal military entry and, hearing the rumour that the Elysée Palace was mined, took up residence in Talleyrand's town house on the Rue Saint-Florentin, conveniently located in the heart of the city. The tsar was now disposed to support, although rather reluctantly, the restoration of the Bourbons, particularly since he was in frequent contact with Talleyrand, the chief conspirator in the city urging their return. Talleyrand's role has often been misread as that of chief architect of the restoration, whereas he was merely an astute consolidator of an already adopted Allied policy. A man of infinite resource, his more demonstrable and positive contribution was to steer the provisional government through the first uncertain days—convening a rump senate on 1 April to approve immediate measures for gaining the confidence of the nation, with guarantees of civil liberties and assurances to officers, bondholders, and owners of property; seeing that he was himself made one of five members to carry on the administration and present a draft constitution; securing a Senate vote to absolve the nation from loyalty to Napoleon and a further vote on the proposed constitution. This put defined limits to the royal power, and it also made clear that neither could the *emigrés* recover their land nor could the church regain its former position. On 6 April the Senate summoned to the throne Louis-Stanislas-Xavier de France, an able man and a devout gastronome, who lay in his Buckinghamshire house of exile, suffering from one of history's most inopportune attacks of gout.

Meanwhile Napoleon waited restlessly at the royal château of Fontainebleau, making and discarding plans, treating repeatedly with Alexander in the first ten days of April, and hoping to salvage for his son a regency under the empress. Alexander was determined to illustrate by Christian forbearance the contrast between Napoleon's entry into Moscow and his own arrival in Paris, and offered to soften his enemy's fate by granting him a kingdom of his own. Napoleon's emissaries, frustrated in most of their demands, were quick to seize this opportunity, and bargained fiercely. They secured from the tsar the offer of Elba, a commitment which might have been averted if Castlereagh and Metternich had reached Paris earlier. A treaty of abdication was drawn up and signed. It embodied the Elba arrangement; a renunciation of the French throne by Napoleon for himself and his family, although he and the empress could retain their rank and titles; the granting to the empress of the Parma duchies; and an annual revenue of 2,000,000 fr. from France to Napoleon, with additional grants to other members of his family and to Josephine (who died several weeks later). In spite of the generosity of these terms, Napoleon, when confronted with defeat, abdication and loss of the throne for his son, resorted to a poison which he had carried since 1812 in a small packet around his neck. It merely made him miserably ill overnight. The next day, 13 April, he summoned sufficient resolve to ratify the Treaty of Fontainebleau. A week later he addressed the Imperial Guard in the court of honour before the château, and departed for the south escorted by foreign officers and wearing at different times a Russian cloak, a white cockade, and an Austrian uniform—to avoid the insults and attacks of former subjects. He had never suffered from romantic impulses to die sword in hand at the head of his troops; and Sir Walter Scott, accustomed for years to think the diabolical worst of Napoleon, found him a disappointing Devil.

With Napoleon out of the way and the Bourbon restoration well begun, the allied statesmen were able to begin the negotiation of peace terms with France. Their hope was to settle the terms before turning to the myriad, non-French problems awaiting action. Through exchanges which appear to have been amicable, terms were soon settled with Talleyrand and signed on 30 May in the treaty known to us as the First Peace of Paris. This rightly famous document contained a preamble and thirty-three regular articles with certain additional, separate and secret terms. It returned France generally to the frontiers of 1 January 1792. Actually numerous adjustments were made which included: the loss of two smallish areas; the addition to France of over a dozen pre-revolutionary 'insulated territories' (the largest of these enclaves being Avignon and its environs); and six separate frontier gains, including a large one straddling the Meuse Valley and another large one lying in the beautiful mountain and lake area just south of Geneva. (The frontier gains did not survive French behaviour in 1815.) The treaty also secured French agreement to free navigation of the Rhine, the enlargement of Holland, the confederating of German states, independence for Switzerland, the handing over of Italian territories to Austria, and the retention of Malta by Great Britain. Plenipotentiaries were to be sent to Vienna within two months to participate in the general European peace congress. The terms were generally those of the 'bases de Troyes' at the Congress of Châtillon, which were here written into international law. By secret articles, France agreed to submit to Allied decisions in the redistribution of territory about to be undertaken at Vienna. Free navigation was to obtain on the Scheldt, most of the former Austrian Netherlands was to pass under the control of Holland, and left bank areas of the Rhine were to be divided among Holland, Prussia and certain German states. In this way a buffer area of formidable dimensions was planned on France's eastern frontier.

With this First Peace of Paris the allies completed the initial stage of the arduous journey toward a restored and balanced state system. Within three months they had bound themselves by the Treaty of Chaumont, occupied Napoleon's capital, sent him to his island kingdom, restored the Bourbons, and written for France a peace treaty free of indemnities, occupation and humiliation—a peace which Talleyrand himself described as showing unique consideration. All in all, it was a brilliant performance, marred importantly only by the Elba blunder; even this had its uses in smoothing the way to abdication and thereby diminishing the threat of civil war in France.

Early in June most of the principal statesmen and sovereigns adjourned to London to celebrate as guests of the British Government the return of peace. A hero's welcome awaited them, especially Tsar Alexander and Field Marshal von Blücher. The Russian leader immensely popular at first but somewhat unnerved by the lack of police protection, soon exhausted his welcome by numerous *gaucheries*, which were astonishing in a person of his gentleness and sensitivity, and which cost him the sympathy of the government. His indiscretions were exceeded only by those of the Grand Duchess Catherine, his sister, who had preceded him to London and caused general dismay by her headstrong ill manners and by meddling with the marriage plans for Princess Charlotte, whose engagement to William of Orange had recently been arranged. For the celebrities so much time went into festivities that little business of the coalition was accomplished or even attempted. On 14 June the Four Powers did agree to transfer the provisional control of Belgian areas to the House of Orange, as recently agreed in Paris. They renewed Chaumont, altering the troop commitments of each to 75,000, and decided they must postpone the assembly in Vienna to September, since Alexander insisted on returning to Russia first.

The most impressive accomplishment of the summer was Castlereagh's negotiated settlement of Anglo-Dutch problems with Hendrik Fagel. They agreed that Britain should retain areas in Guiana seized during the war; that Britain would pay Sweden £1,000,000 for Guadeloupe, which had been promised to Sweden in 1813 but had reverted to France in the First Peace of Paris; that Britain would assume one-half (£3,000,000) of the Dutch debt to Russia; and that Britain would pay Holland £2,000,000 for Cape Colony, also taken by Britain during the war and now to remain in British hands. The Dutch agreed to spend this last sum on barrier fortifications against France. Final details of the frontiers of the new Netherlands were left for the Congress of Vienna.

One may well be amazed at the diplomatic posture of Britain at this point. Her foreign secretary had already secured, months before the opening of the general peace conference at Vienna, the points which he held to be vital to his country's interests—the consolidating alliance at Chaumont which carried over into the post-war period, the return of the Bourbons to France, the placing of Antwerp and surrounding Belgian lands under the friendly House of Orange, appropriate territorial compensation overseas for Britain's share in the victory, the recent financial settlement with Holland, and the consensus on the re-creation of a balanced state system. Castlereagh surely had excellent reasons for confidence as he prepared for the peace conference.

He was lucky to have done so well, for the scene around him bristled with problems. For years French armies had devastated Europe. Behind the glamour of conquest had lain the awful commonplace of pillaged farms, desecrated churches, and hospitals stinking with gangrene. In 1814, the time had come for France itself to receive the same treatment as nearly three-quarters of a million enemy troops crossed onto her soil. In front of them fragments of dissolving French armies plucked their own countryside more severely, according to some observers, than the invaders. Of the latter, the Spaniards, remembering the brutal French occupation, were most ferocious, but were soon dispatched homeward. There remained the Prussian regulars to loot towns and châteaux while the Cossack irregulars, brandishing lances and mounted on dirty ponies, spread terror through the countryside. A miscellany of soldiers, deserters, and released prisoners of war limped from village to village, begging their way homeward. Contributing further to the dislocation were the stagnation of trade and industry, and the loss of merchant shipping.

There were also myriad political uncertainties as Europe waited for its statesmen to revive the state system, determine the size, shape and frontiers of its individual states, establish appropriate regimes for European waterways, create conditions which would favour the re-building of European economic life, set up a sound constitution for a newly confederated Germany, define the relationship of Swiss Cantons to each other and to the rest of Europe, eradicate the slave trade, deal with the special problems of the Pope and the Sultan, and establish a system to protect Europe against the familiar French threat and the new Russian menace. Of less importance, but very vexing, was the problem of resolving the perennial quarrels over diplomatic precedence.

To deal with these accumulated difficulties, September produced a general gathering of the diplomatic clans. To Vienna as guests of Francis I of Austria came King Frederick I of Württemberg, Elector William of Hesse, the Hereditary Grand Duke George of Hesse-Darmstadt, King Maximilian I Joseph of Bavaria, King Frederick VI of Denmark and Karl August, Duke of Weimar and friend of Goethe. The King of Prussia, present himself, was accompanied by his white-haired chancellor, Prince Hardenberg, assisted by the scholarly Humboldt, and a group of experts, among them the prominent statistician, Hoffmann. Alexander I of Russia, taking residence in a splendid apartment in the Hofburg, was supported by the most international group of advisers at the Congress—the Russian Razumovski; Nesselrode, his foreign minister of German extraction; Stein, distinguished reformer and exile from Prussian service; Czartoryski of Poland; and Pozzo di Borgo, Corsican enemy of Bonaparte. It was clear, despite the presence of these men, that the tsar intended to handle many important matters himself.

Louis XVIII did not venture to Vienna. Talleyrand headed the French delegation, settling himself comfortably in the Kaunitz Palace on the Johannesgasse, where his niece, the young and beautiful Comtesse de Périgord, presided as hostess over a household soon renowned for its elegant cuisine. Talleyrand was assisted principally by the Duc de

646

Dalberg, an experienced career official now serving as second pleni-potentiary, and the Comte de La Besnardière, an intelligent, industrious figure who had assisted Caulaincourt at Châtillon. They were supported by a large, fashionable staff. Castlereagh took with him his three principal European ambassadors: Stewart, his half-brother, an eccentric and a fool, to whom he was nevertheless deeply attached; Cathcart, friend of Alexander and ambassador to St Petersburg; and Clancarty, a hard-working official who had been an effective ambassador to the Hague, was devoted to the foreign secretary, and served as his principal assistant. Castlereagh also hired his own embassy staff as insurance against the Austrian spy system, at that time the most efficient in Europe. Metternich, as head of the Austrian delegation, was assisted by von Wessenberg, another diligent career official, by a regular group of assistants and specialists, and particularly by Friedrich von Gentz, a most interesting intellectual and publicist, who served both as secretary to Metternich and as an informal Secretary General of the Congress. Prominent among the lesser statesmen were Wrede, chief diplomatist for Bavaria; Cardinal Consalvi, secretary of state for the Pope; and Münster, able and experienced representative of Hanover.

The Congress served, among other things, as a dazzling festival, celebrating the attempt by aristocracy and royalty to return to the remembered magnificence of the eighteenth century. As such it attracted to Vienna a medley of princes, aristocrats, tourists, beggars, spies and pickpockets. All came to this most musical of European capitals where Haydn and Mozart were not long dead, and Beethoven much alive. The conscientious, conservative and rather ordinary Emperor of Austria, Francis the First, was an extraordinarily generous host, although the Austrian treasury was mightily shaken by the experience. The Festival Committee of the court arranged for its multitude of guests a rich programme of balls, sleighing and skating parties, hunts, gala performances, horse-shows and concerts; and there were many big dinner parties. While much business was, perforce, carried on at these social affairs, the net result was to give the Congress a reputation for frivolity and irresponsibility.

Castlereagh arrived in Vienna on 13 September, to be followed within a few days by the other principal ministers. By the 22nd the four chief spokesmen had quietly determined in their preliminary meetings 'that the conduct of the business must practically rest with the leading Powers'.[1] They wanted not only to confine power to themselves but to do it in such a way that they might avoid outraging the rest of the Congress and also evade summoning it into plenary session. These narrow intentions, slightly broadened by adroit and dramatic objections from Talleyrand and others, produced the simplest organisation of the

---

[1] *B.D.*, p. 193.

Congress imaginable. The Four (later Five) retained control of territorial questions and remained the nerve centre of the conference. Since the First Peace of Paris had summoned the Congress, its signatories (the Four plus Portugal, Spain, Sweden and France) were held to constitute a Committee of Eight, which met numerous times and kept a formal protocol of its proceedings. In late October the Eight established a committee to receive credentials. The formal structure of the Congress was also modestly elaborated with the creation of committees on Swiss affairs, Italian affairs, rivers, precedence, slave trade, and statistics. A committee on the German constitution grew up, but was never an official part of the Congress structure. Plenary sessions were avoided, and Gentz was correct in his cynical saying that the Congress never met officially until the signing of the *Acte finale.*

Diplomatic fireworks did not start until the Russians, who had long remained secretive concerning their specific aims, began to reveal their plan, drafted in August and dominated by the principle of compensations for Russia, Prussia, and Austria. It stood against a unified Germany; gave most of the Duchy of Warsaw to Russia; Posen, Kulm and Saxony to Prussia; and to Austria, parts of south Germany, north Italy, and Illyrian Provinces and Dalmatia. These proposed terms lay at the centre of the biggest and bitterest fight at the Congress, the struggle over the disposal of Poland and Saxony. Although not adjacent, these two territories were tightly linked, primarily because of the tsar's insistence on the basic Russian formula—that Poland should go to Russia and Saxony to Prussia. Since Russian troops occupied both areas, he had scarcely to whisper to be heard with frightening clarity. The emphasis within his formulation lay on the Russian gains, and this meant that early Congress activity was primarily concerned with the Polish half of the formula.

The background of the problem was complicated. As a consequence of the three Partitions of Poland the Russians had been poised after 1795 on the edge of old Catholic Poland which had formed the bulk of the Prussian and Austrian gains of '93 and '95. Then Napoleon, after his victories in 1805-6, had taken this region to create the new Duchy of Warsaw, his satellite outpost in Eastern Europe. The area was especially significant to Poles, because it lay at the geographical heart of Polish culture; here Copernicus had lived, here were Cracow and Warsaw, the great cathedrals and the best land; here in Cracow Poland's kings had been crowned and buried. Although obviously attractive to the Russians, the Duchy territory represented for them a new advance into an area of rich culture. Its retention by Russia and the concomitant denial to Prussia and Austria of their former Polish lands would mean, moreover, that these powers would have to seek adequate compensation elsewhere.

Alexander himself was undoubtedly one of the most puzzling, unpredictable and interesting leaders of his day. Brought up a French sceptic, he had swung strongly toward a deep Christian commitment; a sensitive idealist, he resented and was often unable to cope with the harsh decisions he had to make; a moralist, he was plagued by the awareness of a tacit participation in the murder of his father. He wavered between the cold mechanics of the balance of power, urging proportions appropriate for maintaining the general equilibrium, and flights of idealism, distrusted by the others, in which he spoke of his moral duty to minister to the happiness of the Poles. They were to enjoy a semblance of national existence in a separate Polish kingdom linked with Russia.

To Metternich this type of man was alien, and his fuzzy and emotional policies were anathema. The Austrian minister saw the ideal of nationalism arising from the French Revolution as the greatest menace of that era to the house of Habsburg with its rambling structure of miscellaneous nationalities. A thoroughgoing balance-of-power statesman, content to operate within the tight mechanical assumptions and practices of that system, he supported Castlereagh's general ideas: the enlargement of Holland by the addition to it of the former Austrian Netherlands, the accompanying abandonment by Austria of her traditional defence of the Rhine in favour of Prussia filling the vacuum, and the confederation of Germany under a conservative Austrian presidency. He sought to reconstitute Austrian power, particularly in Dalmatia, the Tyrol, and the Italian lands, and to prevent a preponderating westward expansion of the new Russian menace. To check the latter, he hoped both Prussia and Austria could regain their Polish lands. When confronted with the Russian design, however, Metternich knew that to cede the Duchy lands to Russia would bring the Russian frontier within 175 miles of Vienna. If at the same time Saxony were to be incorporated into Prussia, the latter would add 200 miles to her existing 250 miles of common Austro-Prussian frontier. The Russo-Prussian bloc, already disturbing for Austria, would be positively menacing to her under these new circumstances; and Metternich tended to simplify his policy on this matter into a strategic axiom of risking one-half but not both halves of the Russian formula: if Russia were to secure the Duchy, Prussia could not then have Saxony; or conversely, if Prussia received Saxony, Russia could not have the Duchy.

There was a period during the autumn when it might have been possible to adopt the latter plan and block Russia on the Duchy, but much depended on Castlereagh. Freed by the First Peace of Paris from seeking specific British objectives, he now sought a just equilibrium by working out the barrier system along France's eastern frontier, by sufficiently strengthening central Europe to enable it to resist future encroachment from either east or west, and by appropriately rewarding the major powers for their victory over Napoleon. In a remarkable letter to Wellington on 25 October 1814,[1] he epitomised his reasoning in this way:

Two alternatives alone presented themselves for consideration—a union of the two great German Powers, supported by Great Britain, and thus combining the minor States of Germany, together with Holland, in an intermediary system between Russia and France—or a union of Austria, France, and the Southern States against the Northern Powers, with Russia and Prussia in close alliance.

He strongly favoured the first alternative, although this plan was obviously weakened by the latent rivalry of the two German powers on whose co-operation it depended. He felt that Russian retention of Poland smacked of 'an attempt to revive the system we had all united to destroy, namely one colossal military Power holding two other powerful States in a species of dependence and subjection'.[2] While he supported the ideal of reviving an independent Poland, he thought it unlikely of realisation, and really desired a re-partitioned Duchy whereby Prussia and Austria would regain their former lands and the Russian frontier remain comfortably remote. To secure this generally anti-Russian position, he was prepared to sacrifice Saxony, if need be, to the larger need of checking Russia.

From their earliest meeting in mid-September it was evident that Castlereagh would oppose the tsar's plans for the Duchy. Their arguments are detailed in letters and memoranda which they exchanged in October and November, the British secretary trying to hold Alexander to his 1813 agreement in the Treaty of Reichenbach to re-partition the Duchy, and the tsar arguing both that the treaty was no longer binding and that the equilibrium could be preserved by the Russian plan. With Alexander acting as his own first minister, Castlereagh was in the awkward position of a commoner doing battle with royalty. He was not unpractised in this art, having had frank and extensive exchanges with the tsar at headquarters in the previous winter, and their meetings now were a blood-tingling supplement to the daily routine of the Congress. Although both Castlereagh and Metternich opposed Alexander over the disposal of the Duchy, their weight was easily offset by the solid fact of its occupation by Russia. This circumstance enhanced the importance of Hardenberg of Prussia whose additional weight might well be decisive one way or the other. He had come to Vienna agreeing with Castlereagh's programme to create a series of barriers against future French aggression, prominent among them being the secure establishment of Prussia on the Rhine. He wanted a confederated Germany under dual Austro-Prussian leadership, a partial return of Polish areas to Austria and Prussia, gains for Russia in the Duchy, and

[1] *B.D.*, p. 218. [2] *B.D.*, p. 200.

heavy gains for Prussia in central and west Germany, plus all of Saxony. He was naturally committed to Prussian aggrandisement, because Prussia had suffered maximum humiliation at the hands of Napoleon, but he was not inflexibly bound to any of these areas in accomplishing it. Restoration might involve a return to her former domains, or, depending largely on the extent to which this was not done, might take the form of new lands. It is surprising that Hardenberg should not have felt more strongly about the emphasis, for this was an important crossroads in German history. If restoration took place in Polish territory, the Prussian gaze would fall on alien lands and her policy would tend to bring her into conflict with Russia; if restoration and reward lay primarily inside Germany, her future would be tied more tightly to her own culture and her policy involve her in conflict with Austria.

Hardenberg and Metternich had previously considered the possibility of Metternich supporting the cession of Saxony to Prussia, if the latter would help frustrate Russian designs on Poland. This possibility conformed to the Austrian axiom, and was finally given substance at Vienna when Hardenberg secretly wrote to Metternich in October, promising opposition to the tsar in return for a firm offer of Saxony. Metternich and Castlereagh, although deeply suspicious of the promise, decided to accept it, and the former wrote to Hardenberg to that effect on 22 October. In this letter, described by Gentz as one which gave Metternich 'more grief in three months than he has had in all his life',[1] he made Austrian support for the transfer of Saxony to Prussia conditional upon successful opposition to Russian plans in Poland.

To Castlereagh this marked a notable step toward the realisation of his preferred plan of a strong centre, based on the co-operation of Austria and Prussia. Haste was necessary, because of the impending departure of Alexander on a trip to Hungary, and the three 'conspirators' met on 24 October to discuss their position and draft a joint memorandum proposing the Vistula as the Russian frontier. The tsar, when confronted with the united opposition of the three, erupted in anger, fulminating against both Hardenberg and Metternich before their monarchs. His rage did not shake Francis, but it sufficiently impressed the melancholy and subservient Frederick William to upset the combination. The joint activity of the three powers was effectively dissolved, although Hardenberg was not until 5 November given specific orders by his monarch to withdraw from it. Castlereagh had made an important mistake in allowing the joint opposition to be revealed in his absence, and the tsar carried the day. For several more weeks Castlereagh and Metternich continued to concentrate on the

[1] 'The Vienna Congress', in Prince Richard Metternich, ed., *Memoirs of Prince Metternich, 1773–1815* (London, 1881), vol. II, p. 570.

Polish half of the Russian formula. However, with no further reason for them to hope for appropriate concessions from the tsar, they were compelled to turn to the other half of the formula and block the cession of Saxony to Prussia, even though they had conditionally promised it to Hardenberg in October. There was a general accompanying shift of interest from Poland to Saxony.

The Saxon areas which now came under furious debate were considered to lie at the disposal of the Congress because of Saxony's support of Napoleon and its ruler's tardy conversion to the coalition. This reason made scant sense; so many princes on so many occasions had found it expedient to support Napoleon, that in Talleyrand's famous phrase, it was no more than 'a question of date'. The territory in dispute formed a rough rectangle with a ragged projection flying west toward the Rhine. It was bisected by the Elbe, lay between Brandenburg and Bohemia, and was bordered by Prussian power on virtually its entire northern and eastern boundaries. A relatively prosperous state, it had good wheat land and lush pasturage in the north, with ancient mines and picturesque mountains in the south. Of its cities Dresden was sufficiently far south to be beyond Prussian reach in the event of partition, but Leipzig lay in a more vulnerable location in west central Saxony.

The shift of interest was dramatised by Metternich's formal letter of 10 December 1814 to Hardenberg, refusing to yield Saxony to Prussia. In the resulting frenzy there were bitter recriminations, leading Castlereagh to reiterate to his government his recent warnings of the danger of war. A conflict of Britain with her recent allies, fantastic as it seemed, remained a hideous possibility until well after the Christmas season. Meanwhile a new phase of the Congress began when Hardenberg and Metternich secured Castlereagh's agreement to intervene on the Saxon problem. It came at a most unpromising and discouraging moment, and involved Castlereagh in matters in which he was clearly instructed by the Cabinet to avoid anything that would commit his country to war. He was himself the most European-minded member of it, more keenly aware than his colleagues of the value to them of a sound territorial balance of power on the continent, and was prepared to disregard their official instruction at this critical point in the negotiations. One of the nagging difficulties of the autumn had been the persistent disagreement among the negotiators over the statistical aspects of matters under discussion. Castlereagh proposed to create a separate statistical committee which could, with the help of Hoffmann, the distinguished Prussian statistician, work out an agreed set of figures for areas and the 'souls' that inhabited them. The committee had six sessions between 24 December and 19 January, and its labours were helpful.

For Talleyrand the moment of opportunity had finally arrived. He had come to Vienna in September as the head of the delegation of a defeated power, theoretically excluded from inner decisions by his own signature to the secret articles of the First Peace of Paris, and practically prevented from participation by the success of the leading powers in retaining the initiative themselves. Much has been made of his espousal of 'that sacred principle of legitimacy',[1] which has often, and erroneously, been described as the dominating theme of the peace conference. Talleyrand himself made the matter clear. He came fortified with the most explicit directive of any of the participating statesmen— in the form of the elaborate King's Instructions, conceived by himself and probably drafted by La Besnardière. In it he held legitimacy to be the best device for stabilising the separate entities of the state-system, but found that the creation of a sound balance of power must be the governing conception for Europe as a whole. According to the Instructions, he accepted the perpetual neutrality of Switzerland, he sought to limit Prussian gains in west Germany, to check her power within the new confederation, which itself should not be strong, and to prevent Prussia from regaining her pre-Tilsit power; he wanted to limit Austrian penetration of northern Italy and to contain Russian expansion, either by restoring an independent Poland or by returning to the status of the last partition. It was clearly a traditionally French, balance-of-power position, and equally clearly aimed at generally minimising compensations to the members of the coalition.

Talleyrand at Vienna showed extraordinary virtuosity. Refusing to accept as permanent France's exclusion from the inner meetings of the peace conference, he devoted most of his energy to working his way in. By offering leadership to the disgruntled representatives of the medium-sized and small powers, he was able to harass and embarrass the statesmen of the leading powers. In his eagerness to limit the compensation of Prussia, he stood for denying Saxony to her and thus, in October, annoyed Castlereagh, Hardenberg, and Metternich, who were then deep in their united enterprise. Castlereagh felt that Talleyrand should have co-operated in checking Russia before everything else; Talleyrand, often praised for his prediction of the defeat of Castlereagh and Metternich over Poland, might have prevented that defeat if he had stood with them against the tsar during October. This point, however, remains speculative, and whatever one thinks of his conduct in the autumn, his stock had risen noticeably by wintertime.

Early in December, when Castlereagh wrote to Liverpool particularly discouraging news about the possibility of war, he also suggested that Britain might best act with France in joint intervention or armed mediation. On the 12th Talleyrand sent Metternich a written overture for alliance, and, receiving encouragement, repeated it a week later. Shortly thereafter, the creation of the Statistical Committee served inadvertently

[1] Duc de Broglie, ed., *Memoirs of the Prince de Talleyrand* (London, 1891–2), vol. II, p. 203.

as the point of entry for Talleyrand into the inner councils of the Congress. Arriving unwanted at the first meeting, he successfully resisted expulsion by threatening to withdraw the French delegation from Vienna. Having crossed the threshold, he still had to penetrate the inner sanctum of the Four. The time for that, too, was now at hand.

Castlereagh, although aware of the *rapprochement* between Talleyrand and Metternich, had until Christmas been chary of giving them any explicit indication of his interest in an alliance. However, with the Four Powers still deadlocked over the disposition of Saxony, he finally unbent and indicated that he was now ready both to enter a treaty relationship and to urge the acceptance of Talleyrand within the inner group of ministers. When the Four Powers met on 29 December, Castlereagh and Metternich demanded that Talleyrand be included in the top ministerial council, thereby expanding the Four to Five. Their request evoked highly agitated responses from Hardenberg and Nesselrode, who naturally sought to evade any arrangement giving three votes to their two on the Saxon issue. The Prussian chancellor, usually discreet and usually able through his deafness to avoid hearing what he disliked, not only heard the proposal but was moved to declare in the meeting of 31 December that a refusal to cede Saxony to Prussia was tantamount to war. Castlereagh, stirred to his cold depths, asserted that it might be best to abandon the Congress. The old year went out in an atmosphere of anger, bitterness and frustration, and with former allies staring into the dark abyss of war.

On New Year's Day, when a sudden war move by Prussia was feared, Castlereagh took the decisive step of submitting a draft of an alliance to Metternich and Talleyrand. Their discussions were soon completed, and on 3 January 1815, they signed a Triple Alliance which promised mutual support against an attacker, specified 150,000 troops from France and Austria with an equivalent from Great Britain, and provided for inviting Bavaria, Hanover and the Netherlands to adhere, as they later did. On the same day Nesselrode and Hardenberg tried to secure a compromise on Saxony before France should be included in the Five Power arrangement. When no progress was discernible Hardenberg informed Castlereagh that he would himself call for the inclusion of the French plenipotentiary. The statesmen thus squeezed past the most dangerous period of the winter crisis over Saxony, and this most bitter phase of the Conference was over. Talleyrand reported ecstatically to Louis XVIII: 'Now, Sire, the coalition is dissolved, and for ever. Not only does France no longer stand alone in Europe, but . . . France is in concert with two of the greatest Powers, and three States of the second order'.[1]

---

[1] G. Pallain, ed., *The Correspondence of Prince Talleyrand and King Louis XVIII* (London, 1881), vol. I, p. 242.

It was now clear that compromise could be achieved, although the process of working it out proved to be very difficult. Hardenberg had, to be sure, indicated that an accommodation was possible, but he continued to claim all of Saxony for bargaining purposes. Metternich, now buoyed by the alluring prospect of blocking Prussia, assumed the opposite bargaining stance of refusing the Prussians any part of Saxony. It remained for a hard-pressed and hard-working Castlereagh to draw them toward a suitable compromise. He was considerably helped by the fact that the new western frontier of Poland had been virtually settled on 3 January, when Metternich had placed before the 'Conference of the Four Courts' the Austrian counter-project to the formal Russian proposals of 30 December. This document revealed Austria still to be in strong disagreement with Russia over Saxony, but in complete accord with her on the western boundary of Poland. Their agreement really determined the frontier which was written into the Final Act of the Congress in June. It had the effect of weakening Hardenberg's bargaining position on Saxony because the Russians, having secured their own chief aim, were now less eager to risk war over gains for the Prussian ally. Through use of this advantage Castlereagh secured the tsar's support for compromise on Saxony, and was then able to devote the remainder of January to modifying the intransigence of Metternich and Hardenberg.

From a median position Castlereagh and Talleyrand worked first on Metternich to reduce and confine the Austrian demands. Castlereagh found Francis I belligerent, but, helped by Münster, was able to make satisfactory headway. Metternich responded by placing before the Five Powers on 28 January a formal offer to Prussia of substantial areas of Saxony without Leipzig; and Castlereagh proceeded to confront the Prussians, especially on the latter point. Failing with Hardenberg, he went over the chancellor's head to Frederick William and had the most painful interview of all. Turning to the tsar for help, he secured for Prussia the good offer of Thorn, controlling the middle Vistula, plus surrounding territory. When the Prussians gave way on Leipzig, he hounded them to reduce their demands on the remainder of Saxony, persuaded Hanover to sweeten the prospect by granting moderate cessions to Prussia in central Germany, and then offered on his own a part of the new Netherlands. Hardenberg, after another unsuccessful try for Leipzig, finally settled on 6 February for slightly more than half of Saxony's land, without Leipzig, and for slightly less than half of Saxony's 'souls'. Metternich agreed at once, as did Talleyrand, who had long acted as self-styled champion of the Saxons. The Saxon crisis was over, except for the awkwardness of presenting the details of the partition to the king of that unhappy land, a task which was performed in March by Metternich, Talleyrand and Wellington.

The over-all Prussian gains comprised two other principal areas: the land in the west and that in Poland. The renewal of Prussian power in the Rhineland was substantial; it meant that Prussia came forward with appreciable strength, a matter of unusual significance. The Polish section, although only one-sixth of the Duchy and much less than Prussia's former possessions there, was by no means negligible. It was larger than the gains in Saxony and embraced a useful section of the Vistula, the entire Netze, and over half of the Warta. Together with a previous agreement by Alexander to return part of Poland to Austria, it amounted to a noteworthy reduction of the uncompromising Russian demands of the late autumn. Castlereagh had indeed made a strong return after his apparently severe defeat on Poland.

The solution of the Saxon question made possible numerous decisions which were contingent on it. Bavaria, long in disagreement with Austria over the return of certain areas which had been lost in 1805 and 1809, finally gave way and was compensated in Würzburg and part of the Palatinate. Mainz, coveted by both Bavaria and Prussia, became a confederation fortress under Hessian sovereignty. The former Electorate of Hanover, Britain's outpost in Europe and a recent victim of Napoleon, now emerged as a kingdom and received frontier increments, especially in the west between the Dutch frontier and the Duchy of Oldenburg. These gains gave possession of the lower Ems to Hanover, which already held strong positions on the Elbe and the Weser. England was in the remarkable position, through her sponsorship of the Netherlands, her re-instatement in Hanover and her retention of Heligoland, of having some control over all rivers between France and Denmark.

The evolution of an agreement on the new Germanic Confederation proved particularly slow and difficult. In repeated agreements in the spring of 1814, a confederation had been declared acceptable to the major powers. This conception had been challenged by those patriots, among them Stein, who sought a German Empire, but their dream had faded by the time the Congress opened. At Vienna one of the first decisions of the leading powers had been to leave the drafting of a new German constitution to the Germans themselves. In meetings in October and November 1814, the self-appointed German committee of Austria, Prussia, Bavaria, Württemberg and Hanover discussed various constitutional drafts, and soon reached a stalemate, just as the Four Powers did over the Saxon problem. Disagreement prevailed and for five months meetings were suspended. Upon resumption in the spring of 1815, an Austrian draft initiated progress toward compromise, and agreement—complete in most but not all details—was finally reached early in June. The new Germanic Confederation of thirty-four princes and four free cities would have a Diet under Austrian presidency, with representatives from the member states, and a voting differential. The constitution included stipulations against separate negotiations of the princes in time of war and against their concluding alliances inimical to the good of all. There were no federal arrangements, no common currency or effective executive, and no safeguards of popular liberties. While it created only a weak union, it did bring some order to the political chaos of Germany, and partly realised Castlereagh's dream of the strong centre by drawing both Prussia and Austria into the same structure.

The Netherlands frontier, which had been generally determined in the previous summer and tinkered with more recently, was now carefully completed. In addition to the Belgian provinces, the new kingdom secured Liège and the Duchy of Limburg. The king also received the Duchy of Luxembourg, although it was to remain outside the Netherlands, become a member of the Germanic Confederation, and accommodate a Prussian garrison in the city of Luxembourg itself.

Another Congress stalemate involved Prussia and the Scandinavian powers and derived from the failure of Bernadotte to carry out the financial terms of the Treaty of Kiel of the previous year, by which he was bound to indemnify Denmark for her loss of Norway to Sweden. Britain's spring payment in 1815 to Sweden for Guadeloupe (which reverted to France) broke the impasse and put in motion a triangle of related transfers by which Prussia gave Lauenburg to Denmark, Denmark yielded Norway to Sweden, and Sweden released her bit of Pomerania to Prussia. The changes were particularly distasteful to the Norwegians and particularly important for Sweden. Indeed, for the latter, 1814–15 witnessed the disappearance of the last remnant of her empire on the continent with a consequent elimination of a distracting involvement, and an end to her participation in European wars and alliances.

Metternich largely determined the Italian settlement, a complex affair, stalemated for months and unsolved until May 1815. The central, complicating fact was the alliance of January 1814, between Austria and Joachim Murat, King of Naples, a rash and successful cavalry leader, and husband of Napoleon's youngest sister. Murat had bartered his defection to the coalition for Austrian support of his throne. This daring manoeuvre worked successfully for Murat in 1814, but Metternich, thus committed, found himself entangled with Talleyrand, who sought to oust Murat and restore the legitimate Spanish Bourbon monarch. Metternich resorted to evasions and postponements. Even when pressure at the Congress drove Great Britain, France, and Austria together, and made agreement between the latter two particularly desirable, Metternich contrived further delays. The problem remained until Murat himself solved it during the excitement of the Hundred Days by his further gamble on switching back to

Napoleon and attempting to raise Italy against Austria. We now know that he had no obvious alternative, since Metternich and Castlereagh had already secretly agreed to unseat him. In any event he soon failed, fled to France, later returning to south Italy where he was caught and shot. The Hundred Days considerably hastened the achievement of an Italian settlement by reducing the complicated relations between Murat and Austria to simple hostility, as well as by undercutting French opposition to Austrian policy in the Italian peninsula—thus apparently vindicating Metternich's policy and suggesting how triumphant procrastination can be.

The Italian impasse suddenly yielded; Naples went to the Bourbons, borders of the remaining areas were quickly designated, and a peninsular state-system of eight units was established, four going under the Habsburgs. The Austrian Emperor directly ruled the new Lombardo-Venetian Kingdom. His brother returned to the Grand Duchy of Tuscany; his daughter received the Parma Duchies; and his grandson, the Duchy of Modena. Papal authority was re-established in central Italy, and the strengthened Kingdom of Sardinia in the north-west recovered the island itself, Piedmont, Savoy and Nice, with the addition of Liguria (Genoa). Lucca went to a Parma Bourbon (Chapter XV, pp. 429, 438).

The complex Swiss problems of frontier, constitution and foreign relationship, were generally resolved by March in the special committee which had been created for that purpose. The settlement provided for a loose union among twenty-two cantons and for adjusted frontiers. The powers promised to guarantee Swiss neutrality, a sound and statesmanlike proposal which the Swiss had initiated and now formally enacted in November.

As agreements were reached they were often signed separately with the understanding that they would later be assembled in one comprehensive treaty. The ultimate compilation of 121 articles, garnished with numerous annexes and protocols, was signed as the *Acte finale* by the assembled plenipotentiaries of the powers, great and small, on 9 June 1815. The ceremony was held in the vast Schönbrunn palace, which in that era presided over a country setting beyond the city limits of Vienna. In addition to the territorial arrangements, the treaty embraced a host of items, among them the titles of various German princes, indemnities of one to another, the levy of (or exemption from) transit dues on specified roads, the privileges of drovers and shepherds in areas which had changed hands, navigation rights on rivers traversing different states and the maintenance of towpaths for Europe's economically important rivermen. It also included a solution to the ancient vexations of diplomatic precedence, which were henceforth to be determined first by class (1. ambassadors, legates, and nuncios; 2. envoys and ministers; 3. *chargés d'affaires*) and then by length of assignment. By this simple arrangement European diplomatists gracefully escaped from painful and absurd difficulties.

Considerably less success attended the attempt to secure international action on the slave trade. Great Britain, after a century of riches for her slave merchants shuttling between West Africa and the New World, had recently prohibited the traffic herself, and now sought to suppress the entire trade, which, like that in opium (ironically expanding in that era largely through British initiative), could be dealt with effectively only through international agreement. By the failure to include any solid regulation in the First Peace of Paris, Castlereagh had left his party open to attack from Wilberforce and the powerful anti-slavery movement, with the further consequence that the foreign secretary was particularly eager at Vienna to secure an agreement of substance—motivated more, to be sure, by political pressures than by his own inner impulses. Although many of the powers of the first and second rank accepted the idea of practical regulation, France, Spain and Portugal did not. Castlereagh, by persistent badgering of the Latin delegates, secured a February declaration from the powers that the slave trade was 'repugnant to the principles of humanity and universal morality', and that they agreed in the 'wish of putting an end to a scourge which has so long desolated Africa, degraded Europe, and afflicted humanity'. Portugal accepted abolition north of the equator, but Castlereagh was unable to get more. Inadequate as this was, it did serve as a first step toward agreement which followed in the post-war period. The Hundred Days, oddly enough, soon helped the British cause, because Napoleon outlawed the trade for Frenchmen, and Louis XVIII could not avoid re-affirming his decision.

While the Congress of Vienna was jogging to a close, events of mighty consequence gripped the attention of Europeans. During the night of 6–7 March 1815, the news of Napoleon's escape from Elba arrived in Vienna. He had by that time landed at Antibes and started on the glamorous return which caused French troops, from Grenoble on, to rally once more to his standard. Within two weeks of his departure from Elba, he was installed at the Tuileries and speedily assembling a new government. Louis XVIII had ignominiously fled to Ghent.

In Vienna there was virtually spontaneous agreement that the return of Napoleon was incompatible with the peace of Europe, and on 13 March the eight signatories of the First Peace of Paris signed a joint statement declaring that Napoleon Bonaparte, having 'placed himself outside of civil and social relations, and . . . delivered himself to public hatred', was an outlaw. Plans were swiftly adopted to guard against a new French eruption: British and Hanoverian troops under Wellington were to defend the lower Rhine, Prussians to be in reserve there and hold the mid-Rhine, with Russians and Austrians to the south.

Confronted once again by the French threat, the statesmen at Vienna quickly resumed their familiar posture as partners in a coalition. On 25 March they signalised their return to the principles of Chaumont by agreeing to a document of nine articles in which they reaffirmed the First Peace of Paris and agreed that each of the Four Powers should supply 150,000 troops, that no separate peace could be made, and that the Treaty of Chaumont would continue in effect when the war emergency was over. Great Britain separately agreed to provide subsidies up to £5,000,000. Numerous smaller powers rallied to the coalition, which soon included Hanover, Bavaria, Sardinia, Portugal, Holland, Baden, Saxony and many others. Thus the coalition was re-formed and set in motion with a skill and speed unequalled in European history up to that time. Conditions were, to be sure, ideal for such efficiency: statesmen and soldiers were assembled in Vienna, armies lay at hand, subsidies were soon promised, and a common danger was dramatised by Bonaparte's return.

Napoleon, with his old enemies closing ranks, attempted to split the new coalition, particularly by sending to Alexander the French copy of the secret Treaty of 3 January 1815, which he found in the Tuileries. With the failure of this manoeuvre he turned to the pressing crisis which his return had created. He was all but diplomatically isolated, since only Murat of Naples had rallied to his cause. Moreover, Louis XVIII in one of his few popular moves had abolished conscription and left for Napoleon an army of probably not more than 200,000. The Emperor, swift in the use of emergency preparations and makeshifts, aided by the return of many of his former officers, and appeasing the now stronger liberal sentiment of France by promising a liberal constitution, made ready to attack the coalition. By attempting to deny his enemies time to draw together, he hoped to defeat them separately. His initial moves into the Netherlands gained him precious time which he then unaccountably wasted; Wellington, on assurances of support on his left from the Prussians, chose to stand at Mont St Jean; Napoleon's army on 18 June 1815, in the battle of Waterloo, narrowly failed to dislodge Wellington's and was then routed by the latter, assisted finally by the Prussians, who had been delayed by muddy roads and arrived almost fatally late. The tens of thousands of casualties, French, Prussian, Hanoverian, Dutch and British were a direct consequence of the tsar's blundering generosity in granting Elba to Napoleon.

The new Senate and Legislative Body in Paris defiantly put themselves in permanent session. Napoleon, having fled the battlefield, now considered establishing a tight dictatorship and ruthlessly purging his enemies, only to discard the idea and resign in favour of his son. He was aware that the latter would never have a real opportunity to mount the throne. Louis XVIII, urged on by Wellington and unhampered this time by gout, was back on French soil by 25 June, and four days later the first Prussian troops had appeared on the outskirts of Paris. Blücher, determined to offer the city the alternatives of assault or unconditional surrender, was softened by Wellington, who was inflexible in insisting on mild terms for the French. Capitulation was soon effected through the efforts of Fouché of the police and Davout of the army, both men playing key roles, along with Wellington, in the return of the Bourbons. The allies staged a second triumphal entry into Paris on 7 July, and the next day Louis XVIII was back in the Tuileries.

Napoleon, at Malmaison in late June, had very nearly been caught by the Prussians. Blücher would happily have shot him, but he dropped from Allied view for ten days. During this period he travelled to the west coast port of Rochefort, tried to arrange to escape to the United States on a French boat, found it hopeless in the face of west winds and the British blockade, and surrendered to Captain Maitland of the *Bellerophon*, declaring in his letter to the Prince Regent that he came 'like Themistocles, to throw ... [himself] upon the hospitality of the British people'.[1] He was conveyed to Plymouth, held on board ship while the curious crowded the harbour, and soon taken to his desolate destination on St Helena.

Since many statesmen interpreted the Hundred Days as evidence of the failure of the policy of moderation toward France in the First Peace of Paris, the old demands to weaken her by partition blossomed anew. Some changes evidently had to be made. In mid-July, the allies established a Committee of Four, which met repeatedly during the summer and autumn to formulate the new terms for France. Although the Four agreed on the aim of blunting French power, their summer meetings were saturated with disagreements as to the means. Hardenberg, responsive to pressures from the Prussian generals, represented one extreme by insisting that French power be diminished through the handing over of three historic chains of fortresses—built by Vauban—to Switzerland, the German states and the Netherlands, plus the cession of all of Savoy and Alsace-Lorraine. Castlereagh stuck to the line of moderation. He had wanted and seen achieved the defeat of Napoleon and the return of Louis XVIII. Now, in spite of dissident sentiment in the cabinet, he sought to prevent a vengeful peace. Liverpool, although not fanatic in favouring harshness, did urge on him the need to act against the war criminals. 'Forbearance manifested at the present moment can be considered in no other light than weakness, and not mercy. ... A severe example made of the conspirators who brought

[1] J. Holland Rose, *The Life of Napoleon I*, 6th edn. (London, 1913), vol. II, p. 520.

back Buonaparte could alone have any effect.'[1] Castlereagh disapproved, and merely went through the motions of carrying out his instructions, hoping that the war criminals would prudently absent themselves. He also disapproved of partition of France since it would humiliate and weaken the new government and render the country a less stable unit in the European equilibrium. He would consent to check French power by temporary devices, and hoped that a positive reliance on the principles of Chaumont would help to prevent future trouble. From Wellington he received solid and invaluable support for these policies.

Metternich stood somewhat closer to Castlereagh than to Hardenberg. He believed that the allies should insist on occupation, indemnity, and limited territorial cessions, with the intent of converting France from an offensive to a secure defensive power. Specifically, he felt that her first line of fortresses should either be destroyed or given to neighbouring powers. Castlereagh and Metternich discovered to their great relief that Alexander had returned to Paris in one of his most benevolent moods. With Russian interests not directly involved, the tsar favoured their policy of moderation over the harsh designs of his Prussian ally. He emphasised the unity of the coalition and wanted to renew Chaumont. He had increasingly turned toward religion since 1812, and been through a deeply moving religious experience in the spring of 1815, which made a strong impression on Russian policy throughout the year and which doubtless explains much of his gentleness in this period.

With Alexander, Castlereagh and Wellington in agreement and Metternich not far off, preponderance clearly lay with a policy of moderation. Hardenberg, although isolated, pressed his country's demands vigorously, and Castlereagh had such difficulty in getting Cabinet support that he finally sent his half-brother to London to demand the necessary backing. Hardenberg indicated on 28 August that he would moderate his position, and Alexander, eager to avert a humiliating setback for Prussia, said that he would support moderate territorial cessions from France. By early September the Committee of Four was in substantial agreement. The terms, which they presented to France on 20 September, were disconcertingly rejected by Talleyrand just before he was replaced, but his successor, the Duc de Richelieu, soon accepted a slightly altered version.

Following several weeks of final drafting, on 20 November 1815 the powers finally signed the documents comprising the Second Peace of Paris, with their guarantee of Swiss neutrality and a new Quadruple Alliance. France received, with some modification, the frontiers of 1790, failing to keep the considerably more generous lines of the First Peace of Paris. The most important change was the transfer to Prussia

[1] *B.D.*, pp. 345–6.

of the Saar, although its full economic importance was not yet discovered. The terms also provided for the destruction of the fortress of Huninguen, the occupation of France for three to five years by a force not to exceed 150,000 troops, and the payment of an indemnity of 700 million francs. Earlier, France had been required to surrender most of the art treasures which she had plundered from the rest of Europe.

In the new Quadruple Alliance the Allies agreed to maintain the Second Peace of Paris, to prevent the return of Napoleon, and to stand solidly behind the occupation forces, each signatory power agreeing to supply 60,000 additional troops, or more if necessary. Article VI, in conformity with the spirit of Chaumont, provided for periodic conferences of sovereigns or ministers 'to facilitate and to secure the execution of the present Treaty', to consult upon 'common interests', and to consider 'measures which ... shall be considered the most salutary for the repose and prosperity of Nations, and for the maintenance of the Peace of Europe'. Article VI established the legal basis for the diplomacy by conference of the post-war era, an interesting and noteworthy experiment in international administration. It represented an attempt, by Castlereagh particularly, to carry over into the post-war world some of the experience with coalitions of the leading powers, and it 'marked definitely the ascendancy of the Great Powers and the principle of the European Concert'.[1]

A very different device for shoring up the peace settlement appeared with the tsar's Treaty of the Holy Alliance, which he hoped his fellow monarchs would sign and by which they would make of themselves 'a true and indissoluble fraternity', swearing to base their conduct of foreign affairs on the 'precepts of ... Holy Religion, namely the precepts of Justice, Christian Charity, and Peace, which, far from being applicable only to private concerns, must have an immediate influence on the councils of Princes'. While the tsar ascribed the immediate origins of the Holy Alliance to a February conversation with Castlereagh, his elaboration of the idea owed much to his older interest in the New Testament and something to the influence of Mme de Krüdener, who helped him as a religious mentor in the summer of 1815. Deeply serious as Alexander doubtless was, Metternich and Castlereagh could only greet the project with cynicism. To Liverpool Castlereagh characterised it as 'this piece of sublime mysticism and nonsense'.[2] It was signed by Alexander's fellow sovereigns on 26 September 1815, through fear of his power, as a concession to his exalted mood, and after Metternich had managed to make significant textual changes; but it was not a serious act of statesmanship on their part, nor did it assume any importance in the diplomacy of 1815.

---

[1] Webster, *Congress of Vienna* (London, 1918), p. 143.
[2] *B.D.*, p. 383.

A glance at the territorial provisions of the Final Act of Vienna and the Second Peace of Paris reveals that they followed the twin principles of containment and reciprocal compensation—the former for France, and the latter for her enemies. An arc of containment, conforming markedly to some of the important recommendations of Pitt and Castlereagh, now extended along France's eastern frontier, its chief ingredients being somewhat new and experimental—the expanded Netherlands anchoring the north; the enlargement of Prussia's holdings in the west and the substitution of Prussian for Austrian defence of the Rhine; the strengthening of Bavaria, Baden and Württemberg; the international guarantee of a neutral Switzerland; and the enlarged kingdom of Sardinia to anchor the southern end. By way of Hanover, Britain could join Prussia in backing up the north, while Austria, through her north Italian holdings, could do the same for the south. Thus the territorial allocations provided substantial security against future disturbances of the balance of power by France.

While the frontiers of France herself returned almost exactly to those of 1790, new boundaries were common to her east: Sweden acquired Norway; Austria, extensive territory in Italy; and Russia, most of Poland (before the peace settlement of 1814–15 she had also secured Finland and Bessarabia). To Prussia went Swedish Pomerania and parts of Saxony, Poland and western Germany. Britain retained important overseas areas, secured the expansion of her Dutch client-state and saw Hanover enlarged. Many arrangements which had taken so long to evolve were disappointingly impermanent. Within fifteen years the enlarged Netherlands was breaking up, and the Bourbon Restoration had come to an end in France; two years later Nicholas I had revoked the Polish constitution; soon Hanover's tie with Great Britain was dropped, and the treaty status of Cracow, established at Vienna as a neutral Free City, overthrown. Between 1859 and 1871 both the Italian and German settlements collapsed, with the ejection of Austria from her compensations in Italy, the dissolution of the Germanic Confederation, Austria's concomitant loss of her presidency of the Confederation, and the ordering of the German atoms in a new system under Bismarck. French boundaries were enlarged as a result of arrangements between Napoleon III and Cavour, and later reduced by the German seizure of Alsace and Lorraine. In general, the terms of 1814–15 were modified sooner, oftener and more profoundly than were those in the treaties of Westphalia and Utrecht.

In contrast to these changes, a relatively permanent part of the 1814–15 settlement proved to be the east German frontier between Cracow and the Baltic, although subsequent changes occurred on each side of the line and the line itself did not survive 1914. The union of Norway and Sweden outlived the nineteenth century, as did the acquisition by Britain of Ceylon and Cape Colony. More permanent yet were: the French frontier between Metz and the Channel, although the east side of the line soon passed from Dutch to Belgian control; the arrangements concerning Switzerland, territorial and otherwise, which continue today; the agreement on diplomatic precedence, still operative although now more elaborate; and the retention by Britain of Malta.

The settlement as a whole, unfair in many respects, incomplete in numerous details, destined to be thus endlessly revised, was yet remarkably consistent with the ideal of re-establishing in Europe a balanced state system. Indeed, it represented the last great European peace settlement consciously based on the principles of the balance of power. These principles, soon to be discredited by nineteenth-century liberal criticism, had enjoyed widespread acceptance and application in the eighteenth century, to be followed by large-scale abuse during the generation from 1792 to 1814, and had only recently been restored to a position of honoured usefulness in European statecraft, as is evident in the major decisions of the peace-making: the Bourbon restoration, the moderation of the First Peace of Paris, the use of reciprocal compensation in the distribution of rewards at Vienna, Castlereagh's conception of the strong centre, Metternich's attitude toward joint Russo-Prussian gains, and the guarded moderation of the Second Peace of Paris. The repeated renewals of Chaumont, culminating in the Quadruple Alliance, underlined a concept which derived out of equilibrist experience and envisaged an improved method of preserving the balance of power. The period 1814–15 is indeed one of the best examples of Europe's classical balance of power in operation. Uncounted documents of the period utilise its terminology, acts of all description were justified in equilibrist terms, plans of all and sundry commonly embodied its concepts and aims.

The theory of equilibrium, although clearly dominating the peace settlement, did not pervade it to the exclusion of other conceptions. Legitimacy claimed much support, but even Talleyrand, its high priest at Vienna, regarded it as a subordinate ingredient of the more comprehensive theory of the balance of power. The principle of nationality, violent and disturbing offspring of the French Revolution, had its adherents, notably Stein in his German policies and Alexander in plans for Poland, but gained no significant victories beyond these. State-interest, one of the obvious motivations of powers at the Congress, was a persistent attraction for individual statesmen. Nevertheless, it was generally subordinated to the balance of power, because the exorbitant demands of individuals could be met by group resistance of the other leading statesmen, particularly since the fundamental fact in international relations of the period was the relatively equal power of five states, a condition where no one state could dominate the others.

One of the most interesting problems in interpreting 1814–15 is the evaluation of the relative importance of the leading participants. While earlier generations were content to award top honours to Metternich, it is now harder to argue that any individual dominated, although each of the leading statesmen had his moments of importance and made significant contributions. Alexander assumed responsibility for the direct march on Paris in 1814, joined in giving timely support to moderation in handling France and, by winning on Poland at the Congress of Vienna, moulded virtually the entire Congress settlement and also gave Russia her greatest westward extension of influence up to that time. Hardenberg secured, through fat compensations, the full return of Prussia to her former power, and saw her take over from Austria the responsibility of defending the western frontier of the Germanies. Metternich successfully frustrated the original Russian formula, was very important in preventing Prussia from gaining all of Saxony, and influenced other German decisions. His hand above others shaped the Italian settlement and the re-establishment there of Austrian power. Castlereagh was architect of the Treaty of Chaumont, more influential than any other both in restoring the Bourbons and securing a moderate peace for their new government, author (as Pitt's heir) of the arc of containment on France's eastern frontier, and more useful than any other individual in mediating between Prussia and Austria in the crisis over Saxony during the difficult winter diplomacy at Vienna. He was, in addition, author of the important Quadruple Alliance of 20 November 1815, which provided a really new departure for post-war diplomacy. He was vilified by some and misunderstood by many, but research in this century has demonstrated his genuine distinction.

Thus each, with the exception of Talleyrand, secured large territorial accessions for his country, and Talleyrand gave timely assistance in the restoration of the Bourbons, resourcefully worked his way into the inner deliberations of the Congress, and was to some degree responsible for salvaging part of Saxony. Whatever the verdict on their individual contributions, one should observe how they, in contrast to their heirs in 1919, viewed the continent as a unit and saw its problems as parts of an international whole. They were both a resourceful and a remarkable group of statesmen.

As a group they have occasionally been complimented for establishing a century of peace, and often been castigated for not accepting more bravely the new principle of nationalism. With regard to the former, one may say that, although there was no world war, the century was crowded with lesser, but important wars. Moreover, the absence of a general European war cannot reasonably be attributed to the arrangements made at Vienna and Paris in 1814–15, since many significant parts of those arrangements were soon changed. As to the second point, these statesmen, presiding over an era of transition, were not yet in a position to understand the new forces of democracy and nationalism. In Congress Poland, where the principle of nationalism was applied to a recognisable extent, the arrangements were soon overthrown.

These men had reasonably turned toward the more familiar principles of the system of balance of power. Within that conceptual framework, they performed a series of skilled operations, and made solid contributions in ending the Napoleonic tyranny, granting Europe a breathing spell and giving France sound frontiers. They also made a noteworthy advance in the creation of the system of diplomacy by conference. On the other hand, their experiments were often useless, soon discarded, or hazardous for the next generation. With the exception of Tsar Alexander, their minds did not lift above the orthodox, there was no stunning act of leadership, and no lasting, creative advance toward the future. As the unfolding century soon showed, Europe had been served only moderately well by these able and interesting men.

CHAPTER XXV

INTERNATIONAL RELATIONS, 1815–30

A<small>N</small> attempt has been made in Chapter I (pp. 7–11) to see how the general pattern of the European state system in 1830 differed from that of 1790. The shifting scenes of the war period are described in Chapter IX, and the negotiations leading to the settlement of 1815 in Chapter XXIV. Here it is intended to present in outline the main issues that were implicit in the situation created by that settlement or that came to a head in the years of relative tranquillity that followed it. Most of these issues are touched upon in other chapters concerning particular regions, but they need to be reviewed as elements in a developing total situation as it presented itself to sovereigns, chanceries and foreign ministers. Alexander I could not fix his gaze on Constantinople without remembering Spain and Germany; neither Metternich nor Canning could make a move about Latin America without keeping an eye on the Aegean. Moreover, certain general problems arise concerning the nature and conduct of international relations after 1815. At first, these are closely connected with the experiences, even with the personalities, of the statesmen who made the settlement; all of them, except for Talleyrand, survived in power for some years— Castlereagh and Alexander I until their deaths in 1822 and 1825, and Metternich for almost as many years after 1830 as before it.

But gradually the issues disentangle themselves from the leading actors: by 1831–2, it would not have been difficult to predict the main lines of policy that not only an Austrian but any British, Russian or even French statesman would be most likely to follow. Palmerstonian postures would on the whole prevail in London for a generation; the Emperor Nicholas I had shown his hand at the Treaty of Adrianople in 1829 and in Poland two years later; and the ministers of Louis Philippe, though they might differ in their ideas of what was prudent, were firmly committed (save for the irrepressible Thiers in 1840) to a western alignment and to its corollary, an intention to avoid any major clash with Britain, yet without renouncing some room for manoeuvre. The Prussian government was still to eschew for a generation any really determined initiative of a foreign policy independent of Vienna. Leopold I in Belgium was to steer a shrewd course which gave him an influence among princes much greater than his small power alone would warrant. Secretary Adams and President Monroe had defined the range and limits of American foreign policy in December 1823, though the 'doctrine' which was extracted from the Message was to prove extremely flexible over the years.

Was there ever a 'Congress System' *in action*?[1] It may be argued that there were merely three meetings of sovereigns and ministers, of which the first (at Aix-la-Chapelle in the autumn of 1818) was not much more than a pre-arranged ceremony for winding up the military occupation of France, settling her debts and re-admitting her (with some reservations) among the great Powers; while the second (at Troppau and Laibach in the winter of 1820–1) and the third (at Verona in the autumn of 1822) served rather to focus attention on the differences between the Allies than to resolve them or to compose a system. After that, there is not much until the Congress of Paris (1856) and the Congress of Berlin (1878), both of which were peace-conferences after wars which involved (or nearly involved) more than two Powers; they were not examples of any system for forestalling or adjusting difficulties in time of peace. Between these two, the great changes of 1860, 1866 and 1871 were made without any general congress. Even in the seven years after 1815, no regular machinery for conferences or congresses was devised. The final Article VI of the Quadruple Alliance of 20 November 1815 (Chapter XXIV, p. 663) no more created a working system than did the modern expectation of periodical 'summit' meetings among Allies, and its intention was subject to the same kind of deceptions. A further meeting was already envisaged for the autumn of 1818, but the 'fixed periods' of Article VI were never defined, and the first five articles provided the context—the containment of France. The more effective working 'system' for the next three years was the continuing conference of the ambassadors of the four Powers in Paris.

Yet it is hard to deny that there was initially some *conception* of what might become a system, or at least a method, of consultation among the great Powers. The issues on the agenda in 1818 could probably have been settled by diplomatic correspondence instead, if the principals had not positively desired a conference; and they must have believed in 1820–2 that the method offered at least better prospects of agreement on specific issues than would a less spectacular procedure. Alexander I had not forgotten Czartoryski's ill-defined proposals of 1804 to England for a new system of international law, in which all states should accept an obligation not to go to war without first invoking the mediation of a third party for an inquiry into the causes of the dispute. Castlereagh, for all his apparent insularity, had not forgotten his own association with Pitt's Instructions of 1805, much more severely practical in tone

[1] Sir Charles Webster, *The Foreign Policy of Castlereagh, 1815–22* (London, 1925), p. 56, note, gave reasons for preferring the term 'Conference' after 1815, although contemporaries used both terms in ways which make any clear distinction impossible. Continental historians continue to use 'Congress' for meetings attended by sovereigns at this period, and this usage has some convenience. This chapter's debt is so apparent to that book, and to H. W. V. Temperley, *The Foreign Policy of Canning, 1822–27* (London, 1925), that few references to them will be given.

but touching upon the idea of 'a general agreement and guarantee for the mutual protection and security of different Powers and for the re-establishing a general system of public law in Europe'.[1] Castlereagh was now to abandon the suggestion of a general guarantee, but to make great use of the rest. He believed in the virtue of personal discussion at the highest level among men who had been associated in great events and had at least one purpose in common, that of tranquillity for a season after a generation of wars. The frictions and the superficial frivolities of the Congress of Vienna did not entirely disillusion him. The highest point of his confidence is seen in his letter from Aix-la-Chapelle: '... it really appears to me to be a new discovery in the European government, at once extinguishing the cobwebs with which diplomacy obscures the horizon ... and giving to the counsels of the Great Powers the efficiency and almost the simplicity of a single State.'[2] Yet much of this confidence rested precisely on his success in strictly limiting the scope and purpose of the conference, against the Russian desire to widen it indefinitely. Already, prompted by a cabinet suspicious of entanglements, he was sounding the warning, more emphatically expressed eighteen months later in a famous State Paper (p. 674, below), that England would not be a party to a system of intervention by the great Powers, unasked, in the internal affairs of other States. Nevertheless, in 1818 he was criticising an abuse which could equally arise without summit meetings and he was not denying in principle their usefulness where men who understood each other could make effective decisions. Alexander I could recapture at such a meeting some of that intoxicating sense of 1814–15 that it was his duty to give a lead to Europe. Metternich in turn was attracted to this method for several reasons: because he might more easily adjust his immovable principles to circumstances in personal negotiation than by despatches to perhaps less supple ambassadors; because Alexander in such a setting might be more amenable to reason than when he was feeling and acting as a Russian on his home ground; and because a meeting of sovereigns could be an imposing demonstration of the conservative alliance, against danger from France, danger from the 'parties of movement'—'Jacobins', 'sects', 'liberals'—or even danger from imprudent rulers themselves.

The congresses did not provide a new kind of permanent international machinery, nor even the only possible method of dealing with particular issues arising immediately out of the Vienna settlement. A meeting of sovereigns was one method of maintaining and reasserting this conservative alliance, and the desire to reassert it survived on the Continent the use of this particular method. That is why, perhaps, the name 'Holy Alliance' was attached in mockery by contemporary liberals

[1] Webster, *The Foreign Policy of Castlereagh, 1812–15* (London, 1931), p. 58.
[2] Webster, *Castlereagh, 1815–22*, p.153. Castlereagh to Liverpool, 20 October 1818.

and by later historians to the general attitude of the conservative monarchies. The document drafted for the tsar and signed on 26 September 1815 by himself, the Austrian emperor and the Prussian king, was published in January 1816 and soon adopted by most governments. Not only monarchs were invited to adhere to it. Switzerland did so; and the United States, where the press was at first inclined to applaud its religious tone, eventually declined without any great show of horror. Technically, it had little in common with the objects actually pursued by the continental monarchies in foreign politics over the following years. So far as it was not just a manifesto, it pointed towards a 'general Alliance'—a wider and looser association among rulers than the strictly limited alliance of the victorious great Powers—and it was perhaps intended to give greater scope for Russia to make her influence felt in the world.[1] Certainly, in the next few years the Russian government tried consistently to introduce more States into the general negotiations,[2] and even to bring the United States in as a counterweight to the maritime power of England. In the war of 1812–14 between England and the United States, the tsar had offered himself as a mediator; Castlereagh managed to avoid that, but had to be content with a negative result of this war (Treaty of Ghent, 28 December 1814), in order to free his hands for the Congress at Vienna. Later, he was more successful than Alexander in settling points of friction with the United States, where opinion turned against the Russian disposition to interfere in Spain and Spanish America and to stake claims on the Pacific coast in the north-west. In questions such as these, interests rather than principles dictated the policy of the Russian as of the other monarchies. Yet, symbolically, there was also a 'Holy Alliance' between governments which sought a traditional and religious sanction against any radical disturbance of the aristocratic or patrician social order.

The military power of Russia had been demonstrated in 1813–14, and was not dismantled after the peace-settlement. The tsar's faith and pride in this power was not much shaken, and the fear which it inspired in Europe was not much relieved, by some evidence of disaffection even among officers in crack regiments, or by the inefficiency of a crude and oppressive system of recruitment which an experiment with military farm colonies did nothing to improve (Chapter XVIII, p. 518). Russia's campaigns of 1828–9 against Turkey were to show how difficult

[1] The Russian draft included references to 'the peoples', which were amended, at Metternich's instance, before signature. M. Bourquin, *Histoire de la Sainte Alliance* (Geneva, 1954), pp. 134–5. H. G. Schenk, *The aftermath of the Napoleonic Wars* (London, 1947), pp. 37–8. G. de Bertier de Sauvigny well expounds the uses and abuses of the term 'Holy Alliance' in the English edition of his *Metternich and his Times* (London, 1962), pp. 129–54.

[2] See, for example, the *Correspondance de Pozzo di Borgo . . . et . . . Nessebrode, 1814–18*, 2 vols. (Paris, 1890), and the Russian memorandum of 8 October 1818. The relevant passages are cited by M. Bourquin, *op. cit.*, chs. 11–12.

it was for her to mount and sustain a major striking force outside her own borders; but in the first years after 1815, it seemed as if an incalculable force was at the disposal of one man. In contrast, Austria was plainly in no condition to risk anything more than a punitive expedition into Italy, certainly not a crisis in Turkey; Prussia had not rebuilt a great military machine, and France would soon have been in difficulties in 1823 if her intervention in Spain had not proved to be an almost bloodless parade.

England's maritime supremacy, along with her colonial possessions and prospects, had been secured before the clinch came at Vienna in 1814–15,[1] and Castlereagh had succeeded in keeping them outside the discussion of a European settlement. This enabled him to maintain boldly that 'there is no longer any object which the prince regent can desire to acquire for the British Empire, either of possession or of fame, beyond what Providence has already blessed it with; his only desire is, and must be, to preserve the peace, which in concert with his Allies he has won'.[2] Metternich basically acquiesced in this position, but Alexander I could hardly do so sincerely. Russia had initiated the system of armed neutrality against British sea power in 1780 and again in 1800. In spite of her own weakness at sea, she might hope in time to draw a reviving France and Spain, perhaps Holland and possibly even the United States, into creating globally a balance of power like that which England naturally wished to confine to the continent of Europe. Such a design would involve Russia in theoretically contradictory attitudes—supporting the differing regimes which she believed could alone strengthen these other maritime powers for their role: absolutism in Spain, constitutional monarchy in France and the Netherlands, republican patriotism in the United States. The evidence for a clear and consistently 'realist' policy of this kind is hardly sufficient, and Alexander himself in 1818 rebuked Pozzo di Borgo, his ambassador in Paris, for advocating a specific alignment with France and Spain against England and Austria. But his notion of a 'general alliance' was more than a vaguely religious sentiment; as interpreted by his minister Capodistrias, it amounted to a shift in the balance of power onto a wider stage. It may help to explain Alexander's attempt to woo Holland by marrying his sister to the Dutch crown prince (December 1815); his proposals for disarmament (April 1815), designed to suggest that any pruning of military powers on the continent should be matched by pruning of British naval power; his transfer of some old warships to Spain—

---

[1] Treaties with Portugal (19 February 1810) and Spain (5 July 1814) secured most-favoured treatment for British trade in South America and excluded any revival of the old Franco-Spanish *pacte de famille*. A Treaty with the Netherlands (13 August 1814) kept the Cape and Ceylon for England.

[2] Circular despatch to British missions abroad, 1 January 1816, cited in full by Webster, *op. cit.*, pp. 509–12.

connected with a rumoured but abortive scheme of over-zealous ambassadors to acquire Minorca for Russia (1816–17); his proposal for collective, instead of isolated British, action against the Barbary pirates (May 1818); and, in a larger context, the resentment of all the larger maritime Powers against an extended use of the British navy's claim to rights of visit and search in suppressing the slave trade (1815–19).

With the unrest in Germany and Italy during 1819, and with the electoral successes of the Left in France, Alexander became less interested in a 'general alliance' for redressing the balance of power and more in an *alliance solidaire* against revolution. Of his two chief advisers in foreign affairs since January 1816, Nesselrode was now helping Metternich to move him in this direction (though without Alexander's mystical overtones); but the mobile influence of Capodistrias was only gradually shaken by the events of 1819–21.[1] Capodistrias had some sympathy with the 'parties of movement', and wanted to make it easier for them to become upholders of order like himself. He admired the Alexander whom he had begun to serve ten years earlier. He found Austrian influence everywhere stifling, and England obstructive to his hopes in the Levant. He was probably not innocent of contacts with trouble-makers for Austria. Metternich, touring Italy with his emperor in the spring of 1819, was collecting evidence of intrigues by Russian agents, which were denied by the tsar. Capodistrias had lately passed through Italy on his way to Corfu, and had spoken of discontent under Austrian rule in North Italy and under British rule in the Ionian islands. In Germany, as in Italy, Metternich preferred if possible to manage affairs alone or with Prussia, with moral support from his other allies if he could get it, but without inviting their concerted help. In this he had the full approval of the British Cabinet, which was battling with deep unrest at home but unwilling to take part publicly against it abroad. Here too, Metternich suspected confusion or duplicity in Russian policy. Kotzebue was murdered by a German student for being paid (it was said) by Russia to write against the German liberals; Alexander condemned them as warmly as Metternich could desire, but Metternich was jealous of his influence in some of the German courts,[2] and angry when Capodistrias bitterly criticised in the tsar's name the methods of repression adopted at Metternich's instance by a conference of nine German states at Carlsbad in August and three months later by a larger conference at Vienna.[3]

[1] Already, on 7 September 1819, Metternich was begging Nesselrode privately to counteract the anti-Austrian influence of his colleague. Webster, *op. cit.*, p. 190.

[2] Alexander's wife was sister to the Grand Duke of Baden (who resented certain decisions taken to suit Austrian convenience); and his sister was the widow of the Grand Duke of Oldenburg and now married to the King of Württemberg.

[3] Capodistrias' 'Aperçu des idées de l'Empereur sur les affaires de l'Allemagne', communicated to England 21 November 1819. Webster, *op. cit.*, p. 193.

Concerning Turkey, Alexander did not want to tie his hands for the future, at least while their differences over the Treaty of Belgrade (May 1812) were still unsettled. He had taken pains to deny that his Holy Alliance was in any way a threat to the sultan.[1] But Capodistrias, who had the chief initiative in handling Balkan affairs, was not likely to damp the fires there or to miss any opportunity of promoting, at least by diplomacy, a new deal for the Greeks in particular (Chapter XIX, p. 535). In this region, the tsar would always find the Habsburg monarchy obstructive where its frontiers marched with Turkey in Europe, while British strategical and commercial interests in the Levant, and in Persia too, would usually, though not quite always, obstruct Russian means of pressure on the sultan on that side. The evidence suggests that the events of 1821 presented the Russian government with a situation which it neither planned nor foresaw, nor yet had done much to prevent by any sharp rebukes to some over-zealous agents.

Although Metternich hoped to avoid a public conference about Germany or Italy, he did want moral support from his allies, and pressed during the summer of 1819 for a regular 'point of moral contact' among the ambassadors—if not in London, then perhaps in Vienna (as he doubtless hoped). The British Cabinet rejected all such precautionary measures in advance of any 'overt acts' involving its treaty obligations. Overt acts were soon to show how variously obligations might be interpreted. In Spain, a mutiny of unpaid troops at Cadiz on 1 January 1820 gave the partisans of the Constitution of 1812 the opportunity to proclaim it by seizing power in Madrid in March (Chapter XVI, pp. 448–450). Russia wanted allied intervention (in Capodistrias' view, with the object of imposing a moderate charter on king and insurgents alike); France was inclined to play a leading role, some hoped with the same object and in any case so as to show herself independent of England; Prussia leaned to the Russian suggestion; but Metternich thought that England's reaction would be much more decisive than the tsar's, and showed great caution. This was the situation that produced the British Cabinet's State Paper of 5 May 1820,[2] which pointedly rejected collective intervention as not called for by any direct military danger and as likely to aggravate Spanish feelings. The Alliance was 'never intended as a union for the government of the world or for the superintendence of the internal affairs of other States. . . . No country having a representative system of Government could act upon [such a general principle]. . . . We shall be found in our place when actual danger menaces the system of Europe: but this country cannot and will not

[1] Circular to the other four Powers, 30 March 1816, cited by J. H. Pirenne, *Histoire de la Sainte Alliance*, 2 vols. (Neuchatel, 1945), vol. II, pp. 87–8.

[2] Printed in full in the *Cambridge History of British Foreign Policy* (Cambridge, 1923), vol. II, App. A, pp. 622–33.

act upon abstract and speculative principles of precaution. The Alliance which exists had no such purpose in view in its original formation'.

The immediate effect of this paper was decisive. France acquiesced, and Metternich swallowed its general doctrine for the sake of isolating Russia in this instance. It was not in essence a novel doctrine, and the sharper edge now given to its expression may be partly due to England's special dislike of interference by other Powers in the Peninsula; but the argument that differing forms of government must affect foreign policies was here first clearly stated. Three years later, Canning (who may have had a hand with the rest of the Cabinet in shaping it) used it, by publishing extracts in a different situation and a wider context, in order to strike an attitude against the 'Holy Alliance'. For in the interval other events had made the breach open.

In Portugal, while King John VI was still putting off his return from Brazil, more than twelve years since his flight from the French, a revolutionary movement at Oporto in August 1820 was completed at Lisbon early in October (Chapter XVI, pp. 451-2). Here, Castlereagh's warnings were directed rather against the king's hopes of collective intervention than against any real prospect of it; moreover, he told first the monarchists and then the victorious liberals in turn that they could not expect a renewal of England's guarantee of her old ally against either Spain or the Alliance as a means of propping up any extreme party in Portugal. On King John's return in the summer of 1821, he had to submit to the new Cortes, and a year later his son Dom Pedro made himself a completely independent ruler in Brazil (15 August 1822). Thus the revolutions in Portugal and Brazil were insulated for the moment from any interference by the Alliance.

Meanwhile, if Metternich's compliance over Spain was his reward to England for giving Austria no trouble over Germany, Metternich in turn was rewarded by Castlereagh's positive support for Austria in suppressing revolt in Naples and (for a time) in leaving the sultan free to do so in Greece if he could. The problem was a different one in each of these four regions; in each of them, the reactions of England and Austria were divergent but had this in common—fear of Russian intervention. Unlike the mutiny at Cadiz, the rising in Naples just six months later (July 1820) was unexpected, for there had been no such violent reaction under the restored Bourbon there as in Spain, and the country had appeared to be settling down better than any other part of Italy (Chapter XV, pp. 429-30). But a movement which began among Muratist officers, who resented serving under an Austrian commander, was captured by the Carbonari who forced the king to swear allegiance to the Spanish Constitution of 1812. As usual, the Sicilians in turn rose against rule from Naples, and were bloodily put down. For

43-2

Metternich, if Spain was no more than a bad example, Naples was a direct threat to Austrian control in Italy. And on this ground Castlereagh positively encouraged him to step in alone, both forestalling any Russian move for collective intervention and saving England from the embarrassment of having to stand aside from it in accordance with the principles lately announced in relation to Spain. But Metternich was soon faced by Russian insistence, with some French support, on a formal conference of all the Allies which would also consider the revolutionary problem as a whole. He could not afford, as in Spain, to do nothing, nor could he break with Russia by acting alone. After manoeuvring for a compromise procedure which might satisfy both Russia and England, he had to agree to a conference of sovereigns to which England sent her ambassador at Vienna as a mere observer, without plenipotentiary powers and with instructions to dissent from any collective pronouncements. The French position was ambiguous but eventually nearer to that of England.

Thus the conference which opened at Troppau on 23 October 1820 was not what Metternich had desired, and it was a blow to Castlereagh's hopes, still not quite extinct, of preserving the formal unity of the Alliance. It became a duel for the tsar's mind between Capodistrias, who hoped (as in Spain) to impose a moderate charter on both parties in Naples, and Metternich who found this remedy worse than the disease. In order to circumvent Capodistrias' idea of intervention as a kind of mediation between a sovereign and his subjects, Metternich had to play on Alexander's notion of a religious crusade against the revolutionary spirit. The resulting 'preliminary protocol' (19 November) asserted that States which had undergone revolutionary changes, menacing to other States, would remain excluded from the European Alliance until legal order and stability was assured; that the Allied Powers would refuse recognition to changes brought about by illegal methods; and that, if immediate danger to a neighbour were threatened, they would proceed if necessary from friendly representations to coercive measures in order to bring the offender back into the bosom of the Alliance. Metternich had to agree that Austrian intervention in Naples should be in the name of the Alliance and that the king should be invited to meet an adjourned conference at Laibach in the new year; but there was no mention of mediation, and in the upshot the Carbonari played into Metternich's hands by rejecting any compromise and forcing the king, before he sailed, to swear to the impractical Constitution of 1812. Although Russia, Austria and Prussia had already signed this protocol, they agreed, on the British observer's protest, to treat it as no more than a proposal to the other two; but, before Castlereagh's blunt rejection of it reached Troppau, they followed it up with a confidential circular to their diplomatic representatives (8 December), which reported their decisions as to Naples and repeated many of the unacceptable doctrines as to the nature of the Alliance as if they had been agreed by all five Powers. It also alluded to Spain and Portugal. The gist of this circular was soon known in other capitals and leaked into the *Morning Chronicle* on 15 January 1821. The British Cabinet, under heavy fire at home, had already decided to make its protest public; its answering circular (19 January), was laid before Parliament with supporting documents, and debated in February. Its approval of an Austrian right to intervene in Naples, and its re-assertion of the full harmony and vigour of the Alliance 'upon all points really embraced by Treaty', were ridiculed by the opposition; but its public dissent from the methods of the three courts not only committed British policy for the future but also made a profound and lasting impression abroad.

In the conferences resumed at Laibach on 12 January 1821, the three courts kept on trying to reassert 'the solidarity of the Allied Powers'. With the French they had some success, but the British observer refused to let England's dissent be concealed from the Neapolitans. Before reaching Laibach, the king had repudiated his oath to the Constitution of 1812 and, when an Austrian army restored him to Naples on 24 March, he showed none of the moderation, which Metternich himself now advised, either in Naples or in Sicily. Yet Castlereagh was as much opposed as Metternich to any mediation. His disapproval of collective intervention as a method was genuine, and was to outlast the special need to placate a menacing opposition at home; but this was compatible with relief at the result of intervention. He told Metternich that in Naples 'you would have done better to have acted first and talked afterwards'. He was equally opposed to mediation in Piedmont when an unexpected insurrection at Turin on 10 March led to the resignation of King Victor Emmanuel in favour of his brother (Chapter XV, pp. 433-4). Here Castlereagh was most afraid of French inter-vention, and made no objection when Austrian troops marched in to help the new king restore order. Yet he was disturbed that the tsar still wanted to intervene, or get France to intervene, in Spain, and he could not pass over the final declarations of the sovereigns at Laibach (12 May) which repeated the doctrines of Troppau and announced a further conference next year to report progress in Naples and Piedmont. In principle, the three Powers had placed Spain and Portugal under the ban, although their representatives in Madrid were not for the moment withdrawn. In June Castlereagh reasserted in Parliament the principles of his Circular of 19 January, but made no further direct protest.

Meanwhile, the news of Hypsilántes' adventure in the Principalities and then of the Greek insurrection in the Peloponnese (Chapter XIX, pp. 538-9, 547) reached Laibach before the conference ended.

Capodistrias had the painful duty of drafting the tsar's public disavowal of Russian support for Hypsilántes, but his position was not yet hopeless. Alexander had already at Troppau been talking of the Alliance as the only bulwark against the 'satanic genius' of revolution, which was working everywhere by 'occult methods' to set up the 'reign of evil'. On his return to Russia in June 1821, he ascribed to the Paris Liberals the revolutions in Spain, Portugal and Italy, and now the troubles in European Turkey too, which would have no support from him in spite of past history and popular opinion. He would be faithful to his treaties with the sultan, and to the Alliance. Yet he could hardly do less than protest about the sultan's indiscriminate reprisals against the Greeks in Constantinople, and other measures held to be violations of treaty rights. His ambassador Stroganov, who had already suspended diplomatic intercourse early in June, executed with gusto the instructions (28 June, drafted by Capodistrias), which reached him in July, to demand satisfaction within eight days: already on board a Russian frigate for personal safety, he sailed away on 10 August, as soon as winds allowed.

For the next two years, Metternich concentrated on preventing war by keeping the Greek question separate from Russo-Turkish disputes about treaty rights, preaching to the sultan moderation on the former and strict execution of the latter. In this he was ably seconded by the British ambassador Lord Strangford, whose real services were obscured, in the eyes of Philhellenes, by his extreme Turcophil sentiments. Castlereagh had to rebuke him more than once, but his own view differed from Metternich's only in two ways. First, he was more sceptical about 'conjoint representations upon the Ottoman ministry: they have invariably failed of producing a beneficial effect. The Porte has always looked upon the European Alliance as a league which they viewed with religious as well as political distrust'. Secondly, England had fewer obligations than Austria to Russia, and was less willing even to discuss the possible consequences of a Russo-Turkish war upon the future of Turkey in Europe. With these differences of approach, Castlereagh's meeting with Metternich at Hanover in October 1821 (during a visit with his king) nevertheless produced a close agreement on a parallel but not identical policy towards both tsar and sultan, and above all on eliminating the influence of Capodistrias, whose connection with the Ionian Islands was a special cause of anxiety to the British high commissioner there.[1] No Russian campaign could begin before the spring; intense diplomatic activity filled the interval until the retirement of

---

[1] Yet a private letter of Joseph Planta to Stratford Canning (8 August 1821), printed in Webster, *op. cit.*, pp. 582–4, shows that a personal opinion, even inside the Foreign Office, could already cheerfully contemplate a Russian victory and an independent Greek kingdom under Capodistrias, with the Ionian islands thrown in.

Capodistrias to Switzerland (July 1822) marked the triumph of the tsar's principles over his sentiments. Or so it seemed—but this and other issues were adjourned to the forthcoming conference. Before he died Castlereagh himself could write of 'the progress made by the Greeks towards the formation of a government', and look ahead to their recognition as belligerents and even possibly to 'the creation of a qualified Greek government', but without any British guarantee.

Having been persuaded by his allies not to force the issue in the east, because of mounting dangers in the west, Alexander now embarrassed them by proposing collective armed intervention in Spain on behalf of the king. His offer to send a Russian contingent at once was not taken seriously, but in France a powerful group at court and in the cabinet took the opportunity to lay plans for a French intervention, either in the name of the Alliance or independently. Arms and supplies were already going to the counter-revolutionary parties in Spain, and a French *cordon sanitaire*, spread along the frontier by the summer of 1822, became an 'army of observation' in the autumn. This was less alarming for Austria than the Russian plan, but much more alarming for England because the danger was more real. Thus the Spanish problem, dormant for two years, came to the fore again—just when the question of South American independence was also becoming critical.

The virtual or complete independence of most of South America was already before 1822 generally expected outside Spain (Chapter XXIII). What mattered to the other courts of Europe was that any arrangement should not appear to be a victory for revolution, a humiliation for kings and a bad example to the world. Further, in 1818 Alexander had still been hoping to keep for Spain enough strength to be reckoned in the scales, along with France, against the sea power of England. What mattered to France was the hope of reviving in some way the old Bourbon 'family compact' with Spain. What mattered to England was: first that South American ports should be open to all comers, without special privileges for England or any other State, but allowing, if need be, a 'fair preference' to Spain itself; and secondly that no force or threat of force should be used in any mediation between Spain and her former colonies. These two conditions were among those laid down by the British Cabinet in May 1812 and again in July 1817. Neither was accepted by the Spanish government before or after the revolution of 1820 in Spain itself. For this reason no progress was made in the congresses of 1818 or 1820-1. For the rest, both Castlereagh and Canning held that new republics would be both less congenial to English traditions and also less stable than would new monarchies if such could be set up (as in Brazil). Castlereagh would have preferred Spanish princes, but unwelcome evidence of French designs to promote a

French Bourbon led him to tell the Colombian agent in London (July 1820) that England would recognise any native monarchy.

Neither Castlereagh nor Canning wanted all the credit for recognition of the new nations to go to the United States. Republicans in and out of Congress had long been calling for open recognition; they were incensed by the proceedings of the Alliance in Europe and lately by a Russian *Ukase* (decree) of 28 September 1821, closing to foreign ships the whole Pacific coast down to 51° (almost to Vancouver). Secretary Adams moved cautiously; but in December 1821 the President foreshadowed individual recognition, in May 1822 he was authorised by Congress to send missions at his discretion, and in June he formally received a Colombian representative. At the same time, the British Navigation Acts were being modified so as to admit foreign ships, including those of South America. After a fruitless overture to France and warnings to Spain and the other Powers in May, Castlereagh framed his own instructions (July) for the coming congress, distinguishing three stages in relation to territories where the struggle was already over: commercial recognition *de facto*, already operative; the sending of diplomatic agents; and finally *de jure* recognition which would deny the rights of the former sovereign. Later practice was hardly to support these fine distinctions, at any rate between the second and third stages, but Castlereagh saw the situation as still very fluid. England would try to move in step with her allies, even with a Spain brought to see reason, but would retain 'an independent discretion to act according to circumstances'.

Castlereagh did not decide until the end of July to go himself to the congress, now to be held at Verona, not at Vienna as first planned. On 12 August 1822 he died by his own hand. Five weeks passed before George Canning won the succession; he was indispensable, but feared by enemies at court and among Tory colleagues who had felt the lash of his tongue and distrusted his less than aristocratic origin, his ambition and his versatile genius. Among these was the Duke of Wellington, who had already been named to take Castlereagh's place at Verona. He left a day or two after Canning's appointment, with unchanged instructions. Wellington was a loyal public servant, and continuity was preserved; but England's key position in the great issues affected by naval and commercial power made even a change of style at the Foreign Office a European event. Where Castlereagh made discreet signals, Canning waved a flag—in conversation, in despatches, in Parliament and in public speeches. In all these he far outshone Castlereagh: his political experience was not inferior; in foreign affairs he was equally well informed, but he lacked the personal intimacies born of common experiences. He did not profess or desire to be a European in that sense: 'For Alliance, read England, and you have the clue to my policy'; 'Every country for itself and God for us all' (1823).

Castlereagh had expected that Turkey and Spanish America would be more pressing questions at Verona than Spain or Italy, but the failure of a Spanish royalist *coup* in July, and the determination of France to assert herself in Spain, made this issue overshadow all the rest. In a supplementary instruction (27 September), Canning declared that, 'come what may', England would not be a party to any collective intervention in Spain. In reply to Montmorency's questions, only Russia offered France full support. Austria and Prussia agreed to withdraw their ambassadors from Spain if France should do so, and to give France moral support if war broke out between the two; but in effect they evaded any promise of material help. Finally, all three Powers limited the *casus foederis* to armed attack by Spain on France, direct provocation through propaganda by Spanish agents in France, or violent treatment of the king or his family and their rights of succession. Ten days before he left Verona on 30 November, Wellington dissociated England from these proceedings and said that her minister at Madrid (whose recent posting there was itself an offence to the three courts) would confine himself to 'allaying the ferment which they must occasion'. The result was a diplomatic defeat for Canning. The French government announced its intention (25 December) to act alone and disavowed Montmorency's commitment to the Alliance. The impetuous Chateaubriand, now foreign minister, ignored both the Left's prophecies of mutiny or military disaster, and also the disapproval of England. In reply to the French king's speech from the throne (28 January 1823), Canning threatened France in Parliament (11 February), announced an increase in the fleet and suspended the embargo on sending arms to Spain and Spanish America. But by the end of March the French knew that the British Cabinet did not mean war unless France should attack Portugal or help Spain to recover her colonies. An army of 100,000 men marched to Madrid and finally to Cadiz, and over-turned the revolution almost without bloodshed (April to September 1823). But, although French troops remained in Spain for five years, France was powerless to check the violence of the king's revenge or (as some had hoped) to impose a charter on the French pattern (Chapter XVI, pp. 450-1).

Canning's defiant reaction to this set-back was also the measure of his bounding popularity at home, in spite or because of the known hostility of some of his colleagues and of the king himself. His scornful rejection of the European Alliance—'Areopagus and all that'—was just what many Englishmen wanted to hear. But procedure by means of 'summit' conferences had been killed as much by the waywardness of Alexander and the self-assertion of Chateaubriand as by the gradual progress of England, as it were, from Castlereagh's *'de facto'* dissent from the methods of the Alliance to Canning's *'de jure'* repudiation of its principles. Moreover, for the next few years the 'parties of movement' seemed to be under control in the heart of Europe. Canning was to seek his revenge in fields where there was in any case no hope of an *alliance solidaire:* first in America and Portugal, and then in the Levant.

Canning's first answer to the rumours of French designs in Spanish America was to sound the United States for a joint disclaimer of any territorial ambitions there themselves and a joint warning against those of any other Power (August–September 1823). The American Minister, Richard Rush, welcomed the idea, but on condition that England would first recognise officially the already independent colonies—a condition which American opinion would demand, but one which Canning neither would nor could yet fulfil, for he still hesitated to despair of a voluntary settlement between Spain and her colonies and he could not in any case have carried King and Cabinet for immediate recognition. Next, in the week before news of the fall of Cadiz reached London (3–9 October), Canning pressed the French ambassador, Polignac, into disclaiming any French desire for territory or exclusive advantages, or for any use of force against the colonies. Although Polignac still looked to another conference of the Allies for a settlement, he did not personally reject Canning's suggestion that the United States ought to be consulted.[1] These conversations were known to the Allies in November, but not to Secretary Adams when he was persuading President Monroe to make a bold move.

Adams saw that England could and would prevent Allied interference, and that it would be safe for the president to make independently a far-reaching declaration of policy to his own people. In substance, the Message of 2 December 1823 stated that, since the policy of the Republic was to accept as legitimate all *de facto* governments in Europe and not to interfere in their affairs, so too it would not interfere with existing European colonies or dependencies in America but would not allow any European Power to impose on independent governments, recognised by the United States, the essentially different political system of the Allied Powers—a system which 'our southern brethren', if left to themselves, would surely not adopt. This seemed to make republics the norm, if not the rule, for the American continent; but the sting was in the passage which referred to the Russian *Ukase* of 1821 and went on to rule out future colonisation by any European Powers (Chapter XXII, pp. 591–2 and Chapter XXIII, pp. 637–8). This was a bold claim indeed, at a time when effective occupation by the Republic hardly extended beyond the Mississippi and its frontier with Canada had not been agreed beyond the Rockies. Canning was bound to question this claim, and he did not like the assumption that all independent states in

[1] Full text published by Temperley, *The Foreign Policy of Canning*, pp. 114–18.

America ought to be republics any better than the opposite assumption of the Allied monarchs for Europe; but he welcomed the Message as a death-blow to the Alliance. Though cautious in Parliament, he wrote privately: 'The congress was broken in all its limbs before, but the President's speech gives it the *coup de grâce*'. Alexander's *Ukase* had made nonsense of his supposed desire to use the United States for balancing the power of Britain.

Throughout 1824, Canning refused to take part in the continuing conferences of the other Powers. In March he published his formal refusal of 30 January, along with his record of the conversations with Polignac. When Spain—too late—had opened her colonial trade (as she still saw it) to foreign shipping (February), he did indeed make one more fruitless effort to negotiate peaceful separation, by the doubtful expedient of offering a British guarantee of Cuba to Spain (April). But in July he informed Metternich that the influence of the Continental Powers ceased with the bounds of Europe—a doctrine implicit in British policy since 1814 but now made painfully explicit. In the same month he persuaded the Cabinet to recommend a commercial treaty with Buenos Aires. But he postponed any decisive action while he was collecting information in the former Spanish colonies and building up support at home against determined efforts to discredit him. Finally, after a sharp struggle, the king's speech (7 February 1825) made public the decision, already communicated to Spain at the end of December, to give *de facto* diplomatic recognition to Buenos Aires (Argentina), Mexico and Colombia by means of commercial treaties.[1]

Adams and Canning each understood the sentiments of his own people, but it must be doubtful whether Adams understood those of his 'southern brethren' any better than Canning did. The two men were rivals for the esteem of the former colonies. Both repudiated the 'Holy Alliance' of European monarchs; but, where the Message appealed to something like a 'Holy Alliance' of republican Americans of North and South alike, Canning's appeal was to national interest and sentiment at home, and among Latin Americans to their knowledge that England had the power, as well as the motive, to protect them from interference by the Alliance—or even by the North itself. The actual danger of interference was probably exaggerated: in the Message, by the prominence given to the Russian *Ukase* of 1821; by Canning, in constantly harping upon French designs. But the danger was not imaginary. The moral effect of Monroe's earlier recognition and his Message was in the next few years overshadowed by the practical effectiveness of Canning's diplomacy and British sea power. More-

[1] Without any treaties, British trade with South America had increased tenfold in the past ten years, but treaties were badly needed to protect and regularise it. British exports to the South were now hardly less than to the North.

over, the United States had not, like England, distinctly disclaimed any desire to acquire more territory; although each suspected the other of an interest in Cuba, Canning had offered to guarantee Cuba to Spain. The Panama Congress in 1826 was a fiasco; only four of the new States were represented, and Bolívar's dream of a federal union was shattered; yet at that time the prestige of Britain in South America seemed to be greater than that of the United States. Canning feared an ideological split between a monarchical continent on one side of the Atlantic and a republican continent on the other. He hoped that Britain might provide a bridge between them. His fear and his hope were both intelligible, even if both eventually faded.

The independence of Brazil, with a monarch of the Portuguese dynasty, was less offensive to the courts of Europe, and Canning was anxious to legitimise it with the consent of Portugal. British diplomacy played the chief part in arranging the treaty ratified on 20 November 1825, whereby King John in Lisbon recognised Brazil as an independent empire under his son Dom Pedro. The European Alliance could not object, but soon it suffered a new blow, which Canning clinched at the very moment that he was entering into a separate understanding with Russia about Greece. On the death of King John in Lisbon (March 1826), Dom Pedro renounced his claim to the throne in favour of his infant daughter Maria, and bestowed on Portugal a constitution made in Rio (29 April). Though it was brought to Lisbon by the British minister in Rio, it was not his work. Canning did not much like it, but he supported General Saldanha (a grandson of Pombal) in forcing the regency to take the oath to it, and answered Allied warnings against Portuguese infection of Spain by even more decisive warnings against Spanish interference in Portugal. With the defection of Russia and the embarrassment of France, Metternich could not resist Canning's triumphant argument for respecting a constitution voluntarily granted by a legitimate monarch. Dom Miguel in Vienna half-heartedly obeyed his elder brother Dom Pedro's order from Brazil to swear to the constitution and promise to marry his niece, the infant queen. Canning ensured that this news reached Lisbon just in time to be announced in the regent's opening speech to the new Cortes (30 October). But Portuguese officers, enemies of the new regime and partisans of Dom Miguel's real views, led a force of deserters into Spain, where they were soon being organised under the eyes of the Spanish government (and of the French army still in Spain) for a counter-revolution in Portugal. As soon as Canning could claim that overt acts justified invoking the British treaty guarantee of Portugal against Spain, he announced the despatch of a naval force to the Tagus. In a speech so rhetorical as to risk missing fire, he won at the end a resounding ovation in the Commons with his famous boast: 'I look at the

Indies, and I call in the New World to redress the balance of the Old.'[1]

The timing of Canning's policy in the Mediterranean was closely linked with his Atlantic diplomacy, and it was an even bolder policy because he held fewer trump cards and success was still uncertain when he died. For three years he held aloof from the Greek affair. Capodistrias had been removed from power before the Congress at Verona, and a Greek deputation had not been allowed to come near it. Canning's recognition of the Greeks as belligerents in March 1823 did little more than endorse an expedient already in use for protecting commerce in a region where the Turks had no effective command of the sea. The Austrian and British ambassadors at Constantinople succeeded for the moment in isolating the Russo-Turkish disputes from the Greek question; after meeting Metternich at Czernowitz in October, Alexander agreed to renew relations with Turkey for commercial purposes, and to do nothing about Greece without consulting all his Allies. He invited them to a conference at St Petersburg in the spring to discuss his promised *Mémoire* about Greece. This *Mémoire* (January 1824) proposed dividing Greece into three principalities, with a status like those on the Danube: the Turks would have an annual tribute and garrisons in specified fortresses. To the Allies, this plan seemed a mere device for ensuring the predominance of Russia; to the Greeks it offered autonomy over a much larger area than they could hope to conquer, but their Constitution of 1822 committed them to nothing less than independence. When the plan leaked into a Paris newspaper at the end of May, it was already dead.

Canning's refusal, here as elsewhere, to take part in a conference was here based partly on the argument, already used by Castlereagh, that the Turks would pay no attention to collective pressure not backed by force, and partly on his general antipathy to Metternich, which was fully reciprocated. Yet there were already signs that British neutrality was becoming benevolent towards the Greeks. Both Greek hopes and Metternich's suspicions were indeed unfounded when, early in 1823, a British naval officer had conversations with some Greek leaders, for these were initiated by the high commissioner of the Ionian Islands, no lover of the Greeks, with the object of finding out on what terms they would submit; moreover, in Turkey, unlike South America, British merchants were mostly hostile to the insurgents. But in April Canning rebuked the Levant Company for their pro-Turkish idea of neutrality; in August he wrote (privately, it is true) that, if some vent must be

---

[1] The speech, as reported next day by the *Star* (in close touch with Canning's friends), is given by Temperley, *op. cit.*, pp. 579–85, alongside the corrected version printed in Canning's *Speeches* (London, 1836), where a more extravagant phrase is used: 'I called the New World *into existence* to redress the balance of the Old' (my italics).

found for the Russian army, he would rather it were in Turkey than in Spain; and in January 1824 Sir John Bowring, the Benthamite organiser of the philhellene Greek Committee in London, was favourably impressed by an interview with him.[1] Moreover, the sultan could not understand how the City of London could vote money for Greece, or how Lord Byron, an English peer, could come to spend it there—and his own life too—if the government really felt the friendship which it still professed for Turkey.

The conferences at St Petersburg withered in June 1824. A second series (February to June 1825) made no better progress; Metternich's sudden proposal to abandon mediation and threaten the Turks instead with eventual recognition of Greek independence 'as a measure of fact and necessity' was intended only to show what in the last resort he would prefer rather than the Russian plan, and to force the sultan meanwhile either to offer terms himself or else subdue the Greeks quickly. On the day that these conferences opened (24 February), Muhammad Ali's son Ibrahim landed in the Peloponnese the first division of his army of 10,000 Egyptians, and it seemed that the Greeks could not resist much longer. The isolation of Britain from these conferences did not preclude her from forcible resistance, if need be, to Russian conquests, nor even from British intervention alone on behalf of the Greeks. The last was an attractive notion, and perhaps not impracticable; but the Cabinet would never have agreed to it at this stage, and the Greeks had repudiated any compromise.

A different possibility, that of intervention along with Russia but not with the Alliance, had perhaps been foreshadowed two years earlier when Canning suggested (again privately) that, after the tsar should have renewed full diplomatic relations with Turkey, 'I will talk Greek with him if he pleases.'[2] Now, it seemed to be the only way out. Alexander ceased in August 1825 to discuss the question with his allies. Of Canning's two conditions for 'talking Greek with him'—a Russian ambassador in Constantinople and a disavowal of force—the first was not yet fulfilled and the second never would be; but conditions had changed, for the sultan had brought in the Egyptians to subdue the revolt, and a strong Anglophil party in Greece had lately sent delegates to London, bearing an appeal for British protection, called an 'Act of Submission'. Canning could only tell them that 'there might be a point in the contest when Great Britain would promote a fair and safe compromise', and he issued a new proclamation of neutrality (29–30 September). But early in October Mme de Lieven arrived from St Petersburg, 'a living despatch' bringing 'a little note' from Alexander.

[1] Canning to Bagot, 20 August 1823. Bowring's interview, 10 January 1824. Details in C. W. Crawley, *The Question of Greek Independence* (Cambridge, 1930), pp. 30, 35.
[2] To Bagot, 20 August 1823. Crawley, *op. cit.*, p. 30.

Canning sent Strangford to Russia with instructions (14 October) to 'meet confidence with confidence'; on the 25th Lieven told him that Ibrahim's 'plan for disposing of his conquest is . . . to remove the whole Greek population, carrying them off into slavery in Egypt or elsewhere, and to repeople the country with Egyptians and others of the Mahometan religion'.

Canning would still have preferred to intervene alone, and had just sent his cousin Stratford Canning to Constantinople with instructions to contact the Greek leaders on his way there. But the evidence that Alexander was preparing for war before his death on 1 December, the likelihood that his successor would consult Russian interests alone, and the desperate state of the Greeks—all these suggested that there was no time to lose. Wellington was sent to St Petersburg to congratulate the new tsar on his accession and to follow up the new policy. The evidence for Ibrahim's plan was shadowy, but Canning's willingness to use it as a lever on opinion at home was not unlike his emphasis earlier on French designs in South America and, a little later, on Spanish threats to Portugal. The Anglo-Russian Protocol of 4 April 1826 was grounded not on Ibrahim's plan but on the Greek invitation to England to mediate, forecast by Stratford Canning in January but not confirmed until the end of April. The Protocol gave no hint of the use of force by England, but it contained by implication a threat of it by Russia —an implication which Wellington hardly perceived. Early in May, its text was published in *The Times*, and was as much welcomed by friends of Greece as it had already been condemned by Metternich. Canning himself criticised it as 'not very artistically drawn', and was in any case obliged by Cabinet doubts to move very cautiously. His object was 'to save Greece by the agency of the Russian name upon the fears of Turkey, without a war'. But he found Russia reverting to the Greek question as soon as she had settled by threat of war her other disputes with Turkey, at Akkerman (October 1826). To escape from the charge of being bound hand and foot to Russia, he spent six weeks in Paris in the autumn and persuaded the Bourbon government to take the initiative by producing the first draft (January 1827) of a tripartite Treaty.

In February, Lord Liverpool's illness and retirement caused a Cabinet crisis. Little more could be done until May, a month after Canning had formed a coalition ministry with some of the Whigs, on the resignation of Wellington and some other Tories. The Treaty of London (6 July 1827), as finally drafted after a tussle between Russian eagerness and French delays, omitted any direct threat to withdraw the ambassadors and any promise by England to guarantee the settlement; but it included a secret additional article, pledging the three Powers, if the proposed armistice were not accepted within a month (later reduced to a fortnight), to accredit consuls to the Greeks and to prevent any further collision between the combatants, but without themselves taking any part in the hostilities. The instructions sent to the ambassadors and the admirals a week later did little to elucidate the vagueness of this article; but the interpretation received by Admiral Codrington from Stratford Canning left no doubt in his mind that a settlement was to be imposed on the Turks, by force if necessary, and he found the duty congenial. The ambassadors' final instructions to the admirals prescribed a 'pacific blockade' covering the Peloponnese, part of northern Greece and the 'contiguous' islands, also Samos and (at first) Crete. Meanwhile the unauthorised publication of the whole treaty in *The Times* of 12 July convinced public opinion that Greece was saved.

Canning's last move was an attempt to remove a ground for war by persuading Muhammad Ali independently to withdraw the Egyptian fleet and army; but he died on 8 August before it had failed. The Greeks accepted the armistice, but did not observe it at sea; the Egyptian and Turkish commanders, who were awaiting orders from Constantinople, retaliated by ravages on land, and by trying in vain to break the blockade of the bay of Navarino where their ships were assembled. The French admiral wanted to avoid any clash with the Egyptian fleet, in which a number of his countrymen were serving, but a conference with Ibrahim was indecisive. The Russian squadron, which had left Cronstadt in June, was the last to arrive on the scene, but its commander told Codrington that in his opinion the tsar had already declared war. Codrington, as the senior admiral, made the dispositions for the three squadrons to enter the bay; they were to be ready for battle but not to fire the first shot. His personal view was simple: 'There His Highness's fleet will terminate its hostile career'. The 'battle' which followed on 20 October destroyed most of the Moslem ships. When the news reached Constantinople twelve days later, the ambassadors had no instructions to admit a state of war, or even to depart. The Turks offered to do anything except openly submit to the 'ignominy of a connection with the Greeks', but repudiated the Convention of Akkerman and declared foreign intervention to be contrary to Muhammedan law. Thereupon the three ambassadors departed early in December, and Russia was at war in the spring of 1828. The other two ambassadors returned in June 1829 and joined Austria and Prussia in trying to save Turkey from an expected collapse; but the moderate terms of the Peace of Adrianople were due to the tsar's decision of policy combined with the exhaustion of his army.

Had Canning not become prime minister, the Treaty of London would hardly have been signed in that form; had he lived, it is difficult to imagine how he could have prevented a Russo-Turkish war, unless by forcing the Dardanelles and using the British fleet both to coerce

Turkey and protect her. The problem was too much for the stopgap government which followed on his death, and too much for Wellington who took office in January 1828. The Russians were proposing a temporary occupation of the Danubian Principalities, and a blockade of the Straits at both ends or—better still, since the three Powers would be at war with the Porte—'to penetrate even to Constantinople, there to dictate peace under the walls of the Seraglio'. The first of these measures Russia could and did execute alone, occupying the Principalities for six years; a blockade of the Dardanelles was excluded by British insistence that the Treaty debarred the Russians from making war in the Aegean; the last measure they attempted alone and nearly achieved after two campaigns.

Wellington has been accused of indecision, for he had signed the Protocol without foreseeing all the consequences; but he was not personally a party to the Treaty and, unless Britain was prepared to join in a crusade against Turkey (or to make war on Russia instead), his only weapon was to use delaying tactics: to fulfil the letter of the treaty towards Russia, but not more, and to settle Greece without appearing to be a consistent enemy of Turkey. Metternich agreed with him that a small independent Greece was preferable to a larger Greece which would perhaps be dependent on Russia. Their calculation was perhaps niggardly, and coloured by their distaste for the revolutionary origin of the new State; and, although the minimum execution of the Treaty was ensured by a French army in the Peloponnese (1828–33), it was only Russian arms that compelled the sultan to acquiesce by Article 10 of the Peace of Adrianople (14 September 1829).[1] Nevertheless, the Greeks owed much to Canning's bold initiative in 1826–7, which also helped British interests by putting an end to six years of disorder and piracy in the Levant.

For the Habsburg monarchy, the result was less disastrous than Metternich had expected. Within four years, he reached at Münchengrätz (September 1833) an understanding with Russia over the Balkans, which partly restored the nucleus of the conservative Alliance for the next twenty years. Little has been said in this survey about Prussia, which appeared generally to follow in the wake of Austria. Berlin was as anxious as Vienna not to quarrel openly with Russia, having an even stronger common interest in keeping the Poles quiet. For the rest, Prussia was fully occupied in digesting her recently acquired provinces and quietly consolidating her influence in north Germany. It happened that the chief trouble-spots since 1815 were Mediterranean or Atlantic and not directly interesting to a power without a navy. But it may be

---

[1] For a brief summary of the settlement of Greece to 1832, and of the effects of the Peace generally, see Chapter XIX, pp. 550–1. For Wellington's policy, see Crawley, *op. cit.*, chs. 8–12.

no accident that in August 1829 the Prussian government took one of its few initiatives by sending a general as mediator to help the tsar in coming to terms with the sultan at Adrianople, at a moment when Europe thought that the Russians might soon be in Constantinople.

The Bourbon government in France was disappointed that the eastern crisis in 1829 did not produce a general revision of the Vienna settlement, but it cannot be said that foreign policy was a cause of the fall of Charles X in 1830. In fifteen years France had recovered her status among the continental Powers and had marched into Spain with their blessing though not in their names; with Britain and Russia she had taken part for Greece at Navarino and occupied the Peloponnese in the name of this 'splinter' alliance; and finally, on the eve of revolution at home, she had begun the conquest of Algeria, alone and in the face of strong British disapproval (Volume X, p. 427). That did nothing to save the regime, but Louis Philippe, unlike Louis XVIII, was not handicapped at the start by the shadow of defeat: his difficulty would be to steer a course between self-assertion and restraint in Europe.

Since 1815, the 'conservative Alliance' of the Great Powers had been active for about four years, sick for as long again and moribund by 1825; from 1826–7 a separate triple alliance for a specific purpose had made its full revival impossible. 'Holy Alliances', whether of kings or peoples, were more easily conceived in the early nineteenth century than before 1789, and the dissemination of ideas was quicker and more widespread; but, in practice, governments were not so uniformly conservative, nor peoples so uniformly revolutionary, as to justify an ideological conflict in such simple terms. Statesmen continued to invoke the 'Concert of Europe', and used it to settle without war the affairs of Belgium in 1830–2 and of the Levant in 1839–41. The 'Concert' after 1830, like the Alliance of 1814–20, had the effect of preserving a balance of power, but with less hostility to internal changes and rather more readiness to recognise accomplished facts. It was not, any more than the Alliance, a plan for a supra-national direction of Europe. The problems of governments and peoples were too diverse to be settled by a single formula. An international organisation for preserving peace, difficult at any time, would hardly prosper so long as peoples were in vastly differing stages of development or so long as the prospect of general war did not appear to be in all cases wholly suicidal.

APPENDIX

NOTE ON THE FRENCH REPUBLICAN CALENDAR

This calendar was proposed on 20 September 1793 and adopted on 5 October, (with amendments 24 November), retrospectively as from 22 September 1792, the date of the foundation of the Republic; but for this reason it was never used for the year I. Each month had 30 days. In each month there were three *décades* of 10 days each; the days were Primedi, Duodi, Tridi, Quartidi, Quintidi, Sextidi, Septidi, Octidi, Novidi and Décadi, the last being the official day of rest. At the end of each year five days were added, called *jours complémentaires* or *sansculottides*; and a sixth, called *jour de la Révolution*, was added at the end of each year preceding a leap year (including the year VII, preceding 1800, which was not a leap year in the Gregorian calendar). Consequently, the republican years began on varying dates in September according to the Gregorian calendar, and the succeeding months also. For this reason it is impossible to give concisely a complete concordance, but that will be found in P. Caron, *Manuel pratique pour l'étude de la Révolution française* (1912), pp. 221–69; or (for the years II-VIII only) in the 1947 edition, pp. 281–6. The following tables show the dates covered by each year, and the order of the months, which began on dates varying between the 18th and the 24th.

Years		*Months*	
[an I	22 Sept. 1792–21 Sept. 1793]	Vendémiaire	Sept.-Oct.
an II	22 Sept. 1793–21 Sept. 1794	Brumaire	Oct.-Nov.
an III	22 Sept. 1794–22 Sept. 1795	Frimaire	Nov.-Dec.
an IV	23 Sept. 1795–21 Sept. 1796	Nivôse	Dec.-Jan.
an V	22 Sept. 1796–21 Sept. 1797	Pluviôse	Jan.-Feb.
an VI	22 Sept. 1797–21 Sept. 1798	Ventôse	Feb.-March
an VII	22 Sept. 1798–22 Sept. 1799	Germinal	March-April
an VIII	23 Sept. 1799–22 Sept. 1800	Floréal	April-May
an IX	23 Sept. 1800–22 Sept. 1801	Prairial	May-June
an X	23 Sept. 1801–22 Sept. 1802	Messidor	June-July
an XI	23 Sept. 1802–23 Sept. 1803	Thermidor	July-August
an XII	24 Sept. 1803–22 Sept. 1804	Fructidor	August-Sept.
an XIII	23 Sept. 1804–22 Sept. 1805		
an XIV	23 Sept. 1805–		

Each day of the year was also given a separate name, taken from plants and fruits useful to man, domestic animals, agricultural implements or products used in agriculture. Article 11 of the decree provided that each day was to contain ten hours, each hour 100 'decimal minutes' and each minute 100 'decimal seconds'. A 'decimal clock' was presented to the Convention and placed beneath the tribune under a bust of Marat. But this part of the decree was never put into effect. That the calendar had not only a civic and republican flavour but also a didactic purpose (as part of the programme of 'dechristianisation') is evident from the speeches recorded in the *Archives Parlementaires* for 20 September; 5, 6, 18, 24 October; 5, 7, 24 November 1793. It was remarked that the inauguration of the Republic (22 September 1792) and of the reign of Equality had coincided with the equinox,

APPENDIX

when the sun's rays shone equally on the two poles. It was on 10 November 1793 that the Convention received at the bar a deputation of *sansculottes* demanding the suppression of state stipends for the clergy and bringing with them a classically draped actress impersonating Liberty. The Convention accompanied the procession back to the former Cathedral of Notre Dame in order to show their approval to the people and to sing a hymn to Liberty there.

With the Concordat In April 1802, Sunday was officially restored as the day of rest, and the republican calendar had long ceased to be commonly used when the Gregorian calendar was restored by law as from 1 January 1806 (11 Nivôse, an XIV).

INDEX

Aaland Islands, ceded by Sweden to Russia (1809), 487
Aasen, Ivar, philologist, 494
Aberdeen, George Hamilton, Earl of, statesman, 639
Åbo (now Turku), meeting of Tsar and King of Sweden at (1812), 489
Aboukir, French victory over Turks at (1799), 310
Aboukir Bay, battle of, *see* Nile, battle of the
Abyssinia, *see* Ethiopia
Académie Française, 120
Academies, French Convention abolishes, 119
see also Sciences, Academies of
Acre, besieged by Napoleon (1799), 310, 531
Acte finale of Congress of Vienna (1815), 648, 655, 658, 664
Adam, Rev. William, missionary in India, 568
Adams, John Quincy, American statesman
Federalist, then National Republican, 602, 603
Secretary of State under President Monroe, 88, 591, 595, 637, 668, 682
President, 598, 605
Adams–Onis Treaty, transferring East Florida from Spain to United States (1819), 595
Addington, Henry, Viscount Sidmouth, statesman, 177, 261, 263
views on Spain, 452, 455
Aden, annexed by Britain (1838–9), 10, 532
Admiralty, Board of, 80
Adrianople, Treaty of, between Russia and Turkey (1829), 550, 668, 688–90
clauses affecting Balkan countries, 9, 543, 689
advertisements, and growth of press, 191
Afghanistan, threatens invasion of India, 553, 554
Afrancesados (Spanish collaborators with France)
King Ferdinand as the first of, 444
often liberal-minded, 446, 447, 453
excluded from later office, 449, 451
Africa, economic and political relations of Europe with, 572–90
Africa, Report of Select Committee on British Settlements on the West Coast of (1865), 584
African Association (Association for Promoting the Discovery of the Interior Parts of Africa), 582

Agenda, King Frederick William III's order of church service, 177
agriculture, 31, 33–7
in Austria, 51, 403, 406
in Belgium, 54
in Britain, 6, 43, 44
In France, 56, 329
in Holland, 56
in Hungary, 35, 51, 403
in Italy, 48, 413, 435–6
in Portugal, 442–3
in Prussia, 368–9, 376–8
in Russia, 50
in Scandinavia, 51–2
in Spain, 49, 442–3
'Aid thyself and Heaven will aid thee' Society (France), 189
Ainsworth, Thomas, engineer, 477
Aix-la-Chapelle, Congress of Allies at, (1818), 492, 669, 670
Robert Owen at, 111
Akkerman, Convention of, between Russia and Turkey (1826), 543, 549, 687
repudiated by Turkey, 550, 688
Aksakov, S. T., Slavophil, 540
Alabama, cotton lands of, 594, 596
Alaska, Russian-American Company in, 9
Alba, republic in Piedmont, 416
Albani, J., Cardinal, 174
Albania, Turkish province, 529; mercenaries from, 533
Alexander I, Tsar of Russia
before accession, 502, 503, 505
accession, 259, 506
reign of, 18, 19, 506–21 *passim*
relations with Napoleon, 21–2, 265
sympathetic towards Poland, 503, 512, 516, 649, 665
interested in Lancasterian system of education, 206
convert to biblical mysticism, 169, 192, 516
in final coalition against Napoleon, 639–45 *passim*
at Congress of Vienna, 646–67 *passim*
in international relations (1815–25), 21, 268, 668–74 *passim*
Alexander, Austrian Archduke, Palatine of Hungary, 397, 401
Alexandria
taken by French (1797), 530
occupied by British (1801–3), 263, 533
temporarily re-occupied by British (1807), 533

693

clergy
education of, in Belgium, 463; in France
(1811), 199, (after 1815), 203, 351, 352,
354; in Netherlands, 204
feeling against, 24, 25; in Bavaria, 333; of
Godwin and Shelley, 107; of Paris
Commune (1793), 147; in Restoration
France, 189; in Spain, 441
powers of, curtailed under Concordats,
152, 153, 170
see also Civil Constitution of the Clergy
Clermont (1807), first commercial steamship, 84
Clichyens (royalists and moderates, under
French Directory), 290, 291
Clinton, George, American soldier and
political leader, 603
clove plantations, in Zanzibar and Pemba,
588
coal, and industrial development
in Belgium, 38, 54–5
in England, 32, 38, 40, 44
in France, 56–7
in Germany, 53
coalitions against France, 250
first (1793), 277; crumbles (1795), 254–5,
256
second (1798), 256–8, 292, 310, 419, 530
third (1805), 265–6, 485
fourth (1813), 272, 305, 639–46 *passim*
Cobbett, William, as critic of government,
81, 182
Cobenzl, Count Louis, Austrian statesman,
259
Coblentz, *émigrés* at, 61
Coburg-Saalfeld, Prince F. J., Austrian
general, 277
Cochrane, Thomas, Lord Dundonald
frigate captain, radical M.P., 81
commander of Chilean navy (1817–22),
623, 624, 626
admiral of Brazilian navy (1823–5), 631,
632
admiral of Greek Navy (1827–8), 84, 548
Cockerell, C. R., architect, 228
Cockerill, John, iron-founder, at Seraing,
Belgium, 40, 54, 55, 469
Cockerill, William (father of John), textile-
machinery maker, at Verviers and
Liège, Belgium, 469
Code Napoléon (Civil Code), 298, 299, 319
imposed on occupied countries, 303, 331,
336, 421
retained after 1815, in France, 338, 353;
in Germany, 389, 391; in parts of
Italy, 430
Codrington, Sir Edward, admiral, at
Navarino, 549, 688
coffee, grown in Ceylon, 565

Colebrooke, Sir William, soldier and colonial governor, in Ceylon, 552, 563, 571
Colebrooke-Cameron Commission (1832),
563, 568, 581
Coleridge, Samuel Taylor, poet and philo-
sopher, 91, 103, 109
Collège de France, 121, 137, 569
collèges, secondary schools, 199
collegium philosophicum, at Louvain, for
education of priests, 204, 475–6
Collingwood, Cuthbert, Baron, naval commander, 77, 86, 326
Colloredo-Mansfeld, Franz, Prince of,
tutor of Francis of Austria, 259
chancellor, 399
Collot d'Herbois, J. M., member of *Grand
Comité* of French Convention, 279
Cologne (Köln)
ecclesiastical principality, secularised by
French, 8
Febronian prelate at, 174
'Cologne affair', over mixed marriages
(1837), 175
Colombia, Republic of
New Granada and Venezuela united as,
625
divided, 628
recognised by United States (1822) and
Britain (1825), 637, 680, 683
colombiad, American naval gun, 83
commerce, *see* trade
Committee for General Defence (France),
afterwards for Public Safety (*Grand
Comité*), 279
Committee for General Security (France),
successor to Vigilance Committee, 279,
280, 281, 284
Committee of Legislation (France), successor to much of authority of Committee of Public Safety, 285
Committee of Public Safety (France), previously for General Defence, 279, 281,
283
overthrown by Assembly (1794), 254, 284
communications, 3–4, 37–9, 43, 435
see also railways, roads, semaphore
system, ships
Communist Manifesto (1848), 117
Comoro Islands, French in, 577, 589
Comte, Auguste, philosopher, 15, 113, 118,
123
'Concert of Europe', 663, 690
concert societies, 229–30
Conciliatore, newspaper of Lombard liberal
group (Milan) 191, 431, 435
Concordats, between Papacy and
France (1802), 11, 13, 153–4, 263, 298–9,
301, 319, 322, 323, 468; after 1815,
27, 169, 175, 351

INDEX

INDEX

France (*cont.*)
Hundred Days, 14, 658, 659–61; second Peace of Paris (1815), 342, 661–5
second restoration (1815), 341–2, 661; politics under the Charter, 337–43; '*chambre introuvable*'(1815–16), 343–4; middle-of-the-road government (1816–1820), 344–7; ultra-royalist government (1820–4), 347–9; '*chambre retrouvée*' (1824), 349
reign of Charles X (1824–30), 350–5; intervention in Spain (1823–8), 16, 334, 349, 450, 451, 672, 679, 681, 690; intervention in Greece (1827–33), 354, 550, 689, 690; with Russians and British at Navarino (1827), 549, 690
reign of Louis Philippe (1830–48), 356–66; recognises South American Republics (1830), 638
in Africa, 573, 577, 585–6, 589
in India, 552–8 *passim*
population of, 32, 251, 281
franchise, *see* suffrage
Francia, J. G. R. de, dictator of Paraguay, 619
Francis, Sir Philip, publicist, 102
Francis I, Emperor of Austria (Francis II of Holy Roman Empire)
rule of, 395–400, 403, 472
fears 'Jacobinism', 333
education under, 200, 205
resigns elective title on demise of Holy Roman Empire (1806), 267, 389
father-in-law of Napoleon, 21, 270, 321
host at Congress of Vienna, 647, 651, 655
Francis I, King of Naples, 434
Francis IV, King of Modena, 429, 430, 435, 437
Francis Joseph, heir presumptive to Austrian throne (1835), 405
Frankenberg, Comte J. H. de, Cardinal-Archbishop of Mechlin, 467
Frankfurt, state created by Napoleon, 389
Frankfurt Proposals, offering Napoleon frontiers on Alps, Pyrenees, and Rhine (1813), 272, 305, 639
Franklin, Benjamin, as American 'culture hero', 131
fraternity, 92–3
Fraunhofer, Joseph von, physicist, 144
Frayssinous, Comte D. A. L., French prelate and statesman, 203, 349
Frederick, Crown Prince of Denmark, 482, 485
Frederick VI, King of Denmark, 487, 488, 490, 646
Frederick II ('the Great'), King of Prussia, 373, 375

Frederick William II, King of Prussia, 243, 373, 376
Frederick William III, King of Prussia, 169
accession (1797), 373
suspicious of army reforms, 65, 383
views on education, 127, 208
reforms under, 333, 369, 373, 375
protests to Napoleon at breach of diplomatic immunity, 264
during war of liberation (1813), 384, 385
at Congress of Vienna, 646, 651
and religious affairs (1817), 176–7
Frederick I, King of Saxony, 392
Frederick I, Duke and later King of Württemberg, 391, 646
Fredrikshamn, Treaty of, between Russia and Sweden (1809), 487
freemasons, 24
in Austria, 397; in France, 346; in Italy, 414; among musicians, 237; in Russia, 500–1, 519; in Spain, 190
Freetown, Sierra Leone
settlement of former slaves at, 580, 583, 584
naval base against slave-trade, 581, 584
free trade
Atlantic, 598
desire of merchants for, 58, 477
in Scandinavia (in corn), 482
in Tuscany, 430
Freikorps (mounted volunteers), in Prussian army, 384
Fresnel, Augustin, engineer, 123, 136
Freiberg-im-Sachsen, Academy of Mining at, 140, 388
French Revolution, 11–14, 31, 57, 275–94 *passim*
Babeuf on, 288
Hardenberg and Gneisenau on, 333
Tocqueville's view of, 119
impact of, on Italy, 413–15; on Russia, 500; on writers, 91–106
Napoleon announces completion of, 299
political and social victories of, consolidated, 275; confirmed (in Charter of 1814), 187–8, 305, 338; re-asserted (1830, 1848), 306
Friedland, battle of (1807), 268, 313, 485, 512
Friedrich, C. D., painter, 220
Friends of the Country, economic societies in Spain, 49
Friends of the Muses, Society of (Vienna), 546
Fructidor, *coup d'état* and regime of (1797), 291, 292, 309
fueros, 452, 460
Fullerton, Robert, Governor of Penang, 559
Fulton, Robert, steamship engineer, 84, 141

INDEX

Jemappes, French victory at (1792), 72, 464
Jena, battle of (1806), 268, 326, 376
military aspects of, 66, 70, 75, 313
Jerome, King of Westphalia, *see* Bonaparte, Jerome
Jesuits
suspended in Munich (1783), 390
in reconstruction after 1815, 170
not re-admitted to Tuscany, 430
in France, 189, 203, 352, 353
in Portugal, 441
Jews
in Austria, 409, 411
in Batavian Republic, 465
in Berlin, 386
in France, 97, 299; among followers of Saint-Simon, 114
in Frankfurt, 6
in Papal States, 170, 434
in Turkey, 527, 528
in United States, 97
John VI, King of Portugal, 451, 684
as Prince Regent, takes refuge in Brazil (1807–8), 269, 327, 612
returns to Portugal, 630–1, 675
Johnson, Samuel, interest in Africa of, 98, 573
Johore, Sultan of, 559
Jones, Sir William, of Asiatic Society of Bengal, 552, 569, 570
Joseph, Austrian Archduke, Palatine of Hungary, 401
Joseph II, Habsburg Emperor
reforms of, 252, 373, 376, 395–6, 398; opposed in Austrian Netherlands, 462–3, 467
patron of music, 241
gives privileges to South Slavs, 541
Joseph, King of Naples, then King of Spain, *see* Bonaparte, Joseph
Josephine (*née* Tascher de la Pagerie, widow of Vicomte Alexandre de Beauharnais), wife of Napoleon, 212, 308, 316, 317
divorced, 270, 302
grant to (1814), 643
Joubert, B. C., French general, 294, 310
Jourdan, J. B., French Marshal, 291, 310
Journal des Débats, 185, 188, 345, 350, 354
Journal de l'Empire (*Journal des Débats* renamed, 1805), 185
Journal de Paris, 185
Jovellanos, G. M. de, Spanish statesman and author, 441, 443
Joyce, Valentine, leader of mutiny at Spithead (1797), 87
judicial system
Denmark, 482
France (1799), 297; (1814), 339

Italy (1806), 421
Prussia (1808), 381
Jung-Stilling, J. H., German moralist, 163, 516
Junín, victory of Bolívar at (1824), 627
Junkers, pietism among, 164, 170
Junot, Andache, French general, 320, 335
in Portugal, 612, 335
Greek wife of, 530
Juntas
in Spain, 444–5, 449, 456, 613; central, at Aranjuez, 614, 615, 616
in South America, 616, 619, 620, 621

Kalevala, Finnish folk-epic, 494
Kalisch, Treaty of, between Prussia and Russia (1813), 272, 639
Kandy (Ceylon), British in, 565, 566
Kant, Immanuel, philosopher, 160, 168, 332
views on revolution, 91, 92, 93, 95, 100
successors of, 192
Kara George, Serbian leader, 541, 542, 543
Karamzin, N. M., Russian historian, 19, 514
Karl August, Duke of Weimar, 646
Karl Friedrich, Margrave (later Grand Duke) of Baden, 391
Karlsruhe, technical high school at, 125
Karl Theodor, Elector of Bavaria, 390
Karteria, steam warship, in Greek waters, 84
Kay-Shuttleworth, Sir James, promoter of popular education, 194
Kazan, university of, 511, 518, 200
Kedah, Sultan of, 559
Keith, G. K. Elphinstone, Viscount, admiral, 85, 318
Kellerman, F. C. de, French Marshal, 309
Kentucky, 599, 607; admitted to United States (1792), 594
Key, Francis Scott, author of *Star-Spangled Banner*, 611
Kharkov, university of, 200, 511, 541
Khartum, population of, 534
Kiel, Treaty of (1814), 490, 491; payments to Denmark under, 492, 657
Kildare Place Society, for schools in Ireland, 202
Kilwa, French relations with rulers of, 577
Kirk, Sir John, British consul at Zanzibar, 589
Kisselew, Count Paul, Russian governor of Danubian Principalities, 539
Klaproth, H. J., philologist, 570
Kléber, J. B., French general, 531
Kleist, Heinrich von, poet, 186, 332
Klopstock, F. G., poet and philosopher, 91
Klüppelkrieg against French in Luxembourg (1798), 467

INDEX

languages
 Indo-European, Indo-German, 570
 native, romantic revival of, 304, 476
Lannes, Jean, French Marshal, 318, 320
La Paz, revolt against Spain at (1809), 615
Laplace, Pierre S., Marquis de, mathematician, 28, 121, 123, 124, 132
 minister of interior, president of Senate, 125
La Révellière-Lépeaux, L. M. de, member of first French Directory, 288, 290, 308
latifundia, 37; in Russia, 497; in Spain, 49, 443
Latin, giving way to vernaculars in science, 304
Latouche-Tréville, Louis de, French admiral, 324
Lauenberg, transferred from Prussia to Denmark (1814), 657
Laugier, Abbé M. A., *Essai sur l'Architecture* by, 223, 227
Lavalleja, Antonio de, liberator of Uruguay (1825), 630
Lavoisier, A. L., scientist, 95, 134, 142
law
 codification of, in Austria (1803), 396; in Prussia (1794, 1845), 15; in Russia (1809), 513, 514
 international, 481, 669
Lawrence, Sir Thomas, portrait painter, 216
Lazar, George, teacher of Roumanian, 538
Lebas, Hippolyte, architect, 225
Lebeau, Joseph, Belgian liberal lawyer, 478
Leblanc, Nicolas, chemist, 143
Leclerc, V. E., French general, 261
Ledoux, C. L., architect, 223-4
Ledru-Rollin, A. A., French lawyer and politician, 365
Leeds Mercury, advocate of reform, 183
Lefebvre, P. F. J., French Marshal, 321
Legations, Papal
 detached from Papal States (1797), 151, 156, 255
 returned to Papal States (1815), 430
 hotbed of secret organisations, 434
Legislation, Committee of (France, 1794), 285
Legislative Assembly (France, 1791-2), 13, 62, 68, 252, 253
Legislative Body (*Corps legislatif*) in France (1799), 296; during Hundred Days, 341, 342, 660
Legislative Councils (France, 1795), 287, 288, 291, 292, 293, 295
Leghorn, trade of, 424
Legion of Honour, 301, 319
legitimacy, principle of, 22, 338, 665; support of Pope for, 171; Talleyrand and, 653

Leipzig, 128, 229, 388
 battle of (1813), 273, 305, 333, 490, 639
 disposal of (1814-15), 652, 655
Leipziger Zeitung, 186
Lenz, J. M. R., dramatist, 371
Leo XII (Annibale della Genga), Pope (1823-9), 171, 172, 434
Leoben, Preliminaries of (1797), 309, 416, 438
Leopard, H.M.S., 89
Leopardi, Giacomo, poet, 103
Leopold, Prince of Saxe-Coburg
 offered throne of Greece, 550
 King of Belgium, 18, 668
Leopold II, Habsburg Emperor (1790-2)
 Reichenbach Convention, with Prussia (1790), 252, 463
 pacification under, 396
 death of (1792), 253, 395
Leopold I, Grand Duke of Tuscany (later Emperor as Leopold II, *see above*)
 reforms of, in Tuscany, 425, 430
Leopold II, Grand Duke of Tuscany, 435
Lepeletier, L. M., French republican, 149
Le Père, J. M., French engineer, 533
Lermontov, M. Y., poet and novelist, 108
Leroux, Pierre, socialist reformer, 114
Lesseps, Vicomte Ferdinand de, French vice-consul in Lisbon, 451
Lessing, G. E., critic and dramatist, 97, 168, 371, 372
Letarouilly, P. M., architect, 225
Letourneur, C. L. F. H., member of first French Directory, 288, 289
Levant, the, 525-34
 British interests in, 532-4, 674, 689
 possible French domination of (1799), 256, 265, 529-33, 576
 'Concert of Europe' and (1839-41), 690, see also Turkey, etc.
Levant Company, 685
levée en masse, 62, 122, 291
 see also conscription
Lewis, Frankland, M.P., 42
Lewis, Meriwether, American explorer, 594
Libel Act (1792), 180
liberalism, 12, 31, 58, 192
 economic, 31, 35, 58
 political, in Belgium, 478; in Germany, 16; in Portugal, 454-6; in Spain, 17, 439, 441, 445-6; and the Catholic Church, 173-6, 204
 scientific, in Germany, 128
 theological, 163
Liberia, independent Afro-American republic, 583
liberty, 100, 112, 115
 sought by both revolutionaries and romantics, 94, 103

720

INDEX

National Guards
  French, 61, 281, 285; reorganised (1797), 290; (1815) 342; (1831), 356; (1832), 360
  Cisalpine, 417
nationalism
  associated with romanticism, 94, 99, 190 332, 410
  distinguished from patriotism, 100
  and warfare, 60–1
  under Austrian rule, 407–11
  German, 186, 332, 389
  Italian, 436–7
  Spanish, 333–4
  aroused by Napoleon, 330–4
nationality, principle of, 665
National Road, through Alleghenies to Ohio, 599
National Republican party, United States, 603, 604
National Society for the Education of the Poor (Anglican), 178, 202
National-Zeitung der Deutschen, 186
natural history, encroachment of exact science on, 131, 136
Naturphilosophie, school of, 128
Nautilus, 'plunging boat' (1803), 84
Nauvoo, Illinois, Icarian settlement at, 115
Naval Academy (later Royal Naval College), 85
naval constructors, corps of, 82
Naval Enquiry, Commissions of, 81
Navarino, defeat of Turkish and Egyptian fleets by British, French, and Russian squadrons at (1827), 84, 525, 549, 688, 690
Navarre, Carlism in, 460
navies
  British, 76–8, 80–8, 324, 326; supremacy of, 6, 77, 90, 672; and slave trade, 99, 581, 673
  Chilean, 623
  French, 78–80
  Spanish, 323, 324
  of Sultan of Muscat, 577
  of United States, 89–90
Navigation Acts, British, modified (1822), 680
Navigation Code, British, and United States, 598
Navy Board, 80, 83
Navy Department, United States, 89
'Nazarenes', German colony of, at Rome, 161, 221
Near East and Ottoman Empire, 525–51
Nederlandsche Handel-Maatschappij, 55, 478, 564
Neerwinden, Austrian victory over French at (1793), 464, 465

Neipperg, Count Adam A. von, Austrian general, second husband of Marie Louise of Austria, 429
Nelson, Horatio, Viscount, admiral, 76, 83, 87, 325
  'open' blockade system of, 77
  tactics of breaking enemy's line, 324, 326
  at Battle of Nile, 256, 531
  at Copenhagen, 484
  at Trafalgar, 267, 326, 485
Nesselrode, Karl R., Graf von, adviser of Tsar Alexander I, 18, 673
  at Congress of Vienna, 646, 654
Netherlands, see Austrian Netherlands, Holland, Netherlands (Kingdom of the)
Netherlands, Kingdom of the (Holland and and Belgium)
  proposed by Pitt (1798), 256–7
  formed (1814), 54, 473, with containment of France in mind, 18, 640, 644
  adheres to Triple Alliance (1815), 654
  constitution (1815), 473–4
  Concordat of Pope with (1827; not executed), 170
  divided (1830–1), 7, 664
  see also Belgium, Holland
Neue Zürcher Zeitung, 191
Neufchateau, François de, member of third French Directory, 291
New Granada, Viceroyalty of
  revolt in (1809), and deposition of Viceroy (1810), 615–6
  viceroy reinstated by Spanish army (1816), 621, 622
  united with Venezuela in Republic of Colombia (1819), 625
New Harmony, Owen's settlement in Indiana, 111–2
New Lanark, Owen's textile mills at, 7, 42–3, 111
New Orleans, British defeated by United States forces at (1815), 611
'New Readers' sect in Sweden, 164
New Spain, see Mexico
Newspaper Act (1798), 181, 182
newspapers, see press
newspapers, circulation of
  in Britain, 181
  in Paris (1826), 188–9, 340
  in Prussia (1823, 1830), 191
Newtonian laws, 131–2, 133–4
New York
  as terminus of Liverpool trade, 596
  politics of, 606; suffrage in (1821), 607
  population of, 593, 606
Ney, Michel, French Marshal, 320, 490
  at Waterloo, 70, 313, 314
  execution of, under Louis XVIII, 319, 344, 354